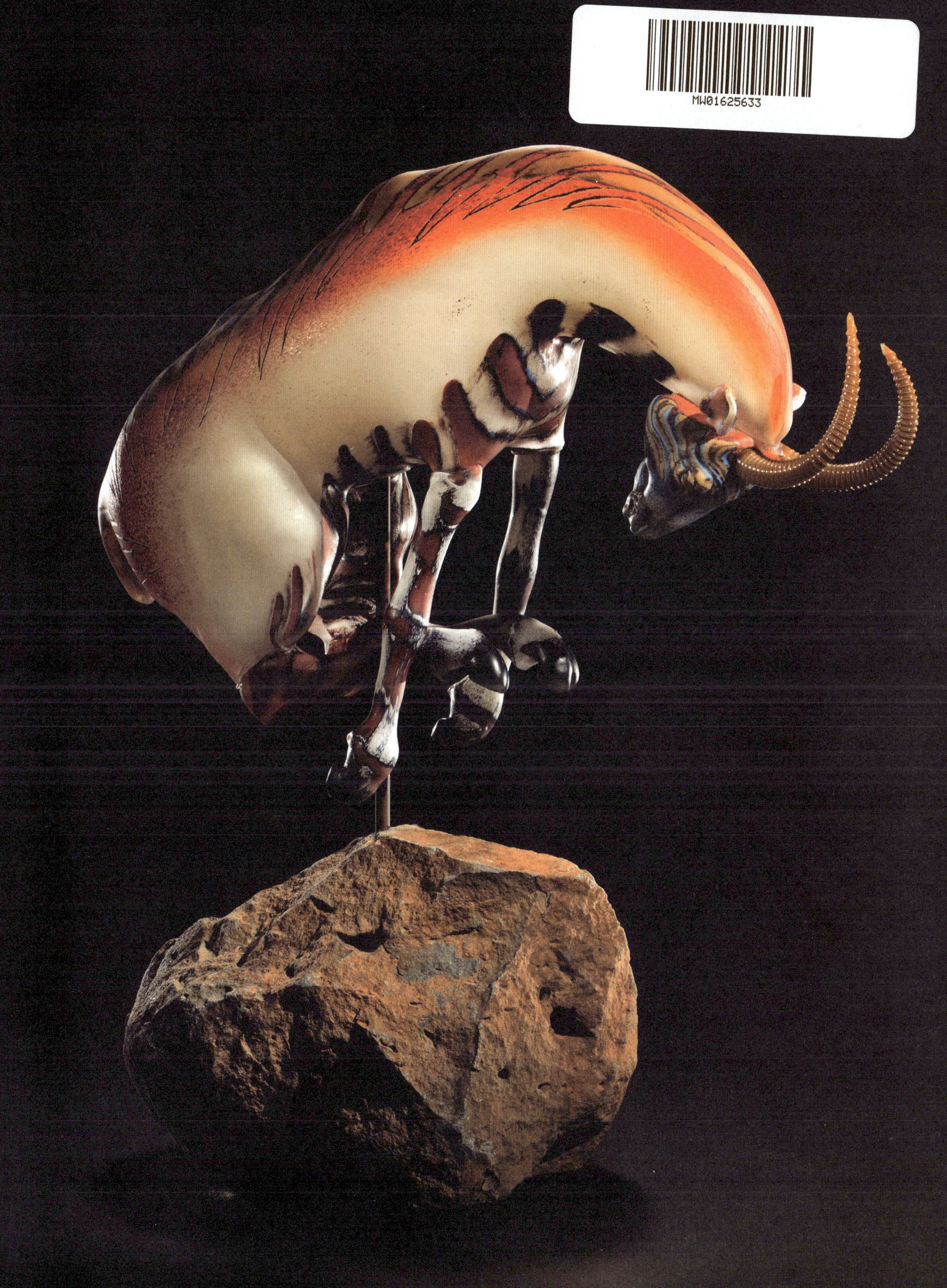

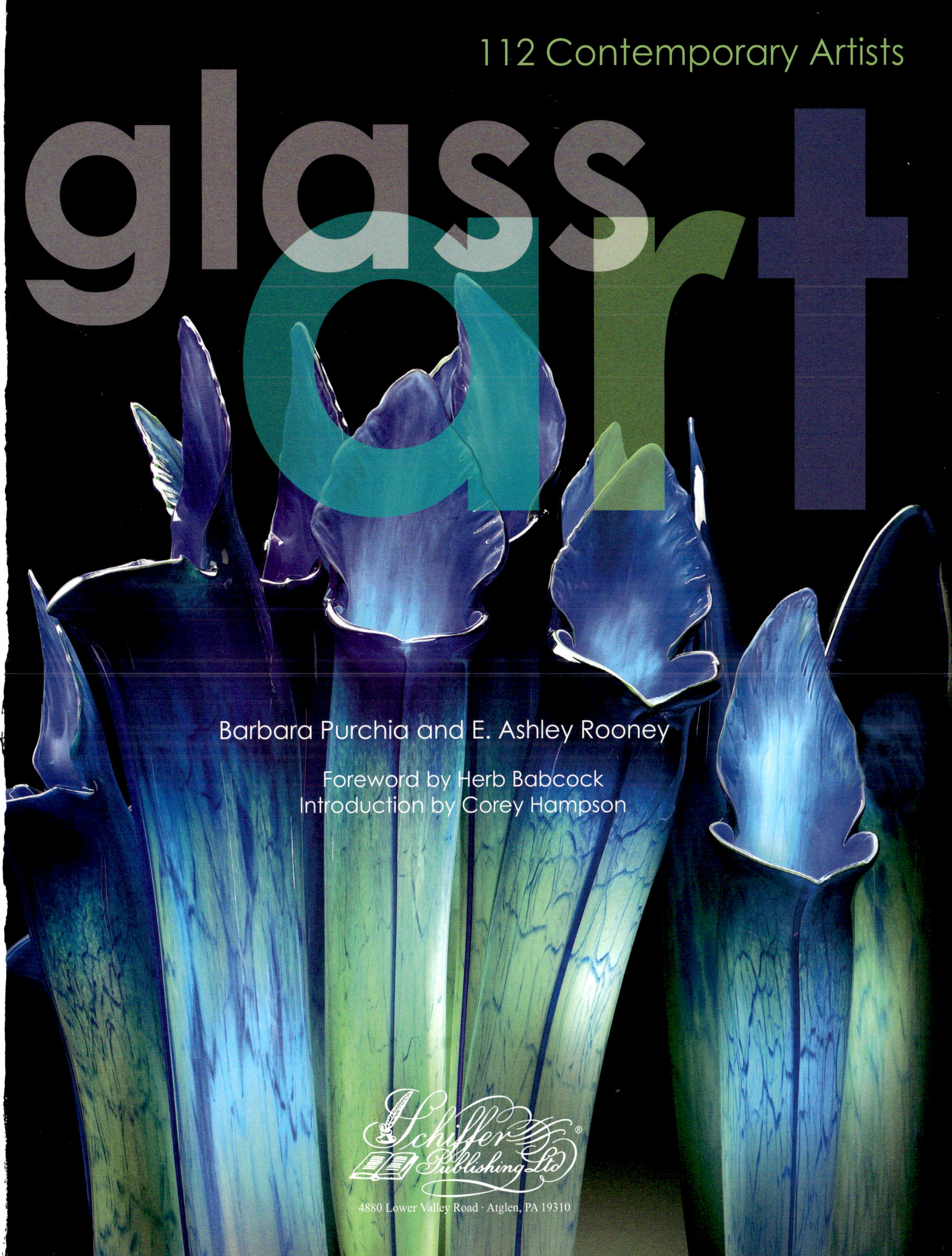
112 Contemporary Artists
glass art
Barbara Purchia and E. Ashley Rooney
Foreword by Herb Babcock
Introduction by Corey Hampson
Schiffer Publishing Ltd
4880 Lower Valley Road · Atglen, PA 19310

Library of Congress Control Number: 2016945354

Designed by Brenda McCallum
Cover design by Brenda McCallum

Type set in Century Gothic/Goudy

Front cover image: Stephan Cox. Front flap: Deanna Clayton (photo by Larry Sanders). Spine: Nao Yamamoto. Front endsheets, clockwise from left: Shane Fero (courtesy of Mary Vogel Photography); Kathleen Mulcahy; Shelley Muzylowski Allen (courtesy of Russell Johnson); John Littleton and Kate Vogel. Back endsheets, clockwise from left: Stephen Gartner and Danielle Blade; David Patchen; Christian Arnold and Laurie Young (courtesy of Screaming Pixel); Carmen Lozar (courtesy of Rick Kessinger Studio). Title page: Jason B. Gamrath (courtesy of Daniel Fox/Lumina Studio). Page 3: Mary Van Cline (courtesy of Douglas Schaible Photography).

ISBN: 978-0-7643-5188-4
Printed in China

Published by Schiffer Publishing, Ltd.
4880 Lower Valley Road
Atglen, PA 19310
Phone: (610) 593-1777; Fax: (610) 593-2002
E-mail: Info@schifferbooks.com
Web: www.schifferbooks.com

Other Schiffer Books by the Author:

Painted Sky: 106 Artists of the Rocky Mountain West, E. Ashley Rooney, ISBN 978-0-7643-4961-4

Artists' Homes and Studios, E. Ashley Rooney, ISBN 978-0-7643-4692-7

Encaustic Art in the Twenty-First Century, Anne Lee and E. Ashley Rooney, ISBN 978-0-7643-5023-8

Other Schiffer Books on Related Subjects:

Art Glass Today 2, Sandra Korinchak, ISBN 978-0-7643-5025-2

Studio Glass in America: A 50 Year Journey, Ferdinand Hampson, ISBN 978-0-7643-4230-1

International Glass Art, Richard Yelle, ISBN 978-0-7643-1834-4

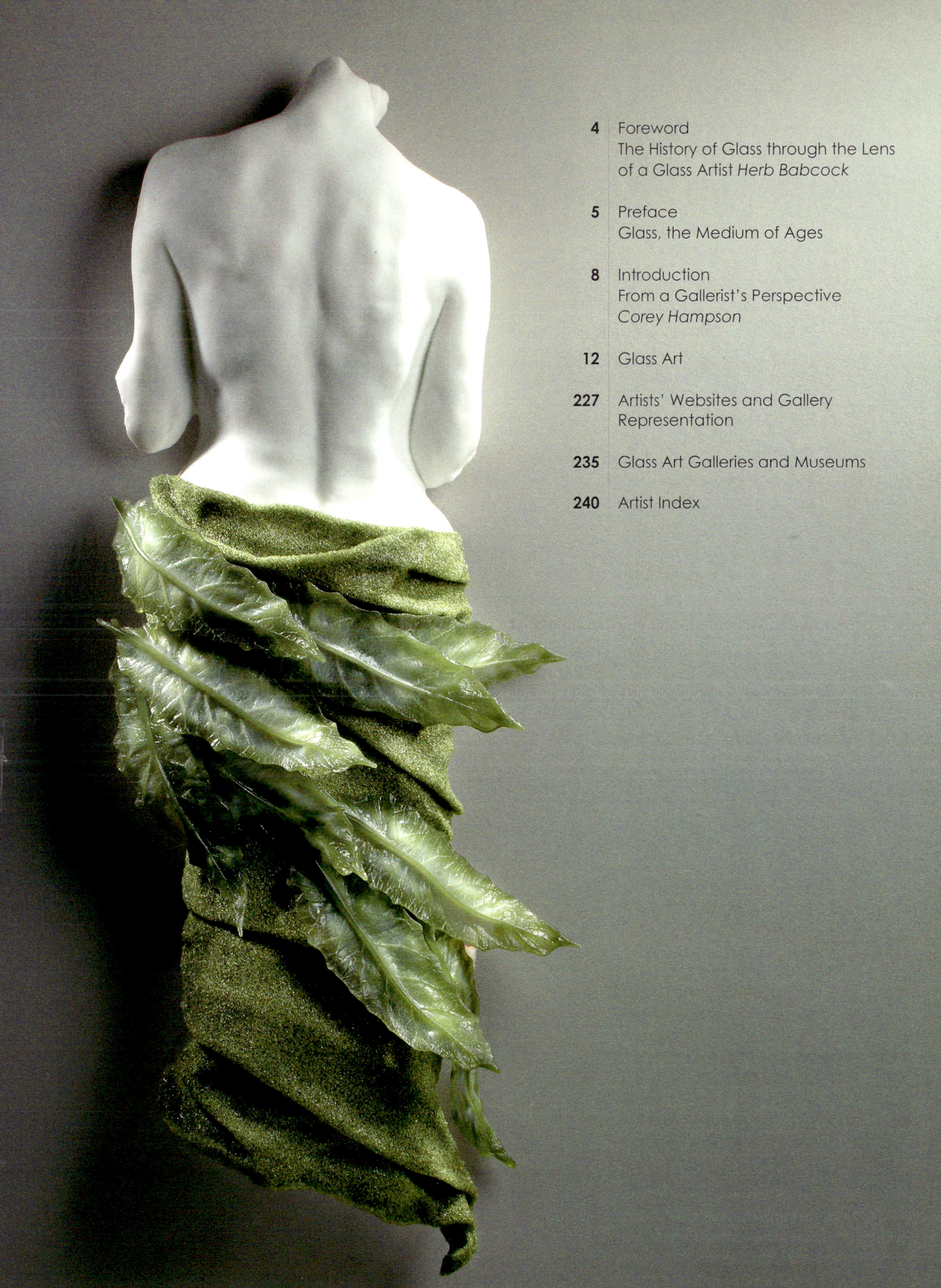

foreword

The History of Glass through the Lens of a Glass Artist

Herb Babcock

In *How We Got to Now: Six Innovations That Made the Modern World,* Steven Johnson identifies six inventions with profound impact: Cold, glass, clean, time, sound, and light. Of the six, he refers to glass as:

> The single most transformative material of the last 1,000 years . . . Glass is now such a central part of our everyday lives . . . we often forget to think of it as an invention. Just think about what glass led to: Spectacles, telescopes, microscopes, TV screens and the fiber optic internet.

Try to imagine the built environment without architectural glass. What more could you possibly do with such a versatile, strong, and, ultimately, seductive material?

You could make art. What other material is so alluring? Glass is thick or thin, refracting or reflecting light, transparent or opaque, crystal clear or color rich, flat or sculptural, fabricated cold or hot. Work "hot" with molten glass, and you have a studio of high drama and theater. Working with fire is never boring; rather, it has danger and excitement. Artists use the medium of glass for any number of reasons, but not because it is easy. Modern art glass requires not only skill and aesthetics, but also some understanding of technology. Silica, lime, soda ash, and fire: the marvel of glass is from this simple mix of elements. More amazing is its accidental discovery.

Either the Egyptians or the Phoenicians probably discovered glass several thousand years ago. Glassmaking evolved in guilds or factories over centuries. In 1962, the American Studio Glass Movement began when Harvey Littleton received support from the Toledo Museum of Art to build a small glass furnace and conduct a workshop there. With that beginning, the movement thrived as colleges introduced glass into their craft departments, and students flocked to summer programs like those at Haystack, Penland, and, eventually, Pilchuck. Simultaneously, glass art, made by individual artists, in small studios, spread rapidly across the world. The phenomenon was enriched as master craftsmen emerged from factories in countries with strong glassmaking traditions and brought their work and experience to the United States.

During the1960s, artists from diverse disciplines began to experiment with glass. The output from small, independent studios was usually crude as artists struggled to learn the medium and tackle the technical problems. We shared our failures and successes; the early years were notable for this generous sharing of information between artists. Sharing continued and expanded with the digital age. Once an artist had a basic level of skill and technical expertise, other life experiences came into play.

I started blowing glass after finishing my BFA in sculpture at The Cleveland Institute of Art. At The Cranbrook Academy of Art, during my MFA sculpture program, I set up a small glass furnace there. My early glass was "hot" sculptured work influenced by minimalist and abstract expressionism.

The 1970s saw artists still working on skills and technology. No one was really a "master" yet. As we learned to control the material, our work became more personal and conceptual both in sculpture and vessels.

The 1980s and 1990s were a time where everything was open to artists; studios welcomed the unique in architecture, lighting, jewelry, etc. In general, this period witnessed more experimentation, where artists utilized even more technique: blown, cold fabrication, solid worked, kiln cast, fused, slumped, lamp, and flat. As each generation of young artists "discovered" glass, a wealth of knowledge and experience flowed to them from those who came before. The beginning of the twenty-first century witnessed more of the non-traditional, with artists of other media including glass in their work or collaborating with glass studios to make art.

Art glass has plenty of momentum. My observations about glass are both generalized yet highly personal. Some artists are sensitive to any dichotomy of "craft" or "fine art," but that just seems rhetorical now. I am a sculptor by education and inclination. Formed in forty years of teaching, my explanation to students is, "A craft object tends to celebrate: an event; a culture; a person. Fine art tends to question: an event; a culture; a person." The perception that fine art must have irony, while craft must have the pretense of beauty, undoubtedly will continue. Artists should not be distracted.

Glass artists continue to benefit from the exchange of knowledge and spirit of collaboration that has persisted for more than fifty years. They are drawn to the medium, the fire, the molten material, and the dance with gravity where every movement counts.

Herb Babcock, Professor Emeritus, College for Creative Studies, maintains an independent sculpture studio. He continues to explore the potential of glass casting and metal fabrication. His work is represented in private collections, public installations, museums, and galleries throughout the world. In addition to his own work, he juries, curates, and lectures.

preface

Glass, the Medium of Ages

I always marvel at all that sparkling, beautiful glass sculpture in the high-end gift shops or museums. To think this material has been in existence for millennia and yet it looks so twenty-first century with its sleek, lustrous durability. One of the first synthetic materials to be made by man, glass is distinctive.

The creation of glass goes far back in time. Initially, glass was used to make small beads, but by around 1450 BCE, Egyptian craftsmen found that they could shape the hot glass into resplendent vessels. The wealthy considered the material valuable. Unfortunately, when the New Kingdom collapsed in approximately 1070 BCE, glassmaking halted. Fortunately, it was rediscovered, and by the first century CE, new glass blowing techniques had revolutionized the ancient glass industry.

Initially, luxury items such as vessels, beads, jewelry, and windows were made from glass. By the Middle Ages, Venice had become the glassmaking center of the western world. Because the furnaces caused frequent fires in the wooden buildings, the city authorities ordered that glassmaking facilities be moved to the island of Murano. That way, too, the authorities could maintain control and ensure that no glassmaking skills or secrets were exported.

But somehow the art and mystery of glassmaking escaped! By the early 1400s, the glass industry in Lauscha, a small German town, was well established. In 1608, the Jamestown colony in Virginia had a small glass factory, which didn't last long, but it marked the beginning of glass manufacturing in America. Two businessmen founded the Waterford Company in Ireland in 1783 to create the finest-quality crystal for drinking vessels and objects of beauty for the home. To this day, however, Murano is still considered the birthplace of the modern art glass movement.

Throughout the Middle Ages, the Catholic Church, which was the only Western European church during this time, built massive cathedrals designed to impress and humble the masses with the power of God. The use of stained glass windows became prevalent, and magnificent windows were created for the great cathedrals.

During the 1800s, the demand for window glass increased substantially. Soon people began to use glass bottles and flasks for alcohol and medicine. By 1858, the screw-top Mason jar for home canning appeared; glass tableware became popular; and the development, manufacture, and use of glass increased rapidly.

Once machines began to produce functional glass items, glass workers could begin to experiment with glass art. By the beginning of the twentieth century, great studios like Tiffany, Lalique, Waterford, and Hoya Crystal began to produce glass art, and institutions such as Corning in New York, the Bauhaus School in Germany, and the Academy of Applied Arts in Prague introduced glassmaking courses. In the mid-twentieth century, the studio glass movement took off with American artists such as Dale Chihuly and Marvin Lipofsky creating unique glass works.

Modern glass studios use a variety of techniques and processes in creating glass artworks, including working glass at room temperature (cold working), stained glass, mosaics, working glass in a torch flame (lampworking), glass beadmaking, glass casting, glass fusing, and, most notably, glass blowing. In addition, many artists combine glass with other materials such as metals, wood, and stone.

The 112 artists exhibited in *Glass Art* reflect the tremendous diversity, depth, and breadth of an ancient material in the twenty-first century. To find them, we did extensive research, checking out galleries, contests, and societies, looking for these twenty-first century artists who spoke to us. We read bios, awards, lists of shows; we wanted those who would bring excitement, passion, and variety to this book. We looked for those who challenged the boundaries of familiar techniques and were on the cutting edge.

We found artists who made panties and kimonos out of glass; those who made towering installations; and artists who made bugs, caterpillars, sea urchins, and beach corals. Glass art obviously brings people together: this book has eight couples and two parent/child pairs. There were those who left their jobs to become glass artists and those who grew up doing it. Many teach; many still do research; and they all work with glass. Certainly, glass is and will continue to be a means through which the artist conveys a contemporary subject matter, while honoring the integrity of a personal voice and creative process. And with this art, our glass is quite full!

Hot Glass. Hot Glass is glass worked in its molten state directly from the furnace, at 2,000 degrees Fahrenheit (1,093.333 Celsius) either by blowing, sculpting, or casting.

In the mid–first century BCE, glassworkers in the region of Syria-Palestine discovered how to inflate hot glass by blowing through a tube. Traditionally and in modern furnace working, the gaffer blows through the tube, slightly inflating the gob, which is then manipulated into the required form by swinging it, rolling it on a marver, or shaping it with tools or in a mold. It is then inflated to the desired size.

Solid sculpted glass is a technique using a solid metal rod to gather the molten glass from the furnace and then shaping it with the use of special tools. While the process is similar to blown glass, no actual blowing takes place in the sculpture. The hot sculpting process tends to make much larger solid pieces of glass art

Cast glass is molten glass that has been poured into a mold and allowed to anneal as a shaped form.

Kiln-Formed Glass. The heat of a kiln is used for processes such as bending, casting, draping, fusing, sagging, slumping, and pate de verre.

Temperatures between 1,100 and 1,700 degrees Fahrenheit (600 to 925 Celsius) are used, mild when compared to working temperatures used for hot glass techniques, which often exceed 2,400 degrees Farenheit (1,320 degrees Celsius). Artists using kiln-formed techniques create a pattern, picture, or design by fitting together and/or stacking colored pieces of glass sheets, stringers (thin rods), and/or frits or powders (ground glass). They then place the result in a kiln, where it fuses and forms a single piece.

Lampworking or Flameworking. This technique involves using a torch or lamp as the only heat source to melt the glass. Once in a molten state, the glass is formed by blowing and shaping it by hand or with tools. In flameworking, one end of the glass tube is heated and closed immediately, after which the worker blows into the other end and manipulates the hot glass. Lampworking is a type of glasswork where a torch or lamp is primarily used to melt the glass. Once in a molten state, the glass is formed by blowing and shaping with tools and hand movements.

Cold Glass. Etching, painting, grinding, and sandblasting glass are examples of cold working techniques. Stained glass and mosaic art, which have been produced for thousands of years, are examples of cold process glass art.

Combined Glass Techniques and Mixed Media. These utilize multiple glass categories and techniques along with other media, such as metals.

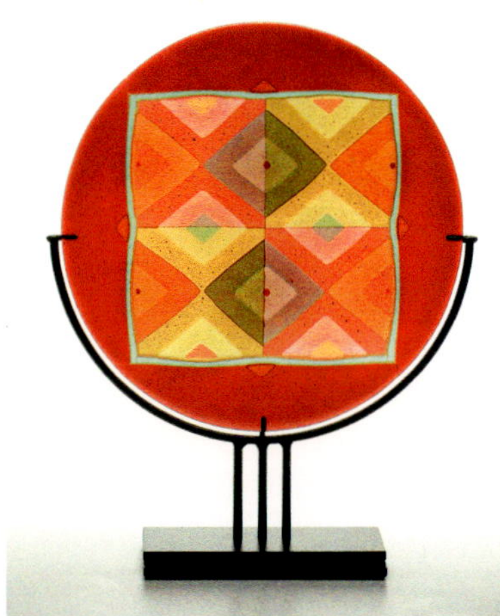

These techniques and processes are often used in describing glass artwork.

Lynn Latimer (courtesy of John Polak Photography).

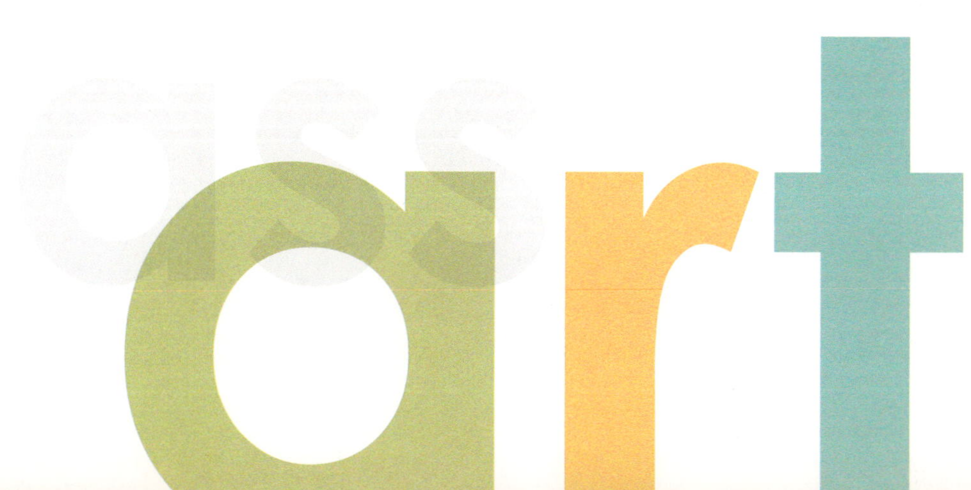

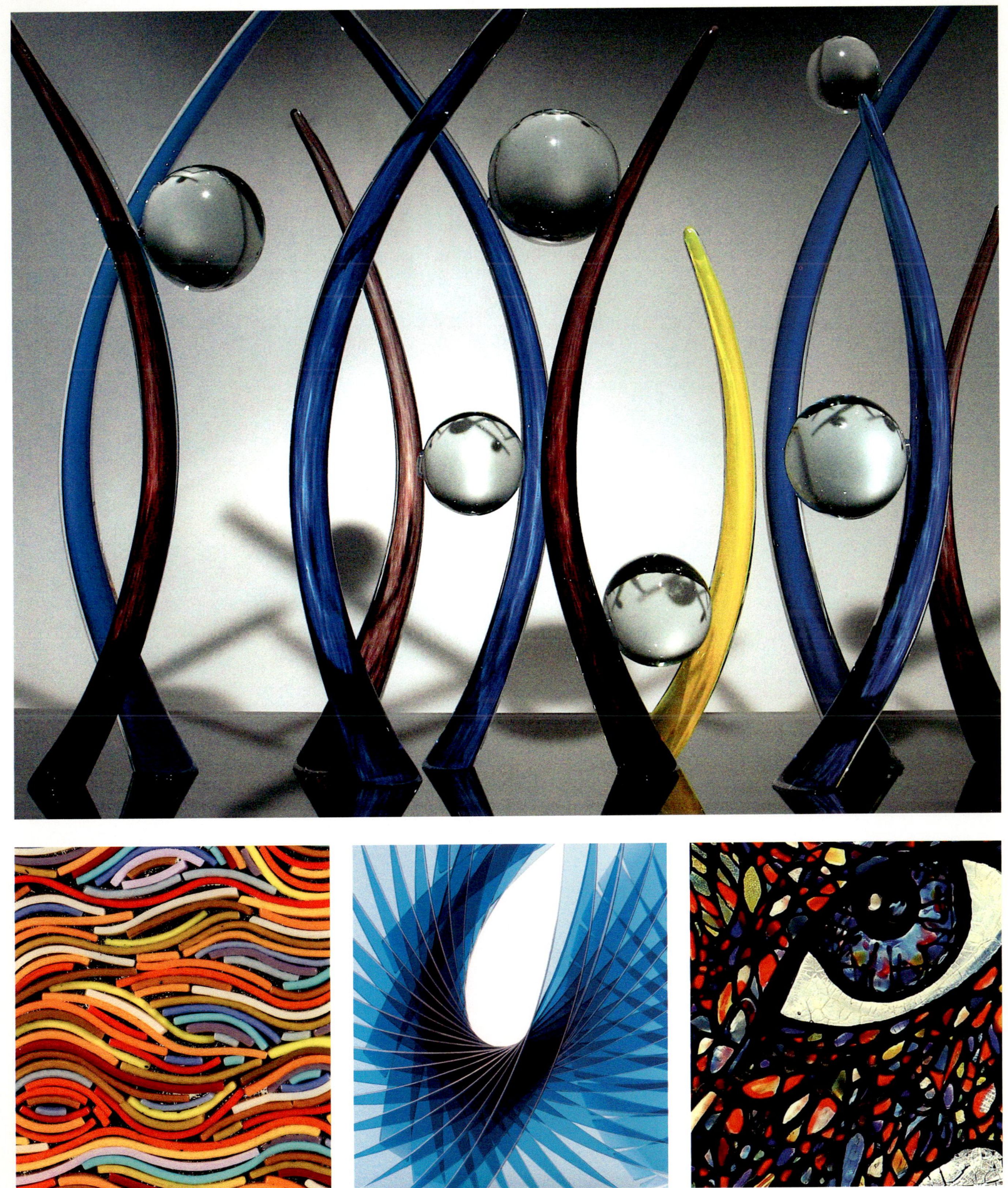

Top: David Patchen; L to R: Eileen Martin (photo: David Terao); Tom Marosz (courtesy of My World Productions); Teresa Young.

Introduction

From a Gallerist's Perspective

Corey Hampson

Glass is a mixture of 80 percent Mother Nature, 10 percent alchemy, and 10 percent magic—a universal blend found eloquently splashed throughout the pages of this book. Early evidence of functional glass has been discovered throughout the world. Use of the material has been around for millennia. Fragments found from ancient civilizations indicate that glass was used to carry or move liquids and was sculpted for prayer. The need for glass was embedded in ancient civilizations, and glass was used during their day-to-day activities. Today, we too depend on glass on a daily basis; whether it's driving in our cars or checking out our appearance, glass has been accepted, often without notice, in our daily routine. However, it was not until recently that artists discovered glass as a material to make art. Once they were exposed to the beauty of glass and began to understand its flexible applications, both the purpose for the material and the art world would never be the same.

Glass as a means for expression encompasses a very broad spectrum based on the variety of techniques, ideas, and uses that have emerged over the years. As the owner of a gallery devoted to artists working with "studio glass," I often use the word "glass" as a generic term. I have learned, however, that the term explains very little to those who want to learn about this new art form. Collectors, most historians, artists, and gallerists have dubbed 1962 as the exact year when artists in the United States experimenting with glass challenged the material and ultimately caused it to take a leap into the unknown. Harvey Littleton and Dominic Labino guided the way by melting some marbles, but, more importantly, they had the vision that artists could use glass to give form to their ideas. This insight spawned a revolution for glass over the next fifty years and later fueled the concept of studio glass as a collectible. Glass art would eventually be accepted into curriculums in colleges, be acquired by museums, and become a part of both significant public institutions and private collections. Reputations of artists, museums, collectors, and galleries would be developed and careers made.

Harvey Littleton explored the world to find answers as to whether glass was a viable material for art. In this pursuit, he stumbled upon Erwin Eisch in Germany. Erwin always thought of himself as a "not so good glassblower." He would paint on glass and stated, "If I paint on the surface . . . do you still consider it glass art?" He brought something to the glass world that distinguished it from other materials. He taught there could be a message beyond the material. This mantra may be why Harvey Littleton coined the term "Technique is cheap." This implied that anybody can learn a trade, but utilizing creativity in a field will give that field life, and with life art will follow.

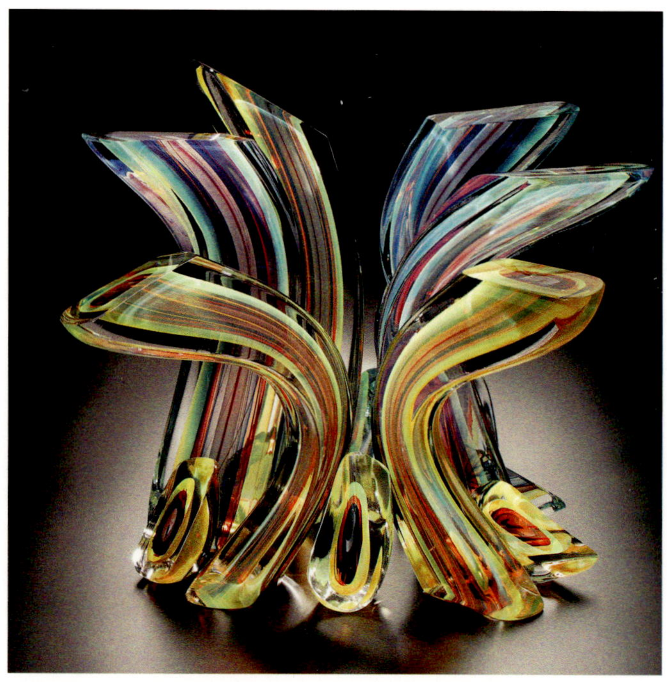

Harvey Littleton's *Yellow Crown* from his *Topological Geometry* series created in 1983 is made from barium/potash glass with multiple cased overlays of Kugler colors: white, ruby, yellow, with red amber lines and an orange center line. The 23" × 28" piece has 12 separate elements. Courtesy of Douglas Schaible Photography.

Fifty years. Middle-aged or still in its infancy? Is studio glass suffering from a mid-life crisis or is it just too young to realize its own potential?

The internationally acclaimed artist Dale Chihuly paved the way for most artists who work with glass. With the advice from his good friend Italio Scanga, he started a major self-promoting marketing campaign. His visions went beyond the glory hole. He created entire cities of glass, private and public installations as well as botanical gardens where his work interacts with each unique habitat. He has created museums devoted to great visual experiences. With the help of philanthropists Anne and John Hauberg, he introduced the world to the Pilchuck School of Glass. Founded in 1971, as a summer school, Pilchuck is a creative learning center situated deep in the rain forest of Washington. Artists can learn and share knowledge while exploring outside of their specialty. It would be difficult to look at the glass world without paying homage to Dale Chihuly and his crew. Dale would find the most talented artists in the world to work on his projects; many artists, including Rich Royal, William Morris, Martin Blank, and Lino Tagliapietra, would go on to develop extraordinary careers.

Generations of maestro (master) glass handlers anchored around the Mediterranean Sea have been working with glass for centuries. Marooned on Murano, glass techniques were passed down through families like ancient cooking recipes. In the late 1970s, Lino Tagliapietra picked up where his brother left off and taught these secret formulas and techniques to artists in the United States. His conquest to educate the world led him to be ostracized for a period of time by the glassblowers of Murano. Ultimately, he helped globalize a better understanding of the material by inspiring many young glassblowers. For his love for the material and a desire to share his talents with anyone who shared his passion, Lino Tagliapietra will forever be revered throughout the world as a true maestro of Murano.

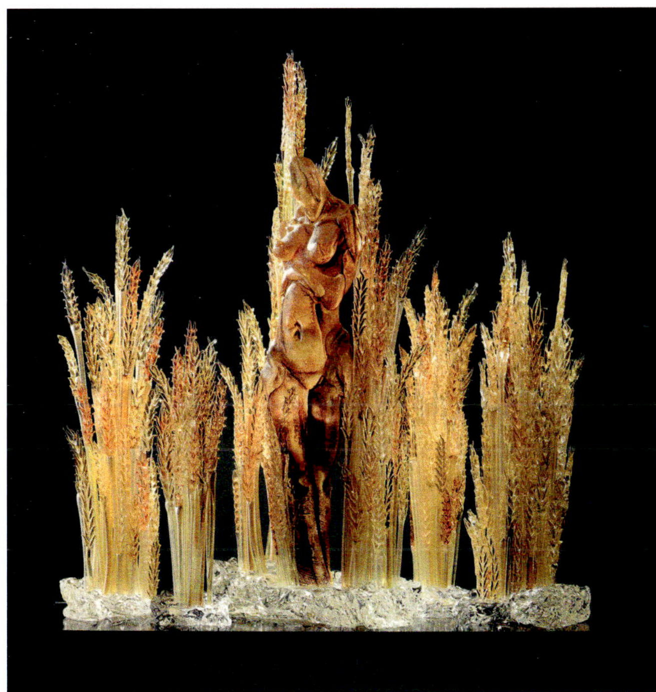

Martin Blank's *Demeter 2014* measures 78" × 43" × 15.5". Martin Blank uses gold/silver leaf on clear and amber hot-sculpted glass wheat stalks to express the beauty, fragility, and preciousness of life. Courtesy of Douglas Schaible Photography.

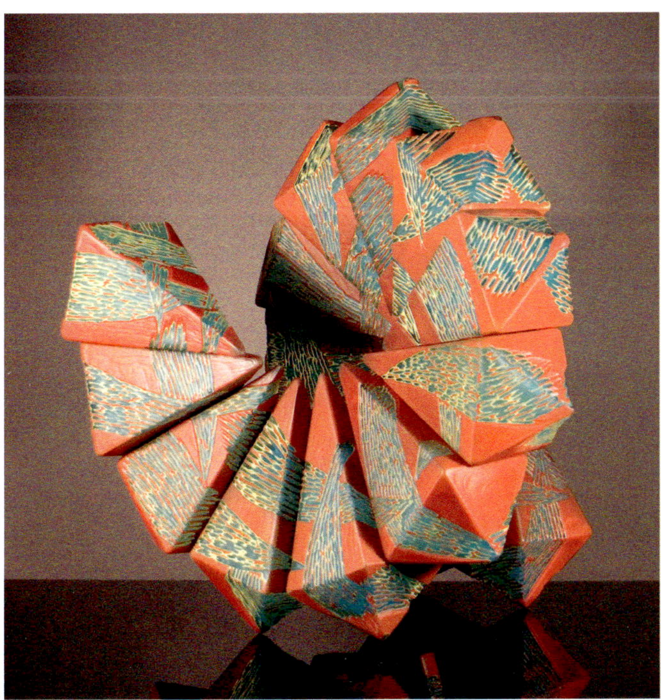

Richard Royal's *Tropical Leopard Skin Scroll*, 2014, is 21" × 21". Each element was made at the end of a blow pipe and heavily cold worked to reveal layers of color beneath the surface. Courtesy of Richard Royal.

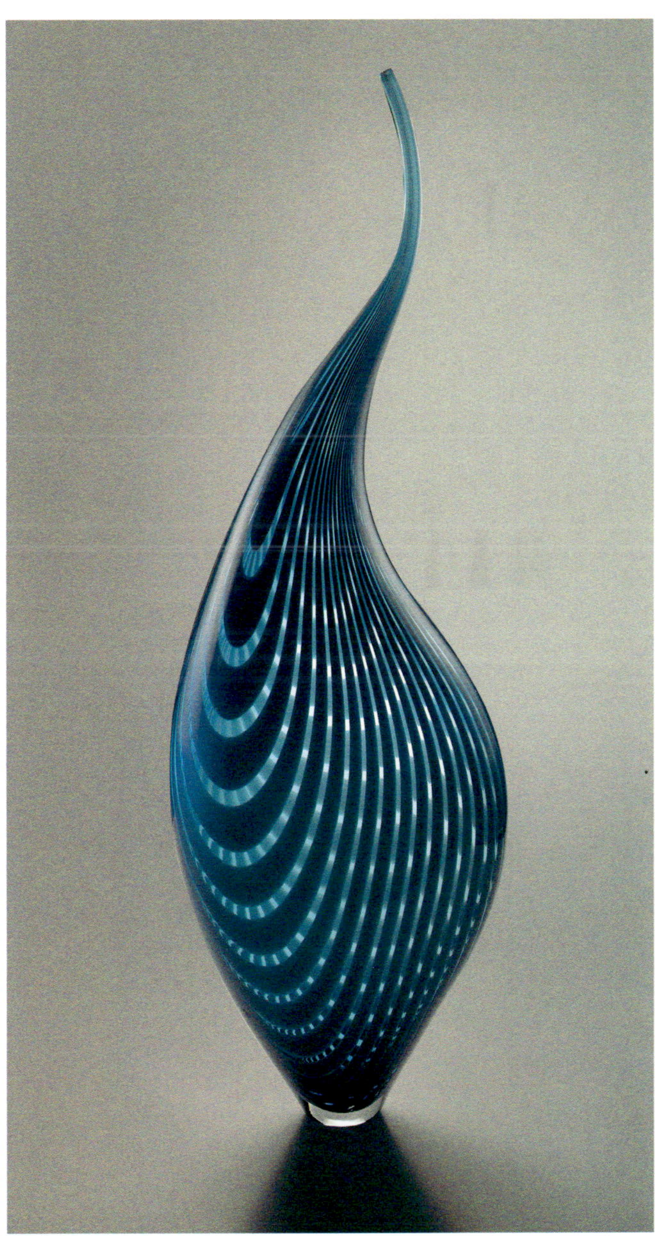

Lino Tagliapietra's *Dinosaur* series created in 1997 measures only 20" high. Work from this series grew in scale, some pieces reaching nearly 70" in height. Courtesy of Daniel Fox/ Lumina Studio.

In the Czech Republic, Jaroslava Brychtova and Professor Stanislav Libensky had an international influence. Breaking boundaries both technically and through subtle political statements, they influenced the world with their teaching and through their sculpture. They are considered by many to be the most important duo in the history of studio glass. Their work may be rugged or geometrical, yet they control both space and volume by utilizing the density of glass. Throughout their life, their collaborations often discretely documented the harshness of living in a country controlled by communism. One of their many successful students is artist Vladimira Klumpar, who blends the rigid structure of industry with organic shapes. Stanislav Libensky and Jaroslava Brychtova permit the viewer to peer into a hole or an open slice and experience a sense of hope. Vladimira internally folds the material as if one should be looking within rather than through. Much like Anish Kapoor's sculpture in Edinburgh titled *Suck*, it's a hole to the unknown where the viewer may explore and look within to stretch the imagination to what might be in, through, or beyond.

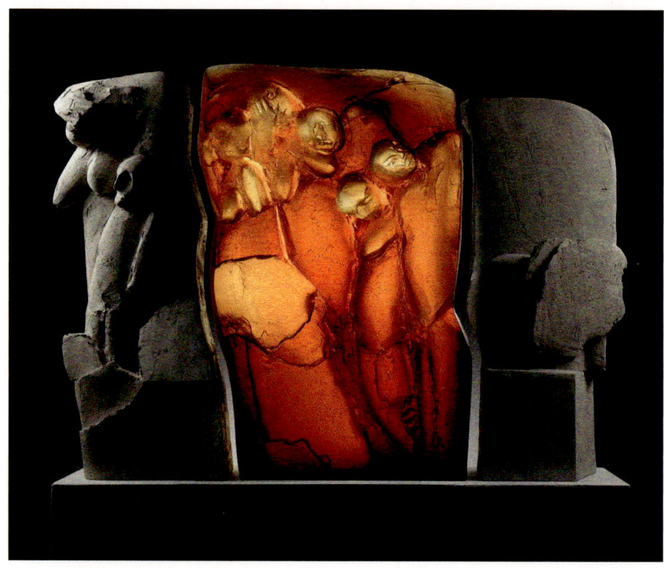

Ann Wolff completed this cast glass and poured concrete sculpture entitled *Notes* in 2014 at 77 years old. The sculpture measures 35.5" × 45.5" and is comprised of three separate elements. Courtesy of Daniel Fox/Lumina Studio.

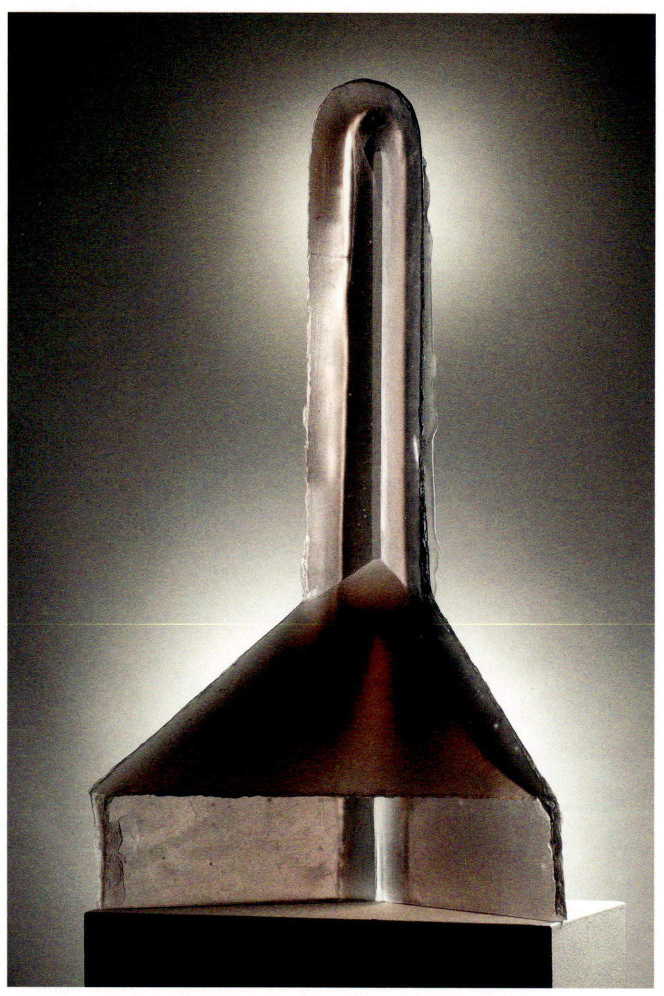

Stanislav Libensky and Jaroslava Brychtova's *Empty Throne II* was created in 1989 and measures 39.5" × 24.5" × 9.5". This piece depicts an empty throne, which is what essentially happened during the Velvet Revolution in the former Czechoslovakia. Courtesy of Douglas Schaible Photography.

In the late 1970s, a young Rhode Island School of Design student decided to leave his life behind in search of the living Libensky legends. He scraped up enough money to get a plane ticket from New York to France. He met up with a colleague, Dan Dailey, who was working with a well-known production company in France, Daum Crystal. The starving artist traveled to visit Erwin Eisch in Germany, who lent him the money to make his way to Novy Bor in the Czech Republic. Stanislav Libensky and Jaroslava Brychtova opened their home and their school to this young student. When the artist came back to the United States, he looked at the world differently. He started to cast work using carbon to imprint the interior, which successfully made a dialogue between the interior and exterior of his industrial-looking cast glass objects. He realized there are few limits to what one can accomplish with this material. On the facing page is an image of Howard Ben Tre's installations (thirty-two separate sculptures) erected throughout the city core of Warrington, England.

In the mid 1990s, Ann Wolff, a former designer for the Kosta Boda glass factory and well known for her richly engraved blown glass vessels, met with Professor Libensky. According to her, the professor convinced her to translate her ideas into cast glass. Early cast work by Ann Wolff somewhat resembles Stanislav Libensky and Jaroslava Brychtova's older work (*Head 1*). Nearly twenty years later at the age of seventy-eight, she is creating the most powerful work of her career. Ann reflects, "Living in Småland, Sweden, which is a rural community, the people are more or less: what you see is what you get." Berlin, where Ann has her studio, is a cosmopolitan melting pot of all types of people from around the world. Her latest body of work concerns the people in Berlin and the façades people wear to mask their identity. Living in Berlin, as in all large urban areas, people build layers for protection and only by continued interaction will they let down their guard to reveal themselves.

A young artist in his early thirties has emerged from the Czech Republic closely following his predecessors with similar uncertainty, angst, and pure love for glass. In 2010, during an annual trade show for glass artists hosted by the Glass Art Society, we stumbled upon a studio that sounded more like a rock concert. This studio hosted hundreds of glassblowers, many of whom were standing on chairs screaming with excitement. We made our way to the front of the crowd, and there was a tall young glassblower working with what appeared to be a molten glass head on the end of his blowpipe. I asked one of the screaming glassblowers, "What is so exciting?" The glassblower enthusiastically replied, "The dude is going into the inside of the head and sculpting the face from within!" We realized then that any glassblower who excited hundreds of glassblowers must be worth looking into. Martin Janecky spends his time between Fairbanks, Alaska, and the Czech Republic. He sculpts his work from the inside out. At first glance, one would think he uses a mold, but his faces are all done "free hand," patiently carved from the inside while hot.

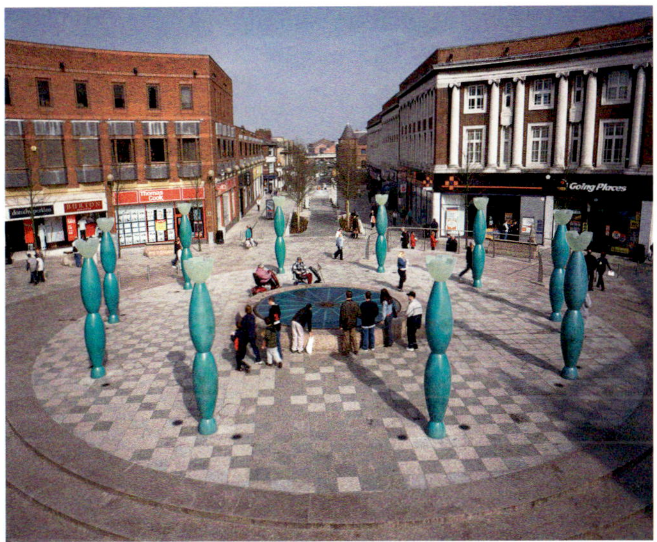

Well of Light, Marketgate. Commission in Warrington Town Centre, Warrington, England, 2002. This installation developed the city core of the city and consists of 32 sculptures created by Howard Ben Tré.

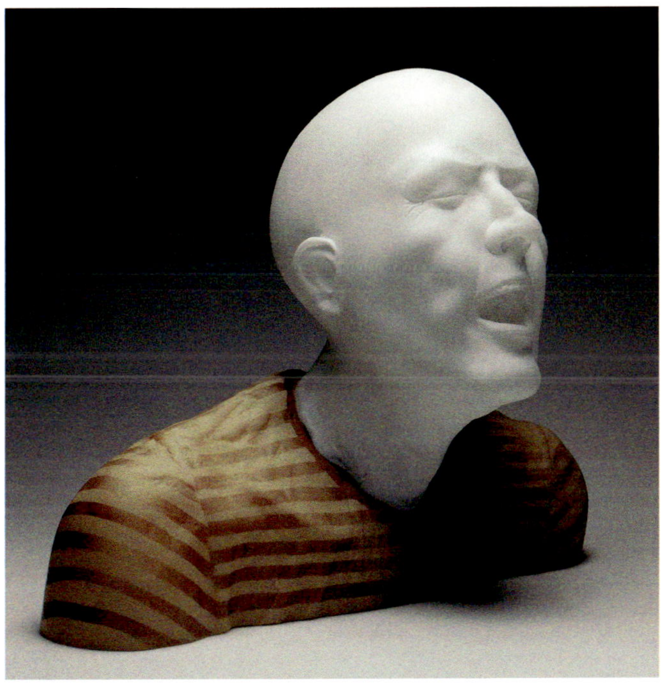

Martin Janecky's *Thom* created in 2014 measures 20" high. The entire bust was created on the end of a blow pipe, and the head was carved hot from inside out. Courtesy of Martin Janecky.

Today, the use of other materials has become prevalent in studio glass. Cristina Bothwell uses ceramic, cement, wood, paint, and found objects mixed in with her pate de verre cast elements to convey her message. Each piece tells a story whether it's a soul rising out to reflect on life or a mother and daughter's unconditional bond. Tim Tate, who is cofounder of the Washington School of Glass, uses cast glass frames to display his looped videos, blurring the definition of studio glass as the glass itself has a function yet the content of the video is narrative. Vivian Wang, a sculptor originally born in China who worked as a fashion designer in New York and as a ceramicist, recently started exploring the use of glass in her artwork. She uses cast glass heads, hands, and feet with heavily detailed and decorated garments to depict children from early Japanese and Chinese dynasties. Each has a story that is told through a subtle expression and magnificently decorated garment.

Artists throughout the world who chose to explore glass over the last fifty years have created some of the most spectacular objects on earth. Whether glass's beauty comes from color, form, or concept, we are utterly and completely seduced by its attributes. Through archeology, glass has helped us discover where we came from and today, through the exploration of expression in art, it will help us identify who we are.

Corey Hampson is currently president and owner of Habatat Galleries, Inc. He has written and published numerous articles about studio glass and curated dozens of museum and art center exhibitions throughout the United States. He hosts the largest and oldest annual studio glass exhibition in the world, the Habatat Galleries International Glass Invitational. Hampson works very closely developing collections for private collectors, museums, and organizations around the world. He currently serves on the National Advisory Board of Directors for the AACG (Art Alliance for Contemporary Glass) and is also the president of the MGCA (Michigan Glass Collecting Alliance).

Christian Arnold & Laurie Young

Melbourne, Victoria, Australia

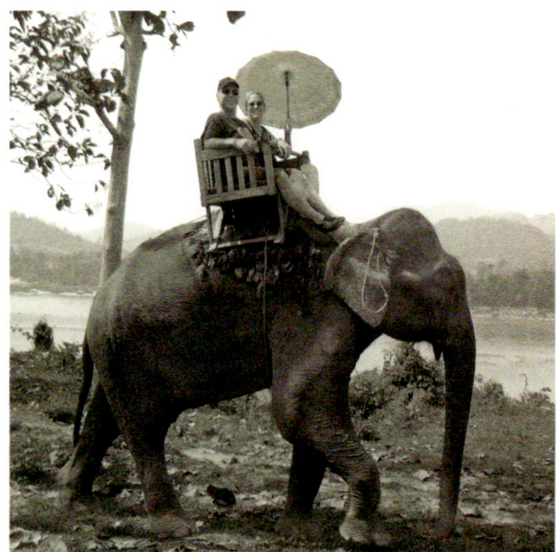

Courtesy of Reza Keikha.

1

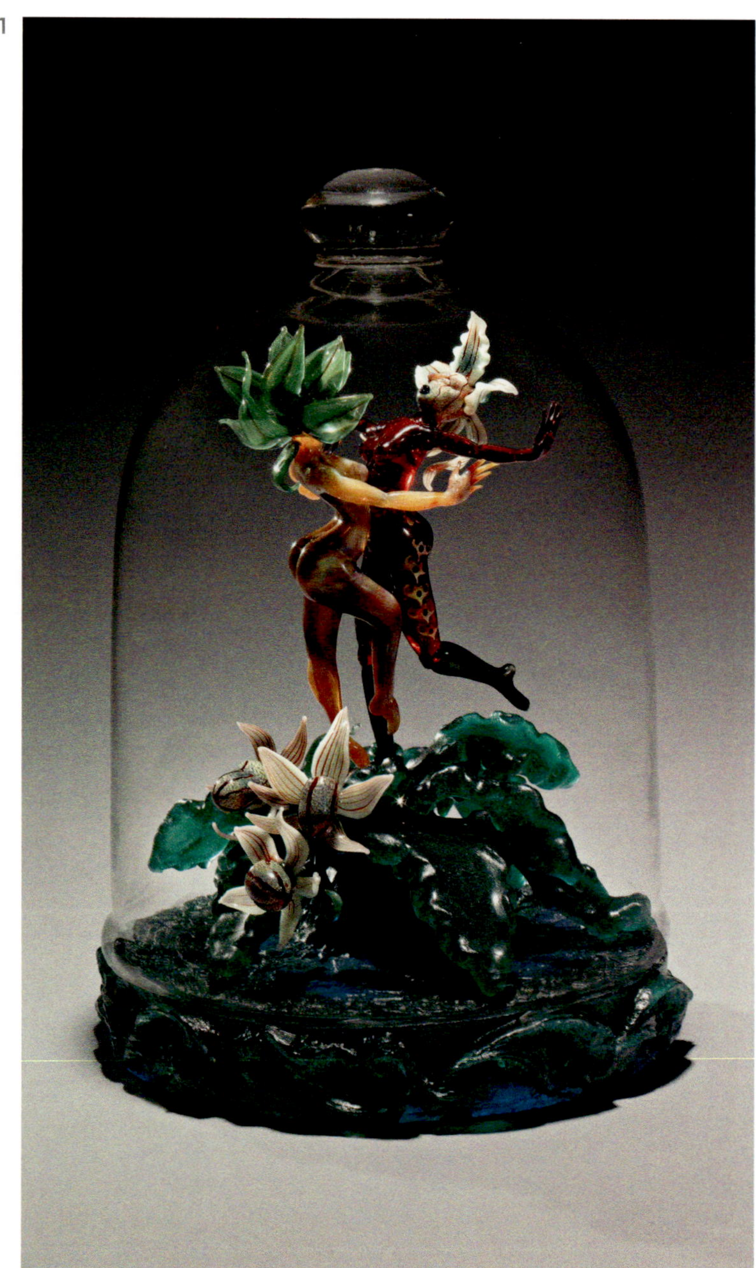

We are university-trained glass artists, engaging mainly in lampwork, cire perdue casting, and pate de verre; we also include furnace work and various other kiln-forming techniques in our repertoire. After we met in 2005, we began working together in a shared studio.

Christian is a flameworking artist. After spending years apprenticed to his father learning the exacting discipline of scientific glass blowing, he eventually broke free to explore his creative side. Earning a masters degree in glass at RMIT University, he quickly carved a niche for himself within the rarefied world of master flameworkers. Laurie has been working with glass for many years, transitioning from flat (stained) glass work, to fusing, to casting, to the torch. After she graduated with honors from the Monash University glass department, she and Chris formed Nudibranch Art Glass.

We draw a lot of inspiration for our work from the world around us, especially the sea (we are keen scuba divers) and from ancient mythology and tribal stories. Laurie's aesthetic is wild and unfettered; Chris comes from the restraint of scientific glass instrument making. Together, we find a middle ground where the joy of creation occurs.

2

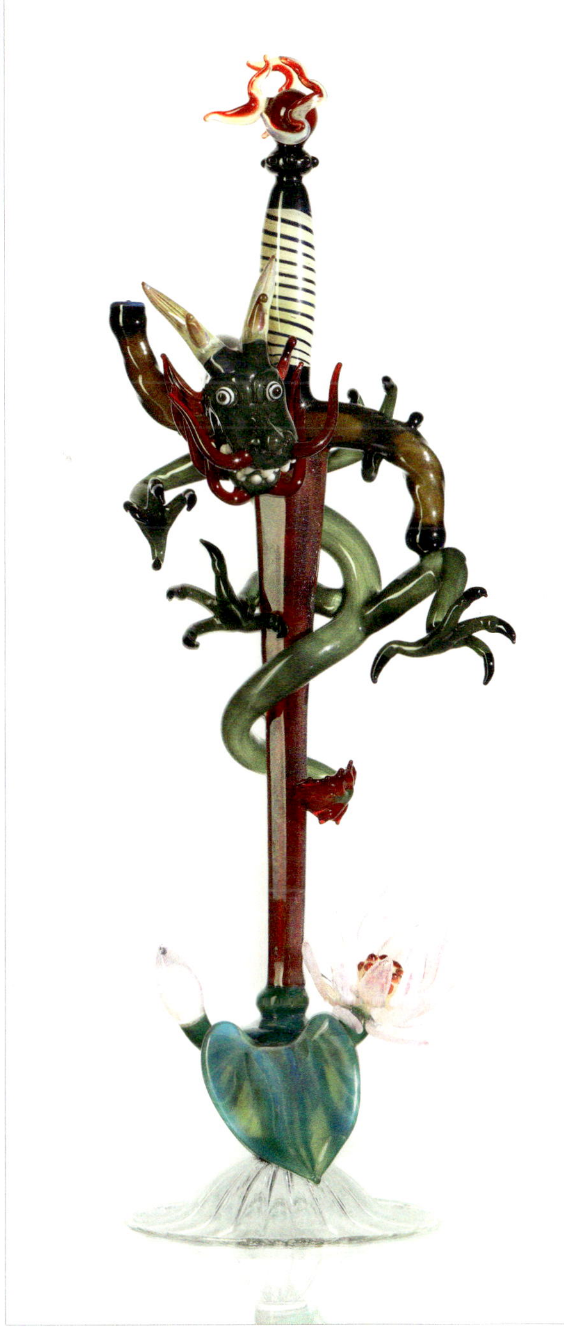

3

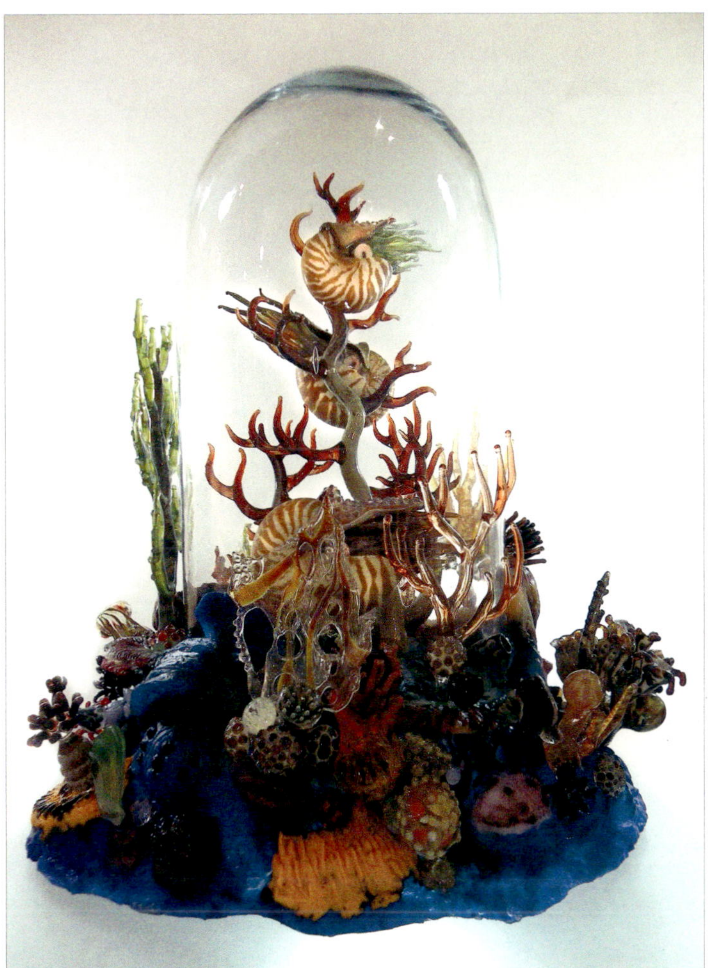

4

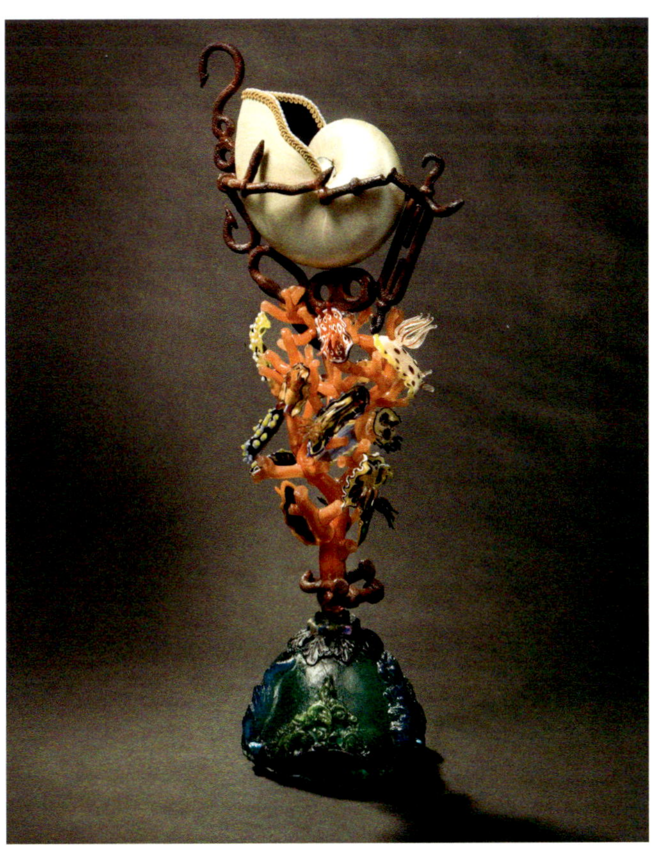

1 *Belladonna and the Mandragora.* Lampwork and lost wax casting. 13.78" × 9.84". 2009. Courtesy of Reza Keikha.

2 *Dragon Tattoo.* Lampwork. 13" × 5.9". 2010. Courtesy of Screaming Pixel.

3 *Nautilus.* Lampwork, lost wax cast and pate de verre. 19.68" × 17.72". 2011. Courtesy of Reza Keikha.

4 *Venus Rising.* Lampwork and lost wax casting. 24.01" × 11.02" × 7.09". 2007. Courtesy of Screaming Pixel.

Herb Babcock

Oxford, Michigan

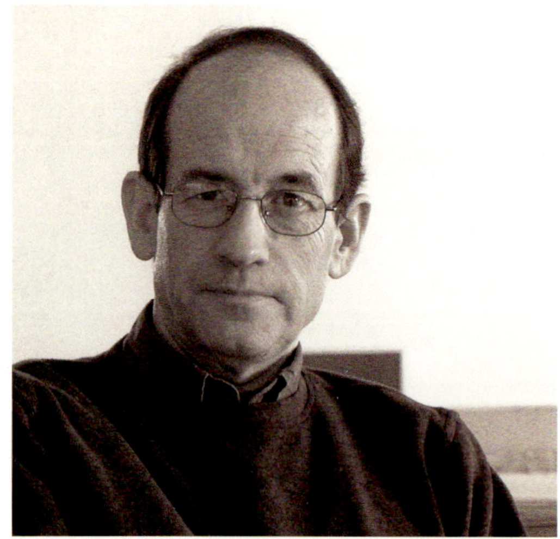

As a sculptor, I know how to forge steel and carve stone. With hot glass, I also use fire to make art. With molten glass, the artist needs a few simple tools along with gravity and viscosity, skill, and unflinching attention. Blown glass is fluid glass; it requires the artist to be agile and precise when handling it. The rewards are immediate results.

This quick gratification originally allowed me to use glass as a distraction from my sculpture. In contrast to the laborious, traditional sculpture process, glass was so seductive and so fast. Over time I saw much more potential for glass in my sculpture. I rarely do any blowing now, but I fabricate glass in many other ways. For a time, I made a series of sculptures using multiple blown glass blocks with steel structures to achieve large-scale work. Eventually, large work was possible when I began to mold bigger, solid castings fabricated with metal.

My current work is the *Pillared* series, which denotes precarious balance and equilibrium. It combines glass, metal, and stone. Glass in sculpture can give light with radiance and color or, with transparency, can represent a visual passage through mass. In *Pillared,* I use metaphor to say, "Pause, turn and reflect on life." The apex of a dance movement is apparent in the sculptural form.

1

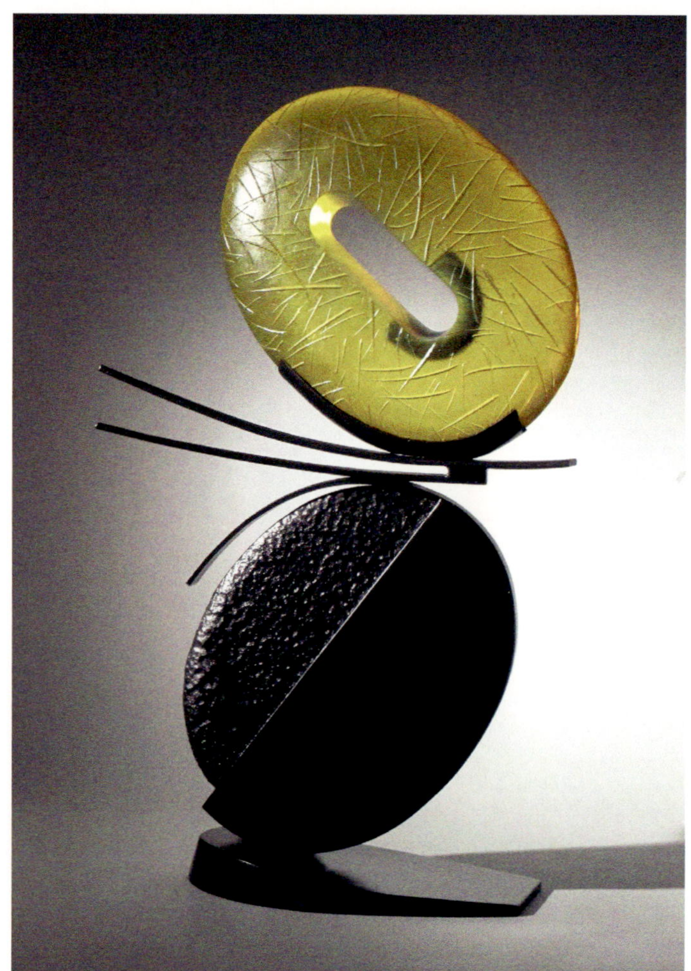

2

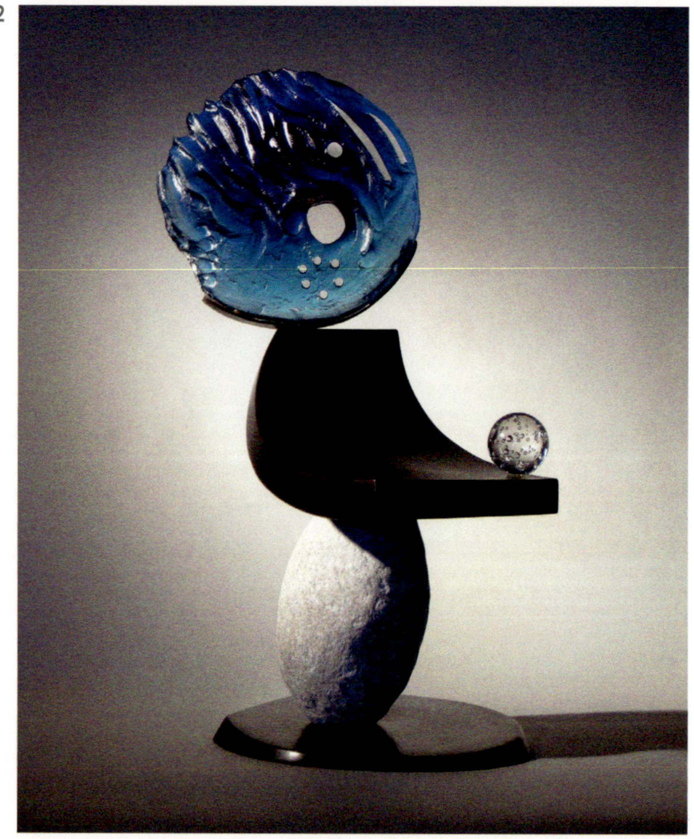

1 *Traveler.* Cast glass and steel.
37.5" × 28" × 17". 2014.

2 *Of Space in Time.* Cast glass and bronze.
34" × 23" × 15". 2013.

3

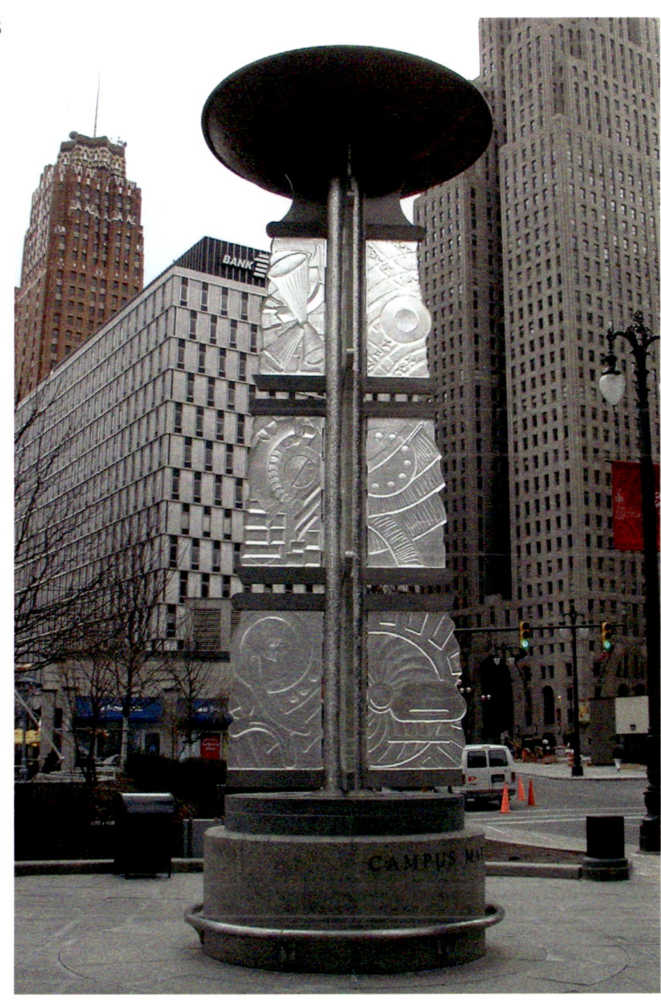

5

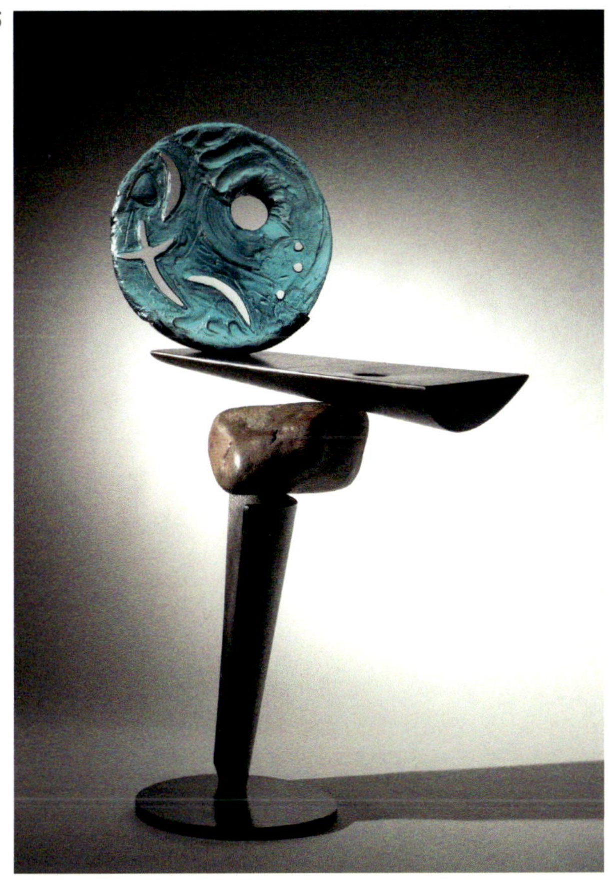

4

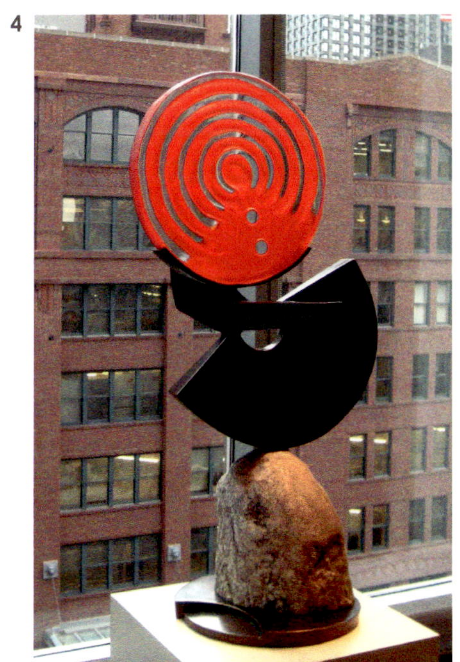

6

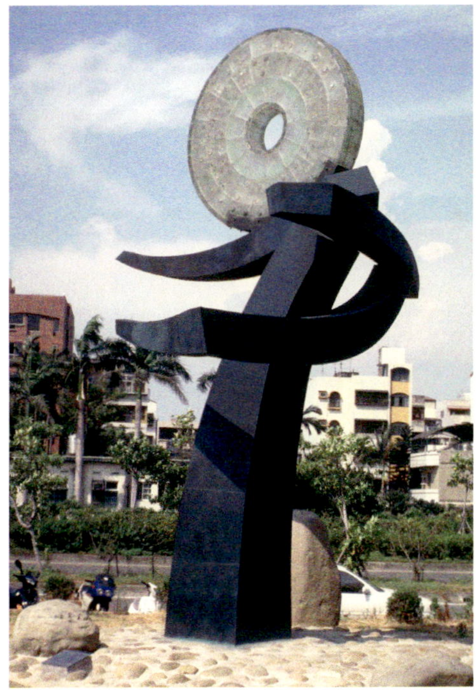

3 *Woodward Marker Tower*. Glass by Babcock. Cast glass, steel, stone, lights, and fire. 22'. Campus Martius, Detroit, Michigan.

4 *Kirkland Pillared*. Cast glass, bronze, and fieldstone. 40" × 22" × 19". 2009.

5 *Cool High Plane*. Cast glass, steel, and fieldstone. 46.5" × 26" × 19". 2013. Kirkland & Ellis LLP, Chicago, Illinois.

6 *Young Bamboo in Wind*. Cast glass, steel, stone, and fiber optics. 22.5'. Hsinchu Culture Center, Hsinchu, Taiwan.

Rhonda Baer

Bethesda, Maryland

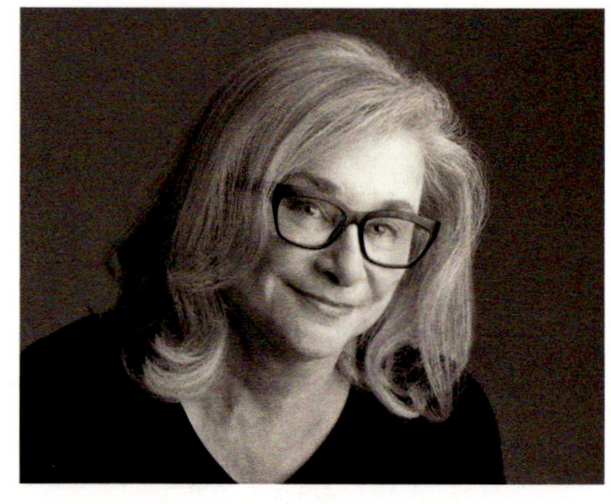

Photo: Harry Pfohl.

Inspired by the Northern Lights phenomenon, I use simple shapes and vibrant shifting tones to create sculptures that explore the interaction of light, movement, color, and form. There is a certain mystery to my optical glass pieces. When you walk around them, the colors diffuse, reflect, and combine to form new colors—or disappear entirely.

1

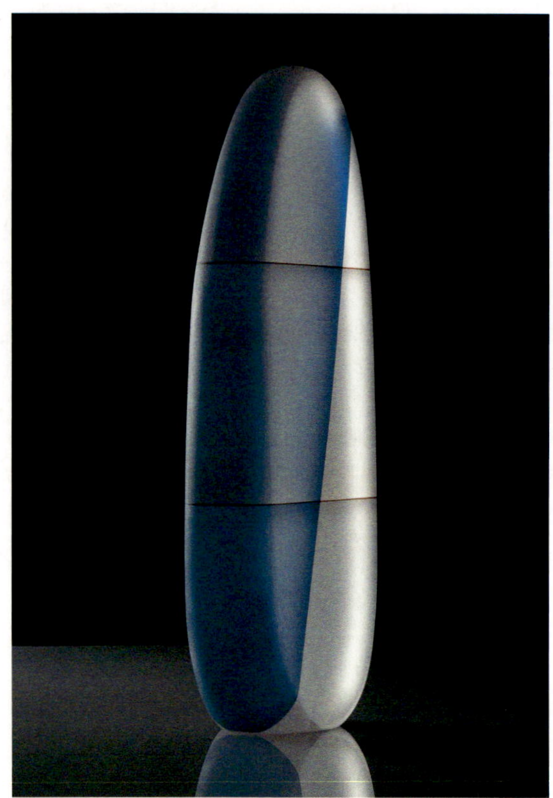

2

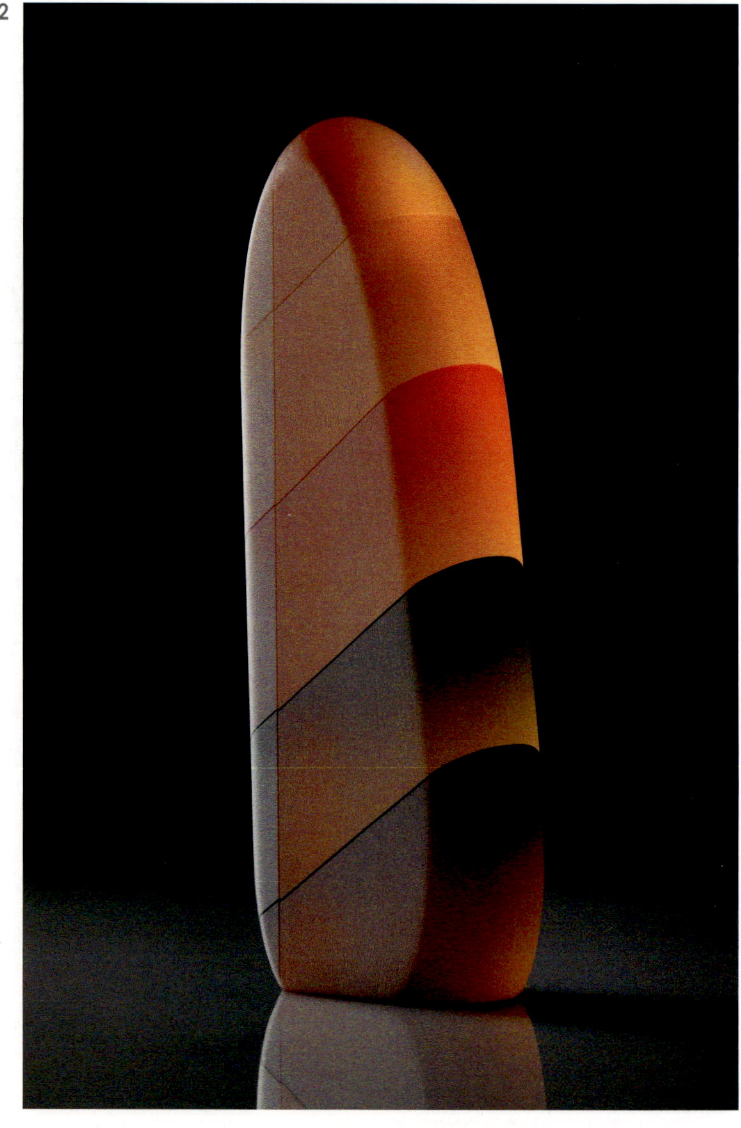

1 *Euclid Alone*. Color laminated and cold worked optical glass. 10" × 1.75" × 4". 2010.

2 *Turning Leaves*. Color laminated and cold worked optical glass. 9" × 1.5" × 3.5". 2011.

3 *Untitled No. 488*. Color laminated and cold worked optical glass. 15.5" × 5.125" × 10.25". 2014.

4 *Untitled No. 494*. Color laminated and cold worked optical glass. 12.75" × 3.25" × 5". 2013.

5 *Untitled No. 486*. Color laminated and cold worked optical glass. 12.5" × 3.75" × 4". 2013.

6 *Untitled No. 496*. Color laminated and cold worked optical glass. 11" × 2" × 5". 2013.

3

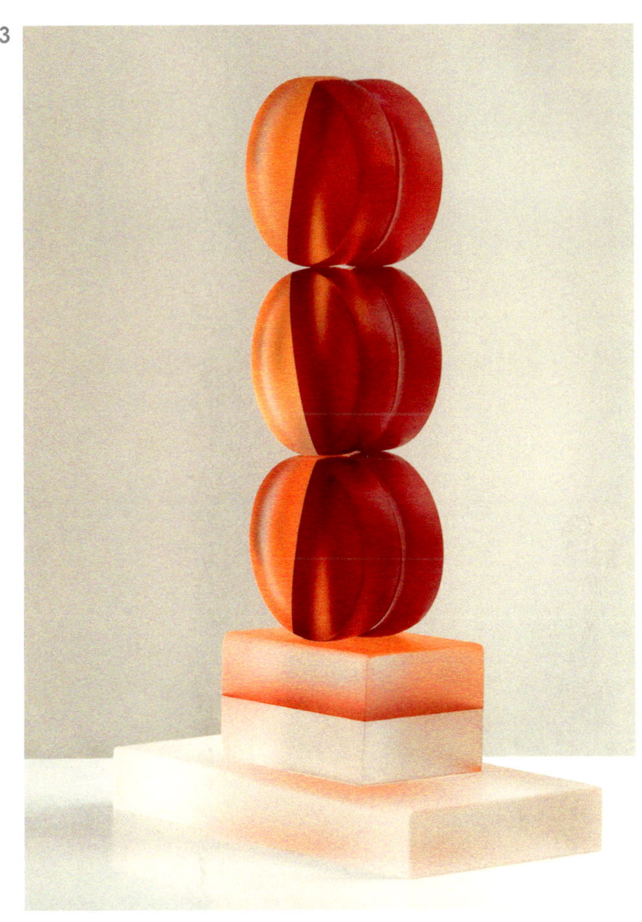

5

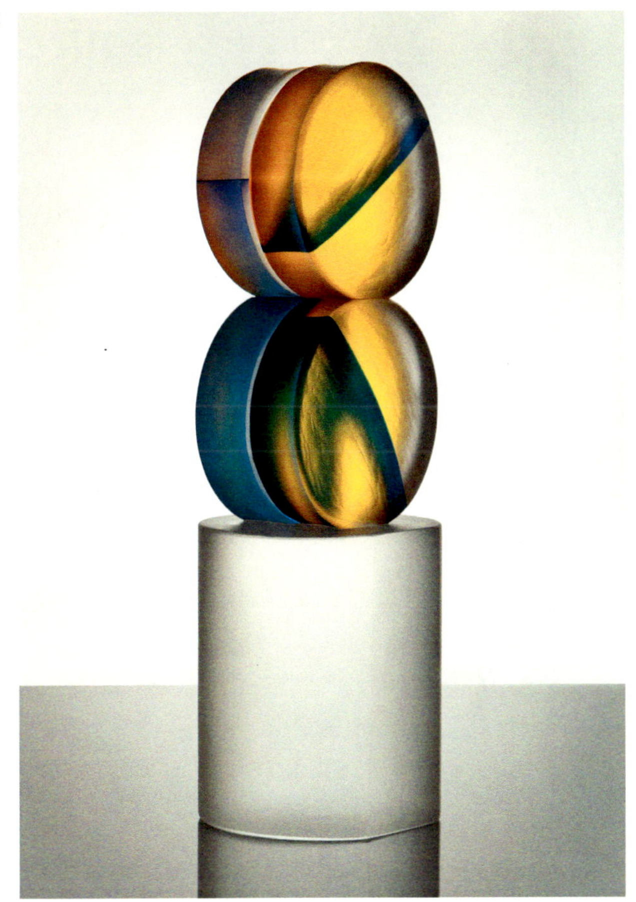

4

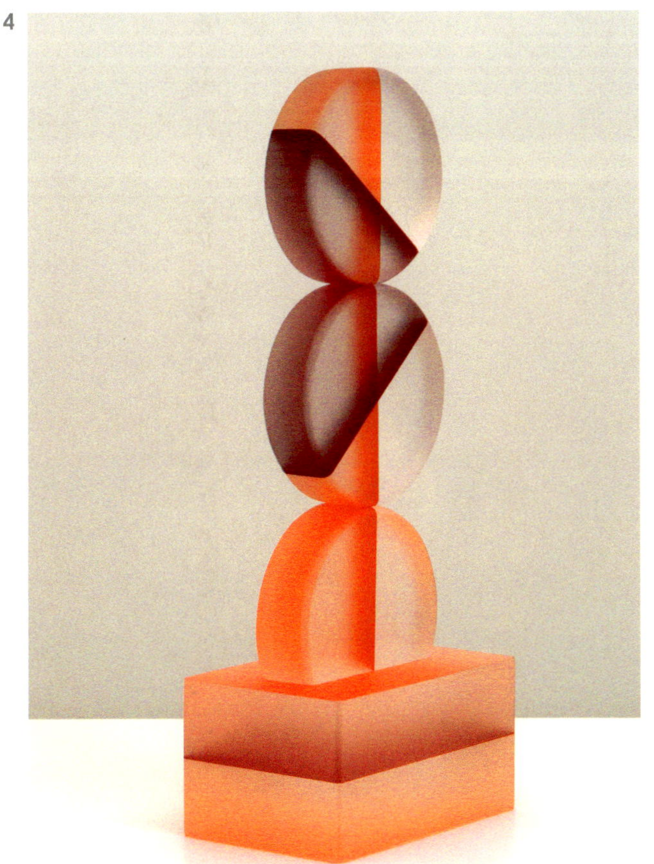

6

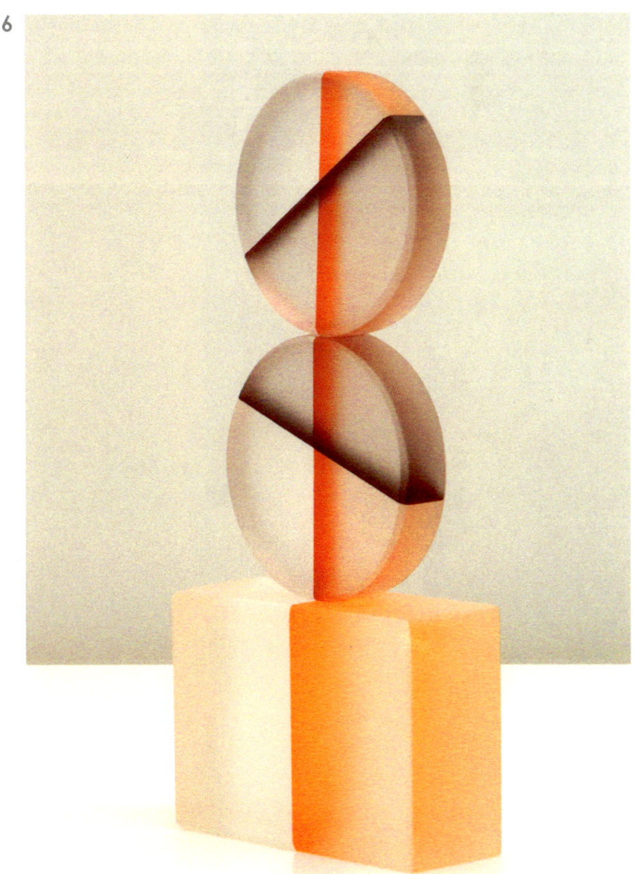

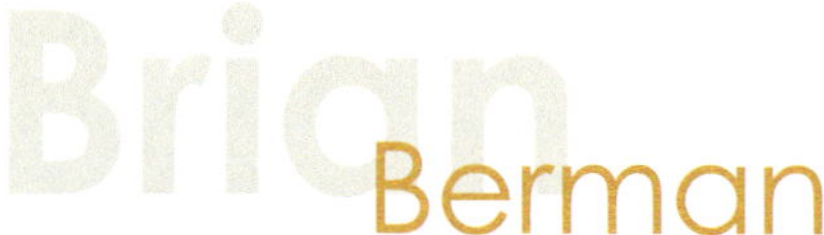

Brian Berman

Ojai, California

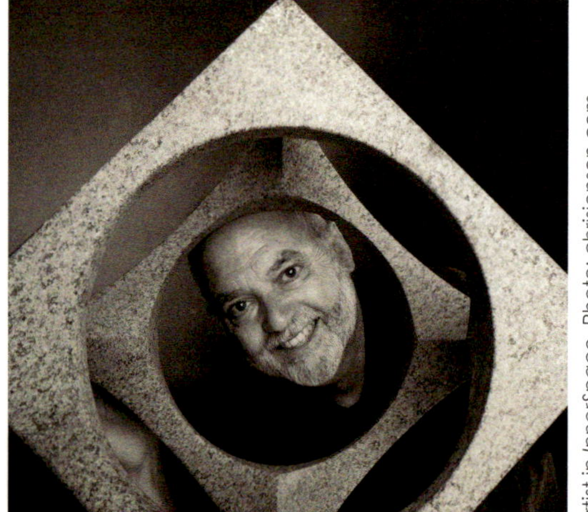

Artist in *InnerSpace*. Photo: chrisjensen.com.

I create timeless sculptures, bringing to the viewer the importance of stillness, serenity, and presence. They instill a calm peaceful sacred space, an environment most valuable in these hurried times. I call my work Art for Peace.

I work with the medium of kiln-cast glass as it reveals a fourth dimension. This inner dimension is metaphorical, for what I love about people is what's on the inside and is most important. As an Artist for Peace and an educator, I teach that peace is an inside job. Cast glass helps me point to the importance of our inner dimension. It is my intention that each sculpture brings healing and renewal to the times we live in as well as a peace message to future generations. May we live peacefully in the knowing of our one shared human family.

1

2

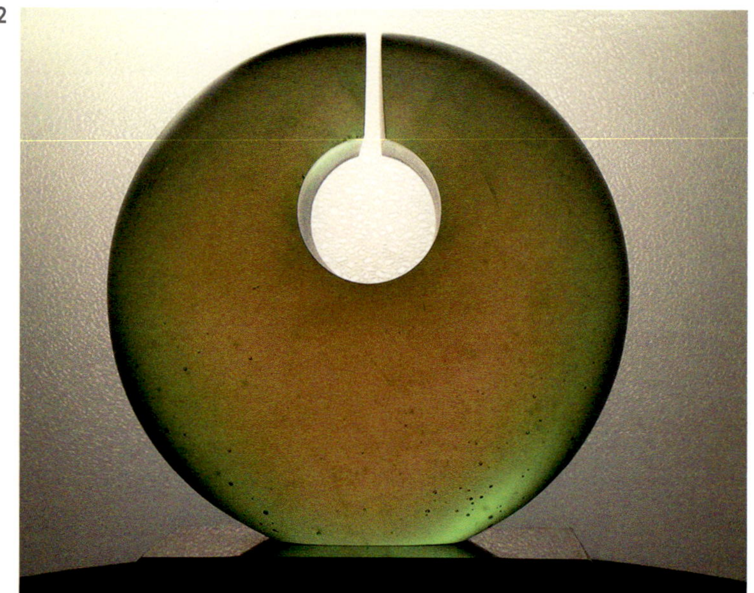

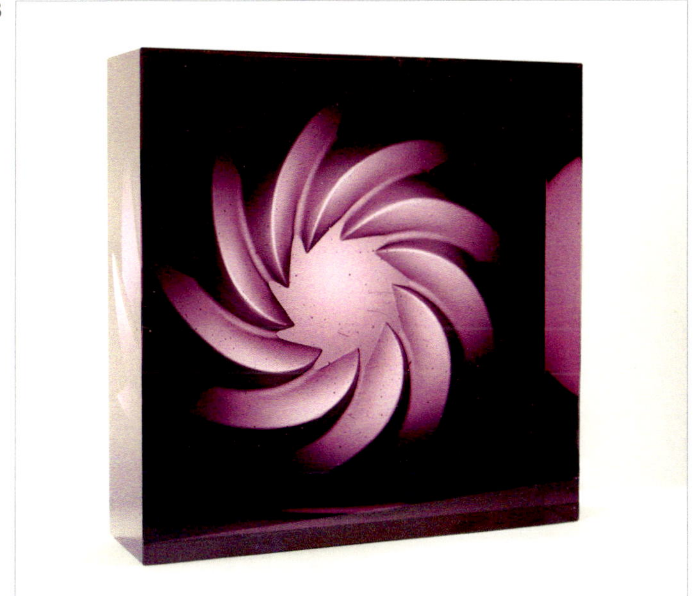

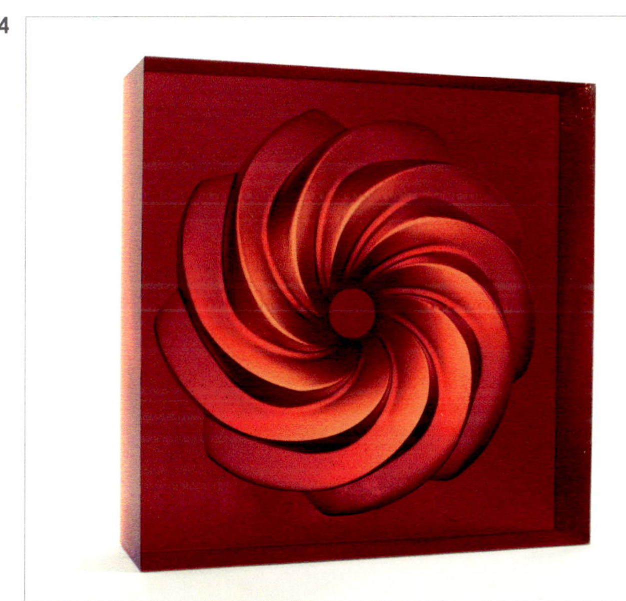

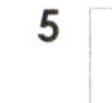

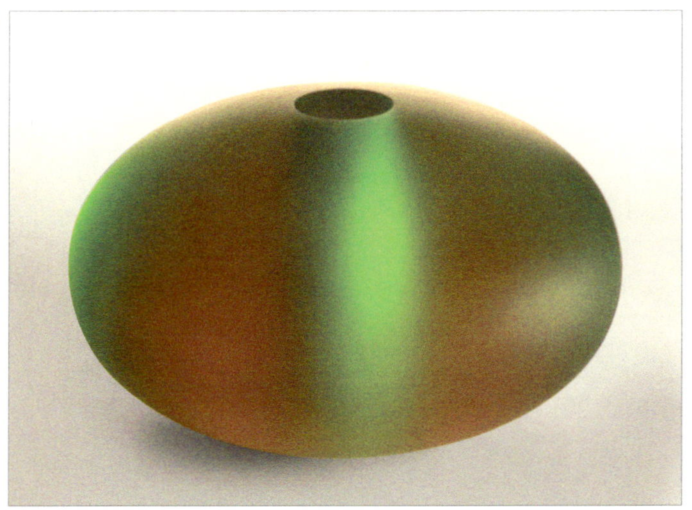

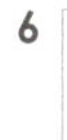

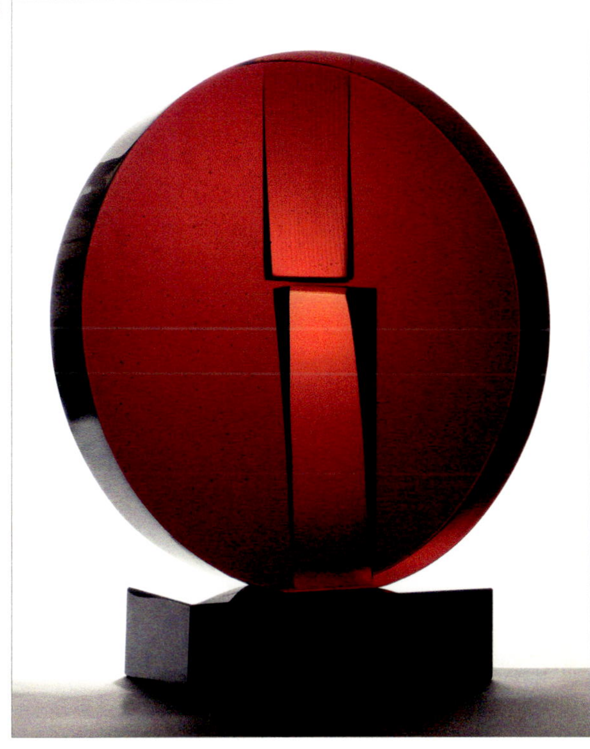

1 *Gateway III*. Kiln cast glass.
17" × 3.5" × 12.5". 2010.

2 *Genesis Glass*. Kiln cast glass.
12" × 6" × 12". 2008.

3 *HOLOS Spiral Portal II*. Kiln cast glass.
12" × 3.25" × 3.25". 2014.

4 *HOLOS Spiral Portal*. Kiln cast glass.
14" × 4" × 14". 2014.

5 *Manna V*. Kiln cast glass.
13" × 7" × 13". 2012.

6 *Light Fall II*. Kiln cast glass/granite.
22" × 6" × 19". 2009.

Tina Betz

Clayville, New York

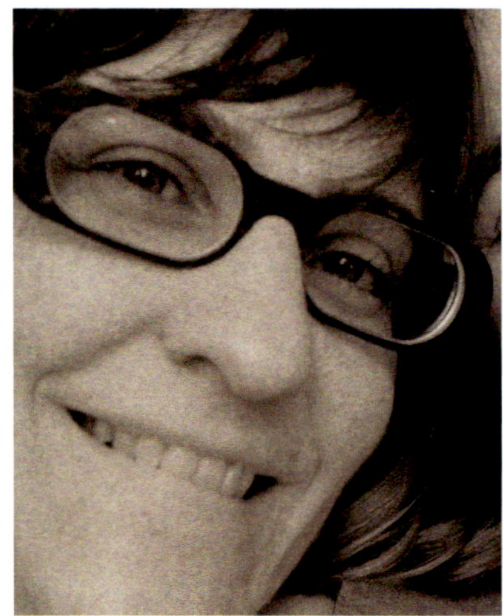

I developed this intricate glass lace-work flameworking technique over many years. I enjoy reproducing identifiable common images to point out their sculptural qualities. I wish to create metaphorical associations using imagery that is, by appearance, fragile and precious, yet in actuality very strong. Therefore, the seemingly fragile way a sculpture is built is appropriate to the ideas behind the work.

I create these sculptures by cutting sheet glass into strips, then pulling them into strands in a flame. Some of the glass is hand-painted with glass enamels, which are fired on, allowing for a painterly and custom color palette. The strands are then fused together with a hand torch, created free form as if they were three-dimensional drawings.

1

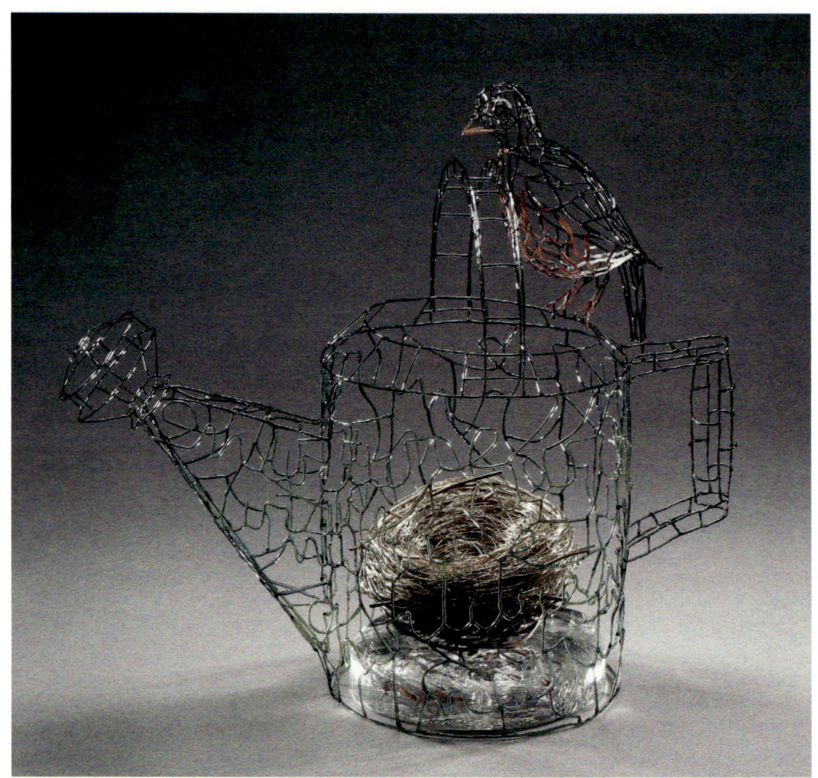

2

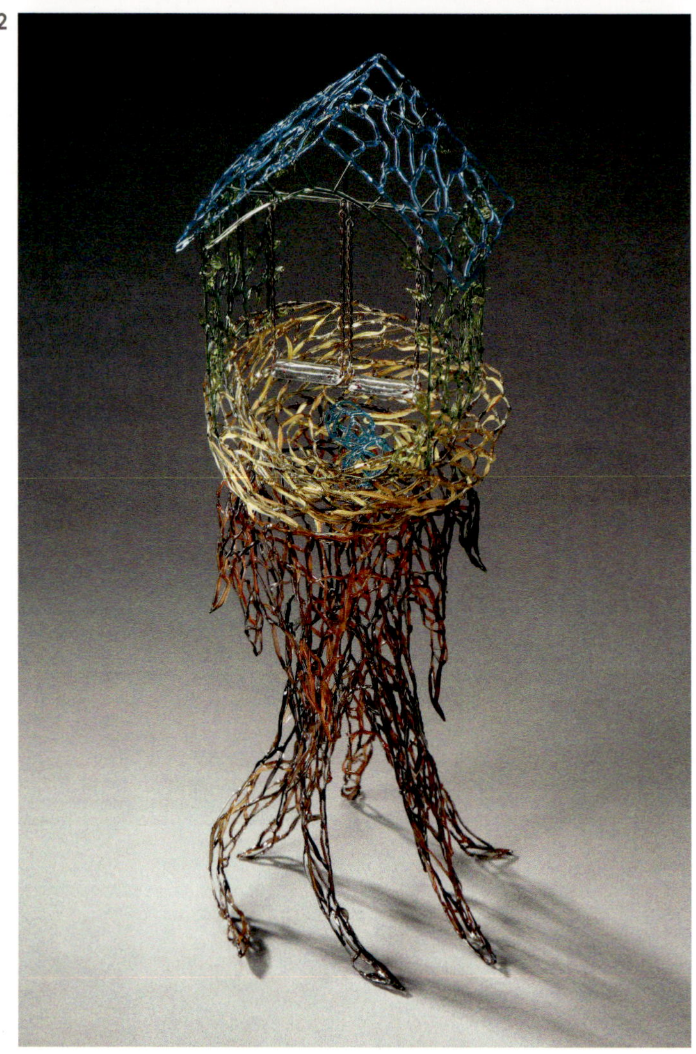

1 *Nurture*. Flameworked glass, cast glass, and brass. 11.5" × 13" × 6". 2004. Courtesy of G. R. Farley.

2 *Planting Deep Roots*. Flameworked enameled glass, fused glass, steel, and copper. 15" × 7" × 6". Courtesy of G. R. Farley.

3

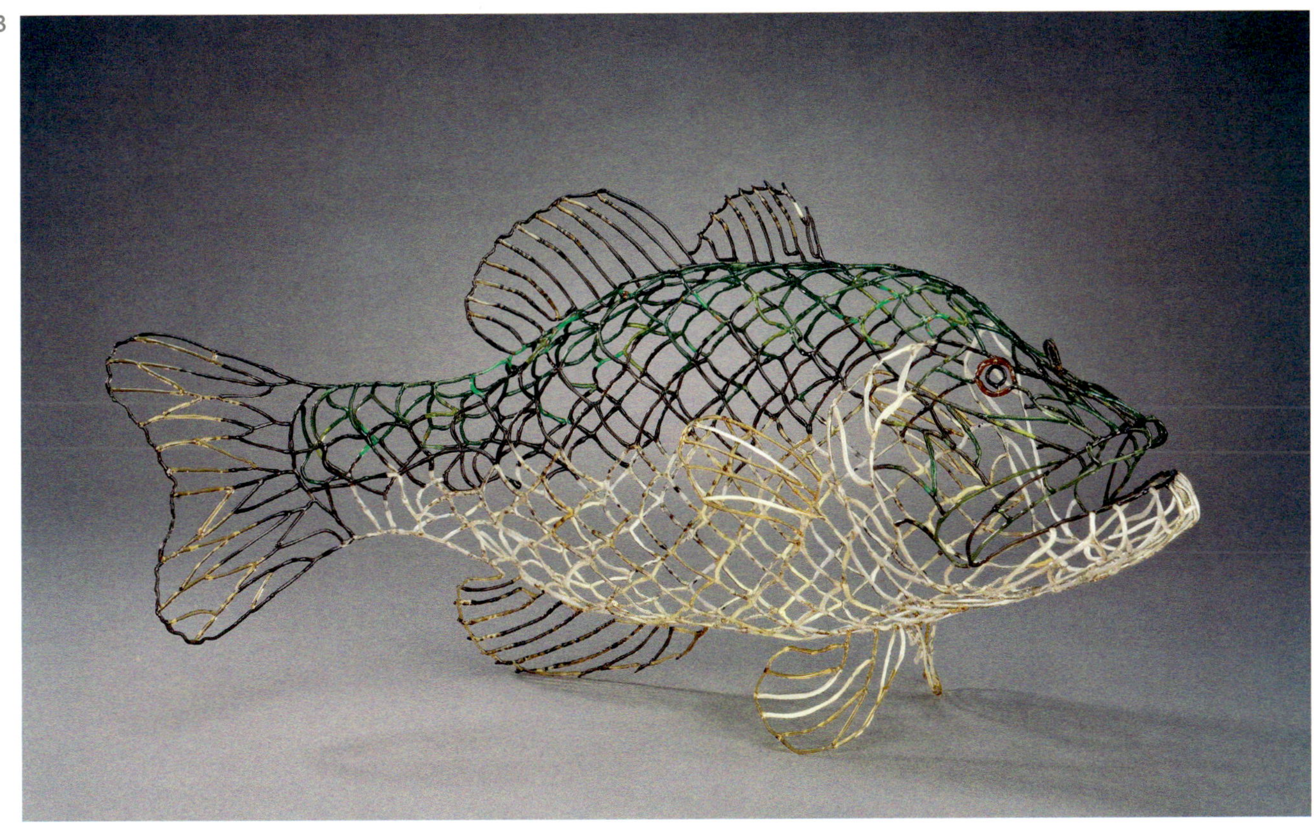

4

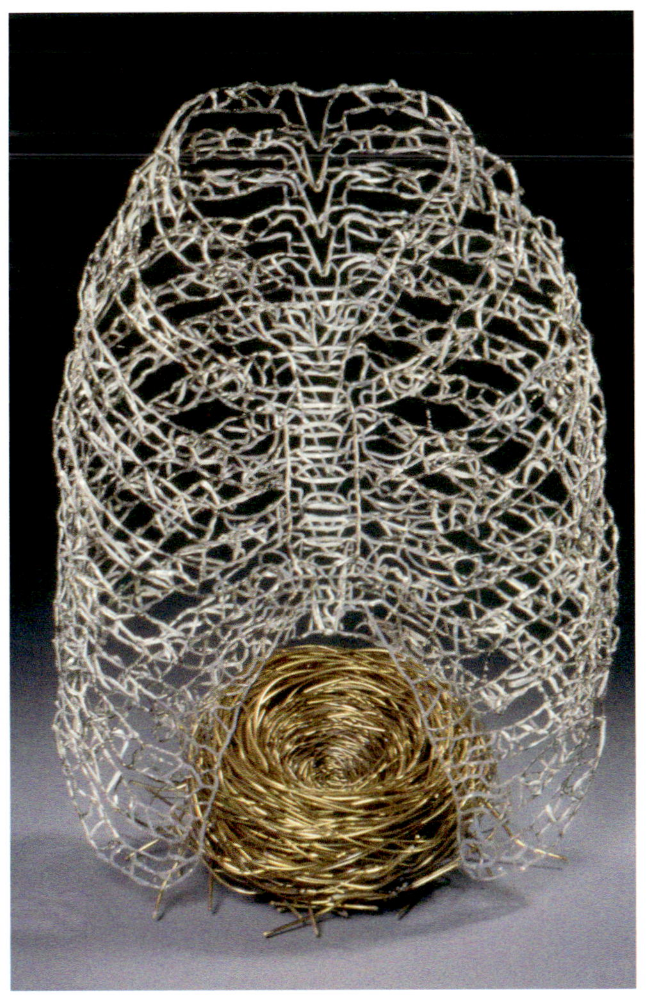

5

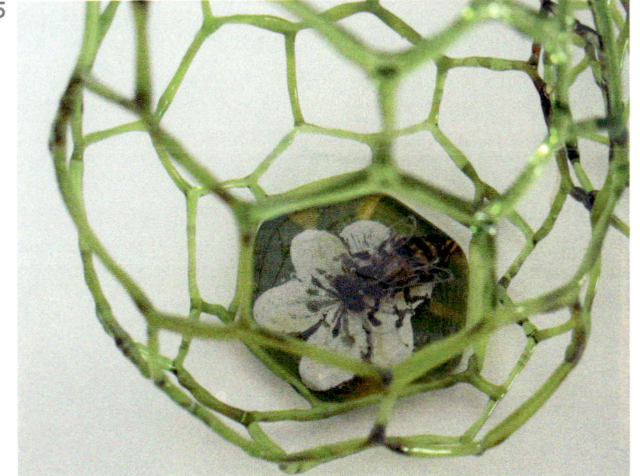

3 *Largemouth Bass (Micropterus salmoides)*. Flameworked and enameled glass. 7.5" × 15" × 7". 2014. Courtesy of G. R. Farley.

4 *Body Baskets (Home is where the heart is)*. Flameworked enameled glass and brass. 16" × 11" × 5". 2000. Courtesy of G. R. Farley.

5 Detail: *Pollinators & Bartlett Pear*. Flameworked enameled glass and fused enameled glass. 5.25" × 9" × 4.75". 2014. Courtesy of G. R. Farley.

Philippa Beveridge

Barcelona, Spain

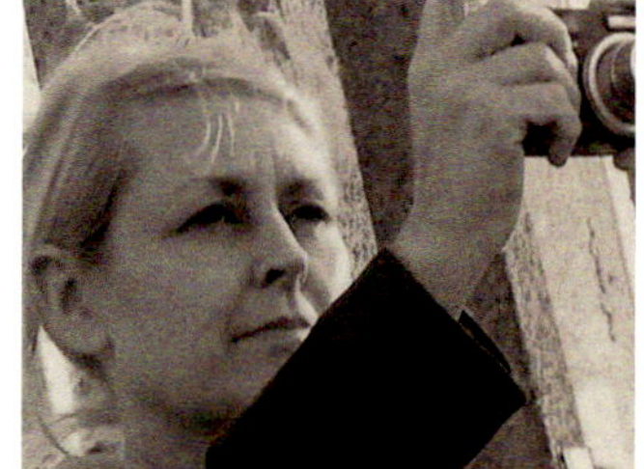

I came to glass through an unconventional route. I studied landscape architecture but was drawn to the world of glass when I moved to Barcelona to study sculpture, painting, and mosaic at the Massana School of Fine Art. In 1994 I founded my studio, La Ventana Indiscreta, where I work on architectural commissions and sculpture in glass. Coming from an architectural background, I've always placed great importance on the installation of my work and how the individual elements are placed within their surroundings.

My work is concerned with time and memory: the fleeting and transitory, absence and displacement, identity and loss. Architectural details, surface decoration, wallpapers, and the natural world are among my sources of inspiration. I draw inspiration from literature, film, and music to add further layers of meaning.

1 *In Flight*. Kiln-formed pate de verre and mixed media. 2011.

2 *The Custodian of Memory*. Kiln-formed, silvered float glass. 25" × 10" × 14". 2008.

3 *The Human Presence in the Absence of a Figure I & II*. Cast glass. 25" × 10" × 14". 2009-2010. Courtesy of Philippe Robin.

4 *Lost and Found* solo show installation shot. Kiln-formed cast glass and mixed media. 2010.

5 *Lost and Found*. Cast glass. 4" × 2" × 5". 2009. Courtesy of Paul Louis.

6 *Lost and Found*. Cast glass. 4" × 2" × 5". 2009. Courtesy of Paul Louis.

1

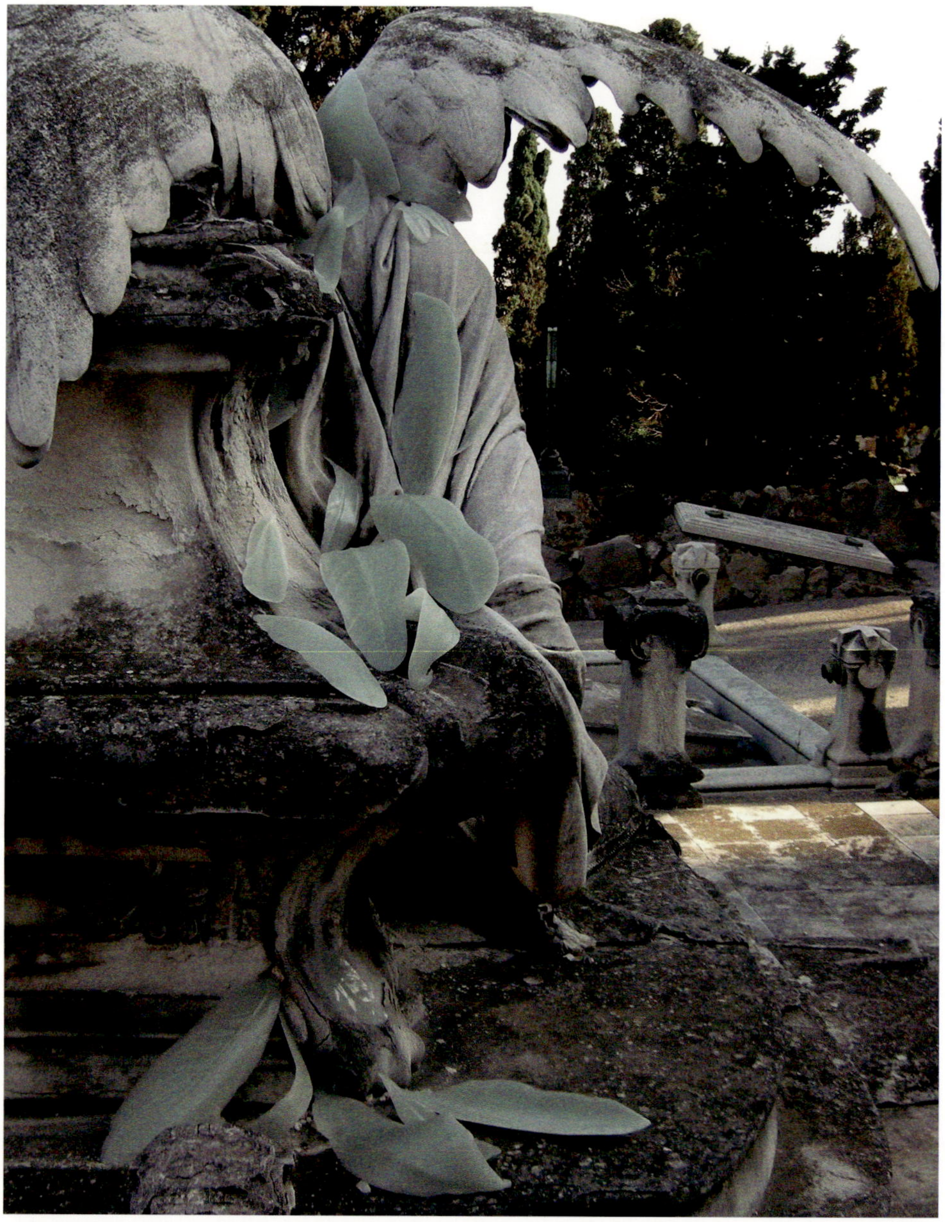

2

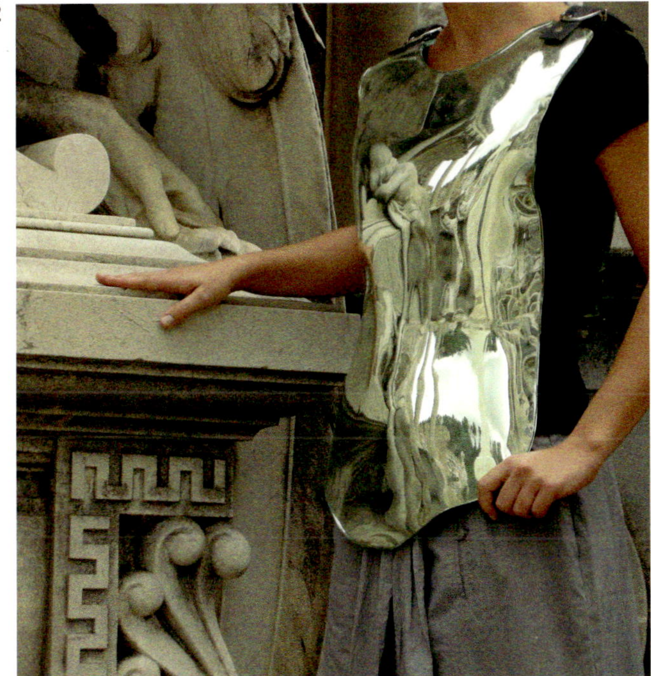

3

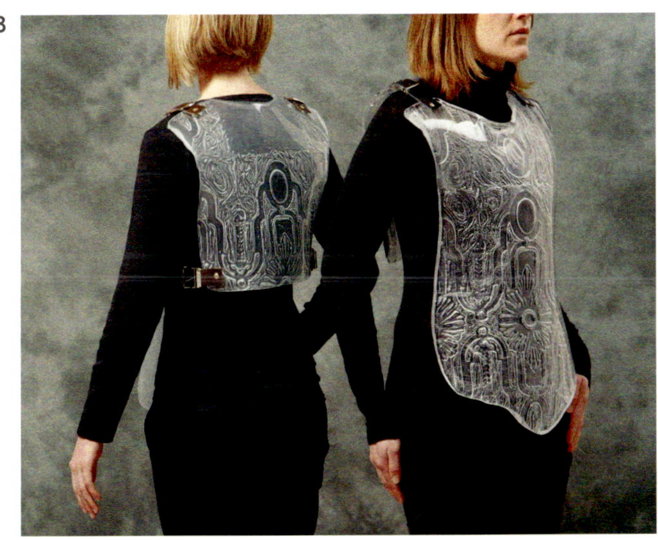

4

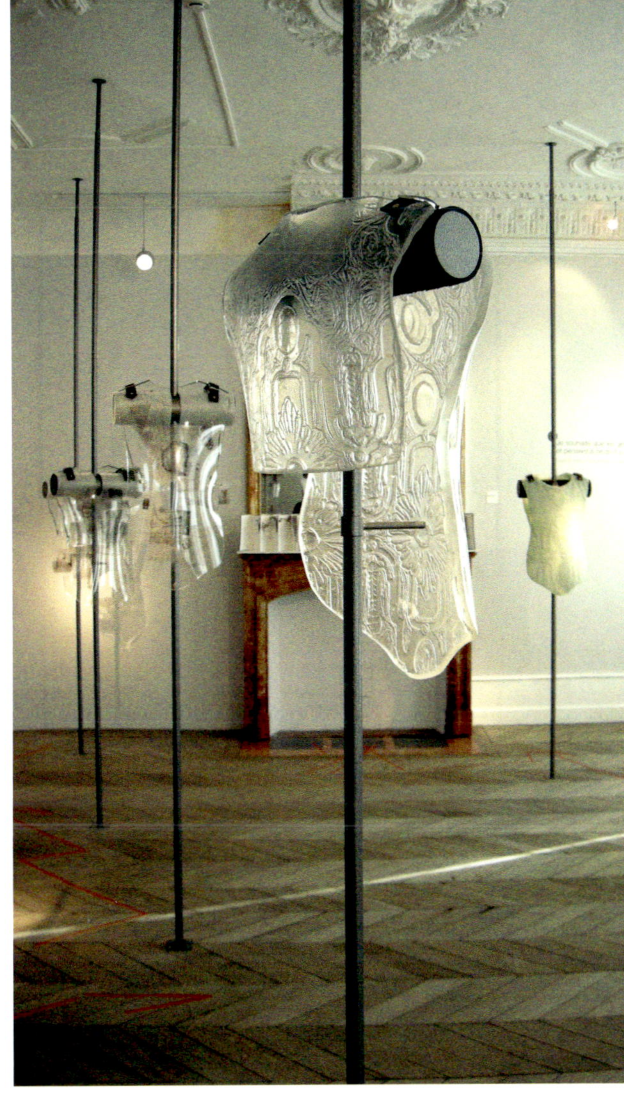

5

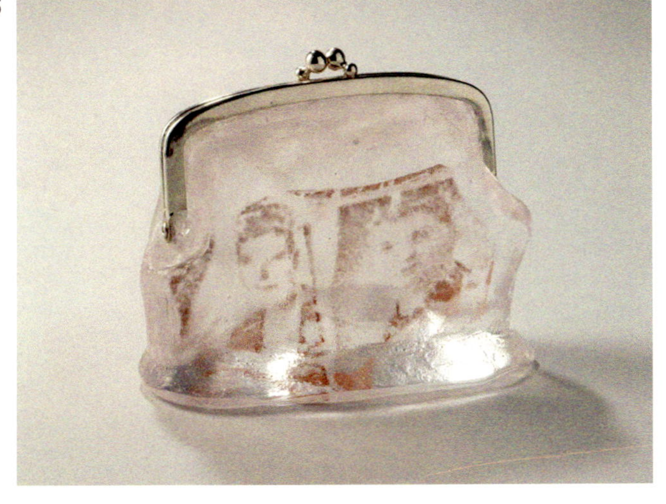

6

Lothar Böttcher

Derdepoort Park, Pretoria, South Africa

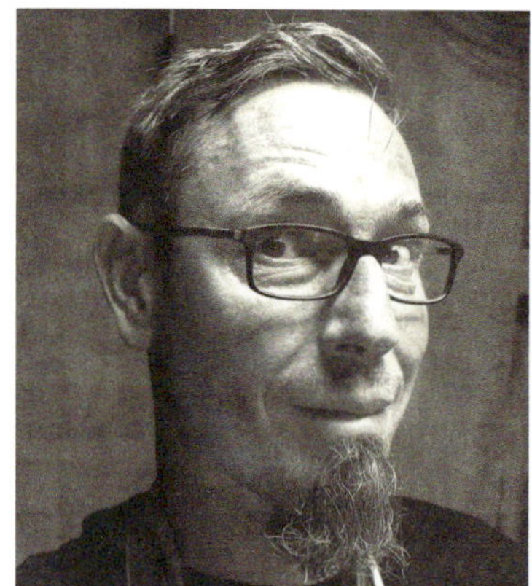

Born in 1973 to German immigrants, I grew up on a small holding outside Pretoria, South Africa. At the Tshwane University of Technology, I was introduced to glass as an expressive medium when the newly established glass department was opened in 1994. In 1997, my passion drove me to specialize at the Staatliche Glasfachschule Hadamar, Germany, learning and perfecting my cold-working abilities under the guidance of masters Josef Welzel and Willie Pistor. In 2001, I returned to South Africa and founded my studio, Obsidian Glass.

Perhaps the only qualified cold worker in sub-Saharan Africa, I am in a unique position, regularly collaborating with local hot shops on projects but mainly concentrating on carved and polished "lenses" as elements in my sculptures. I often incorporate other materials such as steel, wood, or stone to complement and support my works, keeping glass as the focal point.

My lenses can be considered as a visual trope to our consumption of information through social devices. In this exhausting cacophony of informative stimuli, we too often miss the wonders of our immediate surroundings. These carefully cut and polished sculptural lenses intentionally distort, bend, and refract light, enticing the viewer to come closer and experience the contiguous space within and beyond. I call it "music for the eyes."

1

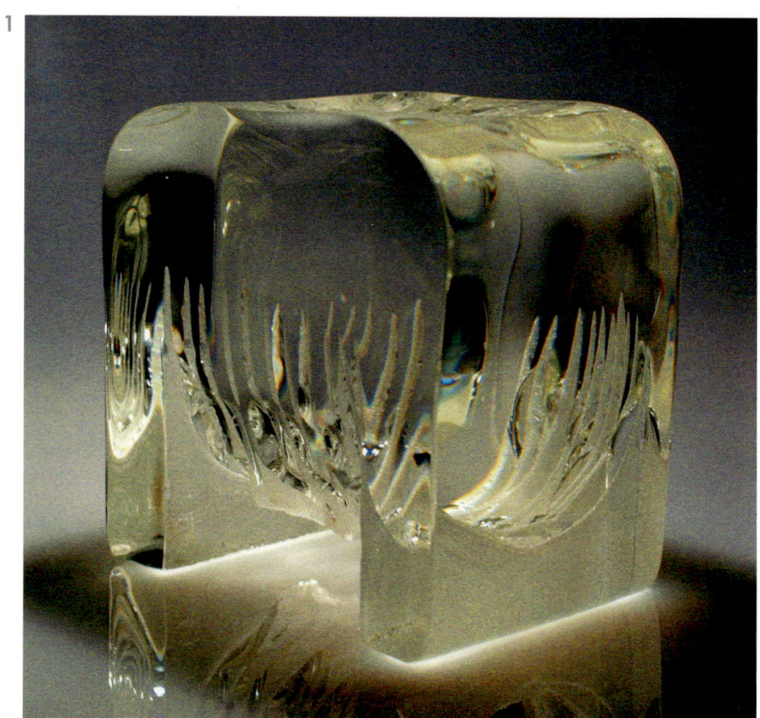

2

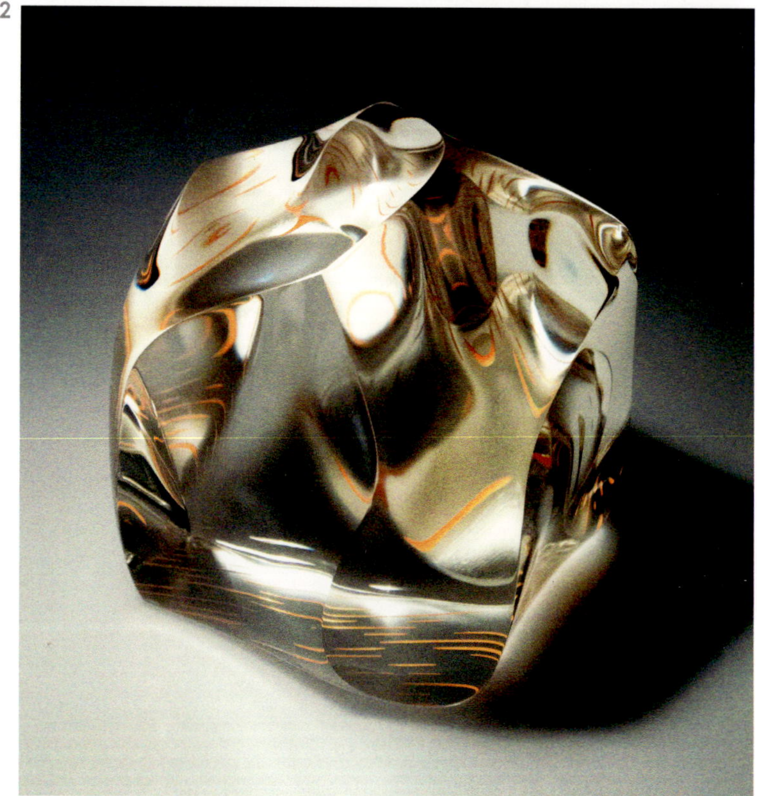

3

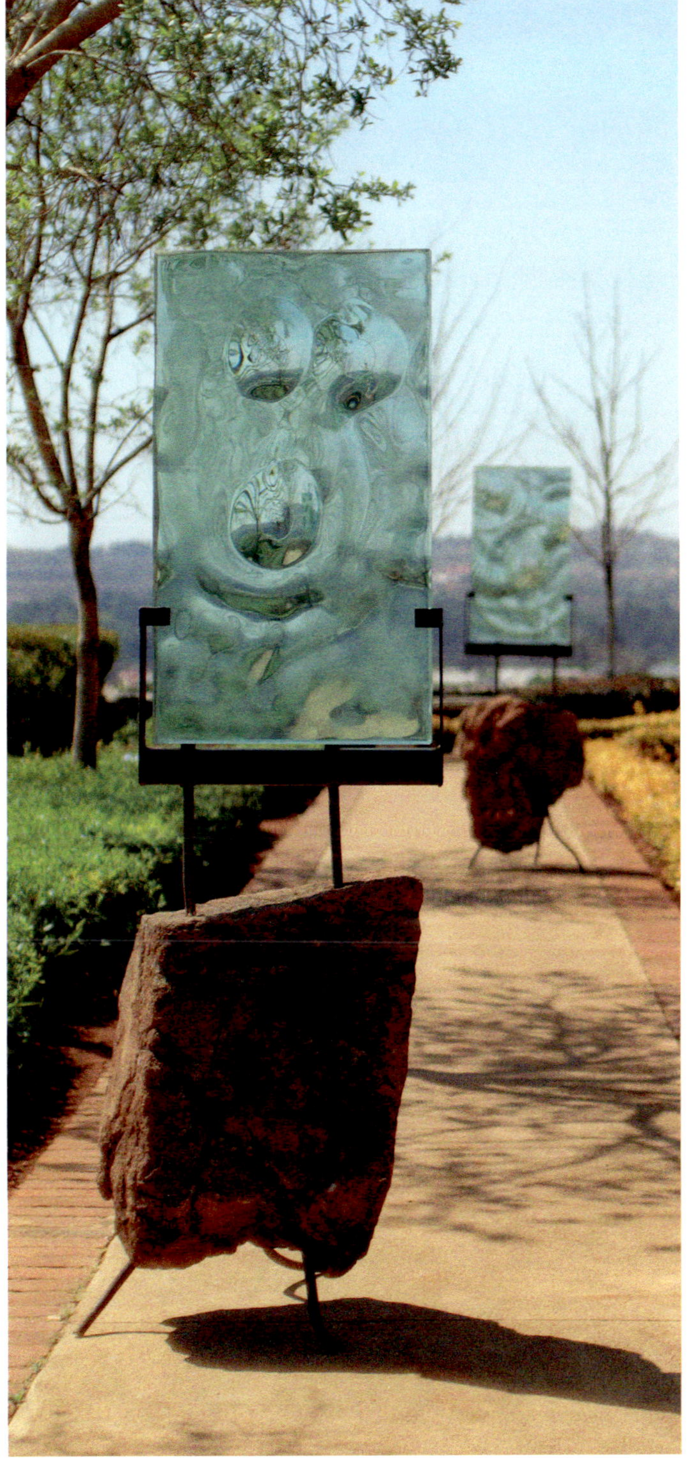

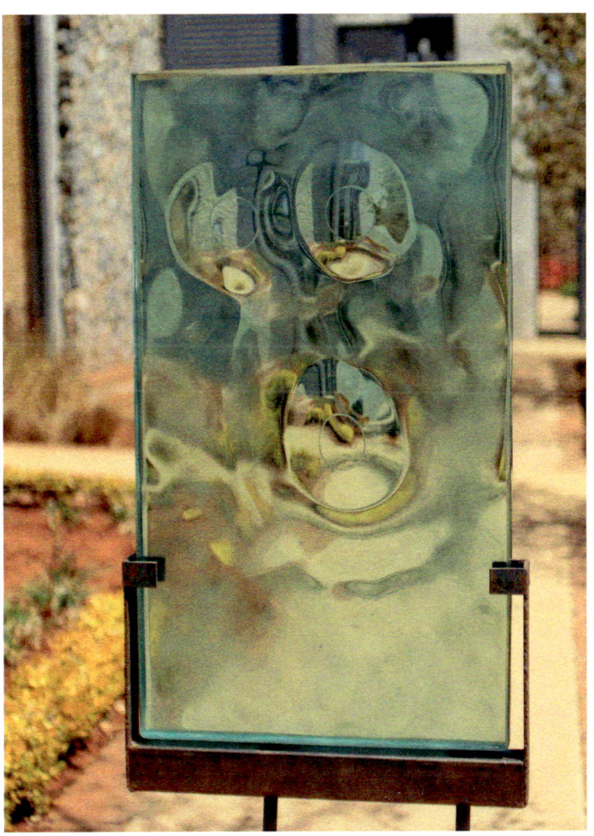

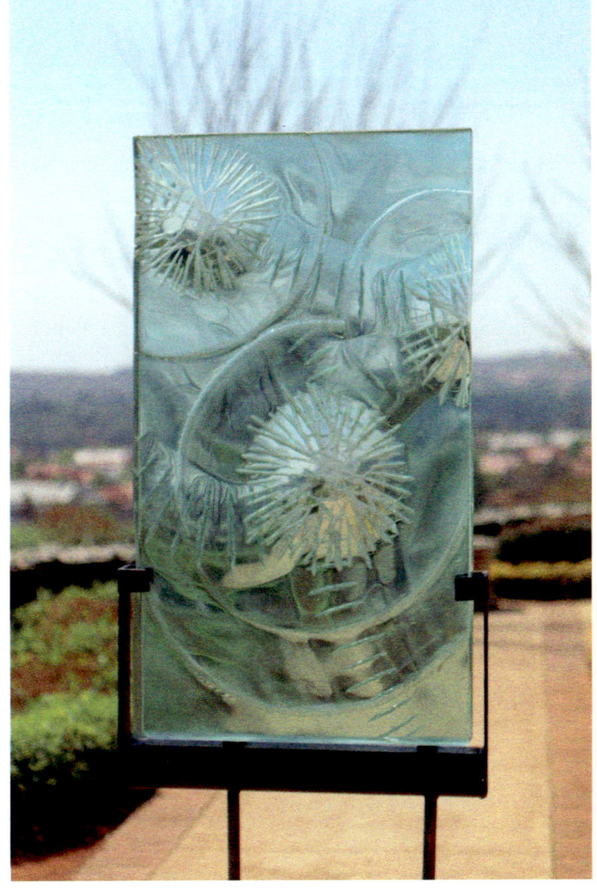

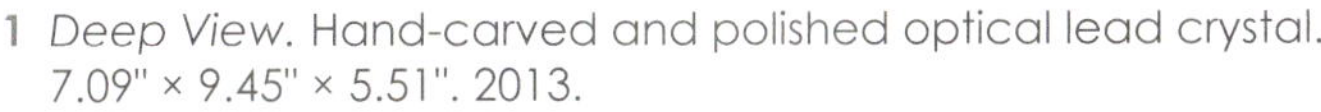

1 *Deep View*. Hand-carved and polished optical lead crystal. 7.09" × 9.45" × 5.51". 2013.

2 *Grid #3*. Hand-carved and polished optical lead crystal. 7.87" × 7.87" × 7.87". 2013.

3 *Sig #1* & *Sig #2*. UV-laminate float glass, hand carved and polished, stone, and steel. 64.96" × 17.72" × 21.65". 2014.

Latchezar Boyadjiev

Novato, California

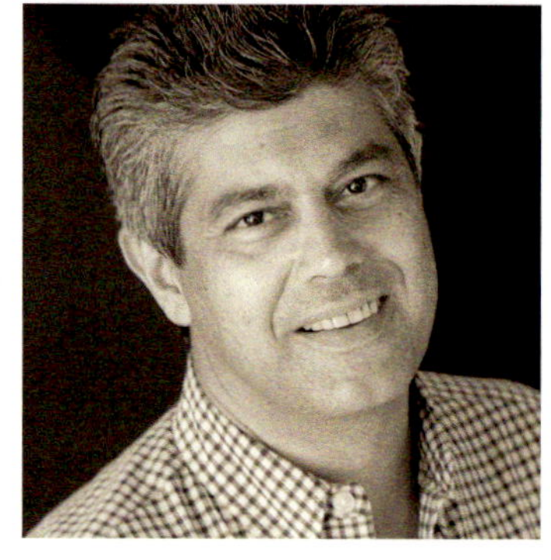

Courtesy of Gary Trignani–AccentsPhoto.com.

I definitely consider my work to be abstract sculpture. Using glass allows me to add another dimension to it: transparency and translucency. I leave one of the planes of my sculptures flat and polished because looking through it allows me to create a lasting impression of a three-dimensional drawing.

Glass offers more than any other material to the creative person. The light coming through the glass defining the texture and composition makes it pure magic, which increases the emotive qualities of the artwork.

1 *Relationship.* Cast glass sculpture. 30" × 5" × 24". 2014.

2 *Torso VII.* Cast glass sculpture. 18" × 4" × 12". 2014.

3 *Torso II.* Cast glass sculpture. 8" × 4" × 12". 2014.

4 *Kiss.* Cast glass sculpture. 15" × 4" × 11". 2013.

5 *Torso V.* Cast glass sculpture. 18" × 4" × 12". 2014.

1

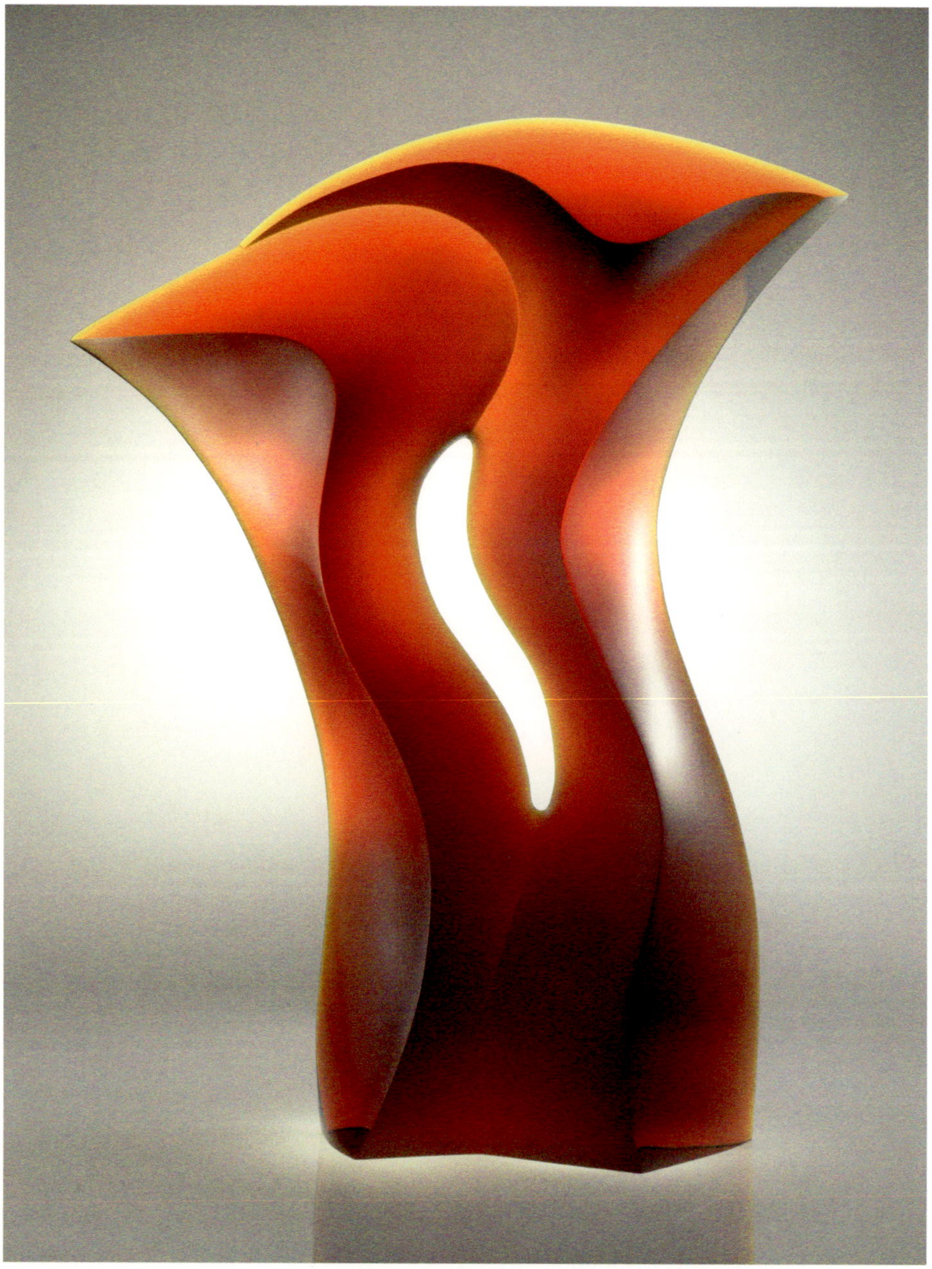

2

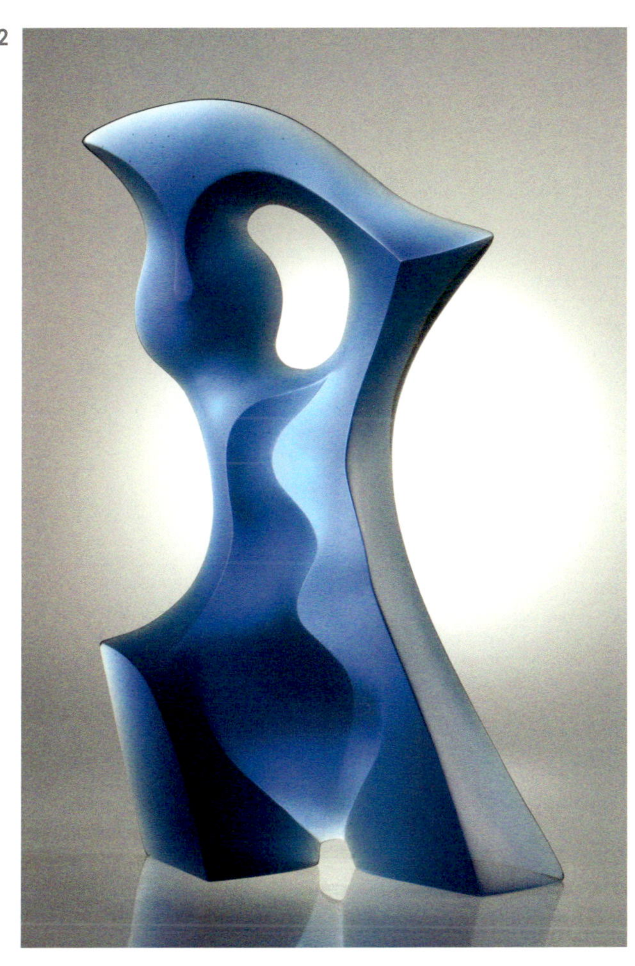

4

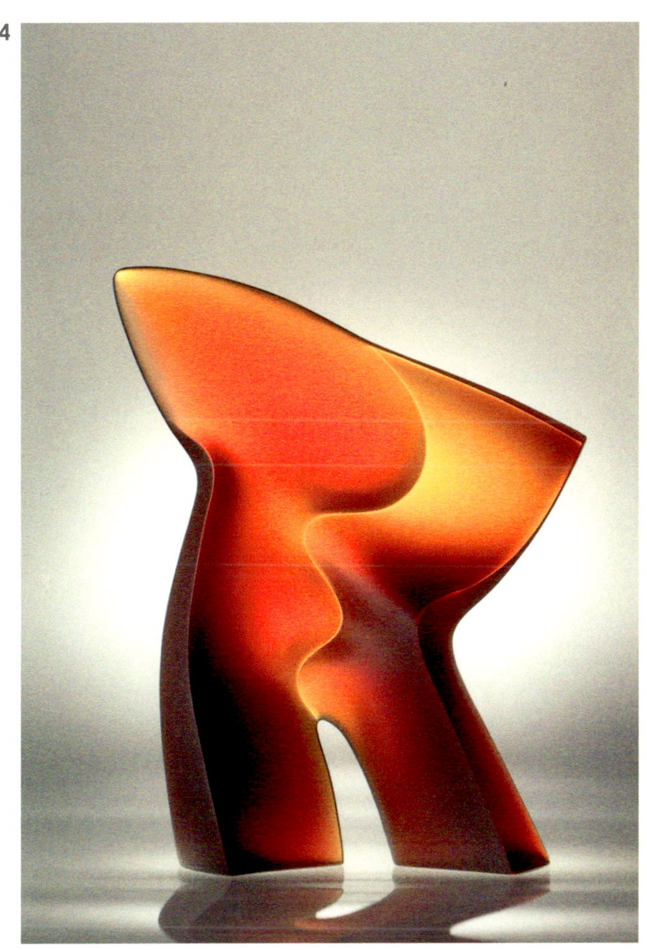

3

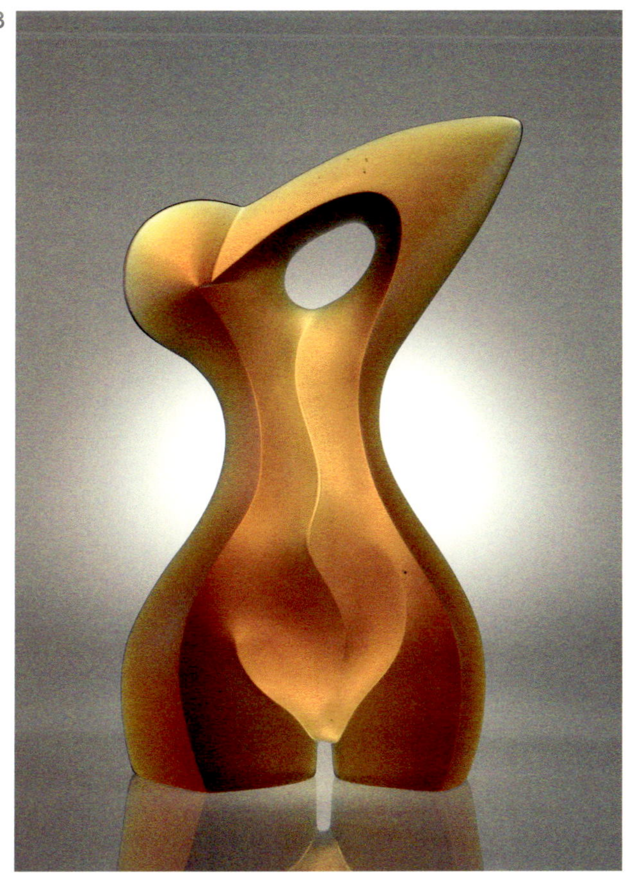

5

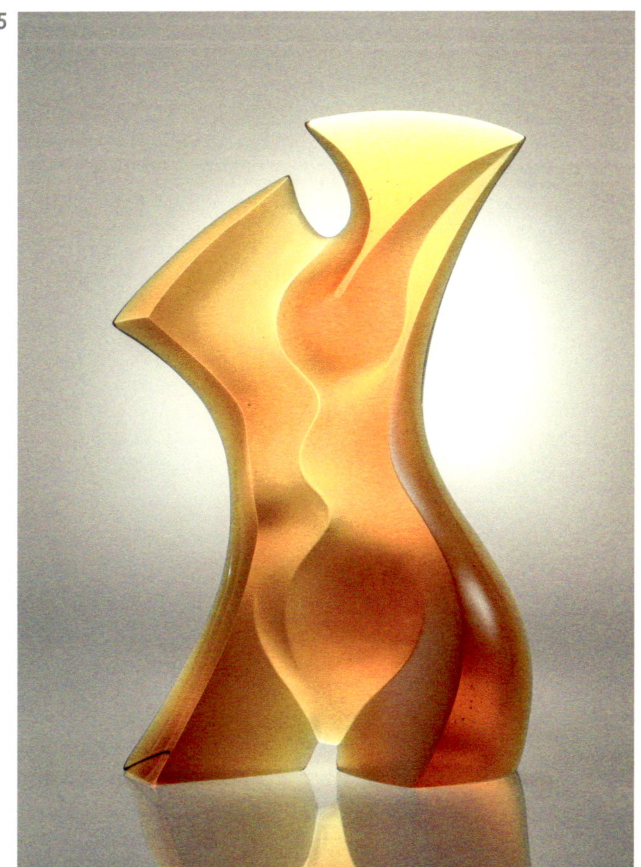

Kathy Bradford

Lyons, Colorado

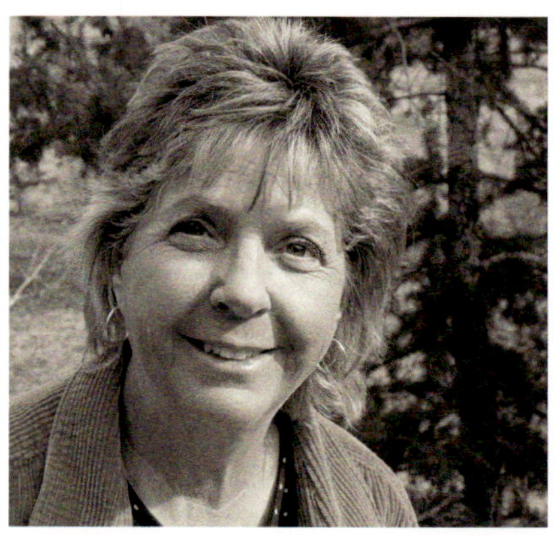

Courtesy of Laird Townsend.

Recognized for sandblast-etched and sand-carved art glass, I have created many large architectural works, both public and private, throughout the country. My fine art degree gave me a good foundation to build innovative and successful art glass used for a variety of purposes.

Much of my work is detailed sandblast carving and etching, with some works combined with independent elements of colorful glass laminated into the design. Made by commission only, each work is original, and I give special attention to the needs of each architectural situation. My designs are whimsical, energetic, and powerful.

1

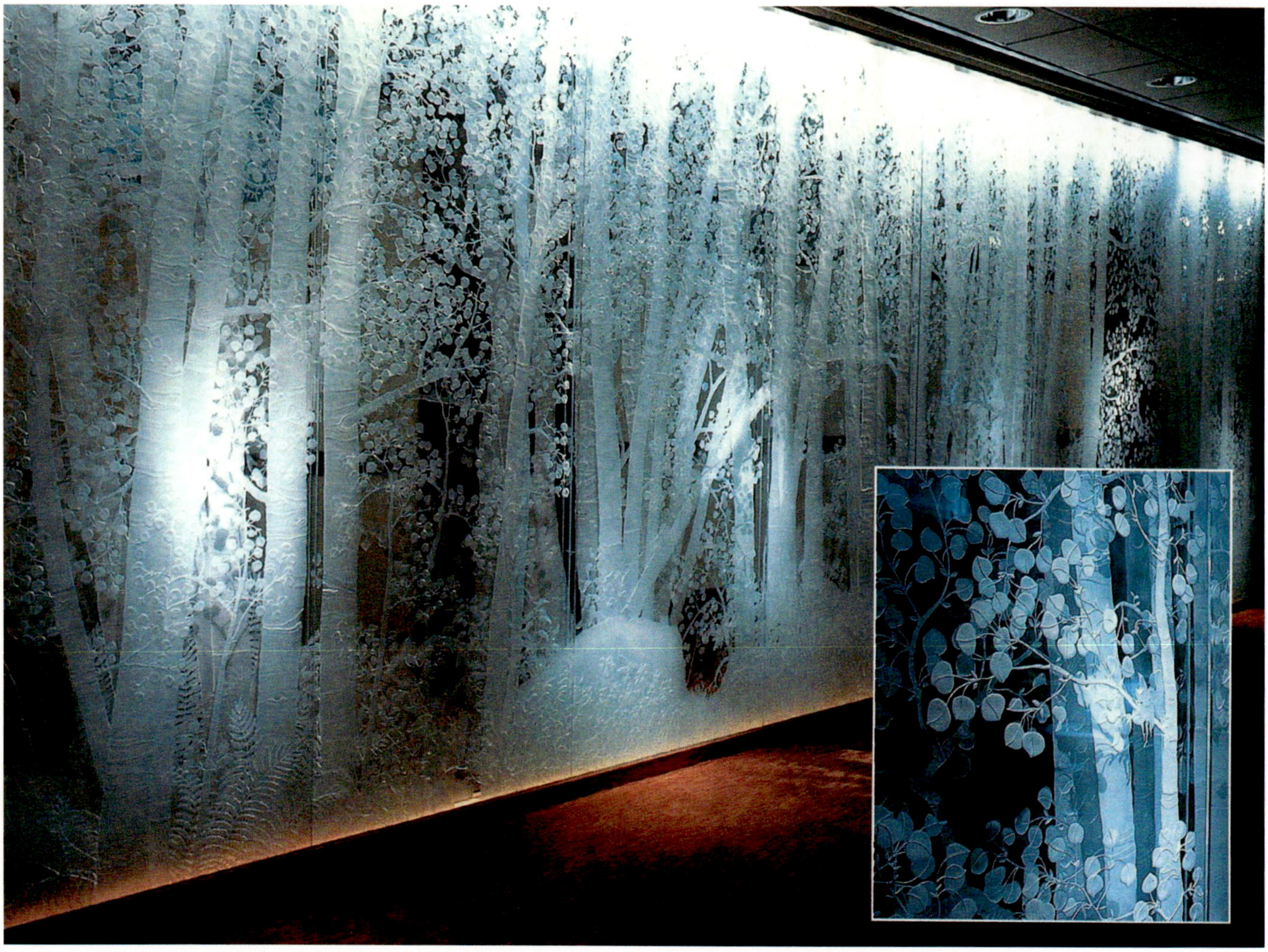

1 *Faces of the Forest.* Sandblast carving and etched triple-layer glass divider wall. 8' × 5" × 21'. 1996. Good Samaritan Hospital, Downers Grove, IL.

2

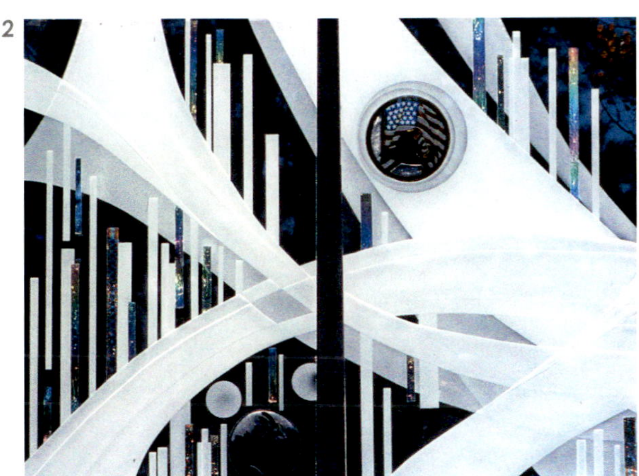

3

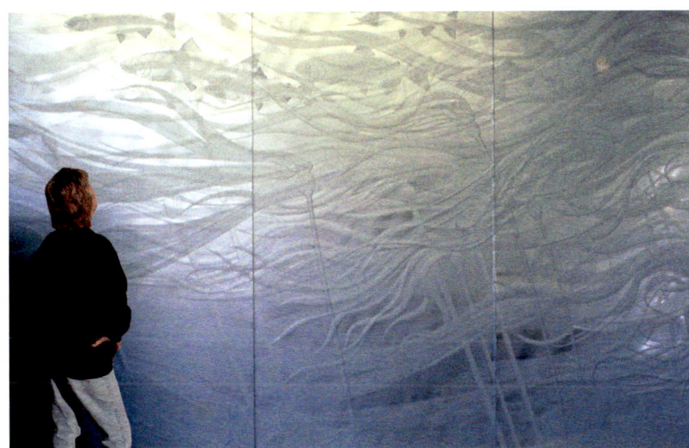

4

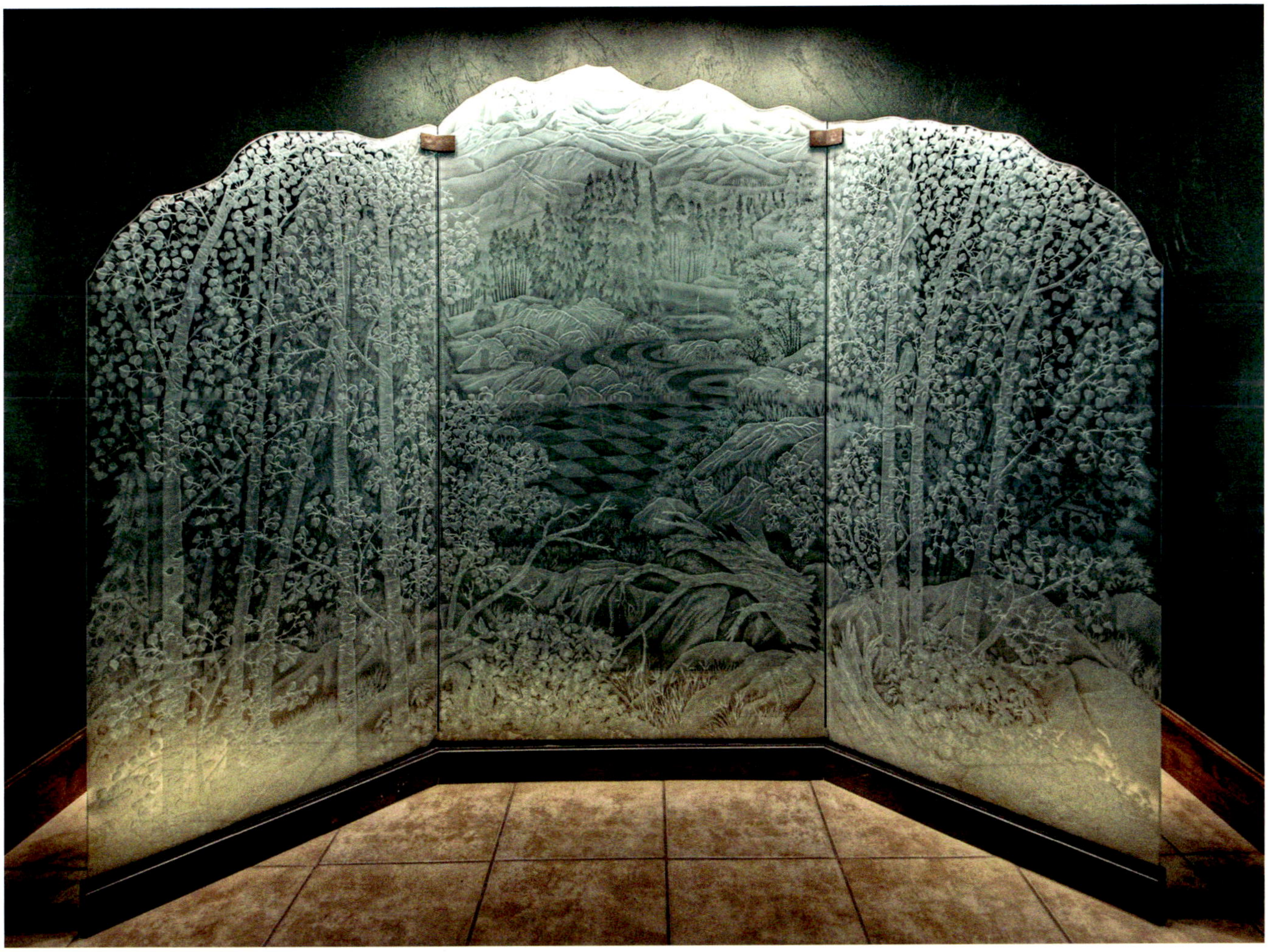

2 *Rhythms of the City*. Sandblast carving and etching with independent elements of dichroic glass. 8' × 12'. 2003.

3 *Cruisin' Through*. Sandblast carving and etching. Multi-layer. 7' × 3" × 11'. 2005.

4 *The Dream Green*. Sandblast carving and etching. 7' × 20' × 10'. 2007. Free standing sculpture. Courtesy of Tim Sutherland.

Rachel Bremner

Oyster Cove, Tasmania, Australia

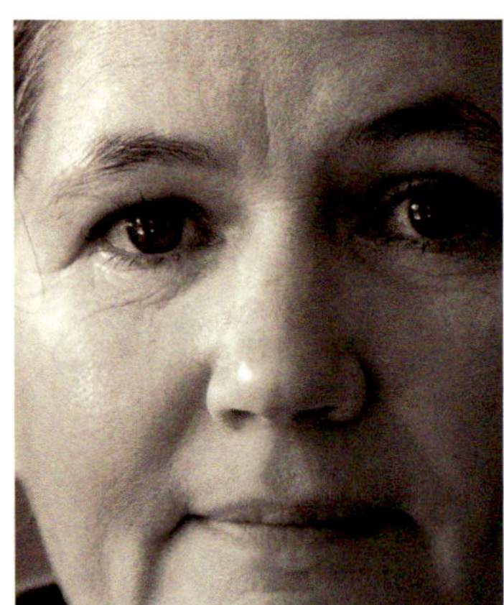

1

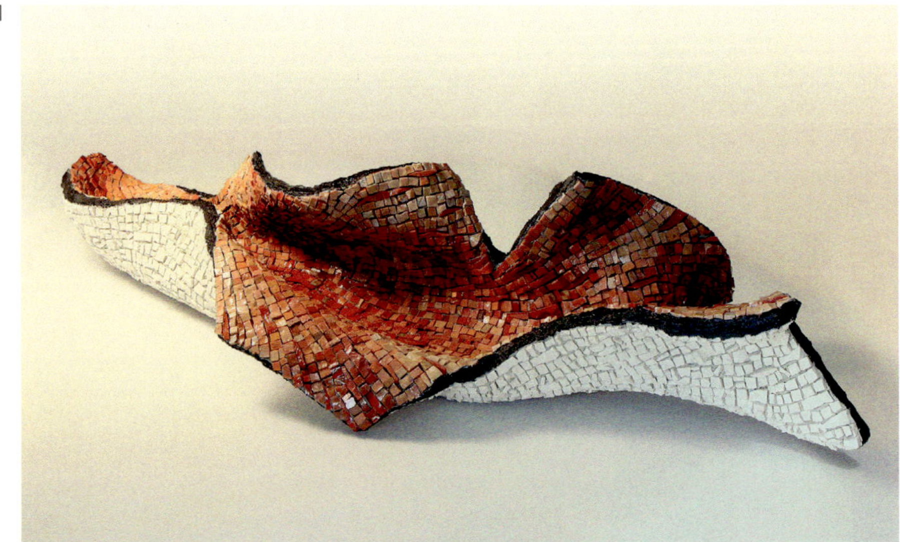

2

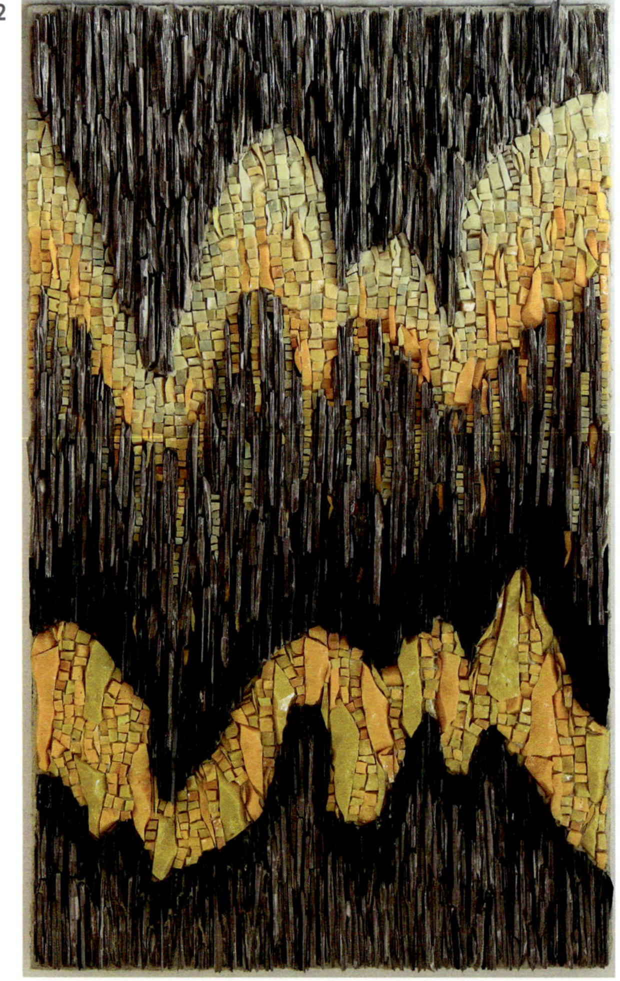

I use a variety of materials for my mosaics but predominantly Orson smalti from Venice and different stones, including slate and marble. I hand cut my tesserae with traditional Italian tools and a beautifully innovative Japanese hardy. Cutting is a time-consuming process but very meditative. I often find inspiration in tiny natural patterns that I develop symbiotically into large designs.

The inherent qualities of my materials and the preparatory process of cutting are fundamental to my expression and most often the starting point for the improvisatory nature of my approach. I like encountering the unexpected, surprises that inspire a new direction, and challenges to my thinking, ultimately surprising myself.

3

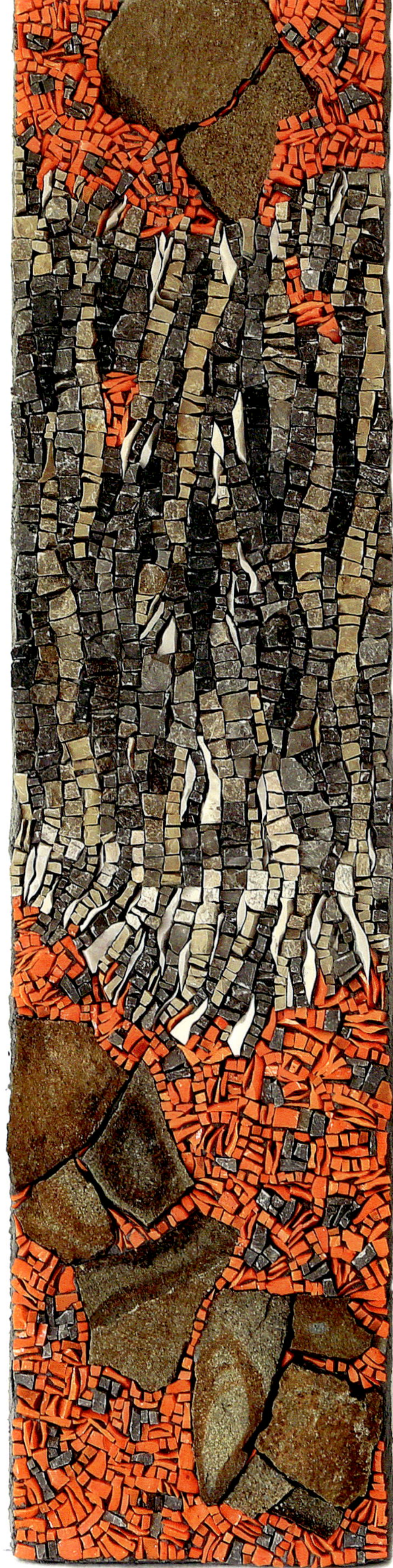

4

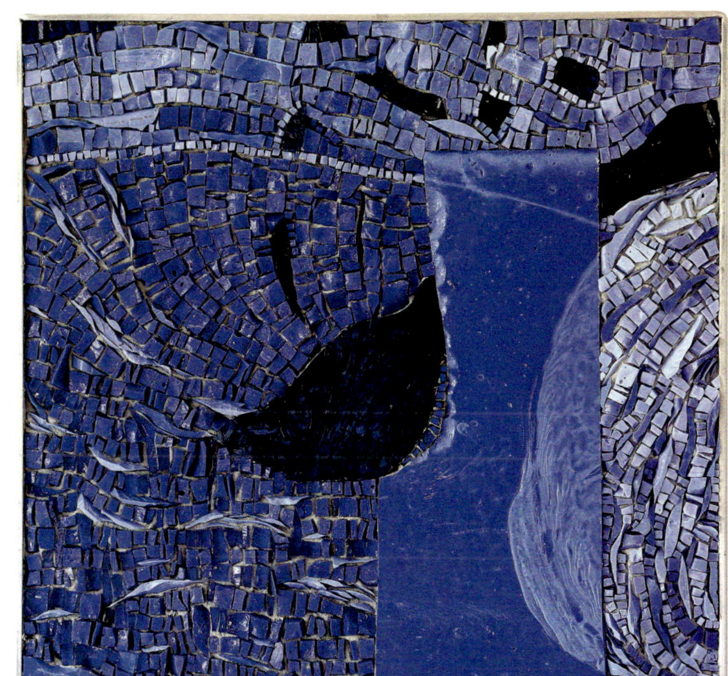

5

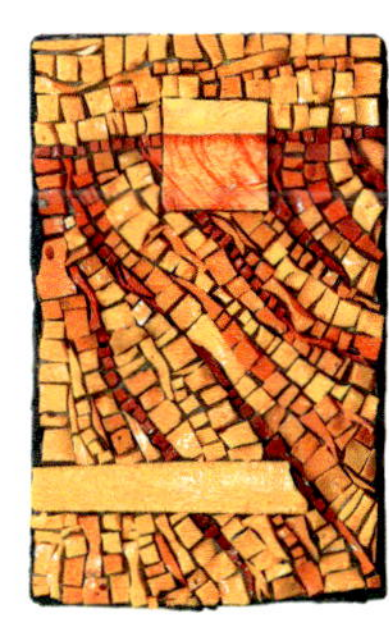

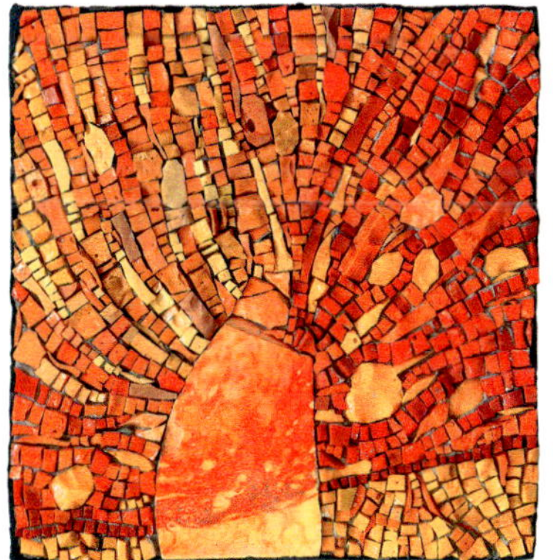

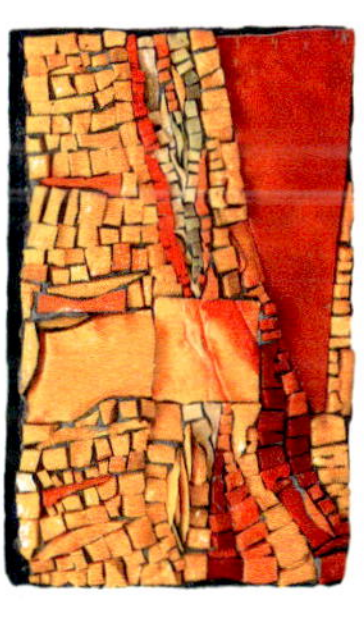

1 *Drift*. Mosaic. 5.9" × 31.5" × 12.6". 2013. Courtesy of John Redeker.

2 *The Inevitability of Emotions no. 3—Up and Down*. Mosaic. 22.83" × 13.39". 2013. Courtesy of John Redeker.

3 *Imagine*. Mosaic. 23.62" × 5.9". 2014. Courtesy of John Redeker.

4 *Blue Moon*. Mosaic. 11.81" × 11.81". 2014. Courtesy of John Redeker.

5 *Sonatina*. Triptych. Mosaic. 7.87" × 16.54". 2013. Courtesy of John Redeker.

Charissa Brock

Portland, Oregon

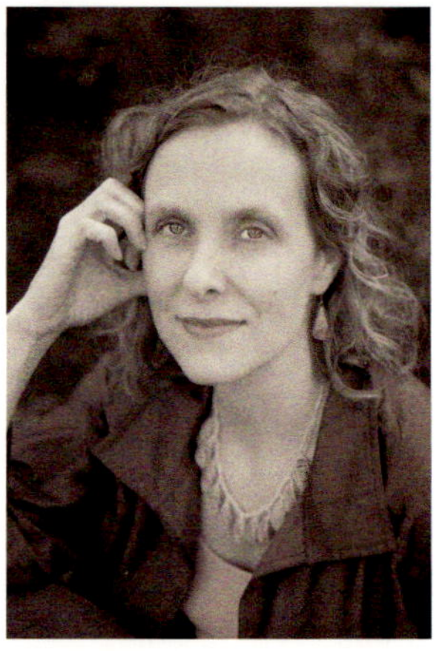

Photo: Dan Kvitka.

Many times in my life I have come upon an archeological artifact, plant, animal, or an insect that at first glance has a questionable yet fascinating identification, origin, or meaning. My mind is at once awed by the mystery and, at the same time, works through my past experiences to try to place meaning on what is in front of me. It is a guessing game, where narrative or meaning is created.

Referencing aspects of objects from the past and forms from nature through the use of tiny sculpted pieces of glass and bamboo, knots, interwoven lines, and stacking techniques, I develop a system for creating a structure. I strive to create that same guessing game for others, allowing them to find their own story in my work.

1

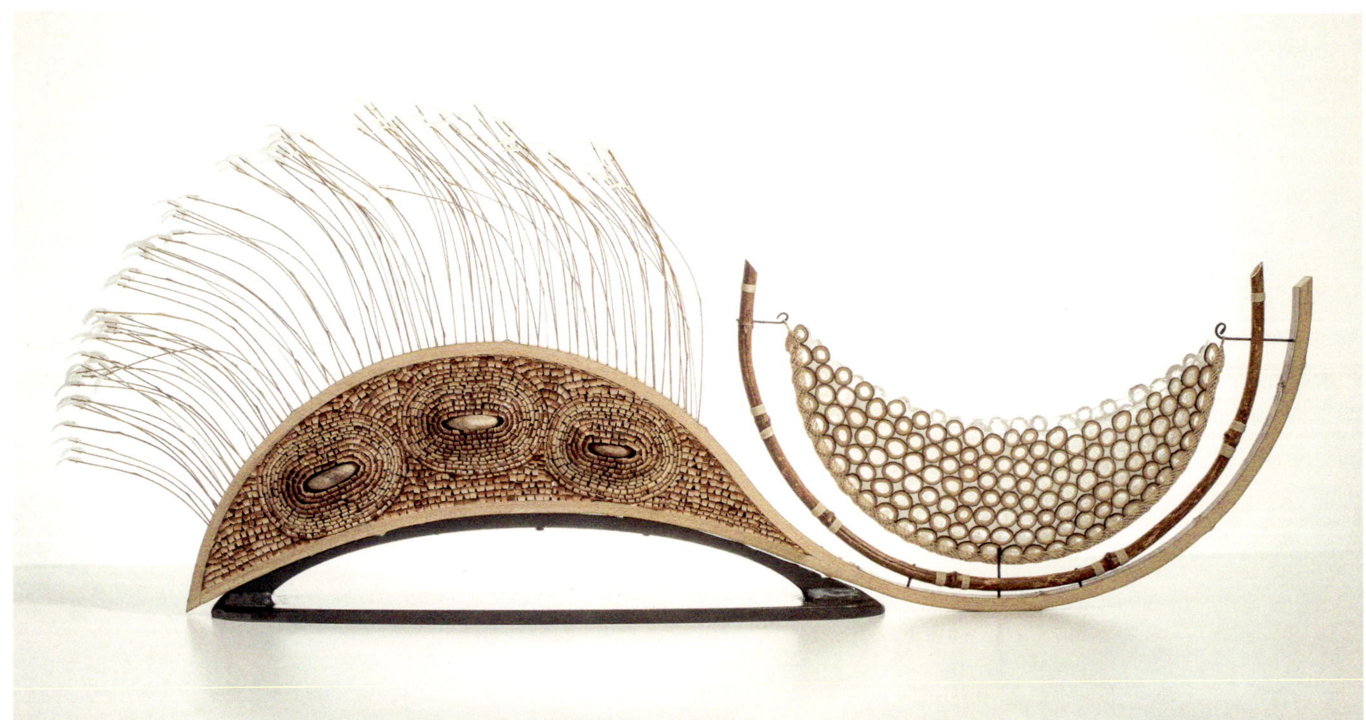

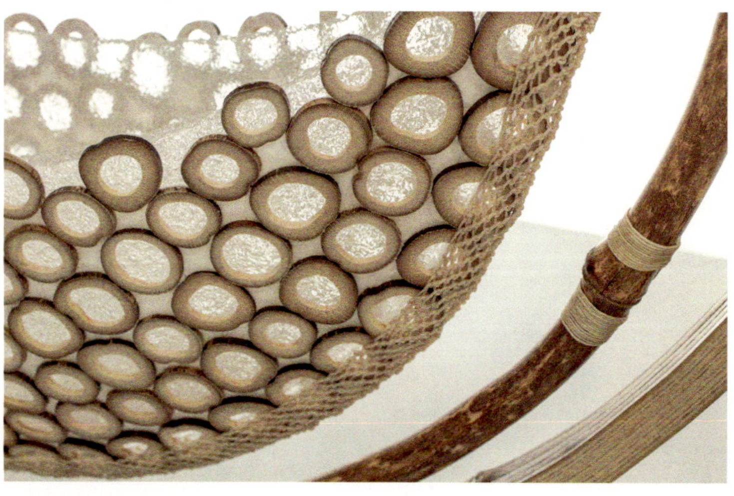

1 *From Land to Sea*. Laminated and stacked tiger bamboo, stone, fused glass frit wafers, knotted waxed linen thread, cast paper, and steel. 26" × 6" × 61". 2014. Photo: Dan Kvitka.

2 *Spira Penna*. Split, bent, and sewn tiger bamboo, fused glass frit wafers, and waxed linen thread. 33" × 13" × 13". 2014. Photo: Dan Kvitka.

3 *Lux Lucis*. Laminated and stacked tiger bamboo, fused glass, cane, knotted waxed linen thread, and steel. 40" × 6.5" × 22". 2014. Photo: Dan Kvitka.

4 *Mille Oculus*. Laminated and stacked tiger bamboo, fused glass, and knotted waxed linen thread. 34" × 6.25" × 26". 2014. Photo: Dan Kvitka.

2

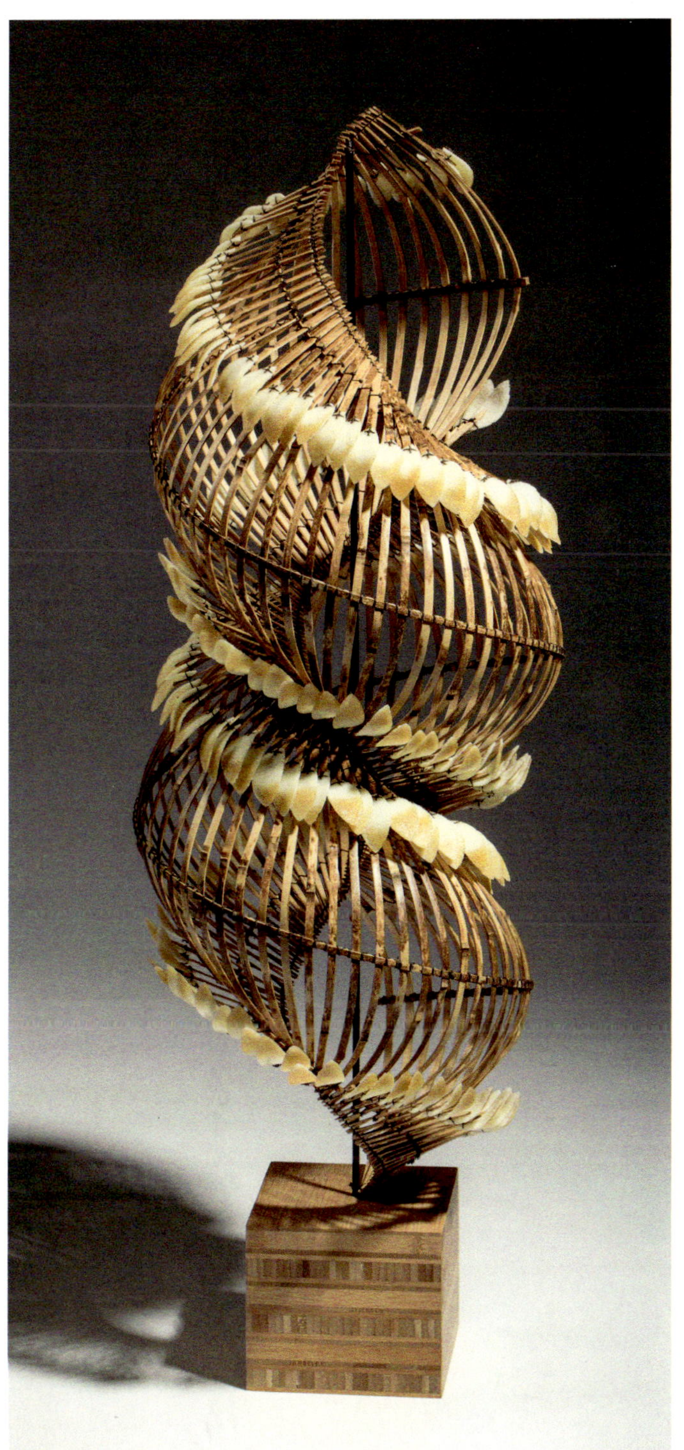

3

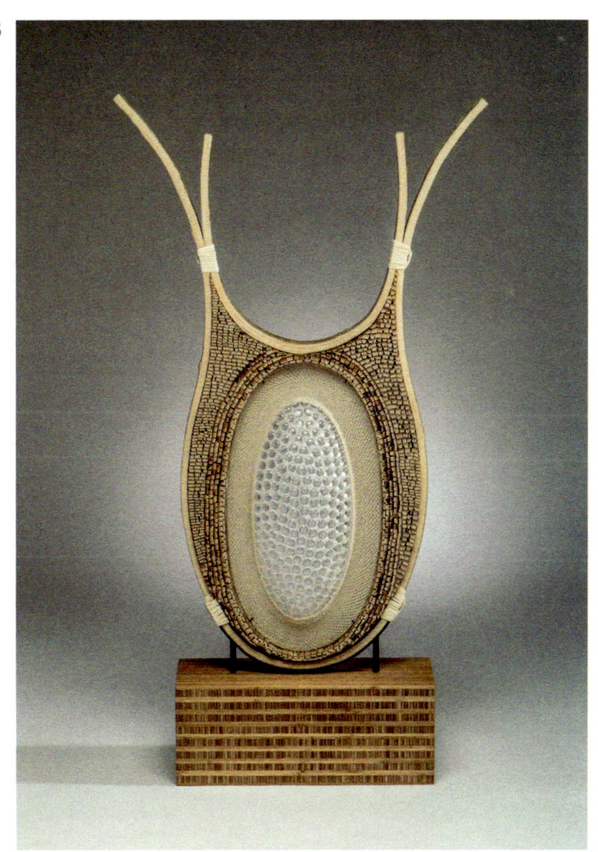

4

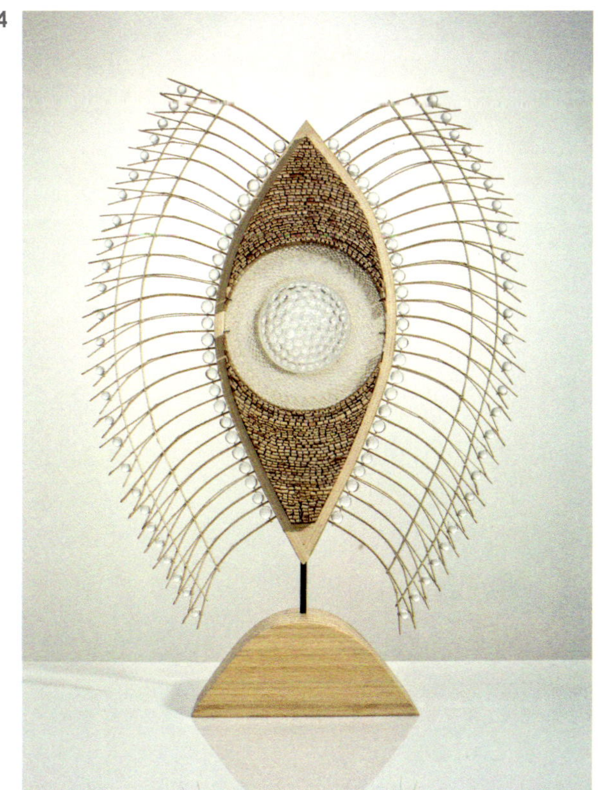

Emily Brock

Corrales, New Mexico

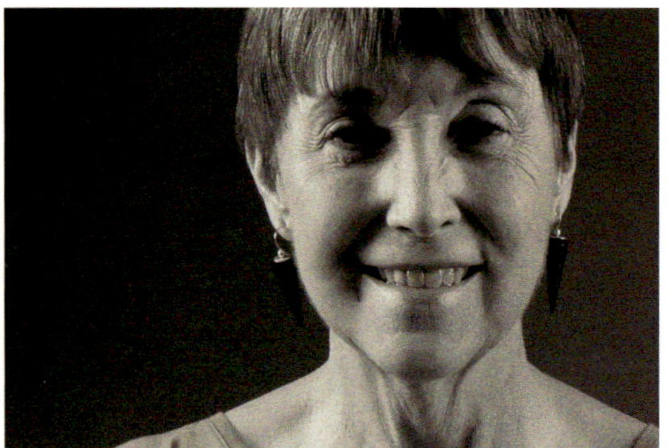

Courtesy of Terry Brock.

After being introduced to glass over three decades ago, I began a primarily self-taught journey of experimentation with this exceptional material. As a narrator of detail, one of my goals has always been to present a smooth transition between what I observe as existing in the real world and my glass representation of it. I absorb cities, homes, diners, libraries, gardens, and everything around me. Then, using a variety of techniques, I construct an environment and create a narrative that references human activity and celebrates our culture.

During the span of my work, this objective has inadvertently led me to become a precise chronicler of amazing and radical changes within our culture in what historically would be regarded as a relatively short period of time. An important aspect of my exploration that has intrigued and inspired me is the versatility of this material that pushes my imagination and expands my abilities. Using my perceptions, I seek to invite and intrigue the viewer.

1 *Rose Diner*. Kilnworked, lampworked, and mixed media. 15.5" × 18" × 13". 2010. Courtesy of Terry Brock.

2 *Flight of Dreams*. Kilnworked, lampworked. 17" × 13.75" × 13.75". 2012. Courtesy of Norman Johnson Photography.

3 *Prelude*. Kilnworked, lampworked. 12.5" × 17" × 15". 2014. Courtesy of Terry Brock.

4 *Culinary Culture*. Kilnworked, lampworked, and mixed media. 16" × 17.5" × 17.5". 2014. Courtesy of Terry Brock.

5 *Tranquil Garden*. Kilnworked, lampworked. 17" × 13.75" × 13.75". 2012. Courtesy of Terry Brock.

1

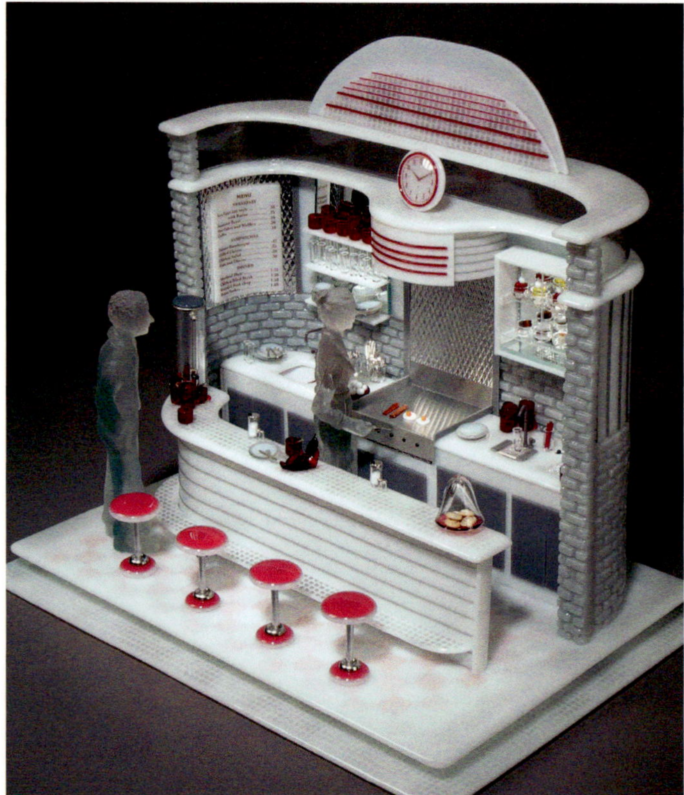

2

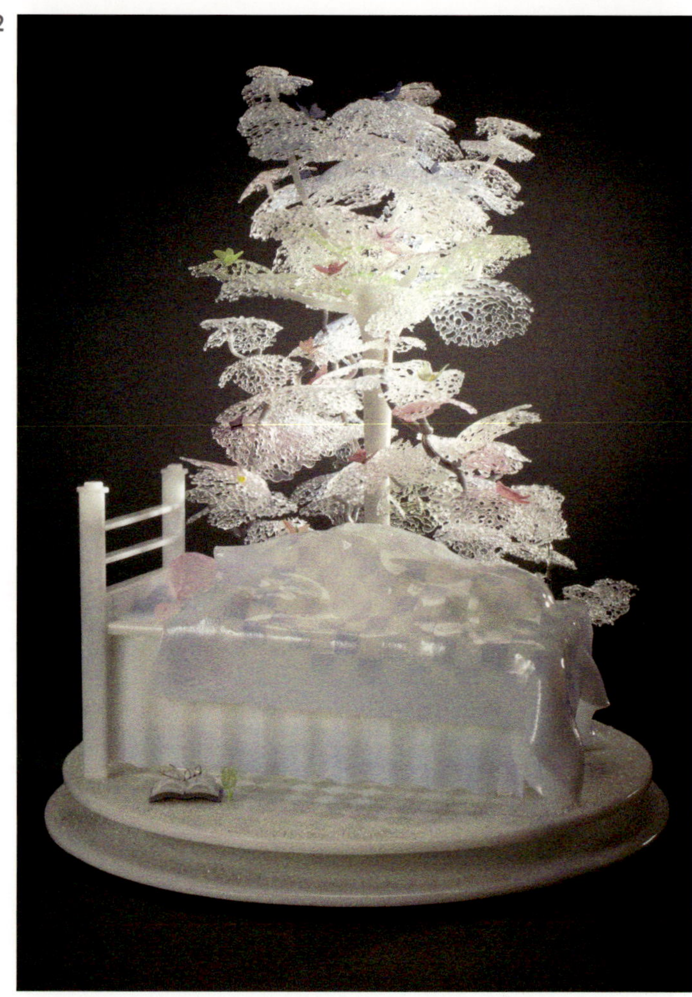

3

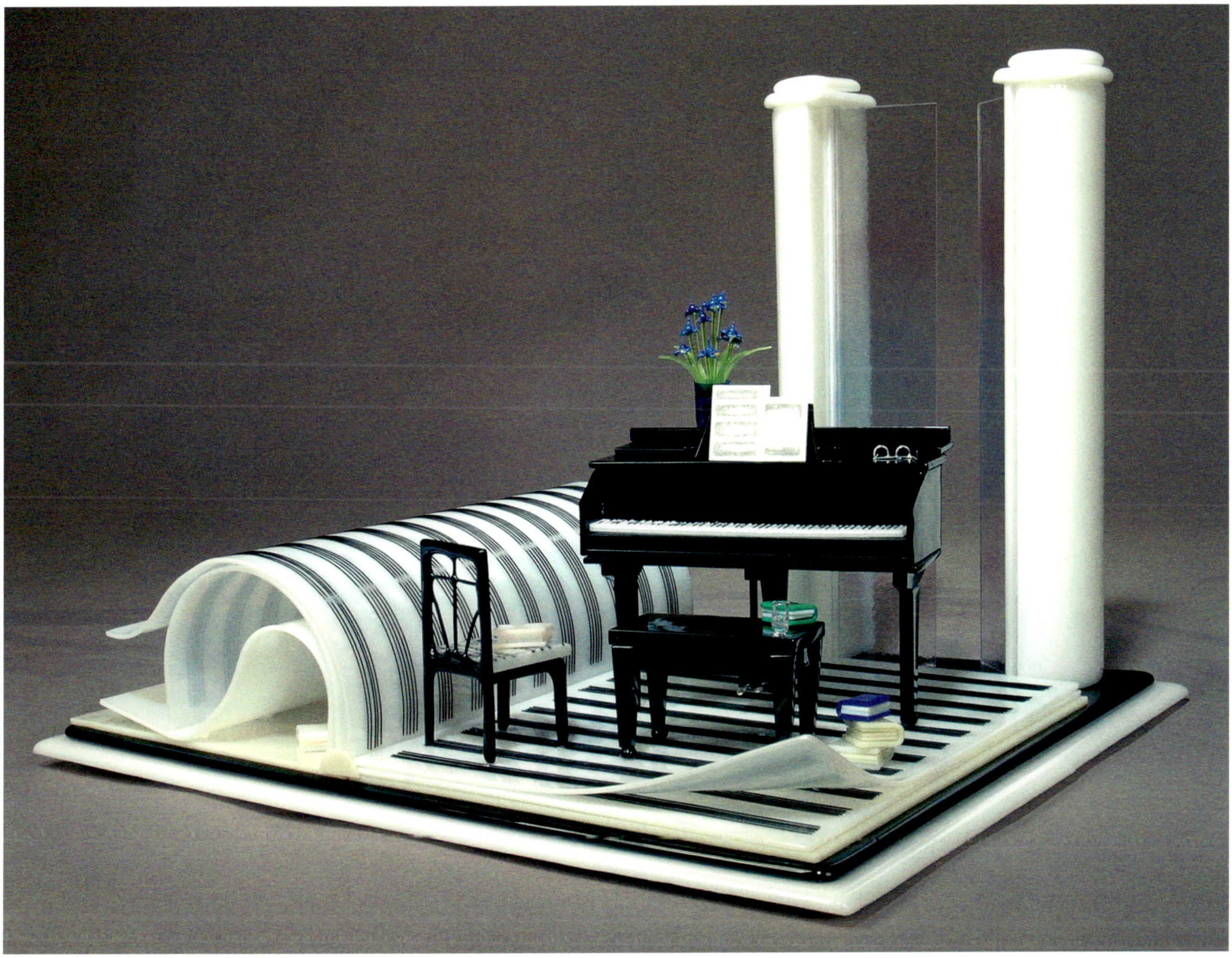

4

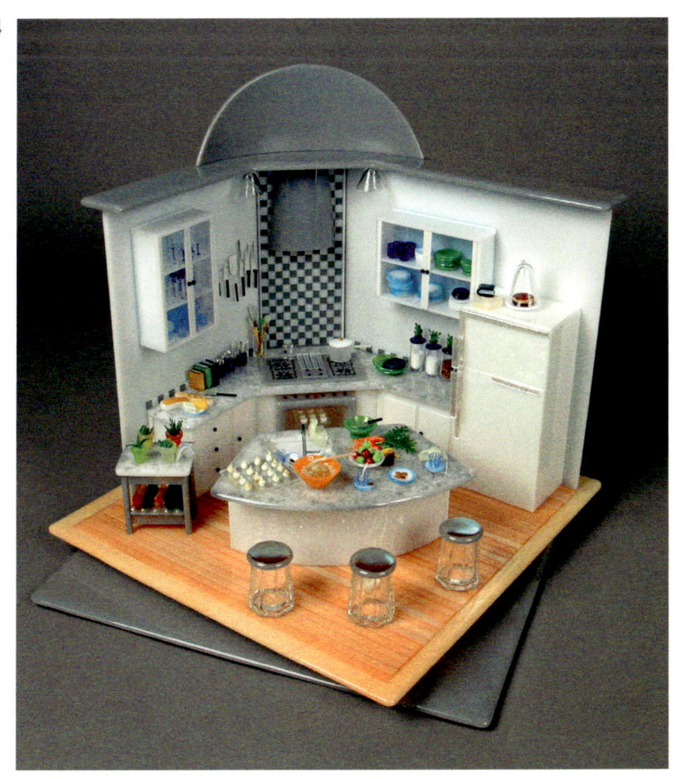

5

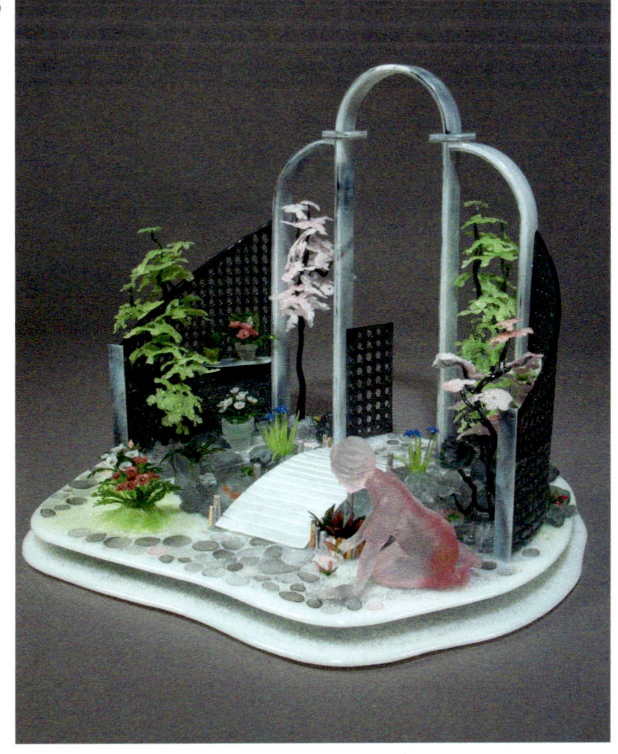

Susan Silver Brown

Scottsdale, Arizona

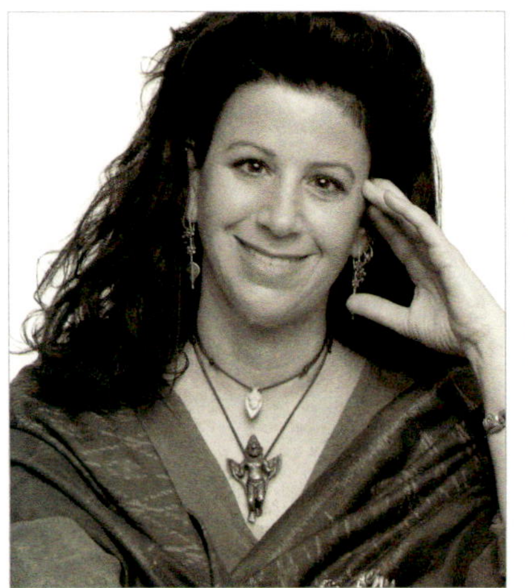

Courtesy of Tim Lanterman Photography.

A cast glass sculptor, I execute my work in the laborious and coveted tradition of Daum and Lalique. I completed undergraduate work at UCLA and went to graduate school in sculpture at the University of Wisconsin, Madison. I studied glass at the Corning Institute as well as at Chihuly's Pilchuck.

My emotive work deals with the spirituality and philosophy of mankind through archetypal, surrealistic, and symbolic images. Using the narrative, I conjure up renewal, hope, and healing. I draw on mythology and a combination of man, animals, and plants to convey these thoughts. The purpose of my visionary artwork is for my viewers to achieve feelings of self-actualization and visual transcendence.

1

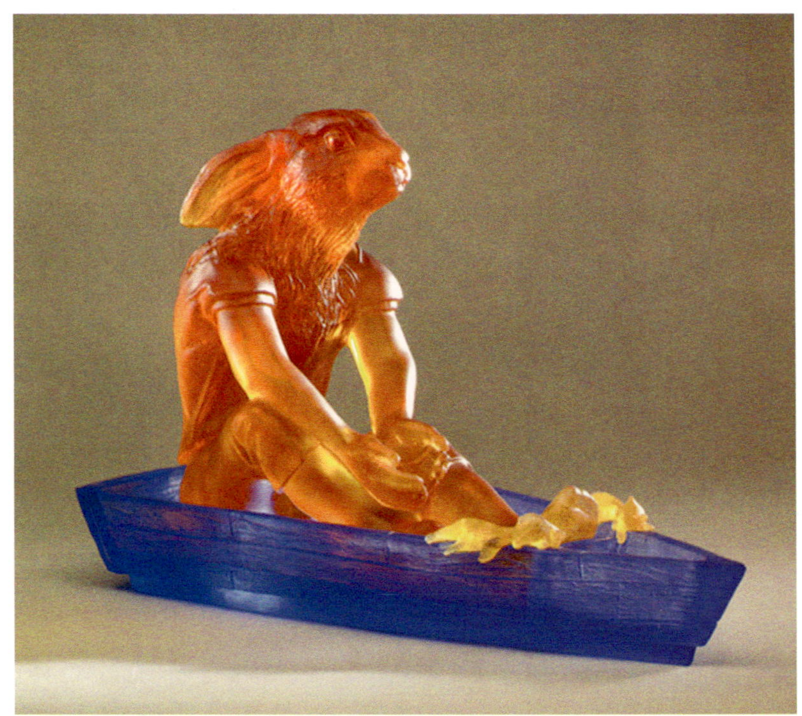

2

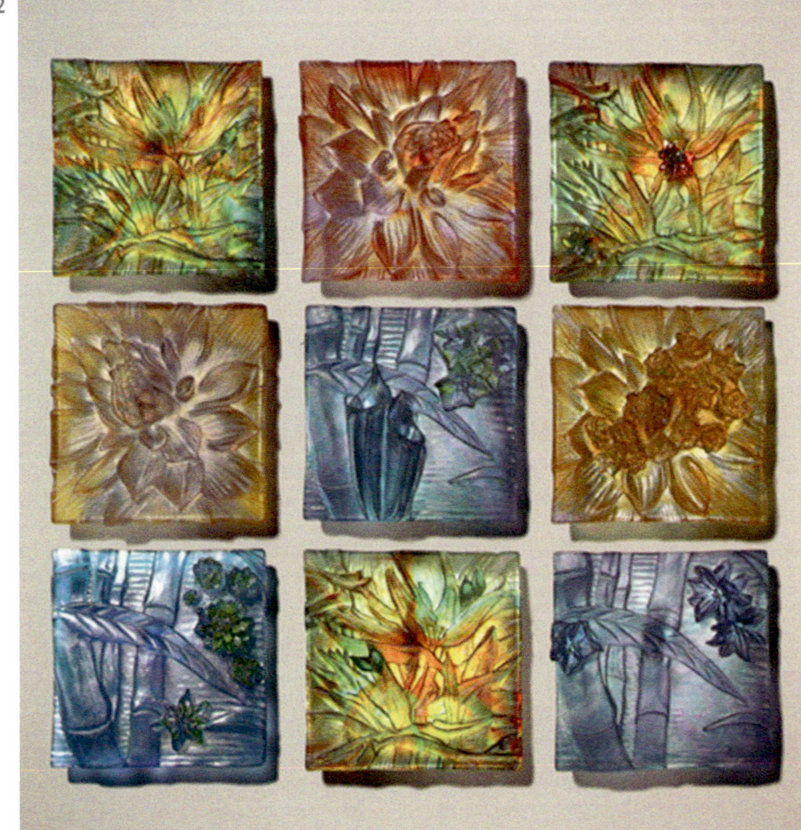

3

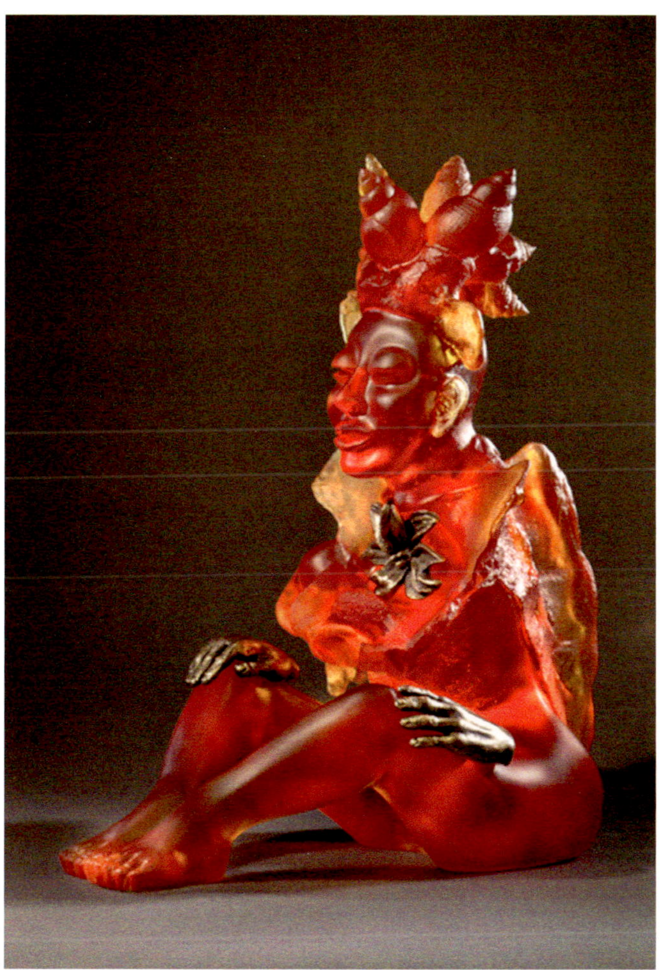

4

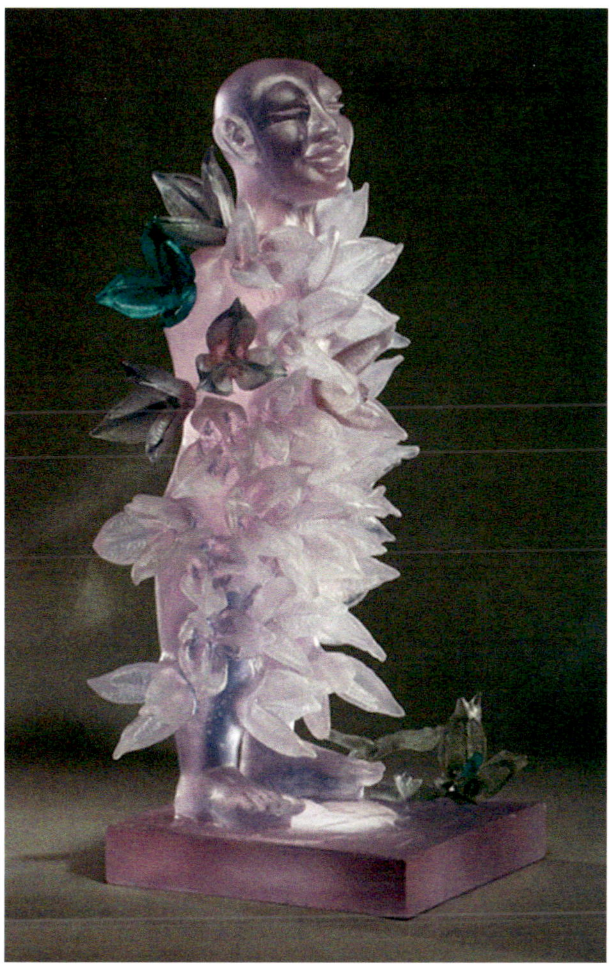

5

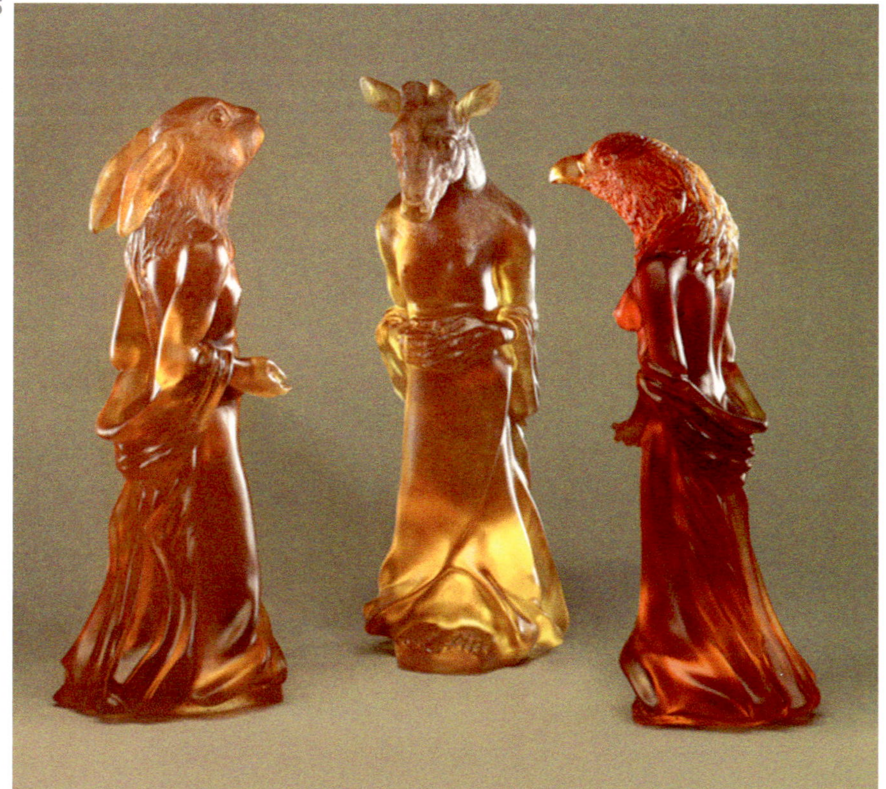

1 *Joy Rider*. Cast lead crystal glass. 19.5" × 8" × 12.5". 2013. Courtesy of Tim Lanterman Photography.

2 *Biophilia "For the Love of Life" Wall Installation*. Cast lead crystal glass, 9 panel wall installation. 4' × 3" × 4'. 2013. Courtesy of Tim Lanterman Photography.

3 *Shambhalla's Illumination of Solace*. Cast lead crystal glass, bronze. 18.5" × 11.5" × 21". 2010. Courtesy of Tim Lanterman Photography.

4 *Daydream Believer*. Cast lead crystal glass. 11" × 11" × 24". 2009. Courtesy of Tim Lanterman Photography.

5 *Animal Whisperers* (group shot). Cast lead crystal glass. 6.5" × 7" × 19" each. 2012. Courtesy of Tim Lanterman Photography.

Roger Buddle

Victor Harbor, South Australia, Australia

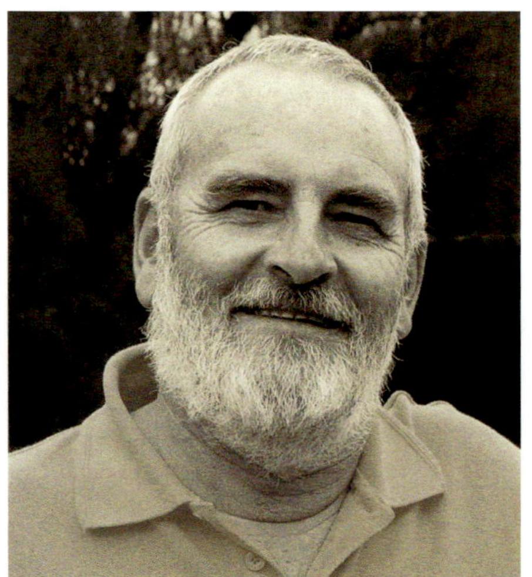

Courtesy of Elizabeth Buddle.

I first became fascinated by glass when I undertook a night class in stained glass work in 1988. I resigned from my job as a computer systems designer and started a small stained glass business but soon wanted more from glass. I studied full time at the University of South Australia and graduated in 1994 with a bachelor of design. My wife and I moved from Adelaide to Victor Harbor and set up a warm glass studio there. My work evolved into two main styles: production work, which helped to pay the bills, and exhibition work, which satisfied my artistic desires. In 2003, I completed a master of visual arts postgraduate degree at the University of South Australia. In 2011, I was awarded an artist in residence position in the remote Gammon Ranges in South Australia, where my wife and I were able to completely immerse ourselves in our passion for wilderness and isolation for three glorious weeks. The body of work produced as a result of this residency, mainly multi-layered wall panels, can be seen on my website.

My work has always tended toward the organic and nature; my *Invitro* series reflects its human aspect. My latest work has been a series of sculptural works based on the fascinating variety of fungi that colonize our planet.

1

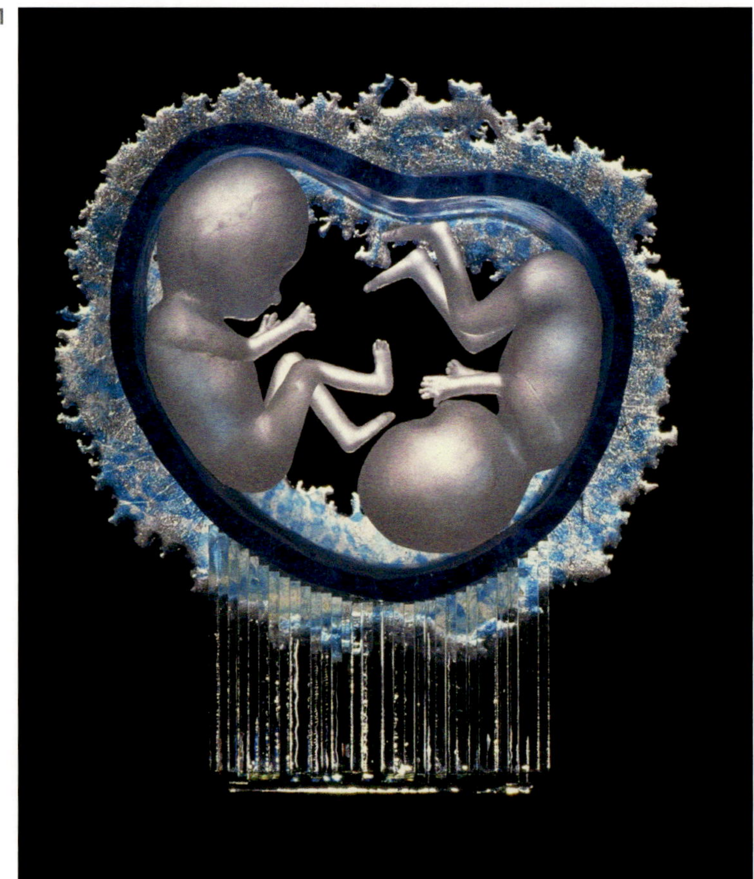

2

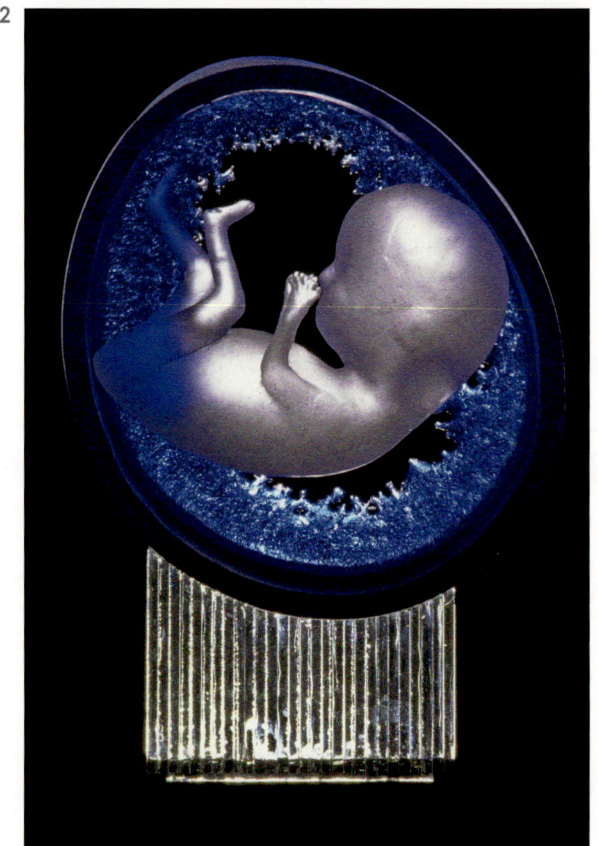

3

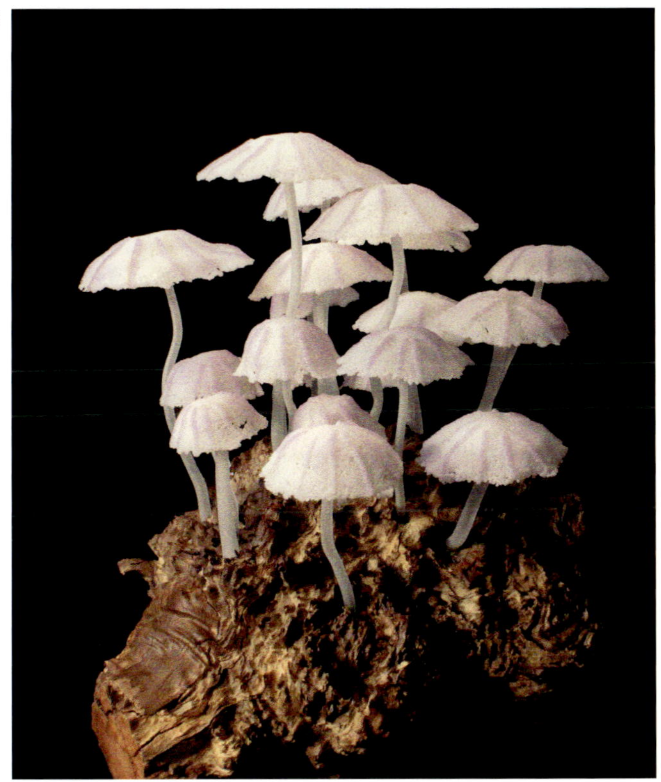

4

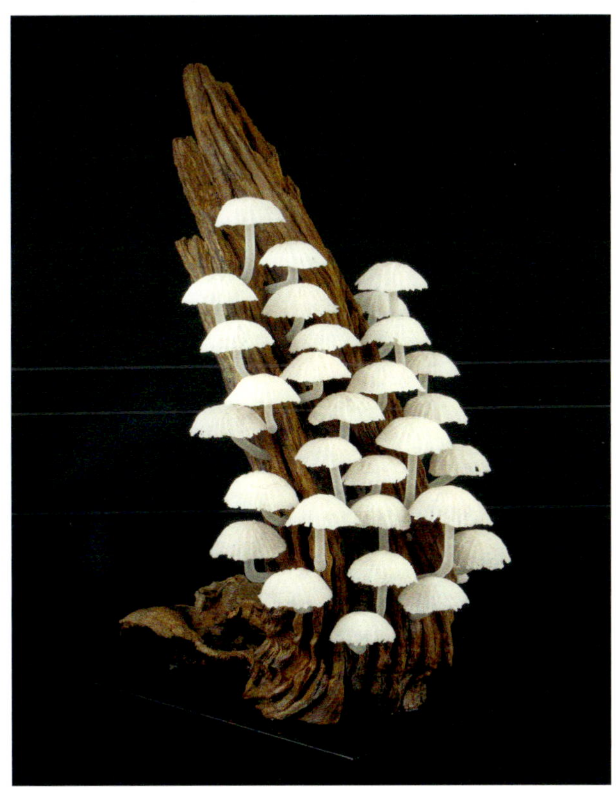

5

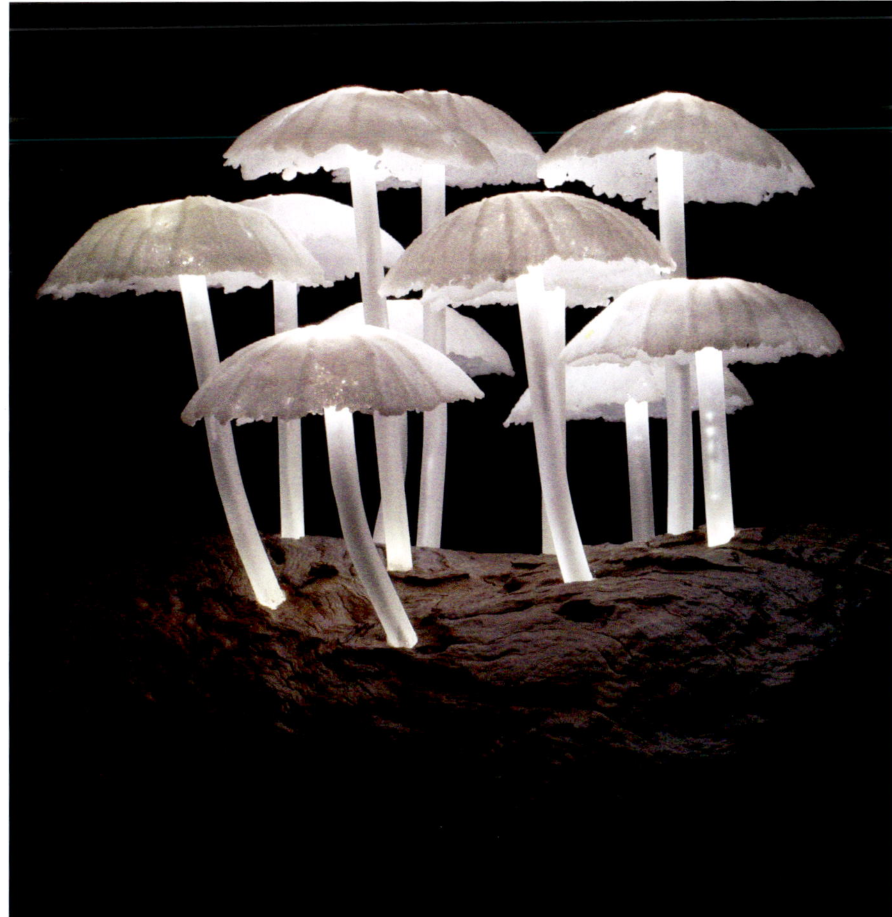

1 *Invitro Twins*. Lost wax cast. 12.6" × 5.51" × 9.84". 2002. Photo: Grant Hancock.

2 *Invitro*. Lost wax kiln-cast. 11.81" × 4.72" × 8.66". 2000. Photo: Grant Hancock.

3 *Toadstools*. Extruded and etched glass stems, cast pate de verre glass caps, and mounted on a prepared mallee stump. 10.63" × 9.84" × 10.63". 2013.

4 *Forest Fungi 2*. Etched glass stems, cast pate de verre glass caps. 15.75" × 7.09" × 11.81". 2014.

5 *Forest Fungi*. Etched glass stems, cast pate de verre glass caps internally lit. 9.06" × 9.45" × 12.6". 2014.

Thor & Jennifer Bueno

Penland, North Carolina

Thor grew up surfing in Southern California and started blowing glass in 1979. He had the privilege of studying with Italo Scanga at the University of California at San Diego, where he received a BFA. As a founding member of The B Team, a performance group that used hot glass, he toured the world performing in public access facilities and universities. In 2004 he earned an MFA in glass from Alfred University.

Jennifer grew up in Seneca, South Carolina, and attended Rhode Island School of Design, where she received a BFA in glass. Her work is conceptual in nature and currently centers on satellite imagery. She has earned two MFAs, one from Bard College in sculpture and one from Alfred University in glass.

We began working together fifteen years ago after meeting at Pilchuck Glass School in Stanwood, Washington. With my background in performance art and hers in conceptual art, we had a lot to talk about. We had a different way of looking at the medium because we didn't always think of glass as utilitarian; it was so much bigger than that! Whether we were working together in the hot shop or independently, we found a shared interest in pushing the boundaries of what was expected from glass. After completing a three-year residency at Penland School of Crafts in the mountains of North Carolina, we settled nearby and set up our studio, where we continue to find inspiration in the natural beauty that surrounds us.

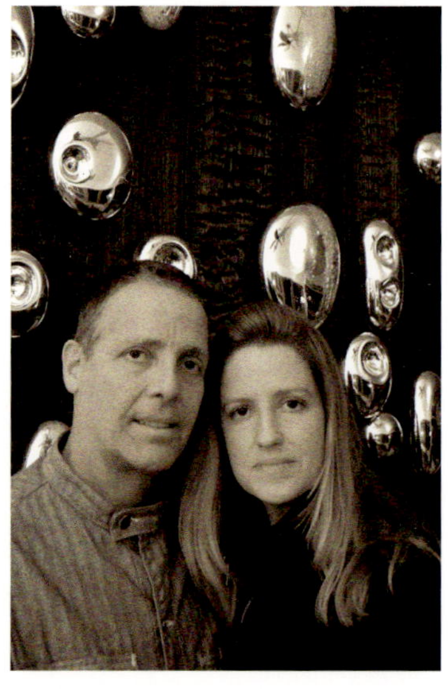

1

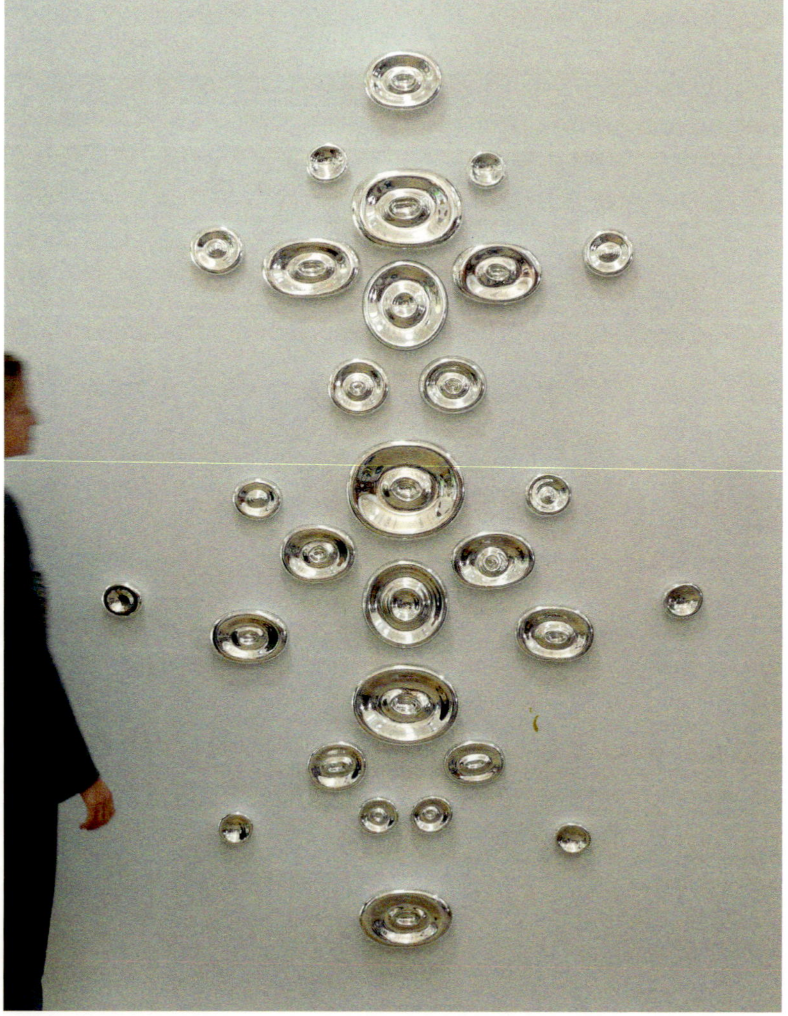

1 *Roar*. Silvered blown glass. 11' × 3" × 4.5'. 2011.

2 *Silvers*. Silvered blown glass. Dimensions variable. 2013. Courtesy of Steve Mann Black Box Photography.

3 *Trailing, Rust, Amber, Ivory and Light*. 12' × 4" × 6'. 2014. Courtesy of Anne Lambert Tracht, Consult Art Inc.

4 *Light Gathered Stones*. Etched and silvered blown glass. 5' × 4" × 3'. 2013. Courtesy of Steve Mann Black Box Photography.

5 *River Stones*. Etched blown glass. 6' × 4" × 4'. 2010. Courtesy of Steve Mann Black Box Photography.

2

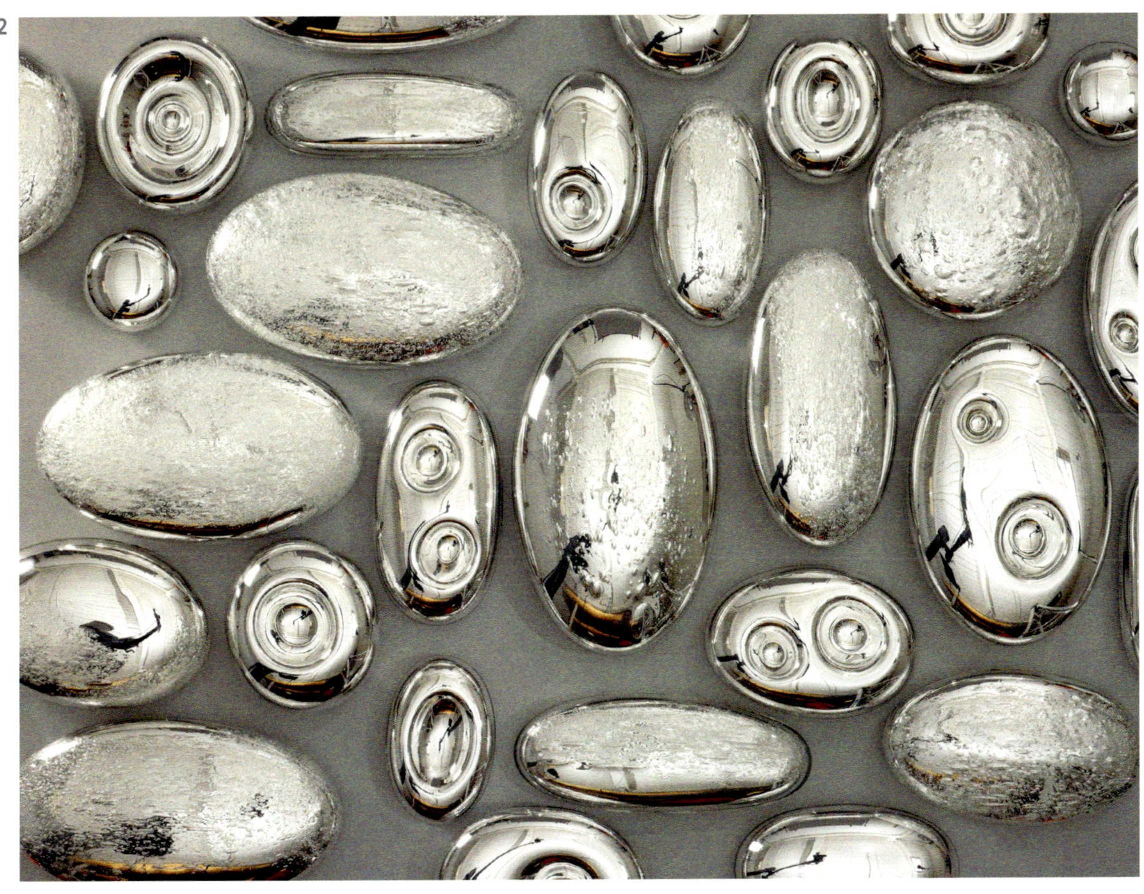

3

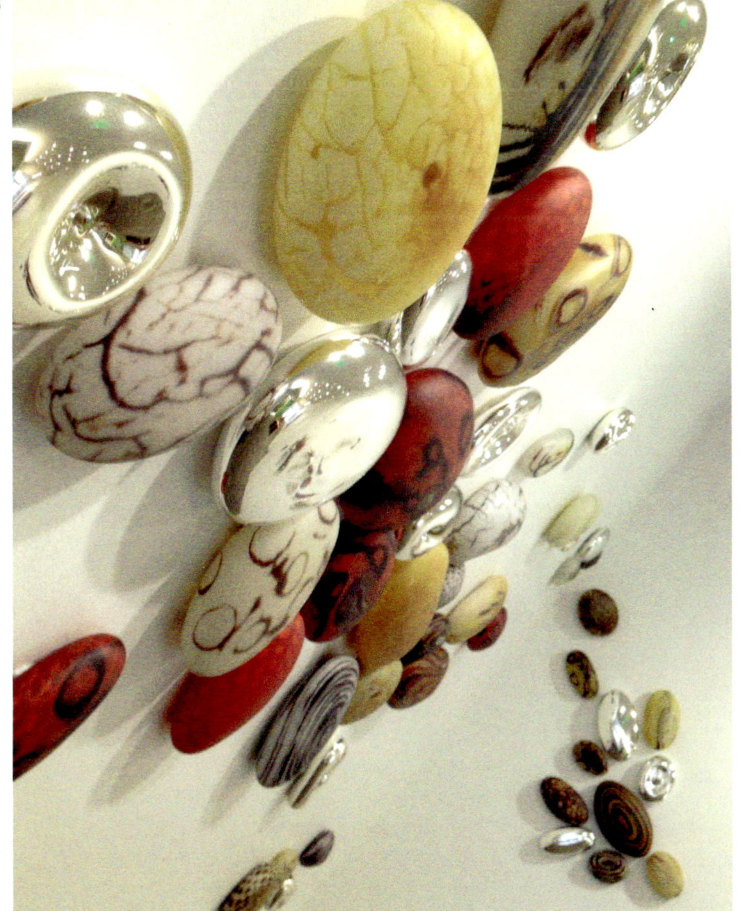

4

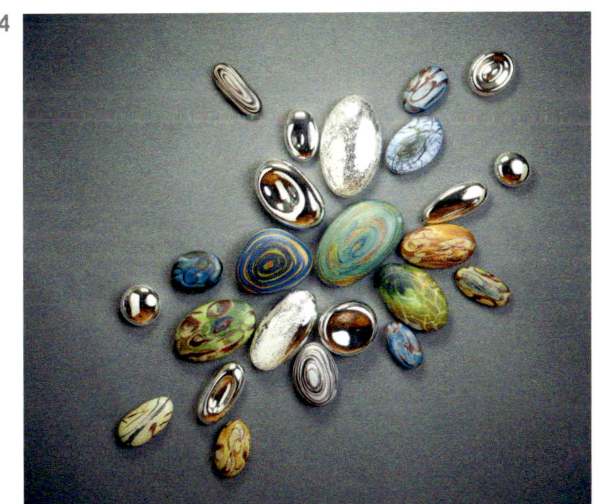

5

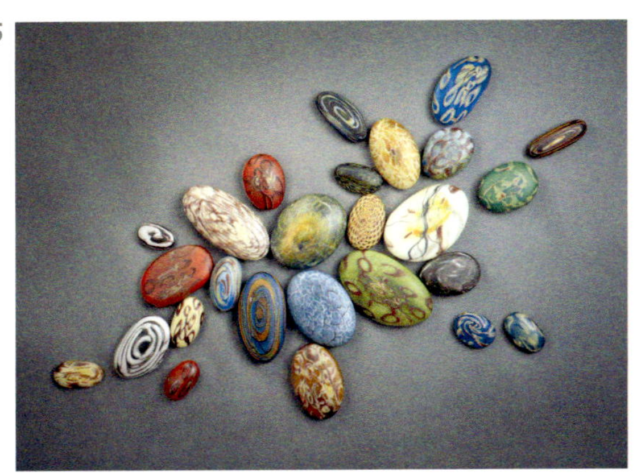

Robert Carlson

Bainbridge Island, Washington

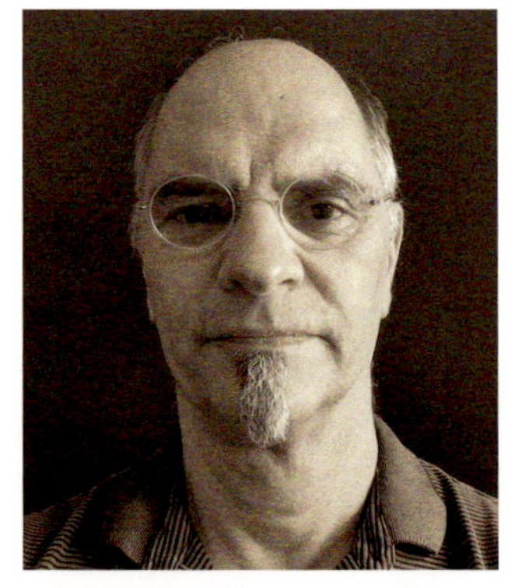

At heart, I am a three-dimensional artist, which is why I love using glass as my medium. The clear glass transmits images through itself, allowing me to turn an object of surfaces into an object with both surfaces and an interior. My pieces are three-dimensional narratives that are meant to be "grokked" as opposed to "understood." Unlike a written narrative, where a linear progression of words slowly brings the reader to the story and ultimately to an understanding, my sculptures present an entire narrative experience in a more immediate visual format. For me, this is the beauty and allure of painted glass sculpture.

While I have always loved the process of glassblowing, my sculptures had to be about more than just the glass and its inherent properties. Painting on glass has allowed me to transform this beautiful and seductive material into narrative sculptures that express the deep inner life that animates all human beings. The glass gives these sculptures form, but the paint gives them meaning, which, I believe, is the most important part of my work.

1

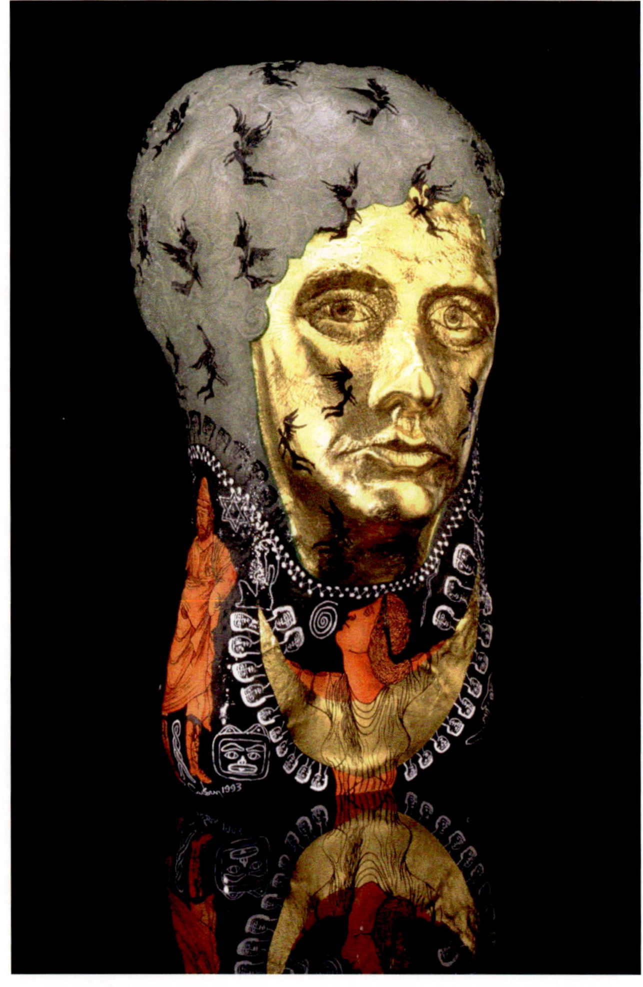

2

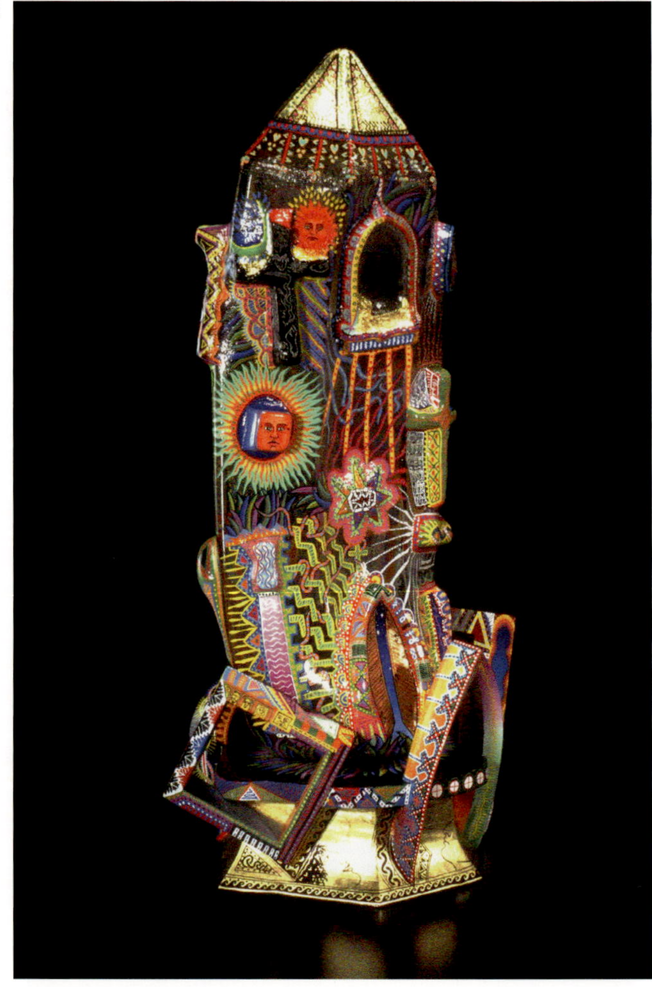

3

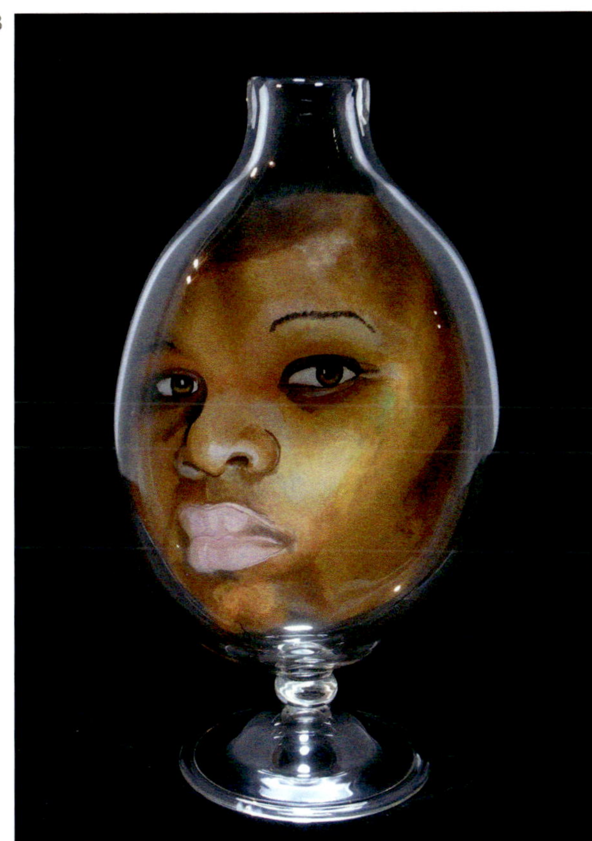

4

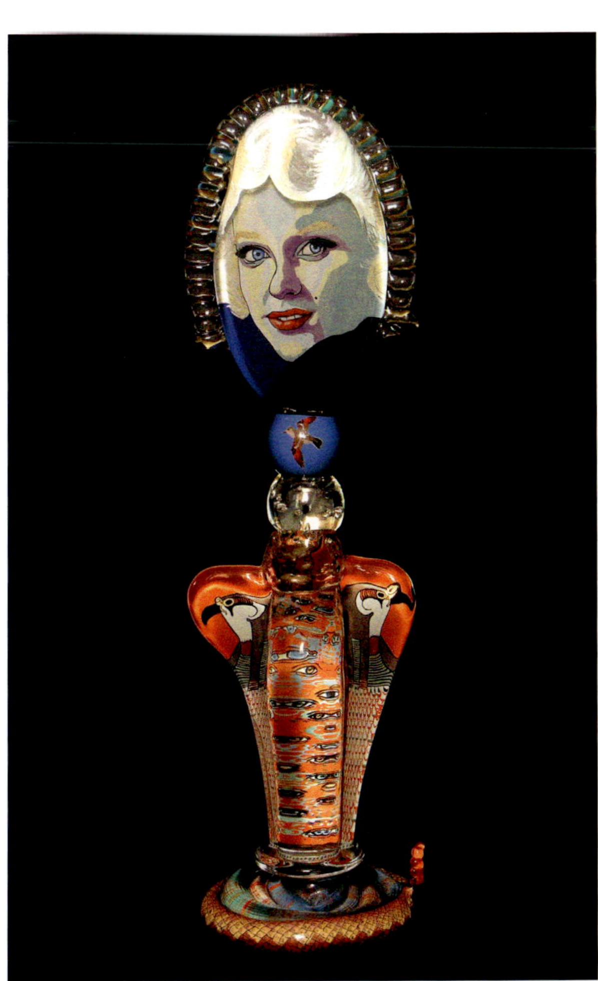

5

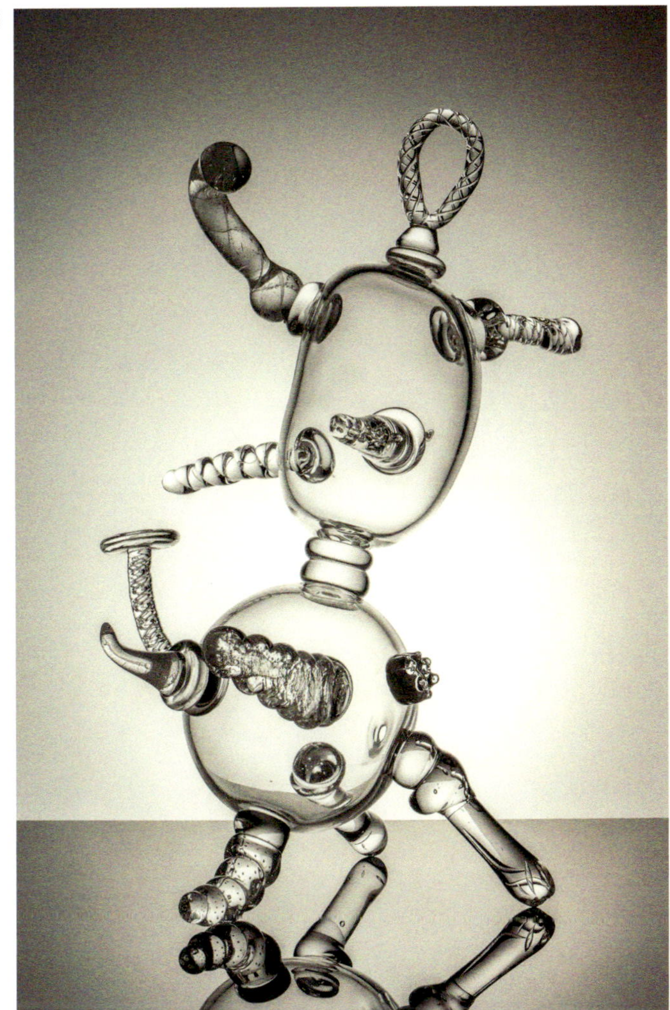

1 *Hephaestus*. Blown glass, enamel paint, and gold leaf. 17" × 10" × 9". 1994. Courtesy of Roger Schreiber, Seattle.

2 *Axis Mundi*. Blown glass, wood, enamel paint, gold leaf, and copper leaf. 16" × 13" × 32". 1996. Courtesy of Roger Schreiber, Seattle.

3 *Injustice Anywhere Is a Threat to Justice Everywhere*. Blown glass, enamel paint, and UV adhesive. 8" × 11" × 20". 2014.

4 *Priestess*. Blown glass, enamel paint, and UV adhesive. 9" × 10" × 34". 2006.

5 *Untitled MV2331b*. Blown glass, UV adhesive. 14" × 14" × 23". 2012. Courtesy of Cameron Karsten.

Robin Cass

Rochester, New York

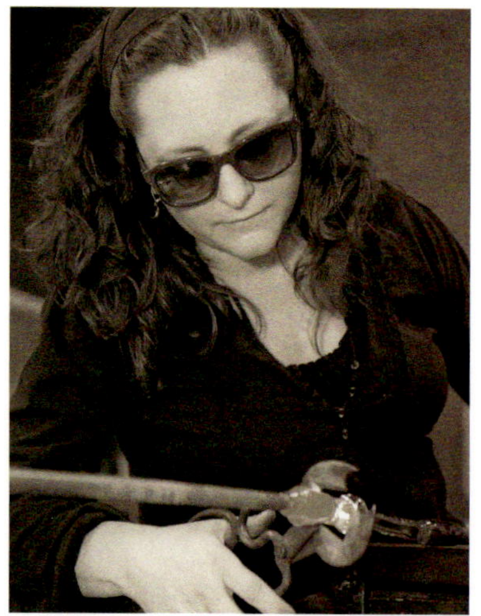

Courtesy of Elizabeth Lamark/RIT Photo Production Services.

I find the sensory elements of various organisms intriguing, especially those features that are light sensitive and perceive form and texture, and those orifices that let matter in or out. I'm interested in how these elements animate a form, how we relate and respond to such features, and use them to figure out what we are dealing with. They can indicate awareness, sensitivity, vulnerability, or even threat.

My inspirations include the botanical photographs of Karl Blossfeldt, the biological engravings of Ernst Haeckel, and the glass scientific models of Leopold and Rudolf Blaschka. I am fascinated by the human inclination to seek out and gather odd and novel objects for personal contemplation and public display, an urge exemplified by the "WunderKammer," or cabinets of curiosities, of Renaissance Europe.

The sense of wonder that one can experience when encountering a mysterious object or being is rare and appealing. Although as humans we are always trying to categorize and define, we still enjoy being challenged by the occasional enigma. I'm often trying to elicit such a response with my work, an enjoyable state of confounded reflection.

1

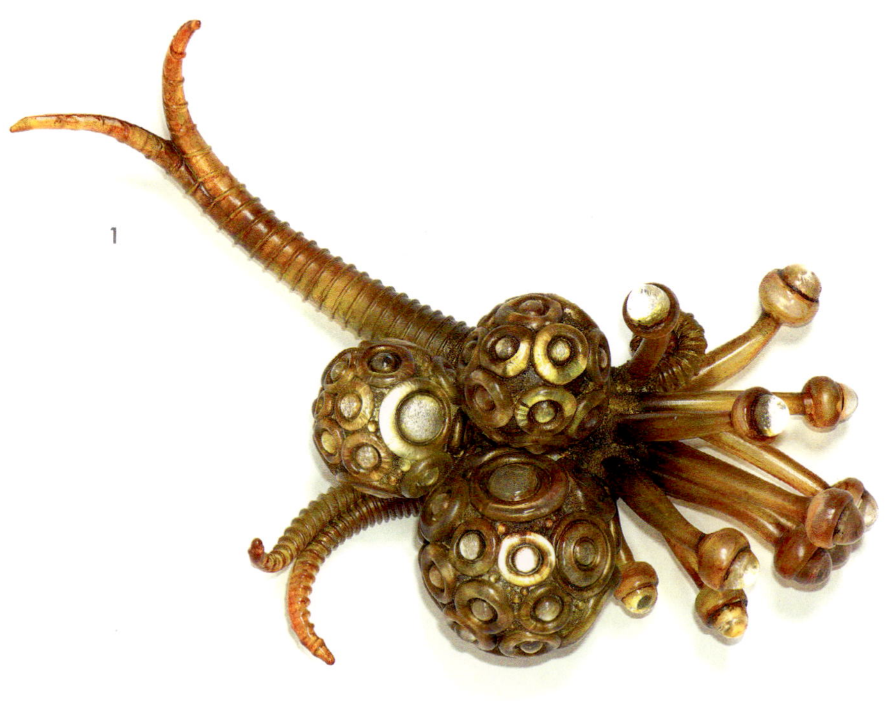

2

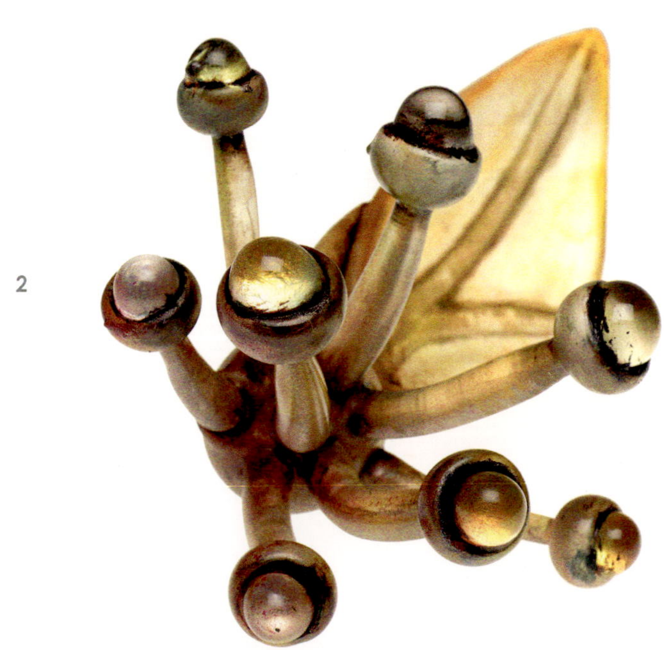

1 *Amber Galactolipid*. From the *Curious Growth* series. Hot-formed glass, silver, and mixed media. 14" × 24" × 8". 2013. Courtesy of Elizabeth Lamark/RIT Photo Production Services.

2 *Minor Pulchella*. From the *Curious Growth* series. Hot-formed glass, silver, and mixed media. 10" × 16" × 8". 2012. Courtesy of Elizabeth Lamark/RIT Photo Production Services.

3

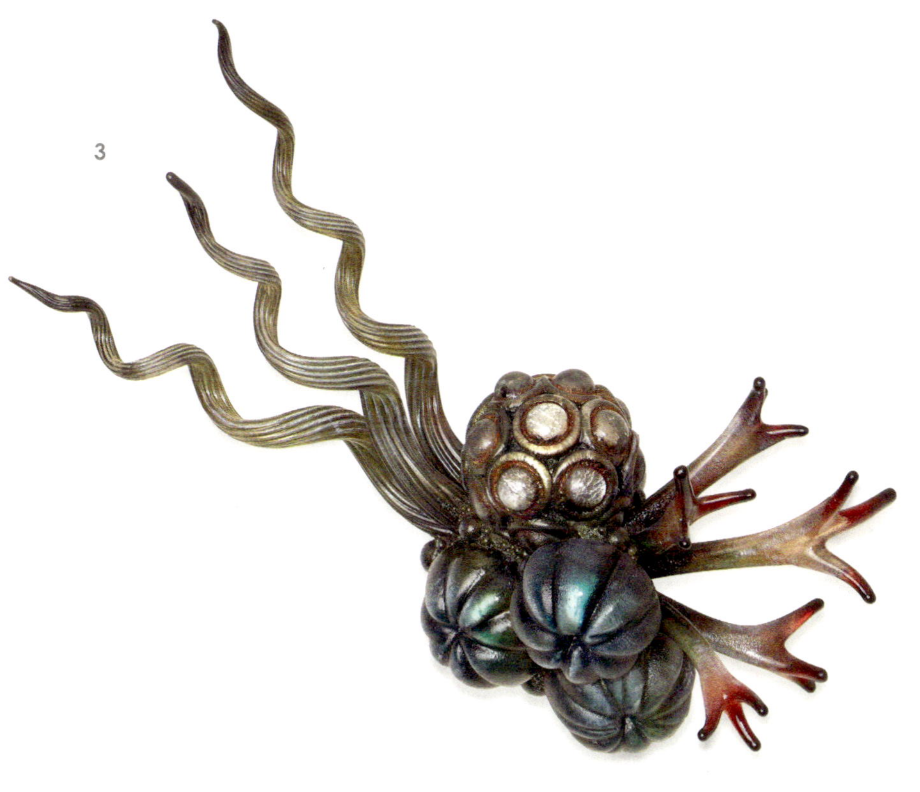

3 *Flagellated Galactolipid*. From the *Curious Growth* series. Hot-formed glass, silver, and mixed media. 14" × 22" × 8". 2012. Courtesy of Elizabeth Lamark/RIT Photo Production Services.

4 *Pilunaria Nutans (mature)*. From the *Curious Growth* series. Hot-formed glass, silver, and mixed media. 11" × 6" × 5". 2014. Courtesy of Elizabeth Lamark/RIT Photo Production Services.

5 *Reclining Perspicalyx*. From the *Curious Growth* series. Hot-formed glass, silver, and mixed media. 5" × 18" × 6". 2014. Courtesy of Elizabeth Lamark/RIT Photo Production Services.

6 *Ocular Cladanthus*. Hot-formed glass, silver, and mixed media. 7" × 18" × 6". 2014. Courtesy of Elizabeth Lamark/RIT Photo Production Services.

4

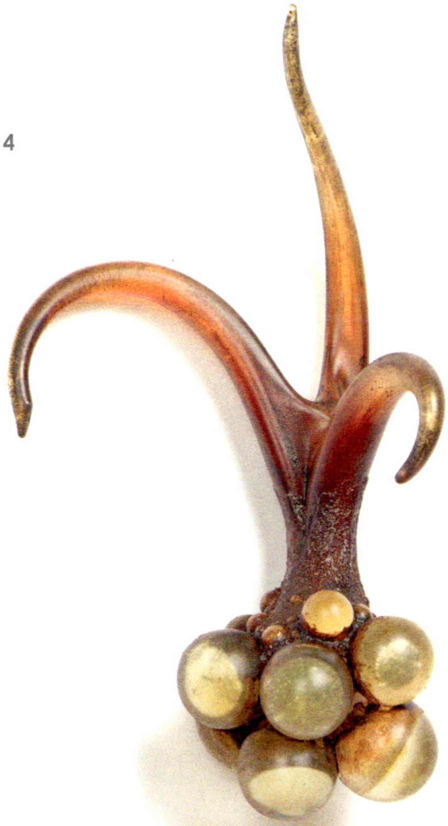

5

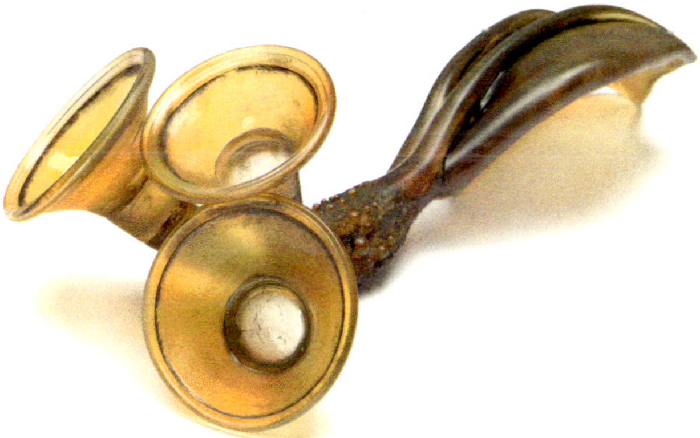

6

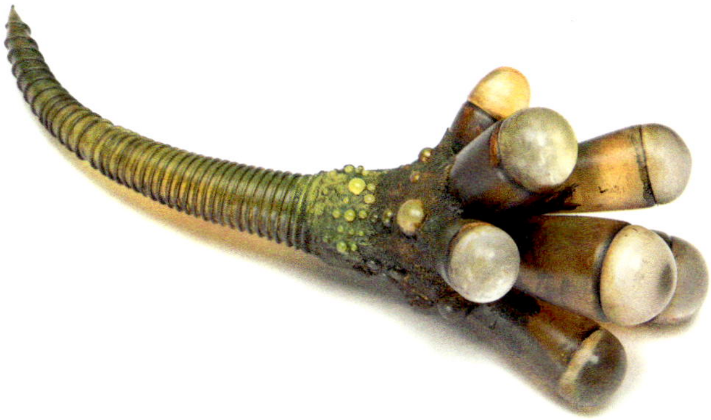

Maryse Chartrand

Montreal, Quebec, Canada

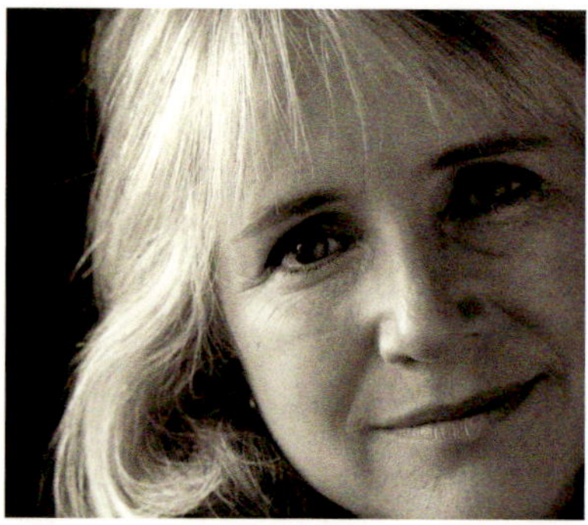

Courtesy of Andréanne Chartrand-Beaudry.

The deeper I dive into the art of glass, the more I'm fascinated with the material's beauty. Glass is solid but fragile, dense but fluid. It hovers between the concrete world and the world of light. Much like a living organism, it contains contradictions, yet maintains harmony and balance. I love to work glass, and I love the way it works me!

Glass is my creative partner. I consider myself an artist but also an explorer. Although my process is sparked by an idea, it is the anticipation of a discovery that really drives me. I want glass to show me the way. And the more it does, the more I find that the final piece underlines the mysterious beauty of life.

1

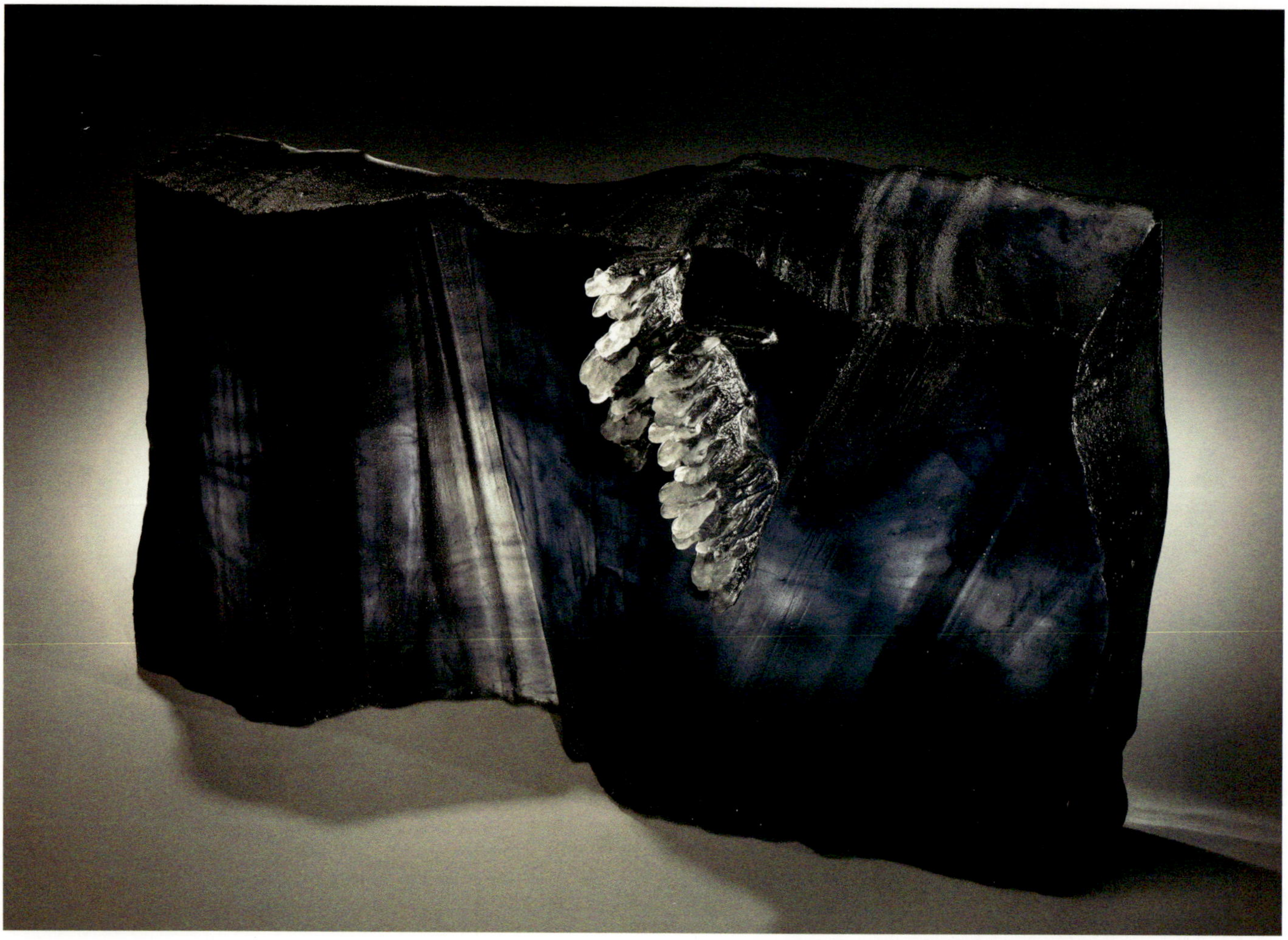

1 *Quiet Strength.* Lost wax cast glass. 10" × 4" × 20". Photo: Michel Dubreuil.

2

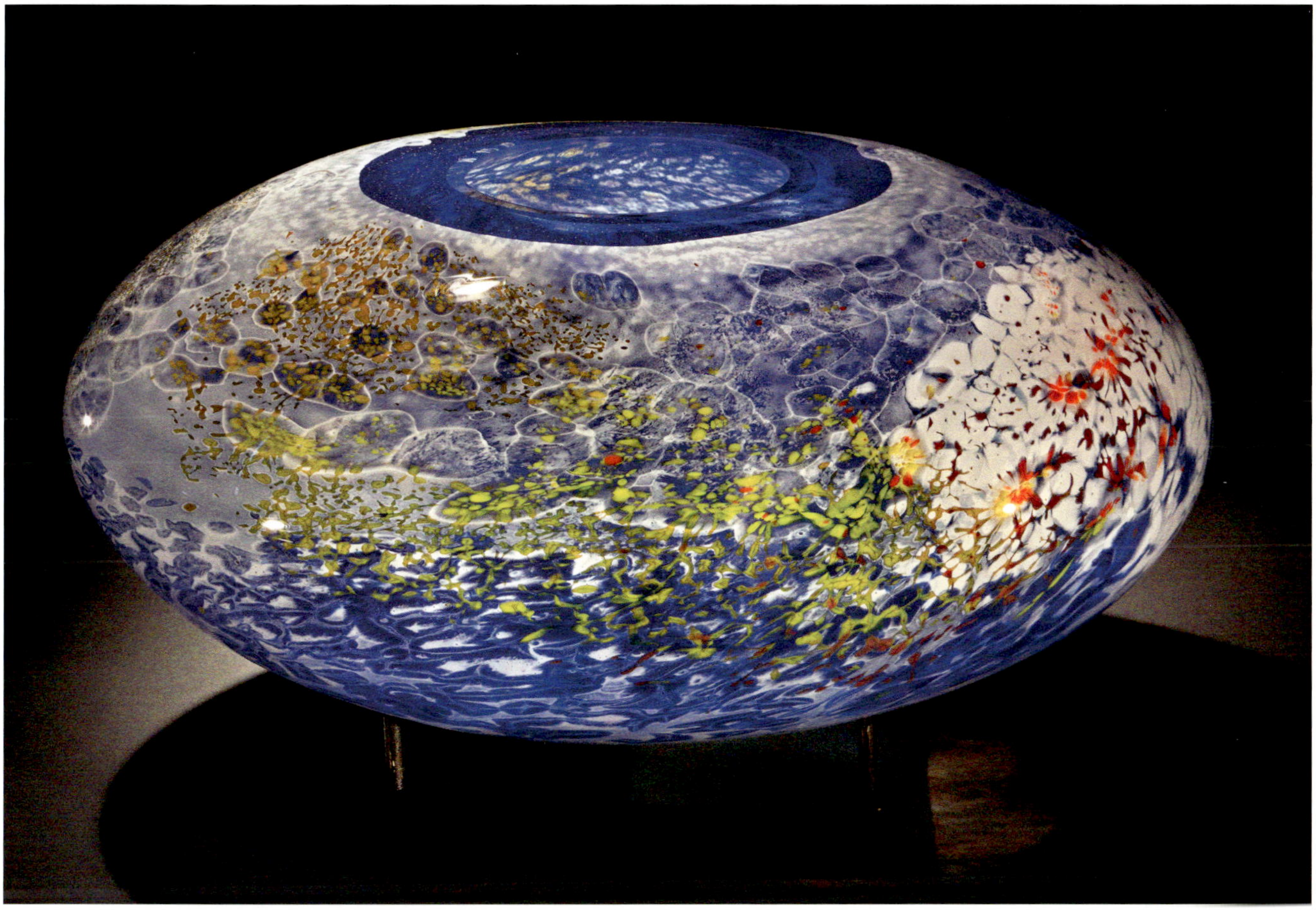

3

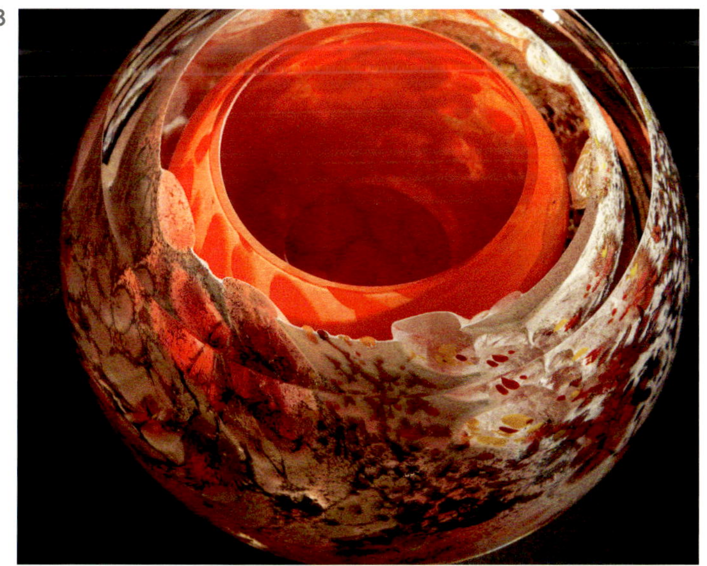

4

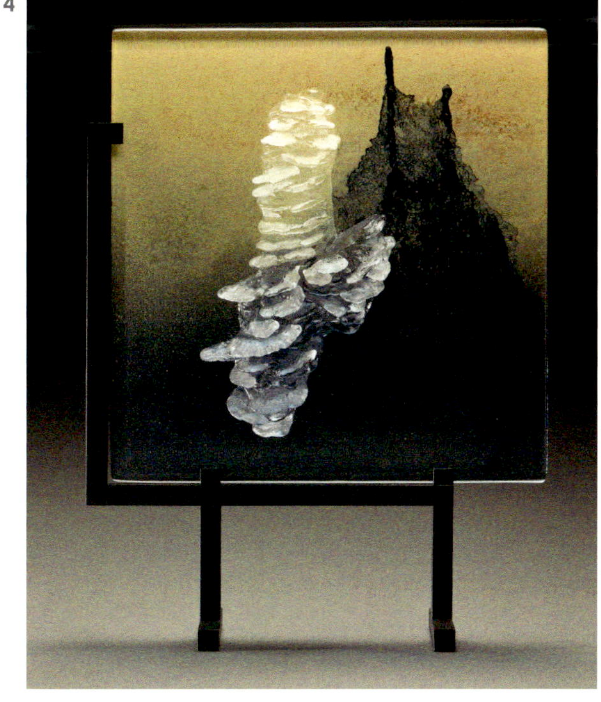

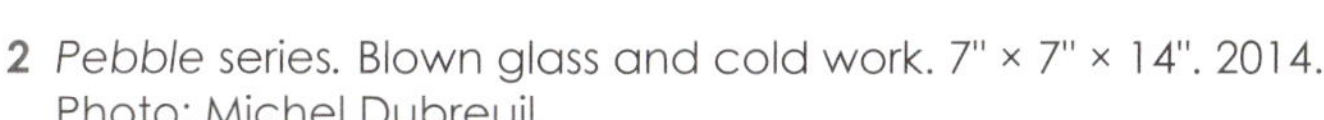

2 *Pebble* series. Blown glass and cold work. 7" × 7" × 14". 2014. Photo: Michel Dubreuil.

3 *Ailleurs* series. Blown glass and cold work. 7" × 7". 2014. Photo: Michel Dubreuil.

4 *Full moon.* Enameled glass and lost wax cast glass with painted brass stand. 11" × 8.5" (with stand). 2013. Photo: Michel Dubreuil.

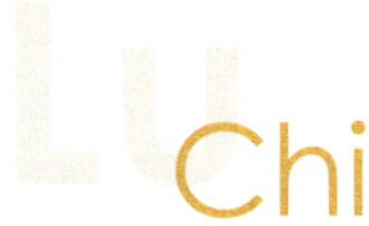

Lu Chi

Shanghai, China

Each of my works is a symphonic poem in glass dedicated to the spirit of Shanghai. I am inspired by the inner tensions of my city's modernity and magnetism. My sculptures are reveries of architectural design, urbanization, and sophisticated lifestyle. At the same time, my works forge a fresh aesthetic that reconciles my Chinese heritage and international experience.

In 2003, I received the first MFA degree in glass art awarded in China from Tsinghua University. In 2007, after I completed my studies in the United States, I became the first professional glass artist in, and set up the first personal glass studio in, mainland China.

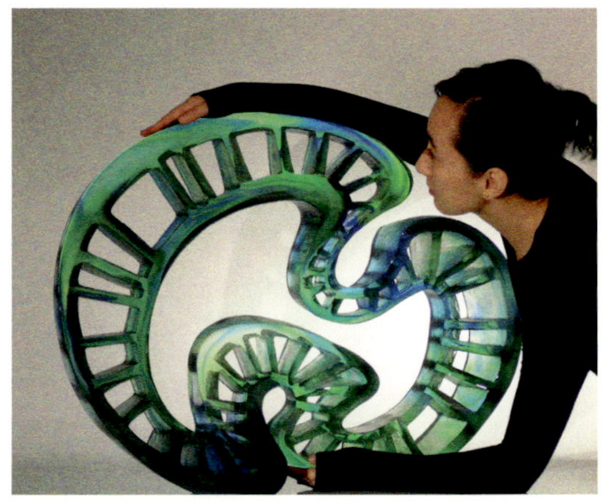

Artist with *Passion*.

1

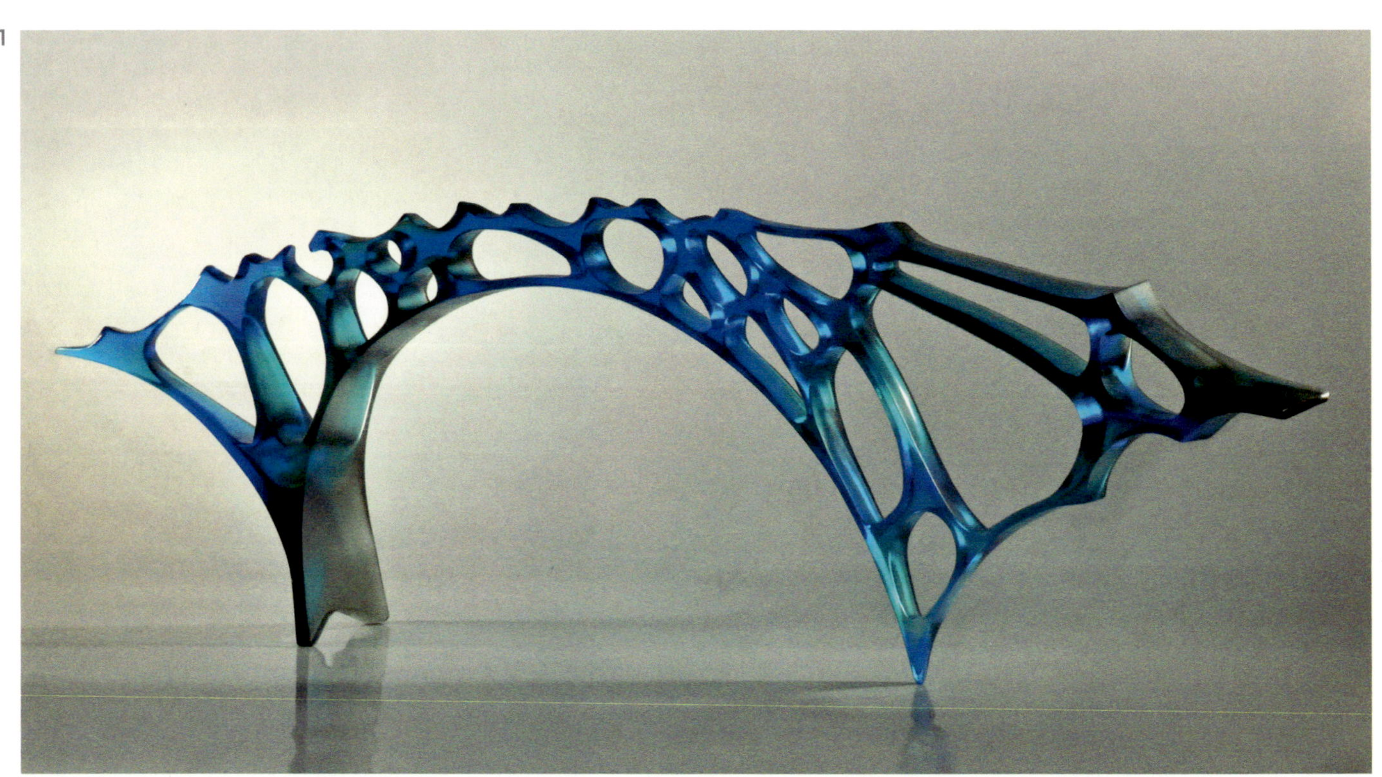

1 *Butterfly Bridge to the Dreamland in Washington DC*. Kiln casting and cold work. 5.3" × 5" × 40.1". 2012.

2

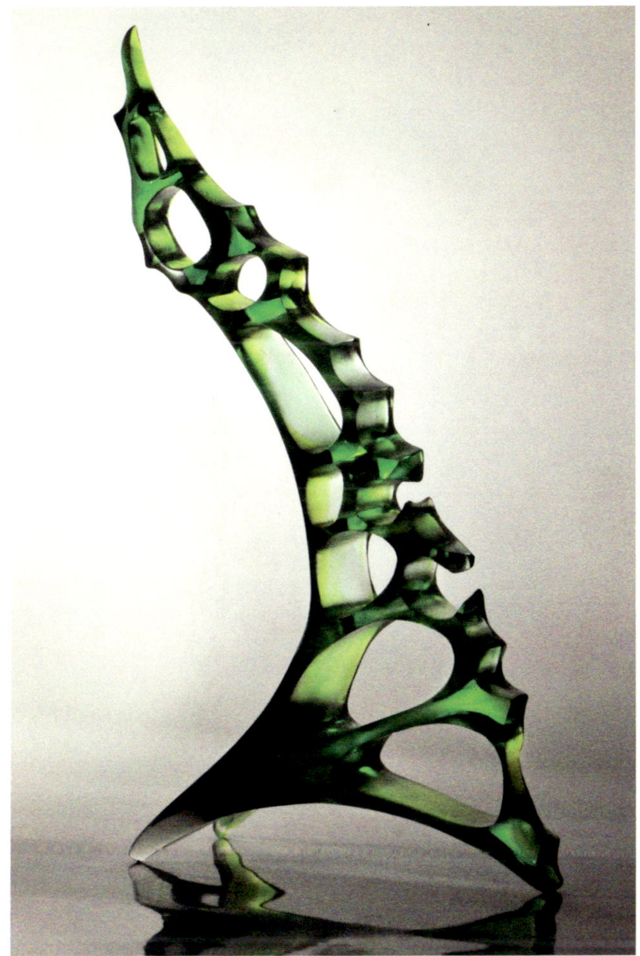

4

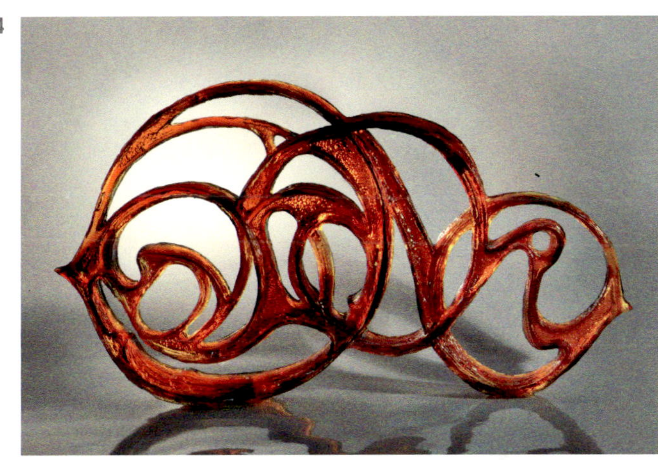

5

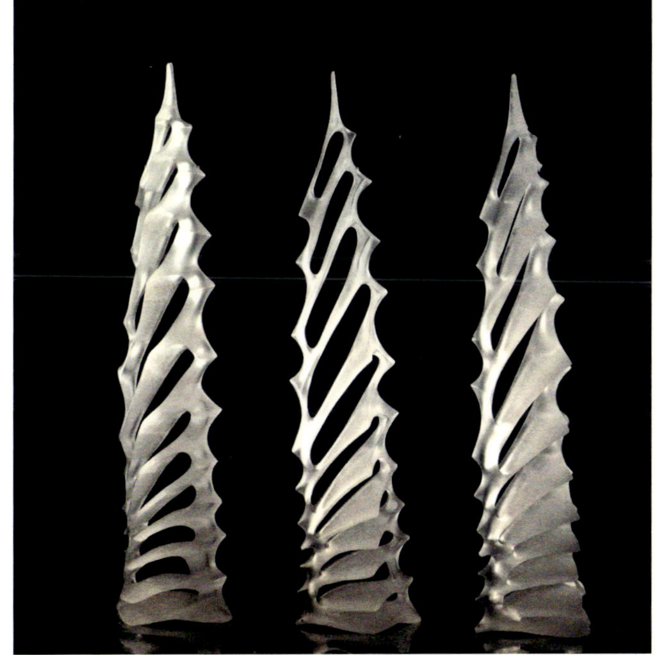

3

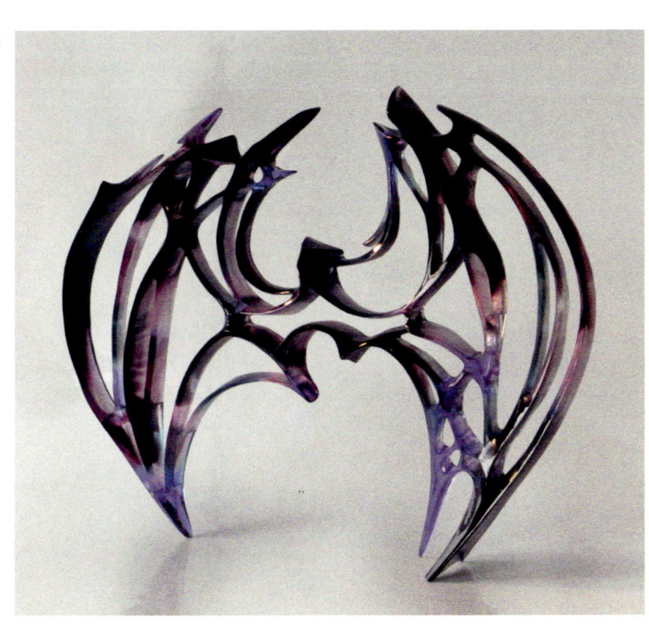

2 *Tango in Paris.* Kiln casting and cold work. 22.4" × 5.1" × 14.6". 2012.

3 *Chicago on Wings.* Kiln casting and cold work. 26" × 7" × 32.7". 2013.

4 *Echo in Verona.* Kiln casting and cold work. 24" × 4.7" × 46.5". 2012.

5 *Heavenscrapers-YunNan.* Kiln casting and cold work. 34.6" × 7" × 8.7". 2012.

Deanna Clayton

Sister Bay, Wisconsin

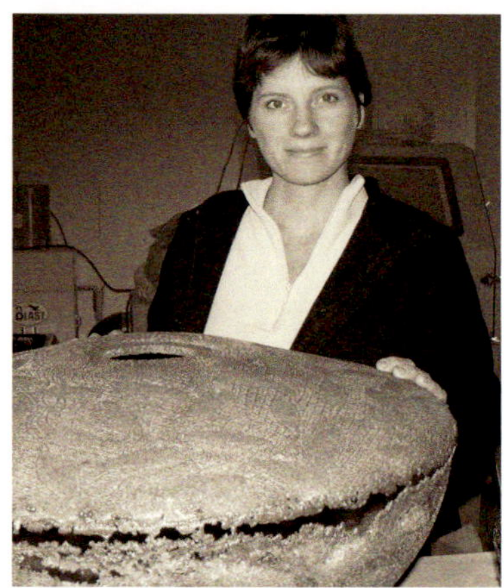

I work in glass with an aesthetic that transcends time and place. My vessels look as though they could have been found in an archeological dig yet are still contemporary in design. I love that the work has a delicate appearance combined with structural integrity.

Pate de verre translates to "paste of glass"; a paste is made with finely crushed glass and gum arabic. I layer the different colors of glass paste in a mold and fire it in a kiln. After the glass is fired and cooled, the pieces are electroplated with copper. This allows the delicate-looking edges to be strong. I then can solder two pieces together and electroplate copper over the solder, making the form whole.

1

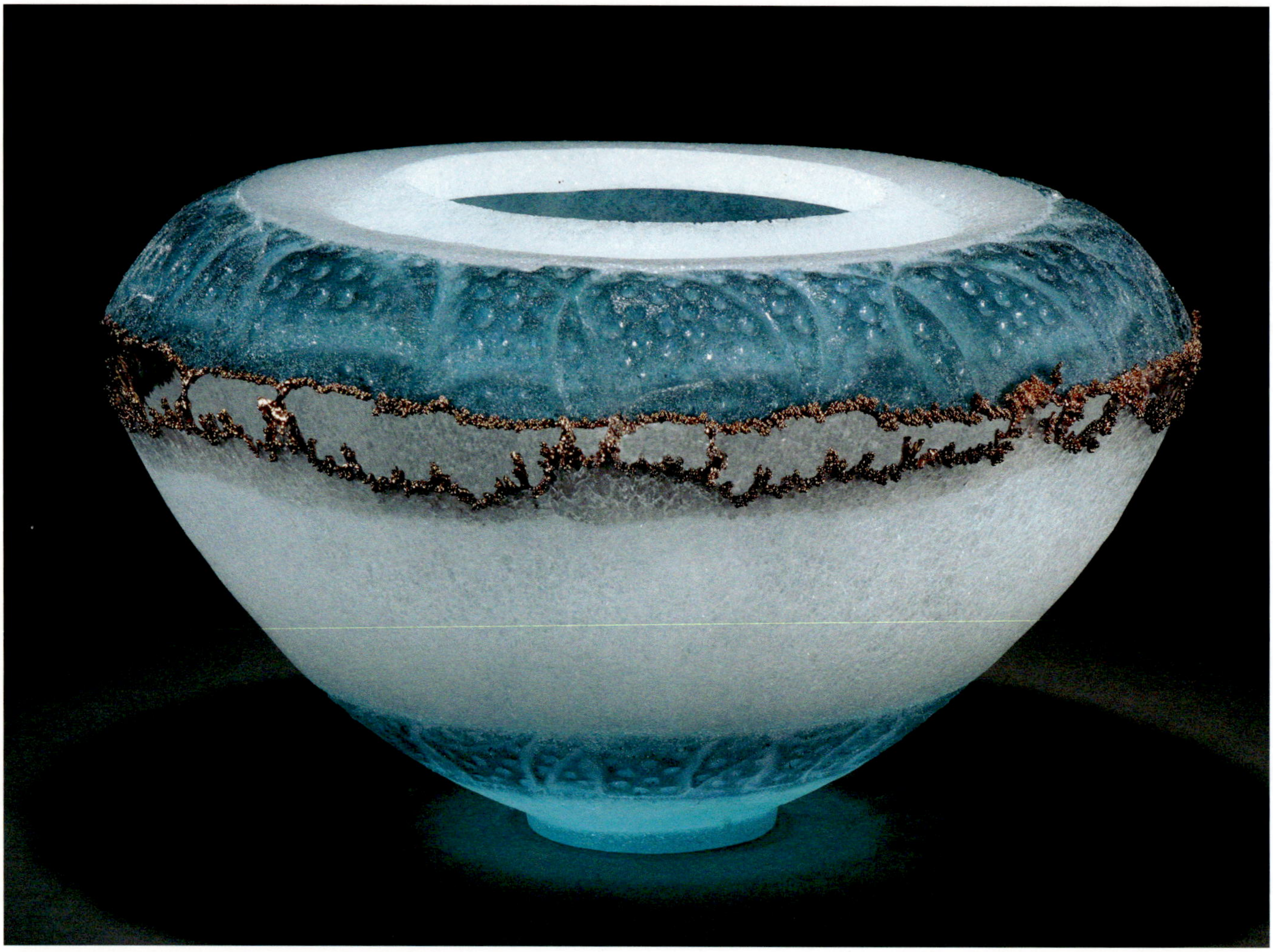

1 *LPGA Trophy*. Pate de verre and electroplated copper. 8" × 13". 2003. Photo by Larry Sanders.

2

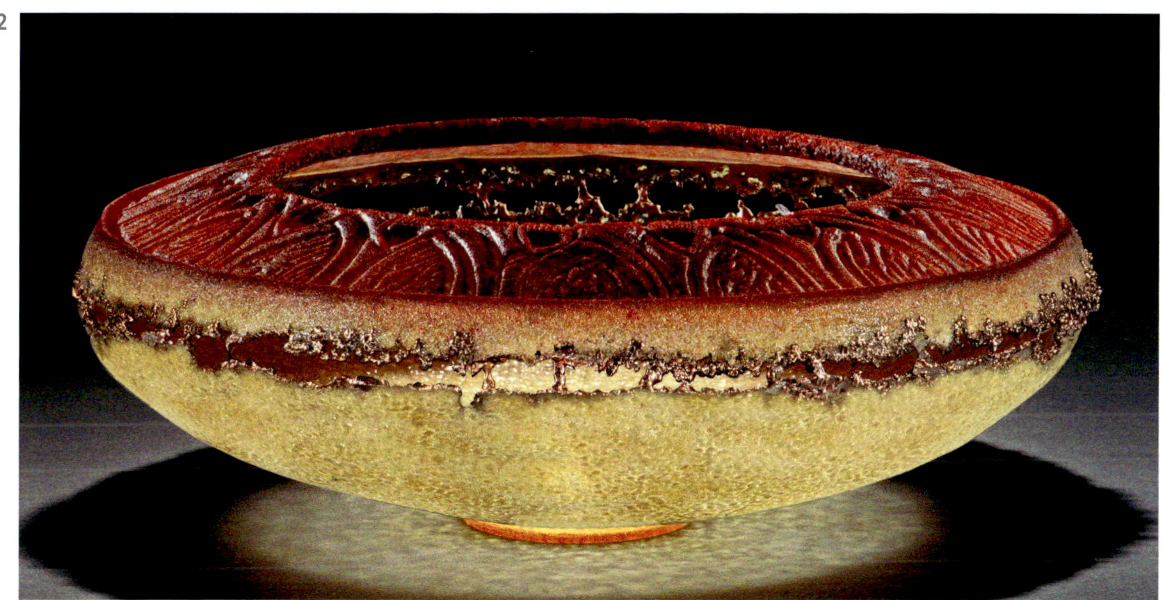

3

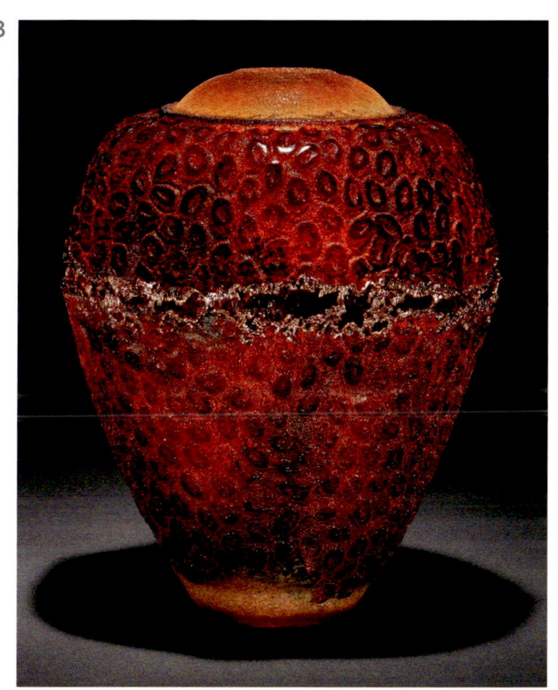

4

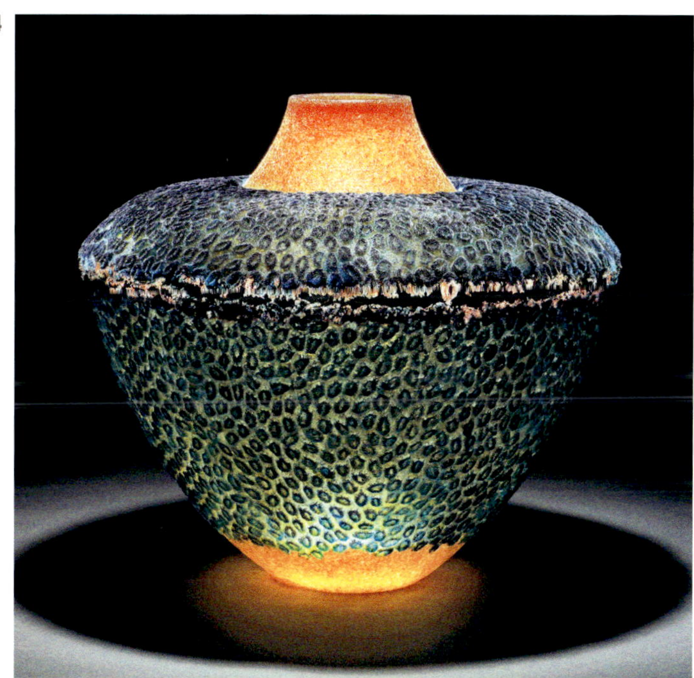

2 *Garnet Vessel.* Pate de verre and electroplated copper. 5" × 18". 2009. Photo by Larry Sanders.

3 *Red Urchin Vessel.* Pate de verre and electroplated copper. 9" × 8". 2011. Photo by Larry Sanders.

4 *Urchin Vessel.* Pate de verre and electroplated copper. 18" × 20". 2010. Photo by Larry Sanders.

5 *Citified Vessel.* Pate de verre and electroplated copper. 15" × 22". 2005. Courtesy of Artistgroup.com.

5

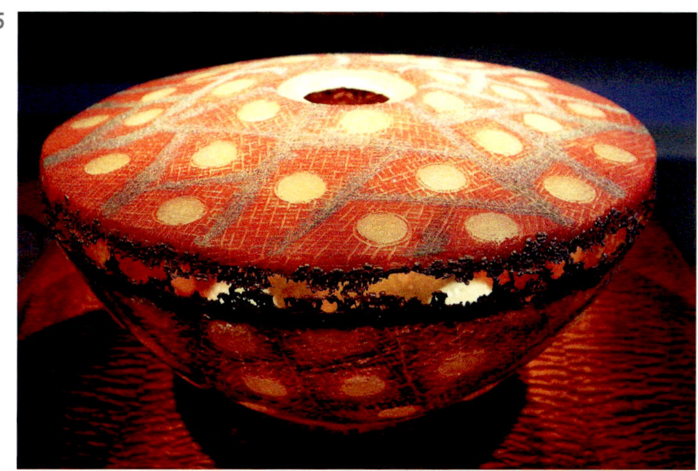

Stephan Cox

River Falls, Wisconsin

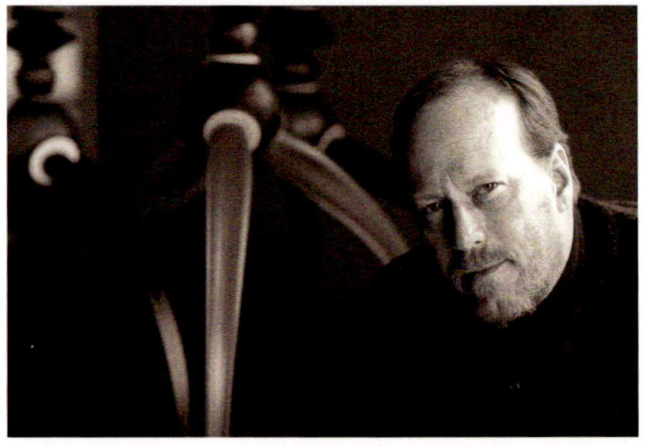

Courtesy of Jane Steinmetz.

The malleable liquidity of glass is endlessly appealing, and I use the interplay of color, form, texture, and light to achieve a compelling frozen moment. After blowing and shaping various elements, I go to my machines, benches, and tables, where—using techniques I've developed that are unique to my work—I cut, carve, and assemble. I prefer to work alone, and this solitary study allows me to distill my thoughts and plans. I have designed and made original art for over forty years, focusing mainly on glass since 1979.

1 *Blue Segments*. Blown and carved glass. 13" × 14". 2005. Courtesy of DCharles Photography.

2 *Black Stingers*. Blown and carved glass. 16" × 16". 2012. Courtesy of DCharles Photography.

3 *Blooming Rockets*. Blown and carved glass. 50" × 20". 2014.

4 *Black Orchid*. Blown and carved glass. 40" × 14". 2007. Courtesy of DCharles Photography.

5 *Swimmer Team*. Blown and carved glass. 29" × 20". 2014.

1

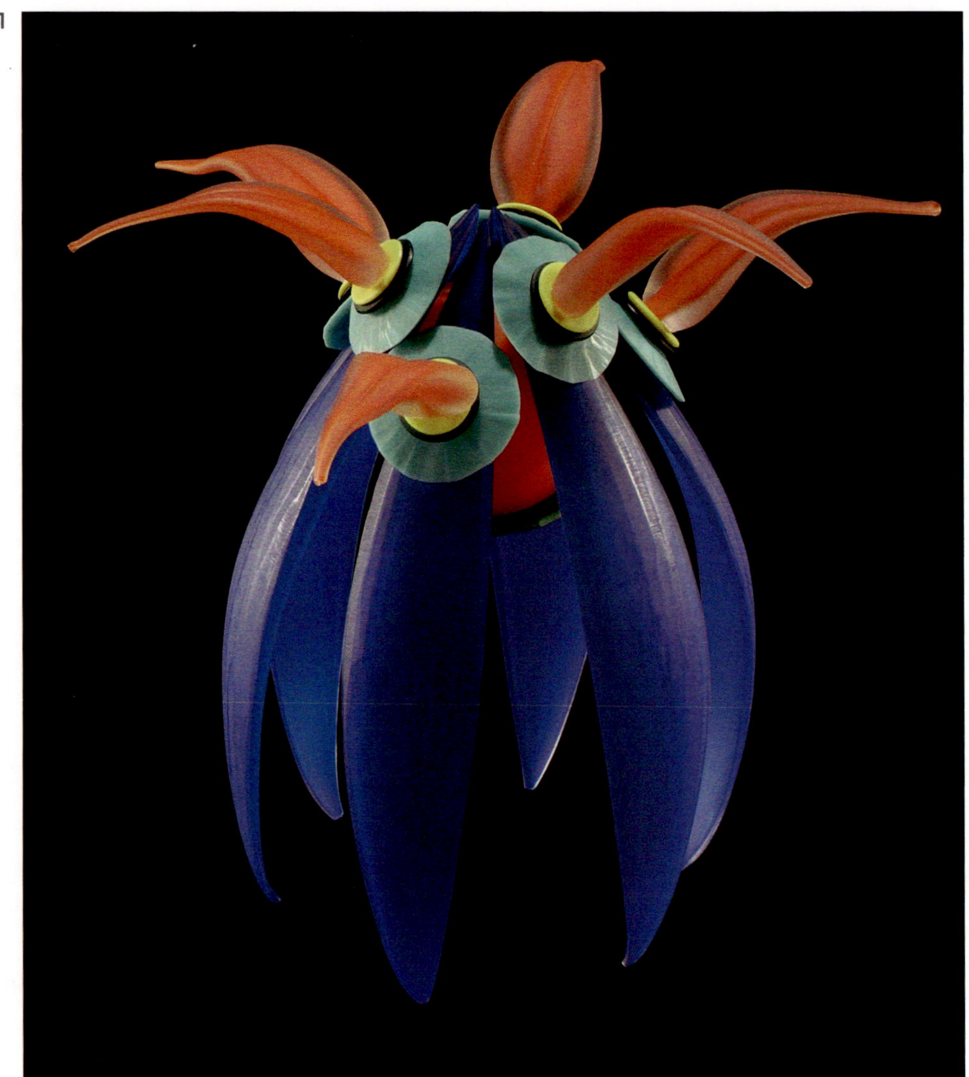

2

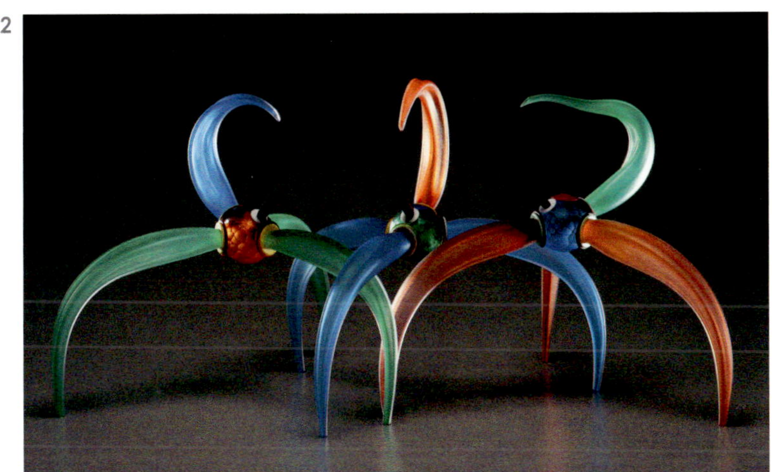

4

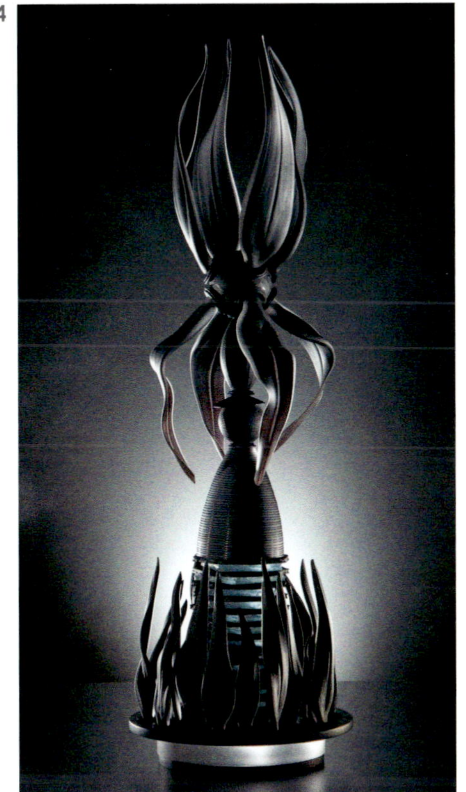

3

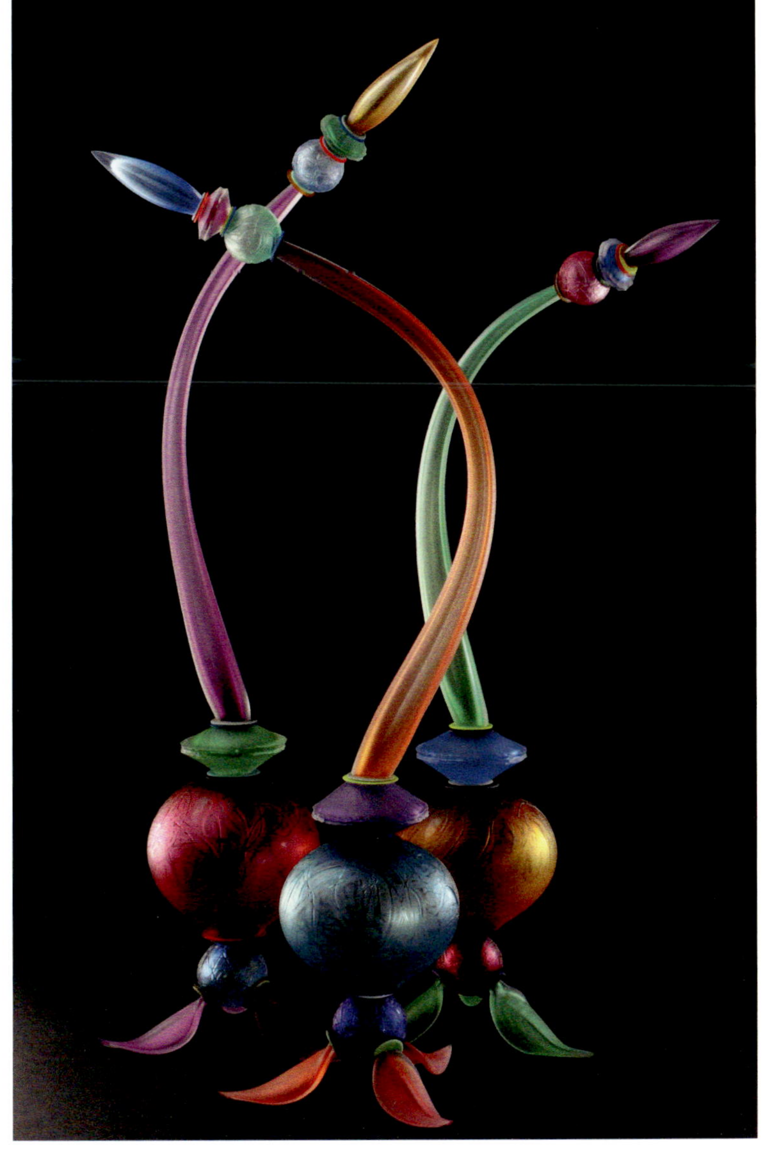

5

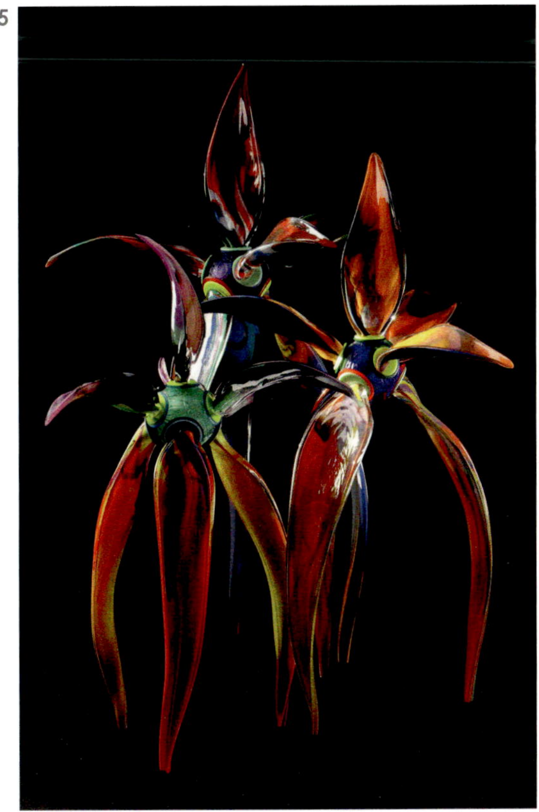

Daniel Cutrone

Elkins Park, Pennsylvania

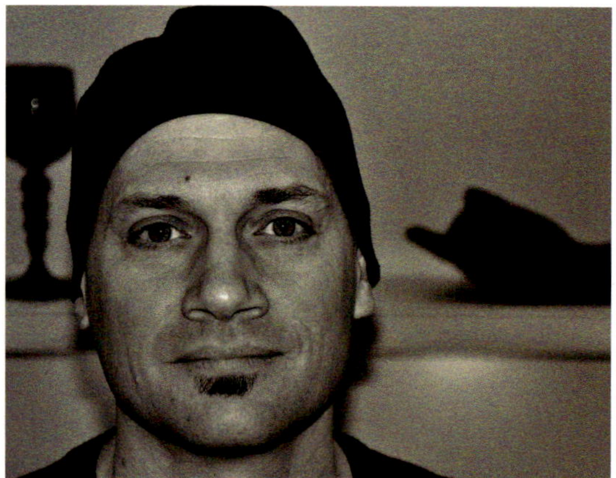

My current work uses CAD (computer aided design) and CAM (computer aided machining) to explore how these new technologies, which have their own language of form making, can be used with traditional glassmaking. I talk to my students about the "What ifs?"—not about certainty. The most fertile ground is one littered with inquiry. It is from this point of view that I begin to tug and pull at the languages of art, craft, and design. What new discourse can be had from the exchange of exciting new vocabulary provided by 3-D technologies and those of traditional glass and art making? It is my belief that relevance and meaning are not derived from a declarative statement but rather from one of inquiry. An aim of my work is to engender a state of inquiry. In particular, my new work investigates the relation between the natural world and a digitally designed one, the handmade and the manufactured.

I am also interested in creating intimacy. It is inquiry, curiosity, and a desire for understanding that moves us to intimacy. I want my work to breathe. I want the viewer to be drawn in to it. I want my work to invite the viewer to consider it from a new point of view, because by changing one's point of view we shape meaning. I believe that we can achieve intimacy through inquiry and experience even if knowledge or understanding remains incomplete.

1 | 2 *Object of Desire: Two*. Blown glass, silvering, and digital PLA print. 99" × 10" × 21". 2014. Courtesy of Matthew Hollerbush.

1

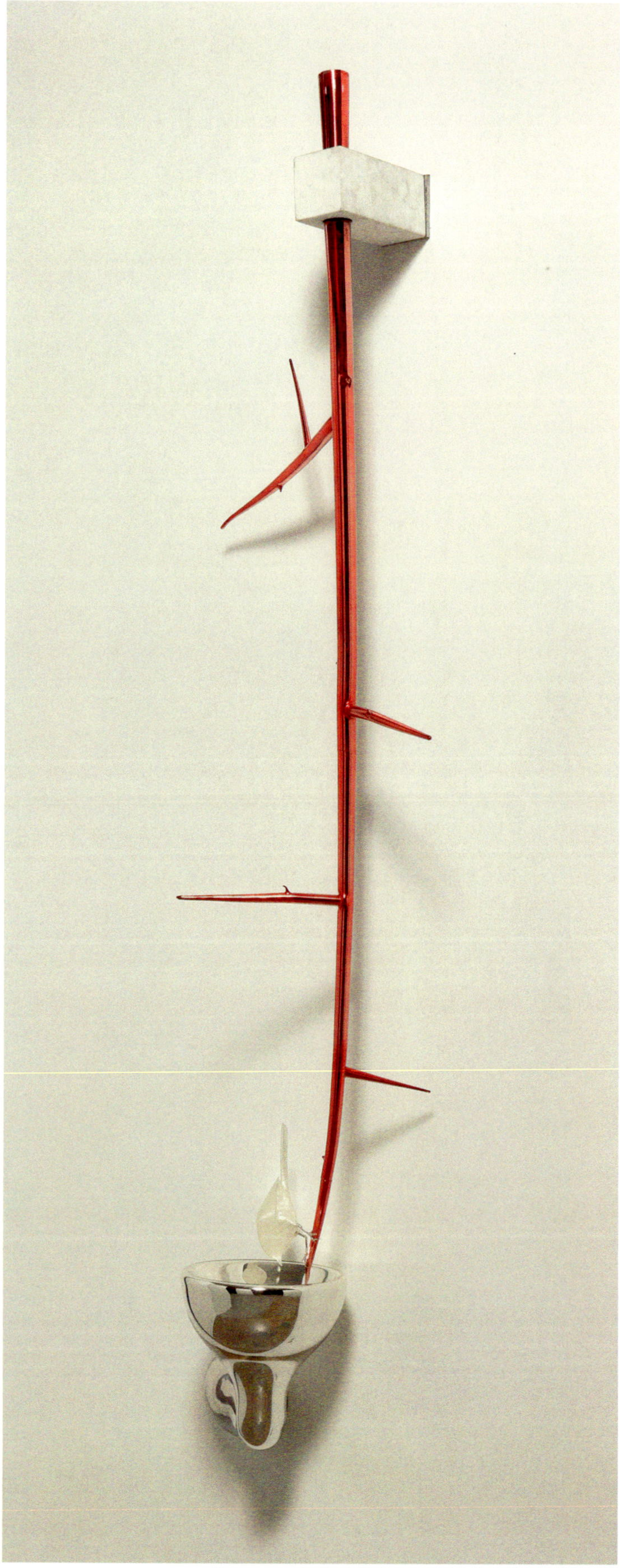

2

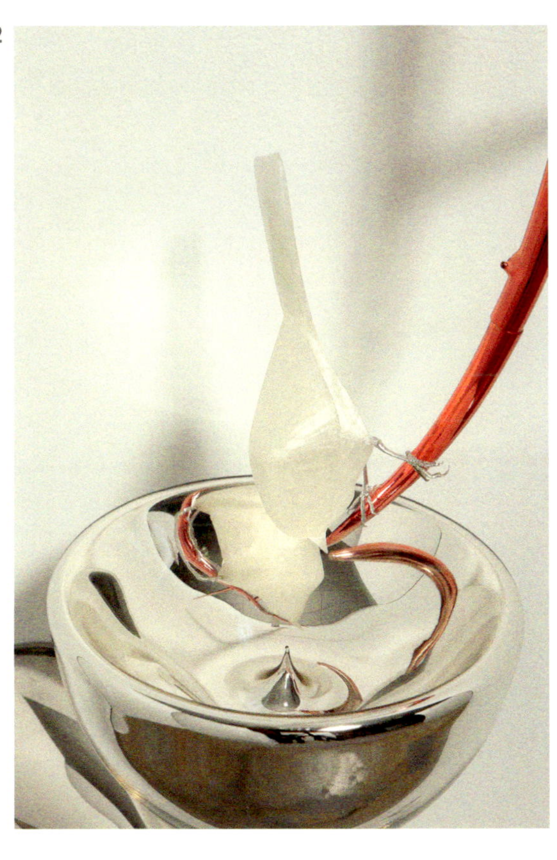

3

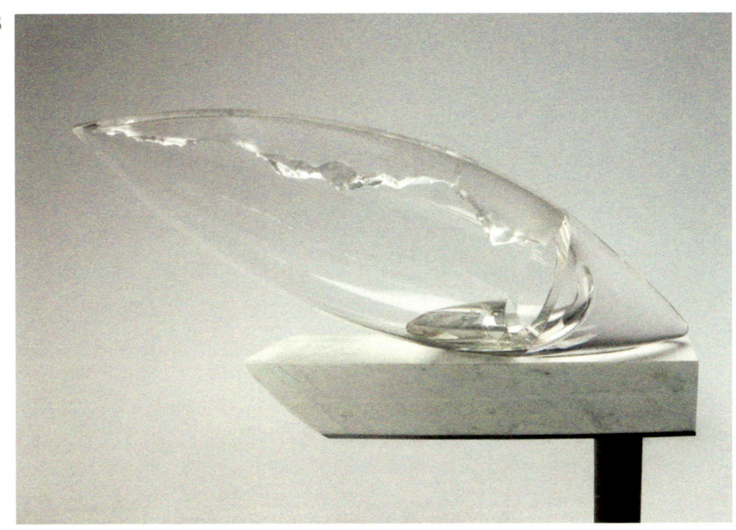

3 Detail from *Object of Desire: Slice of Mt. Everest Inverted.* Blown and cast glass, silvering, stainless steel, and marble. 48" × 16" × 31". 2014. Courtesy of Matthew Hollerbush.

4 *Object of Desire: Slice of Mt. Everest Inverted in Black.* Blown and cast glass, wood, rosin, stainless steel, and marble. 48" × 12". 2014. Courtesy of Matthew Hollerbush.

4

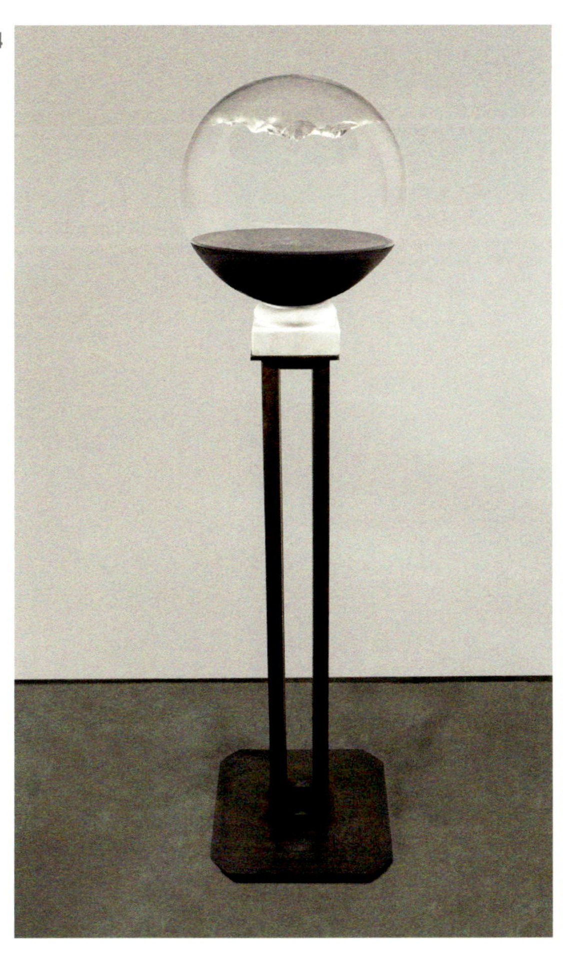

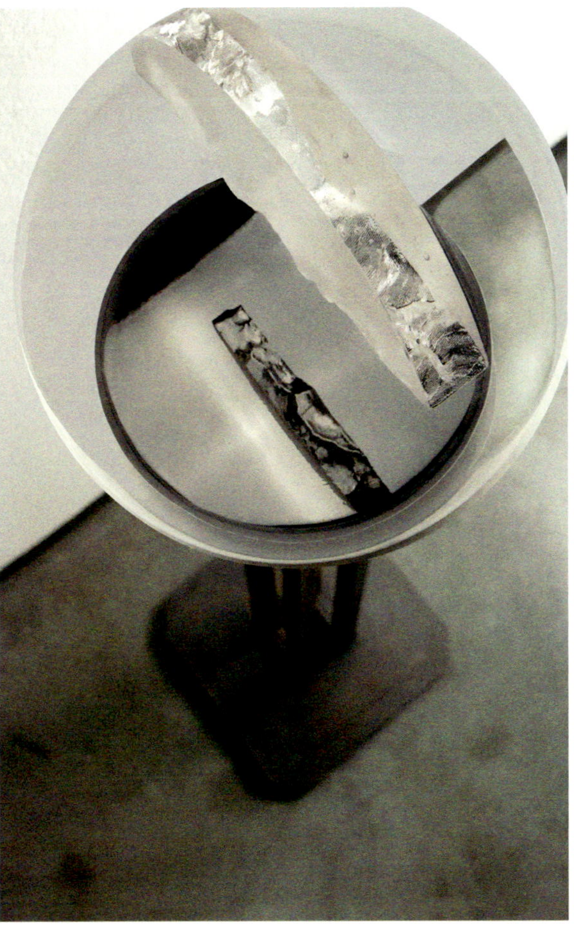

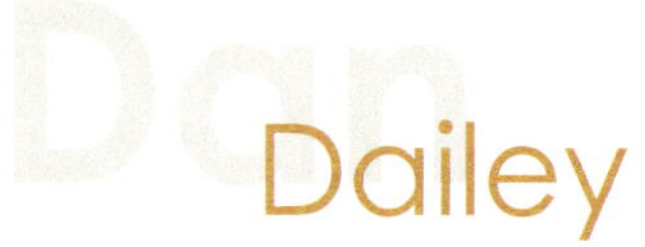

Dailey

Kensington, New Hampshire

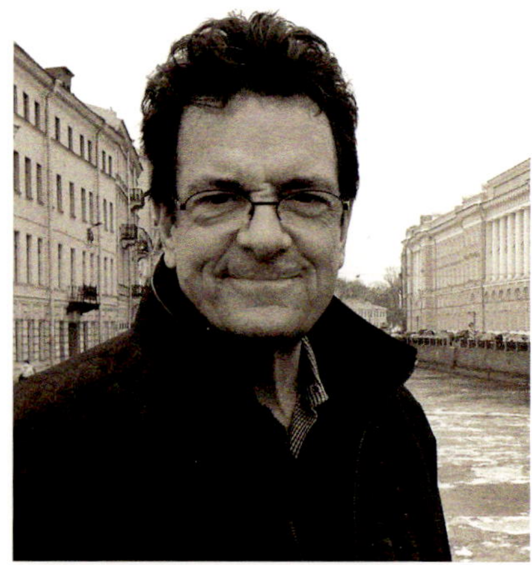

If I had remained satisfied with drawing as the end result of my artistic urge, perhaps I would have employed no format other than the white rectangle. But when I discovered ways of working with 3-D materials and began to gain skills with glass and metal, it was easy to imagine ways of realizing my ideas as functional works in addition to making art for no specific purpose. Eventually, it became natural to move back and forth between sculpture and functional art with little sense of changing my personality or mindset as I conceived new works.

Drawing allows me to put fantasies onto paper with ease, requiring no heavy material processes. Yet, the drawing is always step one for me as I record thoughts quickly from imagination. I can repeat a drawing multiple times and refine my ideas before committing to the long haul of fabrication in demanding materials. When the final work is complete, it has a character unique to the materials and processes, born of the qualities inherent in glass and metal or other mediums incorporated, and the vision of the drawing has been realized.

1

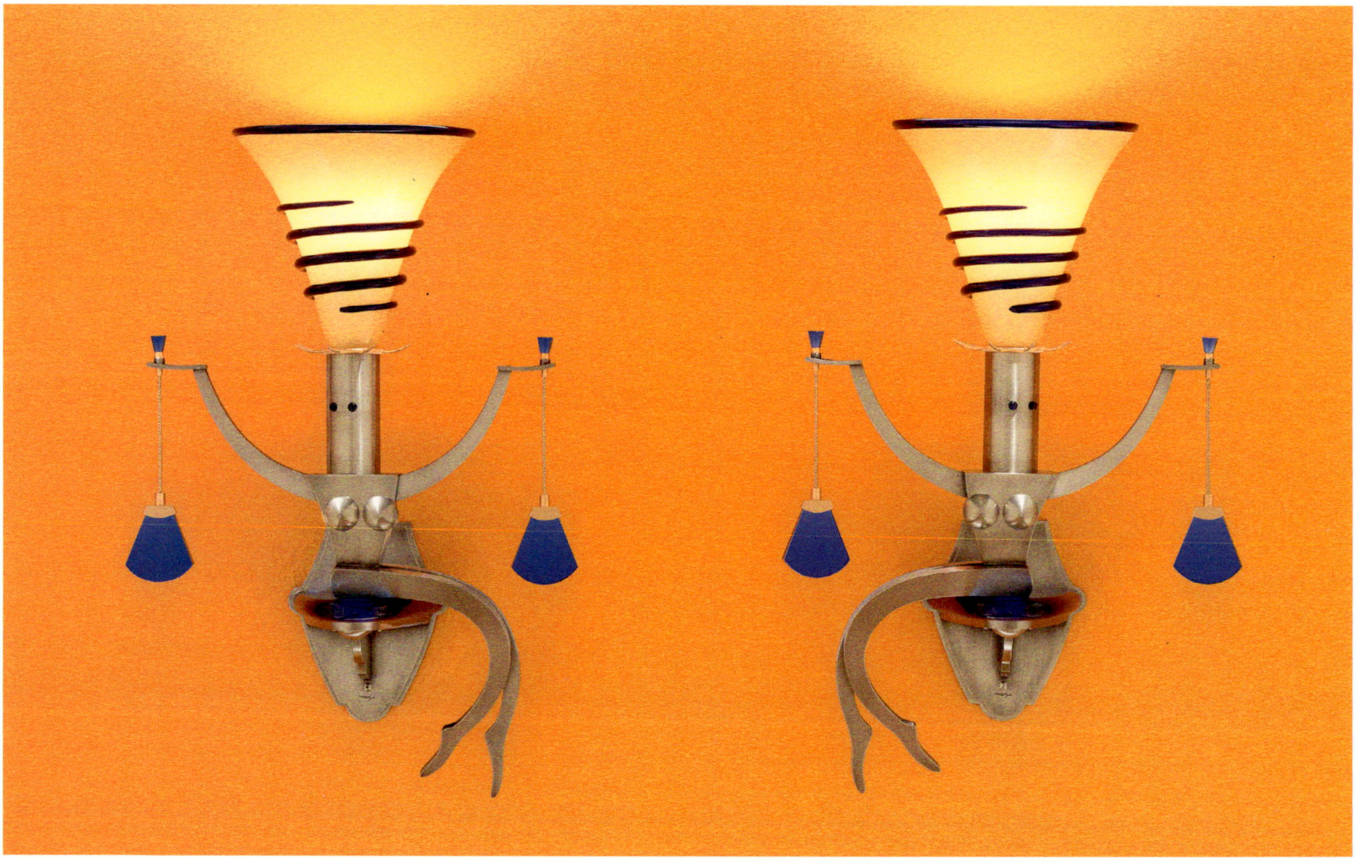

1 *Seated Nudes on Blue Shelves.* Fabricated, patinated, nickel- and gold-plated bronze. Blown glass shades. Pate de verre pendants. Cut and polished glass details. 24" × 15" × 7.5" each. Illuminated sculpture. 2014. Courtesy of © Bill Truslow www.truslowphoto.com.

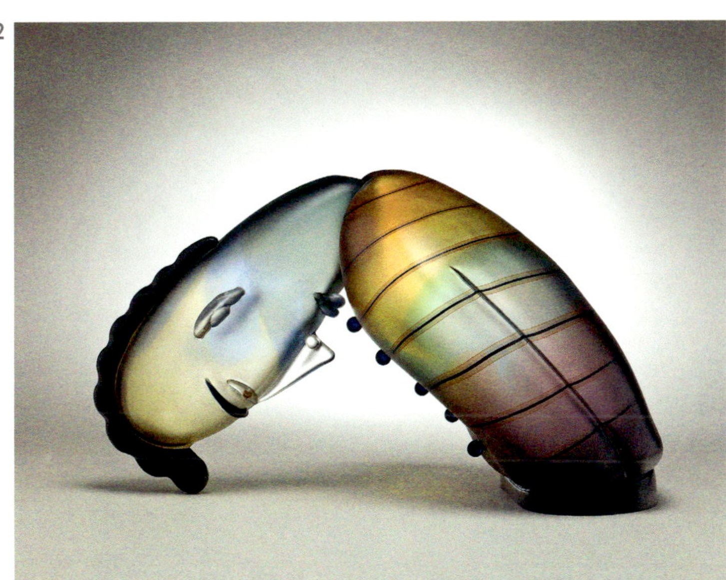

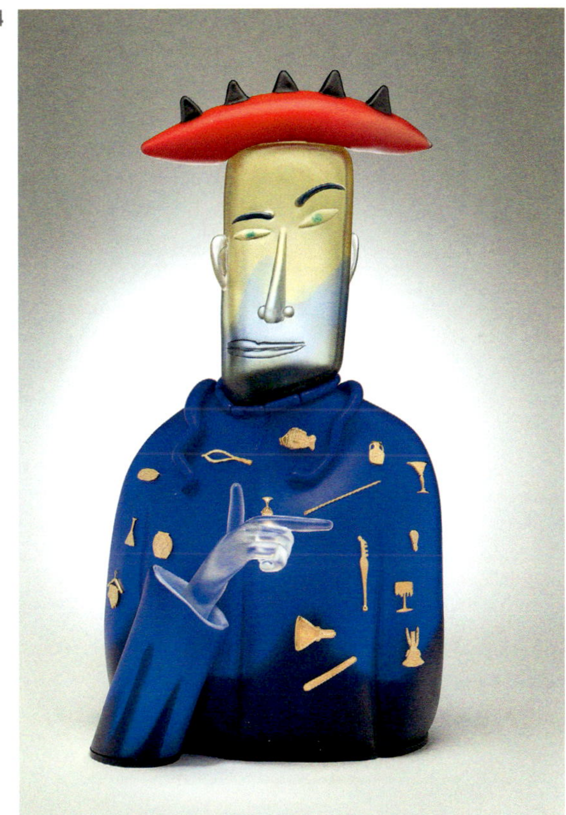

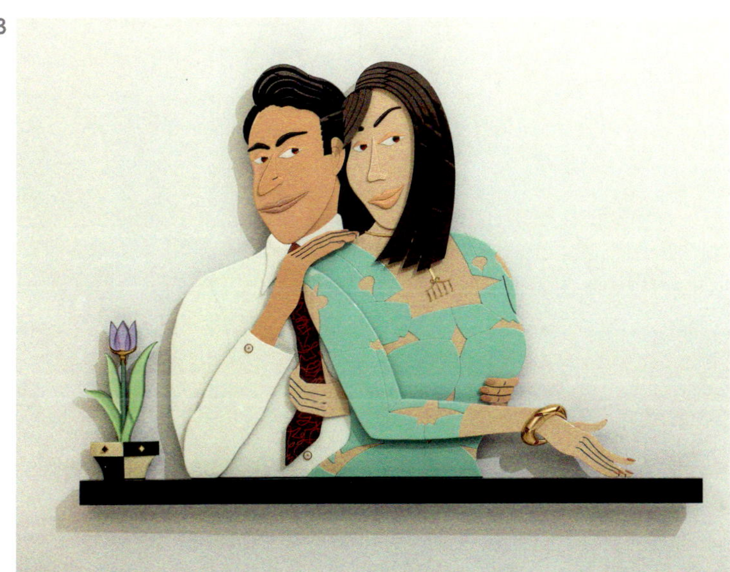

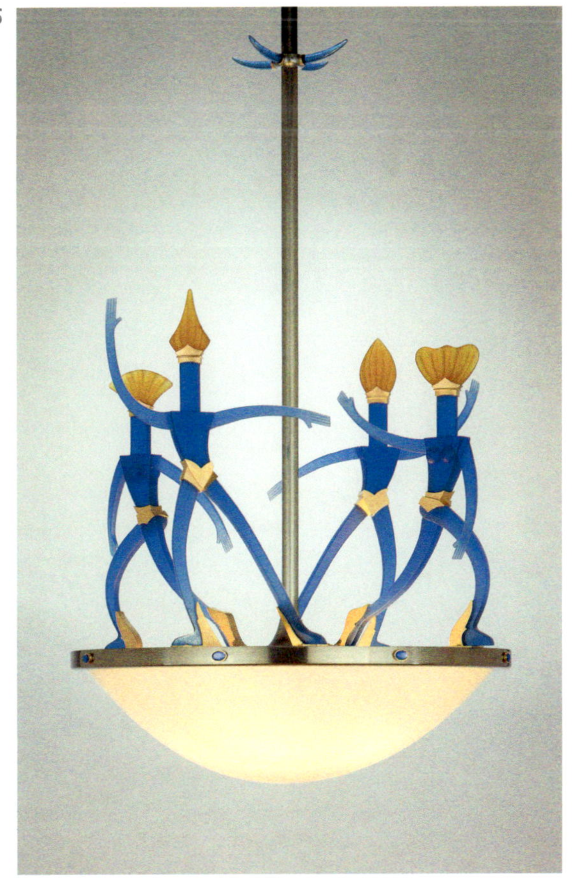

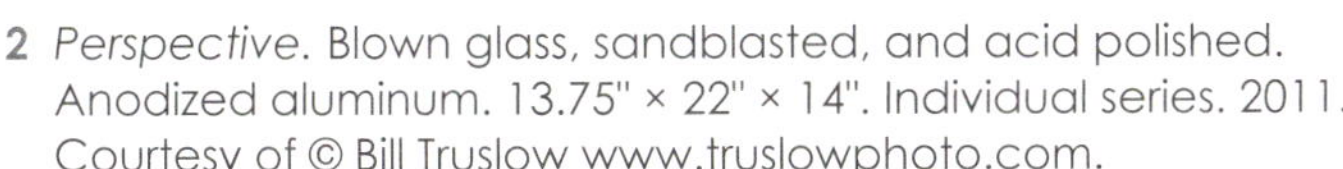

2 *Perspective*. Blown glass, sandblasted, and acid polished. Anodized aluminum. 13.75" × 22" × 14". Individual series. 2011. Courtesy of © Bill Truslow www.truslowphoto.com.

3 *Likewise*. Vitrolite, nickel- and gold-plated brass, anodized aluminum, various glass details, and enamel paint. 31" × 44" × 6". Vitrolite wall mural. 2013. Courtesy of © Bill Truslow www.truslowphoto.com.

4 *Erudite*. Blown glass, sandblasted, and acid polished. Gold-plated bronze medallions. Anodized aluminum. 26.75" × 14.5" × 10.5". Individual series. 2011. Courtesy of © Bill Truslow www.truslowphoto.com.

5 *Celebration*. Fabricated, patinated, nickel- and gold-plated bronze, brass, aluminum- and steel. Slumped glass shade. Sandblasted and acid polished pate de verre glass figures. Lampworked glass details. 32.5" × 30" × 30". Illuminated sculpture. 2014. Courtesy of © Bill Truslow www.truslowphoto.com.

Robert Dane

Heath, Massachusetts

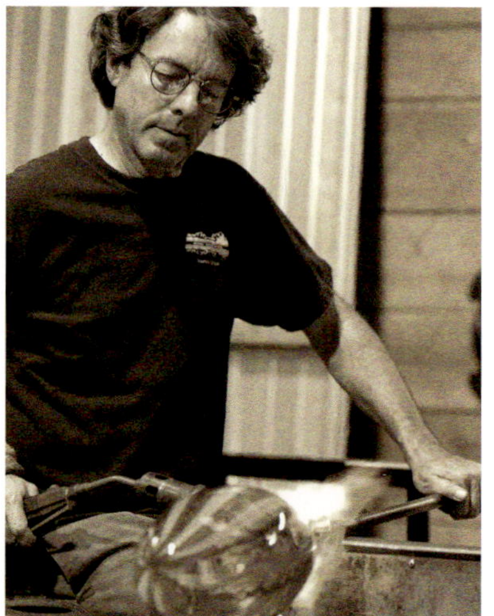

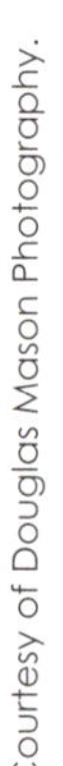
Courtesy of Douglas Mason Photography.

The themes I always focus on are of a continuum revolving around life and growth. There is optimism inherent in my work, which I have tried to reinforce in the face of a seemingly constant barrage of negativity and pessimism coming at us from many sources. The beauty of nature in its many forms continues to inspire me and inform my work. We are often too absorbed by the day to day of our own small existence to visualize and recognize the grand scheme around us. My aim is to celebrate the beauty of the progression of life as it ever unfolds and reveals itself. Music, especially jazz, has always been a major influence in my work, and the titles of my pieces are taken from different tunes. The horn form is a tribute to the improvisational nature of the music and its relationship to the dance of glassblowing.

In 1996, my wife Jayne and I opened the Dane Gallery on Nantucket.

1

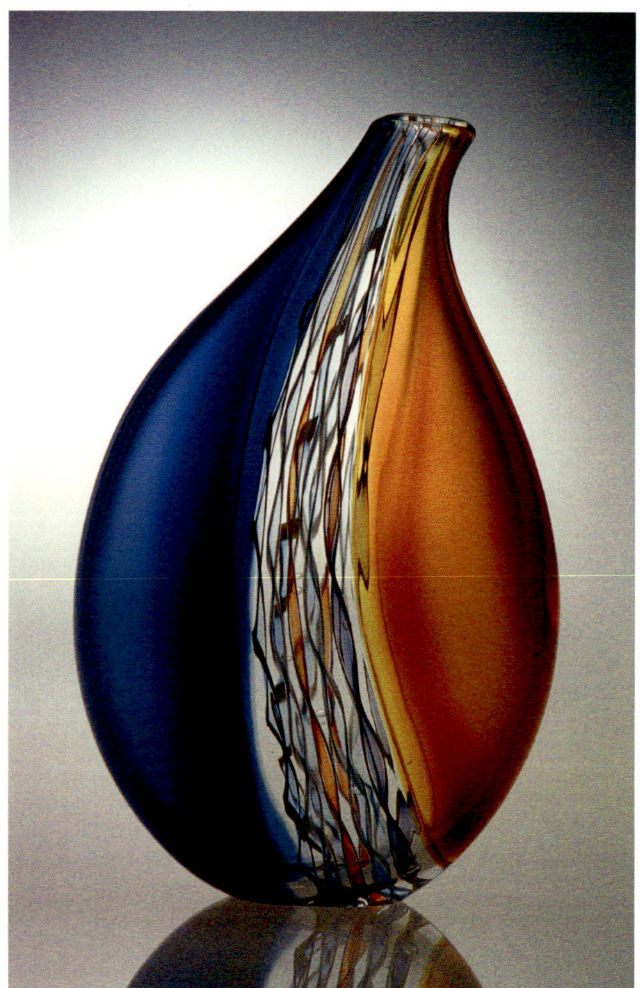

2

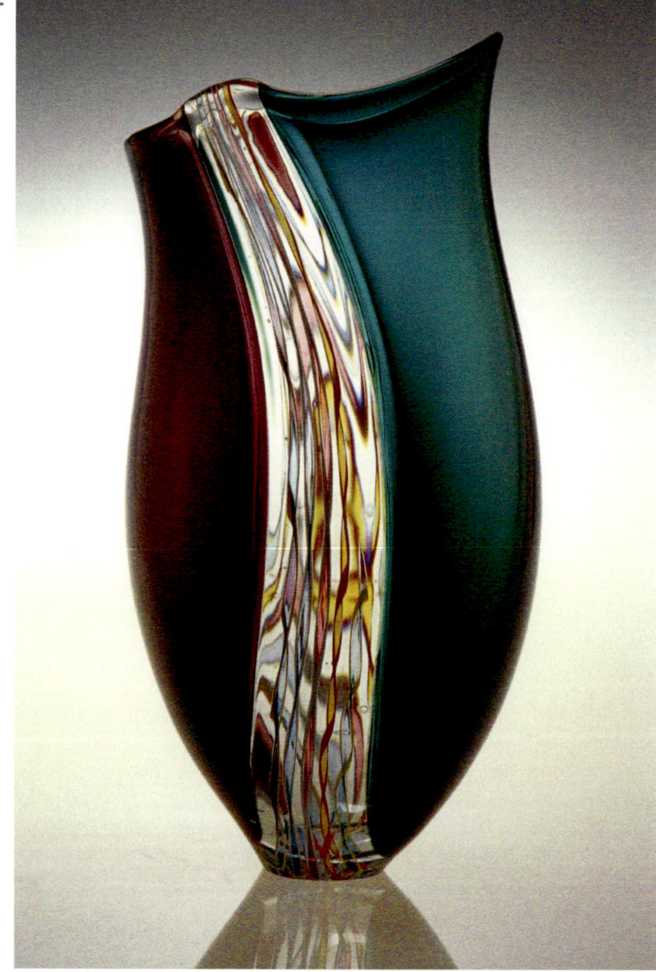

3

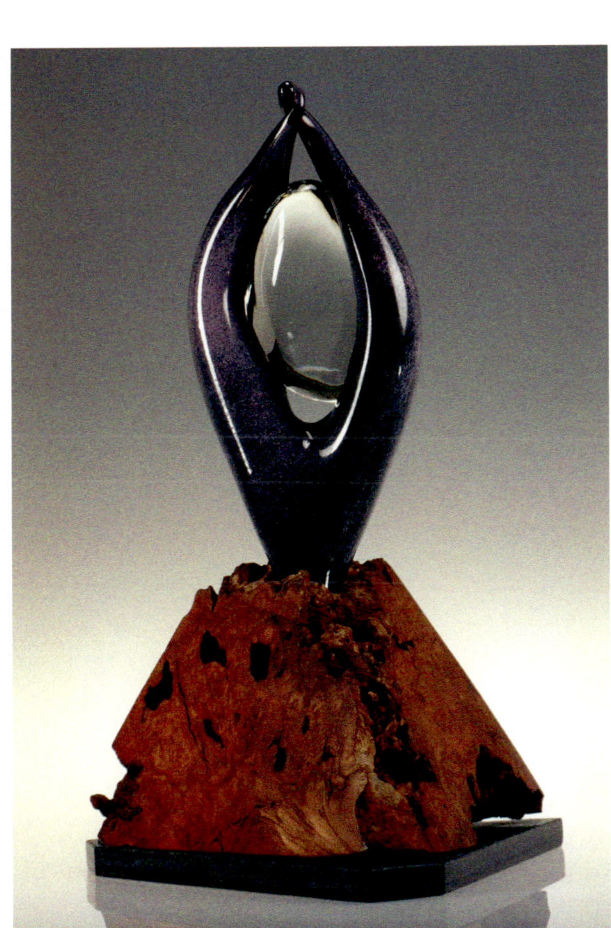

1 *Incalmo Vase with Vertical Cane: Blue Amber*. Blown glass. 16" × 4" × 9". 1998. Courtesy of Turnbull/Boudreau Photography.

2 *Incalmo Vase with Vertical Cane: Purple Teal*. Blown glass. 16" × 8" × 8". 1998. Courtesy of Turnbull/Boudreau Photography.

3 *Rejoice*. Hot sculpted solid glass, cherry wood burl, and mica schist. Assembled with epoxy. 22" × 11" × 9". 2002. Courtesy of Turnbull/Boudreau Photography.

4 *Timbertotem*. Mold blown, optical, cast, and plate glass. Ground and polished and assembled with epoxy. Base and lines painted with enamel. 33.5" × 16" × 9". 1991. Courtesy of Turnbull/Boudreau Photography.

5 *Woodland Dance*. Blown and solid hot sculpted glass and cast glass. Assembled with epoxy. 28" x 22" x 9". 2006.

4

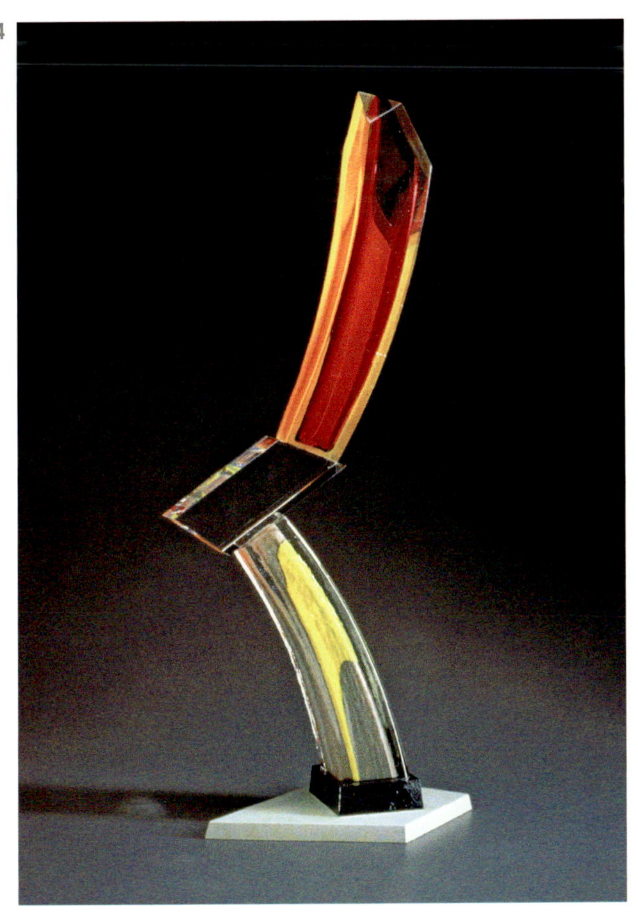

5

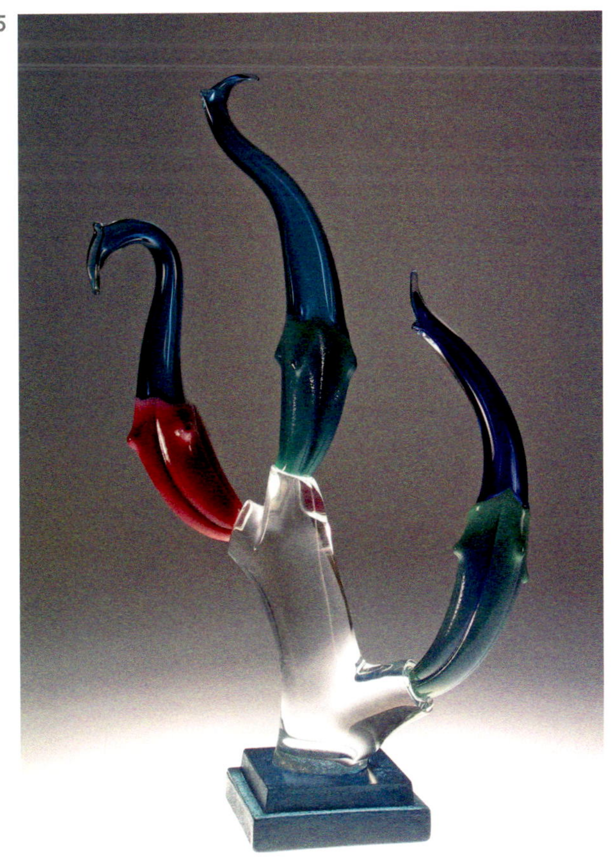

Gerald Davidson

York, Pennsylvania

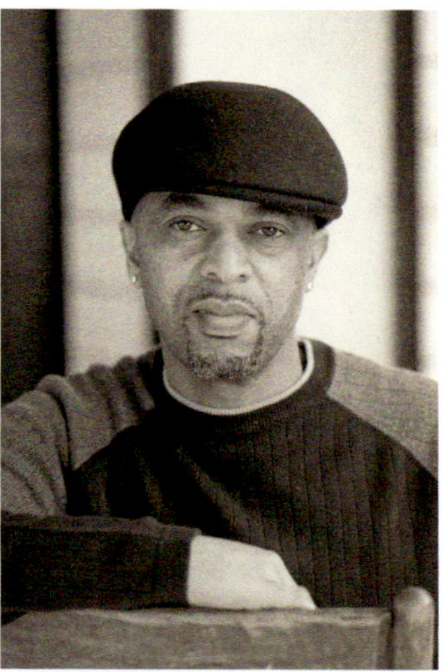

Courtesy of Studio 11 West.

Creating art is my natural way of being in the world. Creating mosaics and stained glass is an intentional choice. I find the work of creating mosaics challenging, engrossing, and thoroughly engaging. Every mosaic I create is a struggle: a personal struggle to slow down and be present one tesserae of glass at a time. A creative struggle, to get every piece of glass just right: the relationship of one piece to the other, and the work as a whole.

Using glass as my primary medium, I am drawn to its complex qualities of texture, striated color, and the interplay of light on each shard. I thrive on experimenting with and exploring new styles, techniques, and use of materials. Therefore, my work is continually evolving. Ultimately, I aim to produce work that draws people in for a closer look by revealing the combined beauty of the materials and the nature of the design concept.

The themes, designs, and colors of my creations are a reflection of my diverse interests, travels, cross-cultural experiences, and background in commercial art. Every country I have lived in—Zimbabwe, South Africa, the United Kingdom, Trinidad, Tobago, and the United States—has influenced me in ways that find expression in my life and art.

1

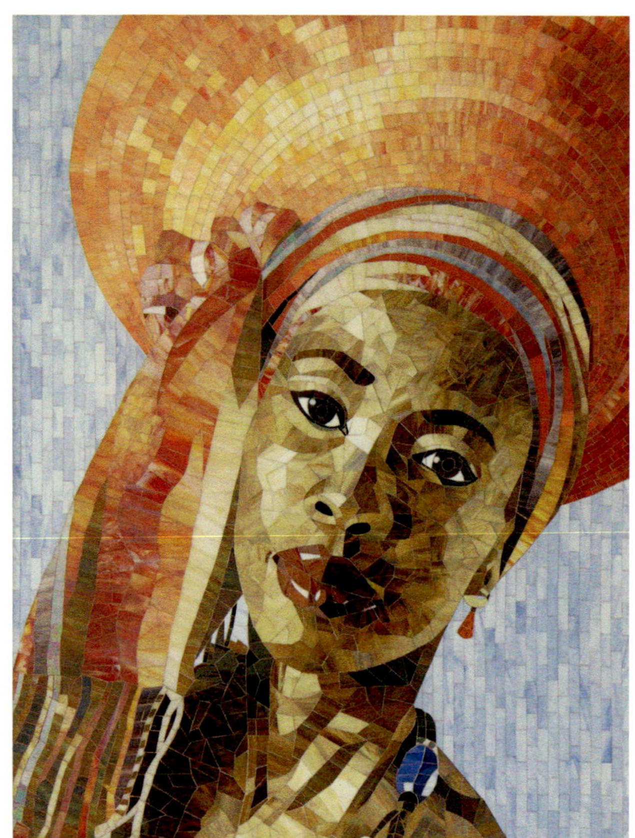

2

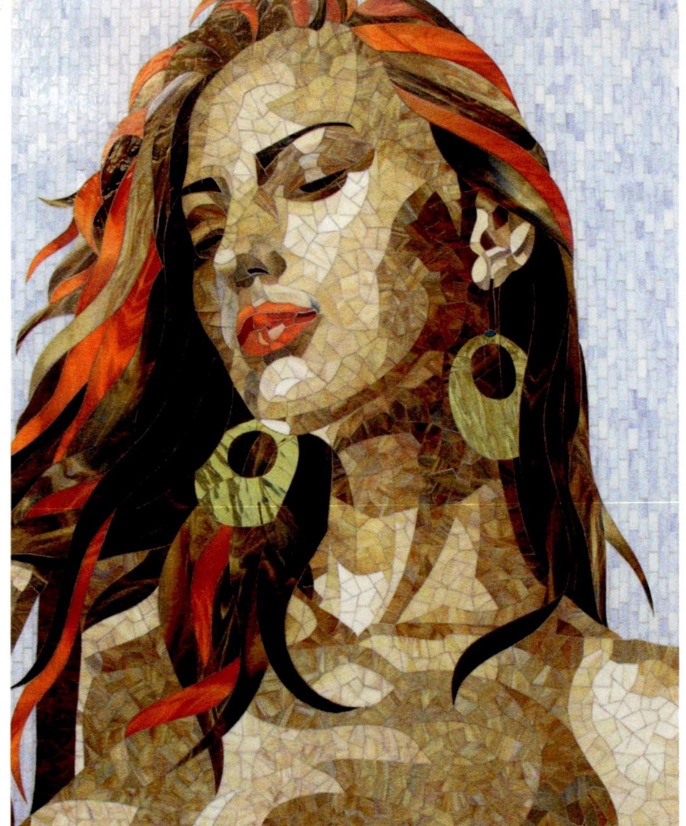

3

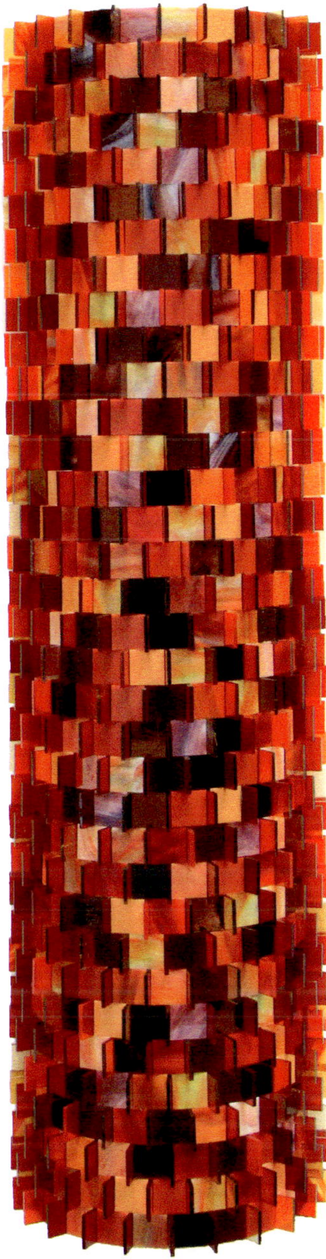

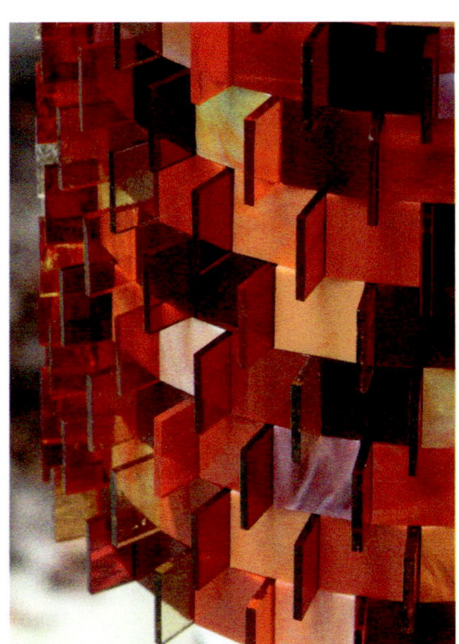

4

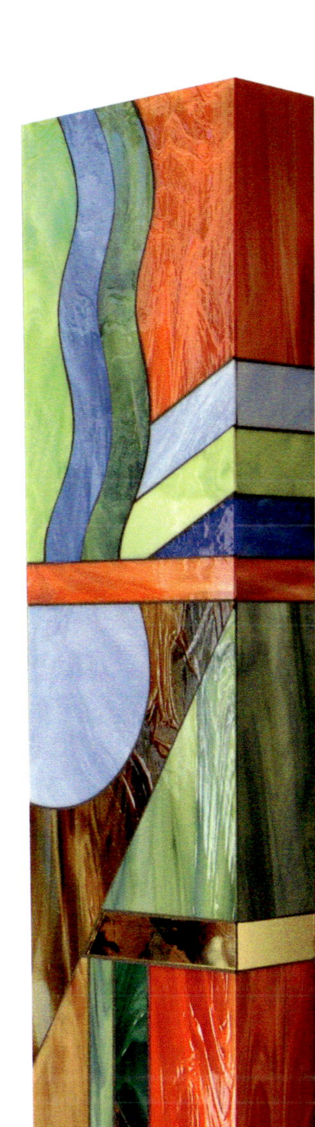

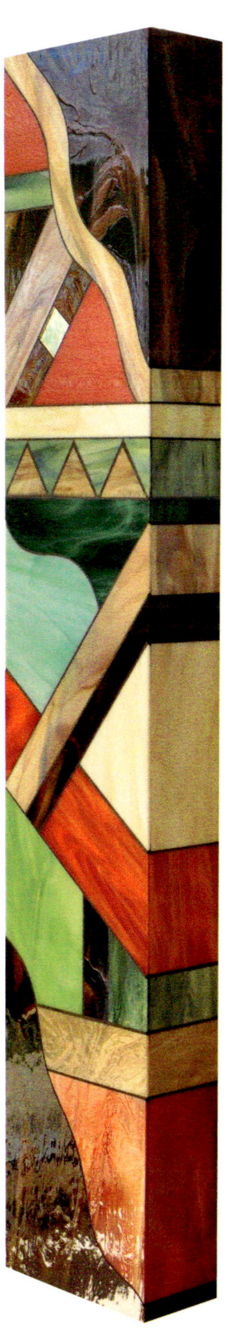

1 *Africa's True Wealth.* Stained glass, kiln-formed glass. 43" × 32". 2012.

2 *Because I Am.* Stained glass, gold waterglass mirror. 45" × 36". 2013.

3 *Reflections in Red.* Opalescent stained glass, cathedral stained glass, and colored mirror. 36" × 10" × 5". 2013.

4 *Tribal Totems.* Stained glass, gold waterglass mirror. 40' × 7" × 3". Ongoing.

Ron Desmett

Oakdale, Pennsylvania

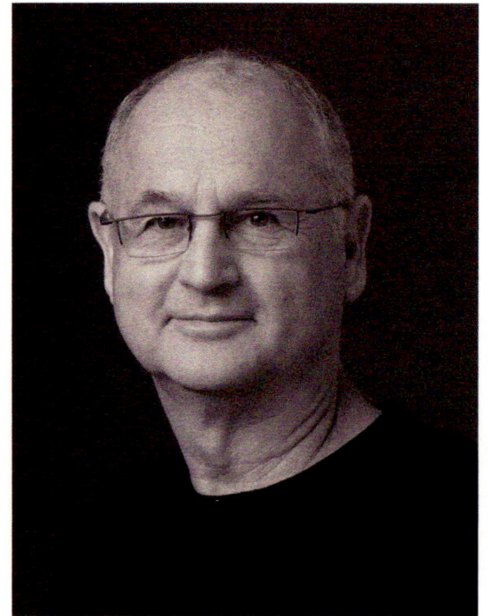

Courtesy of Mark Perrott.

My *Lidded Trunk Vessels* are hulking, often homely, yet captivating in their lack of aesthetic kin. They are black glass blown into hollowed-out and water-soaked segments of tree trunks that are cut to open as a mold. I find these trunks in nature, from fallen rotted ancient trees. You can almost hear the forms breathing. I believe their power comes from defying established criteria for either glasswork or sculpture.

This work led to the replacement of the vessel by a series of abstract shapes that use the tree interior for texture. Some mimic the delicate balance in nature found when taking a canyon walk. A new series takes it one step further, adding non-glass objects to the mix.

1

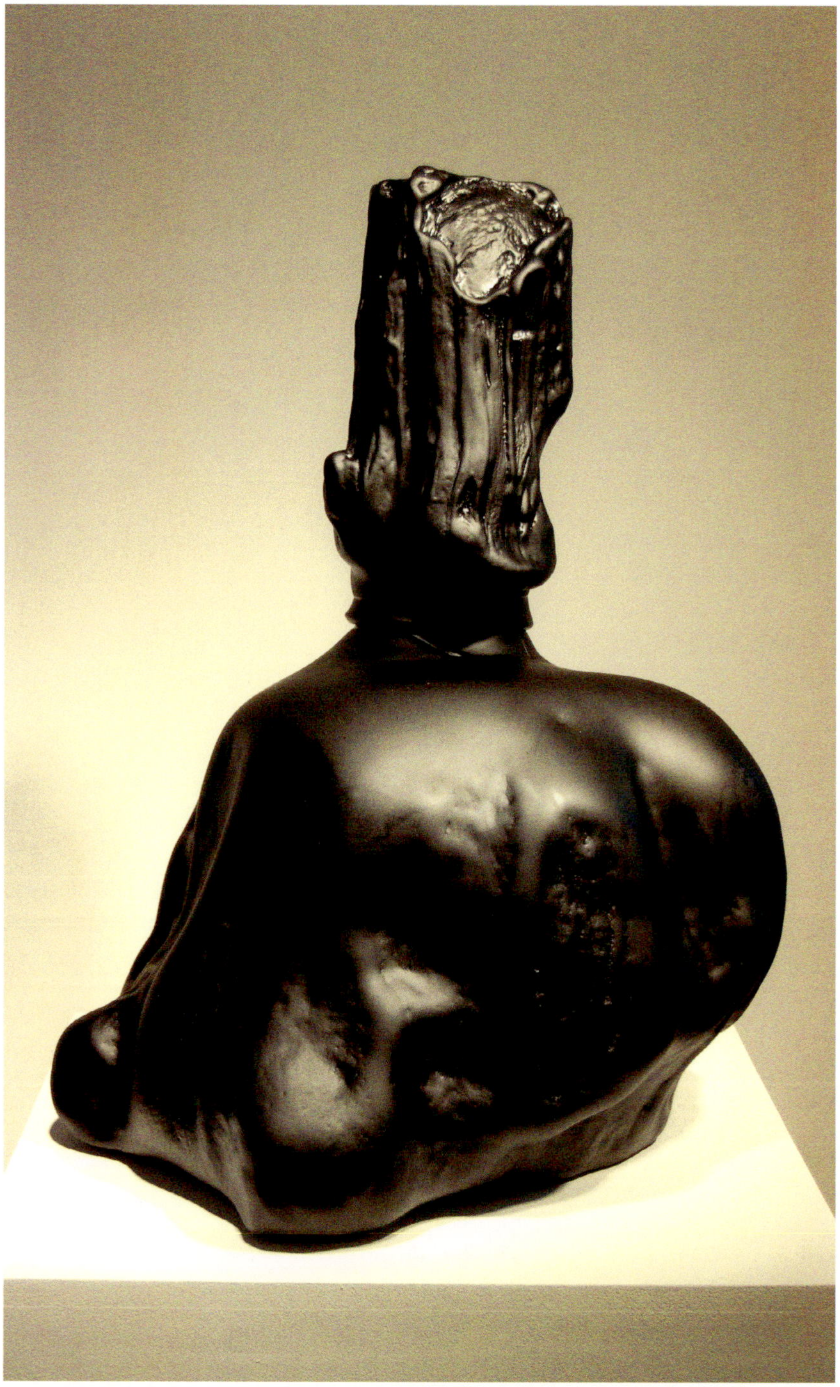

1 *Lidded Trunk Vessel: The King*. Black glass blown into a hollowed tree trunk. Etched and sealed. 34" × 18" × 18". 2010. Courtesy of Jim Judkis.

2 *Breach*. Blown and fabricated black glass. 18" × 16" × 21". 2012. Courtesy of Mark Perrott.

3 *Cairn*. Blown and fabricated black glass and gold leaf. 20" × 18" × 26". 2012. Courtesy of Mark Perrott.

4 *Feast for Small Things*. Blown and etched black glass. 12" × 22" × 22". Courtesy of Mark Perrott.

2

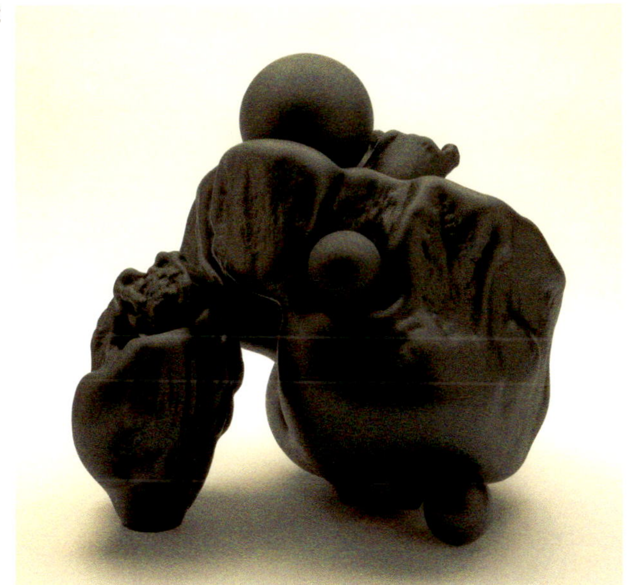

3

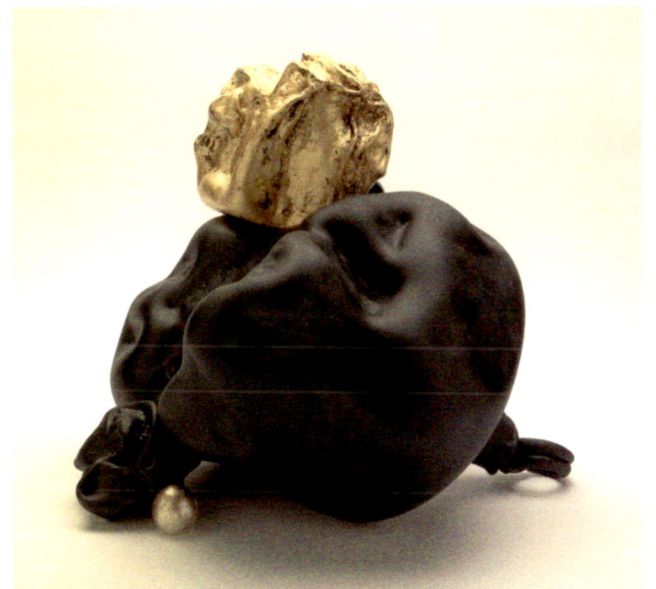

4

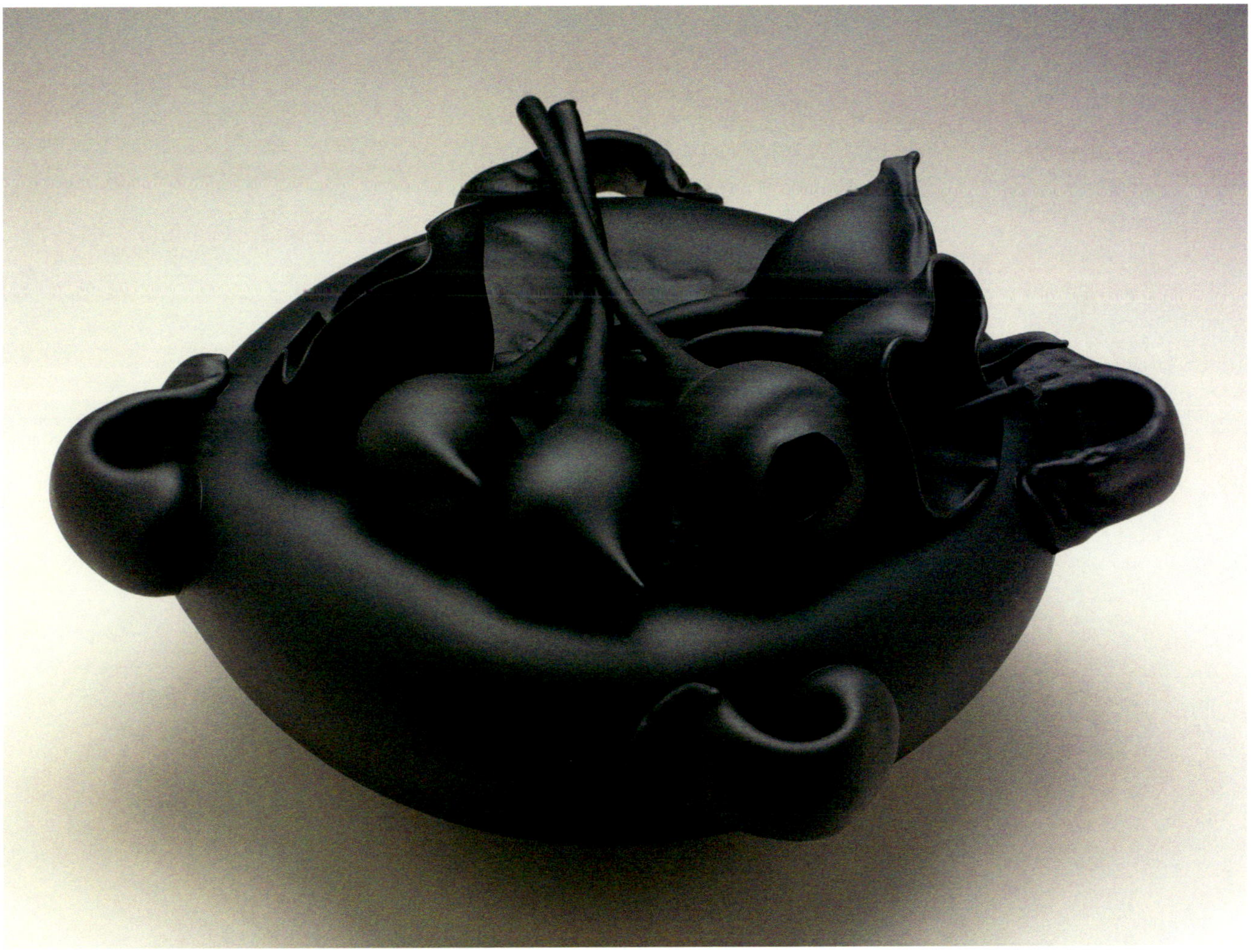

Miriam Di Fiore

Mornico Losana, Pavia, Lombardy, Italy

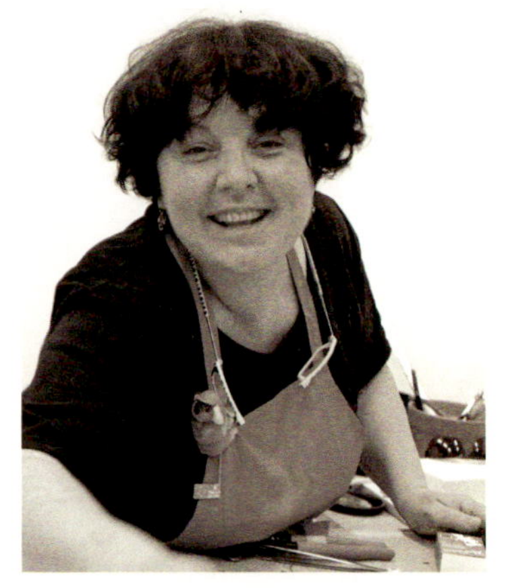

Courtesy of Marc Leib, Art Glass Studio.

The forest has a deep and symbolic meaning for me. A pine forest was around the town where I spent my childhood in Argentina. What I intend to do with my work is not an "interpretation" of the wood, but a simple and respectful translation in glass of a place that is important to me. I connect my landscapes with wooden items. The tree from which the wood comes doesn't exist anymore, but the life it led still moves me.

My technique is a long and complex process that combines soft flameworking and fusing glass with multiple firings. The entire image is created without special help or tools but with my hands and glass.

1

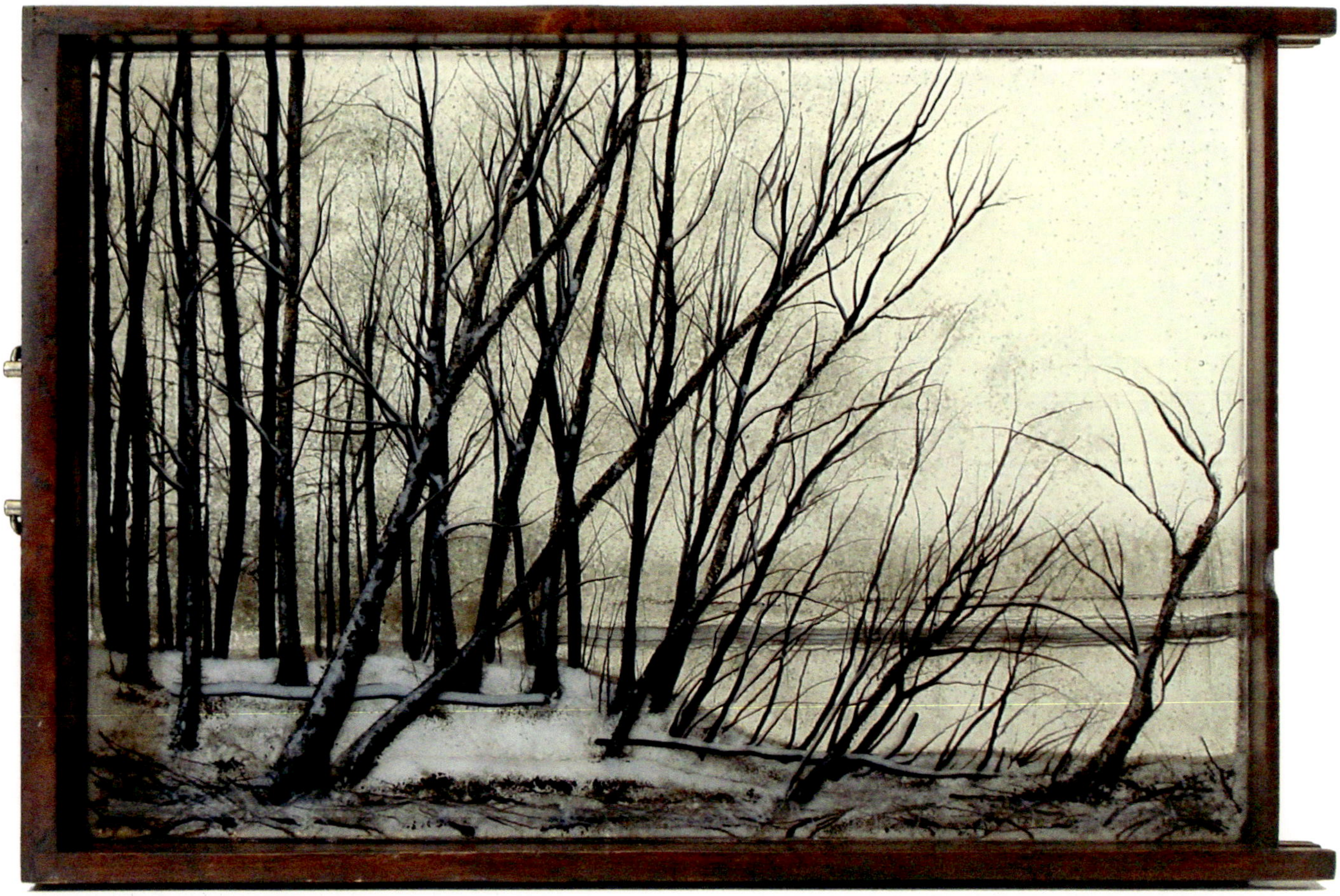

1 *Drawer for My Fifty.* Multi-firing kiln-forming glass. 16" × 4.5" × 24.5". 2012.

2 *Spring Season.* Kiln-forming glass, pate de verre. 36" × 2.7" × 20". 2009.

3 *La Nostalgia Di Mrs. Pavesi (Mrs. Pavesi Homesick).* Multi-firing kiln-forming glass, founded object. 24.5" × 2.25" × 12.5". 2009.

4 *Seed.* Multi-firing kiln-forming glass, kiln casting, and hand polished. 4" × 2.5" × 6". 2008.

5 *Violoncello (Good Bye Song).* Multi-firing kiln-forming glass, kiln cast glass. 42" × 4" × 15". 2006.

2

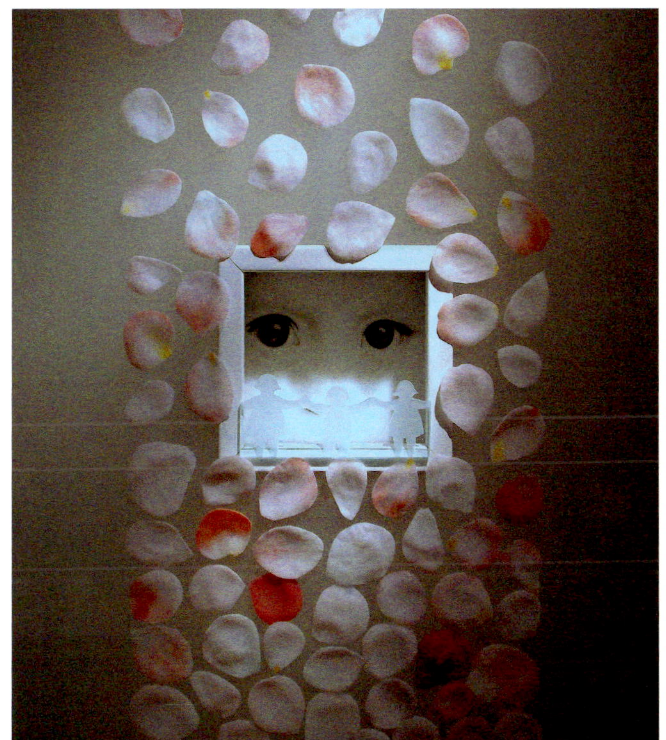

4

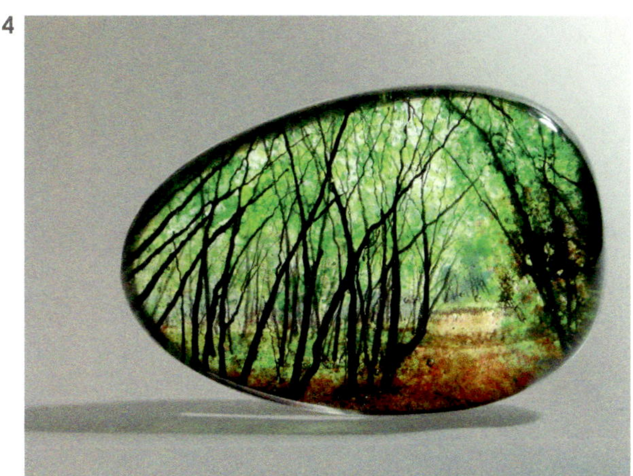

5

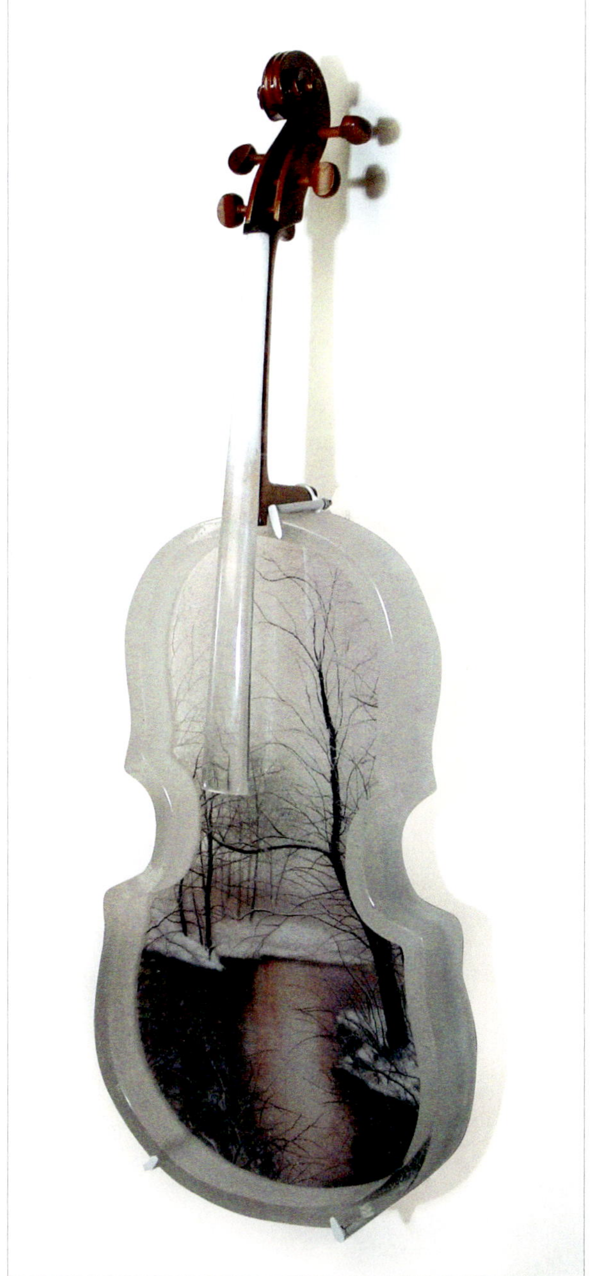

3

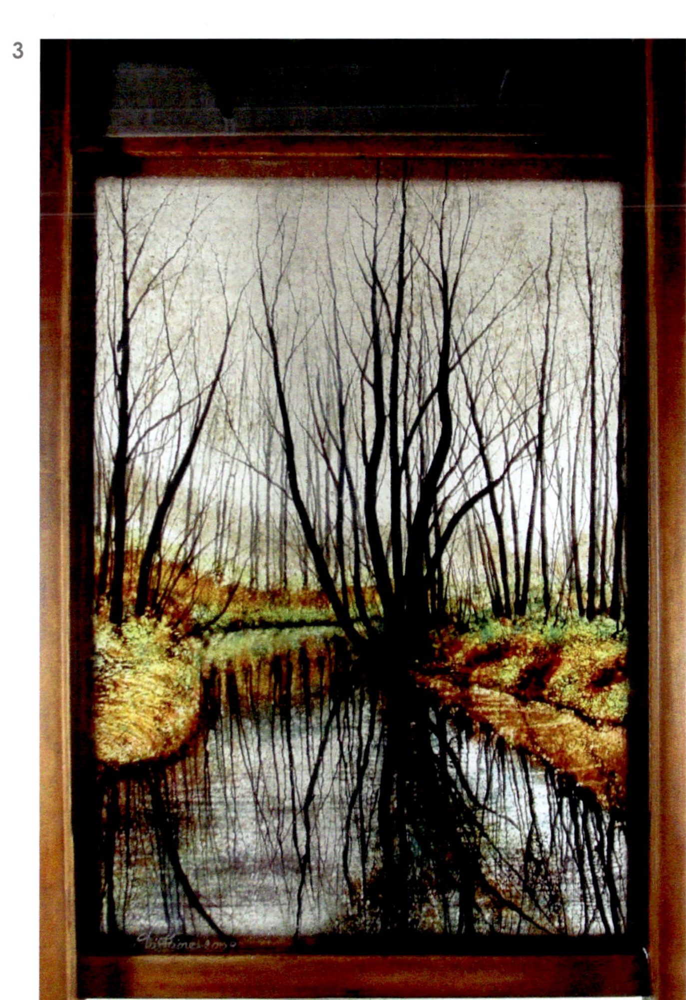

Laura Donefer

Harrowsmith, Ontario, Canada

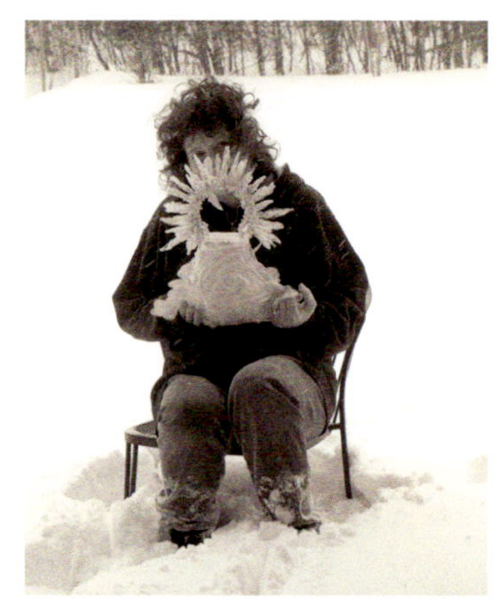

Throughout my artistic career, I have attempted to create heartfelt work with an unbridled passion, seeking to push past the boundaries of traditional glassmaking. Much of my work has been about exploring intense emotion, attempting to portray the human experience from a personal perspective, investigating ideas concerning memory, assault, bereavement, and madness. Known also for my innovative blown and flameworked *Amulet Baskets* initiated after 9/11, I use joy-inducing blasts of color to reinforce a spirit of joie de vivre. Using glass and mixed media, I am seeking to communicate my inner core with the rest of the world, and it has been an amazing journey of invention, determination, and self-discovery.

1

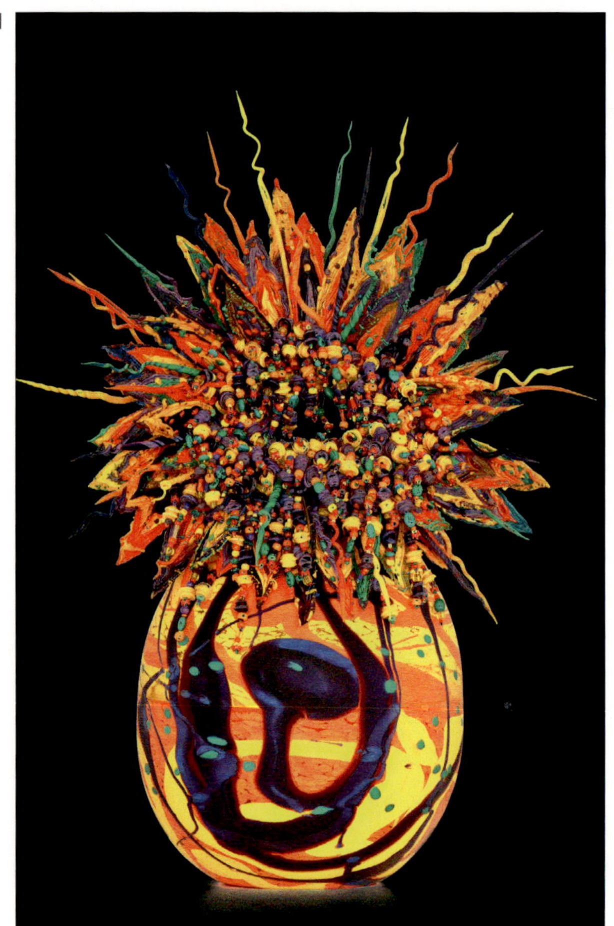

2

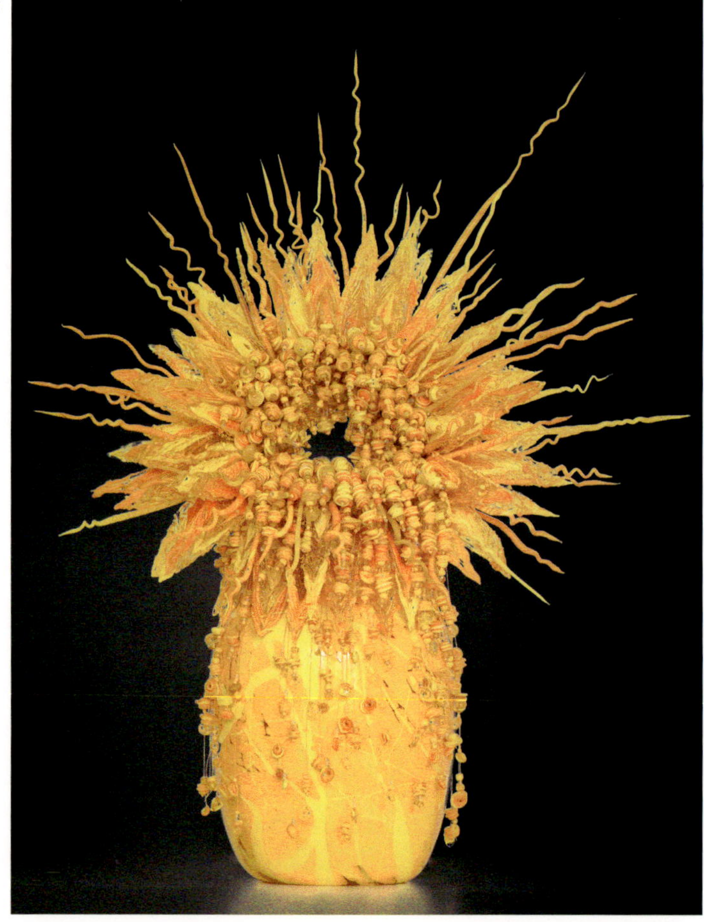

1 *Mardi Gras Amulet Basket.* Blown and flameworked glass/ mixed media. 38 " × 30" × 16". 2012. Courtesy of Steven Wild.

2 *Yellow Heart Amulet Basket.* Blown and flameworked glass/ mixed media. 40" × 40". 2012. Courtesy of Steven Wild.

3

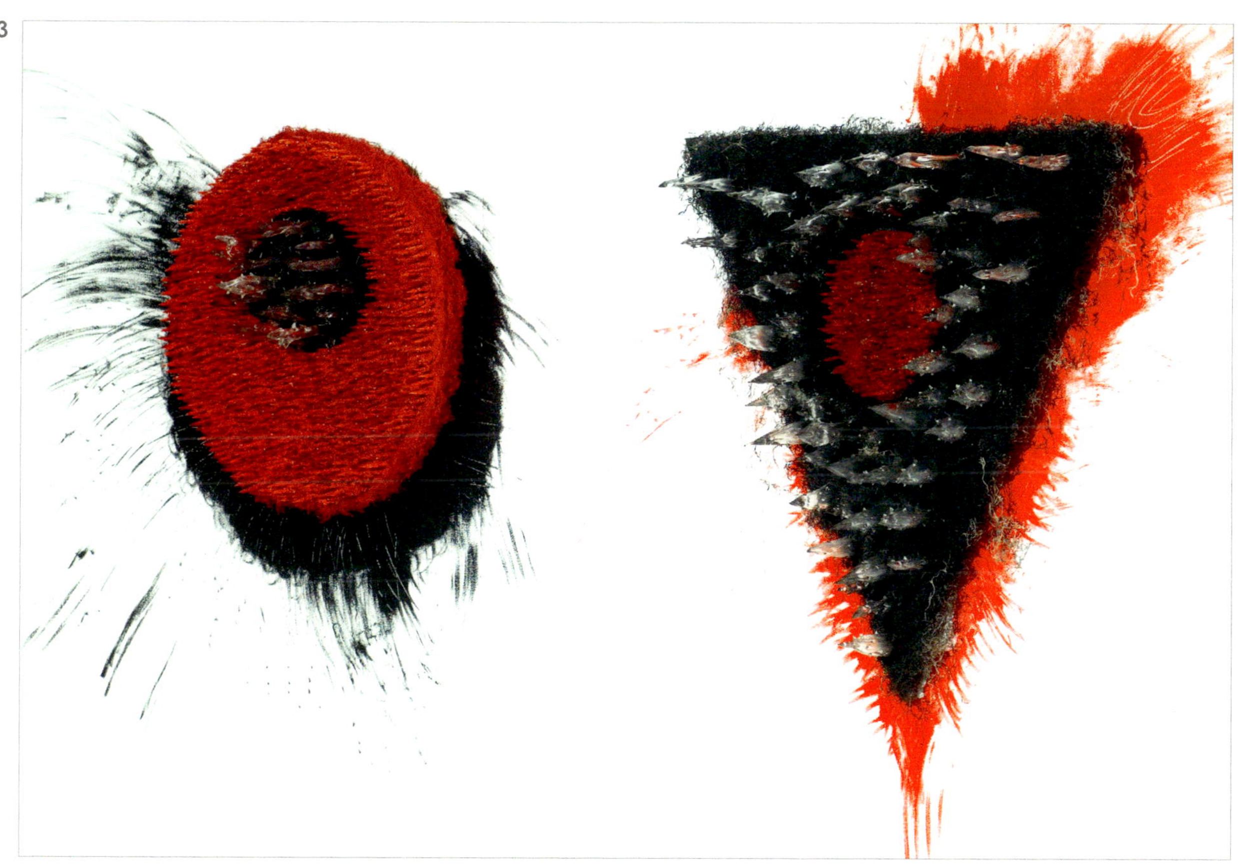

4

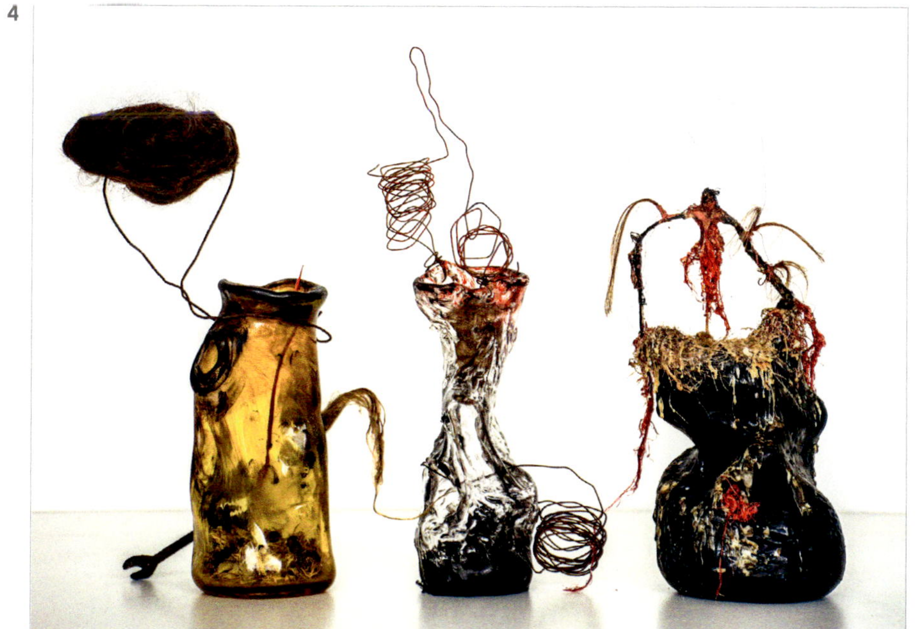

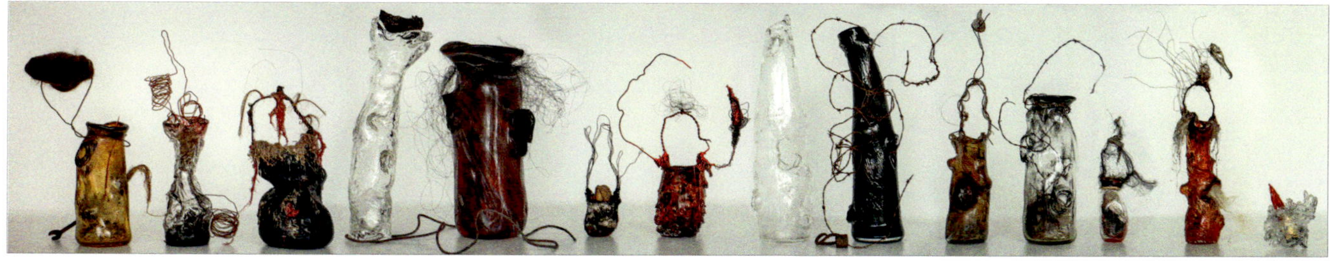

3 *Shields to Ward off Madness* (detail). Blown and cut glass and red flameworked spears/moss, and paint. Each shield approx. 5' × 6'. 2009. Courtesy of Steven Wild.

4 *Beyond the Pale: A Tale of Loss, Longing, and Love*. Installation created for the exhibit "The Human Condition through Glass." Blown glass/mixed media, including hair, wire, wrench, and wax. 4' × 15' × 2'. 2013. Courtesy of Steven Wild.

Dina Priess dos Santos

Buenos Aires, Argentina

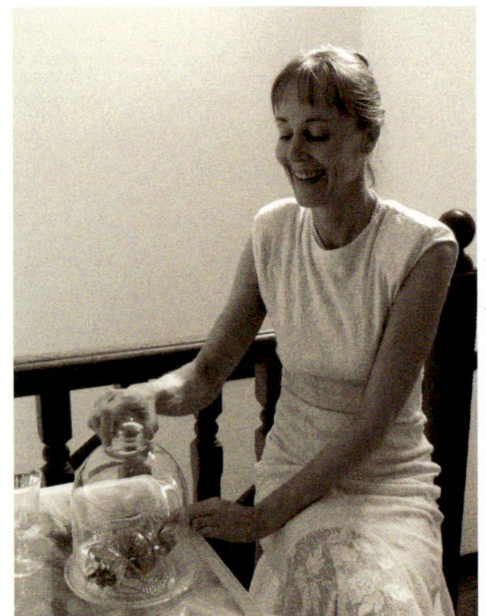

My fascination for glass is expressed in my work with three-dimensional pate de verre casts of organic forms. Traditional methods are used in which I incorporate experimental techniques. Translucent, transparent, and forever changeable, pate de verre lends itself perfectly to illustrating the fragility and subjective perception of our apparently certain reality.

1

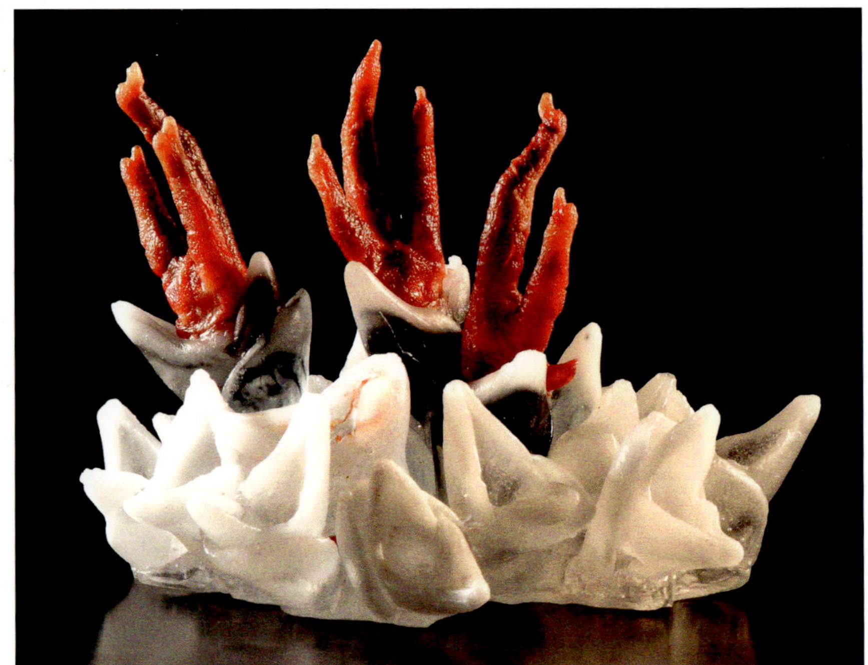

2

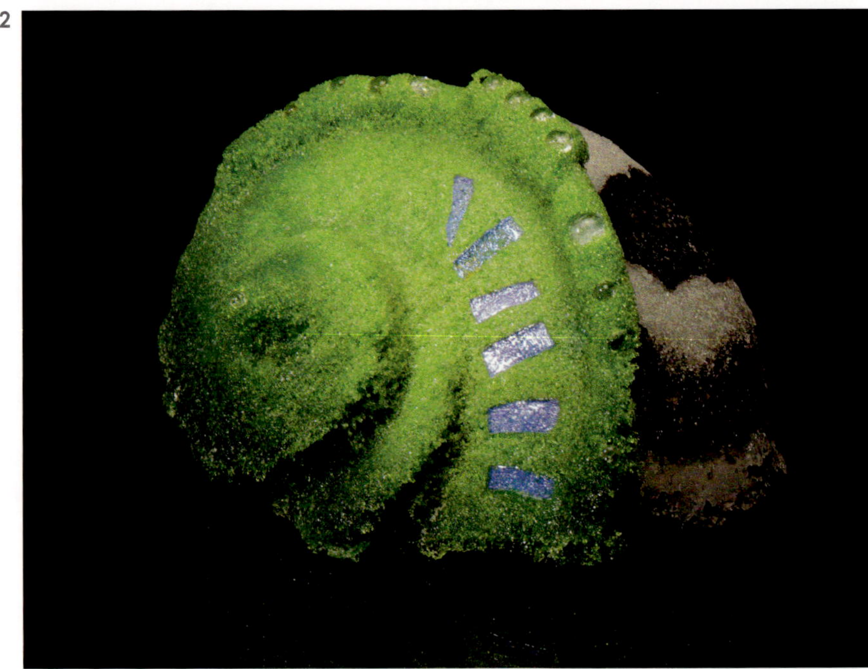

1 *Claw Coral*. Glass, warm glass, and lost wax pate de verre. 7" × 8" × 10". 2013. Courtesy of Eugenio Valentini (www.eugeniovalentini.com).

2 *Colorful*. *Sea Creature* series. Glass, warm glass, and pate de verre. 5 " × 7.5" × 8". 2011. Courtesy of Sebastian Gringauz.

3

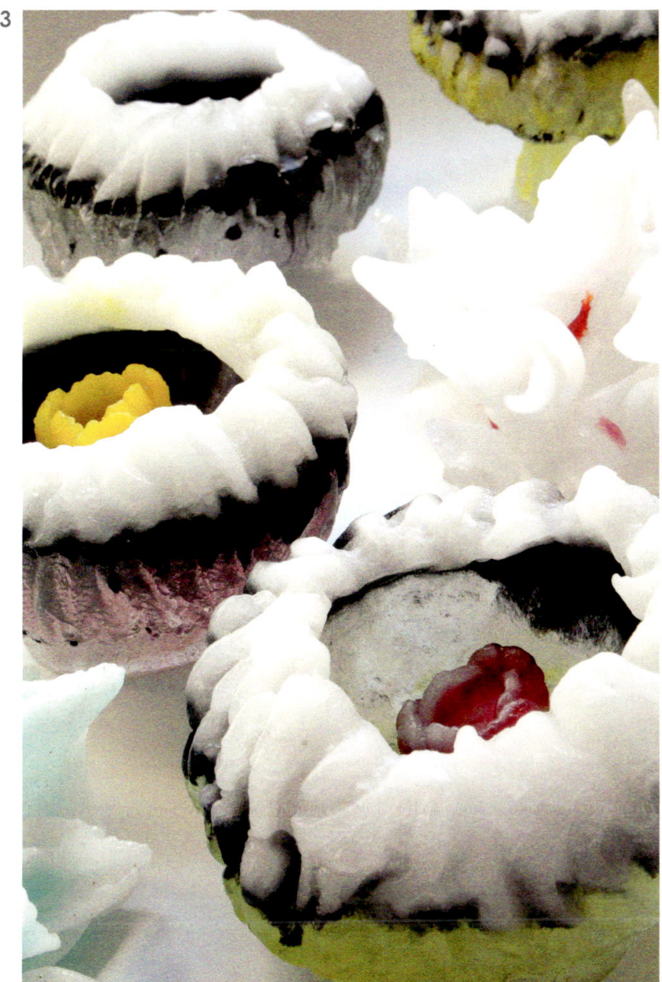

5

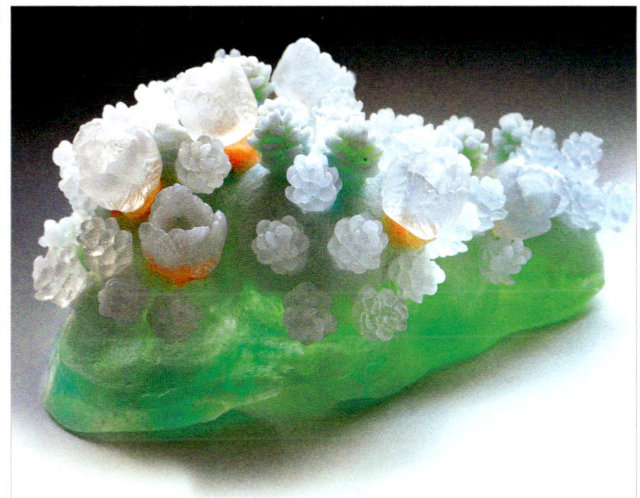

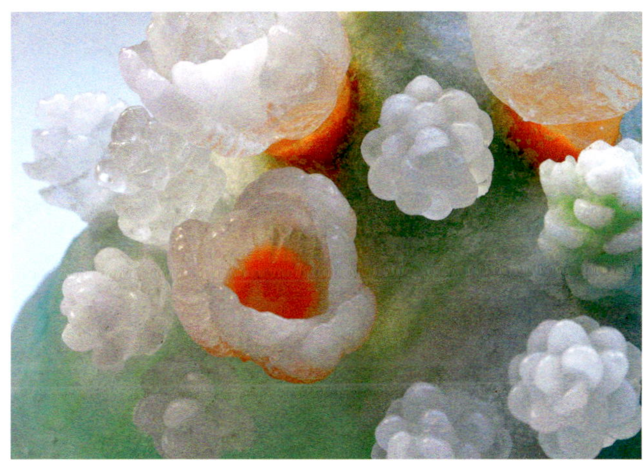

4

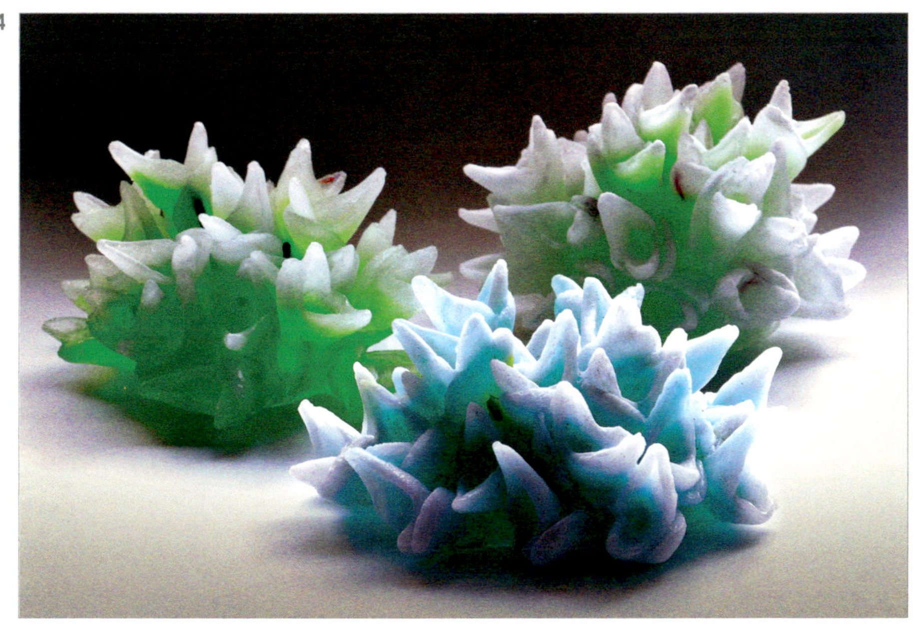

3 *The Reef, Brain Corals.* Glass, warm glass, and lost wax pate de verre. Each approx. 4–6" × 5" × 5". Courtesy of Eugenio Valentini (www.eugeniovalentini.com).

4 *Screaming Corals.* Glass, warm glass, and lost wax pate de verre. Each approx. 5.5" × 9.5" × 9.5". Courtesy of Eugenio Valentini (www.eugeniovalentini.com).

5 *Rangiroa.* Glass, warm glass, and lost wax pate de verre. 7" × 8" × 10". 2013. Courtesy of Eugenio Valentini (www.eugeniovalentini.com).

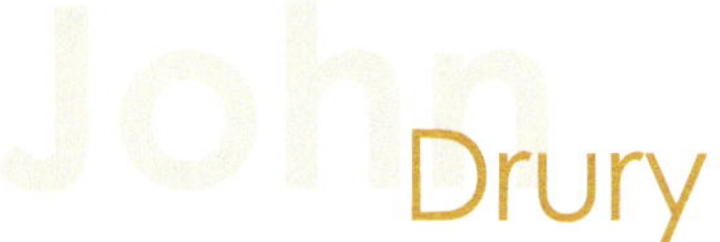

John Drury

Brooklyn, New York

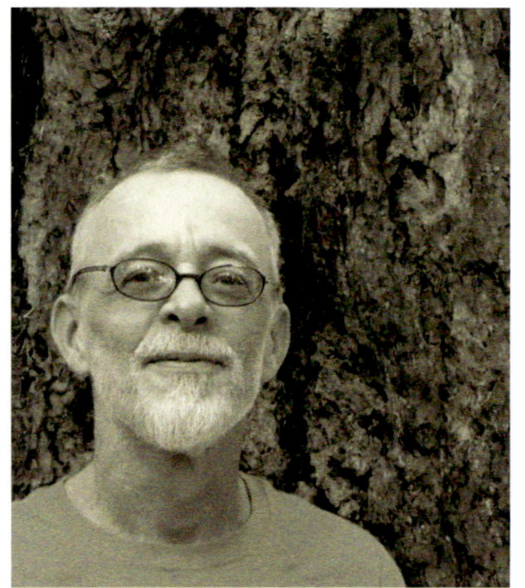

Courtesy of Robbie Miller.

I approach diverse, often common, materials intuitively. Chance, situation, and humor inform my work.

1 *Recycling* series *(Toledo)*. Glass and rubber. 12" × 6.5" × 6.5". 2012.

2 *Orifice*. Glass and foam insulation. 6.5" × 7" × 5". 2014.

3 *Recycling* series *(Toledo)*. Glass and rubber. 4.5" × 4.5" × 4.5". 2012.

4 *Recycling* series *(Pilchuck 1)*. Fired enamel on glass and rubber. 3.5" × 6" × 3.5". 2005.

1

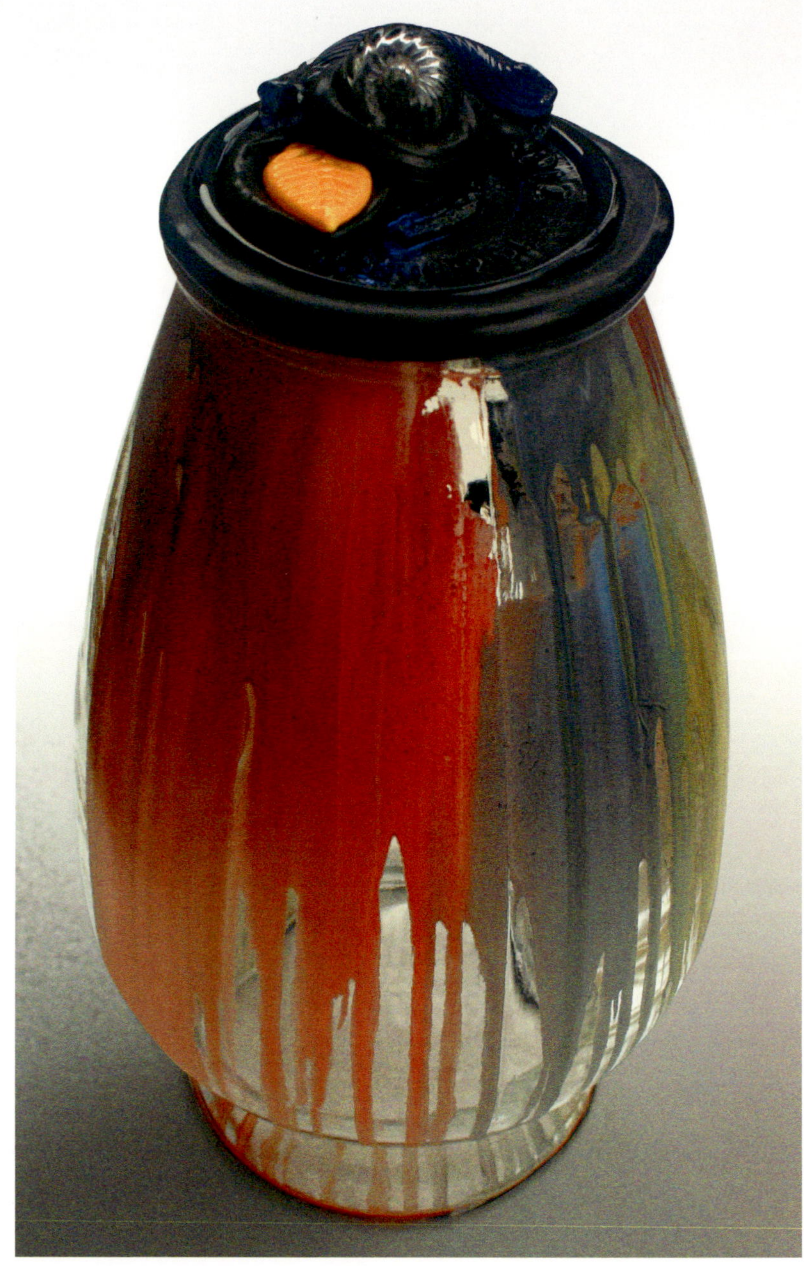

2

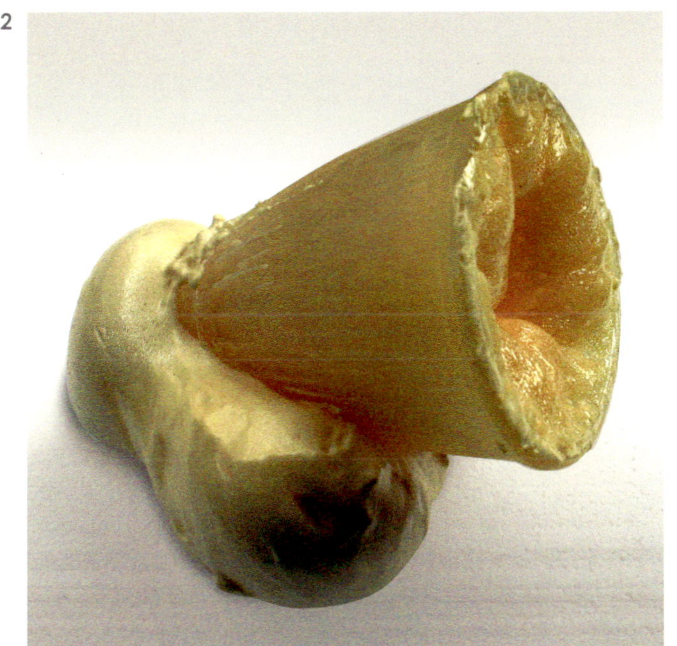

3

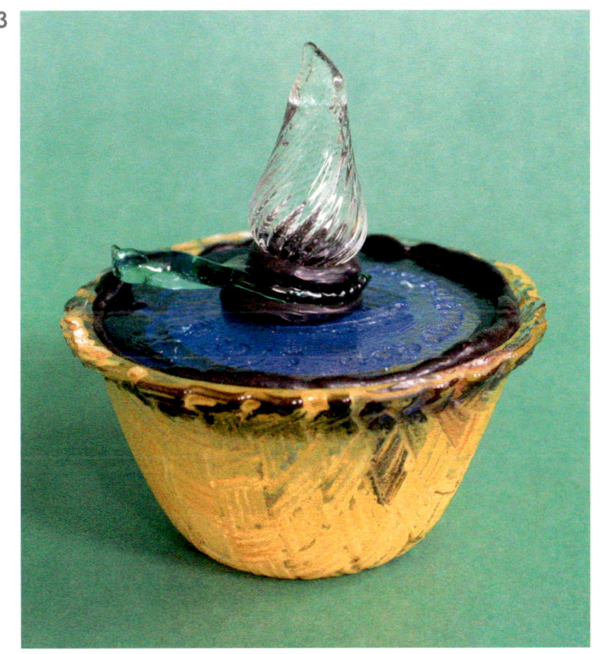

4

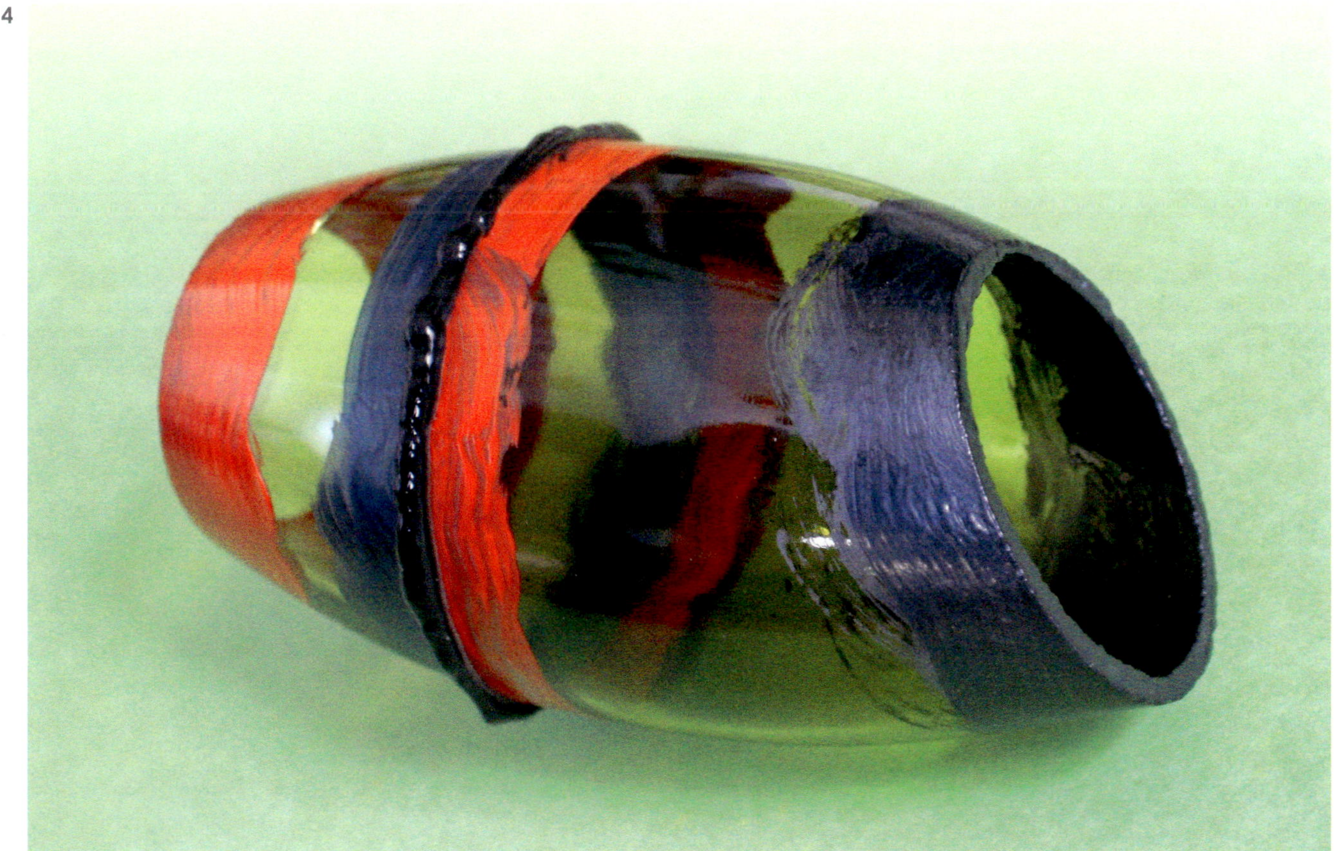

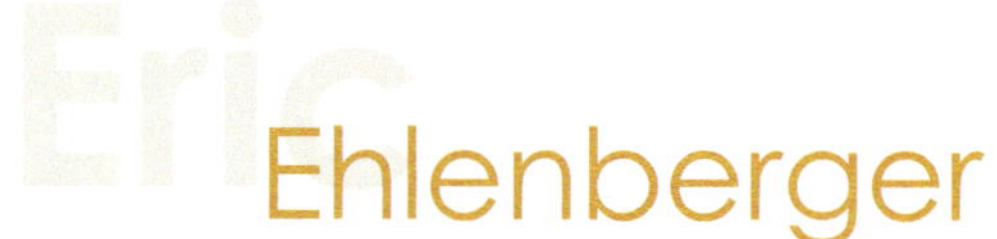

Eric Ehlenberger

New Orleans, Louisiana

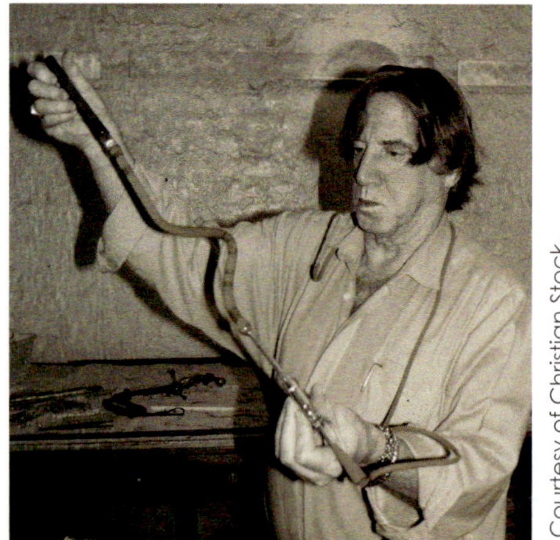

Courtesy of Christian Stock.

My work in neon, metal, and glass evolved from a childhood attraction to prisms, rainbows, and colored lights. It was my later exposure to the impressionist use of color and light to develop mood, the abstract expressionist focus on subjective interpretation, and the Asian culture's aesthetic emphasis on the elegance of simplicity and economy of form that culminated in my drive to make sculpture.

On a basic level, I approach my sculptures as meditations, using neon light with glass and other media to explore the emotional impact of luminous colors, shadows, and simple forms. On a more complex scale, my theme-based *Venusian World* sculptures present a fantasy world with luminous flora and fauna.

1

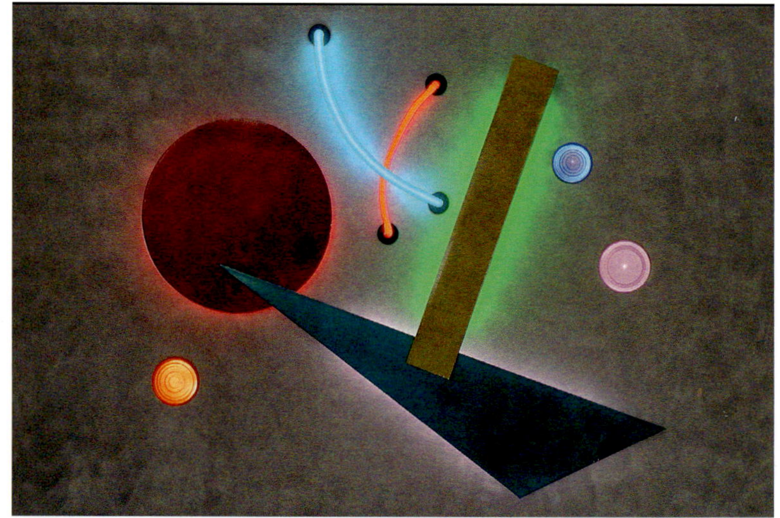

2

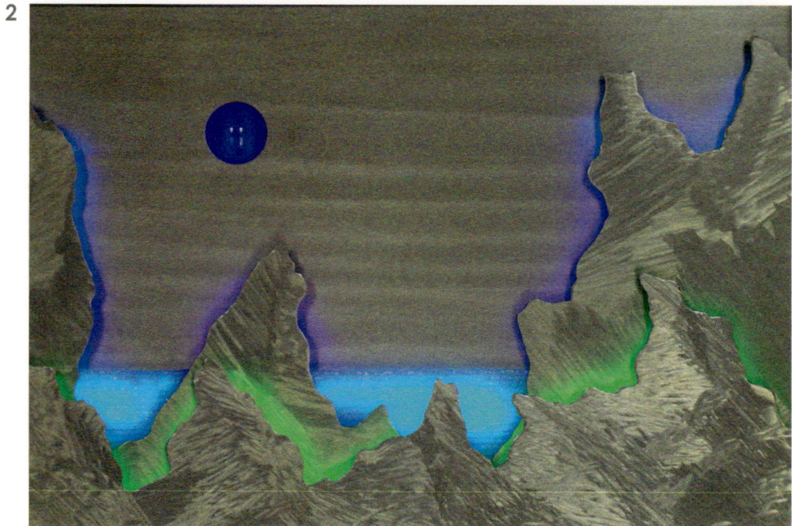

1 *Composition XV.* Aluminum, glass, and neon. 48" × 4" × 32". 2003.

2 *Venusian Landscape XII.* Aluminum, glass, silicone, and neon. 48" × 6" × 32". 2006.

3 *Jellyfish,* group image. Hand-blown glass, and neon. Sizes variable: approx. 16" × 36–40" × 16". 2014. Courtesy of Michel Friang Photography.

4 *Jellyfish,* paired image. Hand-blown glass, and neon. Sizes variable: approx. 16" × 36–40" × 16". 2014. Courtesy of Michel Friang Photography.

5 *Jellyfish,* close-up. Hand-blown glass, and neon. Sizes variable: approx. 16" × 36–40" × 16". 2014. Courtesy of Michel Friang Photography.

3
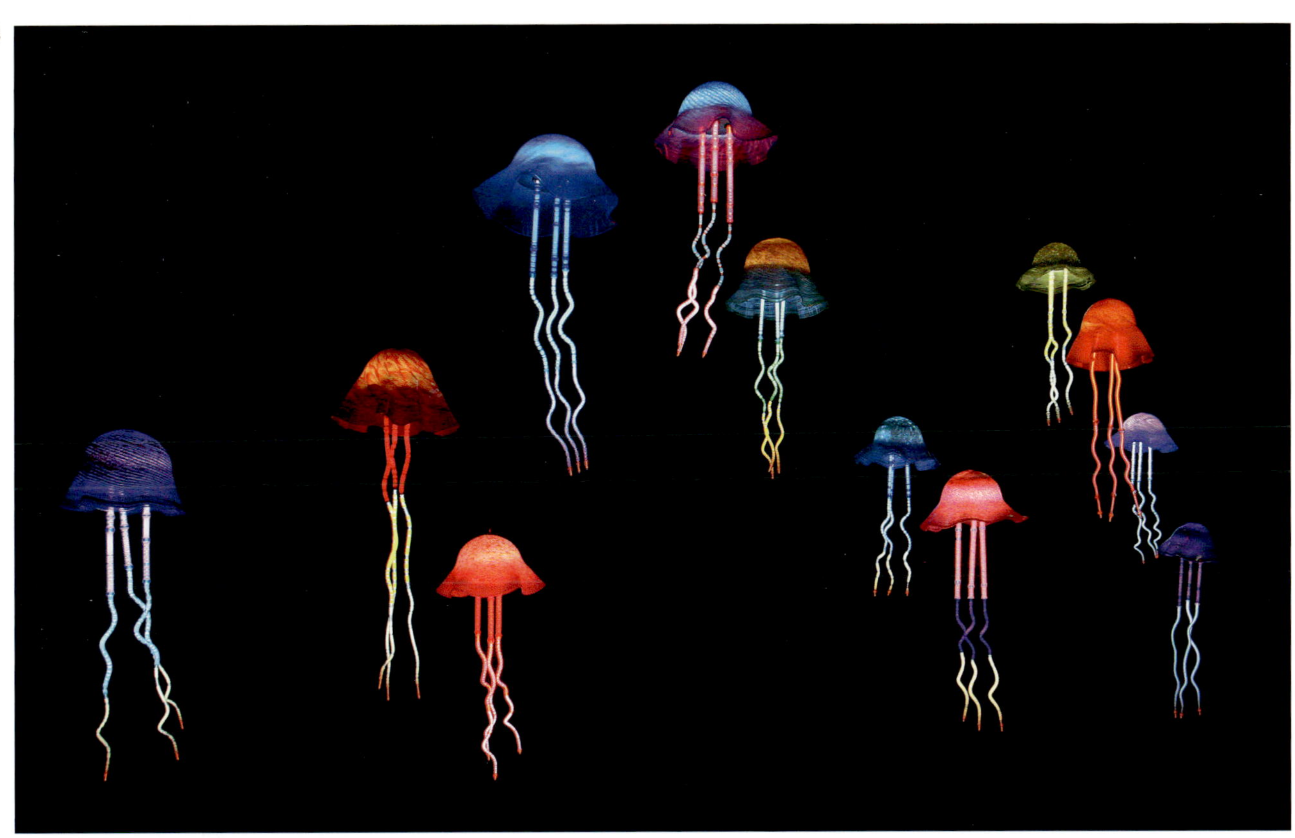

4
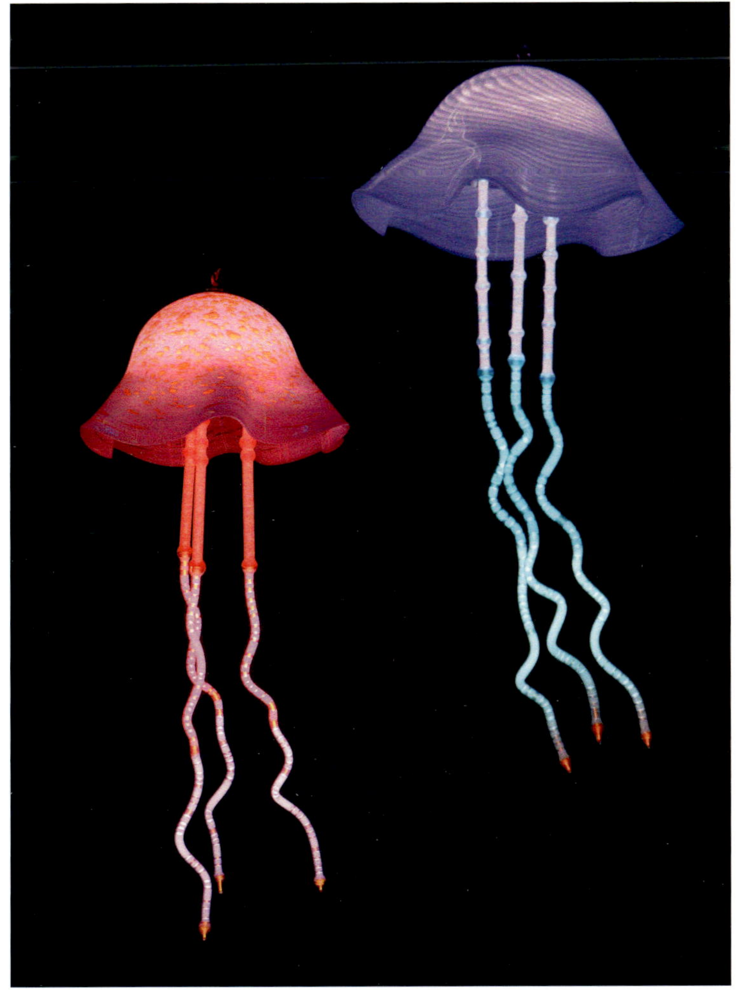

5
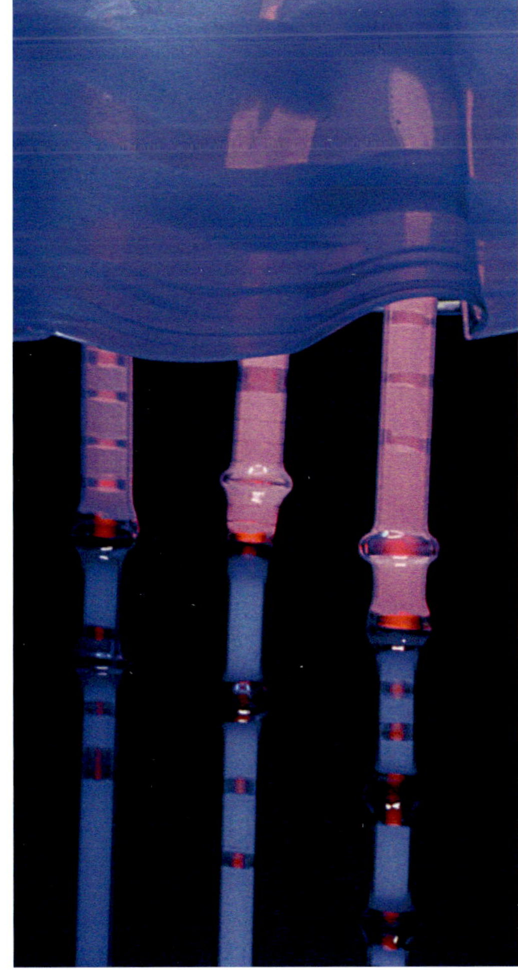

Shane Fero

Penland, North Carolina

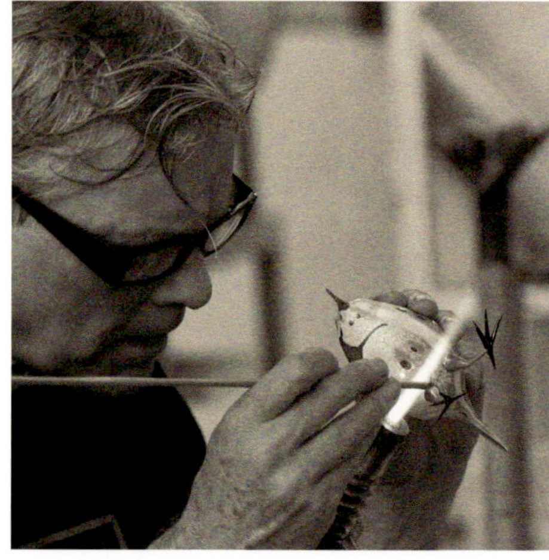

Shane Fero demonstrating at the 10th International Glass Festival, Hsinchu City, Taiwan. 2014. Courtesy of Yon Chun Peng.

During my forty-five-year career, I have been fascinated with and have rendered bird imagery in various forms. This focus has sharpened in the last twelve years with my blown bird series, which is based on techniques of German flameworking. I learned these techniques when I was a young apprentice, although I brought them into a contemporary context in relation to my work. I have always combined bird and human elements in my sculptures, vessel forms, and mixed media pieces.

I began the present bird series after 9/11 to counter the mood and malaise of that time period. Birds have that special metaphysical and spiritual quality, which is reflected in their colors, gestures, song, and flight. I love to imbue humor and character into these pieces, especially in the titles. Recently, I have added to the mix bird prints in the medium of vitreography, printed at Harvey Littleton studios, and paintings in acrylic on canvas.

1

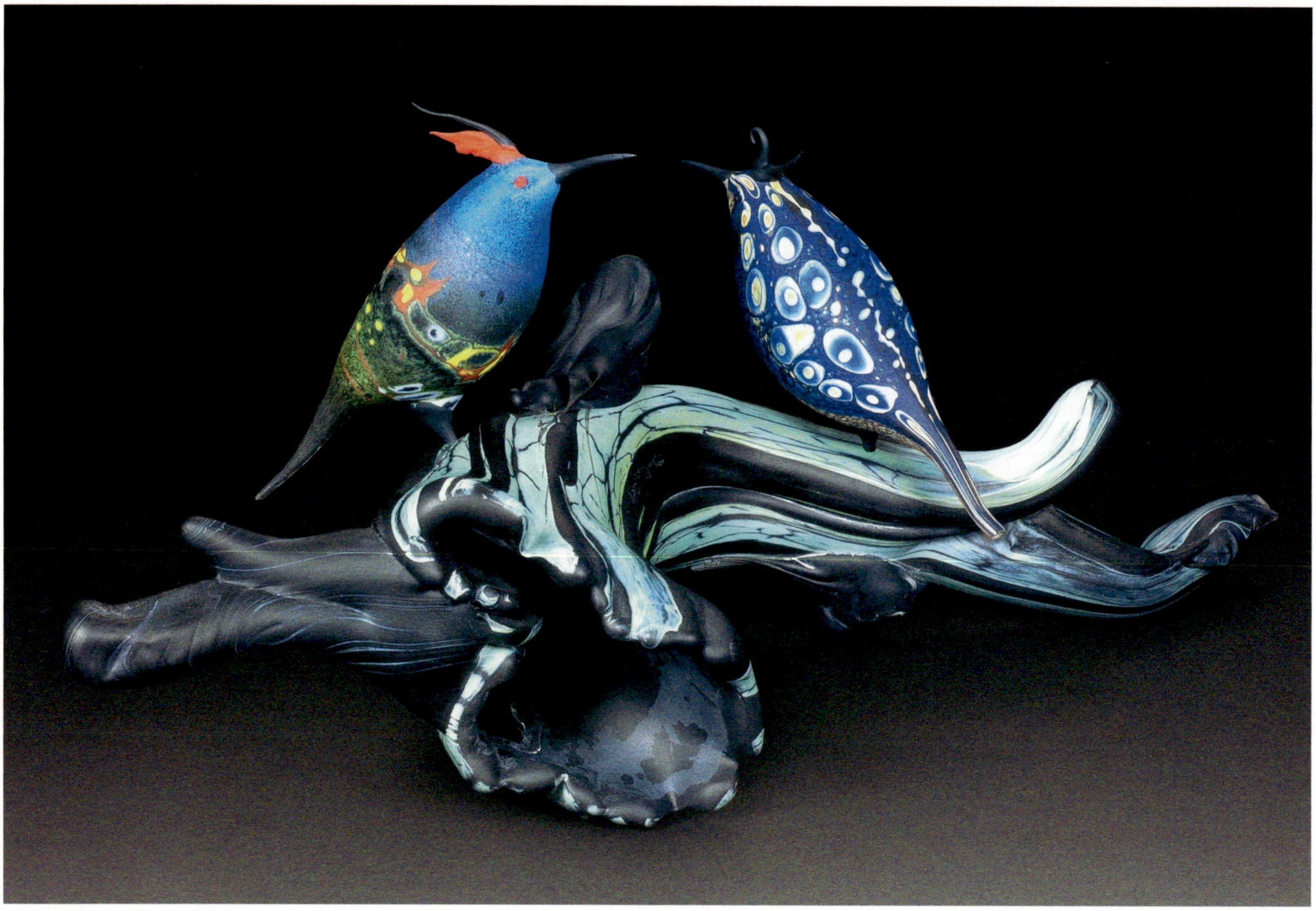

1 *Exotic Hummingbirds on Branch*. Hot and flameworked glass, sandblasted and acid-etched. 7" × 17" × 7". 2012. Branch gaffed by Jeff Mack. Courtesy of Mary Vogel Photography.

2

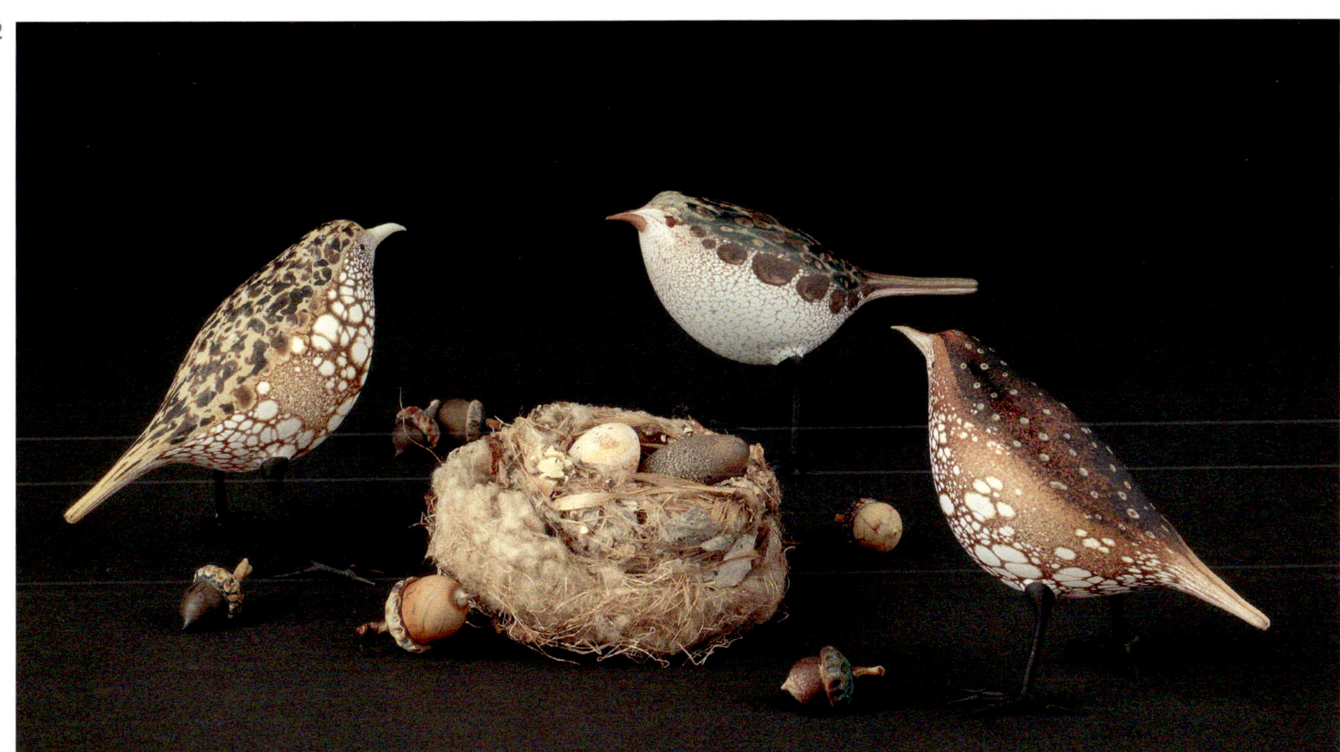

3

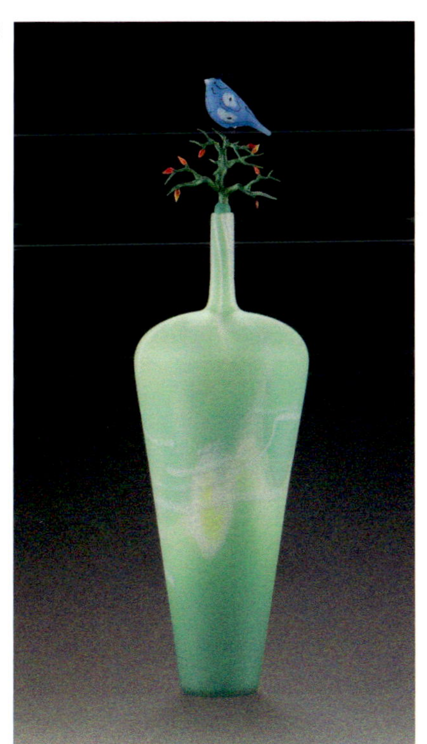

4

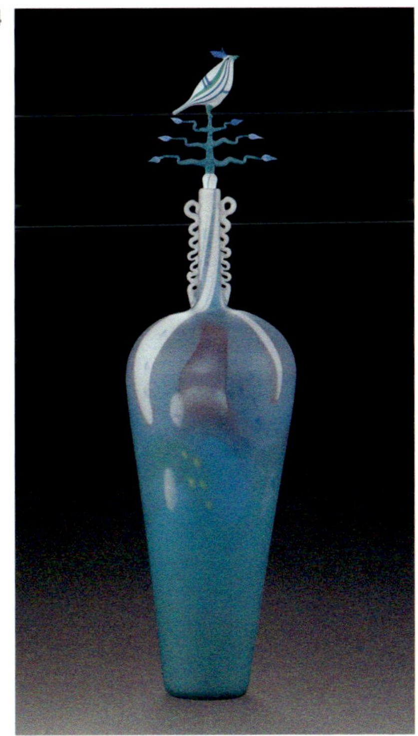

5

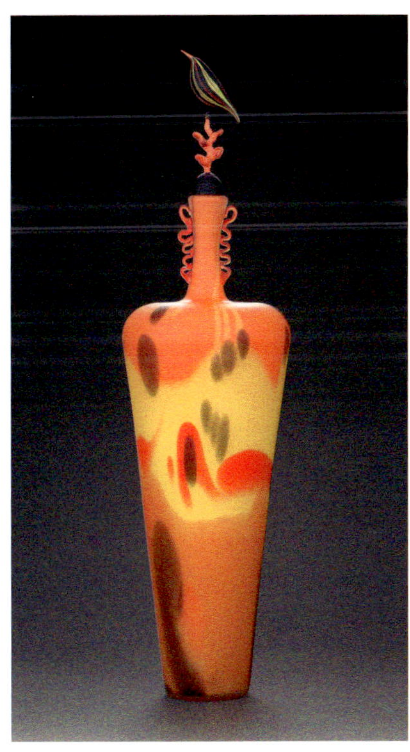

2 *Nesting*. Flameworked glass and acid-etched with manipulated found nest. 4" × 12" × 18". 2014. Courtesy of Mary Vogel Photography.

3 *Autumn into Spring*. Hot and flameworked glass, sandblasted and acid-etched. 23.75" × 6.5" × 6.5". 2012. Bottle gaffed by Pablo Soto. Courtesy of Mary Vogel Photography.

4 *Turquoisa*. Hot and flameworked glass, sandblasted and acid-etched. 24.5" × 6.5" × 6.5". 2012. Bottle gaffed by Pablo Soto. Courtesy of Mary Vogel Photography.

5 *Jack-O-Lantern*. Hot and flameworked glass, sandblasted and acid-etched. 26.25" × 7" × 7". 2012. Bottle gaffed by Pablo Soto. Courtesy of Mary Vogel Photography.

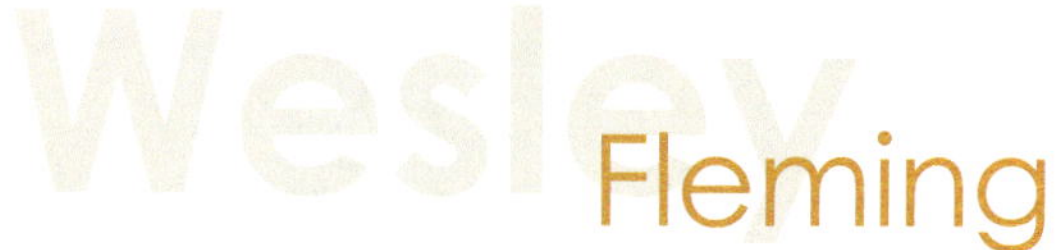

Wesley Fleming

Ashfield, Massachusetts

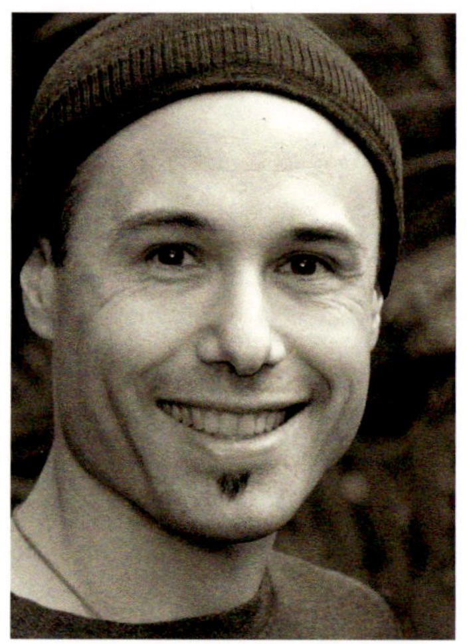

Courtesy of Alana Dunn Photography.

My experience with hot glass began at the furnace in 2001, working for Josh Simpson and the MIT Glass Lab, among others. I have always had an eye for detail and enjoy solitude, so the switch to flameworking was a logical step. In 2005 I studied with Vittorio Costantini and Lucio Bubacco in Murano, learning the Italian technique of glass sculpting. I then focused solely on making glass insects for the next two years. After becoming comfortable with these techniques, I began branching out to other phyla of the animal kingdom.

Growing up in rural western Pennsylvania, I spent my days exploring the space beneath logs and rocks or reading science fiction. Thus the shapes and colors of the natural world, as well as my wacky imagination, are the primary sources for my work. For example, with my glass beetles I try to mimic an actual species by replicating the intricate detail on their legs and thorax. I conjure creatures from my inner reality. In some cases, I merge reality with fantasy through color choice or by referencing mythology.

1

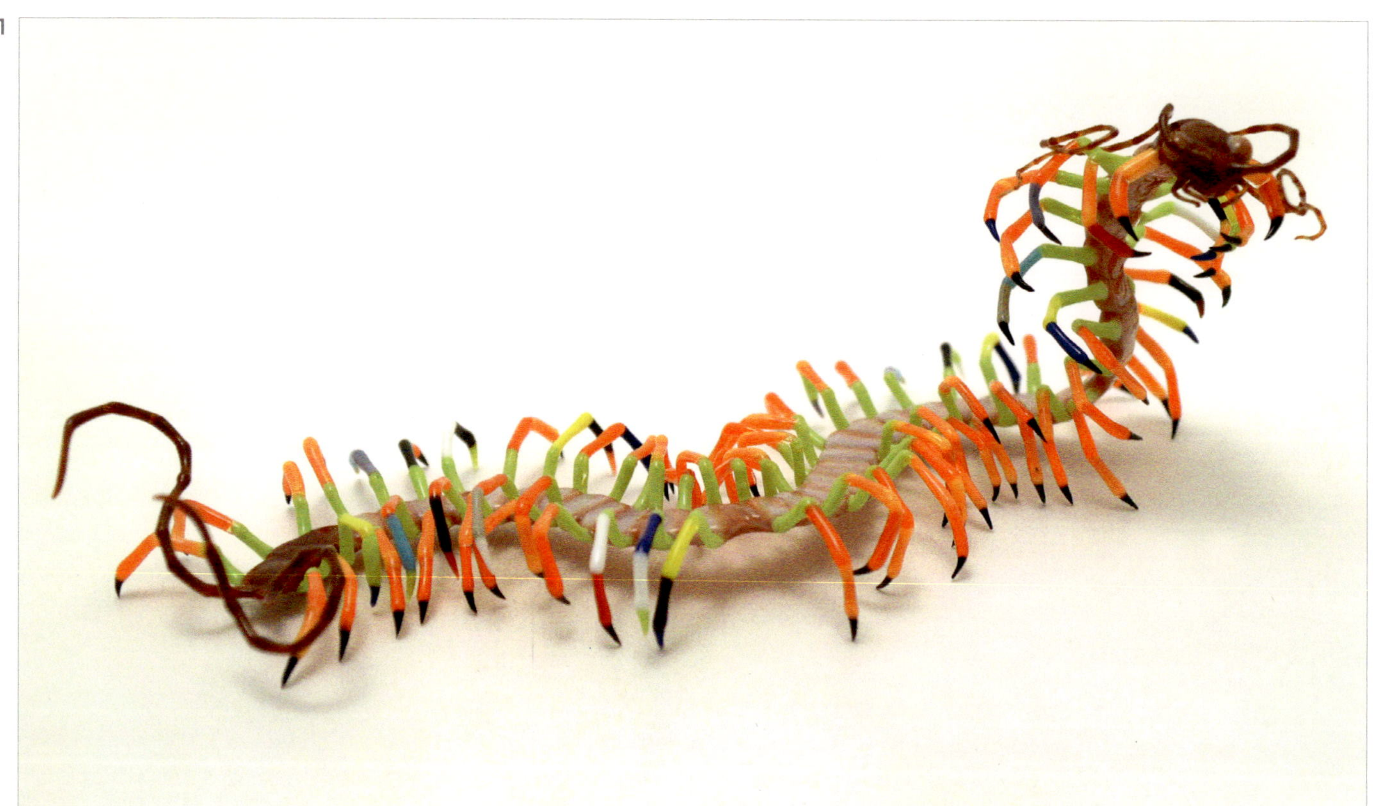

1 *Turning Point*. Flameworked hot glass. 3" × 3" × 8". 2014.

2 *Ladies Night*. Flameworked hot glass. 6" × 3" × 3". 2014.

3 *Hermit Crab with Teapot Shell*. Flameworked hot glass. 3" × 3" × 4". 2013.

4 *Amethyst Warrior Ant*. Flameworked hot glass. 5" × 3" × 3". 2014.

5 *Indigo Mantis with Wasp*. Flameworked hot glass. 4" × 4" × 2". 2014.

2

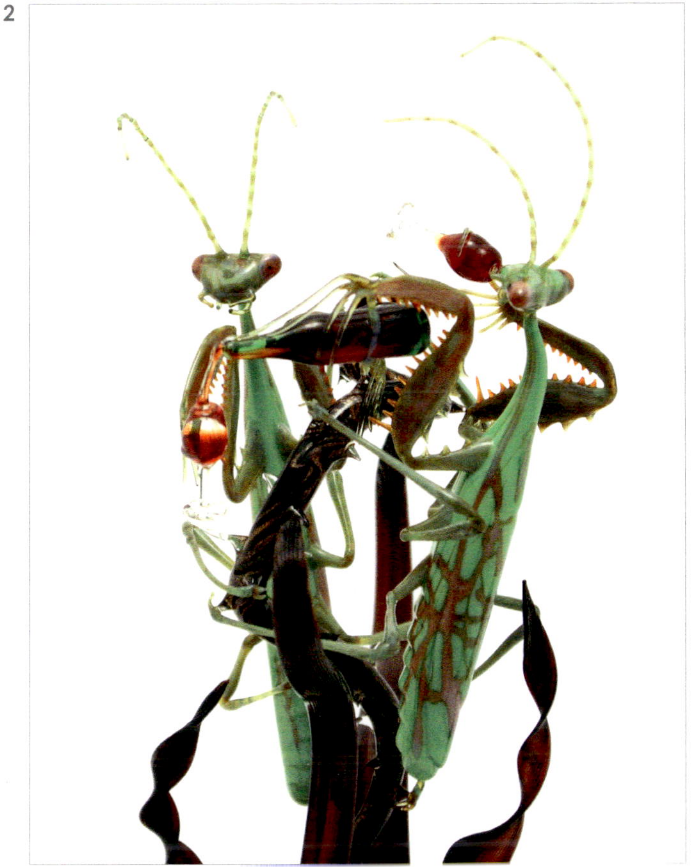

4

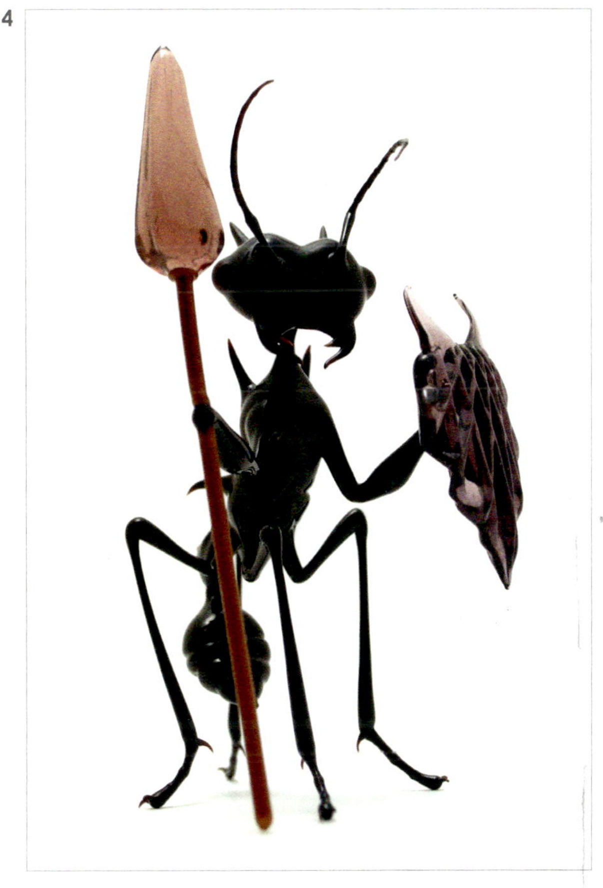

3

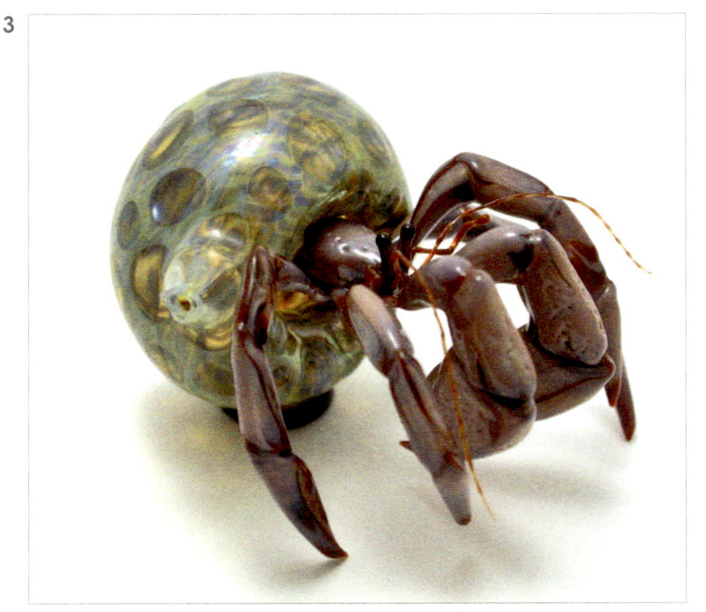

5

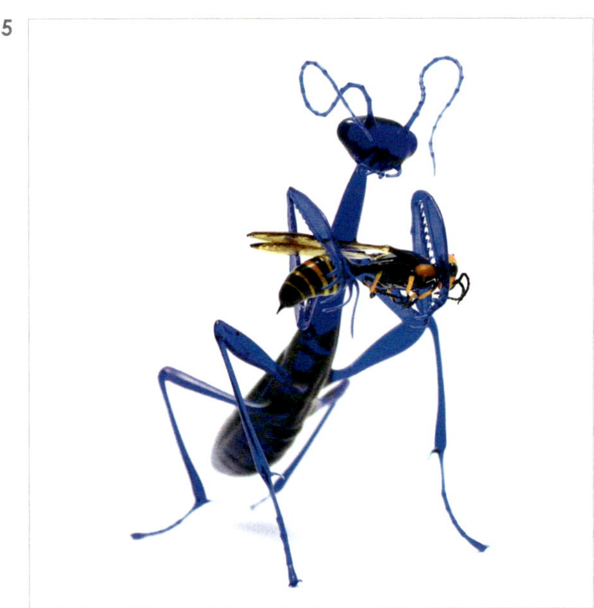

Tom Fuhrman

Oak Ridge, Tennessee

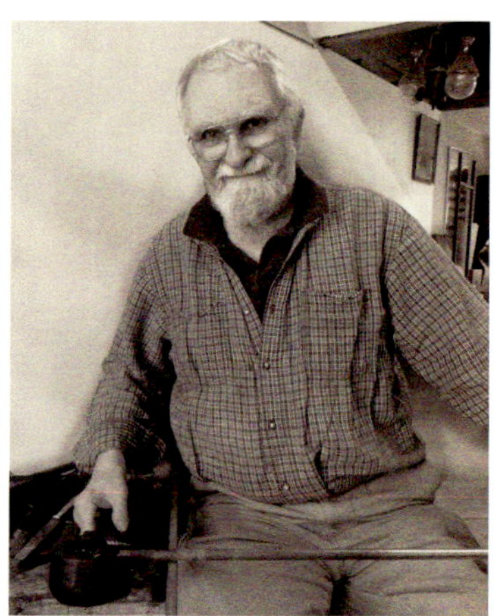

I started my journey with glass with the purchase of a paperweight when I was ten years old. Since then I have been "addicted" to the medium. Over the years, I have worked with all types of glass, including blown, fused, stained, lampworked, polished, laminated, and repurposed glass.

My art is about the light and its interaction with glass. Glass has unique qualities, which allow it to express things that are not possible in other media. It can be reflective, transparent, translucent, opaque, etched, shiny, smooth, rough, sharp, and obsessive to the human eye. I try to use all of the various qualities that result from the glass/light relationship to create exciting assemblages.

1

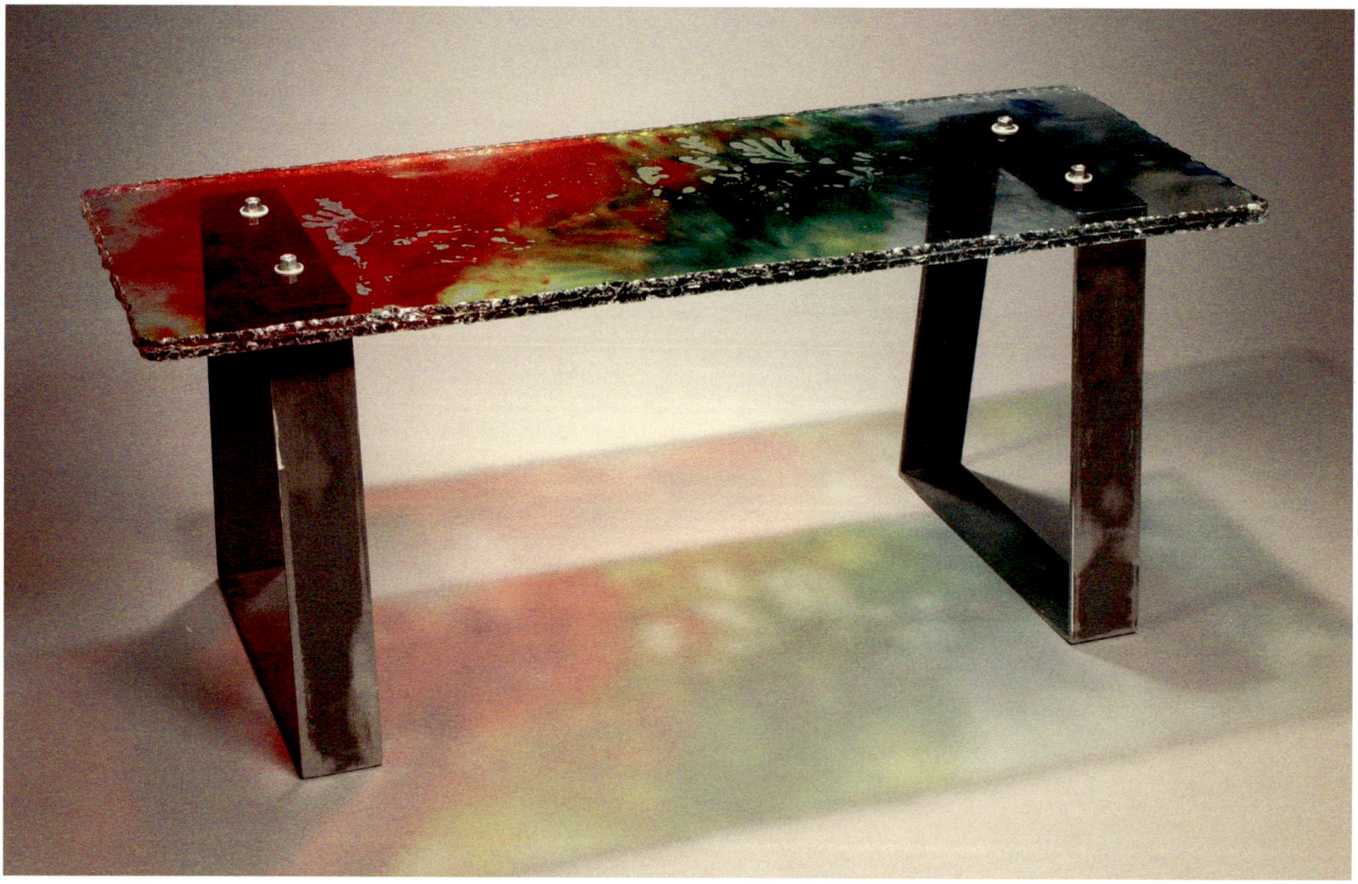

4

2

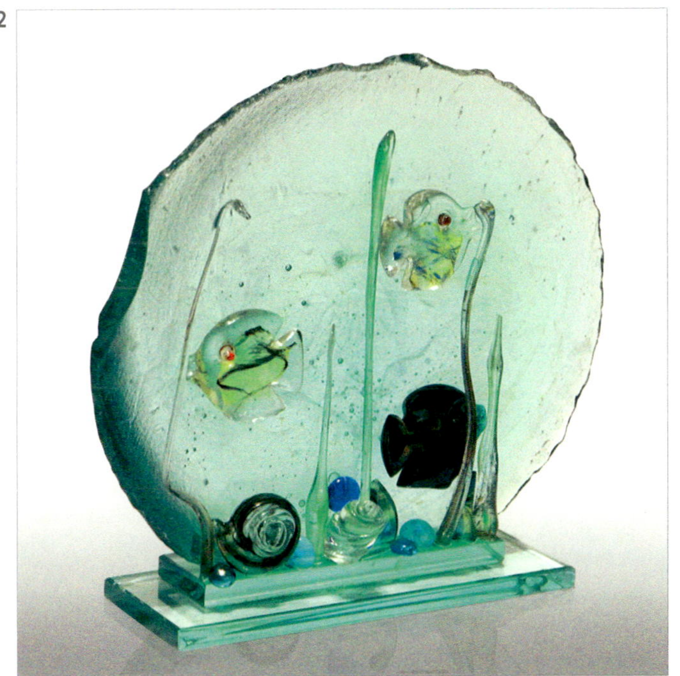

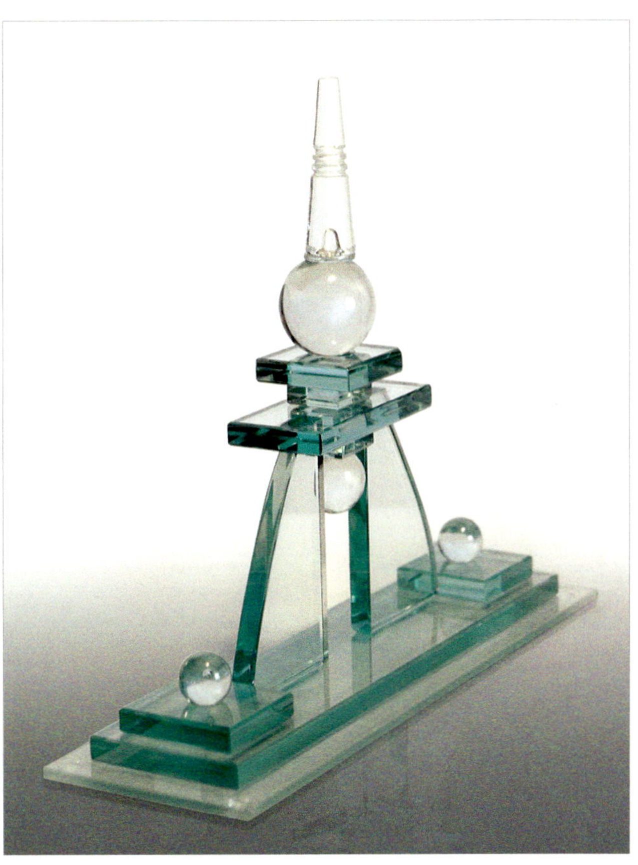

3

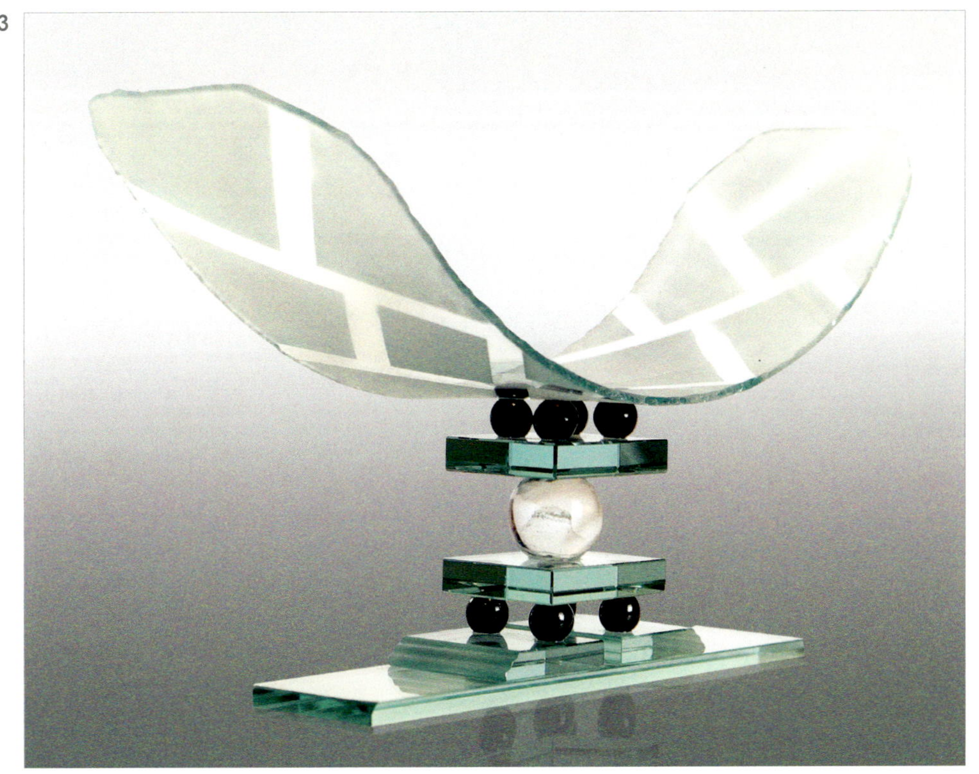

1 *Garden Bench.* Laminated float glass and steel. 16" × 16" × 42". 2012.

2 *Fishscape.* Cast glass, blown glass, lampworked glass, polished float glass, and laminated glass. 14" × 4" × 14". 2011.

3 *Art Deco Wedge.* Kiln-fired float glass, etched float glass, laminated/polished float glass, and blown glass. 22" × 4" × 6". 2009.

4 *Classic Temple Series #4.* Blown glass, polished and laminated float glass. 2008.

Jason B. Gamrath

Seattle, Washington

The most beautiful, extravagant manmade object could never creatively equal the simplest and smallest naturally occurring life form. The purpose of creating this series on a macro scale is to bring to light the beauty that exists within the micro scale of nature. Through the rigors of day-to-day life in an urban setting, I find it all too easy to overlook the natural beauty that has ultimately birthed us as a species. Small plants, although minuscule in comparison to our natural human perspective, are overwhelmingly perplexing when held inches away from one's face. The vast majority of people will seldom grasp this seemingly secret perception of existence. When I scale life forms up to be larger than a person, they can be observed with this perspective from across a room because of their overwhelming physical presence.

It is my hope that when people admire my large-scale renderings, they will become curious and captivated by the hints of realism I incorporate. I encourage people to attempt to observe with the same eyes through which I humbly and graciously experience our natural world.

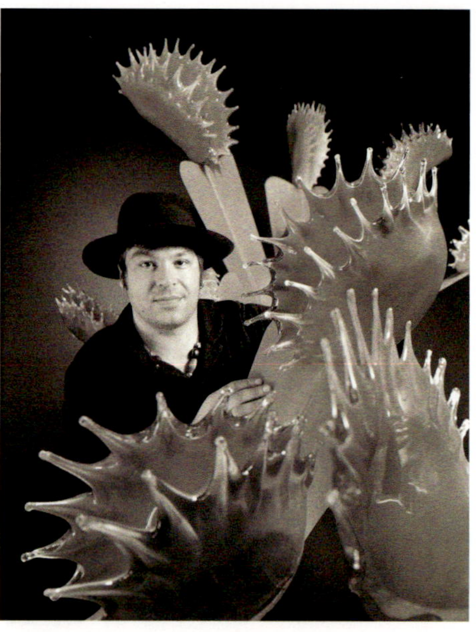

Artist and *Flytrap*. Courtesy of Daniel Fox/Lumina Studio.

1

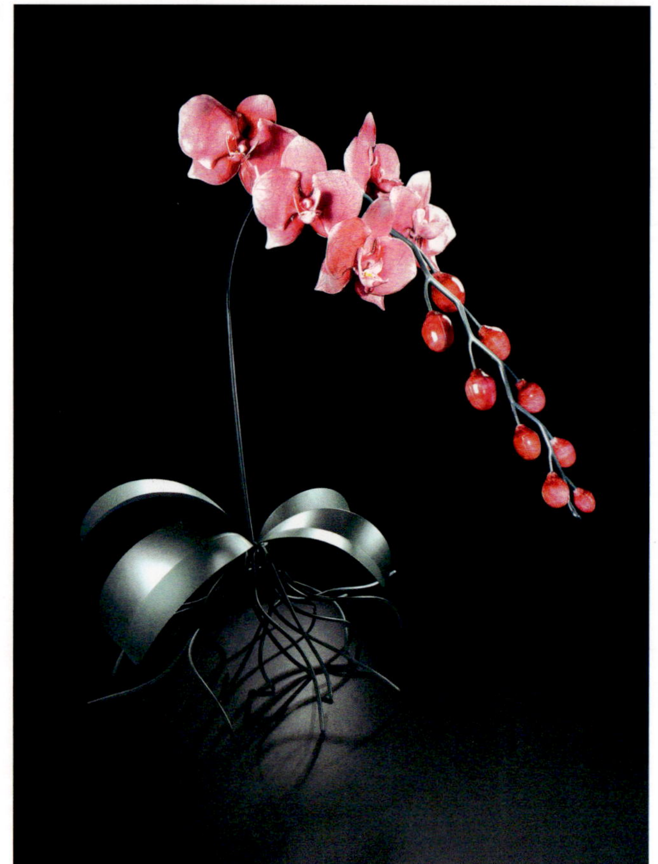

2

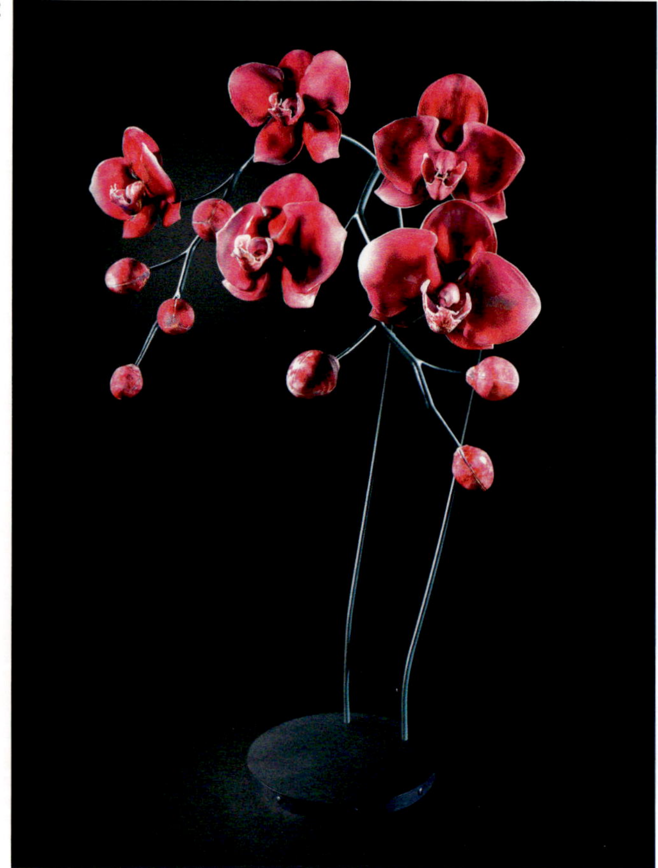

3

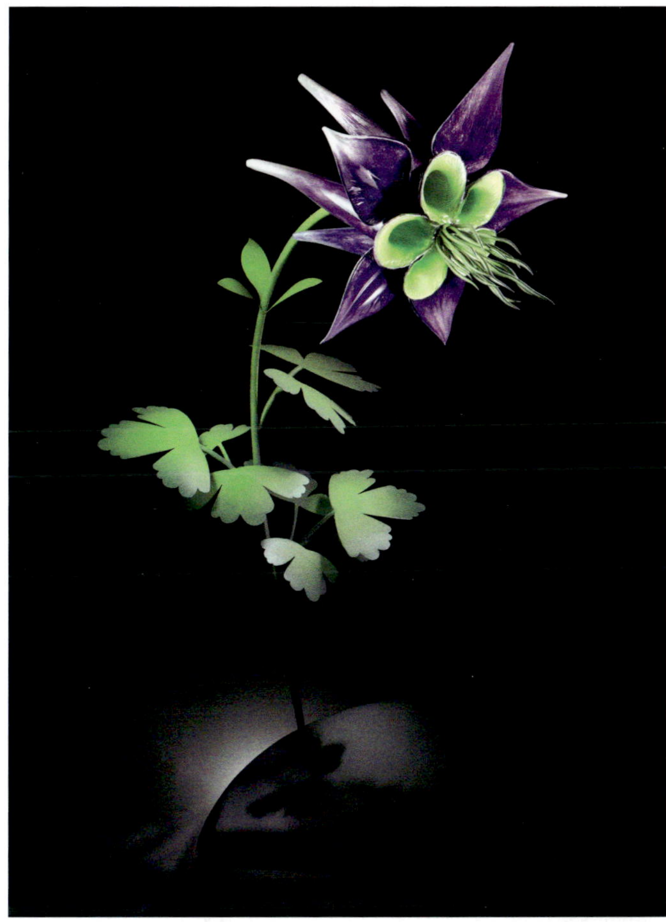

4

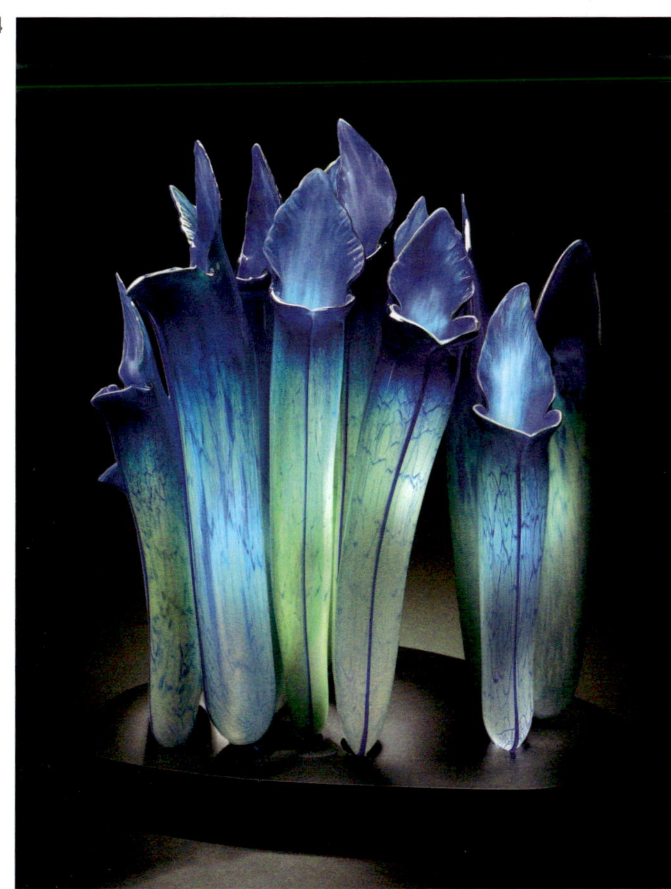

5

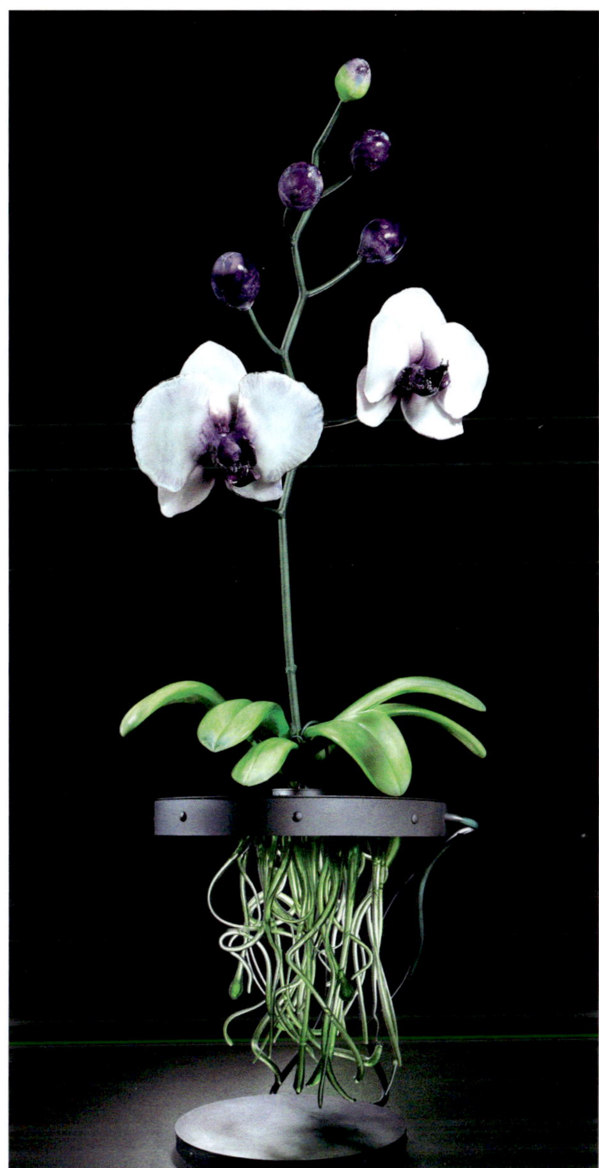

1 *Specimen.* Hot blown/sculpted glass and steel. 108" × 84" × 84". 2014. Courtesy of Daniel Fox/ Lumina Studio.

2 *Arielle.* Hot blown/sculpted glass and steel 96" × 48" × 84". 2012. Courtesy of Daniel Fox/ Lumina Studio.

3 *Veronica.* Hot blown/sculpted glass and steel. 72" × 48" × 36". 2014. Courtesy of Daniel Fox/ Lumina Studio.

4 *Ben.* Hot blown/sculpted glass and steel. 48" × 36" × 48". 2013. Courtesy of Daniel Fox/ Lumina Studio.

5 *Mikaela.* Hot blown/sculpted glass and steel. 144" × 48" × 48". 2012. Courtesy of Daniel Fox/ Lumina Studio.

Stephen Gartner & Danielle Blade

Ashley Falls, Massachusetts

Gartner and Blade Glass is the work of Stephen Gartner and Danielle Blade. Business partners since 1995, we combine our individual ideas, techniques, and experiences to create original works in hand-blown and sculpted glass. Over the past decade, we have been developing a series of pieces that explores our mutual fascination with the use of found objects in the rituals of primitive cultures. In these pieces, we hope to convey a reverence for and an understanding of the value of our natural resources.

Natural elements such as bone, antler, wood, vines, fossils, and rock formations have inspired our signature designs, which include covered vessels and sculptural objects. Our work combines traditional hand-blown technique with innovative color application and original sculpting techniques. Prior to opening our own studio, we studied with prominent American and European glass artists.

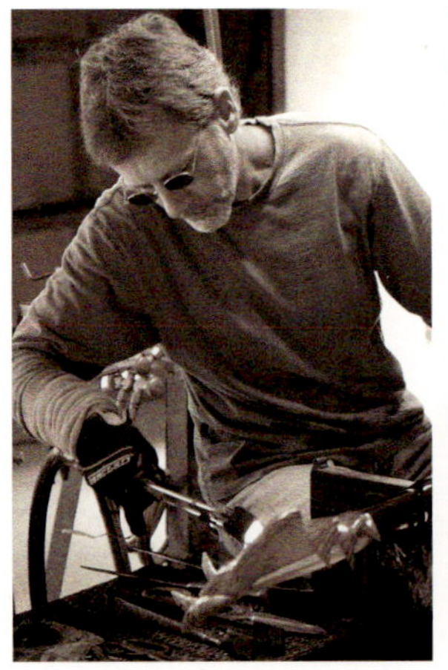

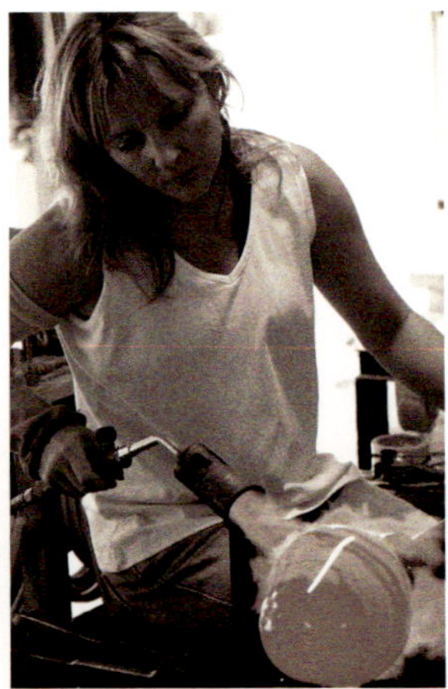

Courtesy of Katie Malone Photography.

1

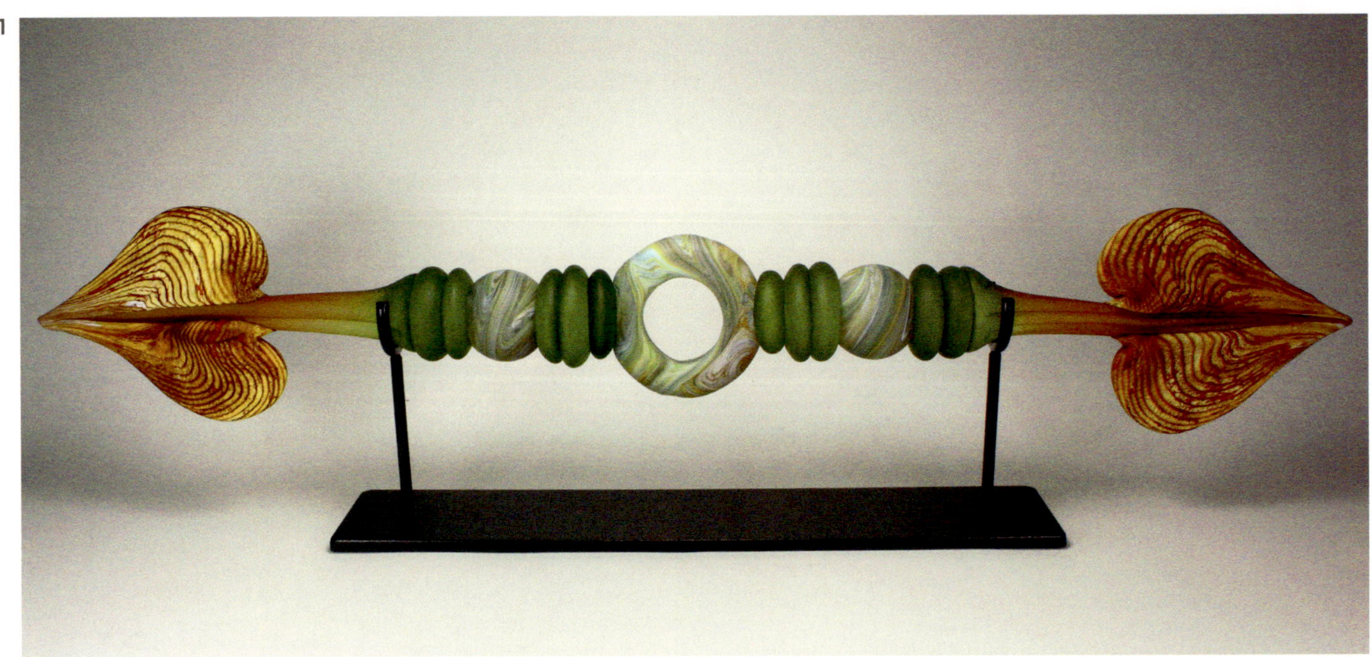

1 *Lime and Tangerine Austral Sculpture with Sphere Inclusions Talisman.* Hot sculpted, cold worked, and sandblasted glass. Hand-forged steel sculpture base. 42" × 7".

2 *Amethyst Strata Covered Bowl.* Hand-blown and hot sculpted glass. 12" × 9". Photo: Jonathan Wallen.

3 *Ruby Arbor Sculpture Pair.* Hot sculpted, sandblasted, and polished glass. 15" × 6". Photo: Jonathan Wallen.

4 *Black Sargasso Sphere*. Hand-blown and hot sculpted glass. 12" × 15".

5 *Amethyst Sage Talisman.* Hot sculpted, cold worked, and sandblasted glass. Hand-forged steel sculpture base. 32" × 10".

2

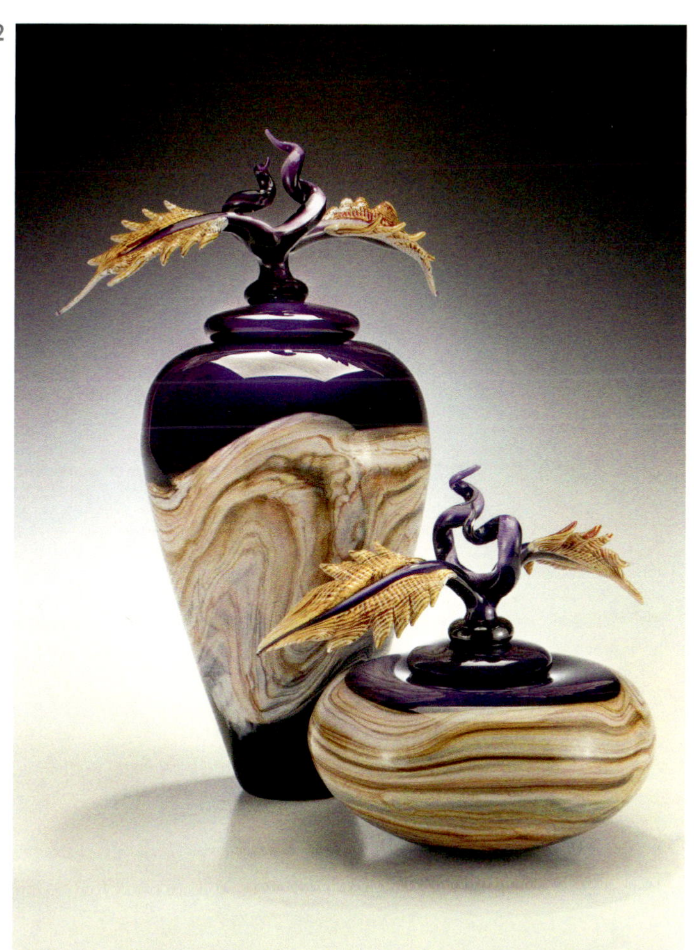

4

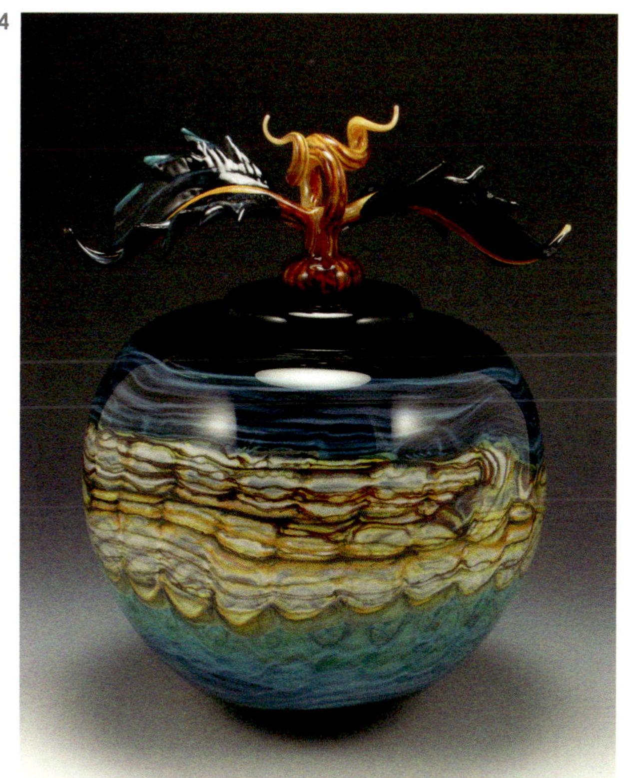

3

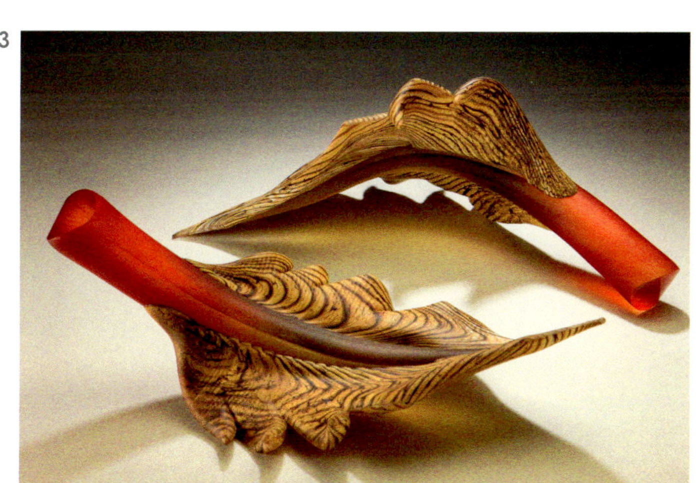

5

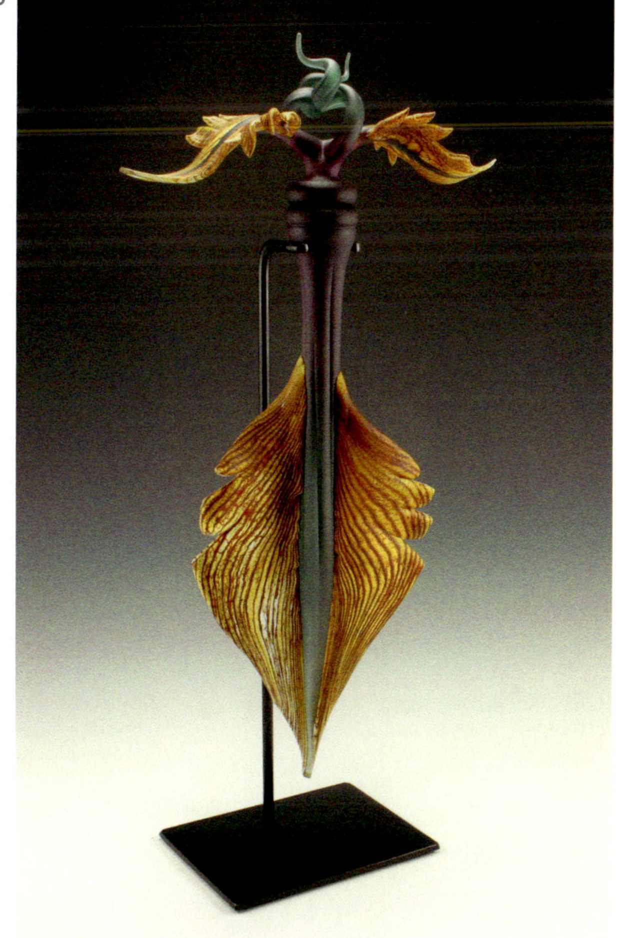

Michael Glancy

Rehoboth, Massachusetts

My sculptures reveal my exacting struggle toward perfection. Drawing inspiration from natural macro- and micro-environments, I translate cellular landscapes into elegant jewel-toned sculptural objects. Made with blown and plate glass, copper, bronze, silver, and gold, my works reference science, biology, molecular physics, and mathematics. My process of electroforming metal and glass is both magical and scientific, so much so that I walk a fine line between alchemy and art.

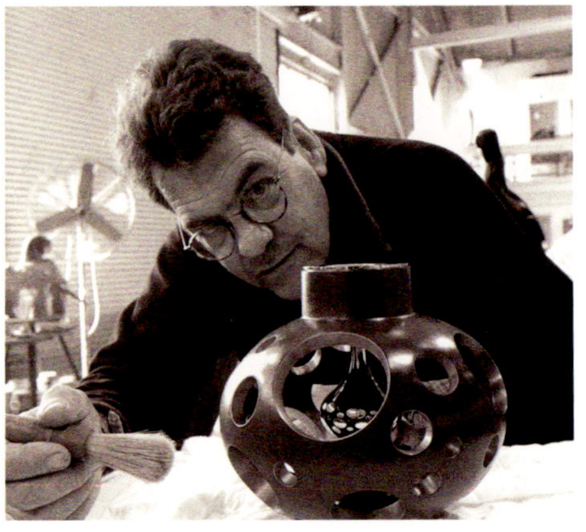

Courtesy of Chris Roque.

1

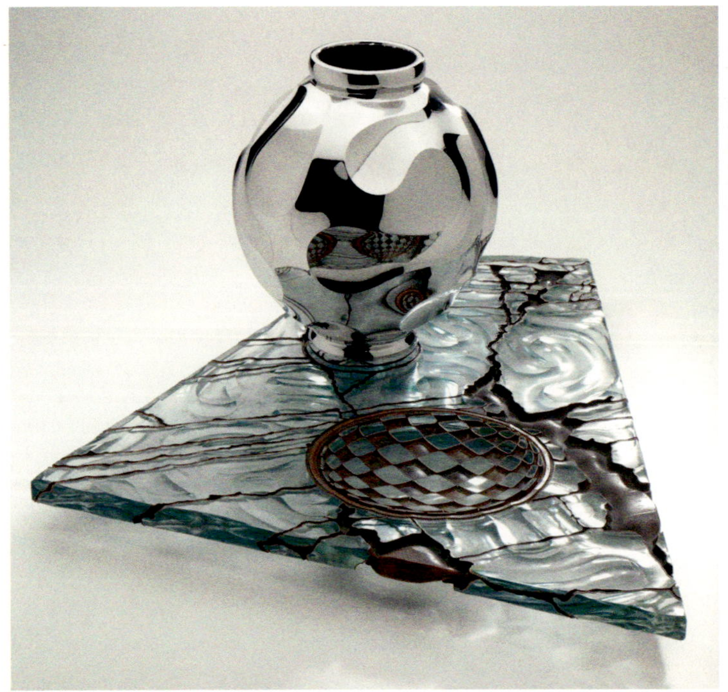

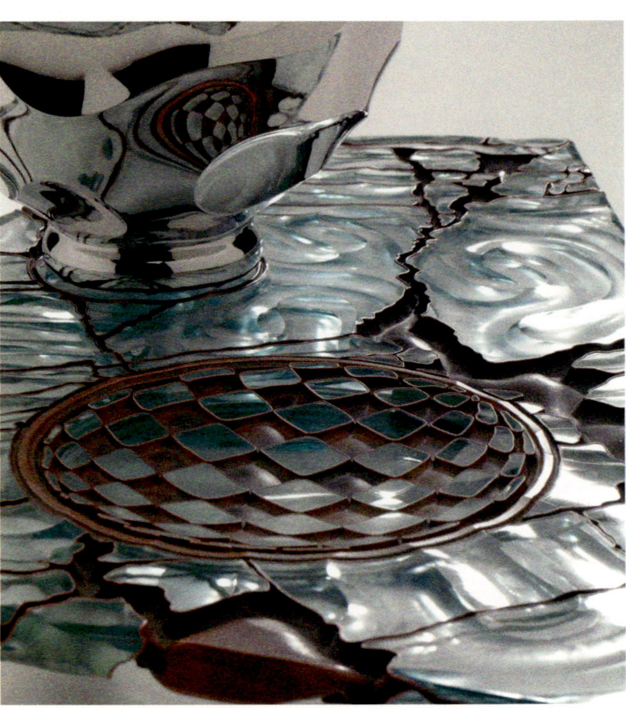

1 *Liquid Landscape.* Mirror polished cast stainless steel object, industrial plate glass, and copper. 10" × 22" × 17". 2010. Photo: Marty Doyle.

2 *Twilight Star X—Indigo.* Cast glass object with engraved lens and interior surface manipulation (Reverse Star X), industrial plate glass, copper, and silver. 14" × 20.5" × 20.5". 2013. Photo: Marty Doyle.

3 *Indigo Inner Jazz.* Cast glass object, copper, and silver. 14.5" × 8" × 9.5". 2011. Photo: Marty Doyle.

4 *Whirling Fusion.* Cast glass object, machined blue industrial plate glass (mfr. Brazil, 1958–1967), copper, and silver. 18" × 23" × 27.75". 2013. Photo: Marty Doyle.

2

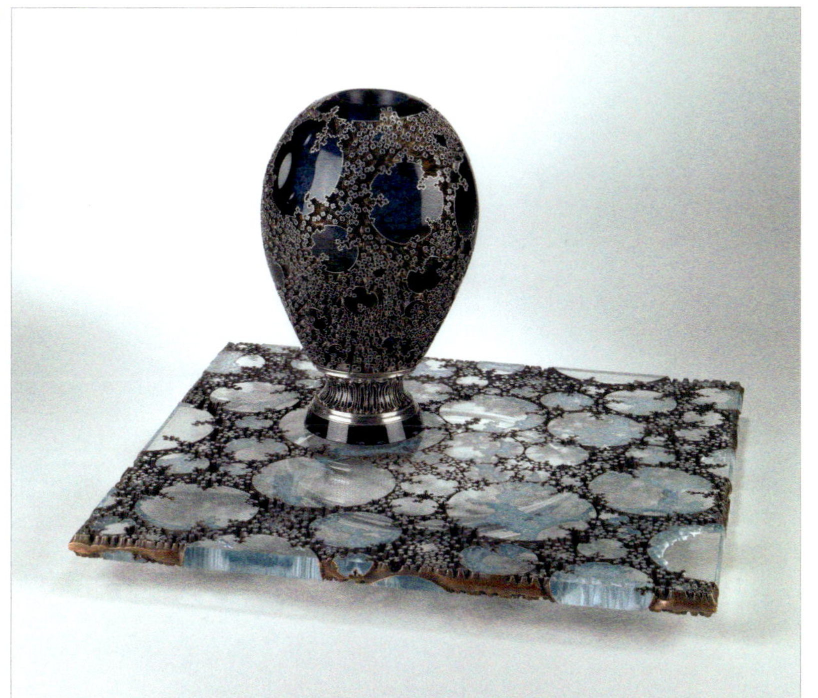

3

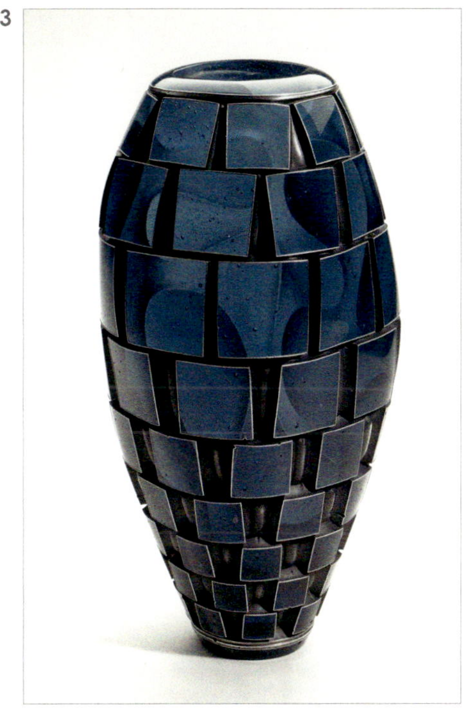

4

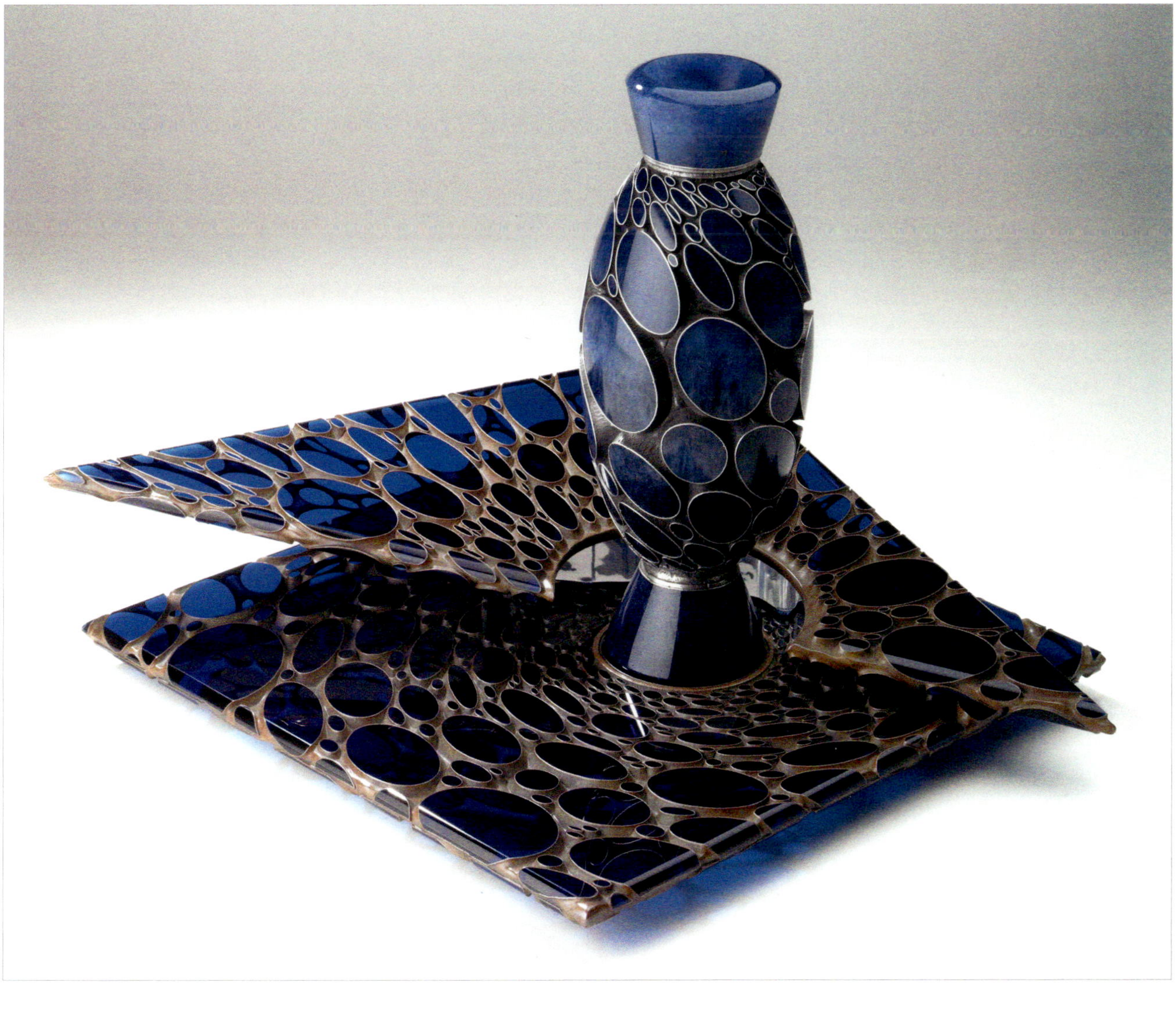

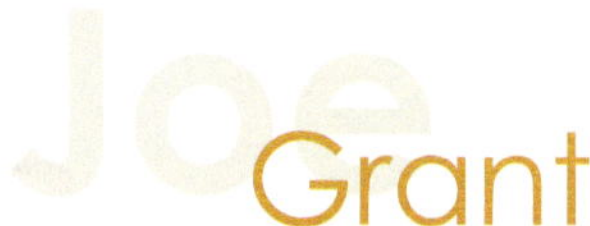

Grant

Elon, North Carolina

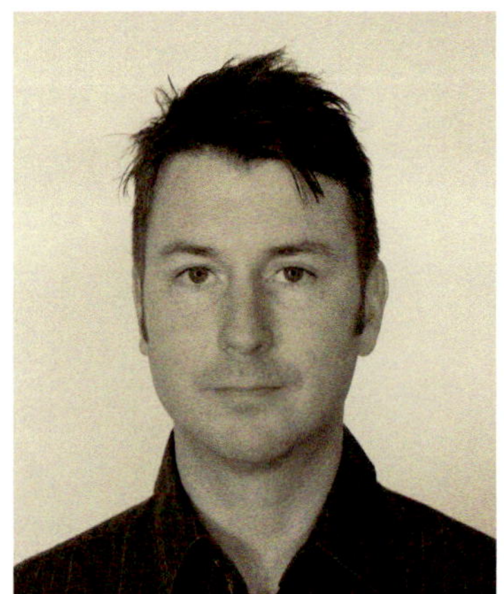

I have exhibited, demonstrated, and taught throughout the United States and abroad. Nature and the cyclical metamorphosis of life that surrounds us inspire me. I draw and paint to explore form and pattern, transforming the images from my research into blown glass using traditional and innovative techniques. They come alive to me in the glass studio, gathering, sifting, marking, shaping, blowing, and stretching, but they are not finished. The forms must be carved to completion, the patterns brought to maturity, and the objects given a place to rest.

1

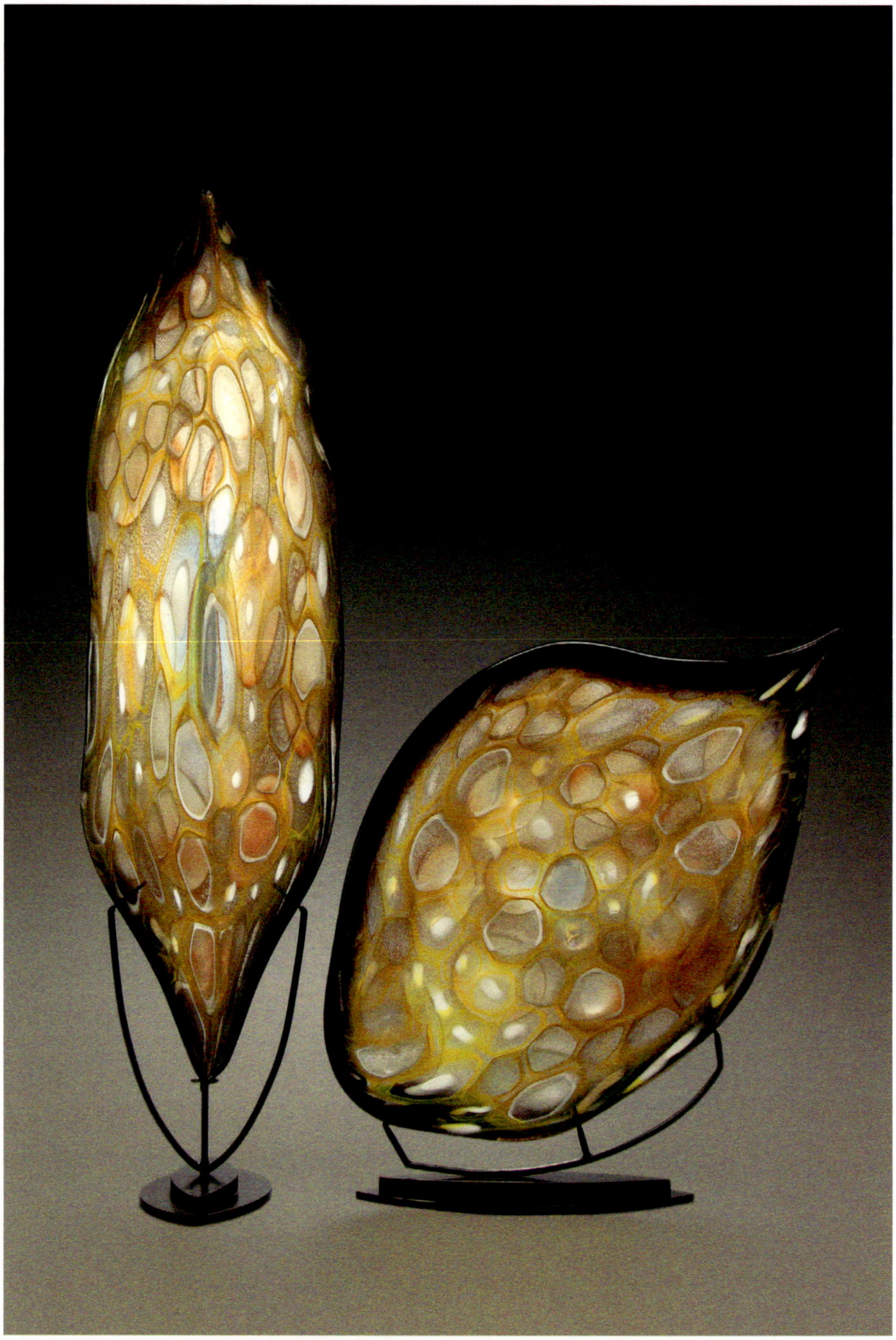

1 *Grand Morphis*. Blown glass and steel. 32" × 11" × 29". 2014. Courtesy of Mary Vogel Photography.

2 *Crystal Heliconious*, Blown glass and steel. 29" × 3" × 22". 2012. Courtesy of Mary Vogel Photography.

3 *Aroura Admiral*. Blown glass and steel. 36" × 3.5" × 25". 2012. Courtesy of Mary Vogel Photography.

4 *Phosphenes*. Blown glass and steel. 13" × 9" × 12". 2014. Courtesy of John Gessner.

5 *Volantes Striated*. Blown glass and steel. 10" × 9" × 14". 2014. Courtesy of Mary Vogel Photography.

2

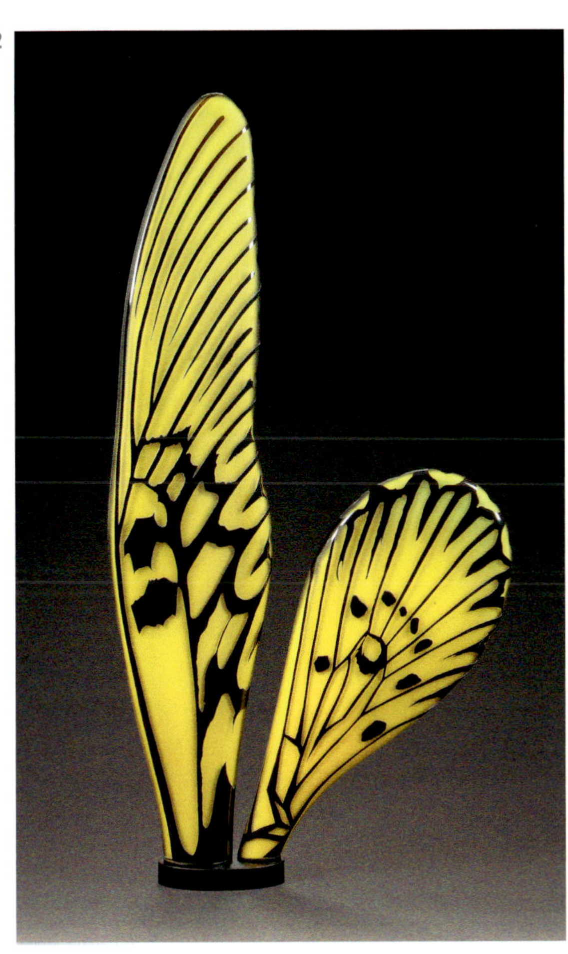

4

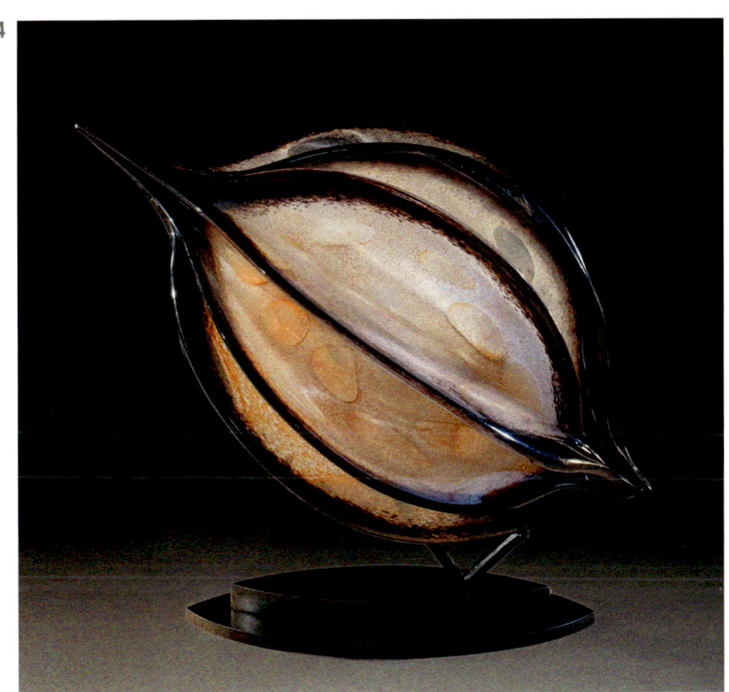

5

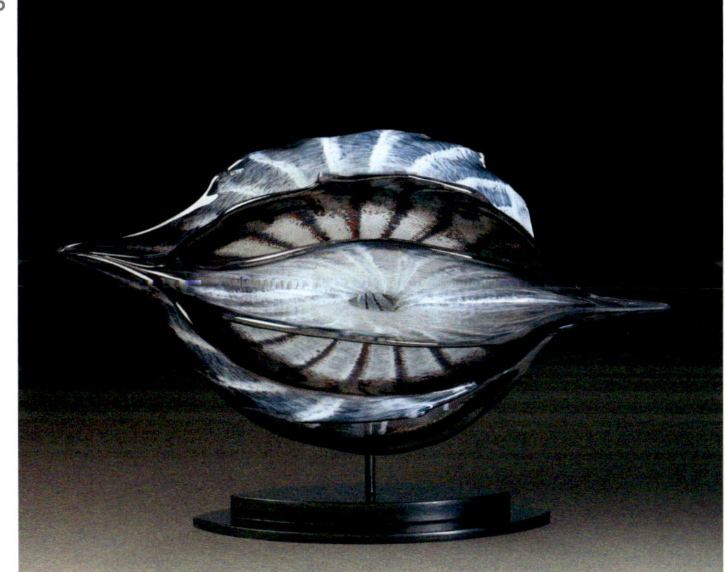

3

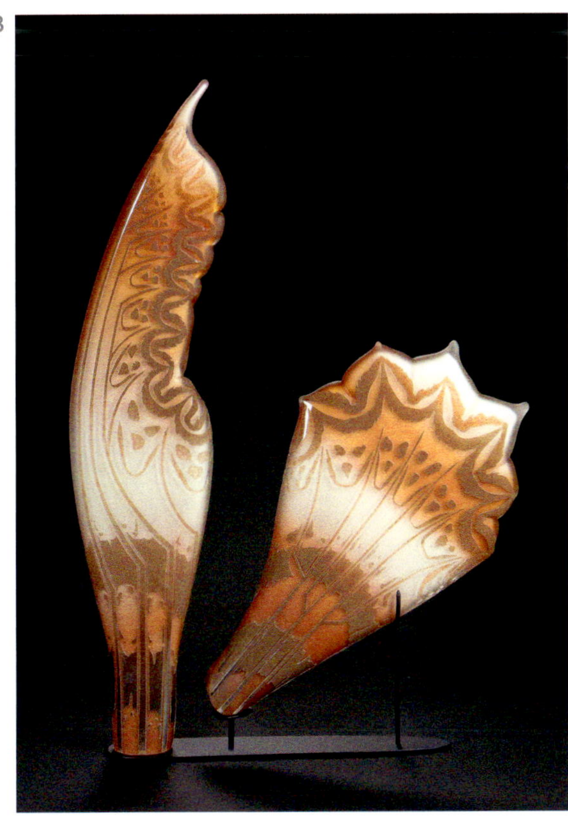

Gabriel Greenlaw

Smithville, Tennessee

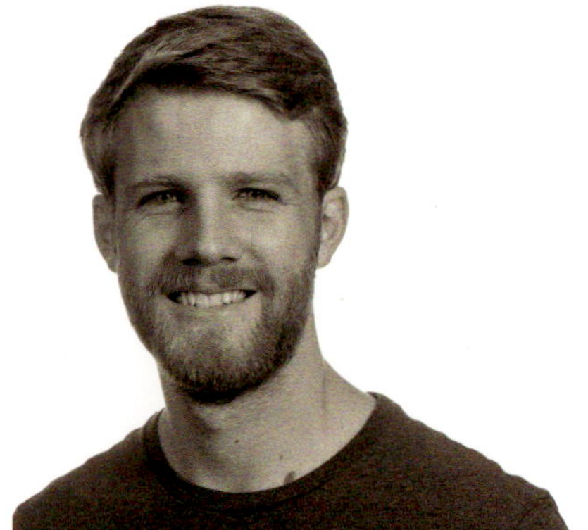

Courtesy of Benjamin Corda.

My current work involves taking small inspirations, such as neurological elements, and expanding them millions if not billions of times larger to where they become an immersive experience for the viewer. The use of glass in my work exploits the innate fragility that is associated with the material, creating an environment of tension and intensity that introduces a visceral sense of life into the material, transcending the visual impact of the composition.

Combined with complex and organic forms, as well as traditionally incompatible materials, my work embodies my internal obsession with drama and precision. I frequently find myself consumed by the act of making: impulsively acting, immersing myself in the process, and becoming obsessed with details that others might never consider.

My goal is to create forms that have a sense of movement and life and are accessible enough to allow the viewer to create their own associations while still preserving my original inspiration. My compositions invoke conversations of growth and expansion, representing my personal evolution as a creative individual. The passion that empowers me to spend sleepless nights in the studio delivers a high degree of craftsmanship and exceptionally resolved work. Throughout my process, I strive to communicate the complexity in the natural world through intricate lines, dense intensity, and the inherent intrigue and tension within the chaos.

1

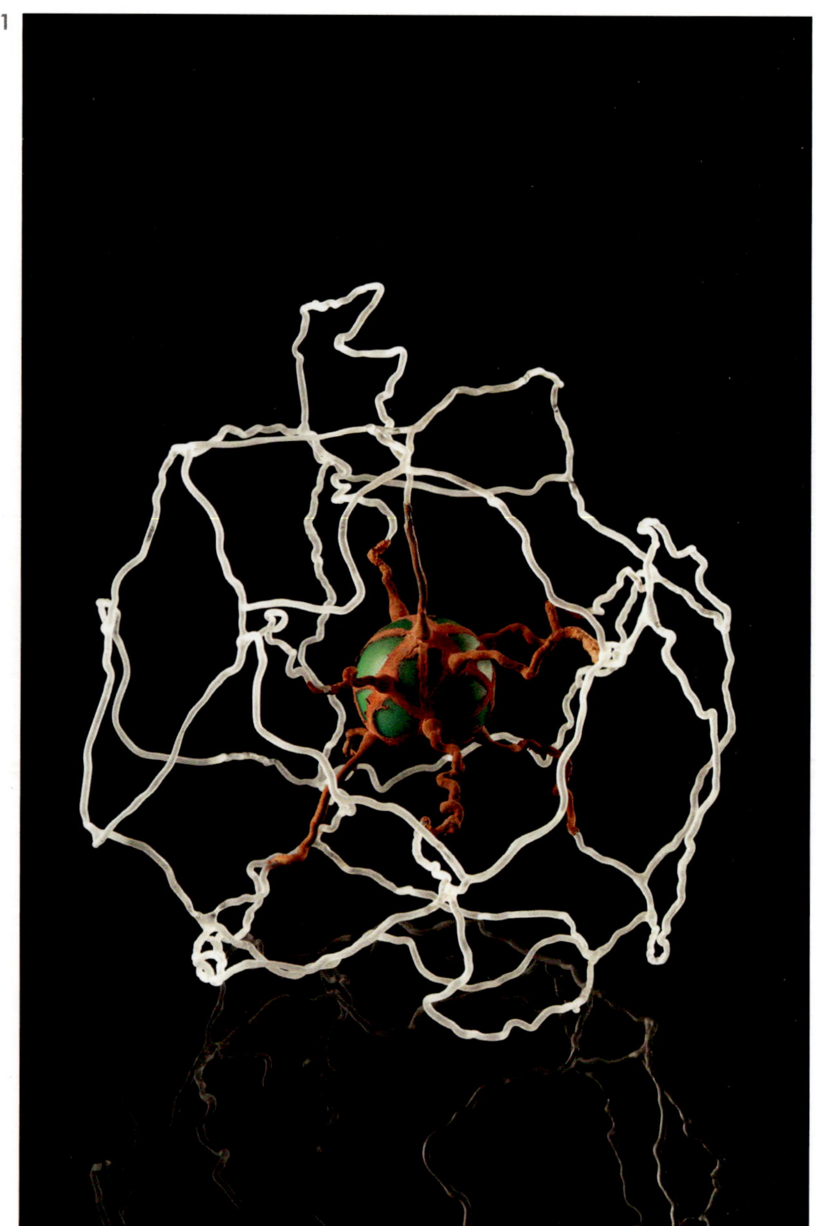

1 *Invasive and Malignant.* Blown and flameworked glass and electroplated copper. 22" × 21" × 23". 2013. Courtesy of Elizabeth Torgerson-Lamark.

2 *Upward Growth.* Blown and flameworked glass. 33" × 13" × 12". 2014. Courtesy of Elizabeth Torgerson-Lamark.

3 *Rooted Axon.* Blown and flameworked glass. 21" × 11" × 11". 2014. Courtesy of Jill Greenlaw.

4 *Motoneuron Expansion.* Blown and flameworked glass. 18" × 18.5" × 28". 2014. Courtesy of Elizabeth Torgerson-Lamark.

2

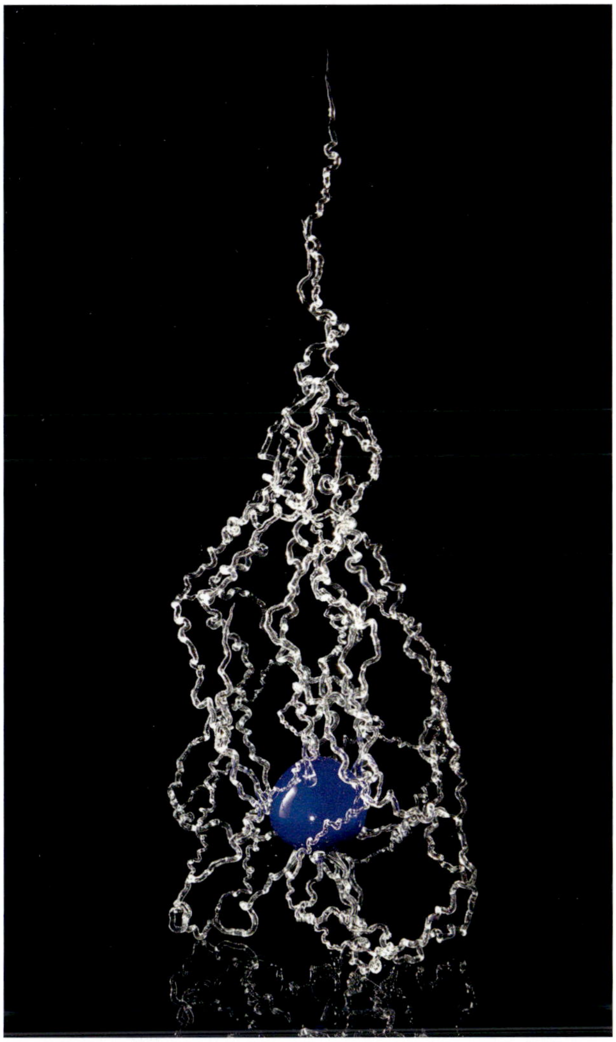

3

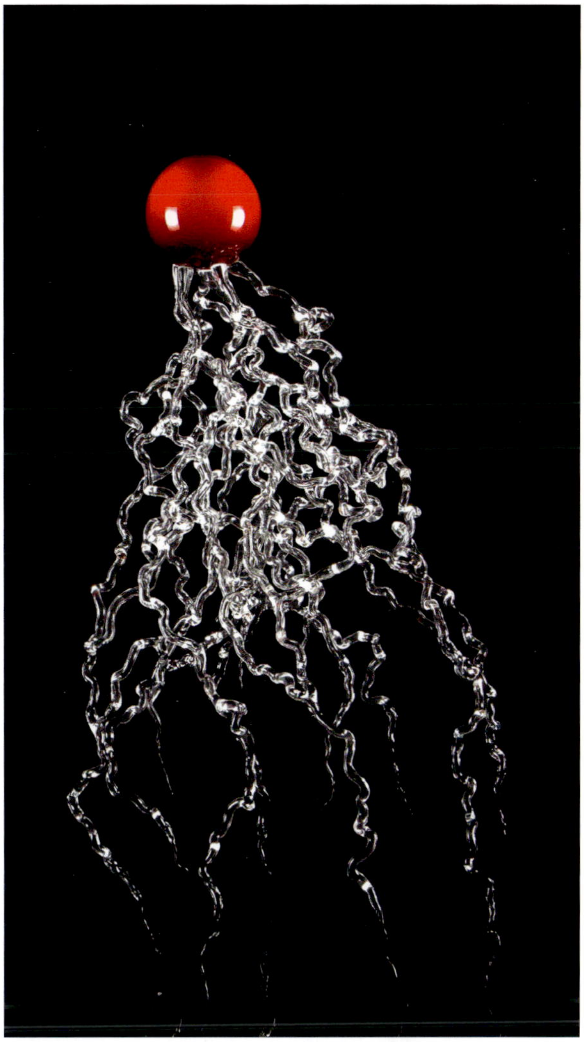

4

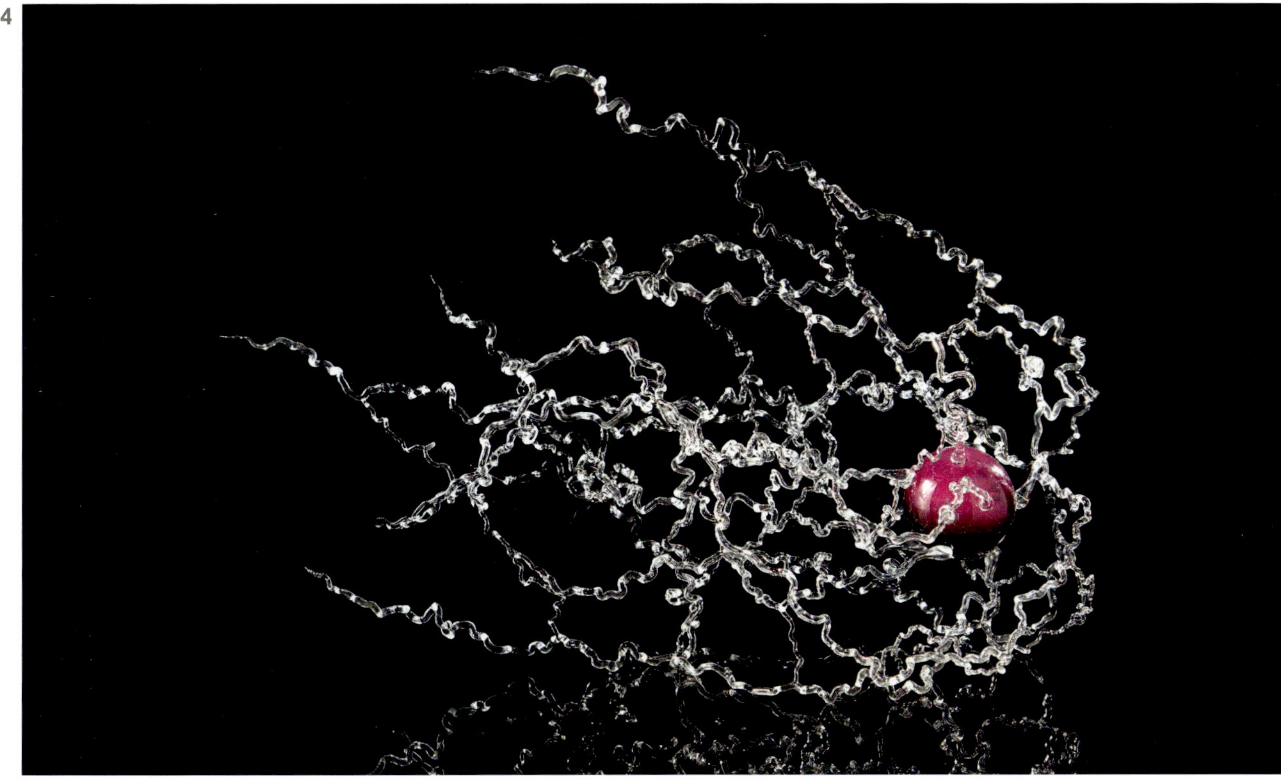

Wilfried Grootens

Kleve, North Rhine-Westphalia, Germany

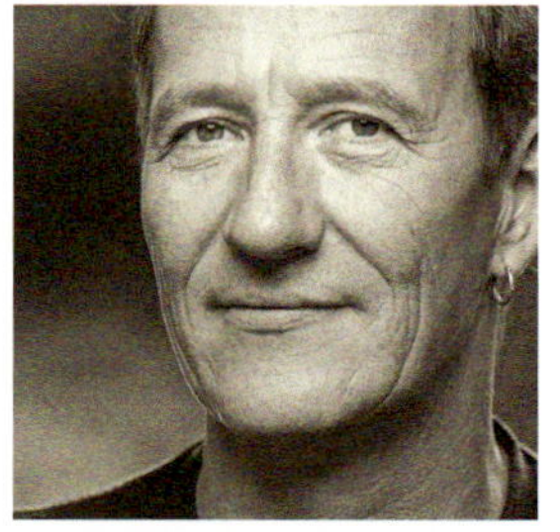

Photo: Norbert Heyl.

Ars gratia artis, art for art's sake.

With my glass painting, I fill transparent, geometric spaces with visual explorations producing surprising variations in forms. Different perspectives on apparent spherical, floating, built-up forms of linear brush strokes reveal to the viewer new perspectives within the object's space.

The following works are from my series *Where the Shark Bubbles Blow*.

1 *Where the Shark Bubbles Blow*. Optifloat, painted, glued, and polished. 8.66" × 8.66" × 8.66". 2014. Photo: Norbert Heyl.

2 *Where the Shark Bubbles Blow*. Optifloat, painted, glued, and polished. 8.66" × 8.66" × 8.66". 2014. Photo: Norbert Heyl.

3 *Where the Shark Bubbles Blow*. Optifloat, painted, glued, polished. 8.66" × 8.66" × 8.66". 2014. Photo: Norbert Heyl.

4 *Where the Shark Bubbles Blow*. Optifloat, painted, glued, and polished. 8.66" × 8.66" × 8.66". 2014. Photo: Norbert Heyl.

5 *Where the Shark Bubbles Blow*. Optifloat, painted, glued, and polished. 8.66" × 8.66" × 8.66". 2014. Photo: Norbert Heyl.

1

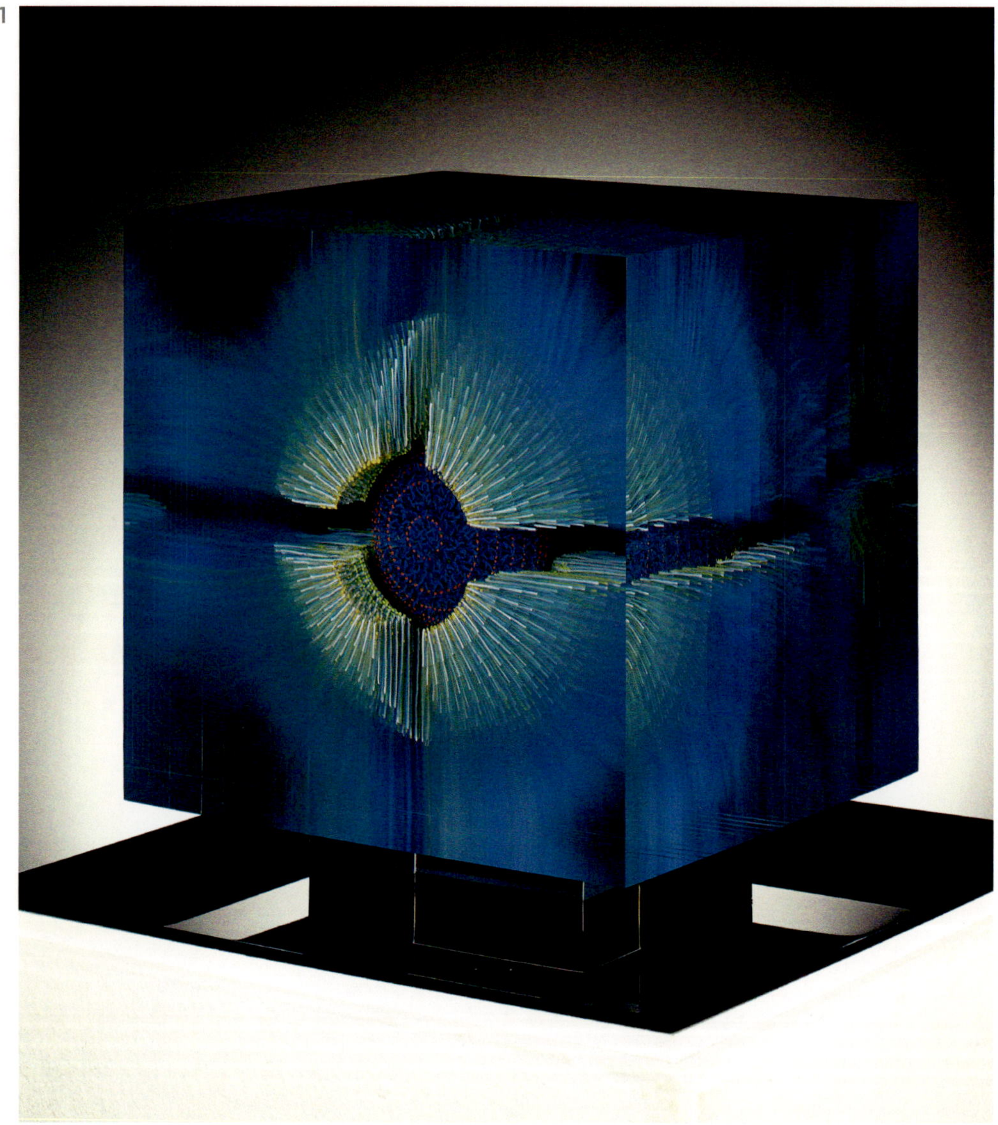

2

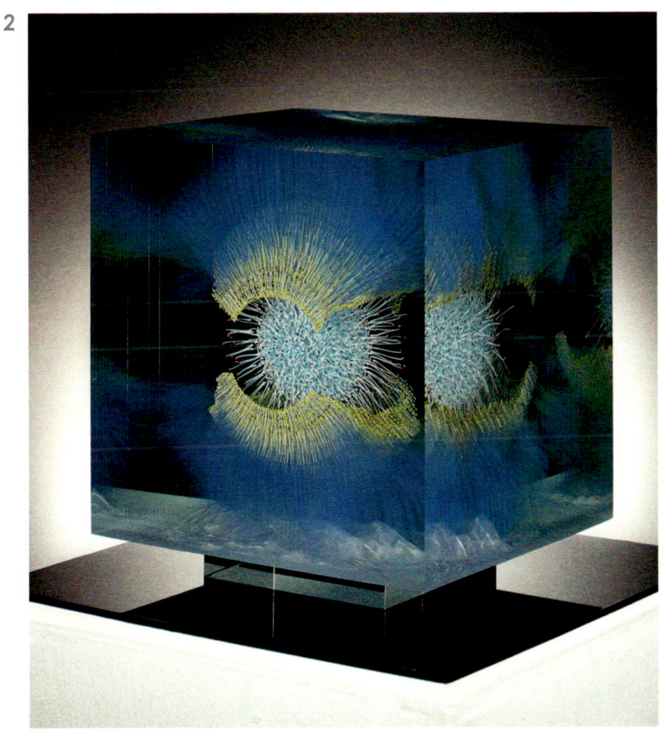

4

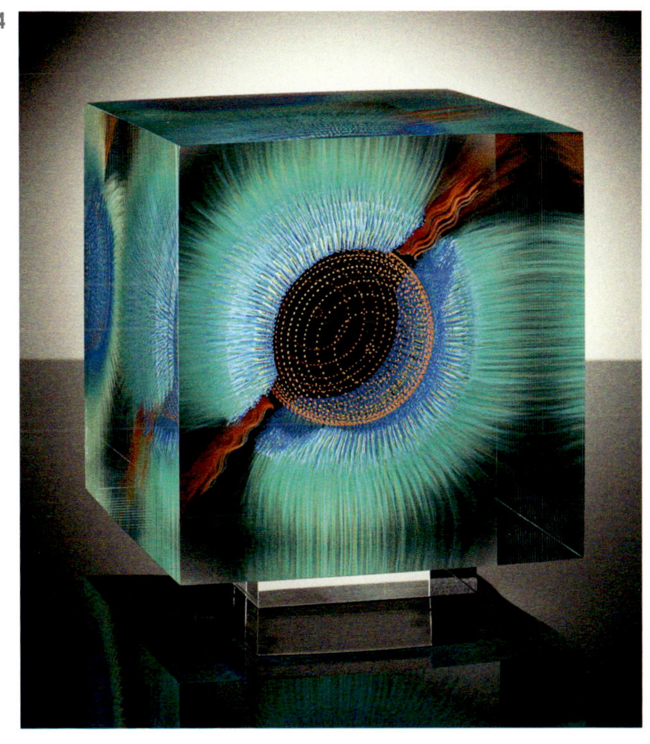

3

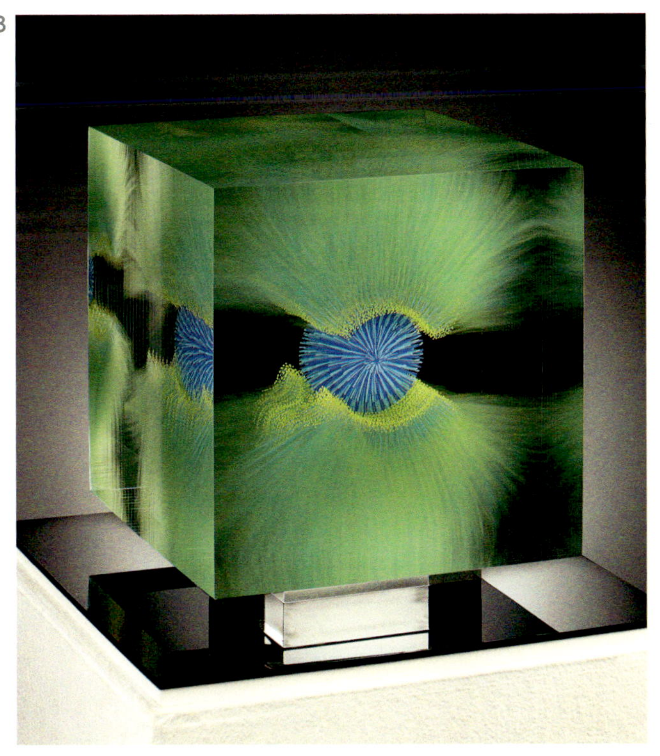

5

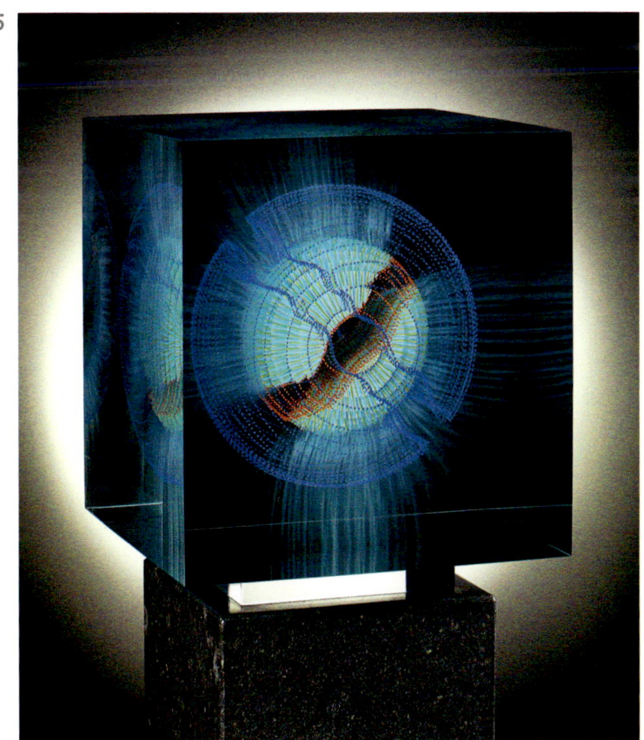

Jaime Guerrero

Los Angeles, California

Before I am an artist, I am a craftsman. My work illustrates the juxtaposition between ancient ideas and contemporary urban issues. I was born and raised in Los Angeles, California, where my Mexican heritage and urban American setting have strongly influenced my ideas. It is important for me to address the social inequities that exist in society while simultaneously staying true to a traditional art-making process.

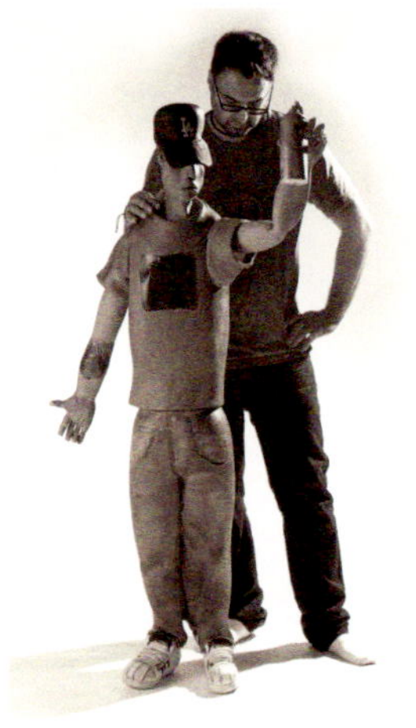

Courtesy of Keay Edwards.

1

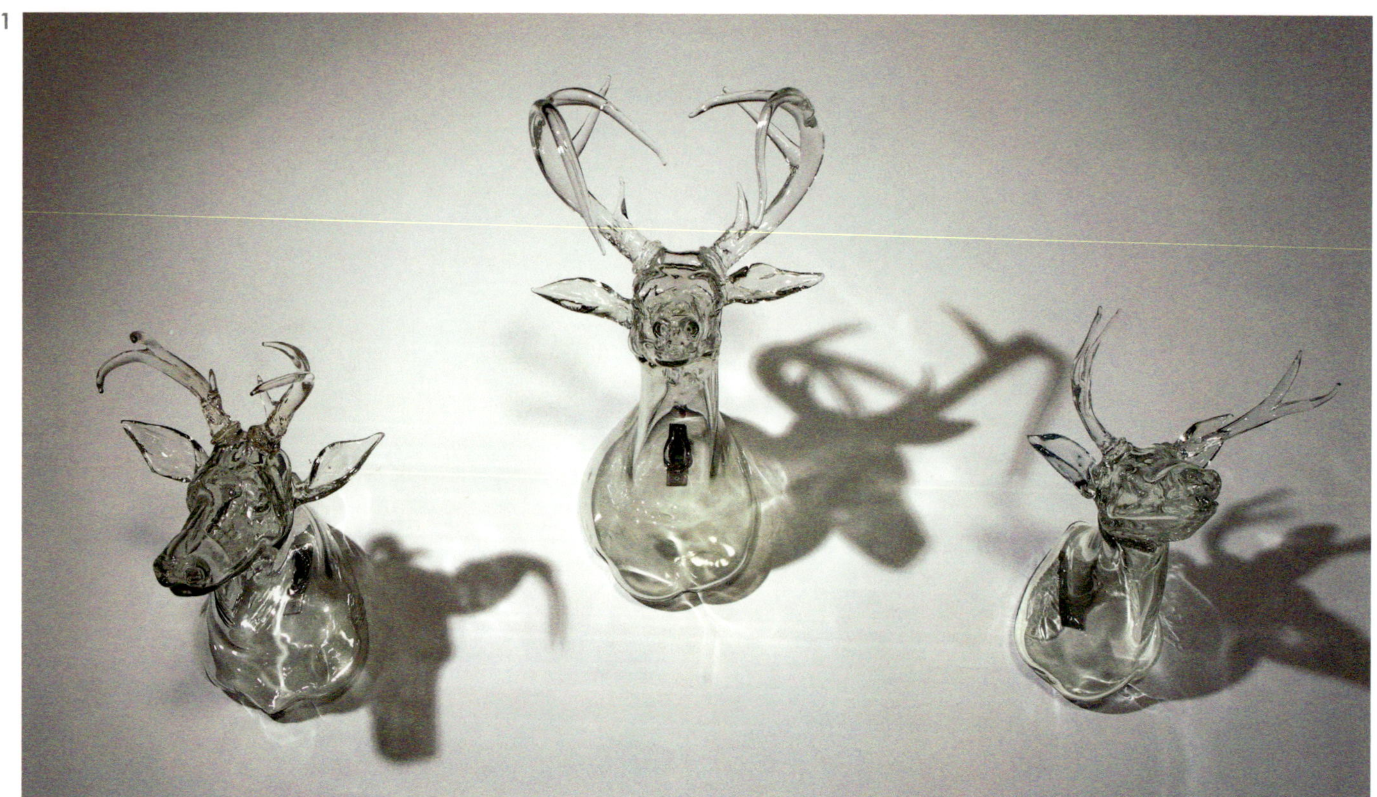

1 *The Hunt*. Hand-sculpted glass. 25" × 29" × 68". 2014. Courtesy of Keay Edwards.

2 *Untitled*. Hand-sculpted glass. 48" × 8" × 83". 2014. Courtesy of Keay Edwards.

3 *Farm Worker*. Hand-sculpted glass. 76" × 14" × 36". Courtesy of Keay Edwards. 2014.

4 *Charros y Sus Caballos*. Hand-sculpted glass. 72" × 30" × 15". 2012. Courtesy of Keay Edwards.

5 *Once Upon a Time*. Hand-sculpted glass. 48" × 24" × 18". 2013. Courtesy of Keay Edwards.

2

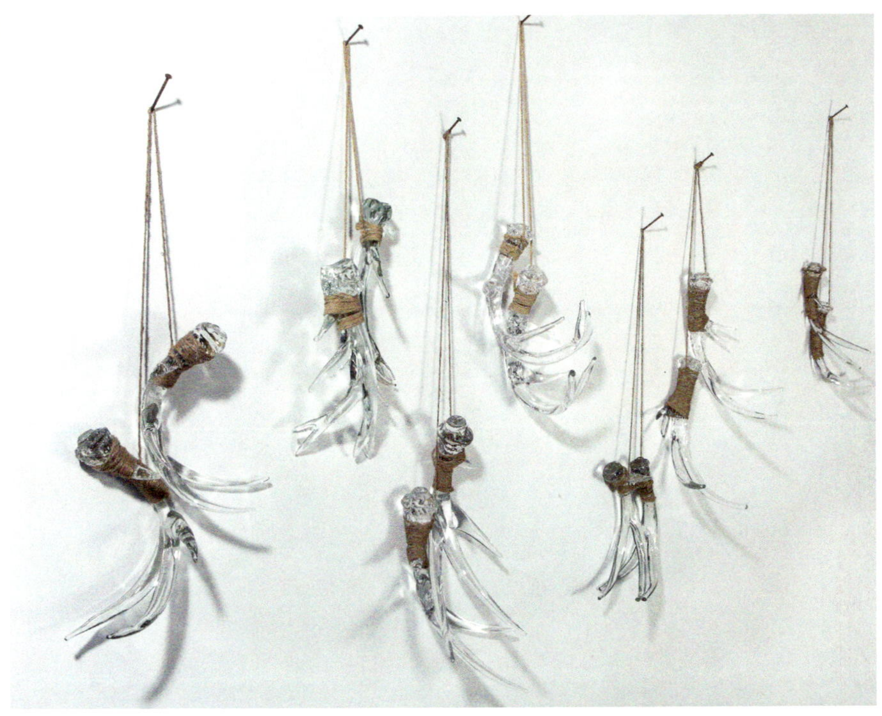

4

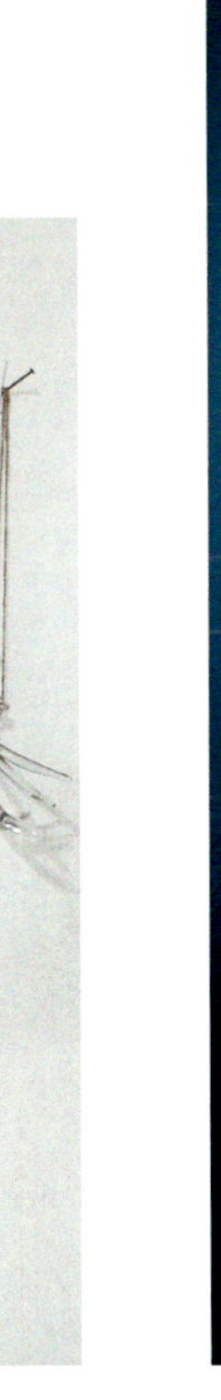

3

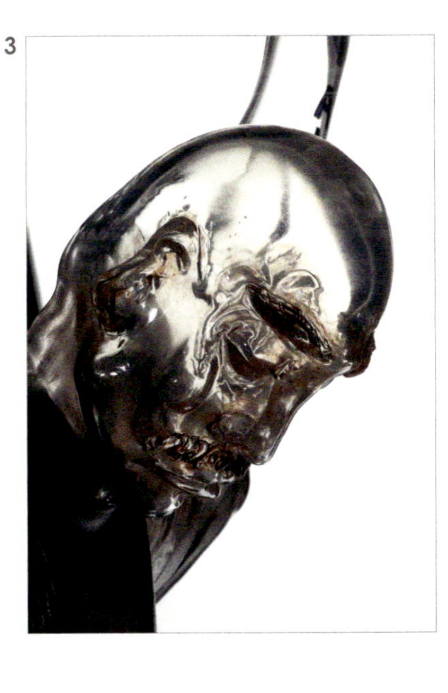

5

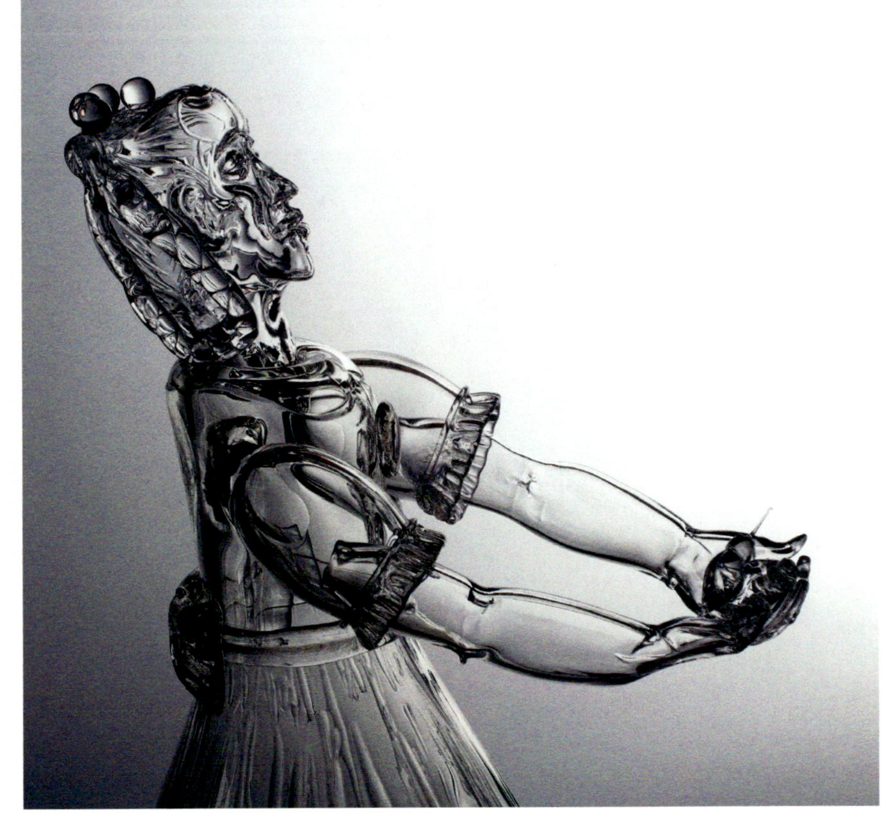

Dorothy Hafner

Norwalk, Connecticut

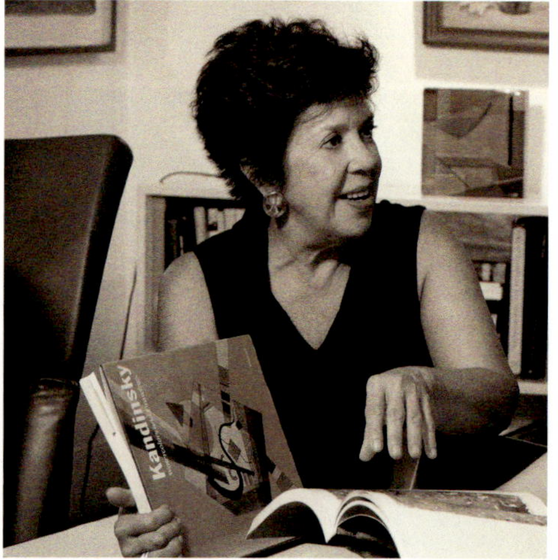

Courtesy of paulrogersphotography.com.

For the first eighteen years of my professional career, I worked in ceramics as both sculptor and industrial designer. My clients included Tiffany & Co. and Rosenthal Porcelain for whom I created signature collections now regarded as icons of the their time. In 1992, I "gifted" myself an artistic sabbatical and soon began my love affair with glass. Immediately, I was taken by its brilliant colors and sparkling transparencies that can be achieved in no other material. Today, I employ my technique of multiple layers of transparent cut-outs, fused together to produce single multi-layered transparent objects, panels, and installations. My inspirations are vast and wide and include my responses to music, dance, scientific imagery, and the varied landscapes to which I travel.

1

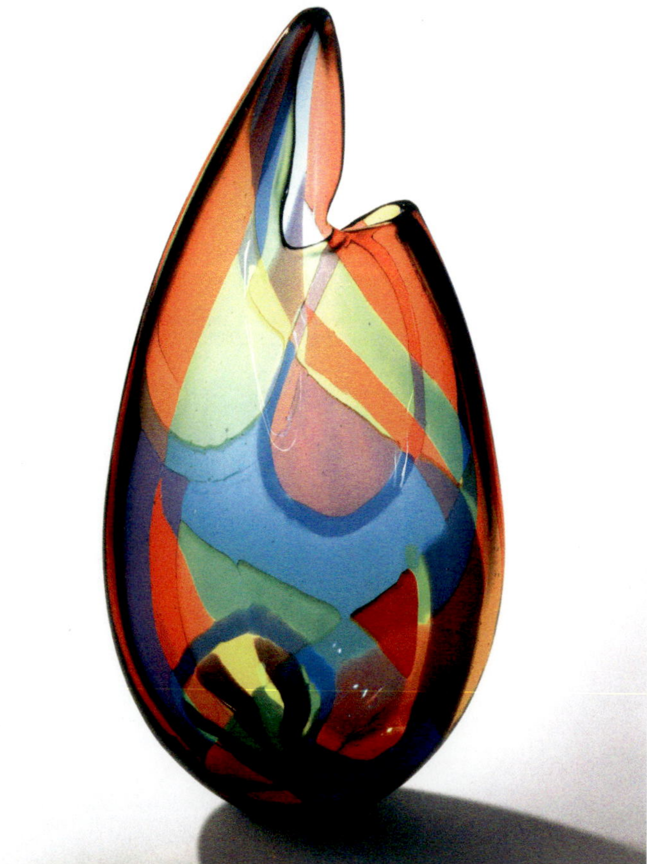

2

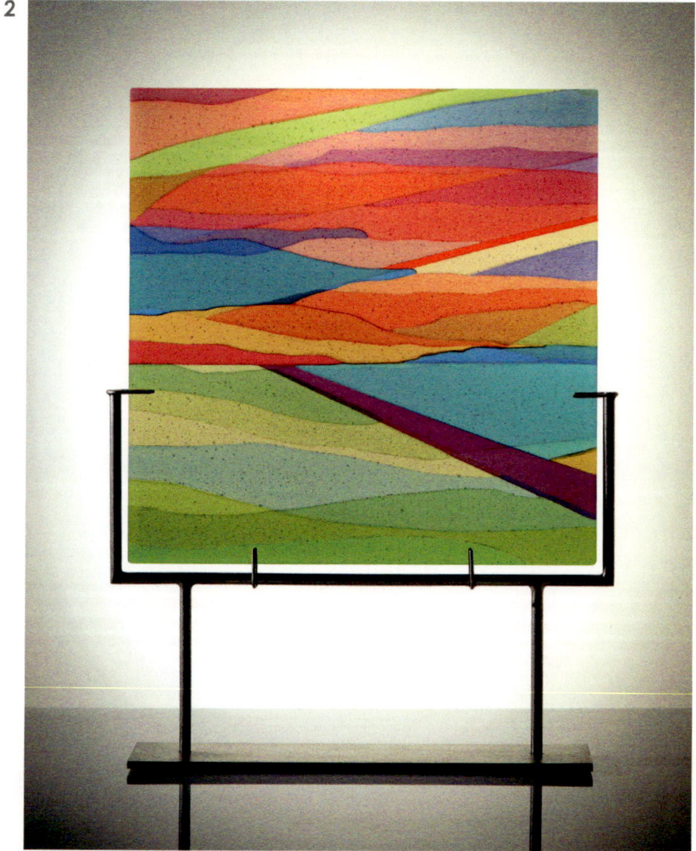

1 *Aurora*. Blown mosaic glass. 18.62" × 10" × 6". © Dorothy Hafner, 1995. All rights reserved. Assisted by Lino Tagliapietra. Collection: Corning Museum of Glass. Photo: George Erml.

2 *Dreamscapes, II*. Multi-layered fused glass, stainless steel. 20" × 16" × 5" (14.5" × 14.5" × 0.62" glass only). © Dorothy Hafner, 2014. All rights reserved.

3

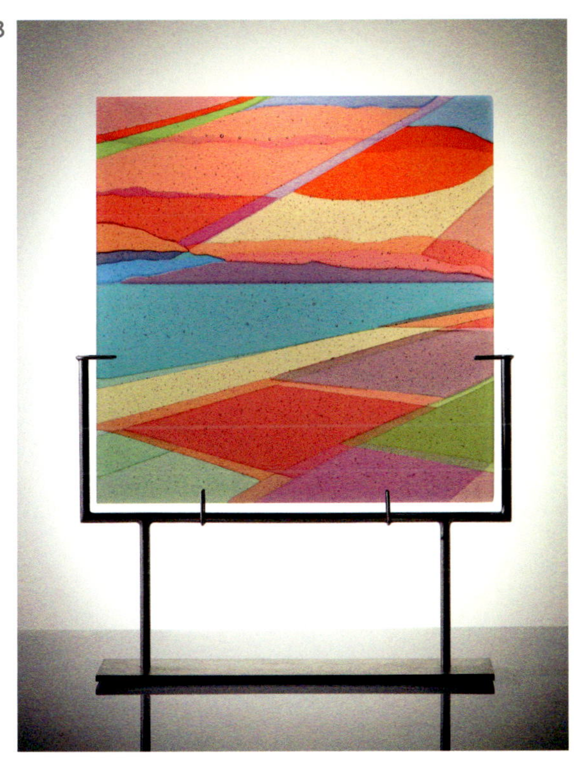

5

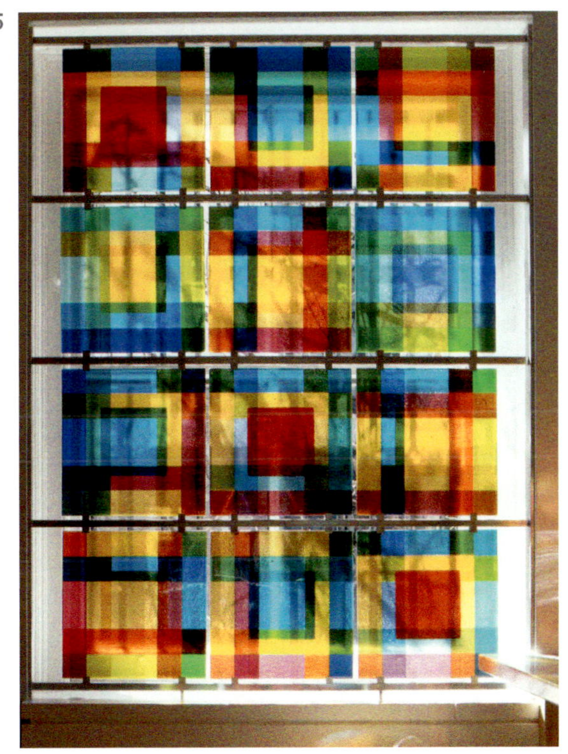

4

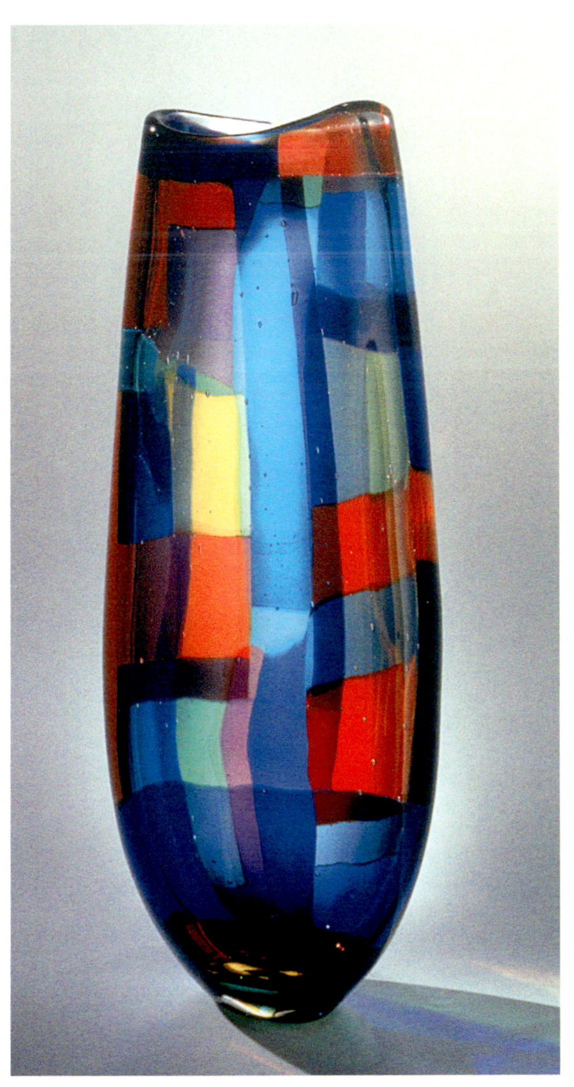

6

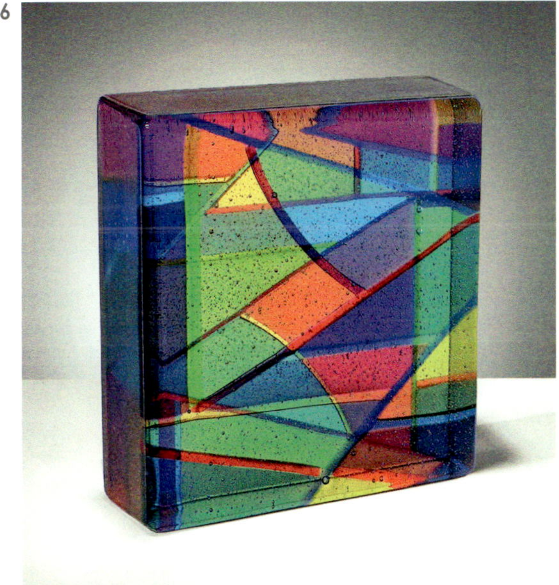

3 *Tulip Fields.* Multi-layered fused glass, stainless steel. 20" × 16" × 5" (14.5" × 14.5" × 0.62" glass only). © Dorothy Hafner, 2014. All rights reserved.

4 *Kashmir.* Blown mosaic glass. 20.5" × 6.5" × 5". © Dorothy Hafner, 1995. All rights reserved. Assisted by Lino Tagliapietra.

5 *Colorways: Brights.* Window installation. 12 fused glass panels, brushed aluminum frame. 5.5' × 4' (glass panels 14.5" × 14.5" × 0.62" each). © Dorothy Hafner, I999. All rights reserved.

6 *Flutter.* Multi-layer fused and kiln formed glass, 22 layers. 8" × 8" × 2.25". © Dorothy Hafner, 2008. All rights reserved.

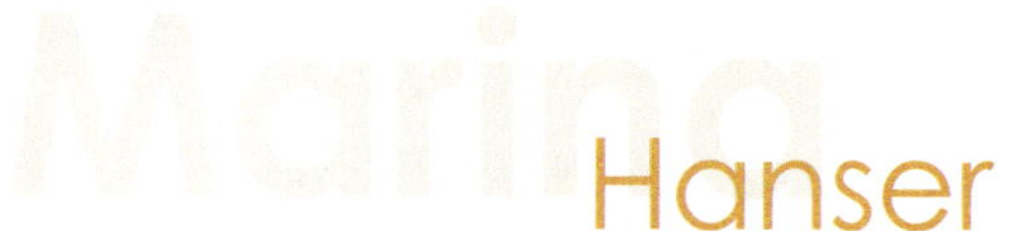

Hanser

Canberra, Australian Capital Territory, Australia

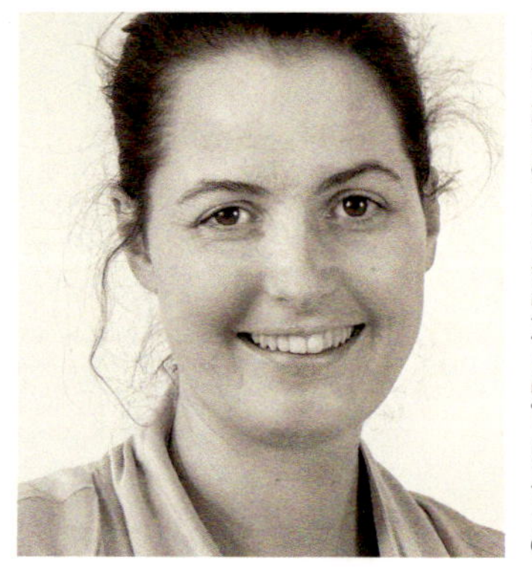

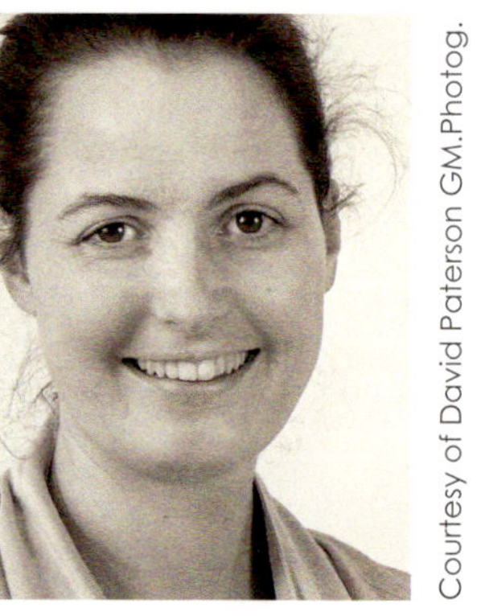

Courtesy of David Paterson GM.Photog.

Notions of grief and the process of healing from psychological wounds inform my glasswork. I have developed a visual language informed by studio-based and contextual research to express notions of healing, transformation, and remembrance.

I work metaphorically with the idea of the wound and healing, drawing from scientific and medical fields, but also from material investigations. The process I have developed transforms glass through various working processes (e.g., grinding and cutting, filling and melting, smoothing, and polishing) to echo the process of trauma and healing. With my work, I aim to reveal what lies hidden within, physical and emotional scars, to trigger emotional responses in the viewer.

1

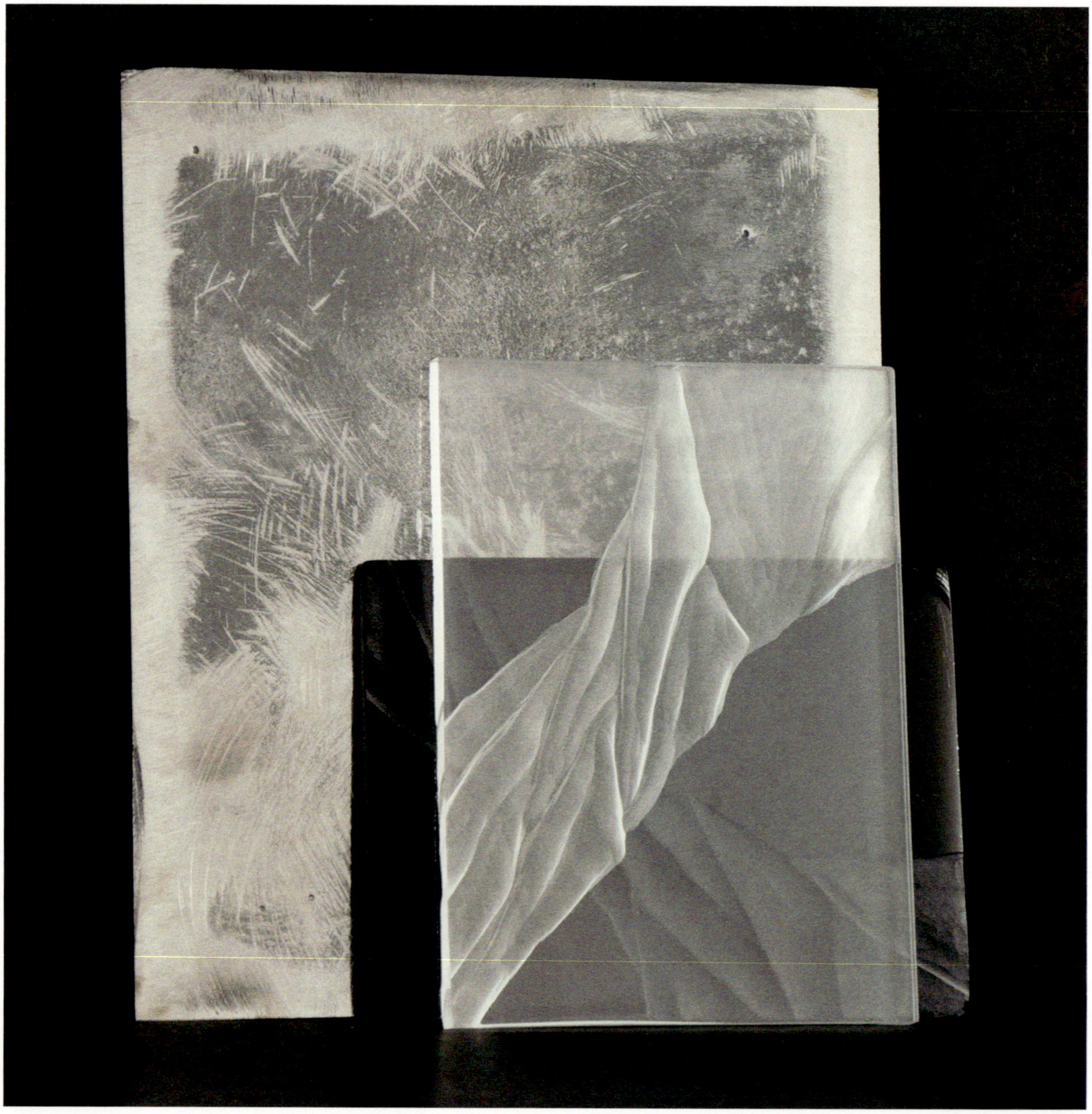

2

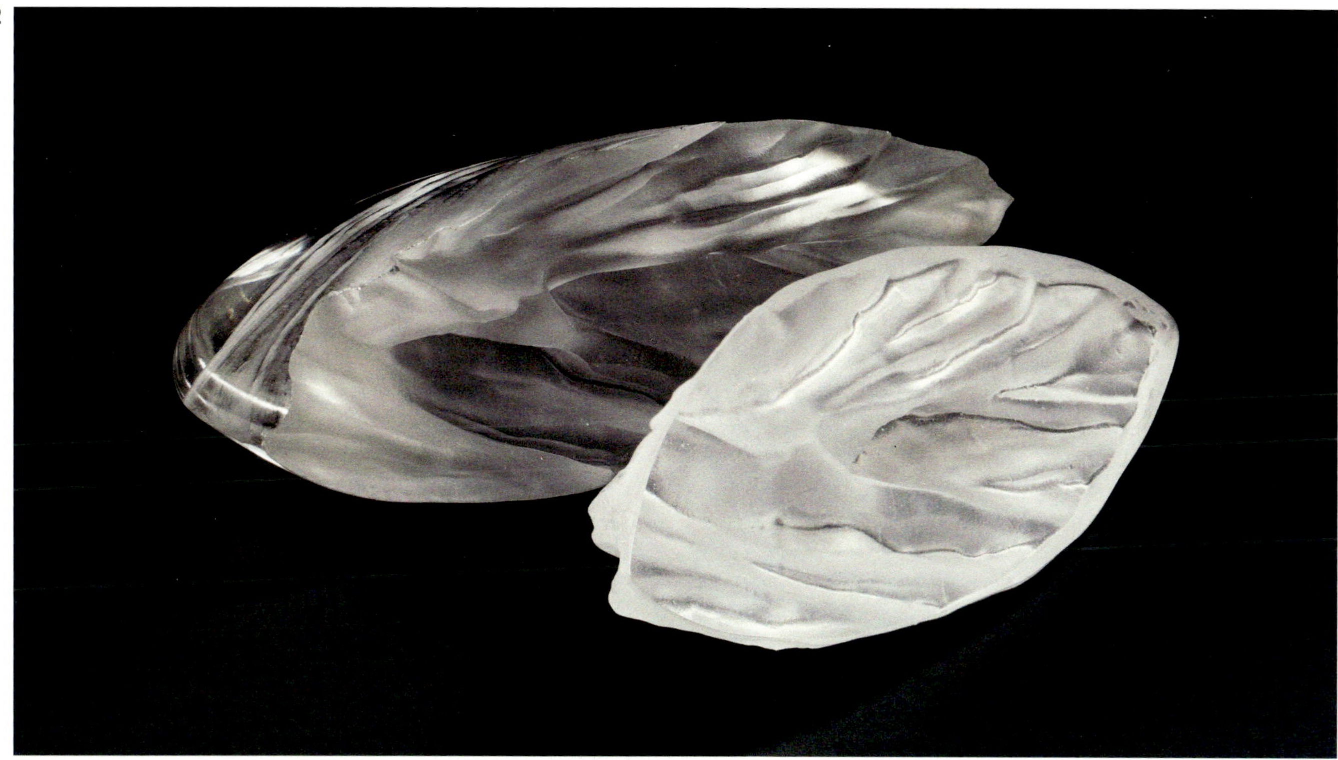

3

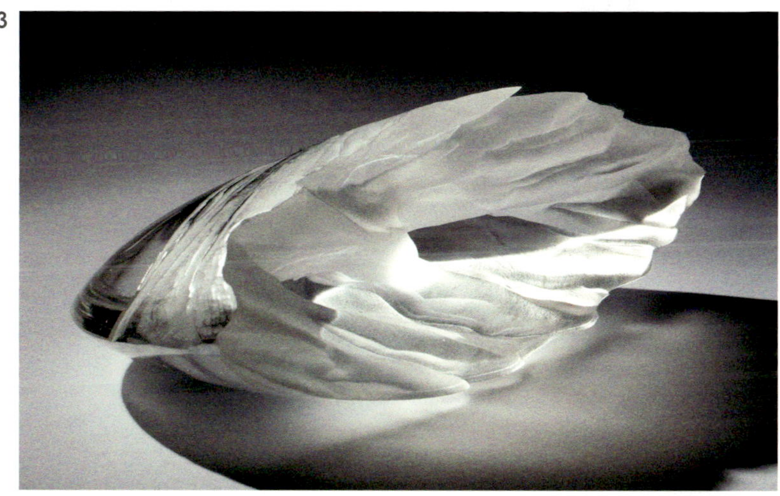

4

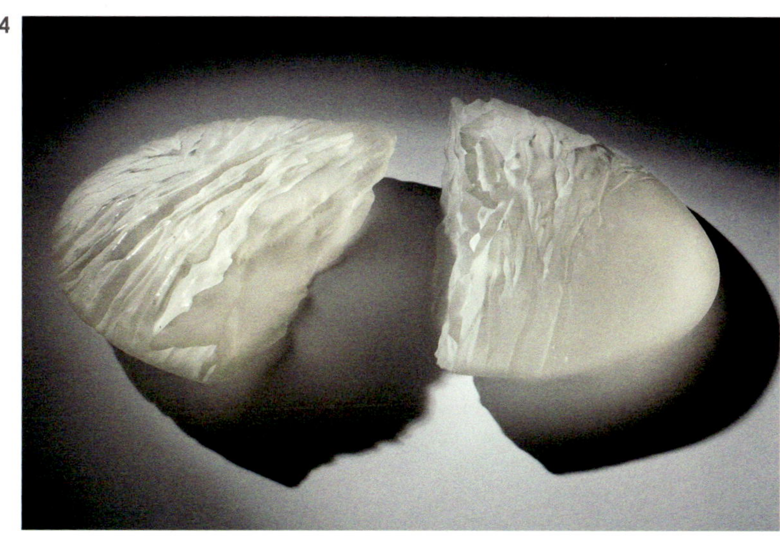

1 *Scar and Wound Study 1*. Carved and cold worked glass panels (set of 2), metal panel. 7.8" × 1.2" × 7". 2012.

2 *Open Wound and Missing Piece*. Cast, carved, sandblasted, and cold worked glass. 3.5" × 11" × 12.2" (2 parts). 2012. Courtesy of David Paterson GM.Photog.

3 *Open Wound*. Cast, carved, sandblasted, and cold worked glass. 3.5" × 11" × 12.2" × 11". 2012. Courtesy of Stuart Hay–ANU Photography.

4 *Zerreisung*. Cast, carved, sandblasted, and cold worked glass. 3.5" × 11" × 17.3". 2012. Courtesy of Stuart Hay–ANU Photography.

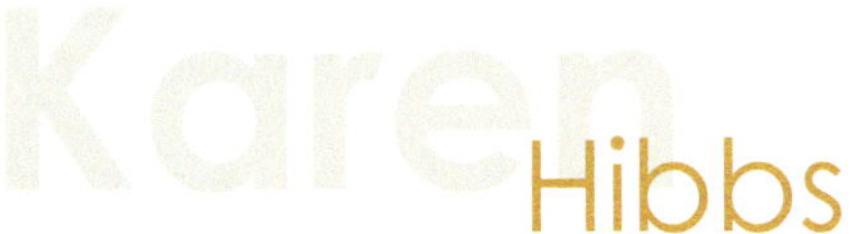

Karen Hibbs

New Haven, Connecticut

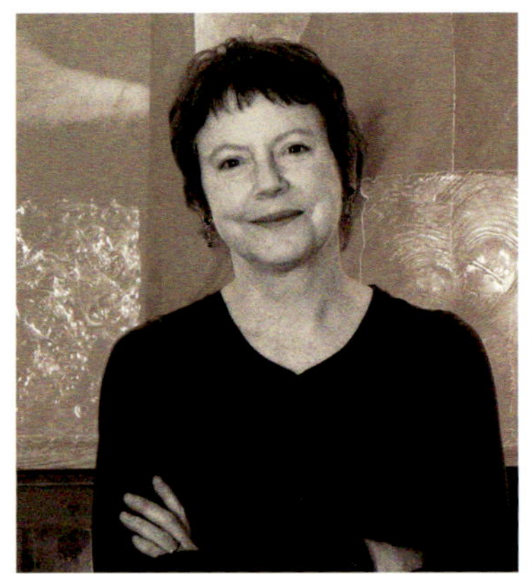

Courtesy of Peter Burton.

For me art is all about composition and the use of interesting objects. Glass is my primary material, with its complex, shifting behavior in light and how well it plays against the more static materials that go into each piece. Whether it is flat or sculptural, glass is always the element that brings life and changeability to each piece. I have worked in this media for over forty years now and am still exploring, still working out new techniques; the possibilities seem endless. Good thing!

1

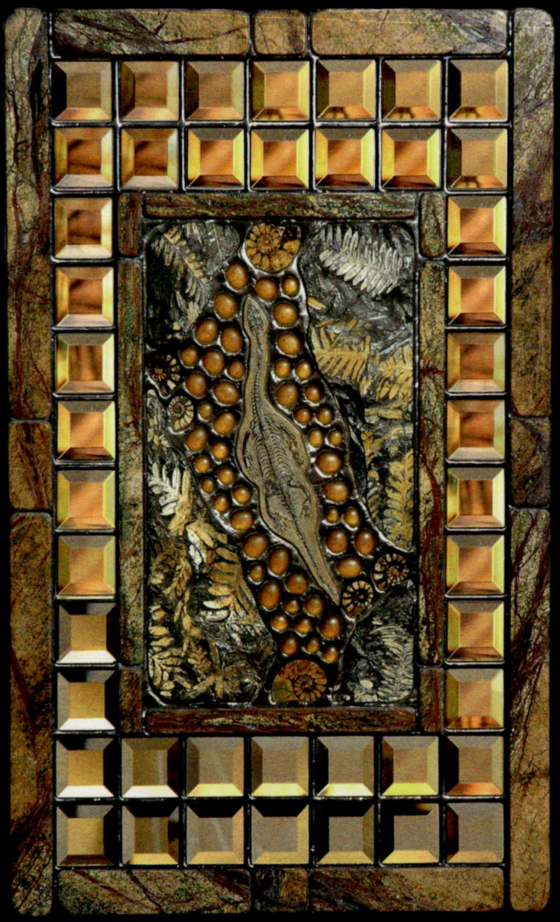

2

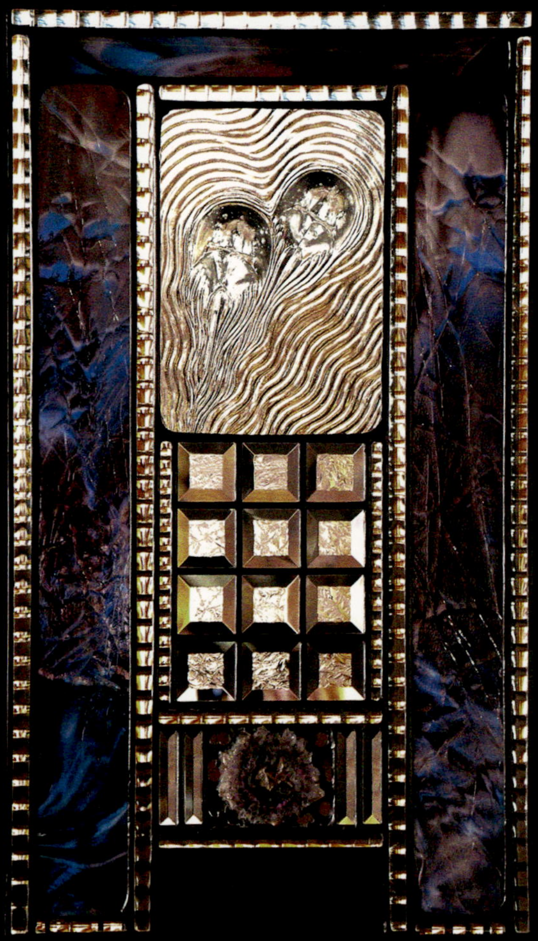

3

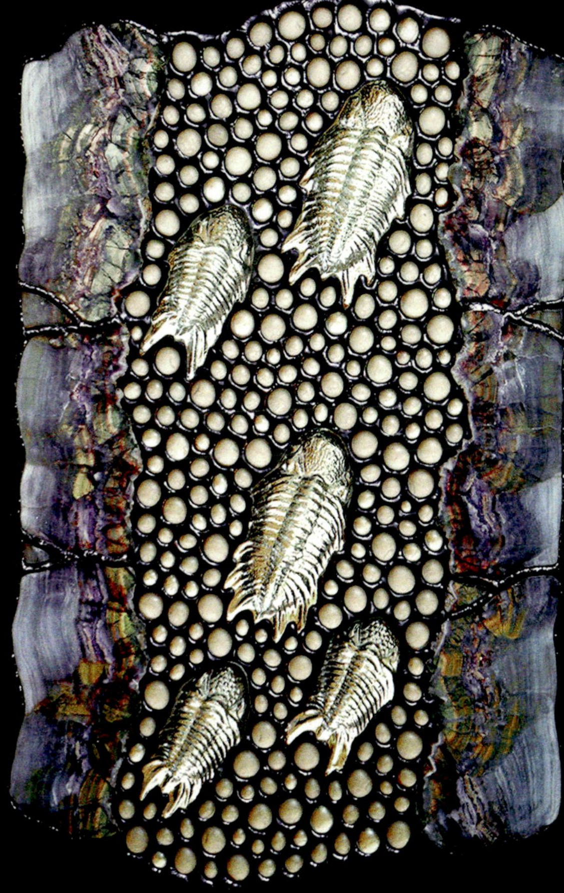

5

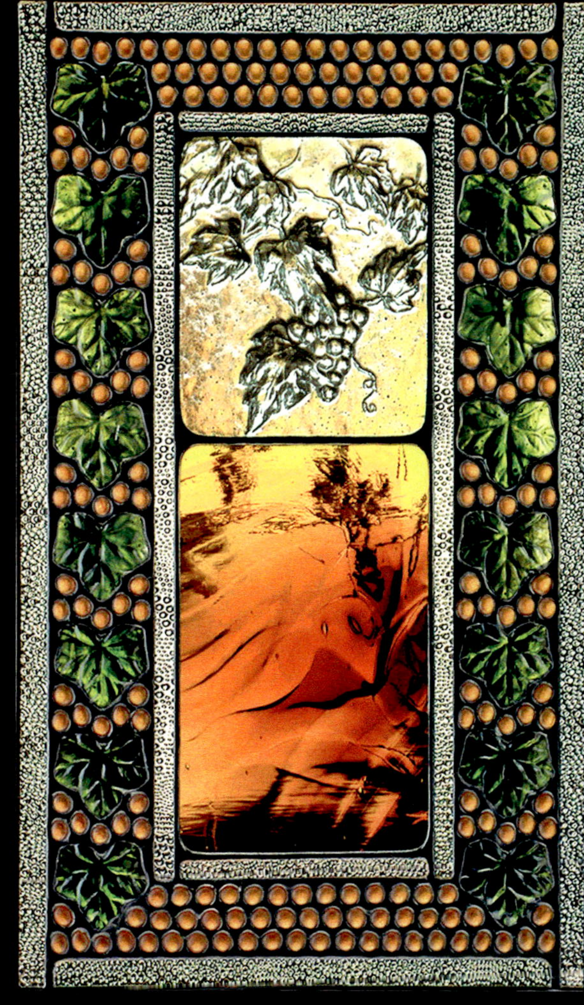

4

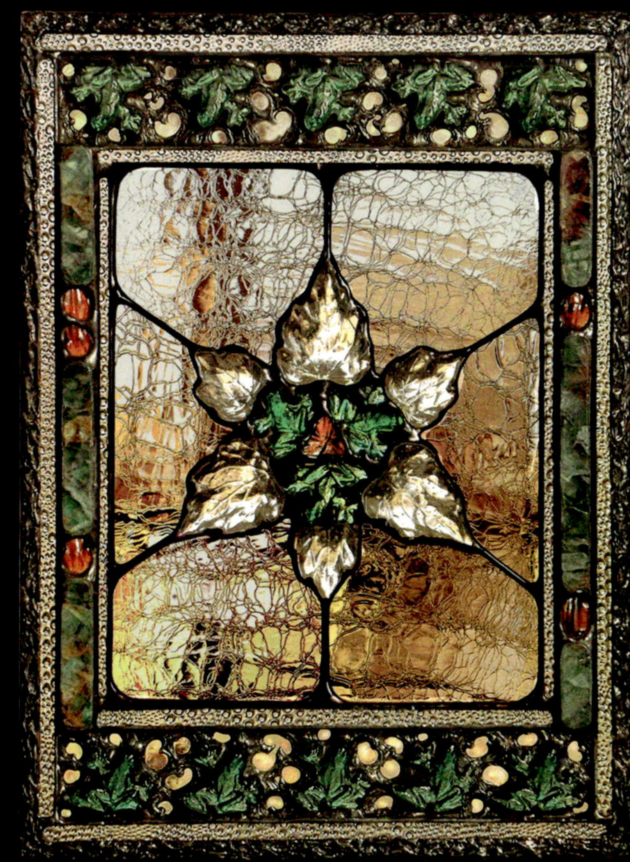

1 *In the Beginning*. Cold worked with stone, fossils, and metals. 28" × 18". 2014. Courtesy of Peter Burton.

2 *Horseshoe Crabs*. Kiln formed, cold worked with metals. 29" × 16". 2002. Courtesy of Peter Burton.

3 *Trilobites*. Kiln formed with stone and metals. 23" × 15". 2007. Courtesy of Peter Burton.

4 *13 Frogs*. Kiln formed, cold worked with stone and sculpted metals. 14" × 19". 2010. Courtesy of Peter Burton.

5 *Grapevine*. Kiln formed, cold worked with metals. 30" × 18". 2001. Courtesy of Peter Burton.

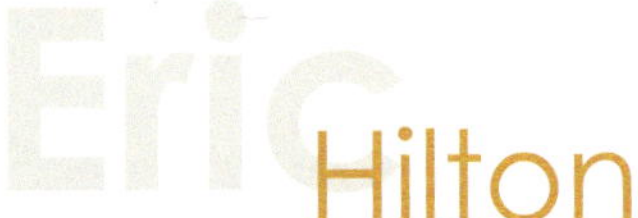

Eric Hilton

Odessa, New York

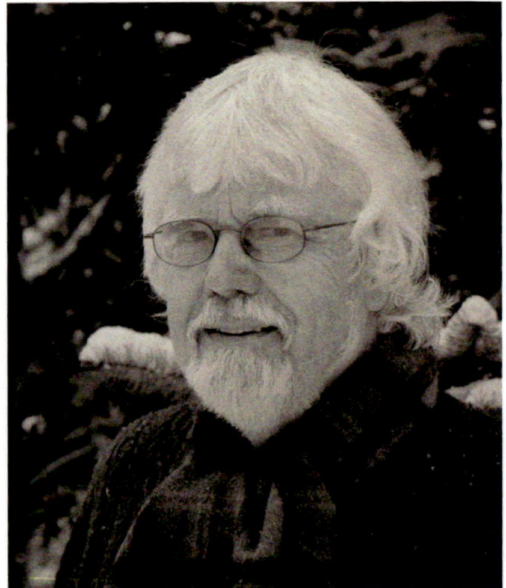

Courtesy of Sarah M. Schantz.

The natural world is always endowing us with gifts. It is said that every tide leaves a present on the beach; hopefully, we are observant enough to see it. I have always been enmeshed somehow in the exploration of the tangled fabric of life's mysteries. I interpret nature's advice in seeking a creative solution to an imaginary problem that beckons to be solved.

It is my belief that creativity is the soul of human consciousness. Art echoes through all human evolution. It gives us avenues of communication with ancestral memories. We are the stuff of stars. Each of my works attempts to tell a story that I hope will have a reciprocity with the viewer.

1

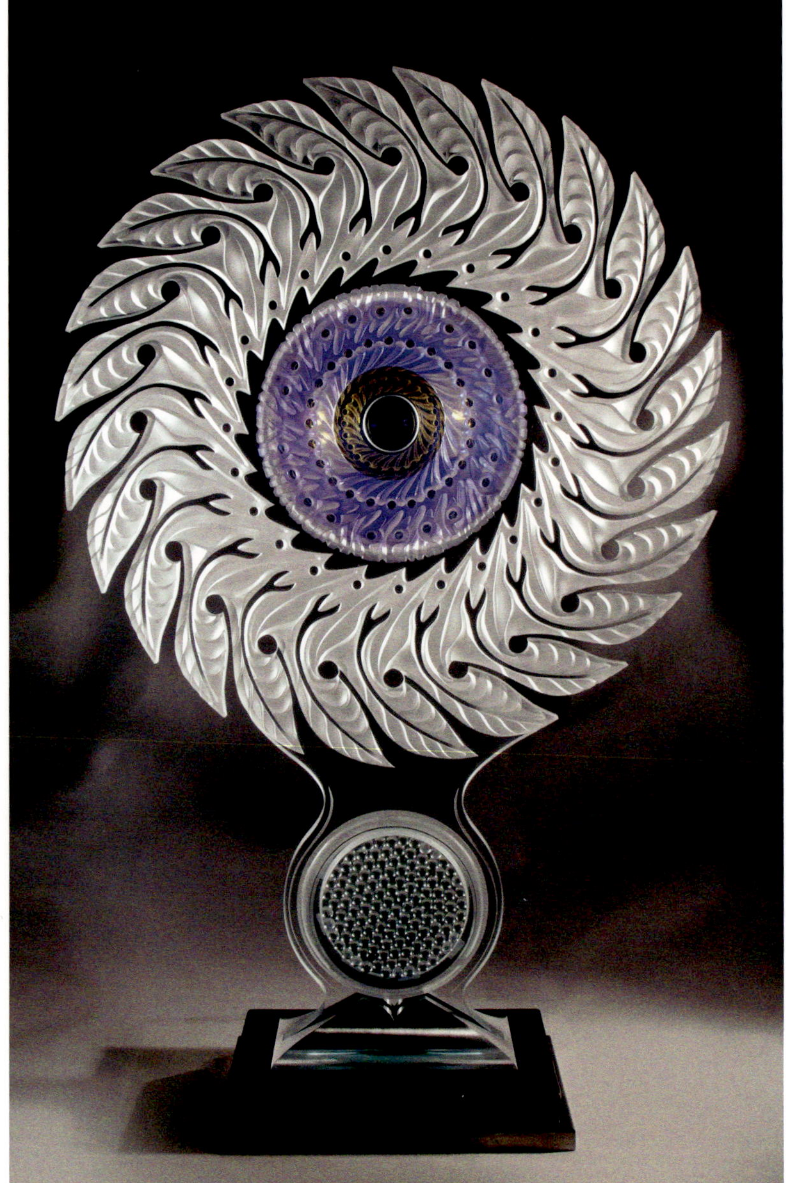

1 *Regeneration.* Waterjet cut, sandblasted, sagged, dichroic filter, and aluminum. 36" × 10" × 24". 2013.

2 *Avian Mysteries.* Cut, engraved, sandblasted, sagged, and stained maple. 12" × 14". 2014.

3 *Cosmic Eyes.* Blown, sandblasted, carved, sagged, and stained maple. 21" × 12" × 12". 2015.

4 *Ark of Life.* Waterjet cut, sandblasted, engraved, and sagged. 27" × 8" × 14". 2014.

5 *Vibration of Life.* Waterjet cut, sandblasted, engraved, sagged, and carved stained maple. 12" × 30" × 30". 2013.

2

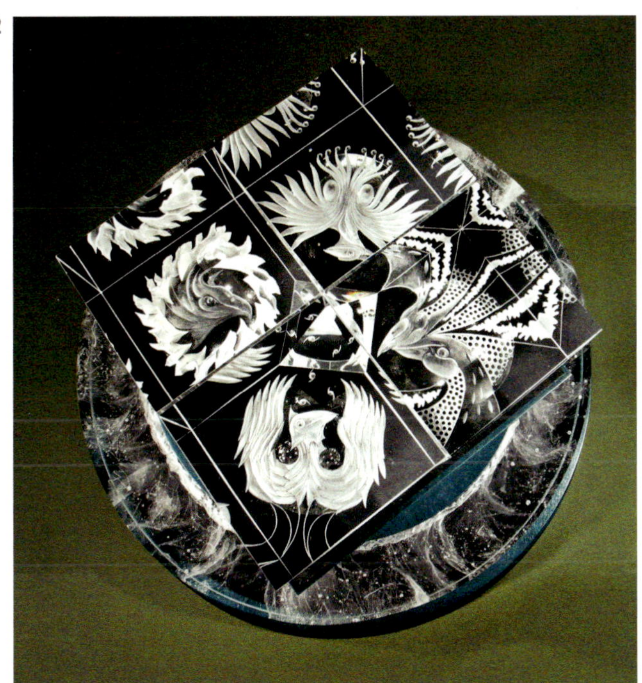

4

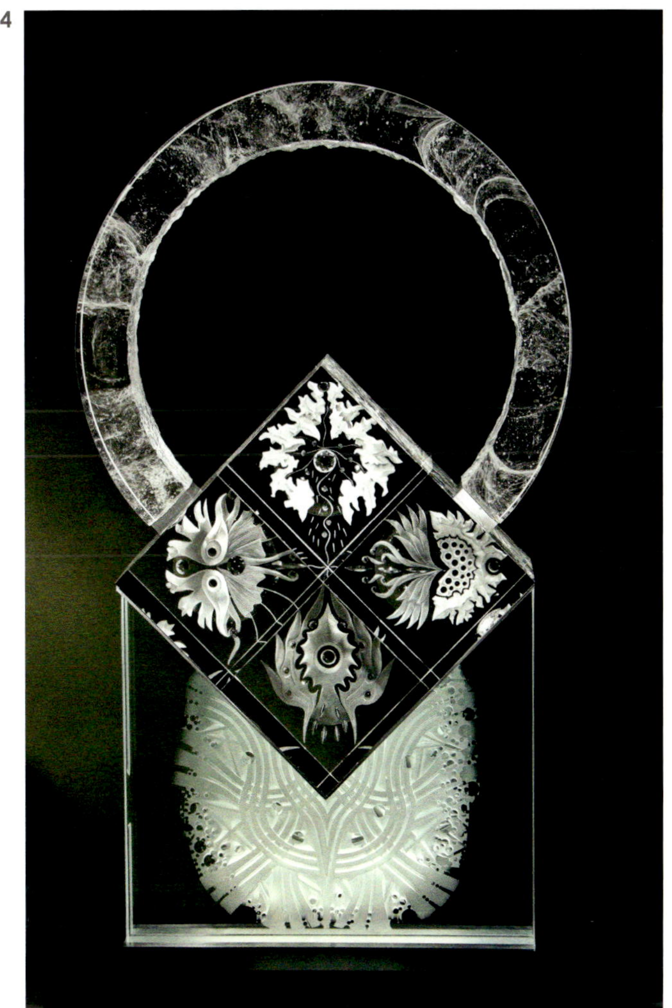

3

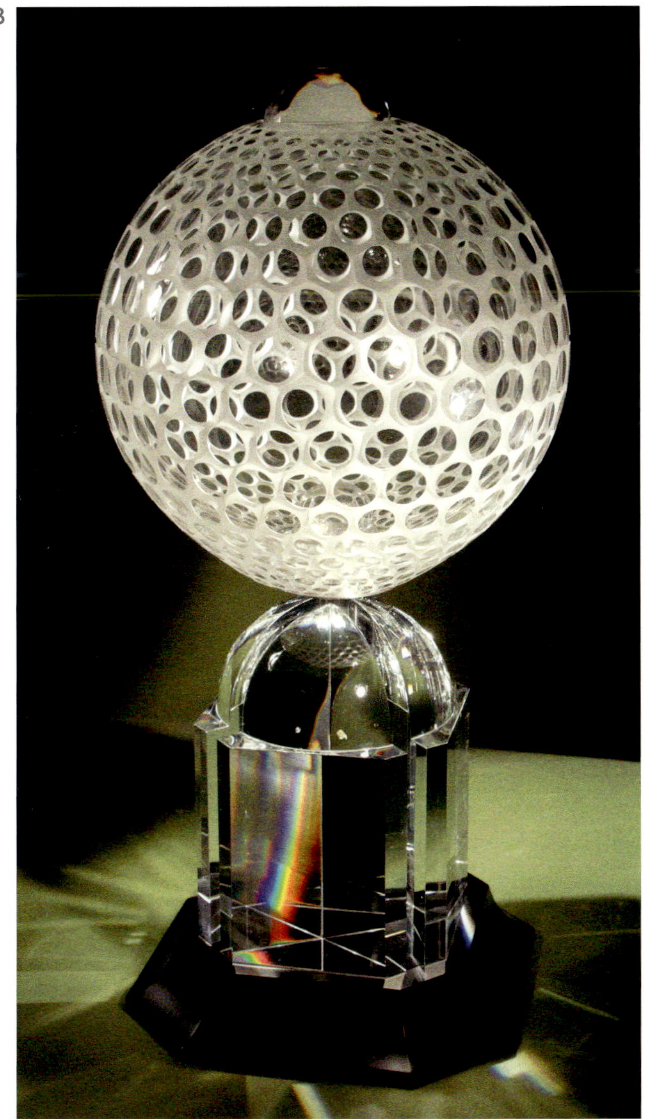

5

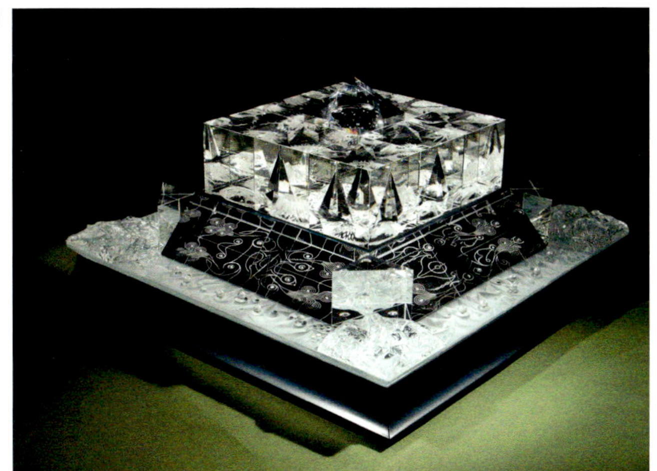

David Huchthausen

Seattle, Washington

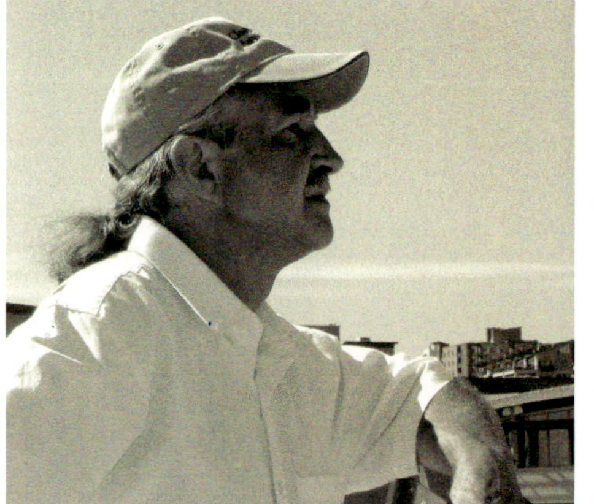

One advantage of having worked as an artist for forty-five years is that you can look back at your older work free of the emotional intensity that enveloped it at the time and see how one series morphed and mutated into the next over the years. The architectural influences and scientific references in my sculpture have always been obvious, yet there are subtler interests permeating the creative process. Projected light, shadow, and internal illusion have been core elements of my work since the 1970s. My ongoing fascination with primitive art and ritual as well as the color and imagery of the many cultural artifacts that I collect persist in finding their way into my thoughts and dreams.

I have always used the full 360-degree circumference of the sculpture, drawing the viewers into the piece as they move around it. I began working with the spheres after reading an article on the theoretical analysis of gravitational fields. It described the three-dimensional universe that we perceive as a holographic projection generated by a two-dimensional field at the edge of infinity. The spheres have no top, bottom, front, or back. They are fully volumetric on every three-dimensional axis, creating a new set of spatial relationships at each axis point.

My work has always been deliberately enigmatic, and I encourage everyone viewing my sculpture to develop his or her own personal response mechanisms. If the work is to have any significance, it must survive outside the realm of my interpretive prose.

1

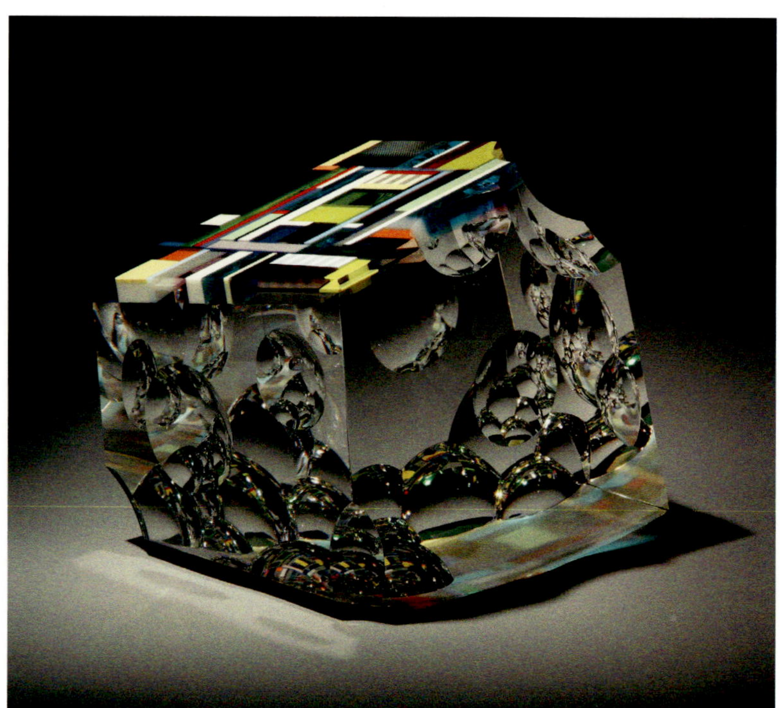

2

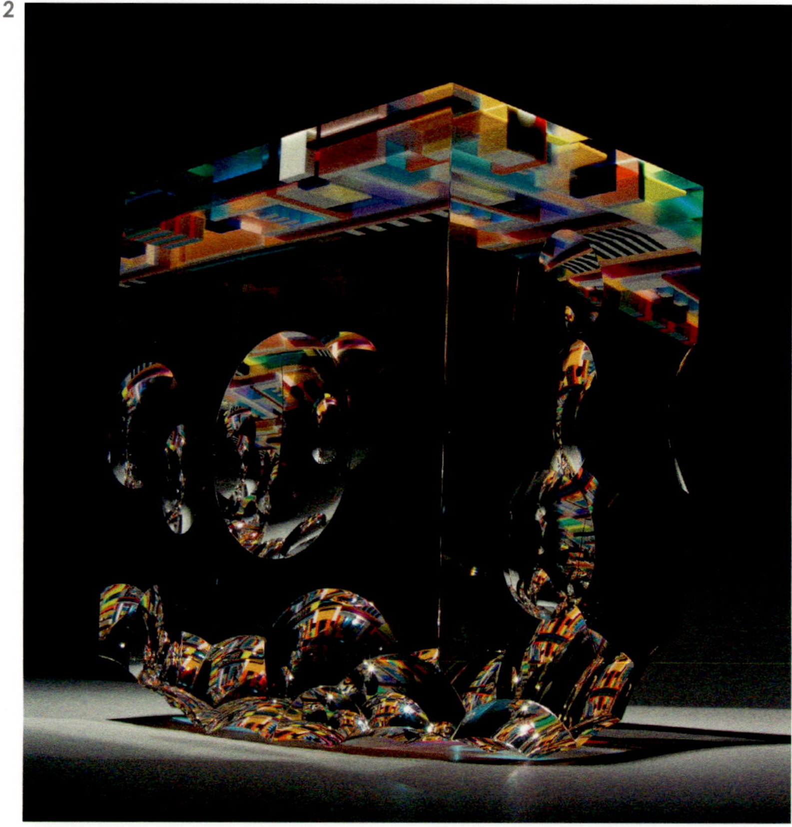

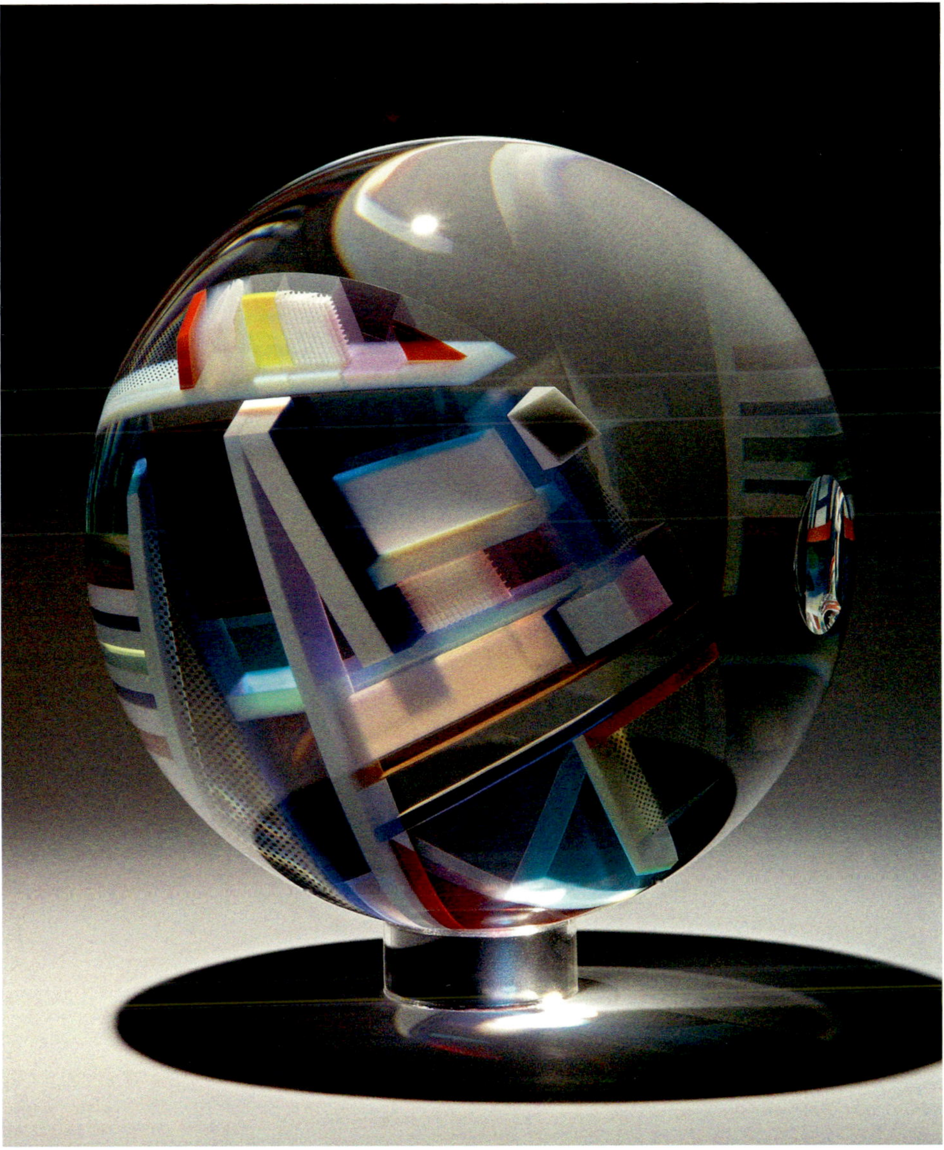

1 *Reliquary for Ray Bradbury*. Fabricated and optically polished glass. 16" × 12" × 11". 2012.

2 *Memory Chamber*. Fabricated and optically polished glass. 12" × 11" × 8". 2013. Photo by Lloyd Shugart

3 *Horizon Line*. Fabricated and optically polished glass. 12" dia. sphere. 2013. Photo by Lloyd Shugart

4 *Echo Chamber*. Fabricated and optically polished glass. 13" × 13" × 9". 2012.

5 *Metropolis*. Fabricated and optically polished glass. 12" × 11" × 7.5". 2014. Photo by Lloyd Shugart

4

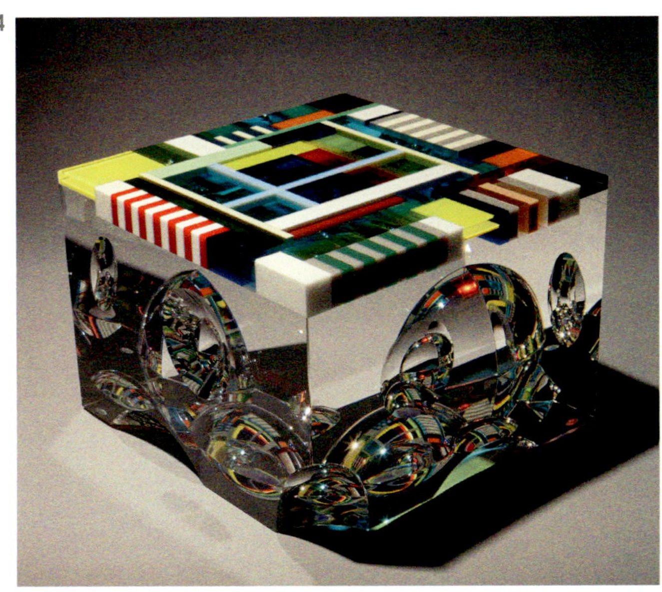

5

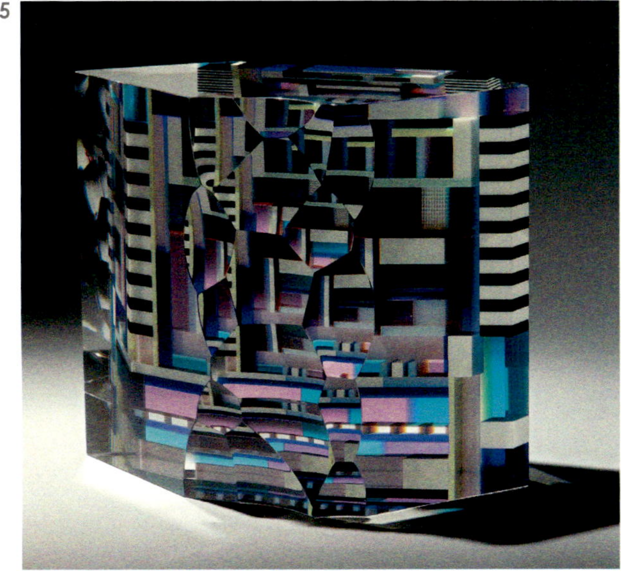

Sidney Hutter

Newton, Massachusetts

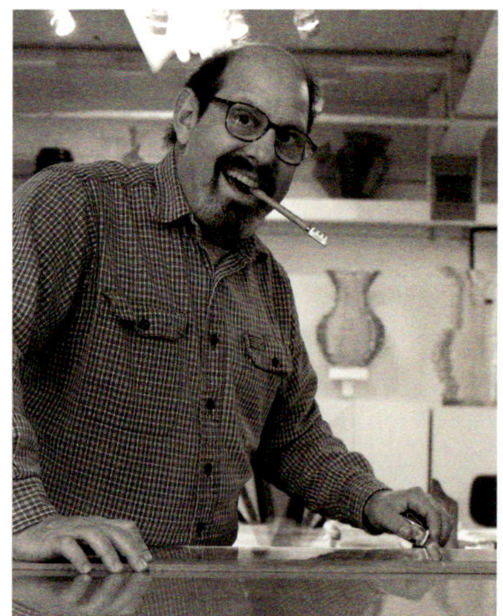

Courtesy of Charles Mayer.

My interest in art, design, and architecture along with a background in glassblowing and fabrication formed the foundation for my work. I make objects that resemble vessels and suggest containment. Volume is described with the exterior silhouette of the structure while the interior holds a landscape of color and light. Each piece is meticulously crafted and sculpted using a combination of rough and highly polished glass surfaces. This, along with the dyed adhesive, allows me to create artistic, three-dimensional paintings—the canvas being dimensional as opposed to flat.

1

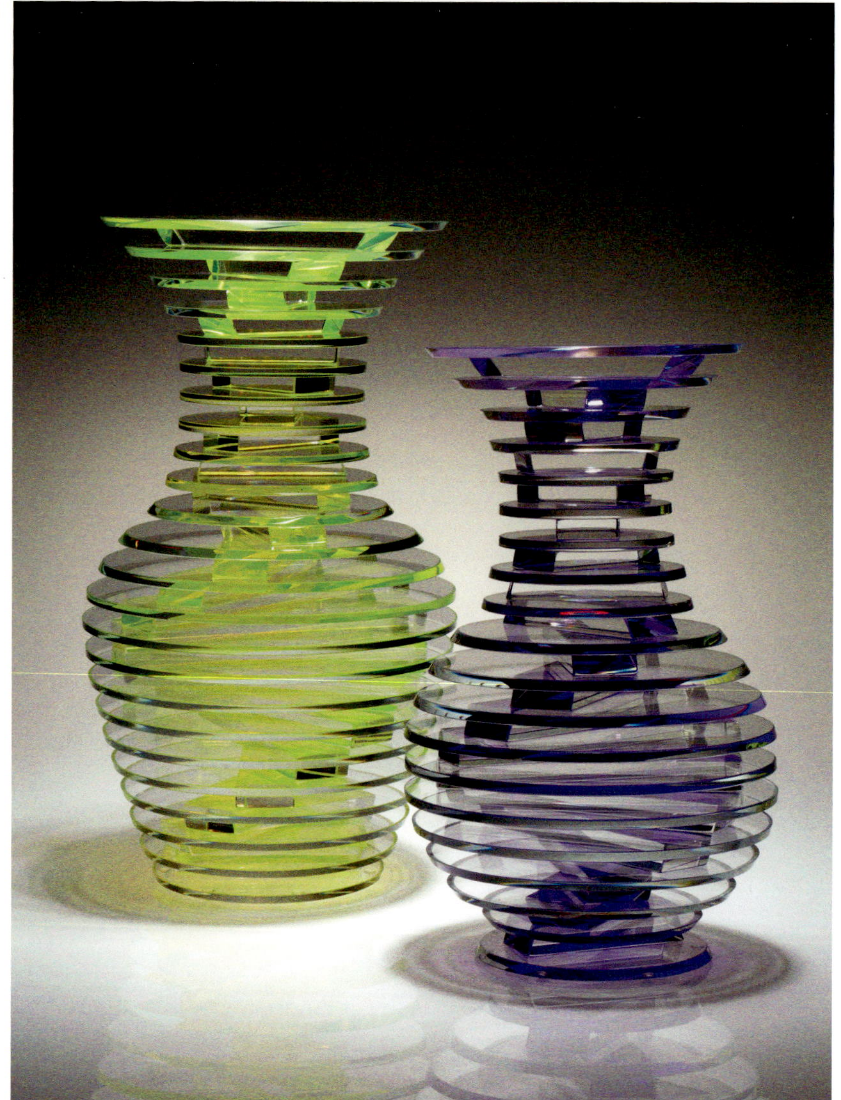

1 *Polished Plate Glass Vase # 32-09*. 16" × 9.25" × 9.25". 2013. *Middy Polished Plate Glass Vase #S2-02*. 12" × 6" × 6". 2013. Polished plate glass laminated with pigmented adhesive. Courtesy of Chris Peaden, Beanstalk Imaging.

2 *Shifting Transmission #7*. Polished plate glass laminated with pigmented adhesive. 15" × 12" × 12". 2014. Courtesy of Chris Peaden, Beanstalk Imaging.

3 *Polished Laminated Plate Glass Vase #17*. Polished plate glass laminated with pigmented adhesive. 18" × 12" × 8". 2005. Courtesy of Chris Peaden, Beanstalk Imaging.

4 *Middy Solid Vase Form #11*. Cut and ground plate glass laminated with pigmented adhesive. 13" × 8.25" × 8.25". 2011. Courtesy of Chris Peaden, Beanstalk Imaging.

5 *Shifting Transmission #6*. Polished plate glass laminated with pigmented adhesive. 14.5" × 7.5" × 10.5". 2014. Courtesy of Chris Peaden, Beanstalk Imaging.

2

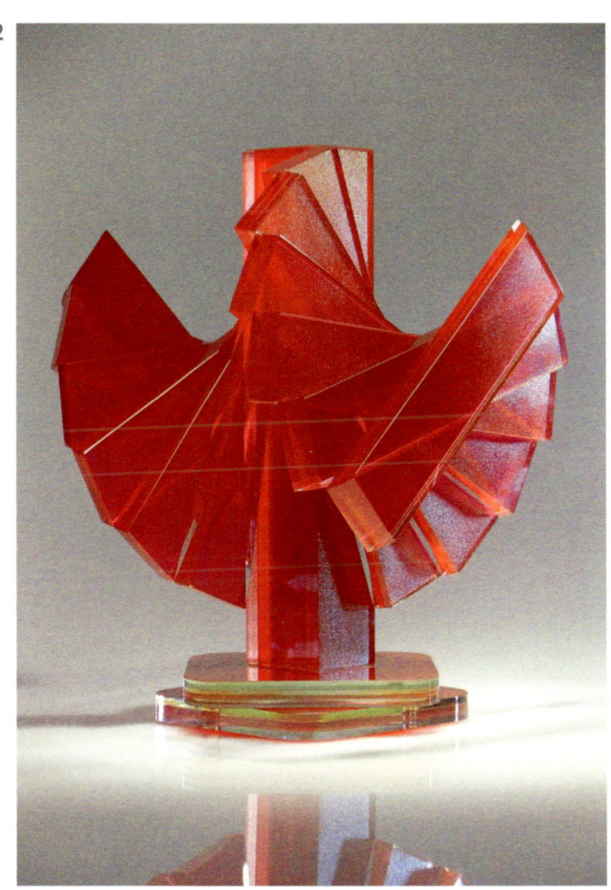

4

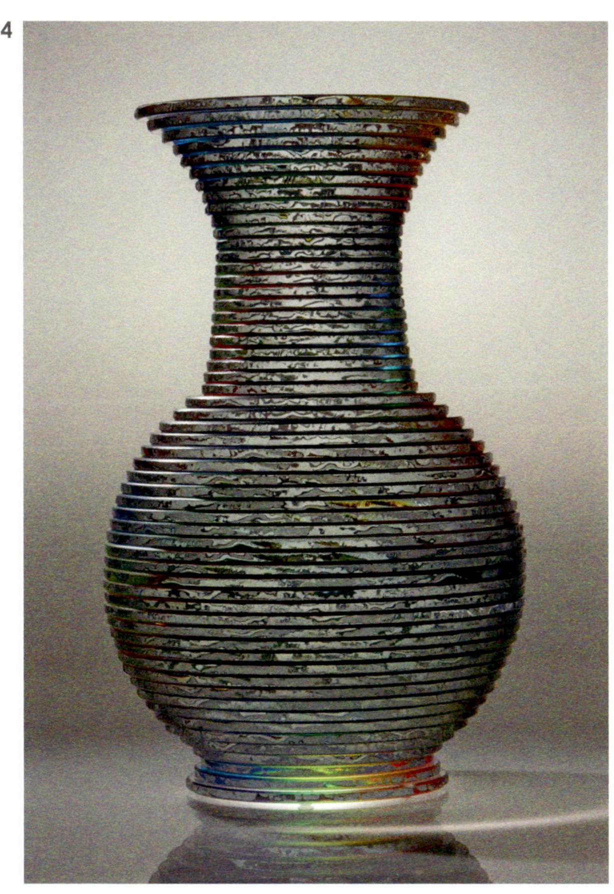

3

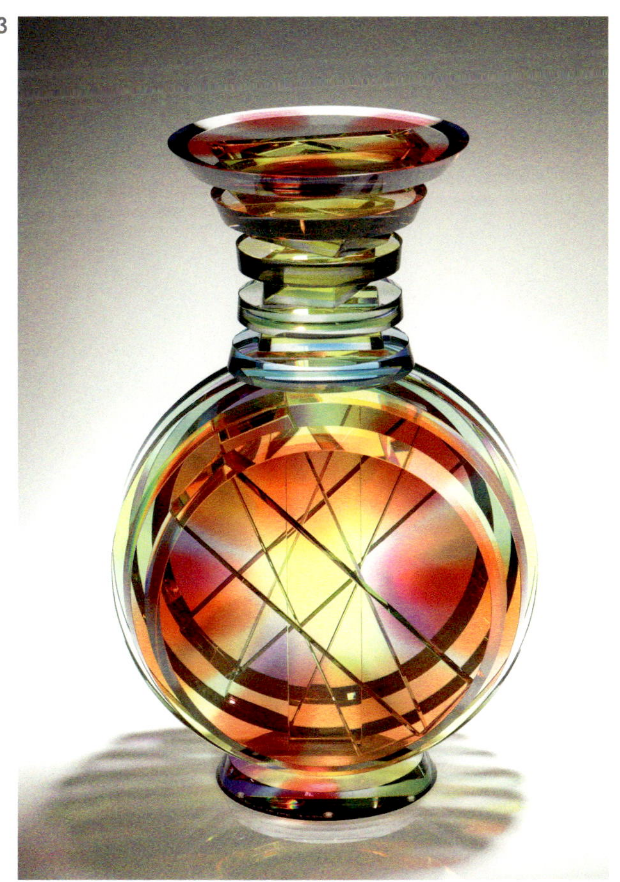

5

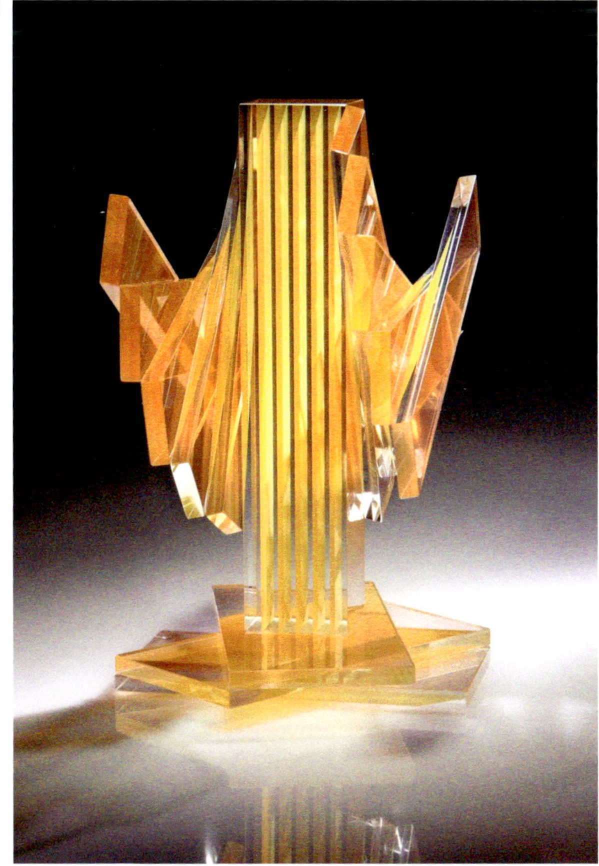

Vlastislav Janáček

Kamenický Šenov, Liberec, Czech Republic

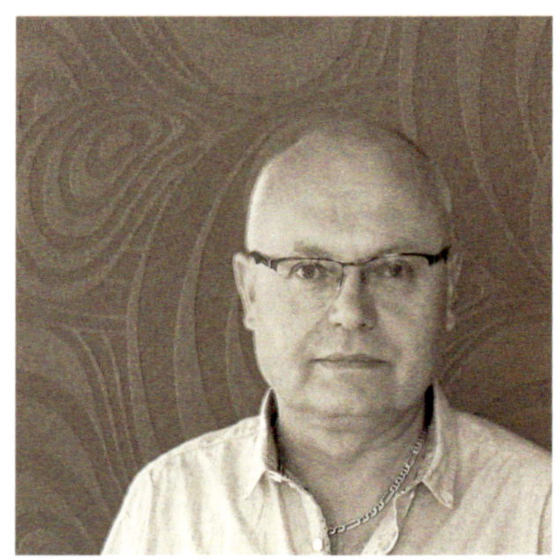

It is very simple to talk about my work; I just love glass.

I am not really looking for the quantity of effects that the material offers; rather, I am trying to discover the inner origin and peculiar world of the glass. My themes come spontaneously. They are everywhere around us: consider the relationship among people, nature, and music. One has only to look and listen.

I will be happy if I manage to touch somebody with my work and bring my feelings and perceptions to the others through my glass objects.

1

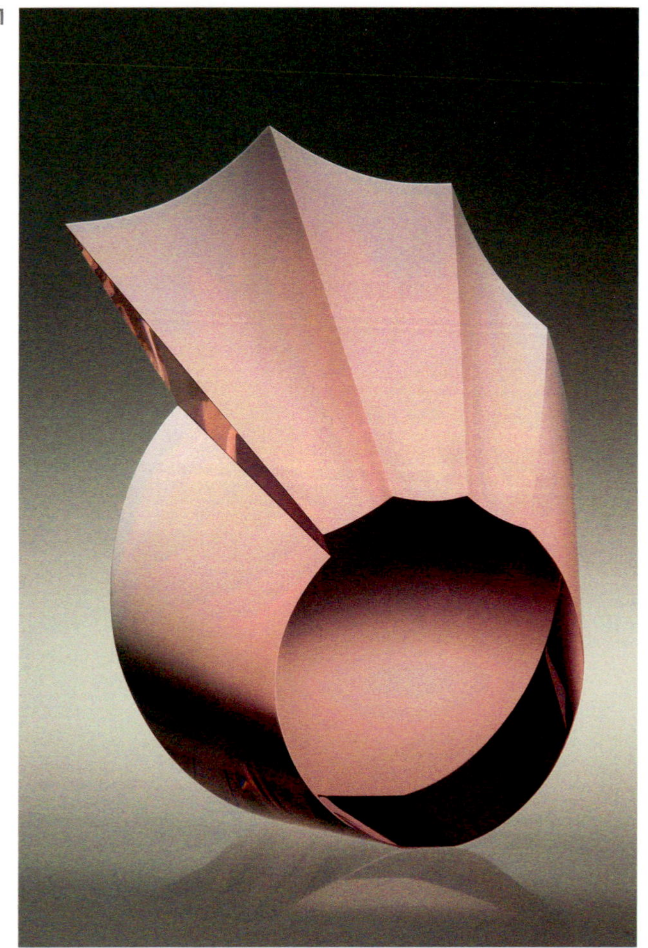

2

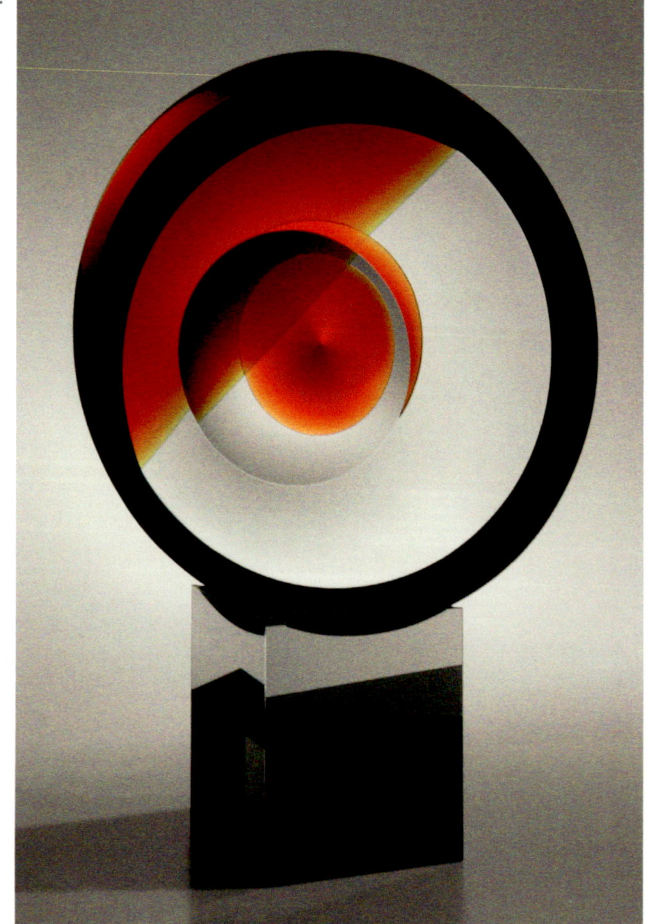

3

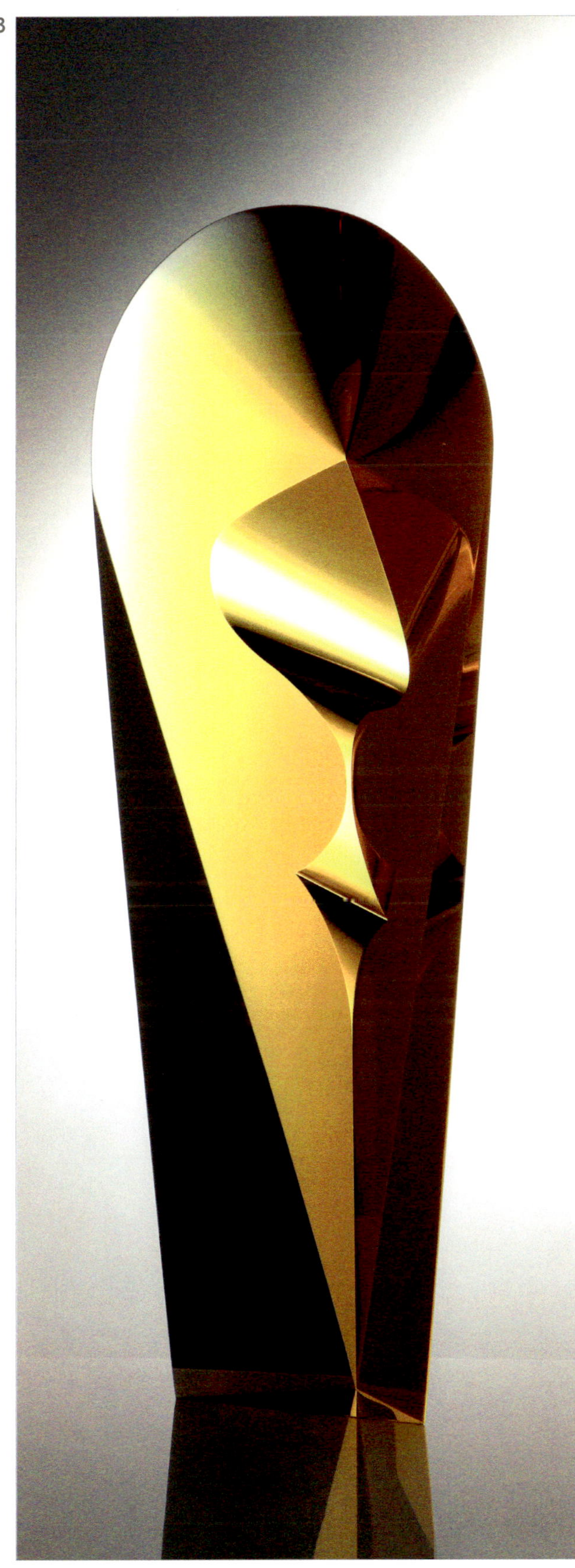

4

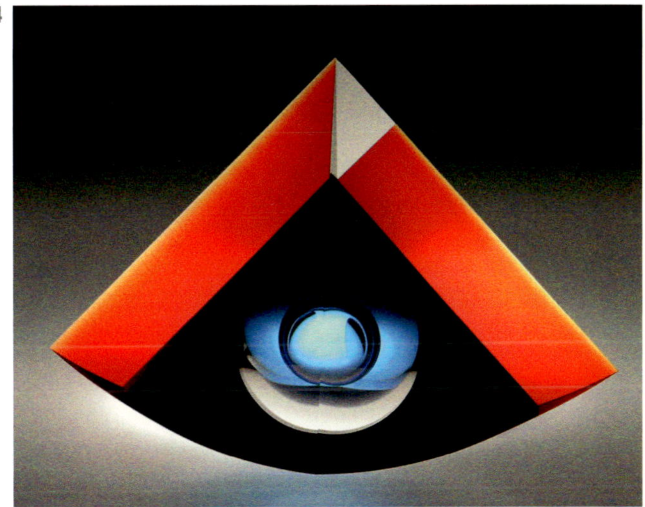

5

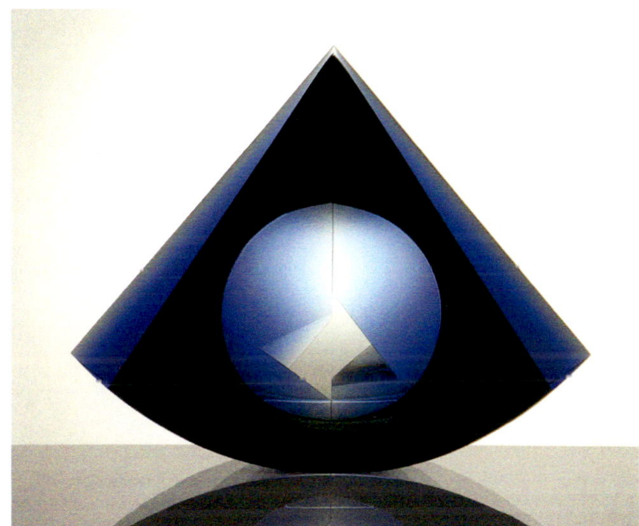

1 *Pink Dragon*. Optic glass, cut and polished. 11.41" × 9.06" × 2.76". 2014. Courtesy of Jiří Koudelka.

2 *Principal*. Optic glass, cut, polished, and glued. 14.17" × 10.23" × 3.94". 2010. Courtesy of Jiří Koudelka.

3 *In a Golden Cage*. Optic glass, cut, polished. 17.72" × 7.09" × 3.15". 2014. Courtesy of Jiří Koudelka.

4 *Twilight*. Optic glass, cut, polished, and glued. 14.57" × 10.23" × 4.33". 2011. Courtesy of Jiří Koudelka.

5 *Midnight Duel*. Optic glass, cut, polished, and glued. 12.60" × 11.81" × 3.15". 2007. Courtesy of Jiří Koudelka.

Elizabeth Johnson

Boulder, Colorado

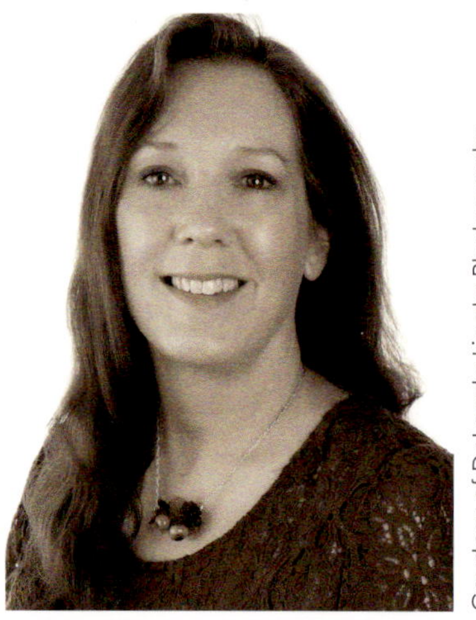

Courtesy of DeLanda Licata Photography.

The fragrance, color, and taste of a raspberry are priceless treasures to me. Connecting with the everyday miracles of nature reminds me that life is a gift and a joy to be savored in each moment.

When I want to capture the fragile beauty of a berry or leaf and freeze it in time, glass is the only possible medium to use. No other art material could so perfectly replicate the voluptuous gloss on a cherry or the way light passes through a flower petal. I want my glass fruit and plants to bring these small wonders home to you, so you can hold them in your hands and appreciate their perfection every time you need a reminder that beauty is everywhere, and that there is joy in even the simplest things.

1

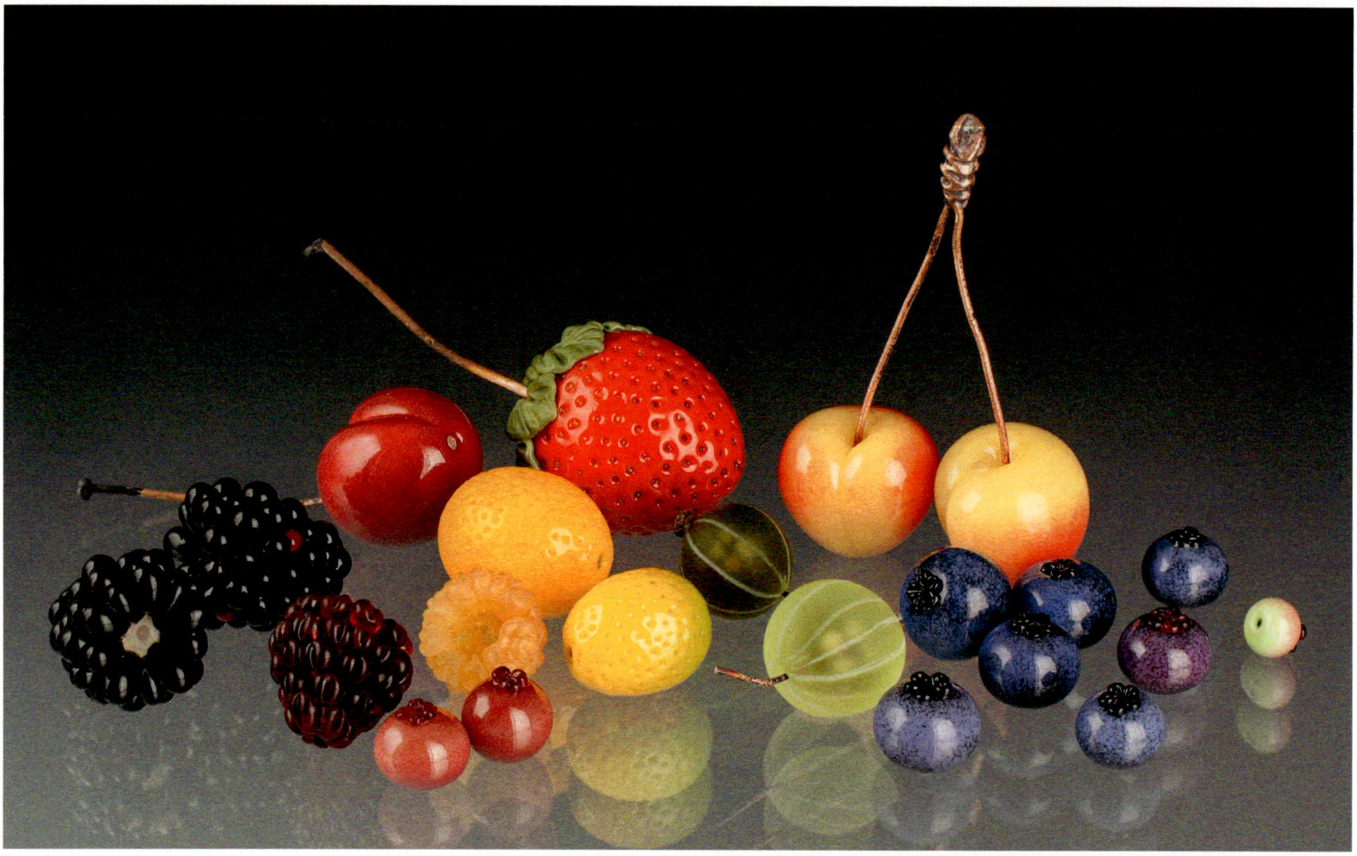

1 *Rainbow Berry Collection*. Lampwork. 1.5" × 8". 2014.

2 *Raspberry Statement Necklace*. Lampwork. 1" × 6" × 8".

3 *Summer of 1985 at Mt. Rainier*. Pate de verre and lampwork. 3" × 9". 2014.

4 *Breakfast #3*. Kiln-formed and lampwork. 1" × 9". 2015.

5 *Rhubarb Leaf*. Pate de verre. 3" × 7". 2013.

2

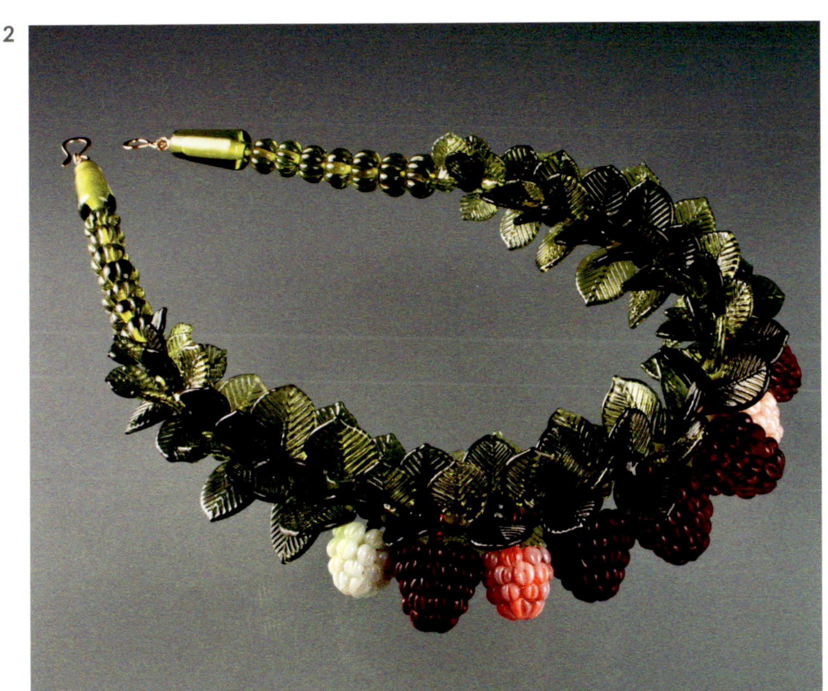

4

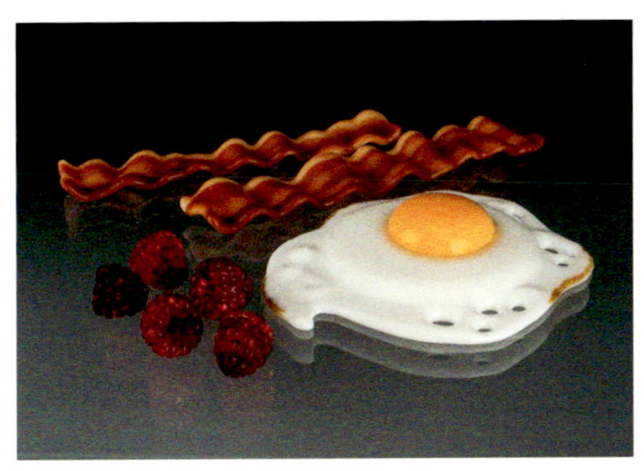

5

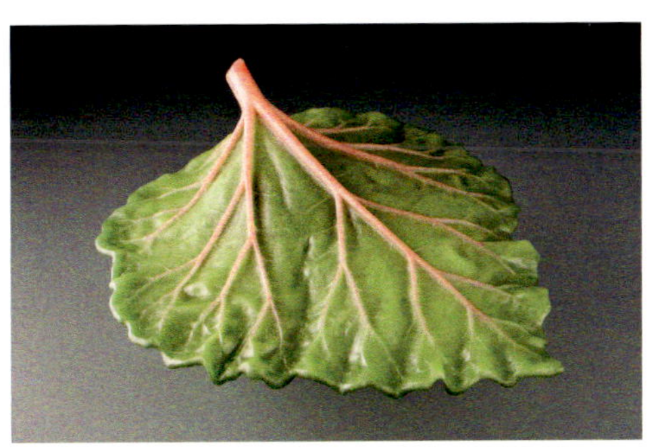

3

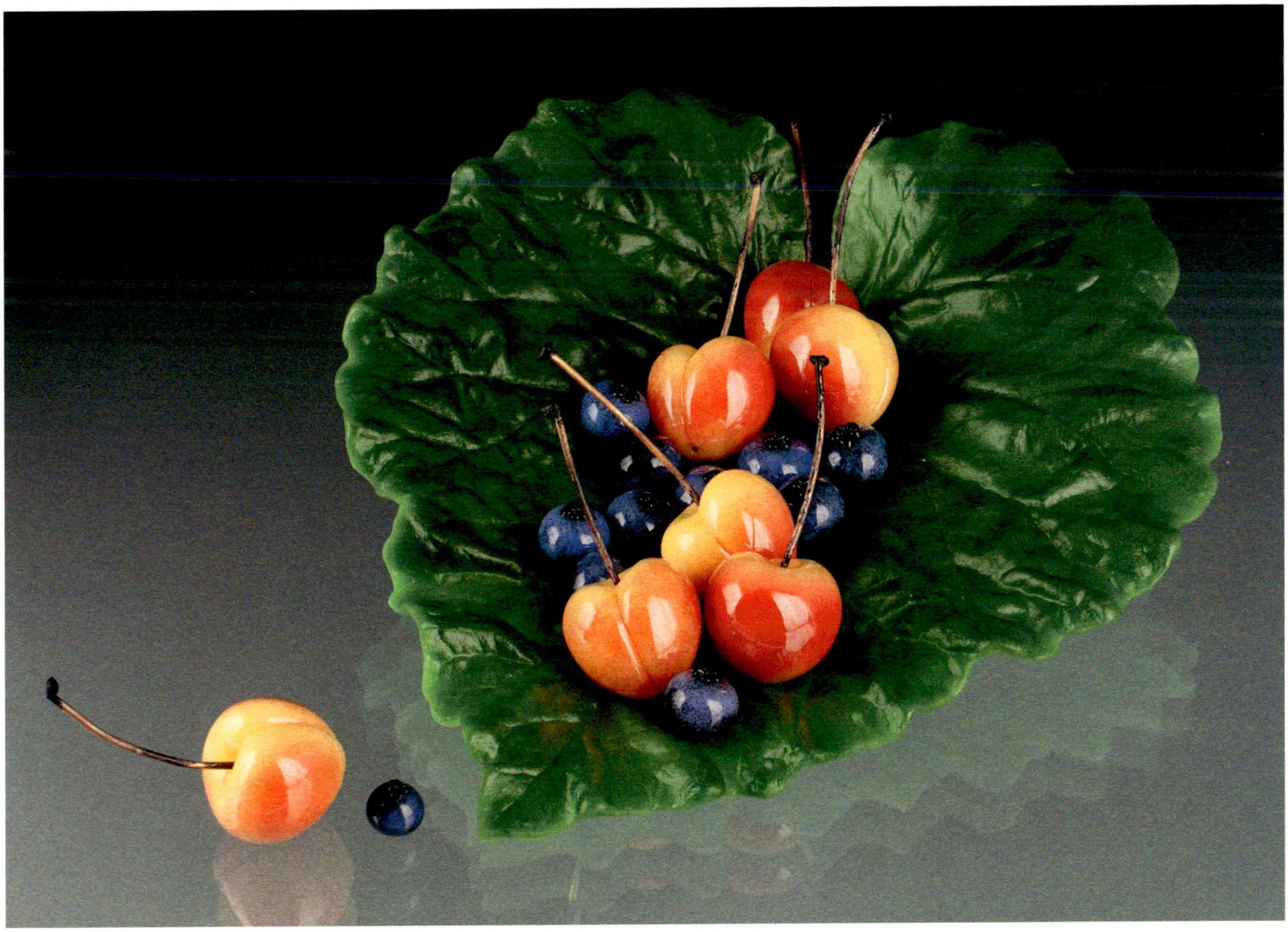

Richard Jolley

Knoxville, Tennessee

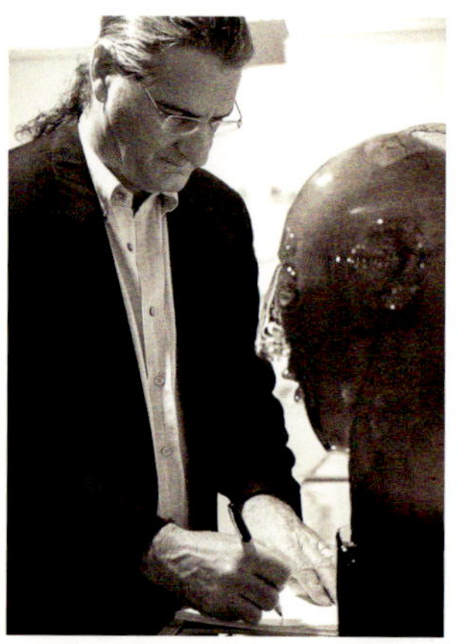

Courtesy of Hei Park.

Relationships, dreams, nature, fulfillment of meaning, love, loss, and the marking of time are the essential elements of the human experience that I address in my art. My work speaks to the importance of maintaining a sense of wonder, both in the natural world we inhabit and toward the larger cosmos of which we are but an infinitesimal part. These universal concerns have captivated the attention of artists, poets, writers, and musicians since the beginning of time, and this will be the case as long as we remain intellectually inquisitive. I observe my universe through a poetic lens—after all, the Greek root of the word *poet* is "maker"!

1

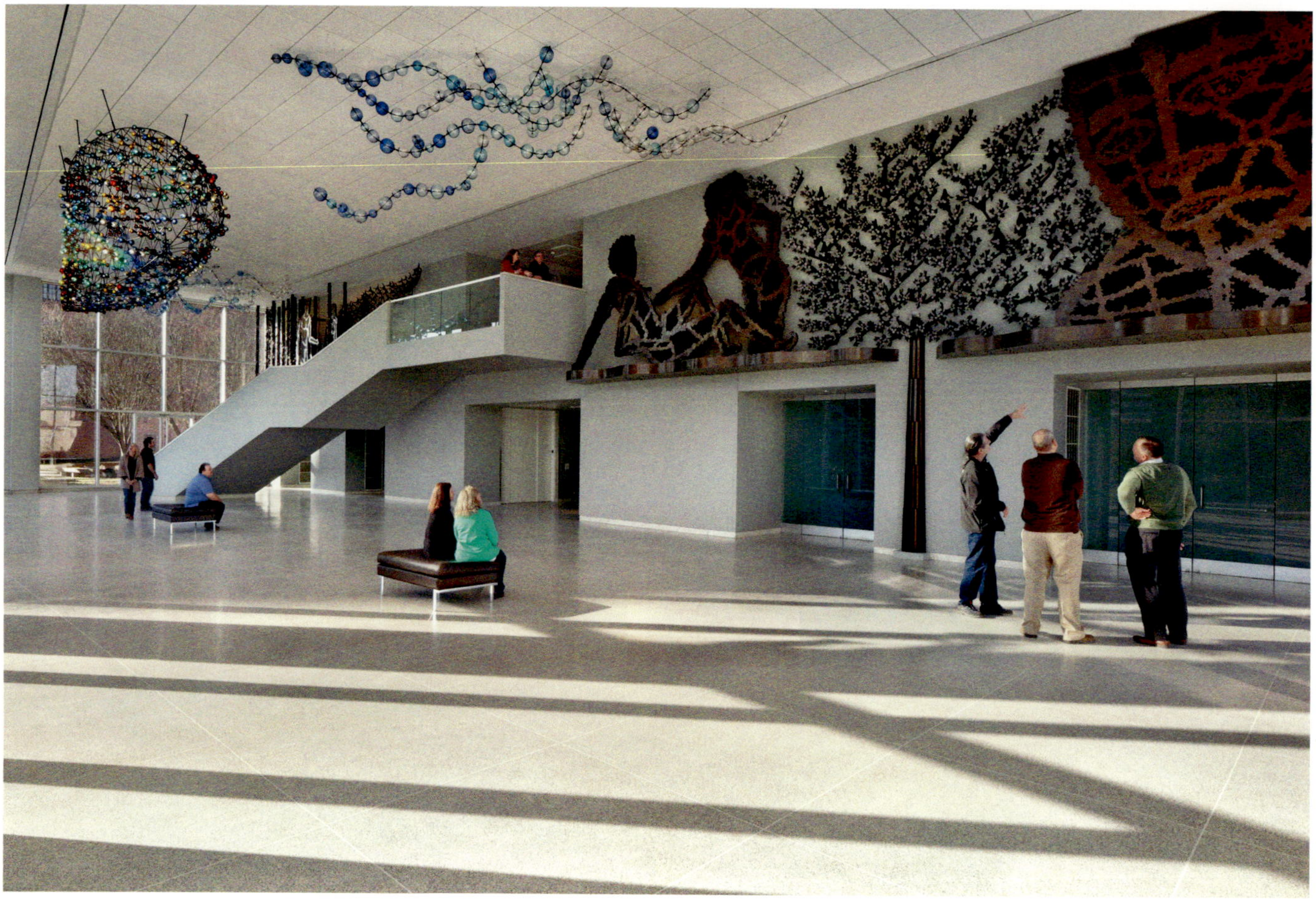

1 *Cycle of Life: Within the Power of Dreams and the Wonder of Infinity.* Permanent installation in the Ann and Steve Bailey Hall, Knoxville Museum of Art, Knoxville, TN. Glass and steel. 22' × 30' × 105'. 2009-2014. © 2013 Elizabeth Felicella.

2

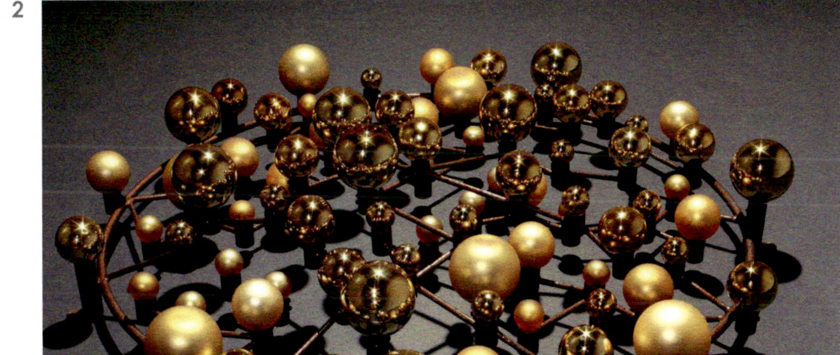

4

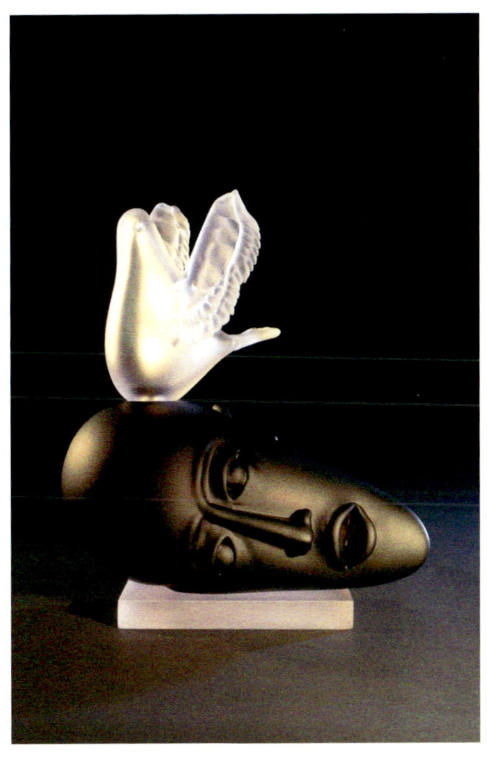

3

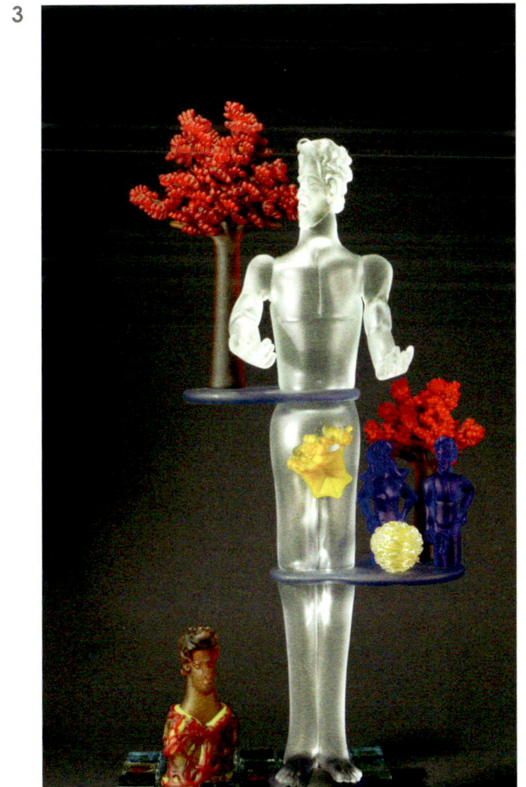

5

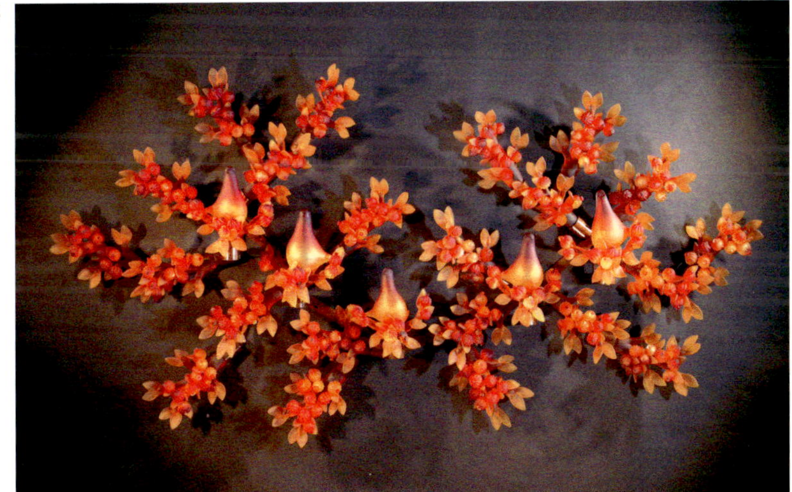

2 *Golden Disk.* Furnace-formed glass and steel. 41" × 9" × 40". 2014.

3 *Translating Substance #33.* Furnace-formed glass fabricated. 56" × 23" × 33". 2008.

4 *Suspended in Dreams #10.* Furnace-formed glass. 20" × 11" × 17". 2013.

5 *Five Fade Doves with Blush Pomegranates.* Furnace-formed glass and steel. 52" × 11" × 104". 2014.

Saman Kalantari

Bolzano, South Tyrol, Italy

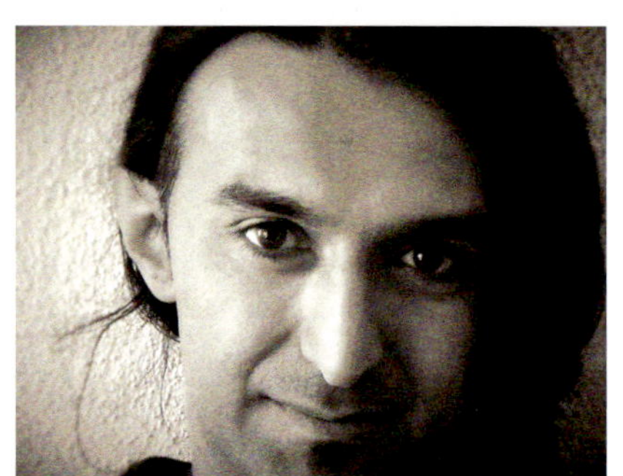

I use glass to explain the consistency, continuity, fragility, mortality, and subtleness of human beings, nature, and life. I try to express what different materials have in common or in contrast with each other and how they react when they revert to their origins. I think of wastes as an artistic material, the presence of something residual, and processes of things that happened or have been.

1

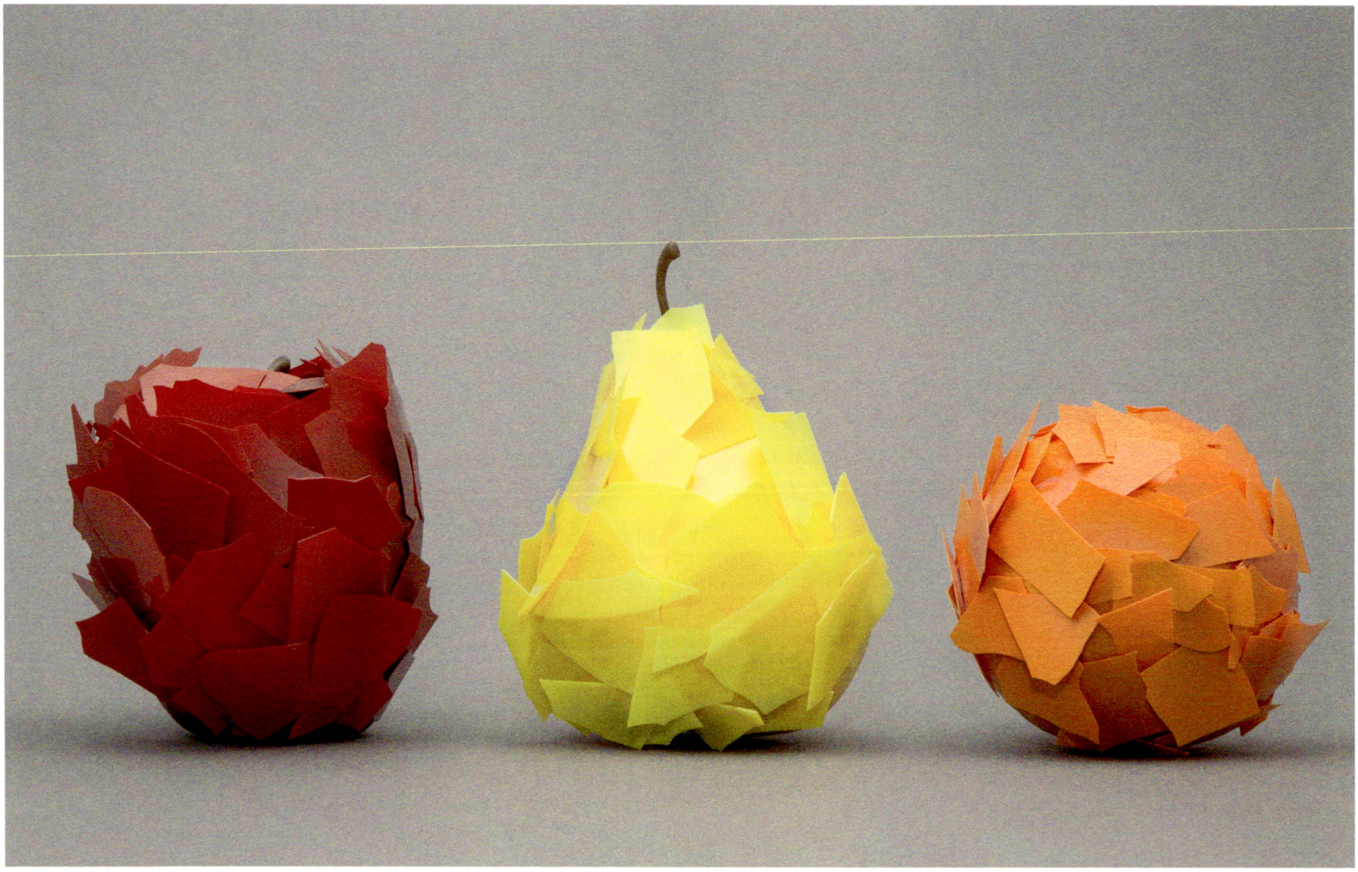

1 *Dynamic Still Life*. Glass confetti. Variable dimensions (life size). 2014. Courtesy of Silvia Giovanelli.

2 *Childhood Games*. Paper-thin pate de verre. 20" × 6" × 15". 2010.

3 *Still Life*. Paper-thin pate de verre. Variable dimensions (largest 20", highest 32").

4 *Touch*. Paper-thin pate de verre. Variable dimensions (largest 16" × 16" × 20"). 2014. Photo by Monica A. Amundsen.

2

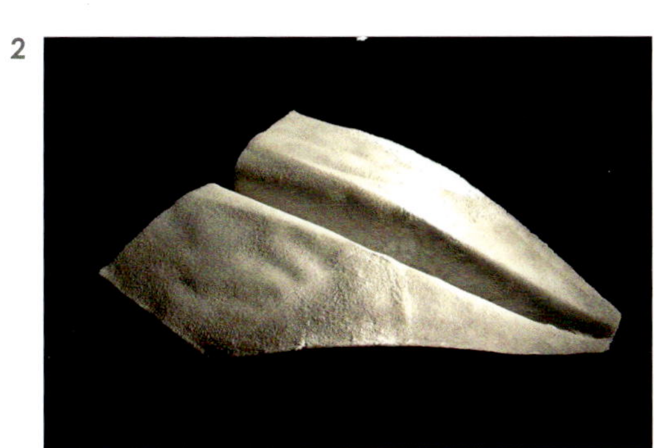

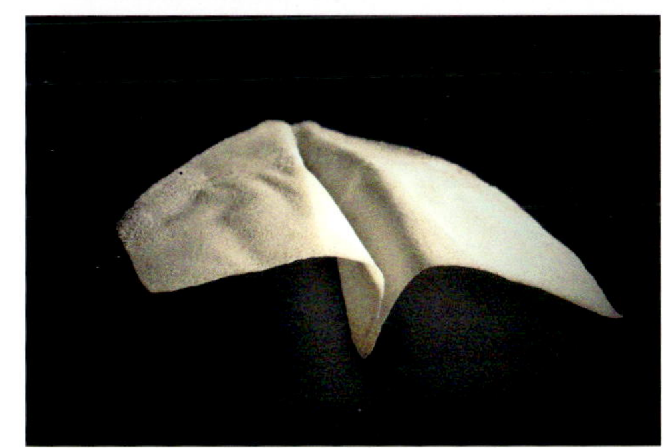

4

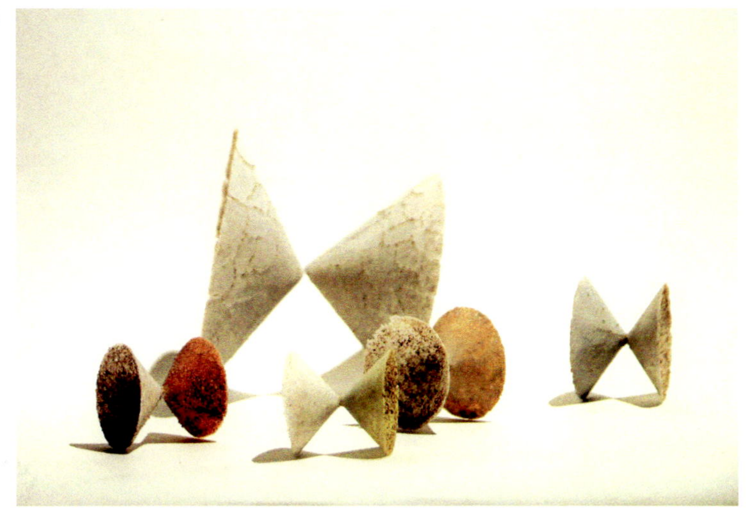

3

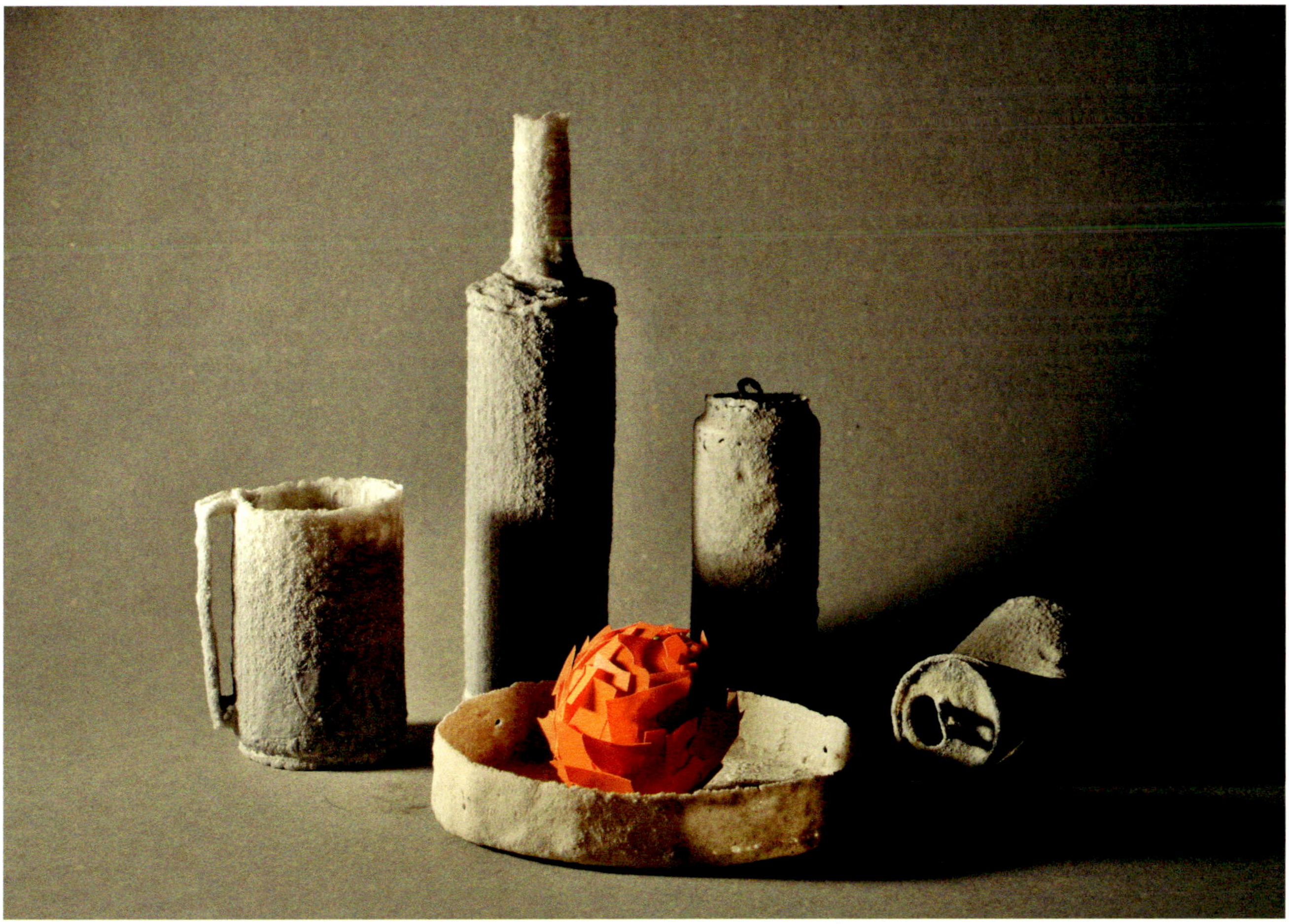

Sonia King

Dallas, Texas

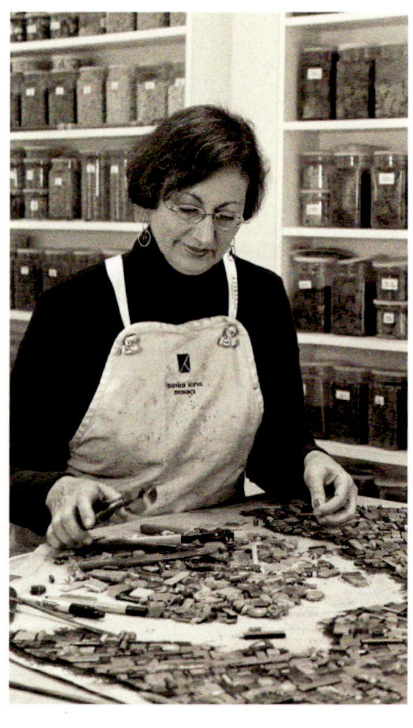
Courtesy of Terri Glanger Photography.

Mosaic's constant interplay between intellectual stimulation and the tactile pleasure of shaping and placing each piece keeps me in the studio. It's up to me and my ability to master the materials and create a work that captures something elusive.

I work with a complex mix of materials using the tesserae, interstices, and andamento to create environments that are complex and serene, positive and negative. Much happens in the "spaces between," just as much of life is in the gaps. It's like trying to hear the silence between musical notes, straining to catch what I have no evidence exists.

Technically, I'm exploring two challenges with the goal of intensifying the viewers' experience. One is creating a sense of serenity from a complex blend of varying materials, shapes, spaces, scale, and reflectivity. The second involves reducing mosaic to its purest expression, freeing the elements to interact tessera-to-tessera. I work to create art that demonstrates the power of my personal expression, heart and soul and emotion; art that can only be created at this particular point in my artistic journey; art that has the power and impact resulting from the intense and intimate struggle between the medium and my vision. The work is engrossing, consuming, and challenging, and I wouldn't do anything else!

1

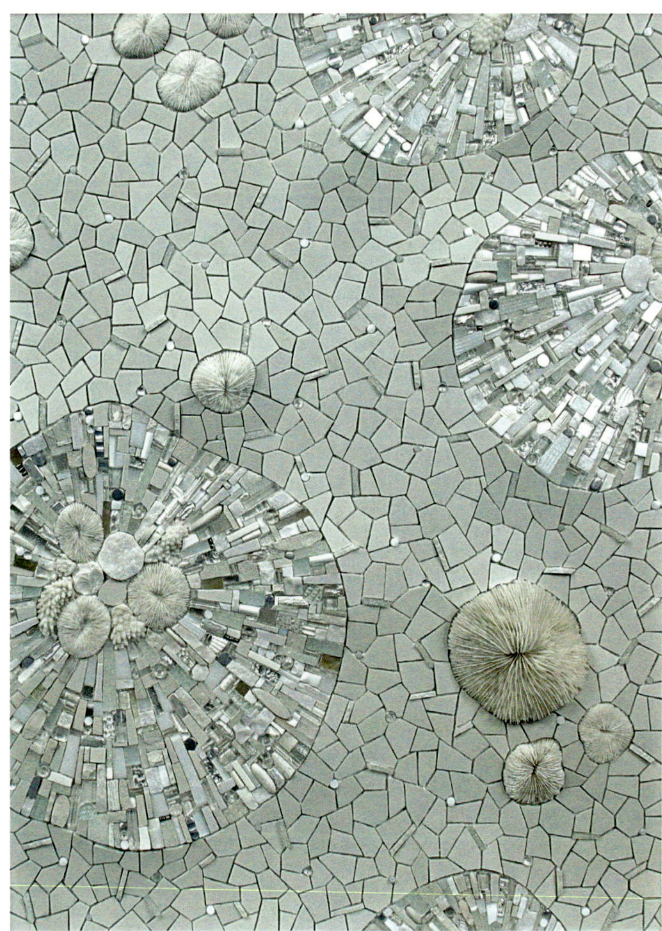

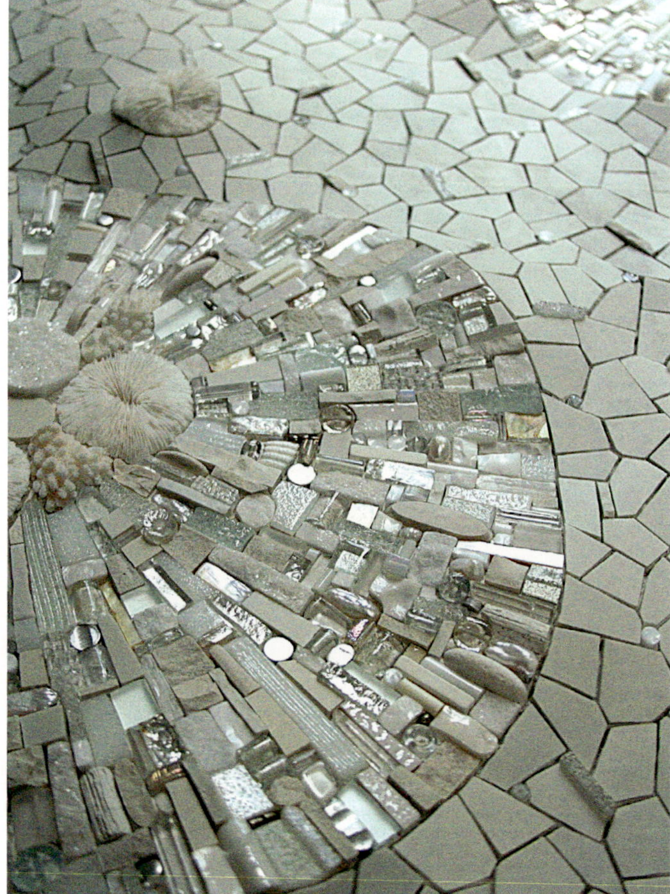

2

3

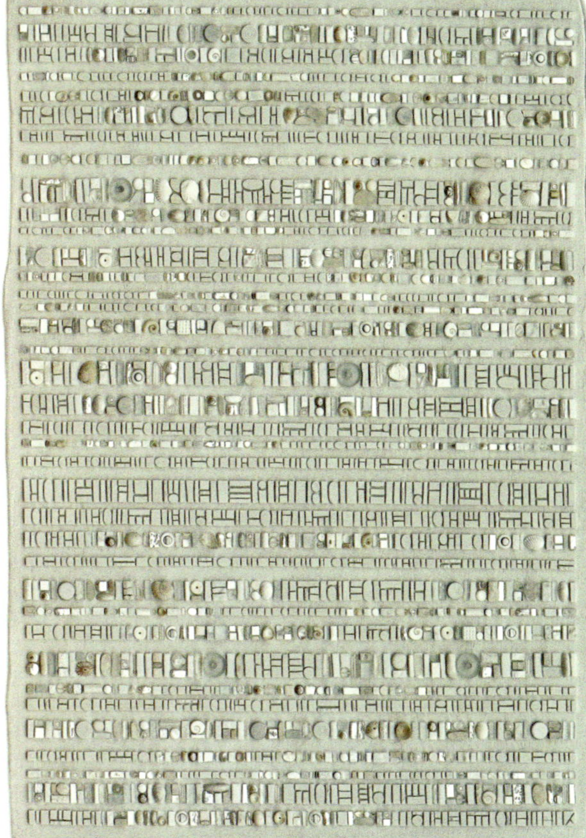

1 *Permafrost.* Glass, ceramic, coral, white gold, smalti, quartz, silver, marble, rock crystal, seashell, pearls, aluminum, selenite, abalone, and pebbles. Direct over hand-formed, undulating surface. 24" × 18". 2009.

2 *Depthfinder.* Glass, ceramic, Paua shell, golds, smalti, turquoise, malachite, labradorite, pebbles, chrysocolla, crystals, pearls, beach glass, amazonite, stainless steel, and abalone. 24" × 18". 2011.

3 *Coded Message: Invisible Ink.* Glass, ceramic, white gold, smalti, quartz, silver, marble, rock crystal, seashell, pearls, aluminum, selenite, abalone, pebbles, stainless steel, bone, coral, fluorite, dinosaur bone, and mirror. Applied without visible adhesive on a hand-formed substrate. 36" × 26". 2012.

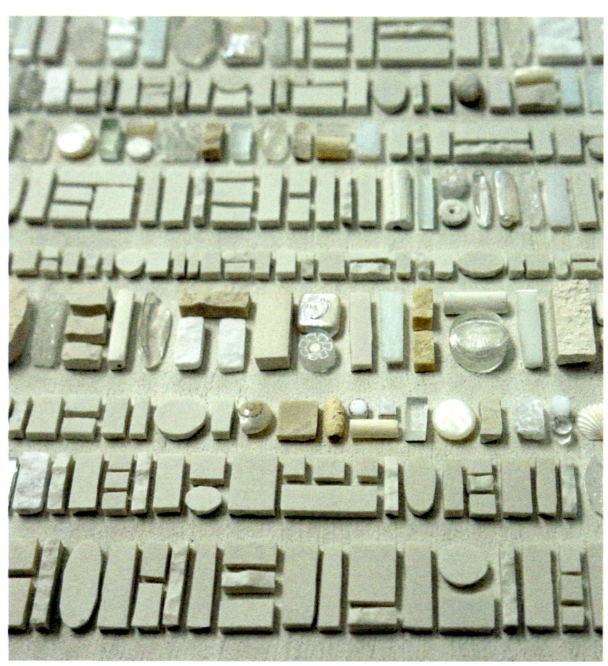

Connie Kolman

Sudbury, Massachusetts

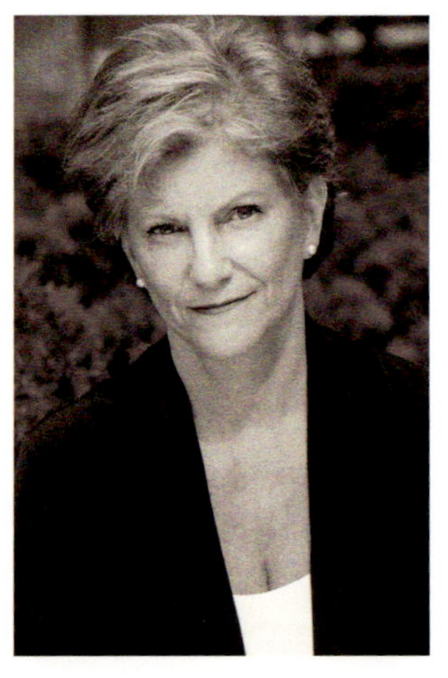
Courtesy of Eric Levin.

My first piece of glasswork was created in my kitchen when I was an interior designer. My client was looking for a unique centerpiece. Initially, it was a hobby, a passion that drew on my natural creativity. That passion led to creating a distinctive approach to glassmaking based on a decoupage technique I've refined over the years using resins, foils, papers, and paints. My work is commissioned as framed artwork, wall panels, screens, table inserts and surrounds, and stand-alone pieces. Using a repertoire of colors, textures, and patterns, no two pieces are alike yet all are distinctly and immediately recognized as "Kolman."

I became an interior designer after attending the Boston Architectural College. In 2011, I founded Kolman to focus on my art full time. Even though my studio is based in Sudbury, Massachusetts, my artwork has traveled the globe in a very short time and been incorporated into private residential designs as well as public spaces such as healthcare facilities, hotels, and restaurants.

1

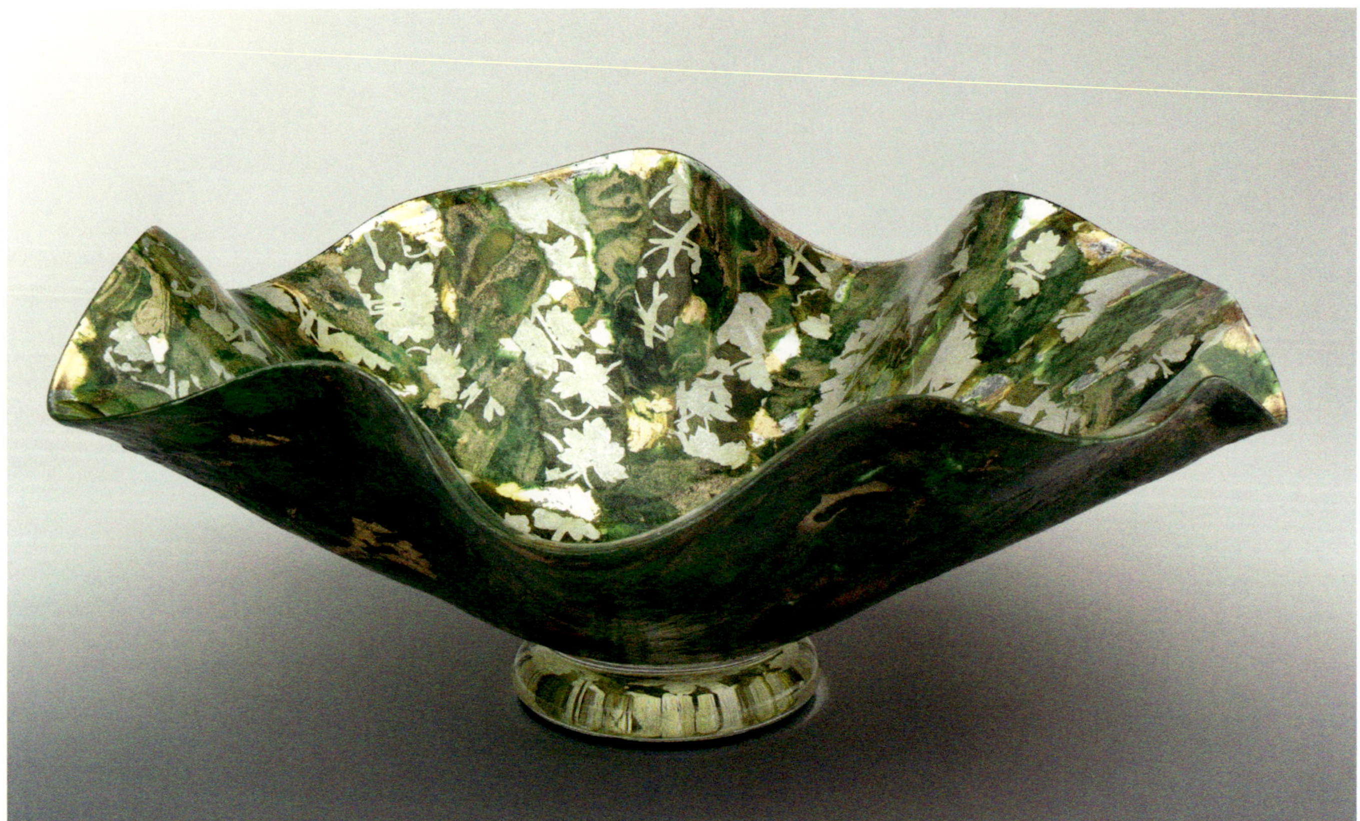

1 *Meadow Bowl*. Mixed media/glass. 17" × 5.5". 2012. Courtesy of FayFoto Boston.

2 *North Hill Turquoise*. Mixed media/glass. 48" × 0.25" × 36". 2013. Courtesy of Jessica Delaney Photography.

3 *Barn Door*. Mixed media/glass. 85" × 0.375" × 40.25". 2014. Courtesy of Greg Premru.

4 *Schraffts*. Mixed media/glass. 1 Panel: 48" × 0.25" × 36"; 2 Panels: 48" × 0.25" × 24". 2014. Bench made by Ray Bachand. Courtesy of Greg Premru.

5 *Charlestown Wall*. Mixed media/glass. 6 panels: 96" × 0.25" × 48". 2013. Courtesy of Greg Premru.

2

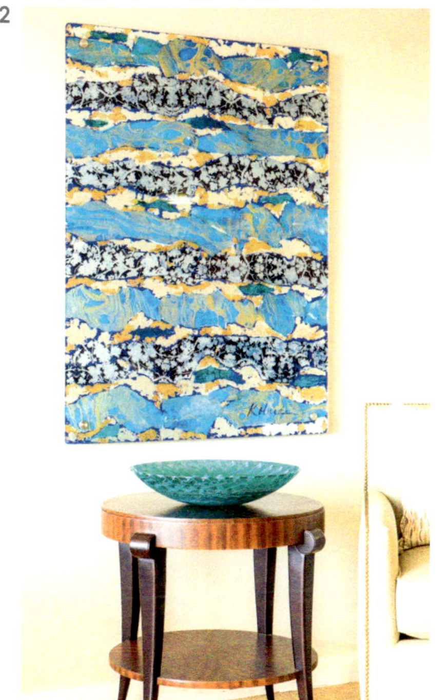

3

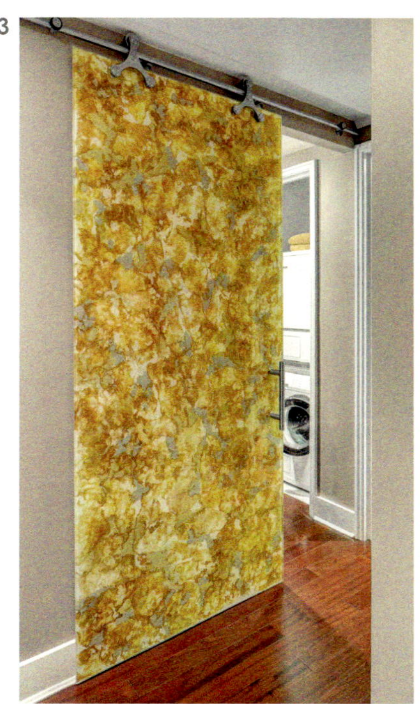

4

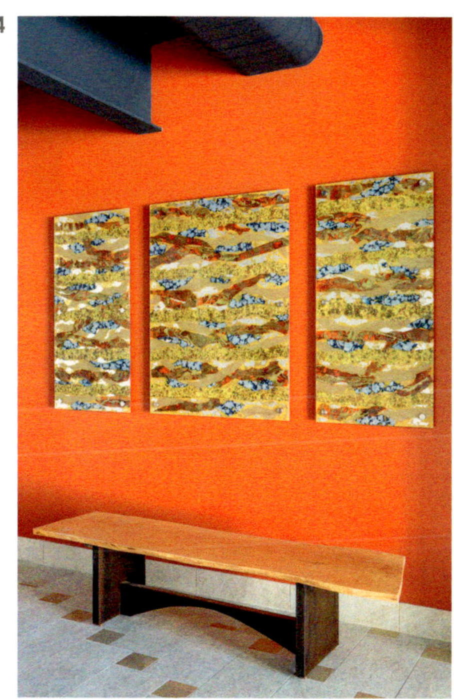

5

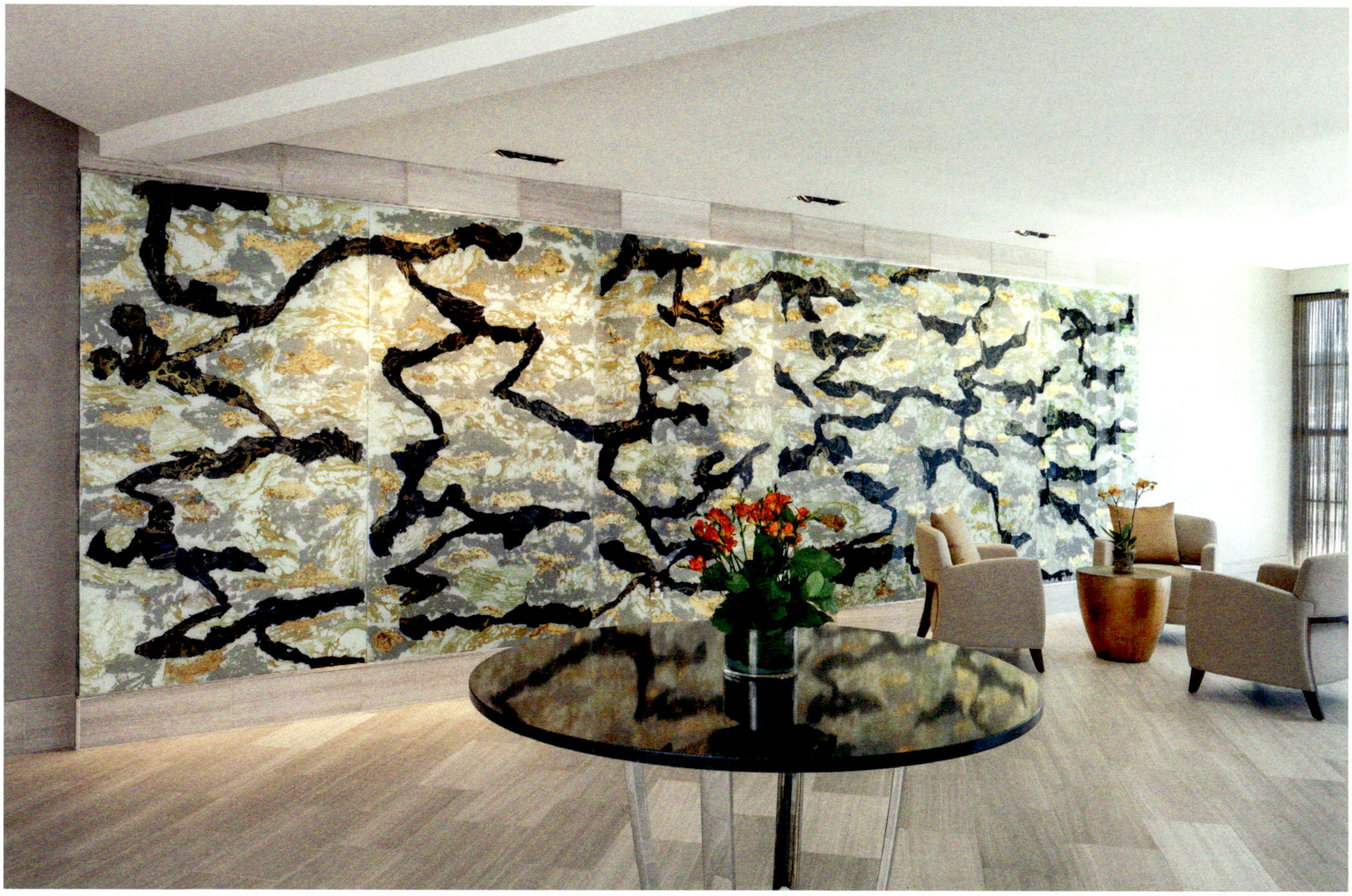

Lynn Latimer

Easthampton, Massachusetts

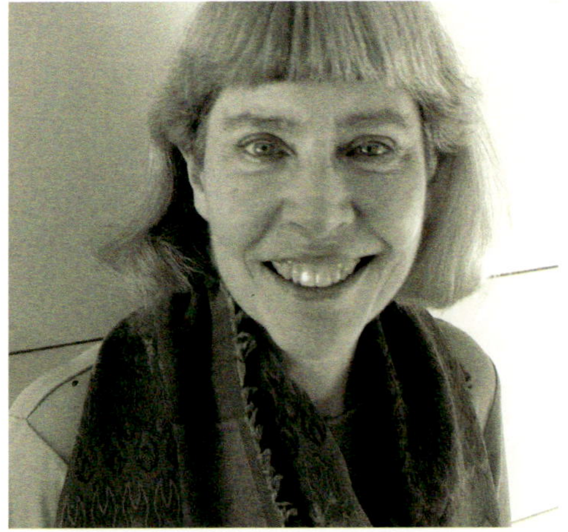

Courtesy of Michael LaMothe.

I began working in glass under the guidance of Dale Chihuly at the Rhode Island School of Design, graduated with a BFA in painting, and started Latimer Glass Studio in 1976.

Born of a love for the drawn line and color, my interest lies in exploring rich and subtle palettes and integrating rhythm, line, and pattern with the luminosity of glass. My panels contain influences of tribal textiles, the balance of Japanese gardens, the nonverbal movement of dance: something primal, reflective, and restorative.

I arrange layers of colored glass into a complex three-dimensional pattern, crisp and architectural in appearance. In the kiln, heat and gravity finish the drawing, moving the composition into place; colors meld, spaces narrow, straight lines undulate, adding a delicate fluidity to the design. If I have done my job right, the glass draws you in and offers a deeply satisfying visceral experience: it is enlivening.

1 *Diamonds*. Warm. 21.5" × 18". 2006. Courtesy of John Polak Photography.

2 *Orange/Lavender Linework*. Warm. 25" × 22". 2008.Courtesy of John Polak Photography.

1

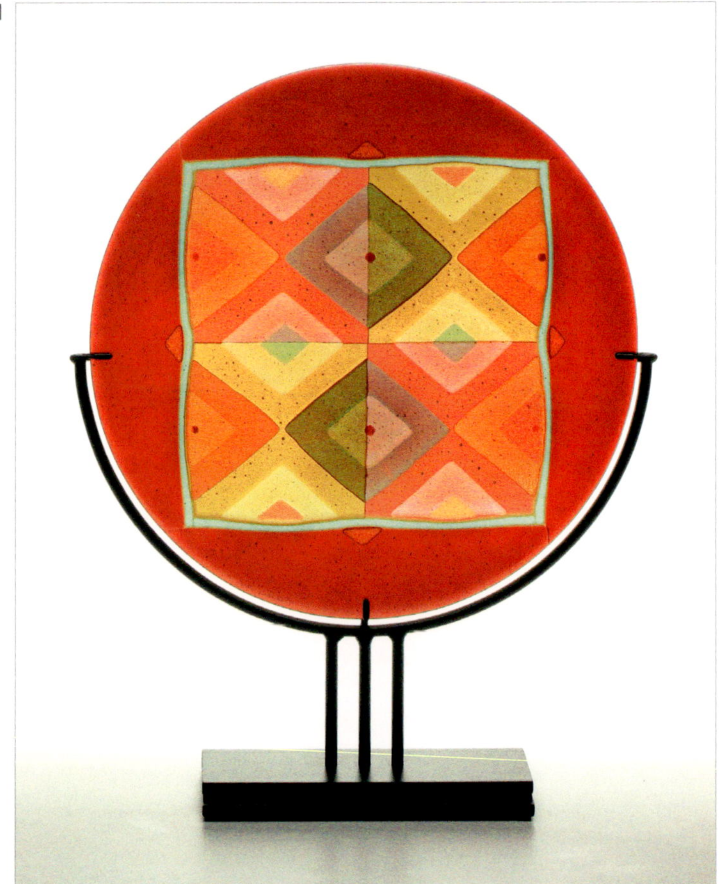

2

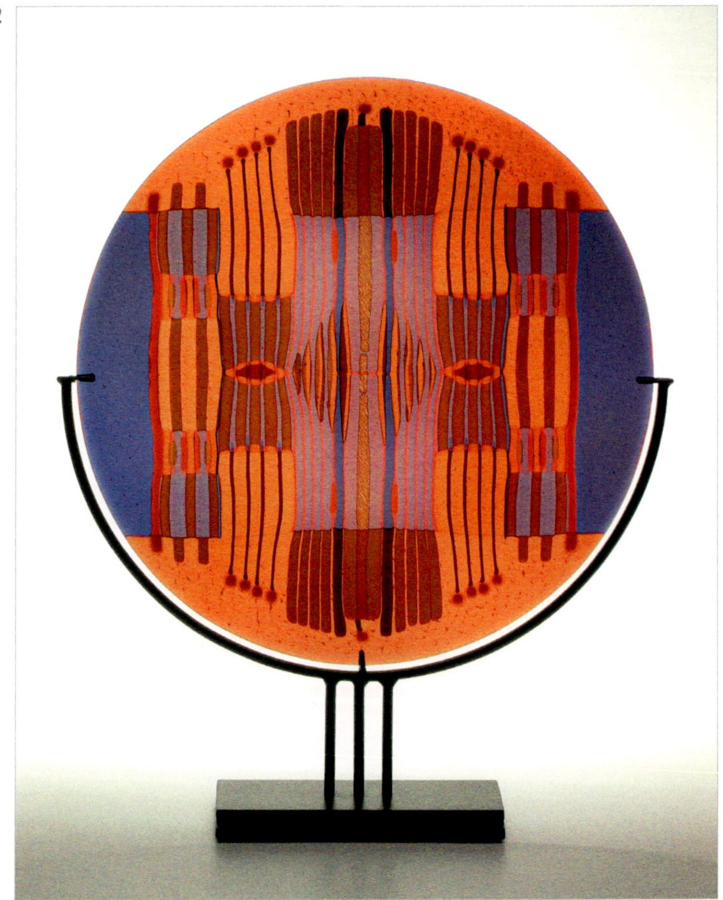

3

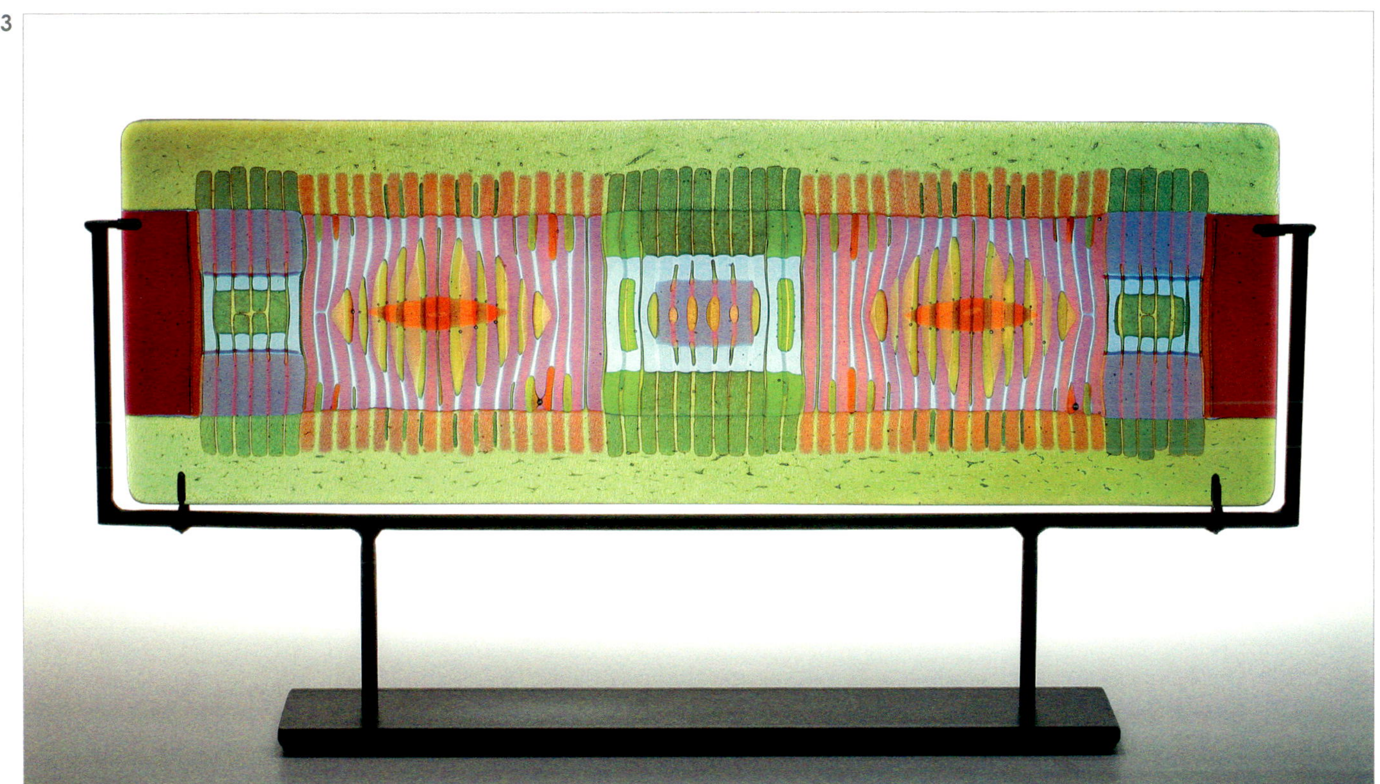

4

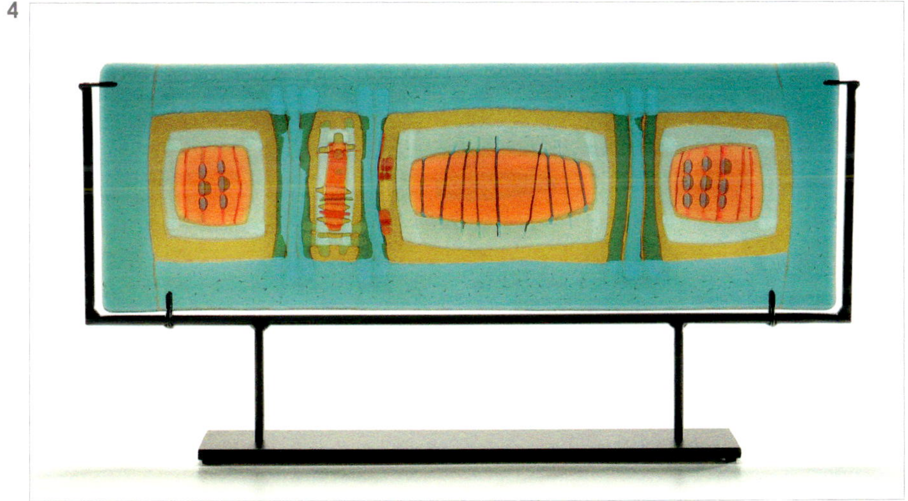

5

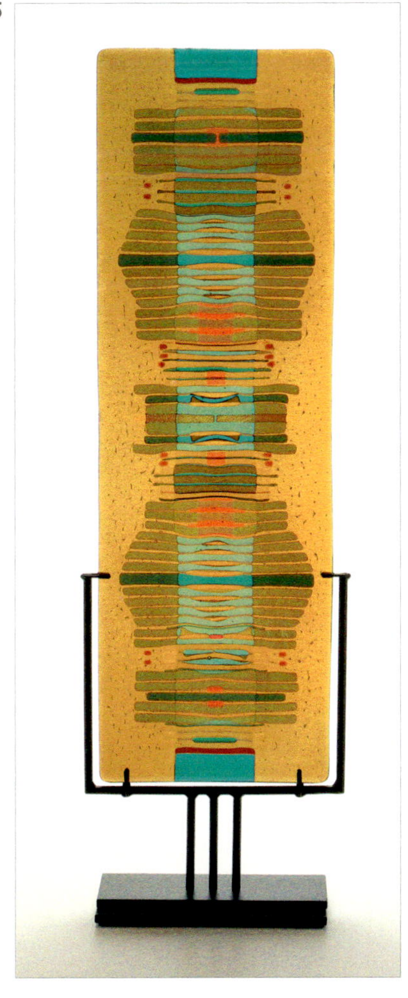

3 *Olive/Lavender Linework*. Warm. 13.5" × 28". 2010. Courtesy of John Polak Photography.

4 *Tribal Study #3*. Warm. 13.5" × 28". 2007. Courtesy of John Polak Photography.

5 *Amber/Aqua Linework*. Warm. 36.5" × 12". 2011. Courtesy of John Polak Photography.

K. William LeQuier

Readsboro, Vermont

I look to nature for my inspiration and use the dynamic elements of wind and water as a source. Sandblasting is a method of carving glass that enables me to create sculptures reminiscent of the elemental forces of nature. It allows me to quickly carve glass, transforming it. Hard edges are softened, and raised areas melt away under the blast from pressurized air and abrasive.

I use plate glass to construct my sculptures. A readily available material, plate glass comes in many thicknesses and is characterized by a pale green color. I use this material in an unconventional way by carving and laminating plates together in a complex assemblage that is no longer recognizable as plate glass yet still retains the translucent quality of glass.

Although my sculptures are three-dimensional, they have a linear quality. The quality of a line can convey much emotion. My sculptures all begin with sketches, and I try to emulate the freedom and spontaneity of the sketch in the three-dimensional work, using the linear quality to express energy and emotion. The resulting sculptures are both powerful and fluid, capturing the harmonious and erratic forces found in nature.

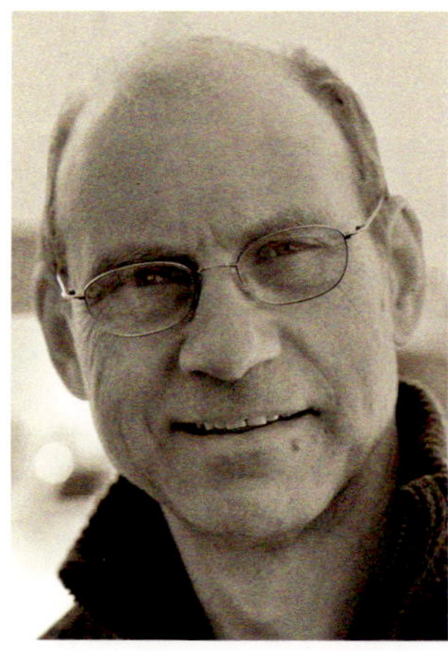

Courtesy of gray photo.

1

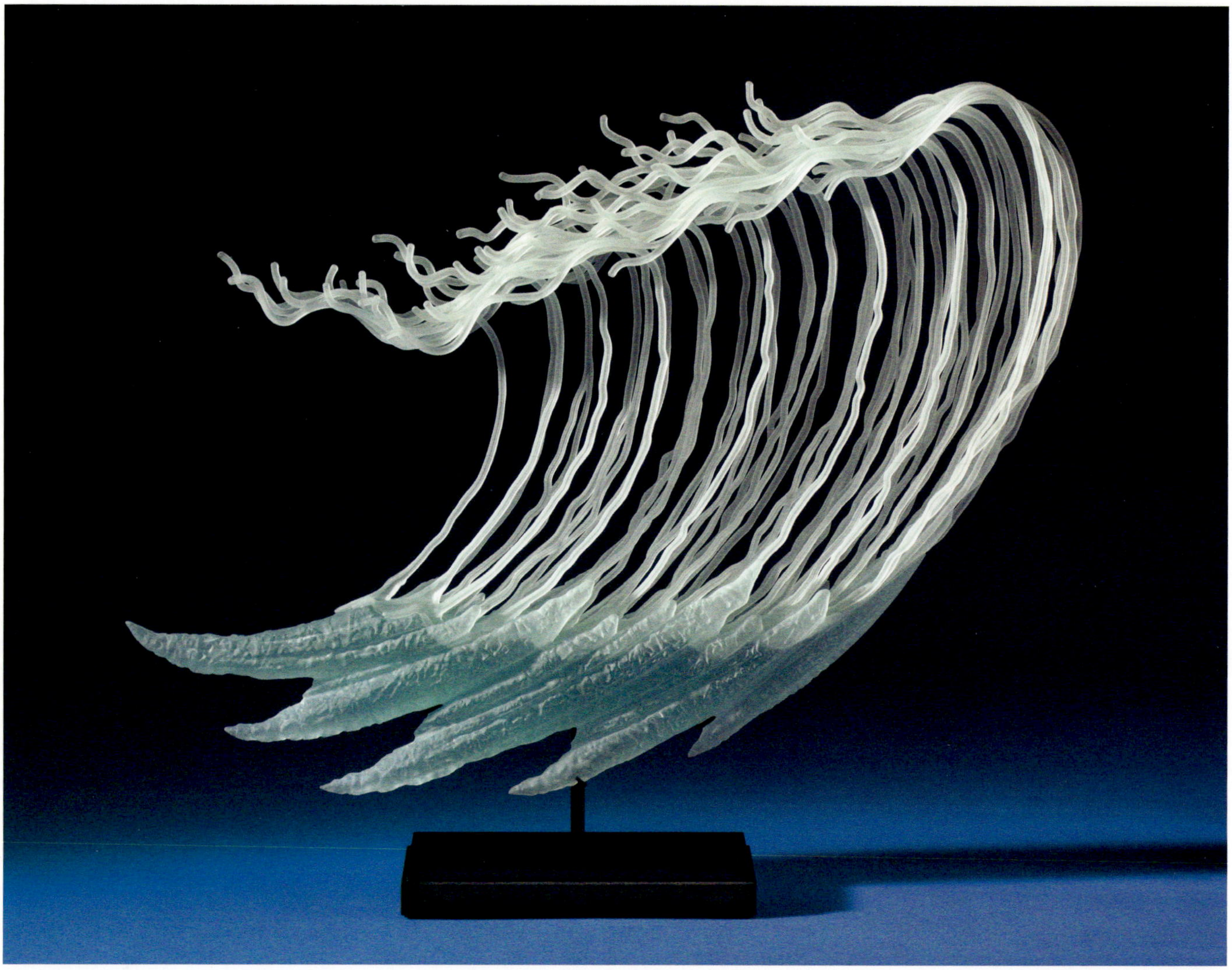

2

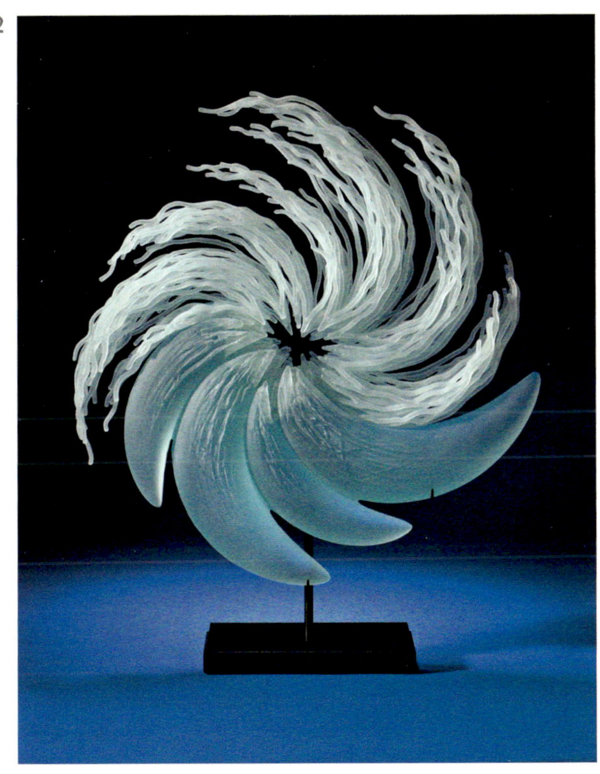

3

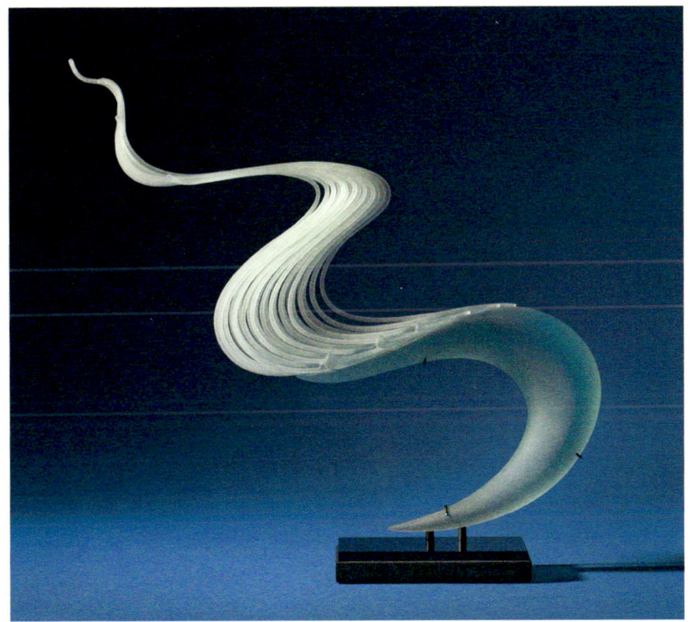

4

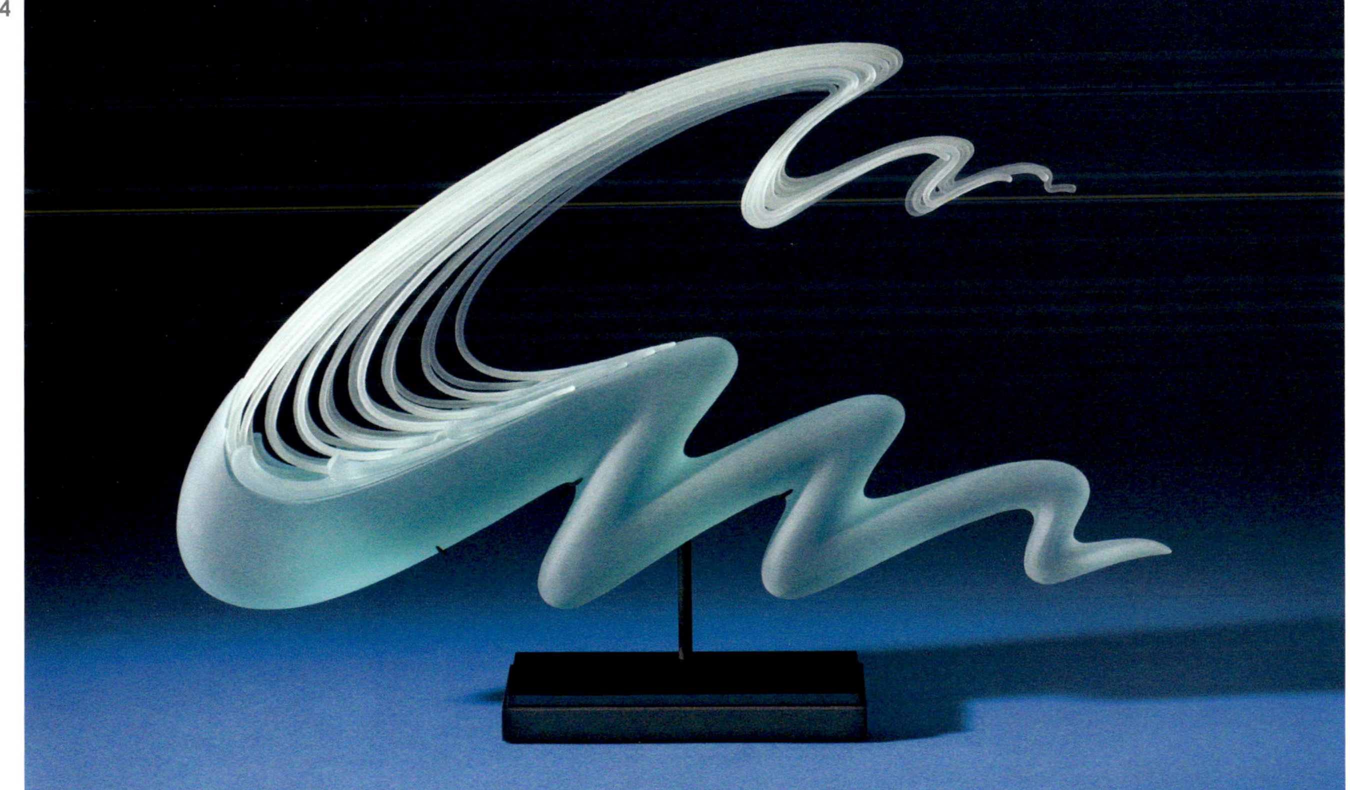

1 *Curl no. 5*. Carved laminated glass. 19" × 23". 2011. Courtesy of groy photo.

2 *Maelstrom*. Carved laminated glass. 21" × 18". 2010. Courtesy of groy photo.

3 *Ascending Rhythm and Blue*. Carved laminated glass. 20" × 21". 2014. Courtesy of groy photo.

4 *Impulse*. Carved laminated glass. 16" × 24". 2011. Courtesy of groy photo.

Robert Levin

Burnsville, North Carolina

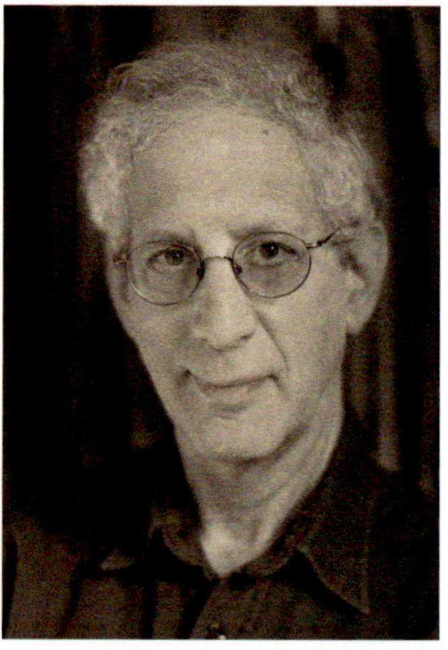

Courtesy of Frederick Park.

I was originally attracted to hot glass because of its liquid qualities and sense of immediacy. I try to capture its inherent properties: elegance, fluidity, and whimsy. I make my own colored glasses and often frost the glass to emphasize the overall form of each piece. Recently, I have minimized the color and have been working mainly with black glass.

I find that various aspects of my work take on personal connotations for me. This usually does not happen consciously; I may be looking at a completed piece and see something new in it—about myself or my work. This dialogue with my work has become very important to me. I view many of my pieces as extensions of this dialogue and as analogies for my attempt to integrate the various facets of my life into some sort of harmony. This all has something to do with possibilities for change and transformation, both with the material and within the person doing the creating. The approaches I use are eclectic and personal at the same time—sort of a blend of Late Venetian and Early Neurotic.

1

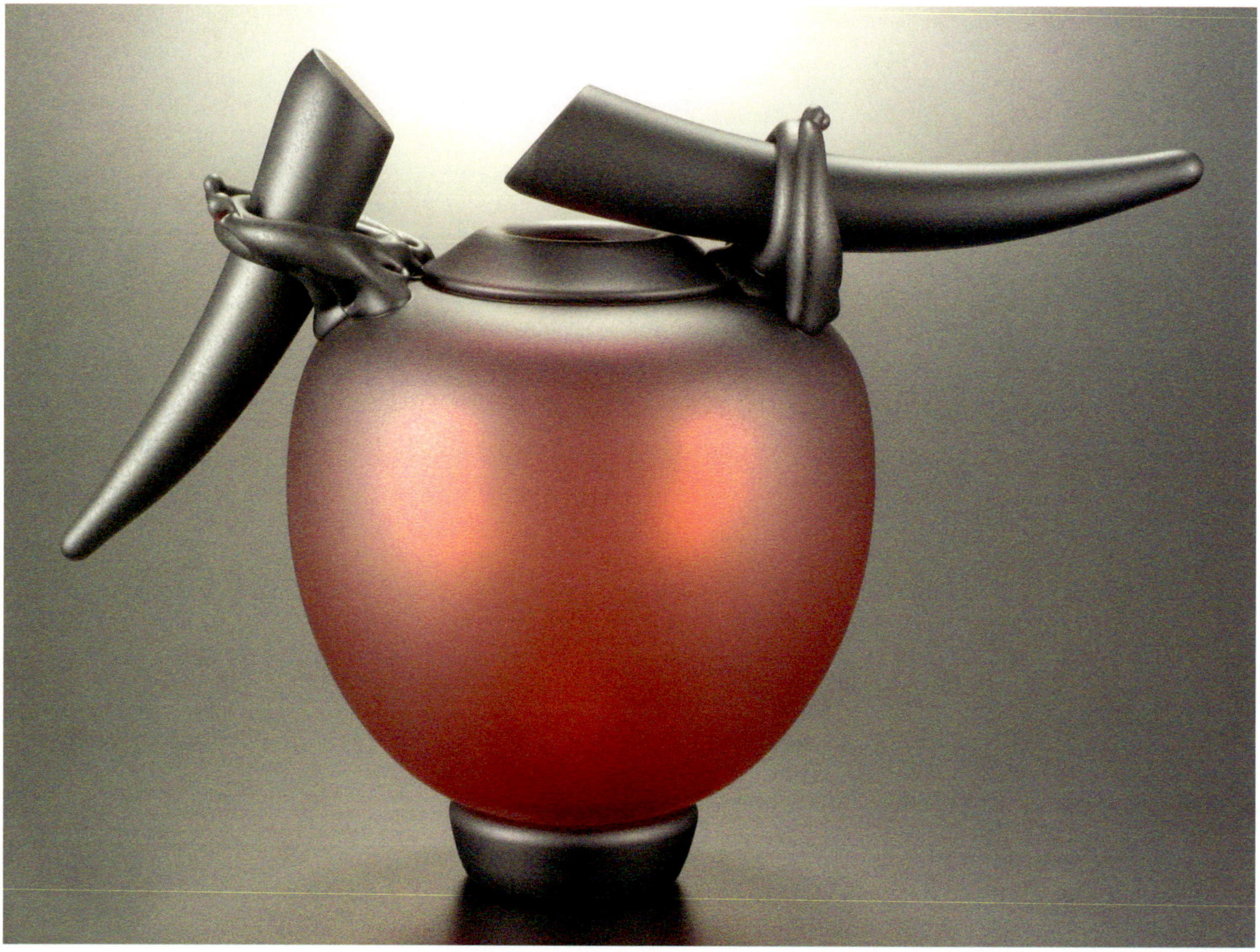

1 *Red Vase with 2 Horns*. Hand-blown glass, frosted. 7" × 4.5" × 10". 2014.

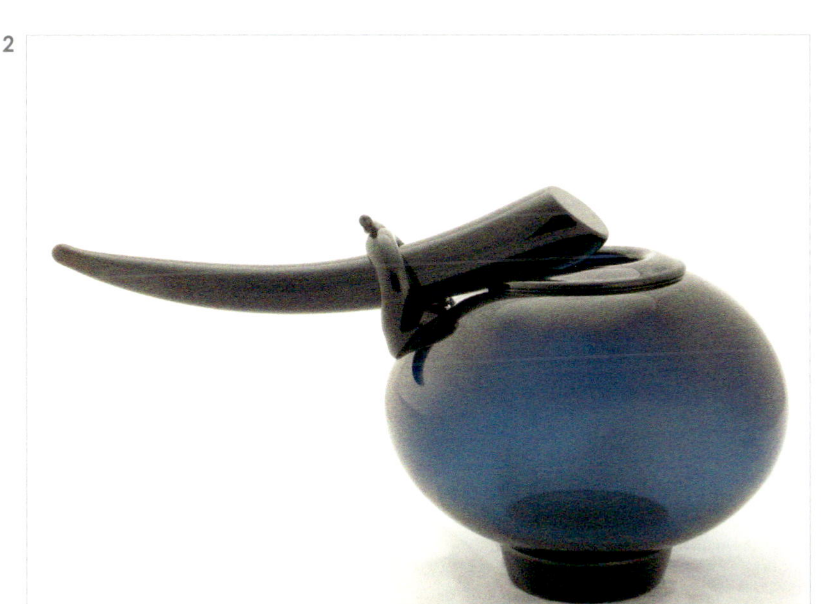

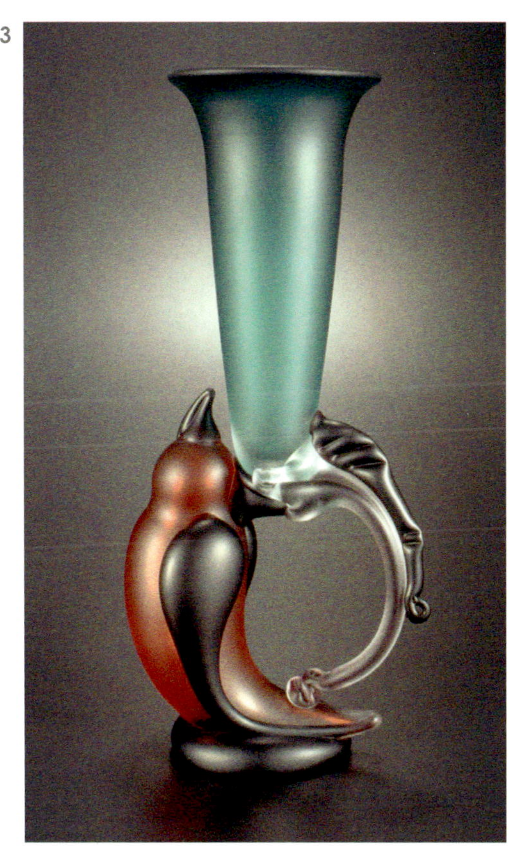

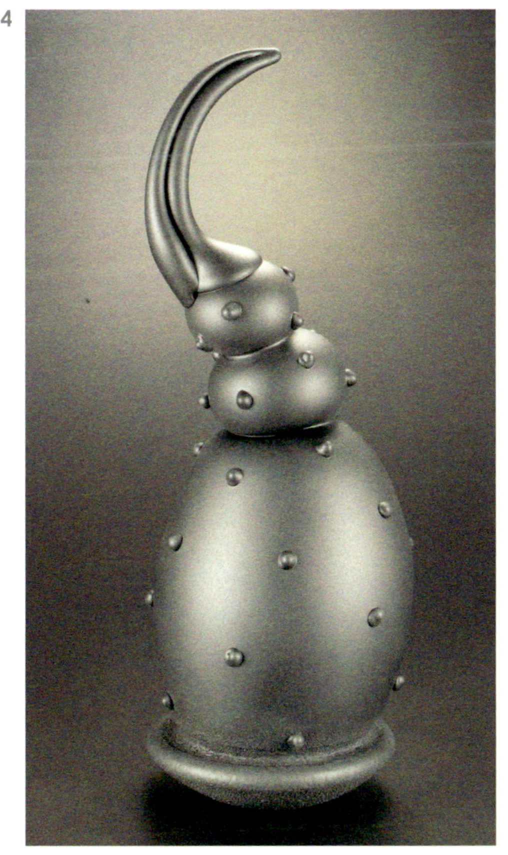

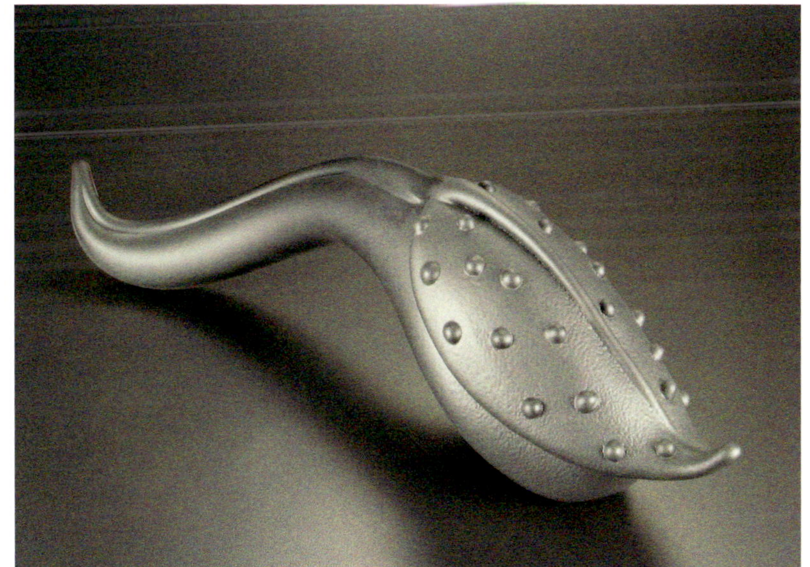

2 *Blue Vase with Horn*. Hand-blown glass. 5.5" × 5.5" × 10.5". 2014.

3 *Bird Goblet*. Hand-blown glass, frosted. 14". 2007.

4 *Black Bumpy Thing #22*. Hand-blown glass, frosted. 13" × 4" × 5". 2013.

5 *Black Bumpy Thing #25*. Hand-blown glass, frosted. 4.5" × 16". 2013.

Steve Linn

Claret, France

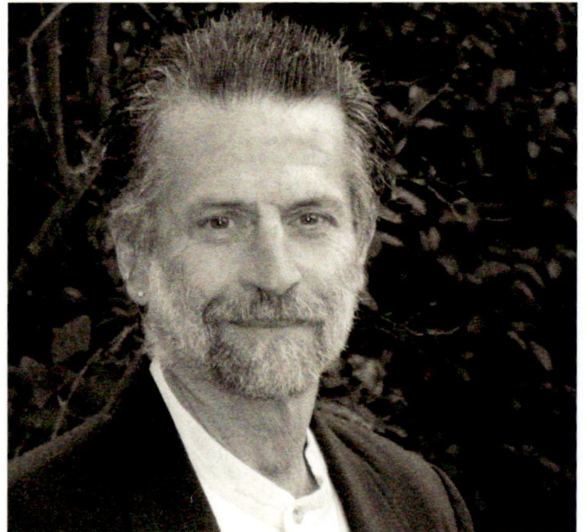

Photo: Karen Lehrer.

Over the past number of years, my work has been principally about artists and other creative people who have done wonderful things. Discovering the poetry of those lives and inventive minds in pursuit of their various disciplines has allowed me to experience in a vague, vicarious sense the different time frames and geographical locations that these characters inhabit and to imagine their intellectual process in order to enhance my own. Not losing sight of the fact that I am a sculptor, my objective is to combine these emotional experiences with the principles of design to create a well-crafted image that reveals the full depth of the character and is a work of art unto itself.

I thank my father Max Linn, my mentors, and the influence of radio dramas during my childhood for fueling my Promethean juices.

1

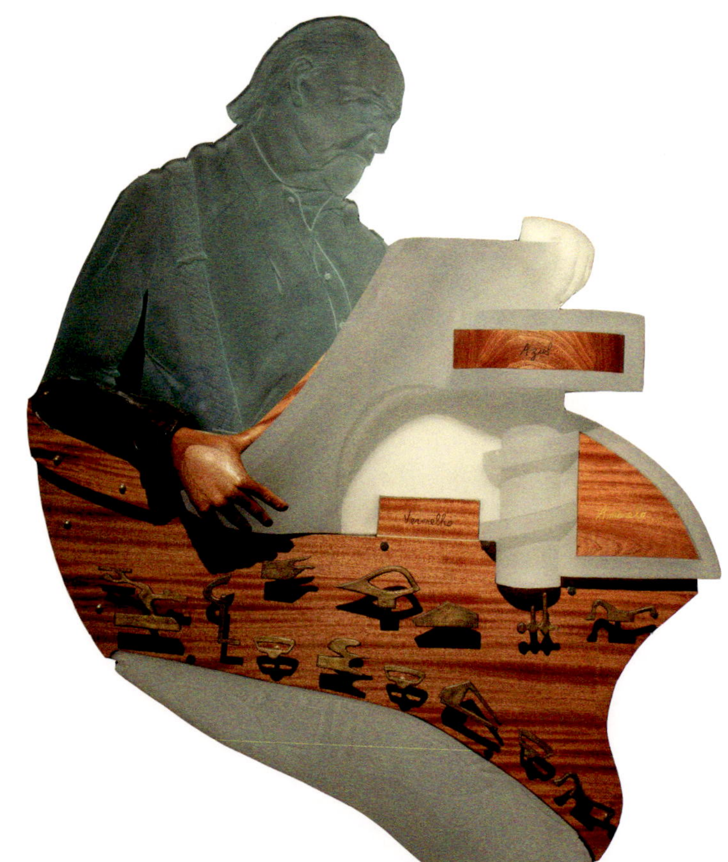

2

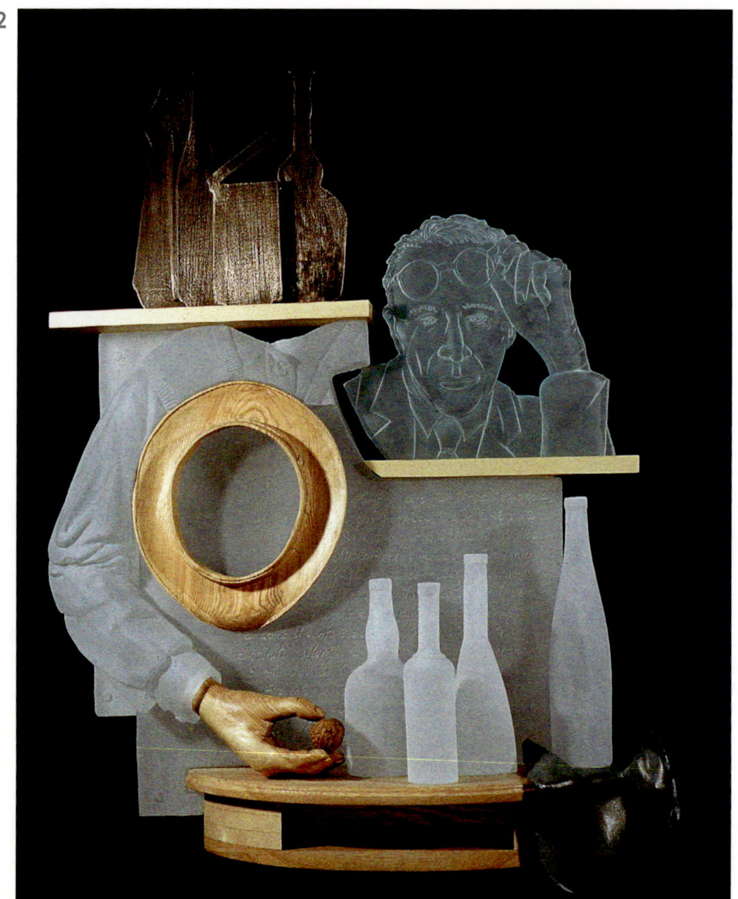

1 *To Swoop Soar and Surprise* (Oscar Neimeyer). Kiln cast glass, sandblasted carved glass, bronze, and wood. 50.39" × 8.66" × 43.30". 2013. Courtesy of Eric Hilton.

2 *L'Infinito* (Georgio Morandi). Kiln cast glass, sandblasted carved glass, bronze, and wood. 42.91" × 11.81" × 34.65". 2009.

3

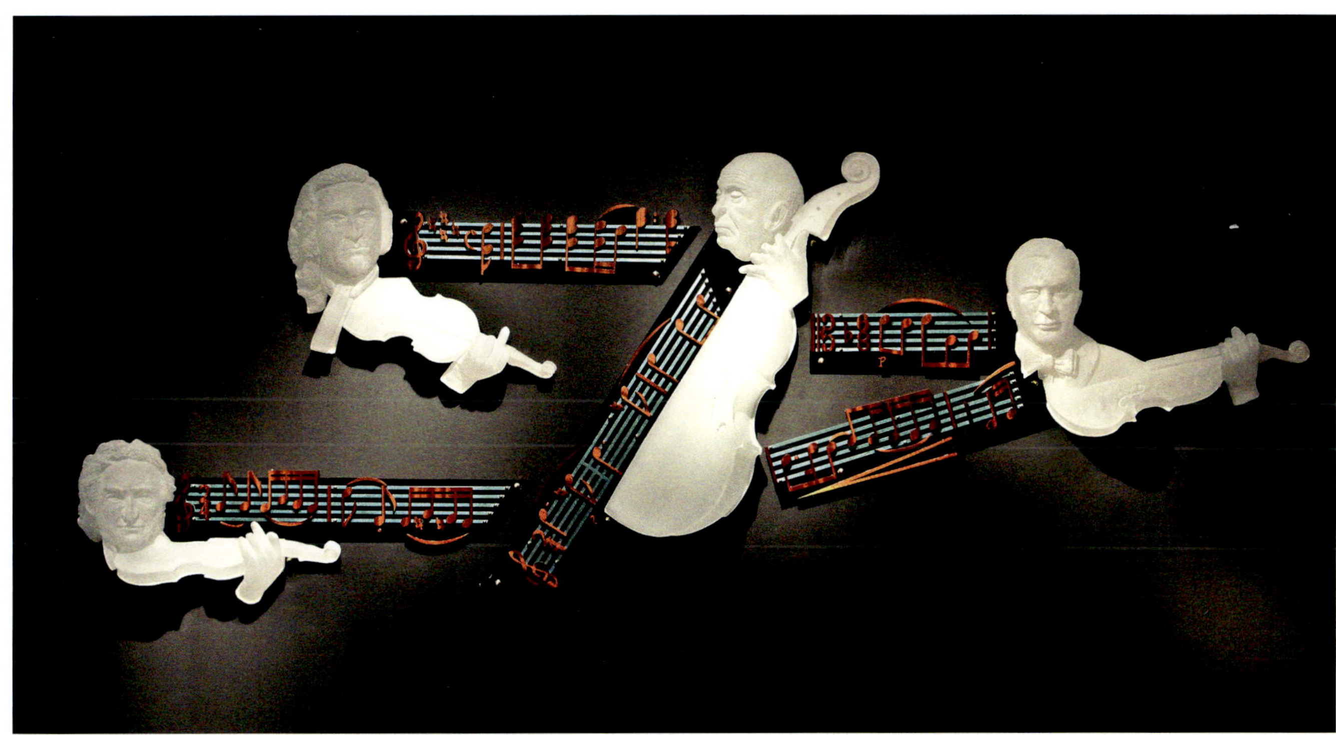

4

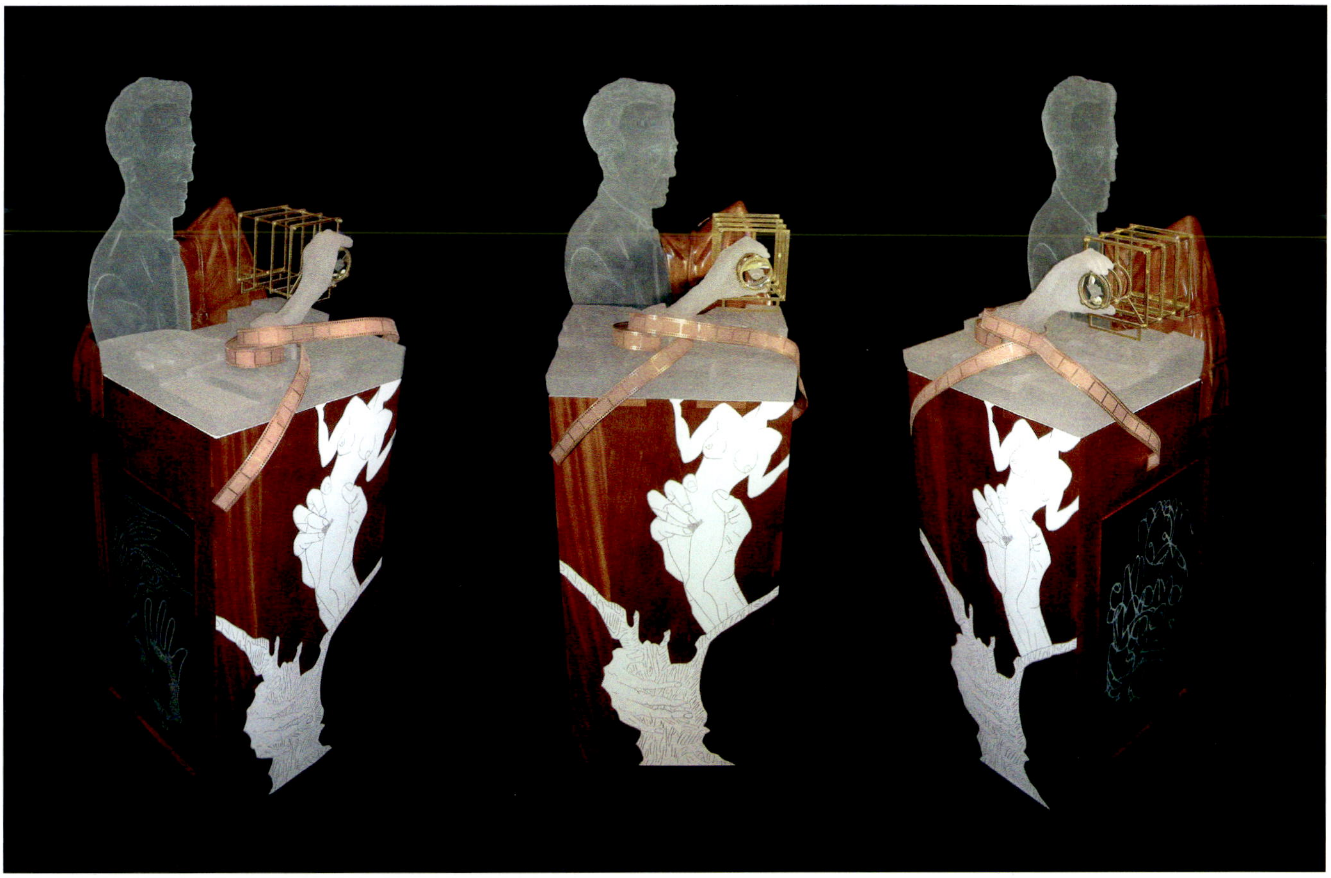

3 *Imaginary Quartet* (Vivaldi, Paganini, Casals, Hindemith). Kiln cast glass, laser cut steel, and wood. 47.24" × 6.69" × 118.11". 2014. Courtesy of Eric Hilton.

4 *Occupations and Evasions* (Man Ray). Kiln cast glass, sandblasted carved glass, brass, copper wood, and pencil on white paint. 62.2" × 21.65" × 19.69". 2010.

Marvin B. Lipofsky

Berkeley, California

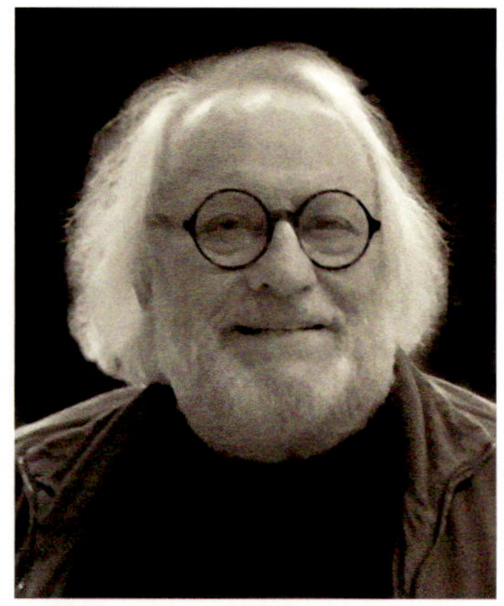

In 1962, I began my graduate studies in the sculpture department at the University of Wisconsin, Madison. My first class was in the ceramics studio. When I arrived, Harvey Littleton was encouraging the students to blow glass for the first time. Purely by chance, I became part of that first group of students.

My personal approach has been non-traditional as I developed my art in more abstract forms using the properties of glass. I accepted the sensual qualities of glass, allowing it to move as it would naturally. I experimented with sandblasting, silver mirroring, copper plating, fuming, metal inclusions; I used molds, painting, and flocking the glass to push the material to what I saw as its limits.

In 1970, I had invitations to work in European factories and studios and started working there with their teams. I decided to embrace the industrial techniques and adjust them to my aesthetic, if possible. Since then, I have been invited to work in over fifty factories and studios around the world.

My sculptures were also influenced by the surrounding seasonal colors, landscape, culture, and feelings of my environment. This has been an important element to my creative process, incorporating my experience as I traveled to such places as Finland, Italy, the Czech Republic, Russia, China, Hungary, Australia, Japan, and across the United States. I always work as part of the blowing team, setting up color and handling molds. I then finish it in my Berkeley studio, doing the cold working by myself.

Intuition, discovery, chance, trial and error, and a passion for the medium are the elements that have driven my life in glass, alongside the international fellowship that developed over the past fifty-three years.

1

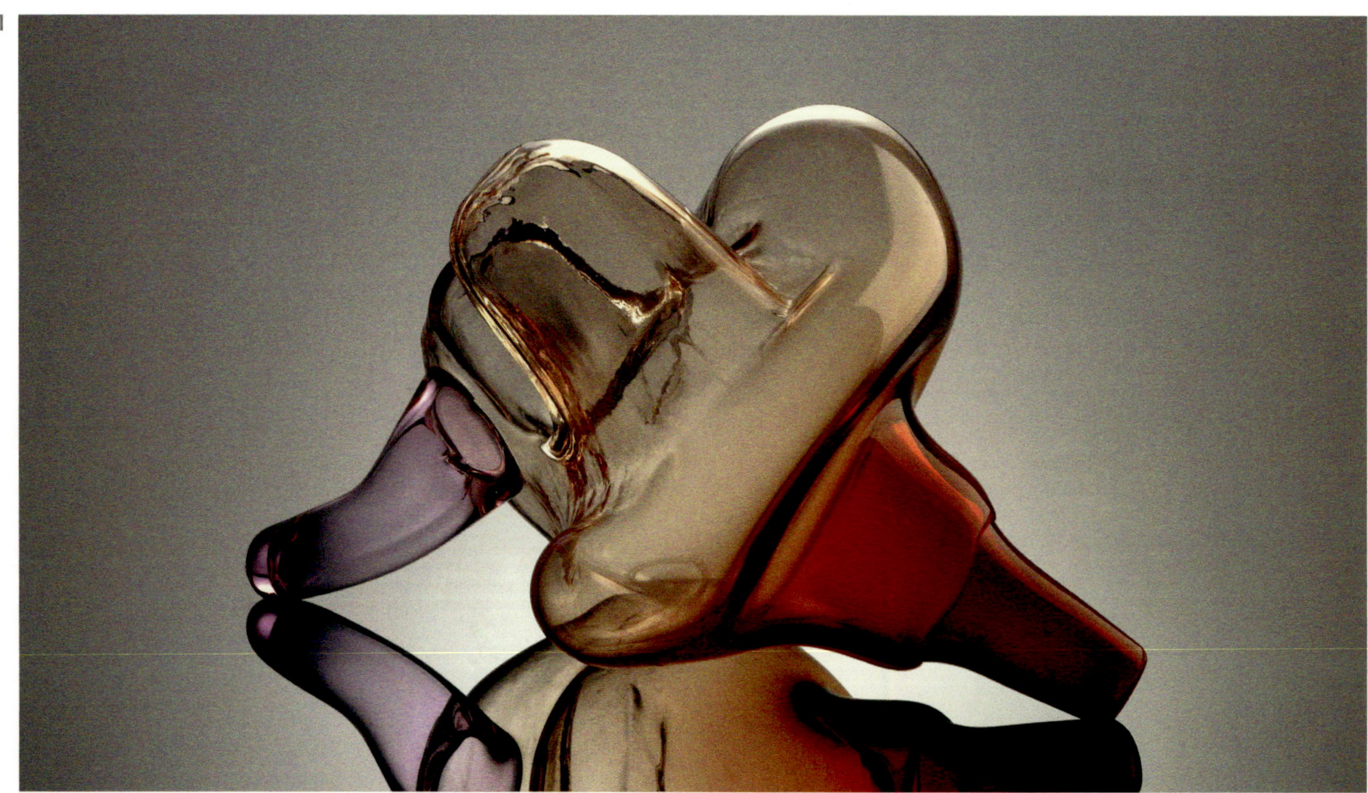

2

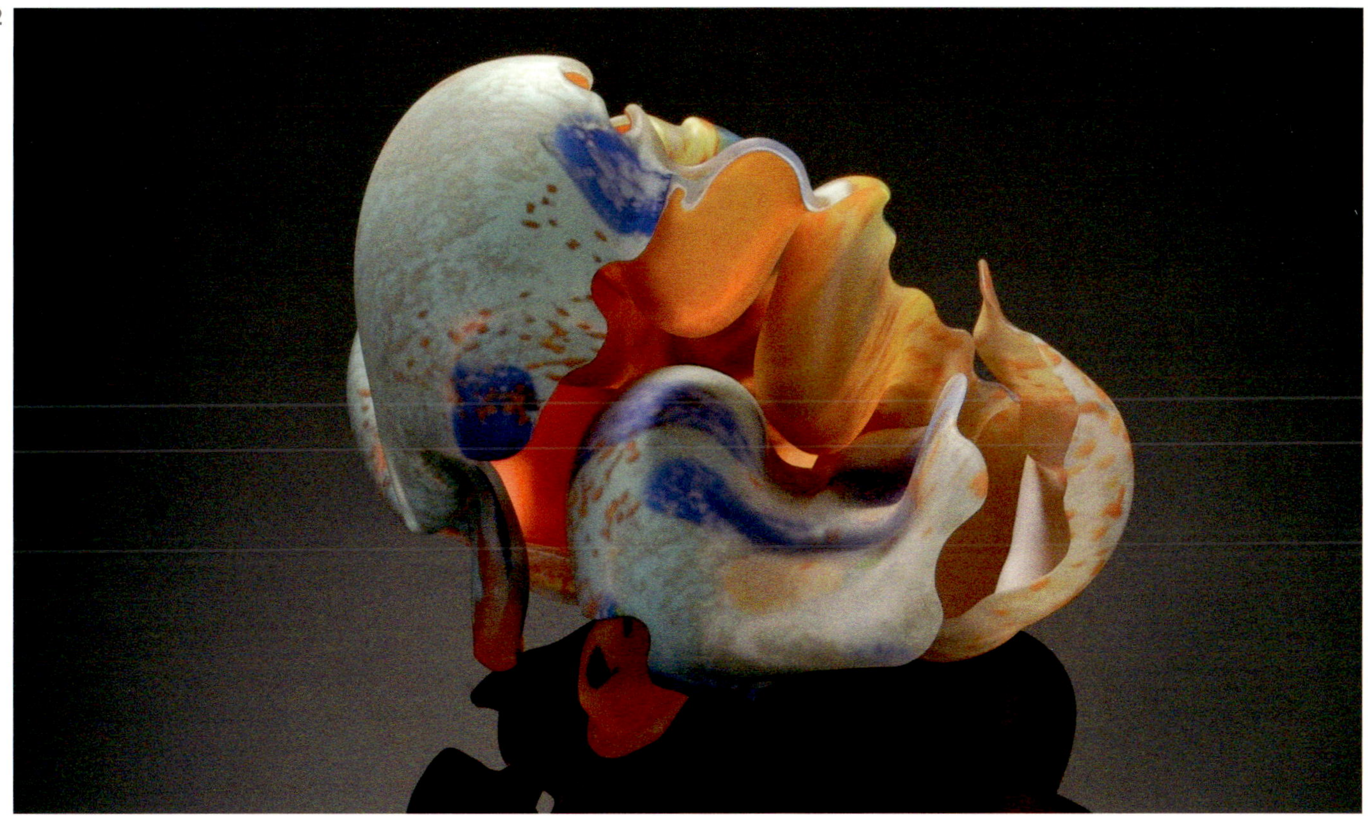

3

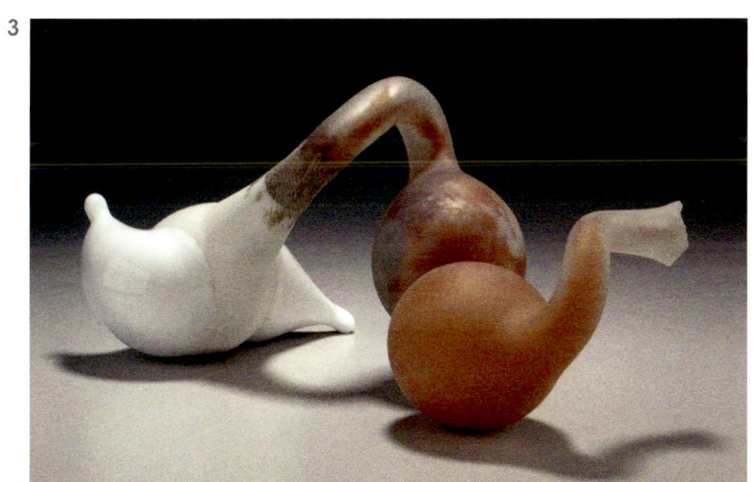

4

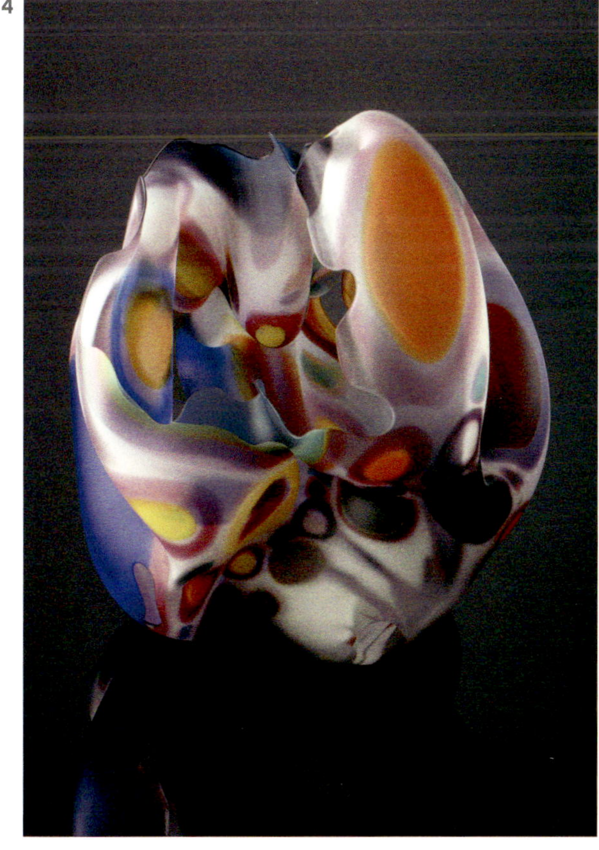

1 *Suomi-Finland Series 1970 #1*. Blown at Nuutajarvi Factory, Finland, with help from Jaakko Niemi. 11" × 19" × 11". 1970. Courtesy of M. Lee Fatherree, Oakland, CA.

2 *Russian Group 2006–7 #4*. Blown at the First International Symposium of Art Glass, Gus-Khrustalny, Vladimir Region, Russia with help from Valdimir Zakharov and Boris Arbusov. 11.5" × 13.5" × 11.5". 2007. Courtesy of M. Lee Fatherree, Oakland, CA.

3 *Small California Loop Series #7*. Blown at UC Berkeley. 8.5" × 18" × 9". 1978. Courtesy of M. Lee Fatherree, Oakland, CA.

4 *Kentucky Series 2000-01 #8*. Blown at Centre College, Centre College, Danville, Kentucky, with help from Steve Powell, Brooke, Paul, Brent, and students. 16" × 17" × 17". 2001. Courtesy of M. Lee Fatherree, Oakland, CA.

John & Kate Littleton Vogel

Bakersville, North Carolina

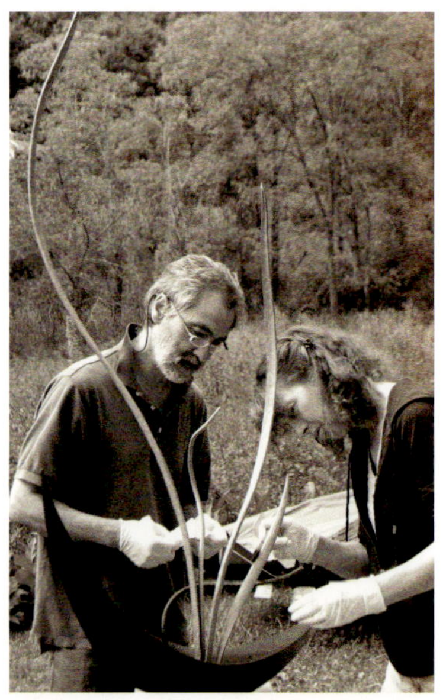

When people see something beautiful, why does it resonate with them? What are they responding to? Our collaboration is grounded in the many discussions that we have about questions like this and about our connection to the world. In our latest pieces, we have been creating work that touches the place of quiet, still, and awe that we feel when we are confronted with the beauty of nature.

Meditation in Pink and Yellow grew out of the *What Do We Hold?* series, where we looked at what is precious to us. The flower was built from wax one petal at a time. This allowed us to slow down and be part of the process of creation; there, we entered a dream world, and a thing of solitude and beauty emerged.

Our work is a result of collaboration, changed from what either one of us would make without the other. We discuss all the formal elements: scale, proportion, line, negative and positive space, and color. Yet in the end, although these things play a part in what we create and what we find beautiful, beauty is not an intellectual exercise. We connect with it on a much deeper emotional level, and it is that place we strive to reach.

1

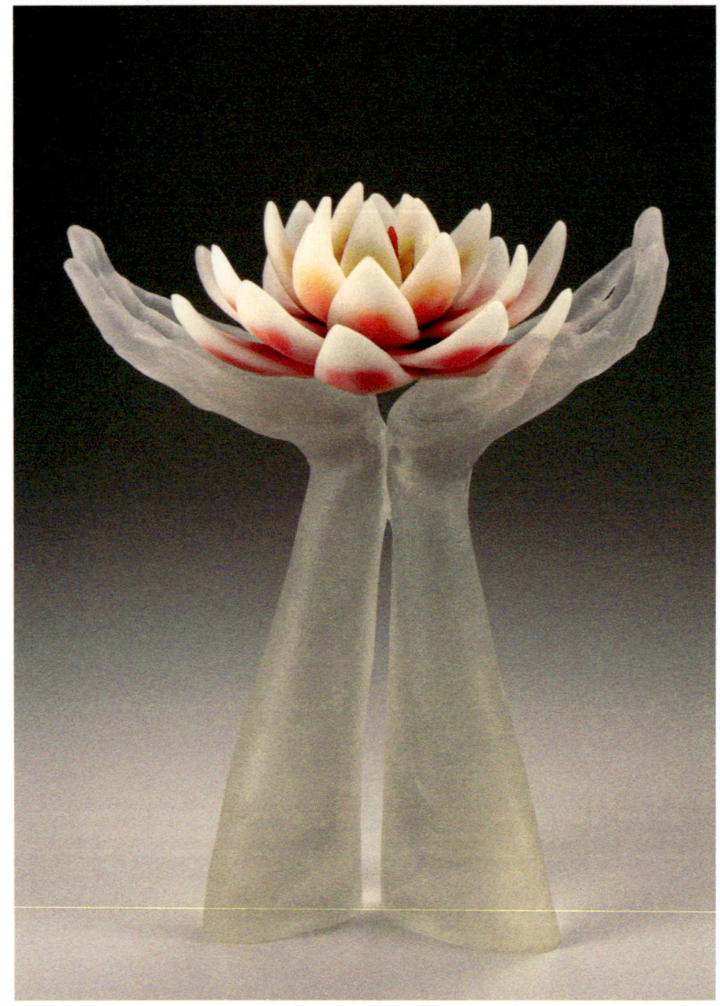

2

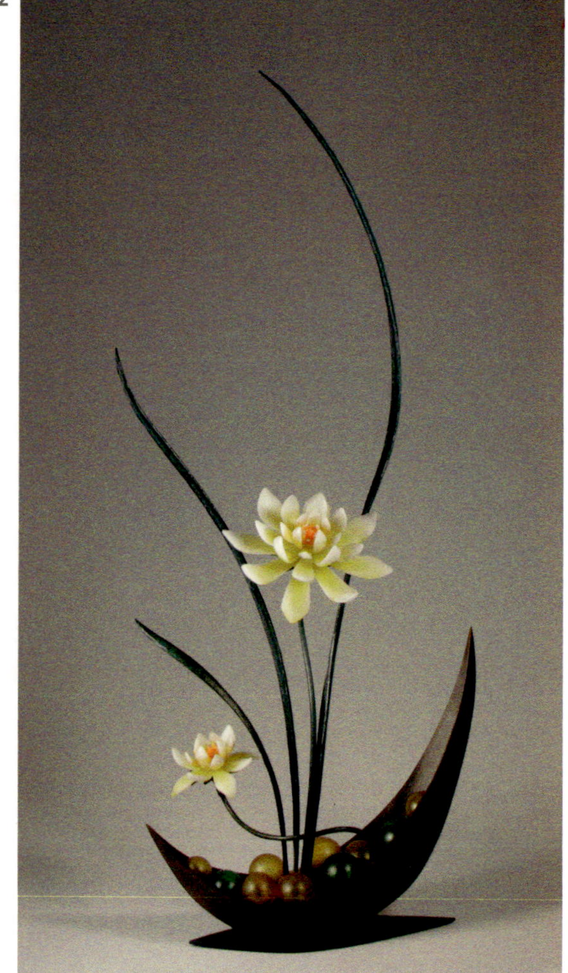

3

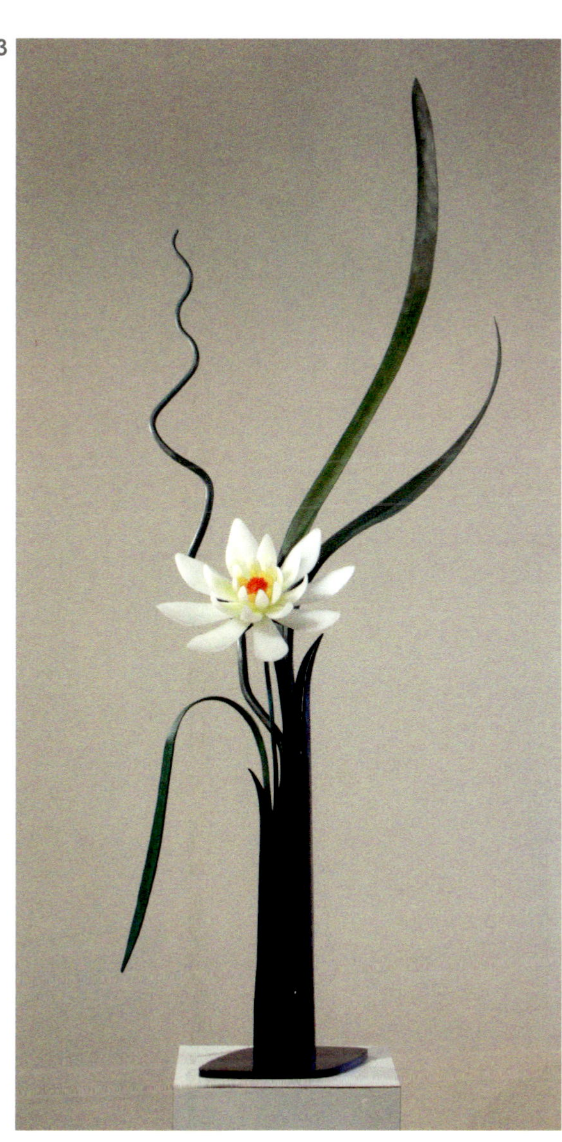

1 *Meditation in Pink and Yellow*. Cast glass. 14" × 7.5" × 10.75". 2013.

2 *Ikebana Inspiration*. Glass and steel. 53.5" × 21.75". 2013.

3 *Ikebana Inspired*. Cast glass and steel. 60" × 21.5" × 25". 2014.

4 *Succulent Flower*. Cast glass. 9.25" × 8.25" × 14.5". 2014.

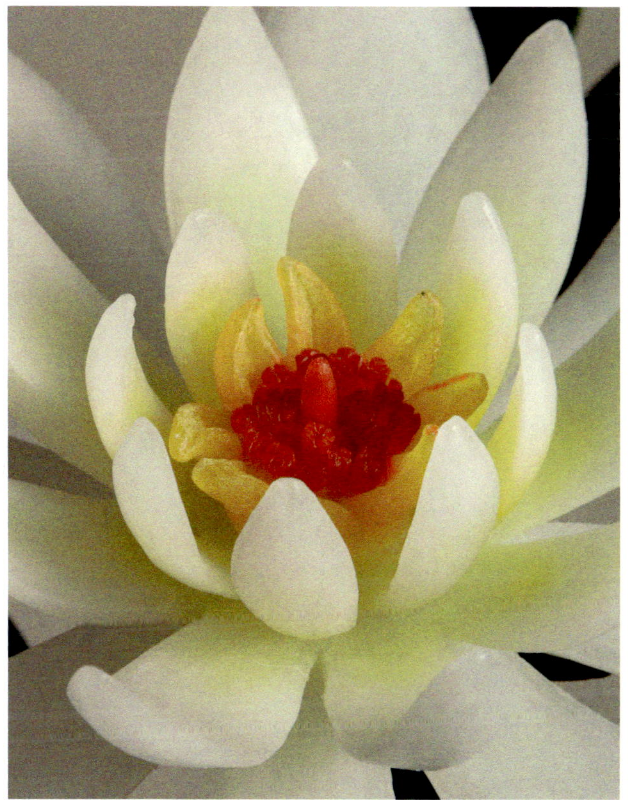

4

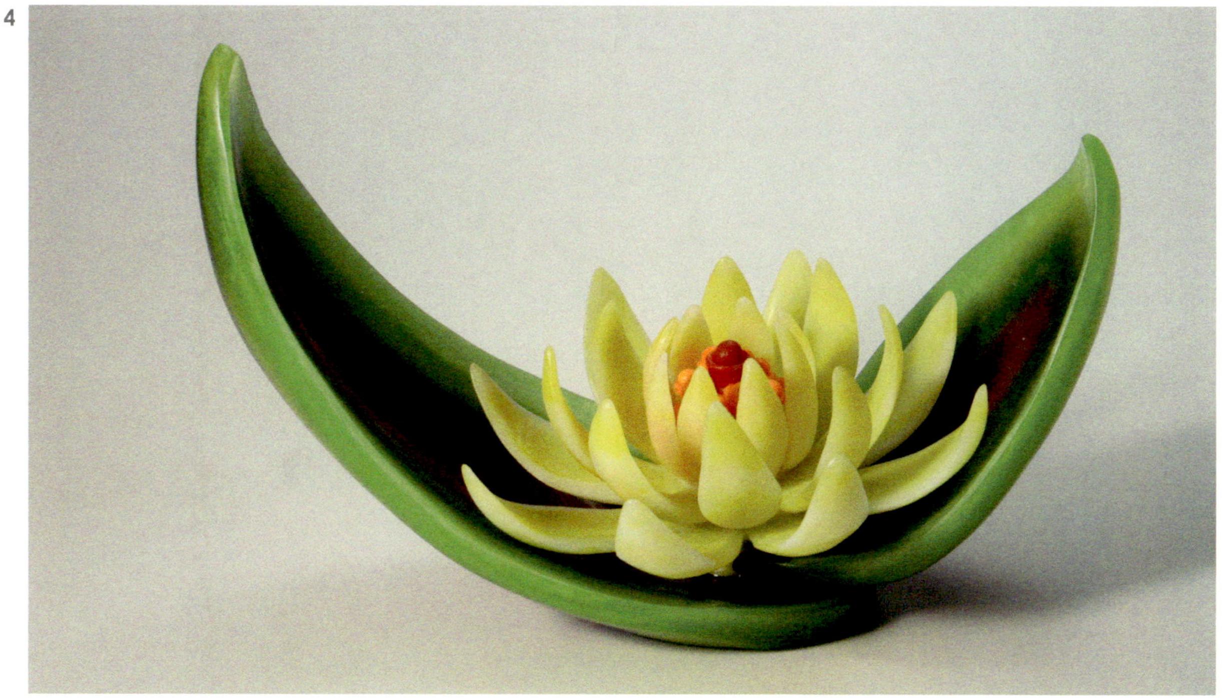

Carmen Lozar

Normal, Illinois

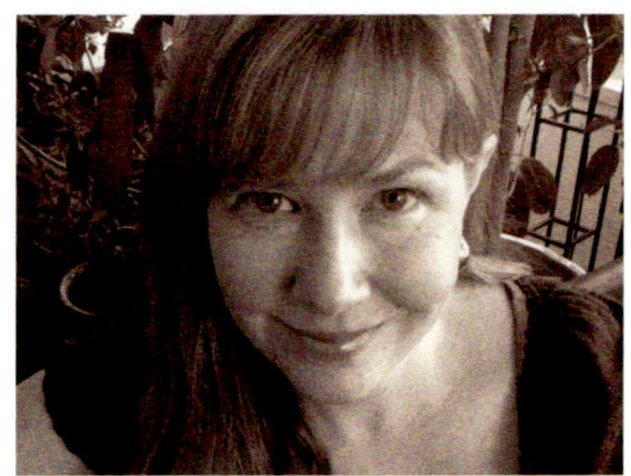

My pieces follow the trail of daily life and seek to transform the mundane into the fantastic. Each piece is an expansion on a reality, a tall tale of what might have started as an everyday interaction. I embrace the absurd and extraordinary, provoking the imagination into wakefulness.

1

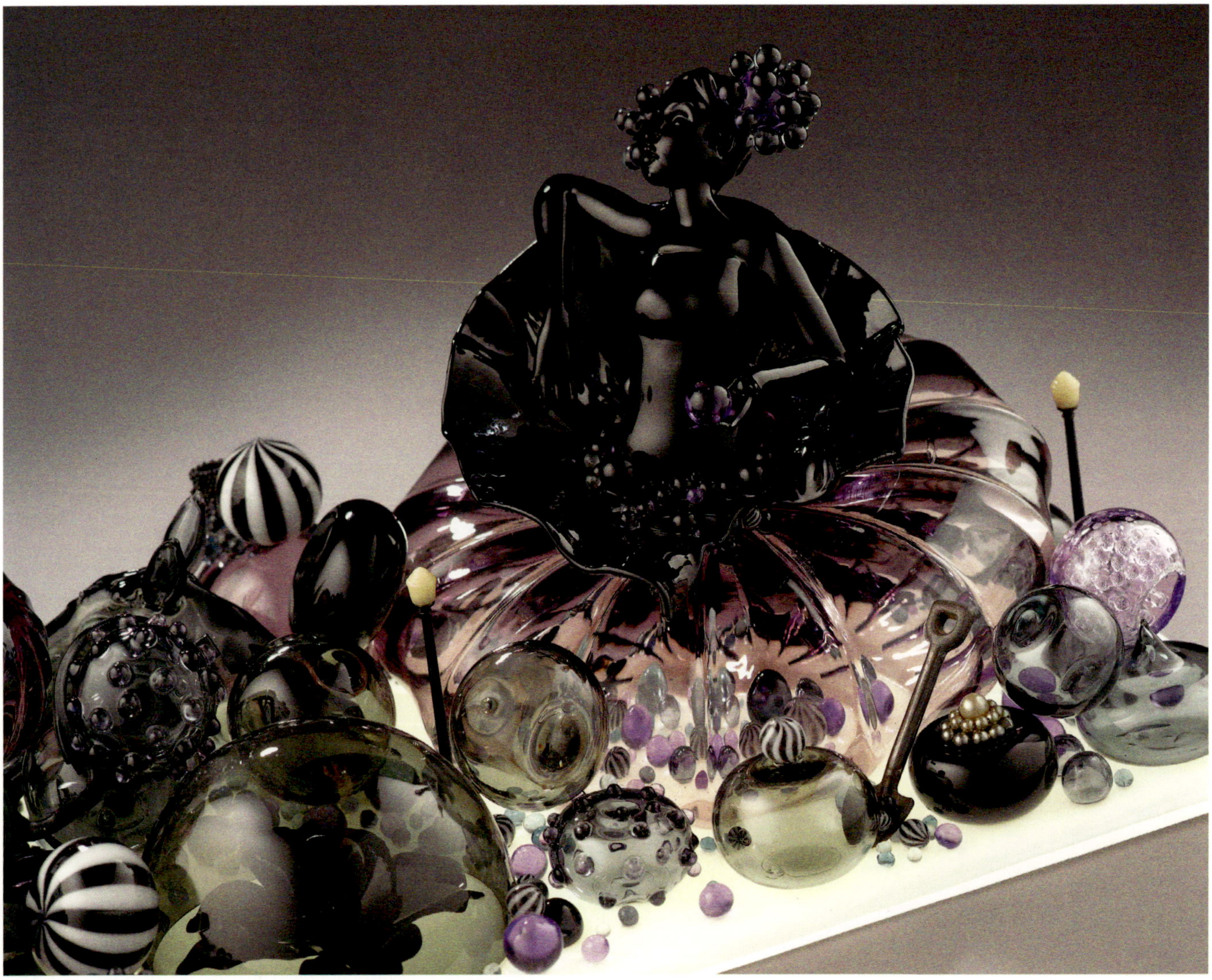

1 *Night*. Flameworked, blown, fused glass, and found objects. 8" × 16" × 9.5". 2013. Courtesy of Rick Kessinger Studio.

2

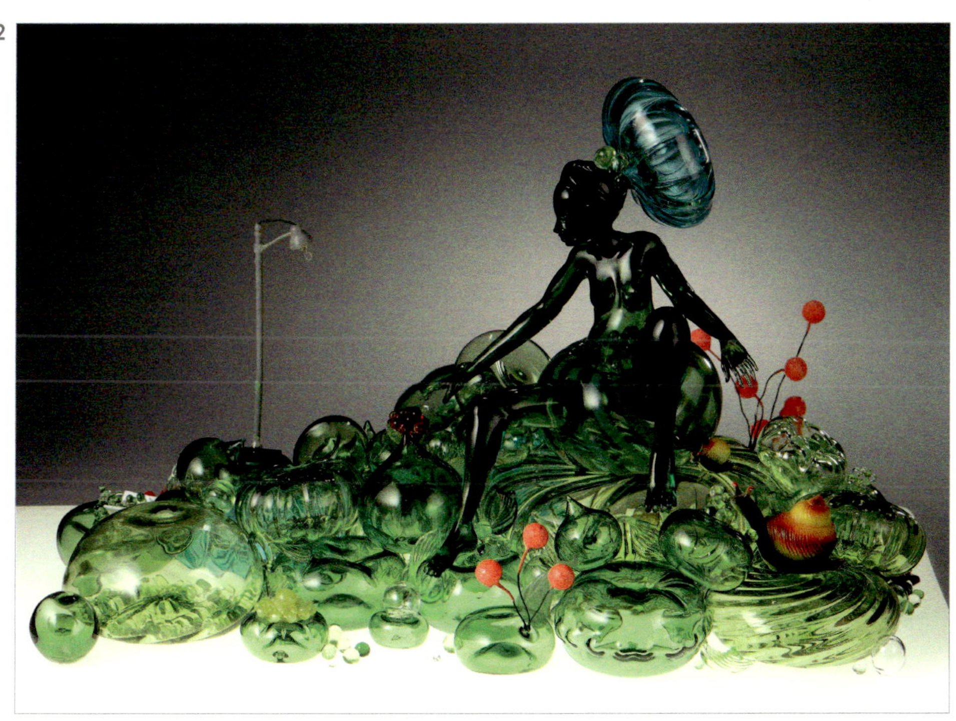

3

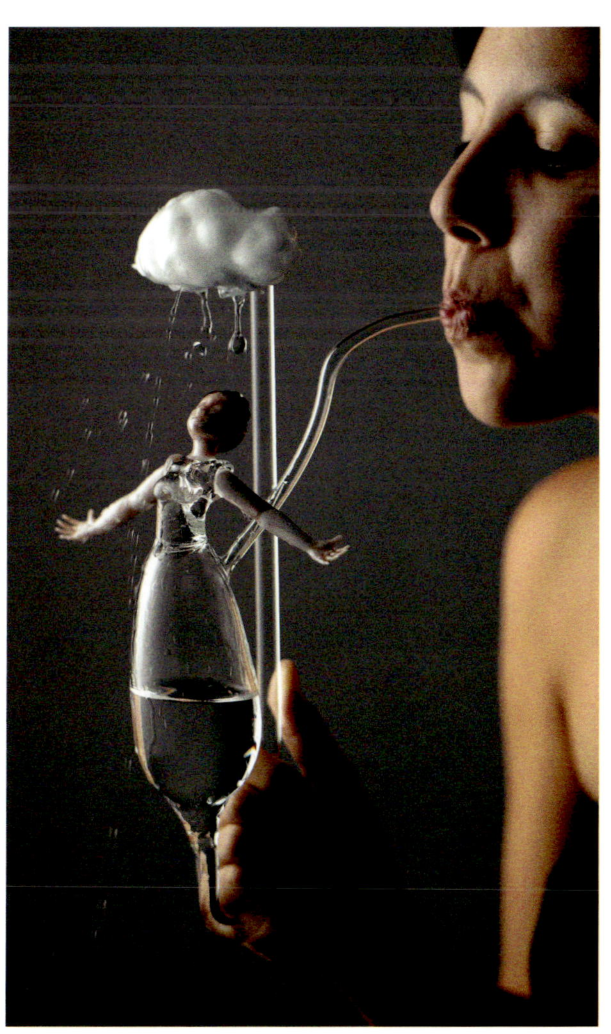

4

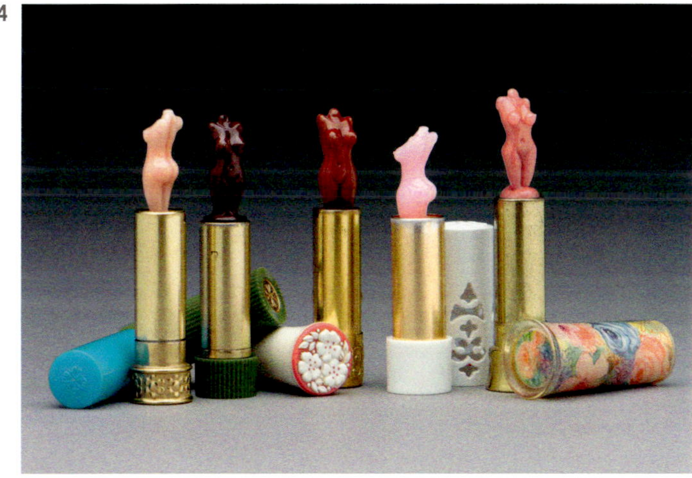

5

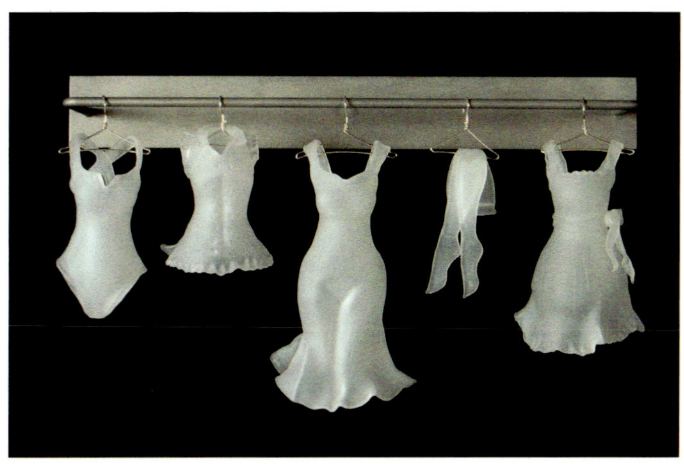

2 *Summer*. Flameworked, blown, fused glass, and found objects. 12" × 12" × 19". 2013. Courtesy of Rick Kessinger Studio.

3 *Shower*. Flameworked glass and water. 19" × 6" × 6". 2011. Courtesy of Rick Kessinger Studio.

4 *Lipsticks*. Flameworked glass and vintage cases. 3.5". 2012. Courtesy of Rick Kessinger Studio.

5 *Dress Set*. Flameworked glass and metal. 7.5" × 4" × 12". 2007. Courtesy of Victoria's Photographics.

Tanya Lyons

Montreal, Quebec, Canada

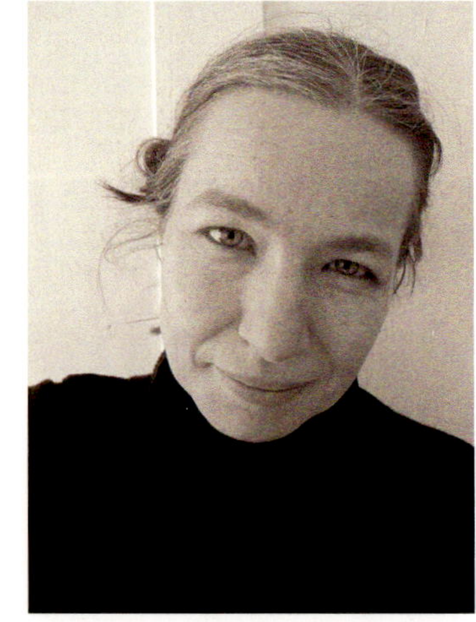

I have always been a gatherer, collecting objects, moments, and memories. As I move through life, I take traces with me, from the places I walk and the people I meet. When I unexpectedly entered into glass, I discovered a material that had a life of its own, rich with qualities and full of endless possibilities to reflect life. I fell in love with clear glass and the strength it held.

I started making life-size glass dresses to express the idea of changing how you feel as simply as changing your clothes. They look at how our clothing can be a shell or a shield, drawing in or pushing away those who surround us. As a continuation in this concept and theme of clothing, I decided to reflect back on my time living in Japan, and made metal mesh and glass kimonos that hang on the wall. The kimono has been worn traditionally for a long time, giving a great history and tradition to the form as well as making it a perfect canvas to express thoughts and conceptual landscapes.

I have studied glass in Canada, Finland, and Japan.

1

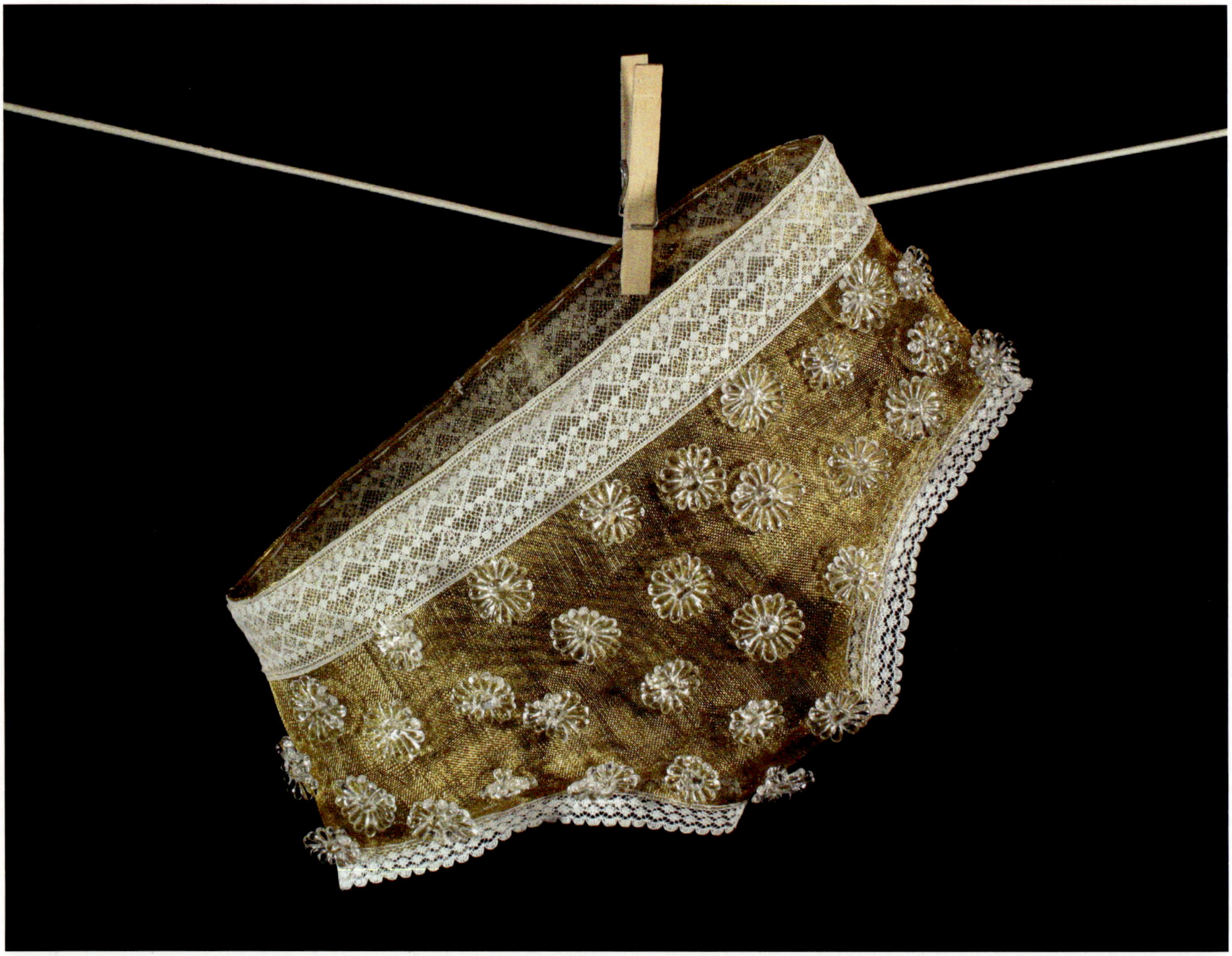

2

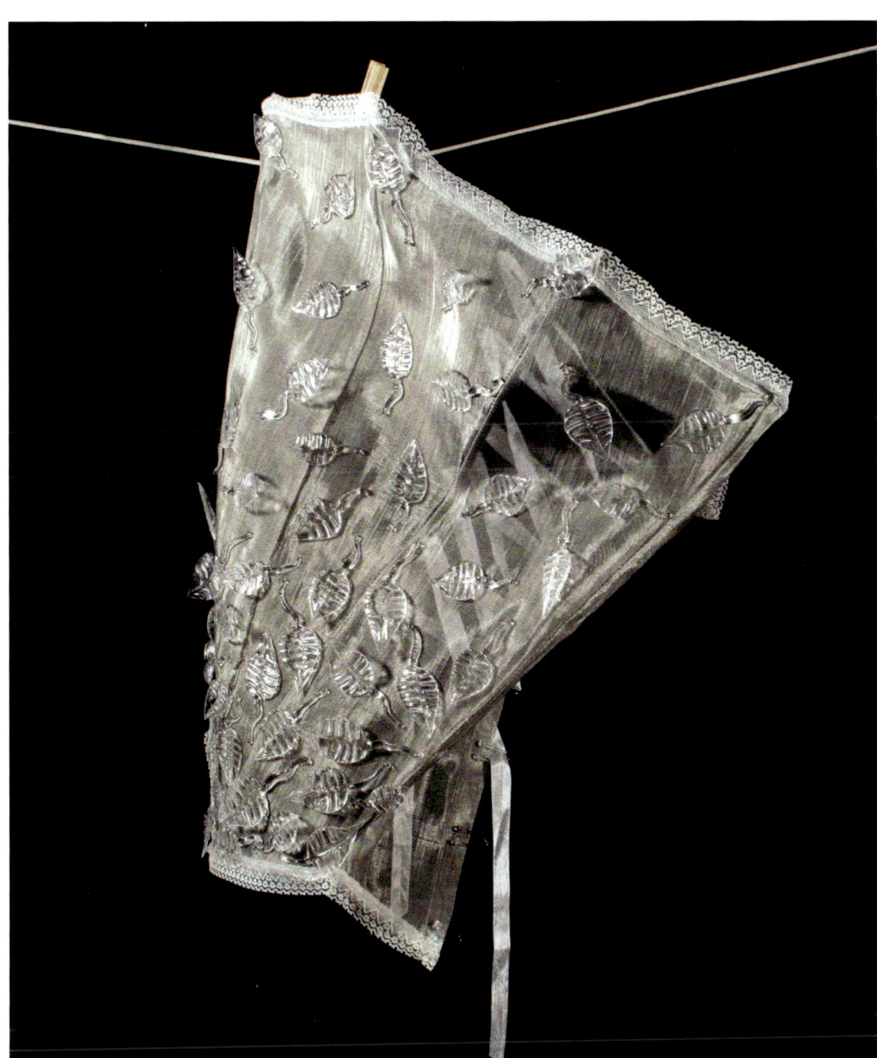

3

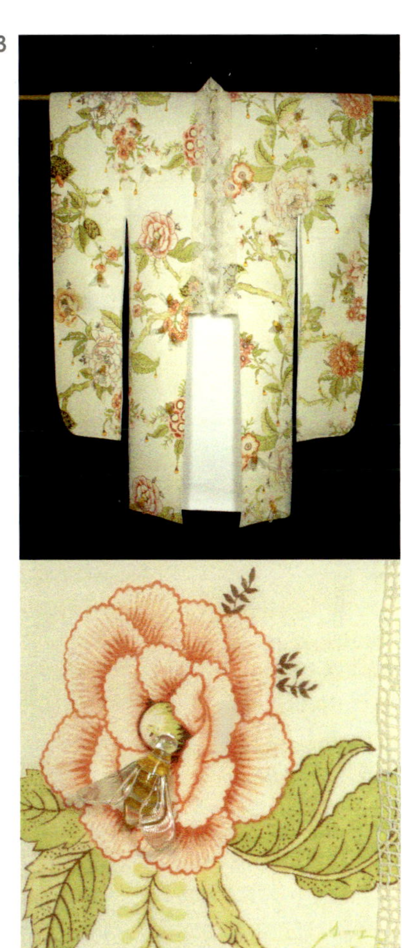

1 *Daisy Panties*. Flameworked glass, brass mesh, and vintage lace. 6" × 3" × 12.5". 2014. Courtesy of Steven Wild.

2 *Camouflage*. Flameworked glass, stainless mesh, and textiles.16" × 5" × 10". 2014. Courtesy of Steven Wild.

3 *Survival*. Flameworked glass, pillowcase, lace, and paper. 42" × 4" × 32". 2014.

4 *Sasayaki* (whisper). Flameworked glass, stainless mesh, and lace with bamboo. 51.5" × 4" × 51.5". 2011.

4

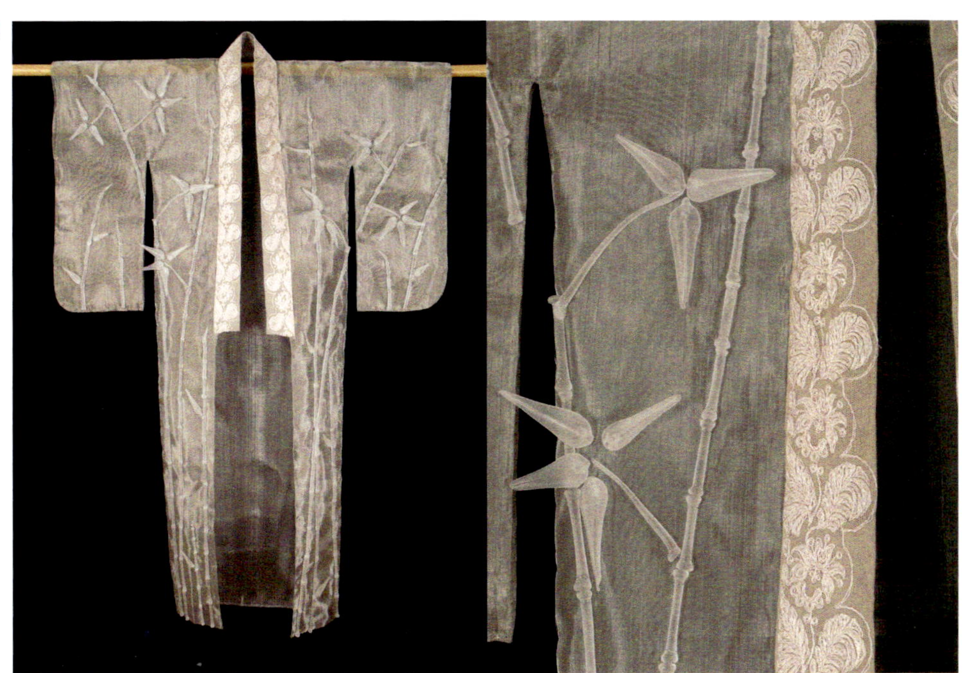

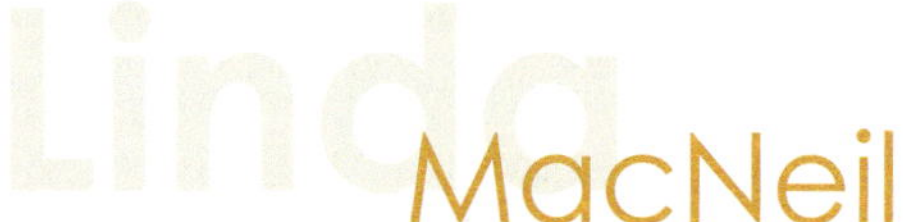

Linda MacNeil

Kensington, New Hampshire

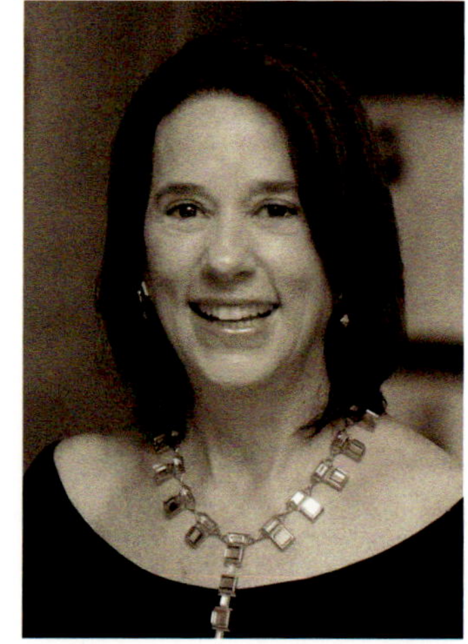

Courtesy of Robert Braunfeld www.cameraeye.smugmug.com.

In these times of glittering mass-produced jewelry, abundant gold and diamond replicas of traditional design in jewelry stores presented in hundreds of ways to everyone everywhere, I am compelled to turn in a different direction and create unique works. The process of design that requires skill and emphasizes quality in the finished works attracts me most, and I strive to develop my art in ways similar to great masters of the past. Even as I intend to be myself and remain aware of contemporary art and the highly developed world we live in, there are important lessons and examples for me in history.

Recently, I spent time at the State Hermitage Museum in St. Petersburg, Russia. I was given a tour of works made with gold, precious stones, and a variety of luxurious materials in combination for ceremonial and religious purposes or for royal indulgence. Many visitors to the museum were also enamored of these works, and I was humbled by the accomplishments of those who created the masterpieces on view. This experience charged me to return to my studio and improve on my own work with renewed energy. Perhaps some of the techniques they employed are now lost to history, but there are elements of their ambitious and meticulous processes that have influenced my thinking.

1 *Mesh Necklace*. Acid polished light blue and clear glass. White diamonds. Polished 14k white gold. 2.5" × 2.375" × 0.5". 2013. Courtesy of © Bill Truslow www.truslowphoto.com.

2 *Sublime*. Acid-polished transparent red, aqua, and yellow mirrored glass. Polished 18k gold with granulation. 3.75" × 2" × 0.5". Brooch Series 2013. Courtesy of © Bill Truslow www.truslowphoto.com.

3 *Ruby Bliss*. Acid-polished aqua pate de verre and red glass. Polished cream and black vitrolite. 24k gold-plated brass. Brooch: 2.5" × 1.25" × 0.625". Floral Necklace 2004. Courtesy of © Bill Truslow www.truslowphoto.com.

4 *Remarkable*. Acid-polished transparent cobalt blue and red/orange mirrored glass. Polished ivory and black vitrolite glass. 14k rhodium-plated white gold. 4" × 2" × 0.75". Brooch Series 2013. Courtesy of © Bill Truslow www.truslowphoto.com.

5 *Neck Collar*. Acid-polished clear, blue transparent glass, chartreuse and yellow transparent mirrored glass, polished yellow, black and ivory vitrolite glass, gold plated. Collar: 5.5" diameter. Pendant: 4.25" × 3.75". 2013. Courtesy of © Bill Truslow www.truslowphoto.com.

1

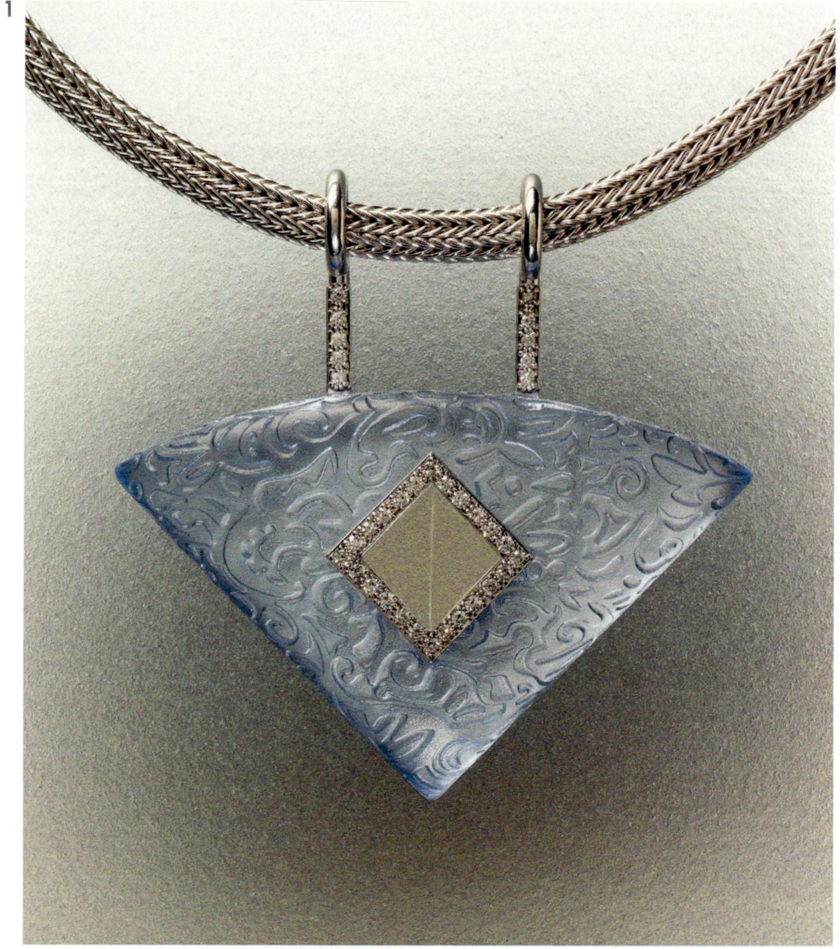

2

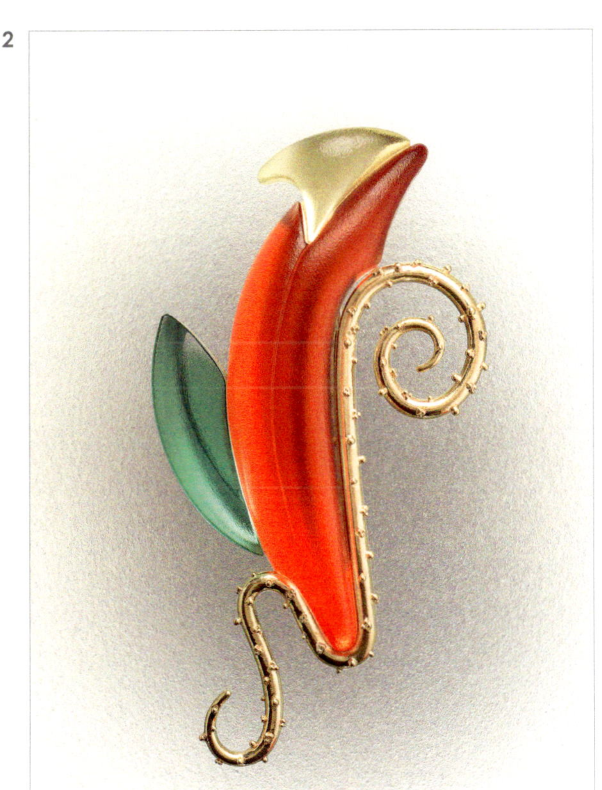

4

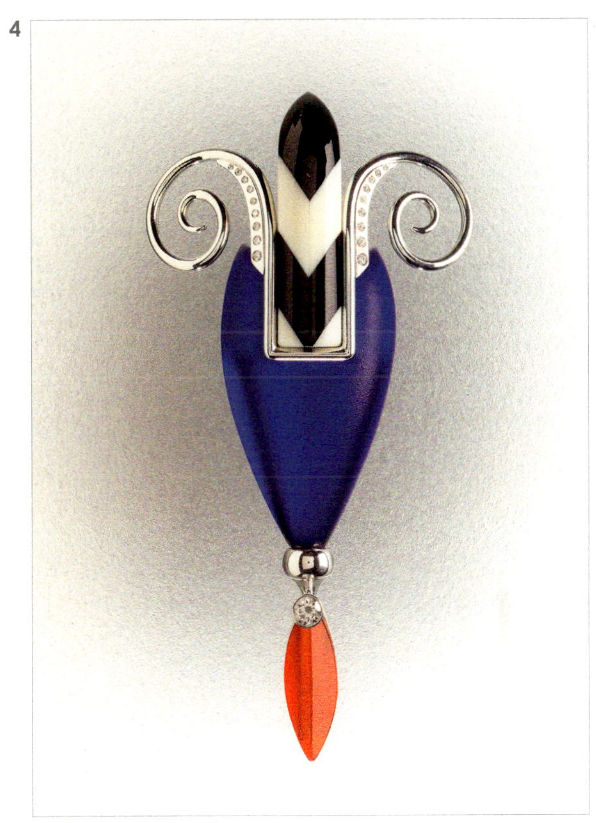

3

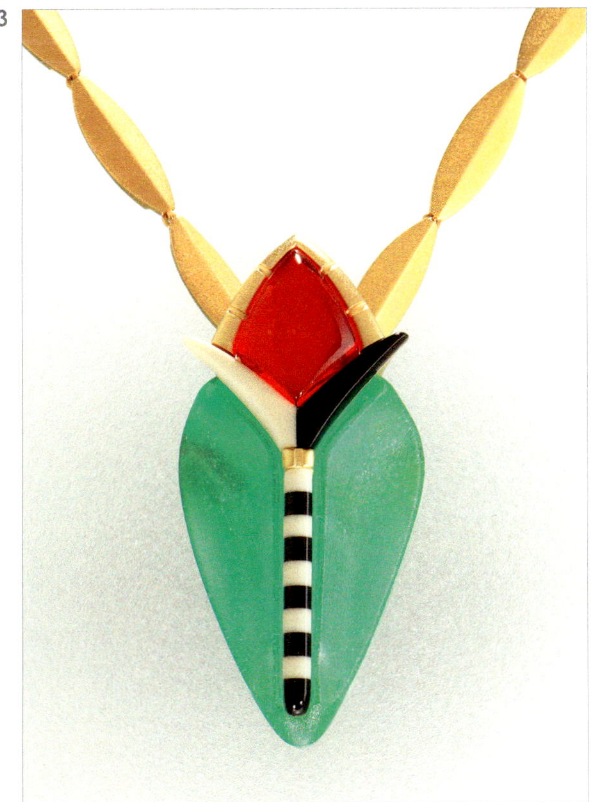

5

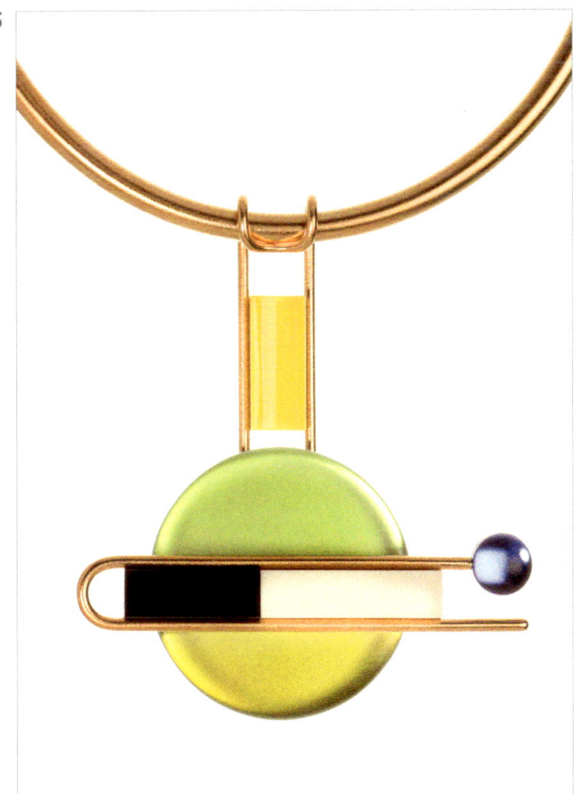

Caroline Madden

Carrick-on-Shannon, County Leitrim, Ireland

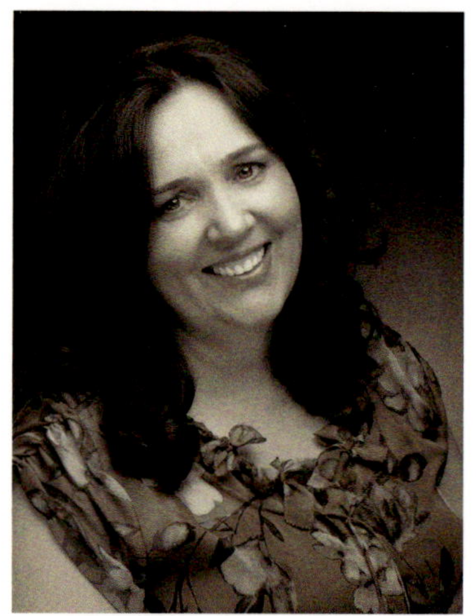

Courtesy of Trendphotography.ie.

The focus of my research is to understand how human perception is constructed and sustained. I use symbolic language to represent emotional sensations for which I can find no rational linguistic expression. My completed works range from large site-specific installations to limited editions.

The site-specific project *Cycles* is a confluence of concepts relating to the physical and historical landscape of the Sculpture Parklands, at Lough Boora. The underlying theme of *Cycles* is man's relationship to the land, as one of sovereignty, rather than displacement and tenancy. *Shattered Cycles* is one in a body of work created through an exploration of the construct of conventional love. *Lost in Translation* is an allegorical work referencing purity, majesty, and transformation, drawn from the Irish legend of the Children of Lir.

1

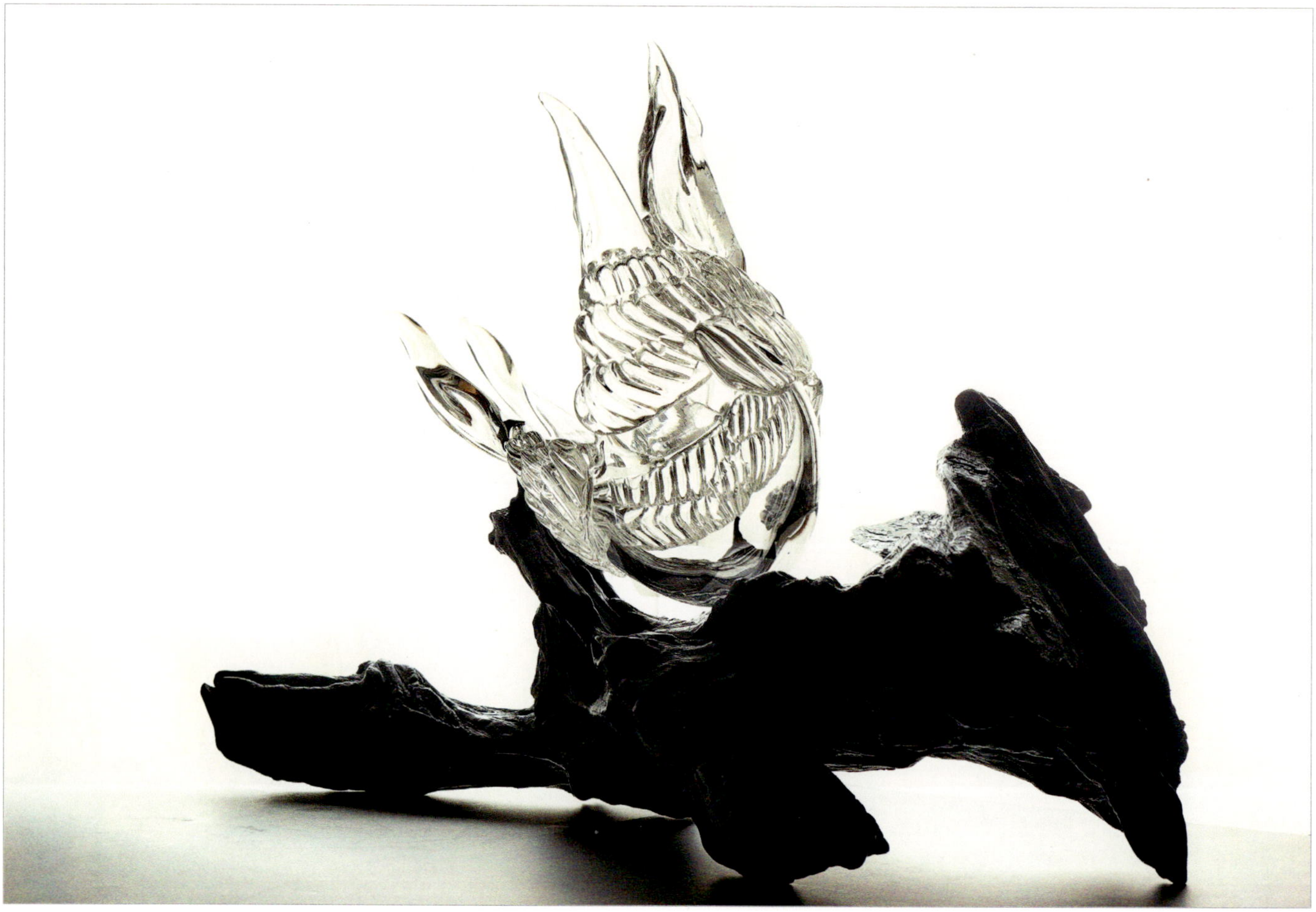

1 *Fallen II*. Blown and solid worked glass on bog oak. 28" × 36" × 24". 2011. Courtesy of Philip Lauterbach.

2

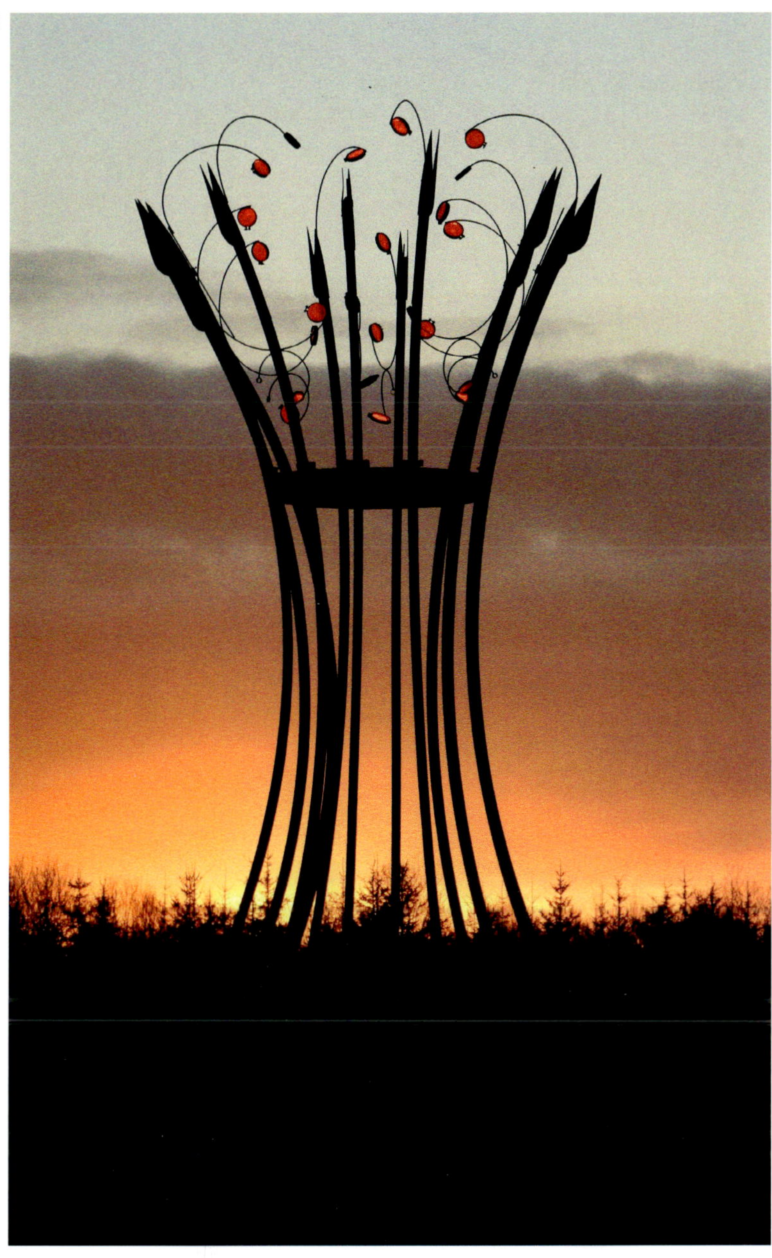

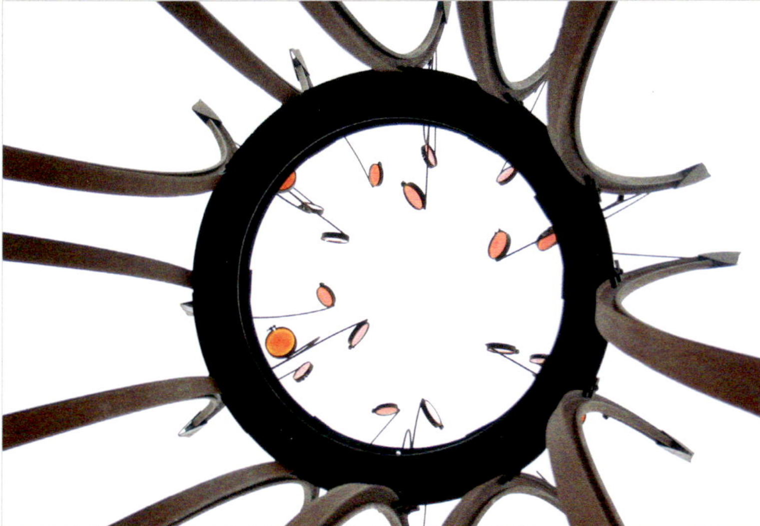

3

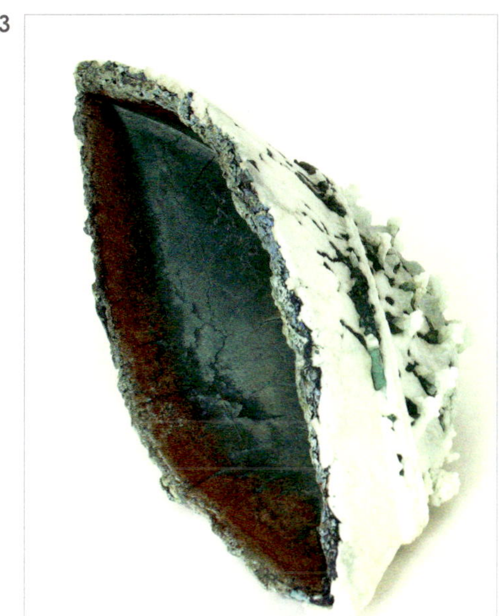

4

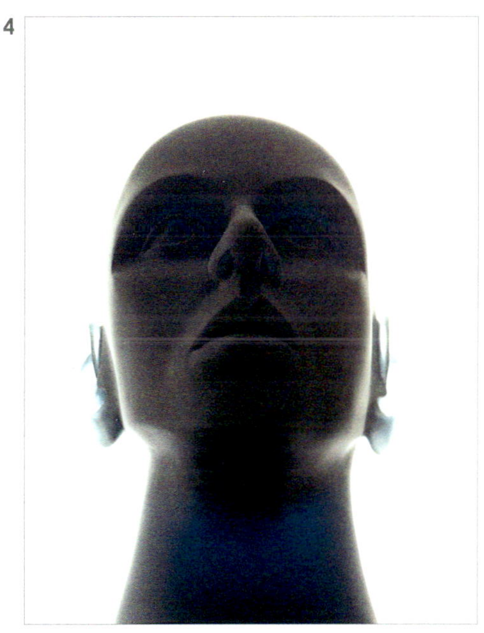

2 *Cycles*. Cast glass and steel. 18' × 8'. 2006. Courtesy of Thomas Egan.

3 *Shattered Cycle*. Cast glass. 18.11" × 36.22" × 15.75". 2002. Courtesy of Philip Lauterbach.

4 *Lost in Translation*. Cast glass. 14.17" × 12.99" × 7.87". 2012. Courtesy of Philip Lauterbach.

Tom Marosz

Spring Valley, California

My art is the culmination of some of the best and worst times of my life combined with the mastery of skills, of craft, and the attempt to manipulate light in ways that no one expects. My fascination with light has been a lifelong pursuit that is evident in every piece I make. When I start a new piece, my desire is to control the light and, therefore, the appearance of the piece in a way that beckons the viewer to see more around the corner and be surprised at each turn. Much of my artistic journey stems from my desire to produce pleasing shapes that flow, reflect, and refract the light, like that little spot on the horizon that catches your eye, making you keep looking back to watch it dance on the edge. I strive for technical perfection and attention to detail on every piece, knowing full well I may never reach that goal, but the journey is part of the fun.

In working with glass over the years, I have found it has many different personalities and properties. It is versatile, frustrating, beautiful, surprising, and sometimes unpredictable. My inspiration comes from my desire to continually investigate new techniques and stretch the abilities of glass. The end result is so satisfying! I love working with glass knowing that one wrong move could send the piece flying into many pieces on the floor or create one rare gem ready to be displayed on its pedestal!

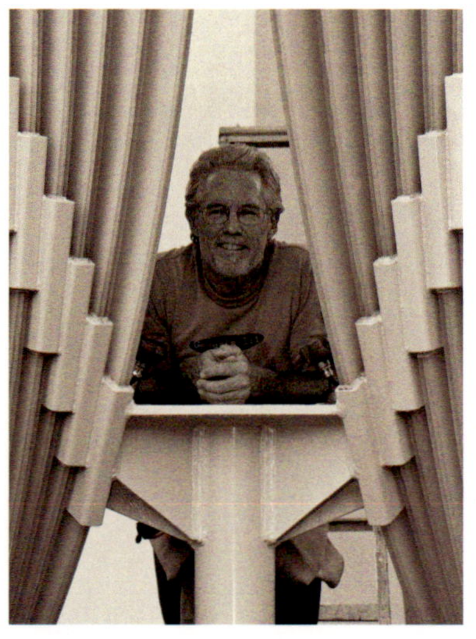

Courtesy of Patrick Riley, Benstreet Photography.

1

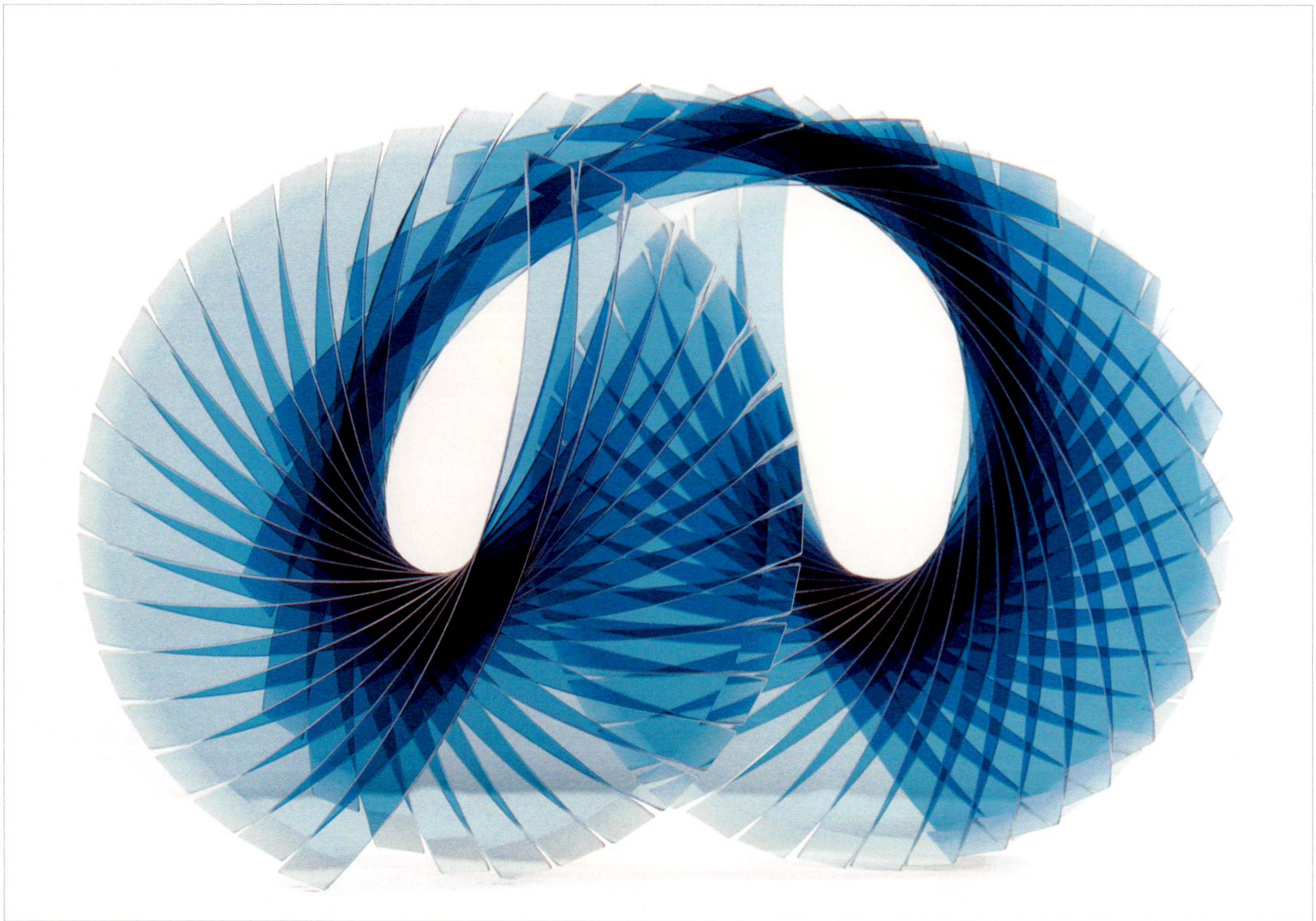

2

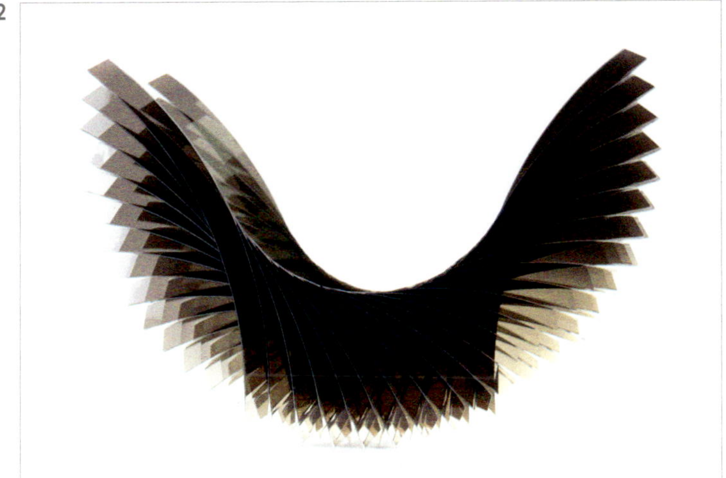

3

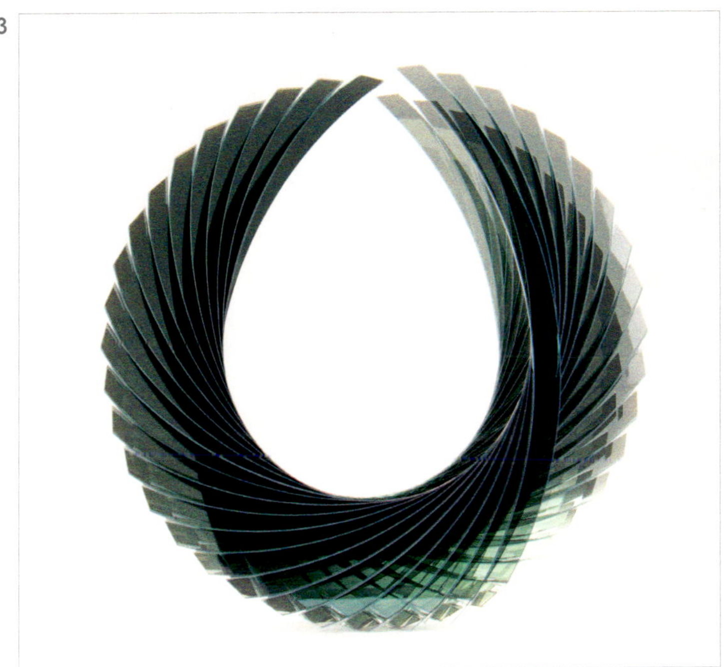

4

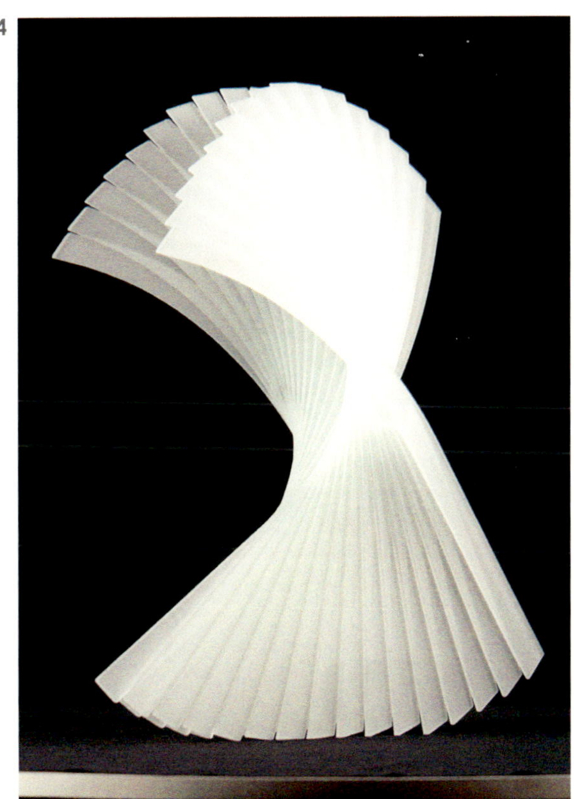

5

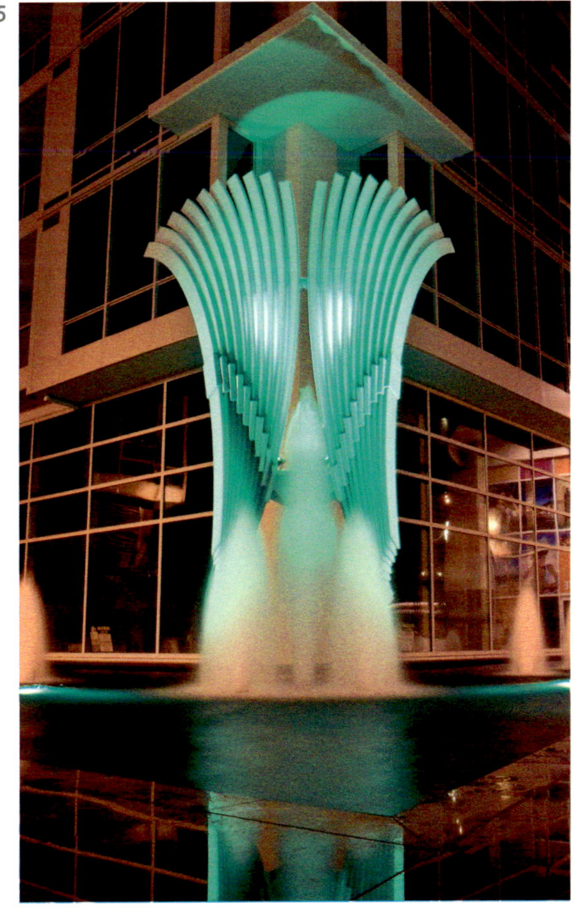

1 *Riptide*. 11" × 24" × 12". 2015. Courtesy of My World Productions.

2 *Blue Monk*. Cold glass. 13" × 34" × 20". 2014. Courtesy of Patrick Riley, Benstreet Photography.

3 *Ella*. Cold glass. 25" × 25" × 11". 2014. Courtesy of Patrick Riley, Benstreet Photography.

4 *Heidi's Thoughts*. 24" × 18" × 9". 2015.

5 *Vantage Pointe Wings*. Cold glass and lighting. 18' × 10' × 8'. 2009. Courtesy of Patrick Riley, Benstreet Photography.

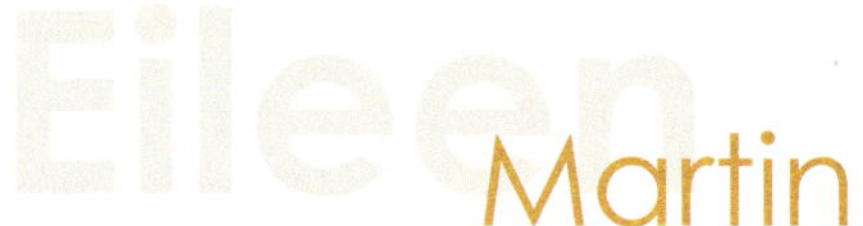

Eileen Martin

Silver Spring, Maryland

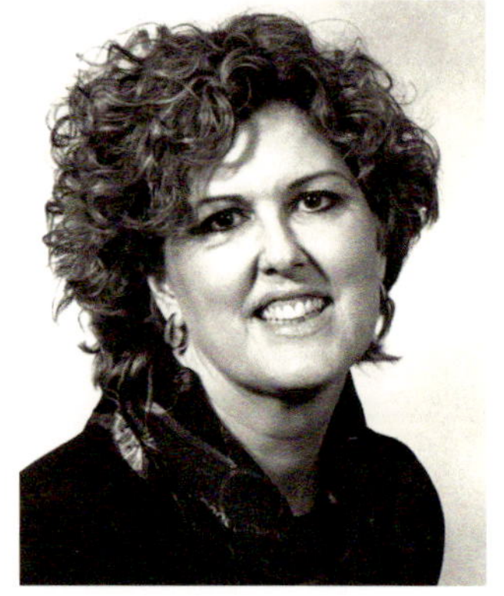

Courtesy of Mario E. Quiroz-Servellón.

I find that most things, people, or thoughts are constructed in layers. Non-organic matter is created with small building blocks on top of other building blocks, ergo, layers. People and other organic matter, too. Even more interesting are thoughts—elusive, intangible, yet still constructed in the same way—building snippets upon glimpses. I am entranced with the idea of how different things look on the surface, but when you peel away layers you see many unique and often surprising views. I find that glass is my medium of choice to unveil, reveal, and otherwise showcase these layers.

1

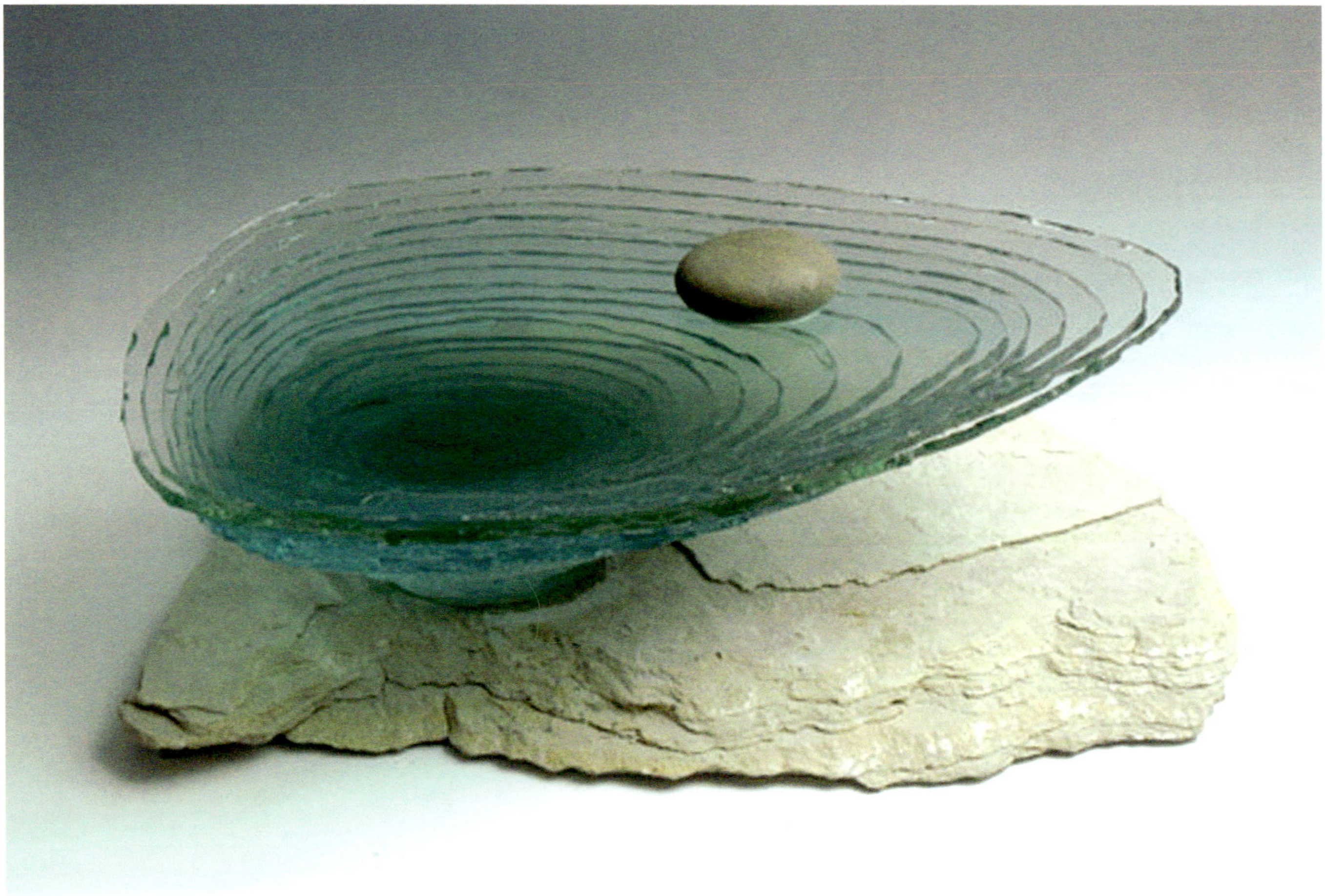

2

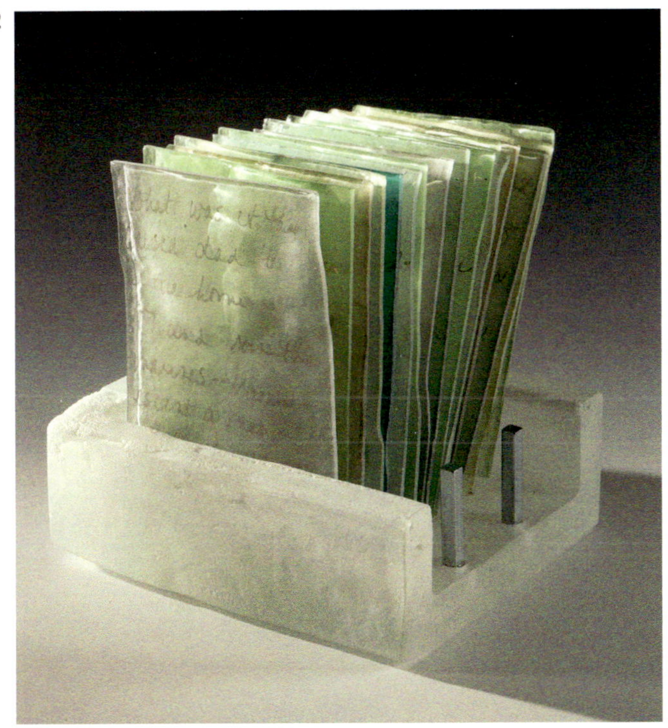

3

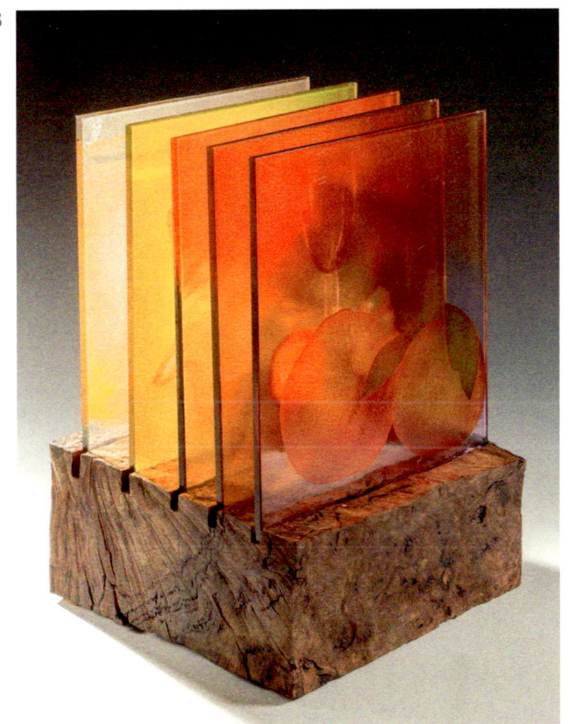

4

1 *Authority Issues*. Laminated float glass set on Arizona limestone, inset river stone. 7" × 16" × 10". 2010. Courtesy of Gregory R. Staley.

2 *Book Study #14*. Cast glass, slumped and sandblasted glass, gold text, and steel rod. 8.5" × 6" × 7". 2013. Photo: David Terao.

3 *Layered Still Life*. Oil painted images on float glass, and eucalyptus base. 11" × 8" × 8.5". 2013. Photo: David Terao.

4 *Down the Path Unbidden*. Slumped glass strips, tack fused. 11" × 1.5" × 14.5". 2012. Photo: David Terao.

5 *Undertow*. Slumped glass strips, fused. 8" × 3" × 37". 2013. Photo: David Terao.

5

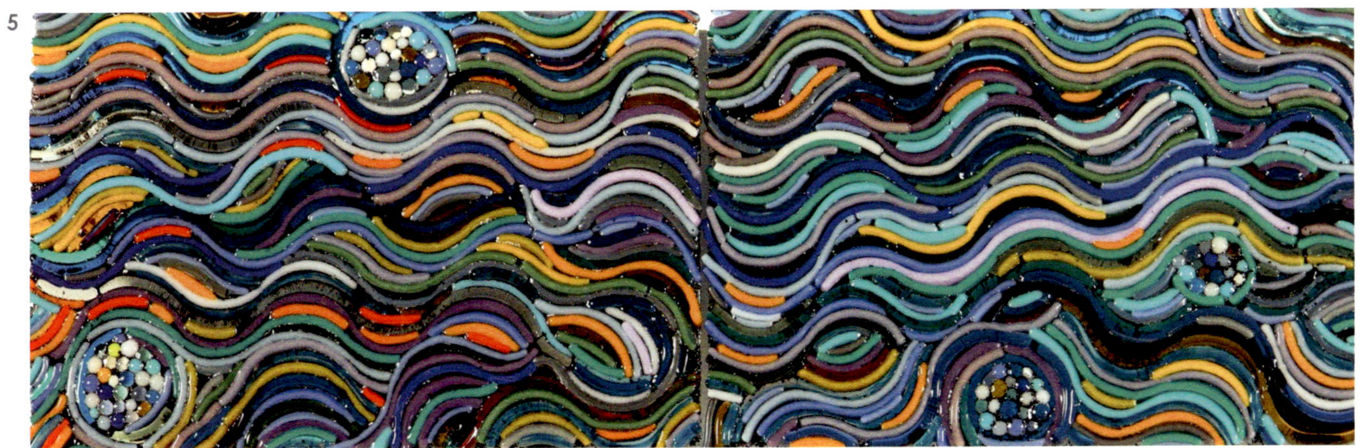

Lin McJunkin

Conway, Washington

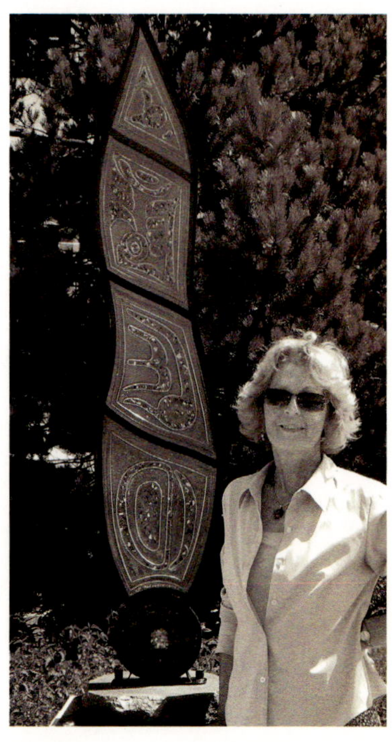

Artist with *Kelp Totem IV: Orca.*

I strive to please two very different audiences with my glass and metal sculpture. Public art commissions demand large, sturdy pieces to showcase their themes. This work must also withstand local weather conditions and potential abuse by "the unsupervised general public." To meet these criteria, I employ heat to kiln-carve (emboss) designs into the back of thick glass panels cut to fit the sculpture's final shape. Fired in the kiln over designs cut from fireproof pattern paper, the glass slumps over the pattern and retains the design on the back of the glass. These patterns are often my interpretation of traditional designs used by local Native Americans, which provide strong details for my depiction of natural and human history.

In another re-interpretation of tradition, I employ an enlarged version of an ancient glass technique called pate de verre to form my smaller, more intimate gallery pieces, often with environmental themes.

With their more protected environments, galleries allow me to indulge in the more delicate work of forming sculptural elements from quarter-inch recycled or new glass chunks and colored glass powders mixed with a binder to form a thick paste. I press this paste into a mold and fire it in the kiln to around 1,400° F (760° C). The heated glass drops down in the mold, leaving long, spiky edges. It is these edges that I find so intriguing for the danger inherent in their beauty.

1 *Bitterroot Totem: Eagle.* Kiln-carved and pate de verre glass, steel. 52" × 10" × 16".

2 *Etching*. Pate de verre glass, steel, and stone. 23" × 11" × 18". 2015. Courtesy of KP-Studios.com.

3 *Convoluted*. Pate de verre glass, steel. 22" × 5" × 13". 2015. Courtesy of KP-Studios.com.

1

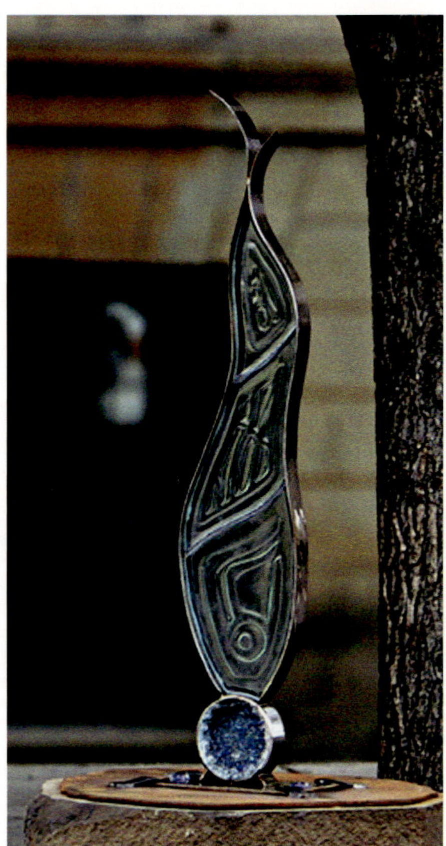

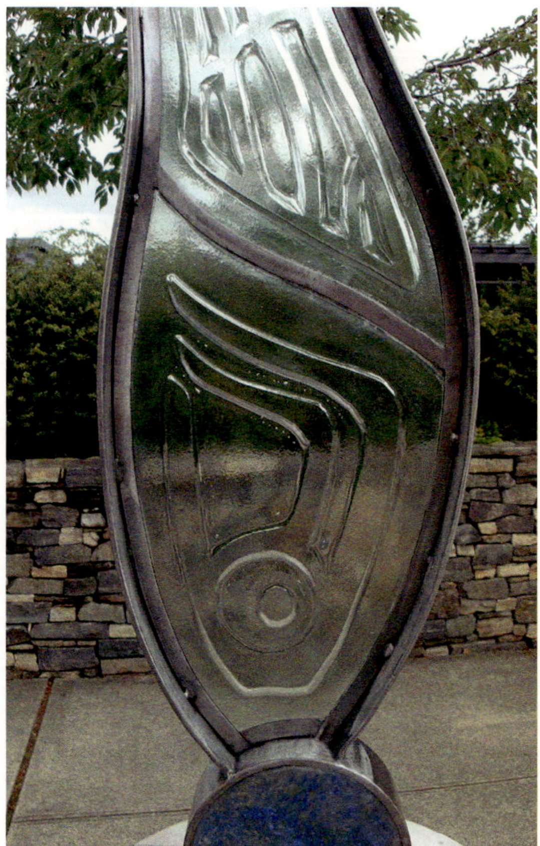

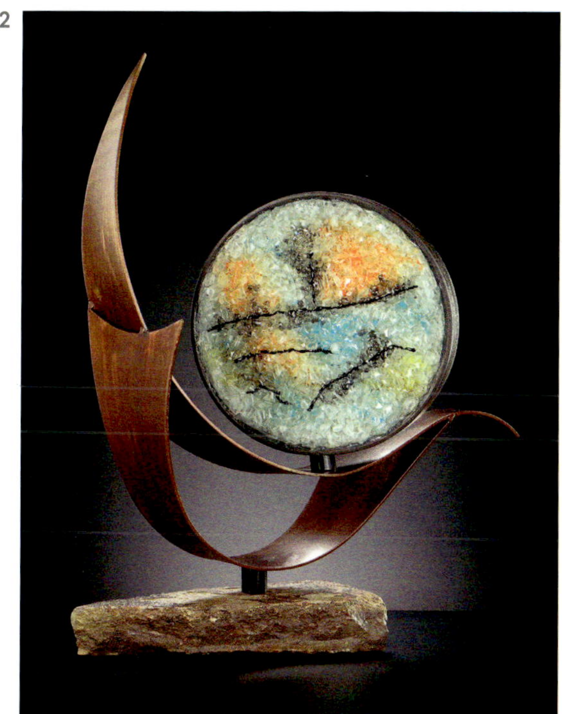

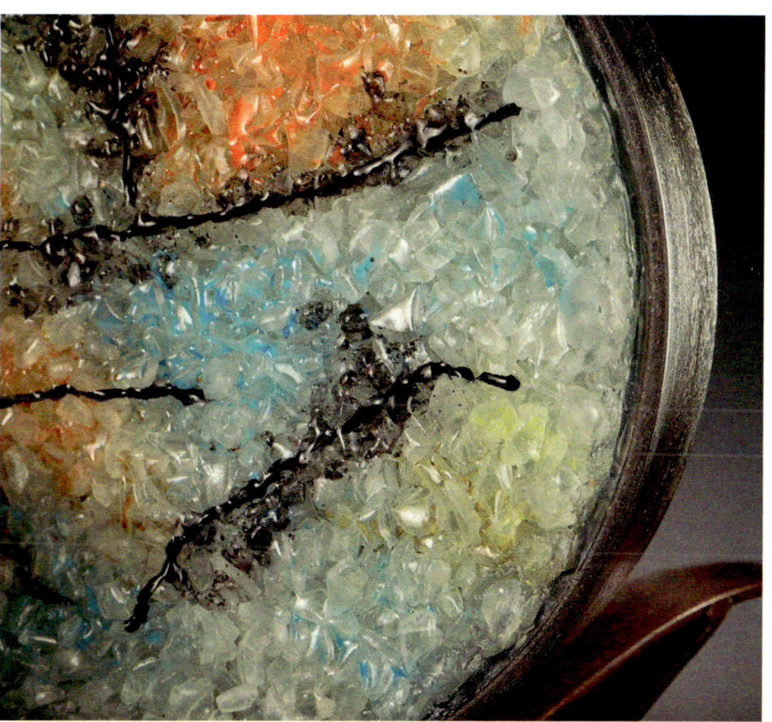

3

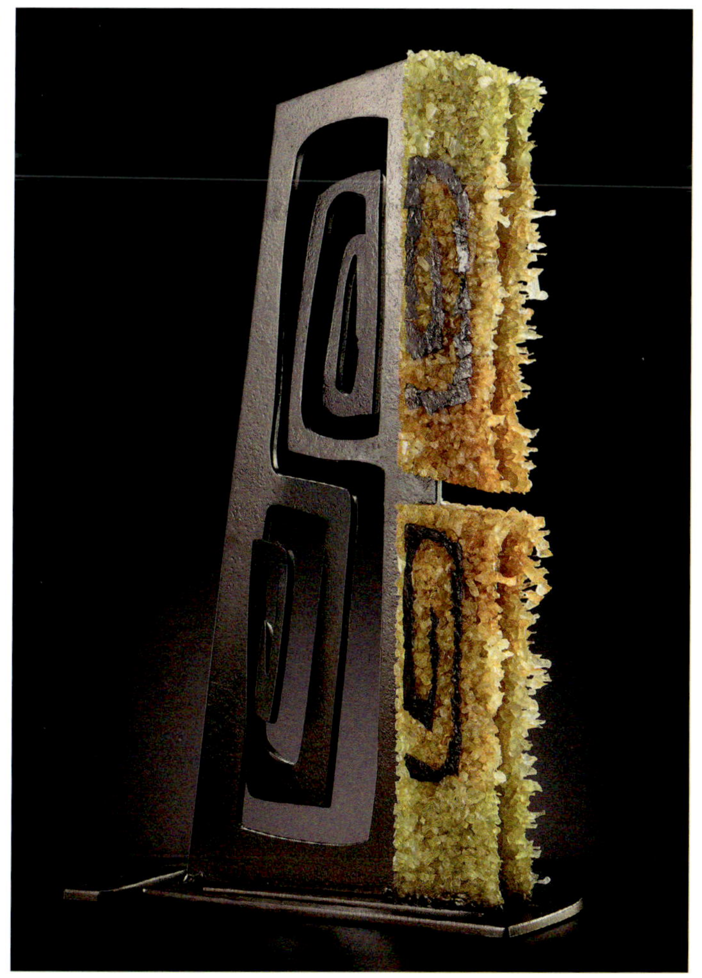

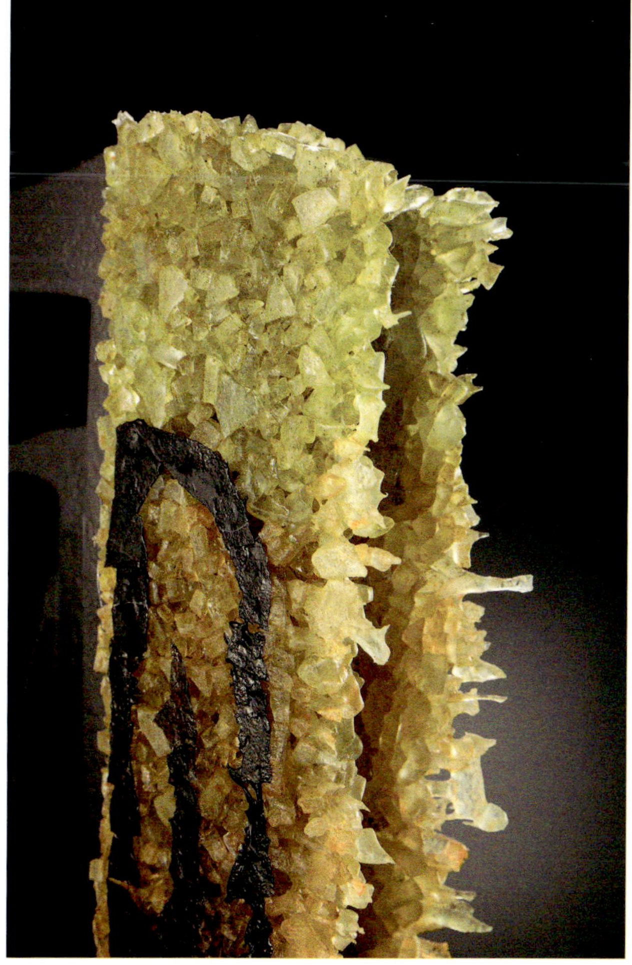

Elizabeth Ryland Mears

Fairfax Station, Virginia

I love plants. During my pre-med studies, I took a lot of botany classes, as I was fascinated by the structure of plants, both inside and out. The house I grew up in was filled with plants in the winter and surrounded by vegetables and ornamentals in the summer. I live in the woods of Virginia and have always tended my own gardens there. Connection to the earth is a part of life. Now I express my relationship to my inner and outer worlds through the images of plant forms in my glass sculpture.

I teach and have written two books describing the techniques I use: *Flameworking* and *Penland Book of Glass*. I love to write and, when photographing, look for the dramatic. Everything has come together in the *Glass Book* series.

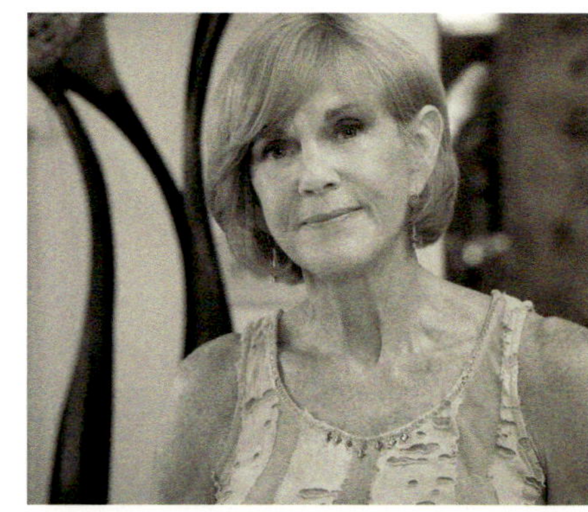

Courtesy of Pete Duvall / Anything Photographic.

1

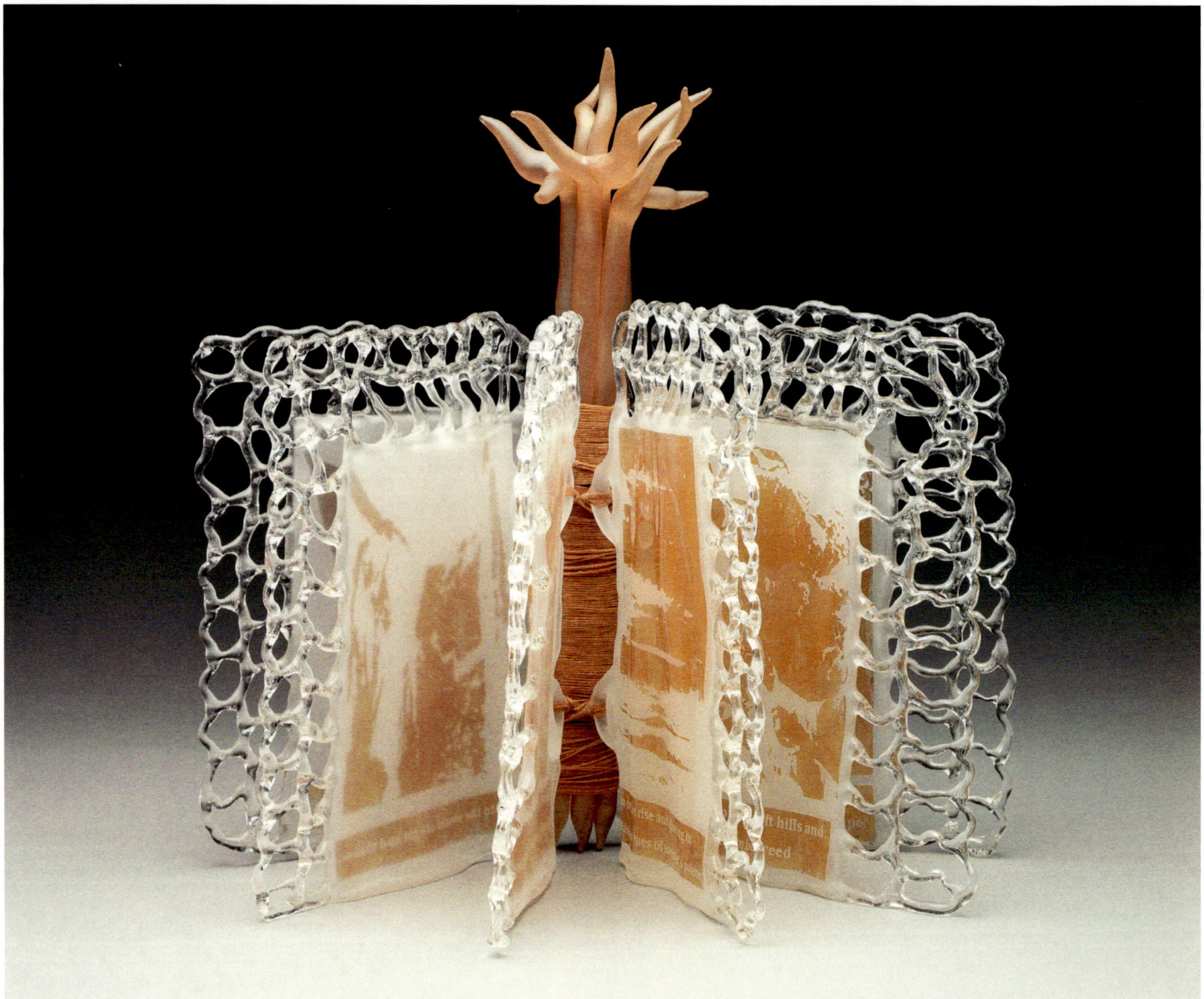

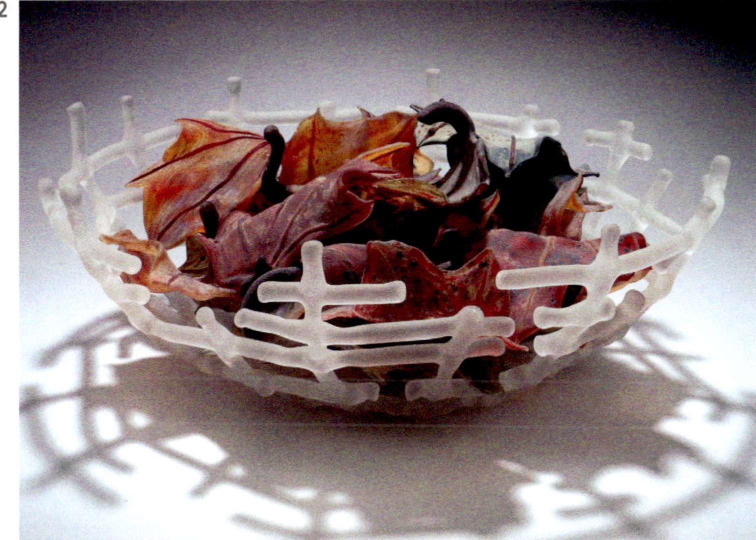

3

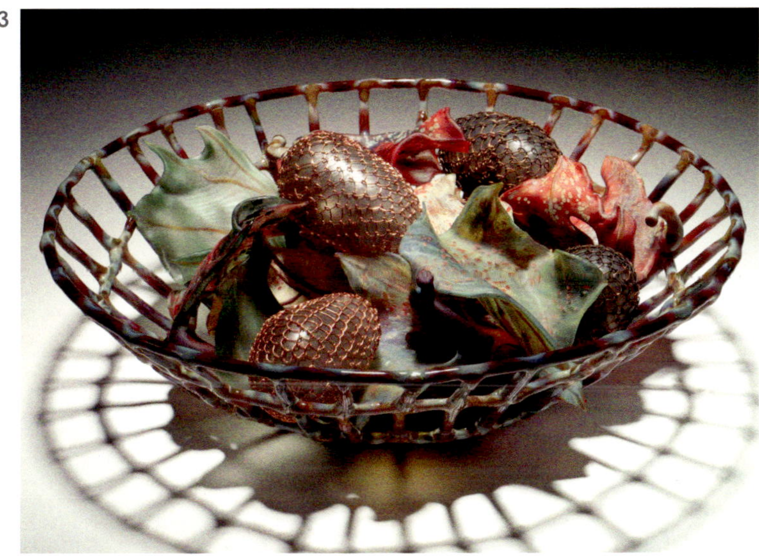

4

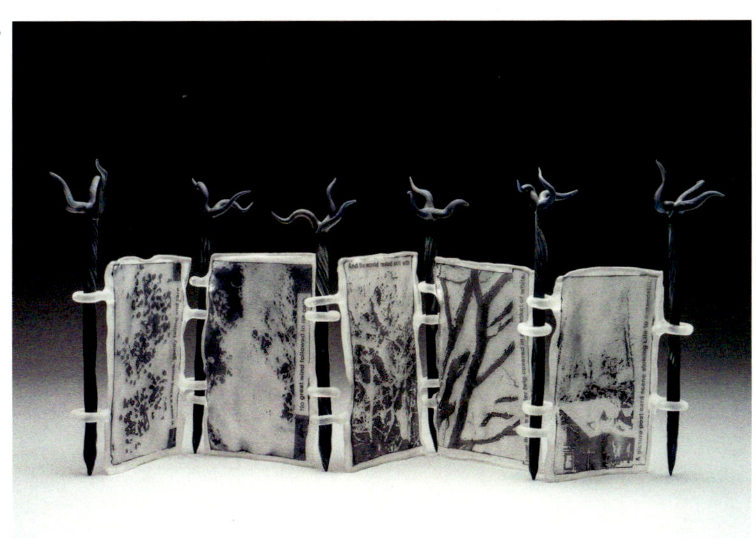

5

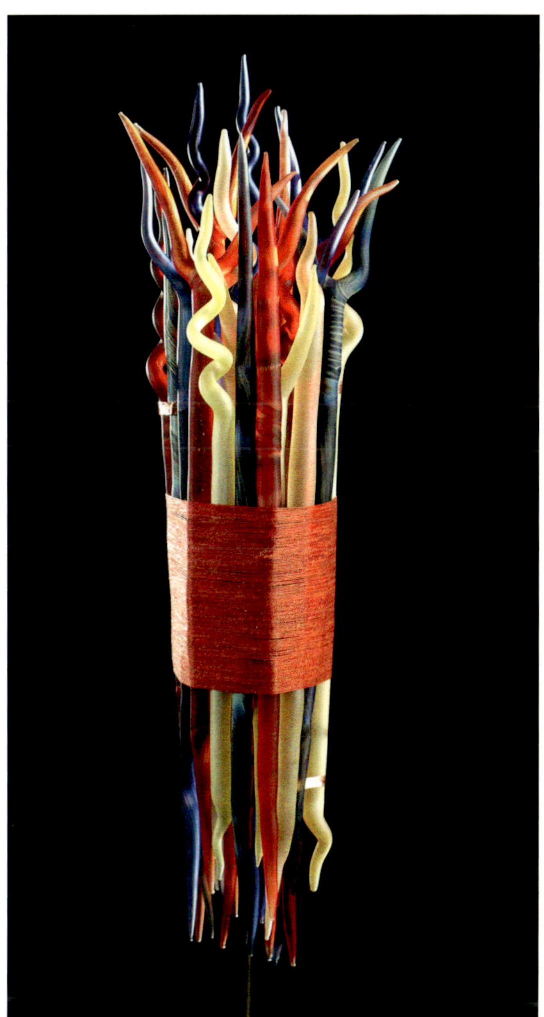

1 *View From Above*. Flameworked, sandblasted, mixed media, personal poetry, and photography. 10" × 8" × 12". 2014. Courtesy of Pete Duvall / Anything Photographic.

2 *Bowl of Autumn*. Flameworked, sandblasted. 5" × 12" × 12". 2013. Courtesy of Pete Duvall / Anything Photographic.

3 *Bowl of Past Dreams and Future Hopes*. Flameworked, sandblasted, and mixed media. 5" × 12". 2013. Courtesy of Pete Duvall / Anything Photographic.

4 *February Snow*. Flameworked, sandblasted, personal poetry and photographs. 9" × 4" × 16". 2014. Courtesy of Pete Duvall / Anything Photographic.

5 *Bundle of Sunrise*. Flameworked, sandblasted, and mixed media. 19" × 6" × 8". 2013. Courtesy of Pete Duvall / Anything Photographic.

Robert Mickelsen

Mims, Florida

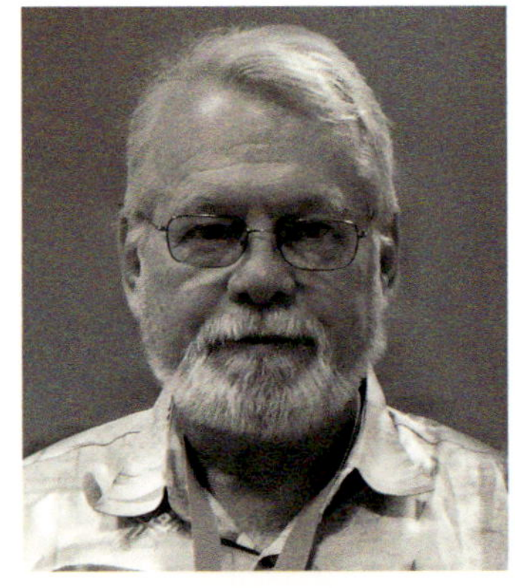

I am primarily interested in the personal expression of ideas and feelings and how the resulting sculptures fit into the environment of our lives. I believe strongly in the uniqueness of my own vision and strive to express it in the purest and most honest way possible. This often means stepping completely away from the traditional forms that have always been associated with my chosen medium (glass) and embracing forms, materials, and techniques that are not only non-traditional but even controversial. I believe in breaking rules to achieve what I want and revel in the disapproval this approach often generates.

The objects I create are narratives—personal vignettes that reveal the secrets of my innermost thoughts. These are often mysteries even to me until the creative process reveals them, and so the work becomes a form of self-discovery. The work provides me with a path to understanding things that I otherwise would not be aware of and to sharing them with others who can then identify those things within themselves.

1

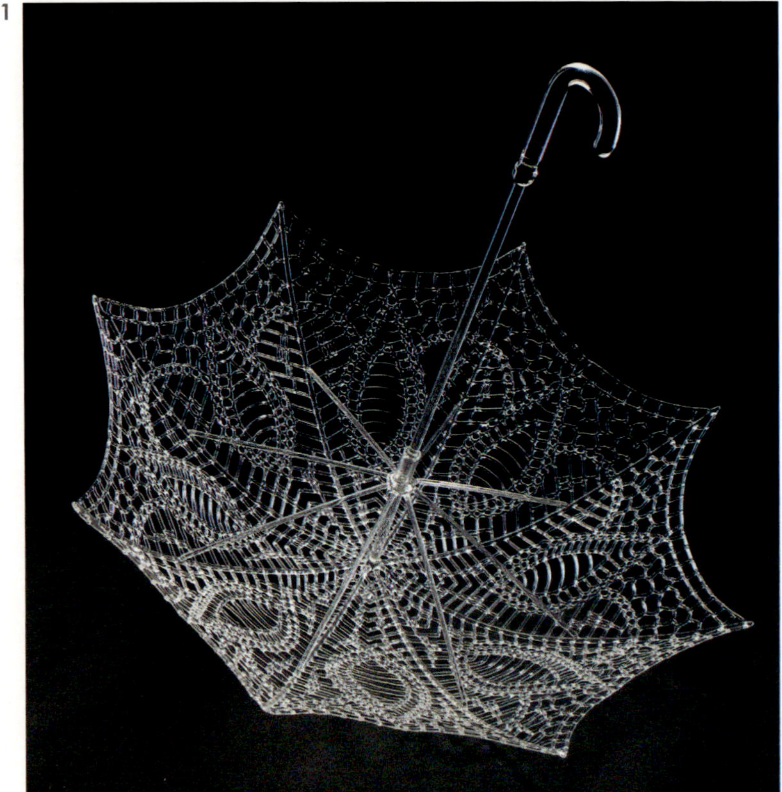

2

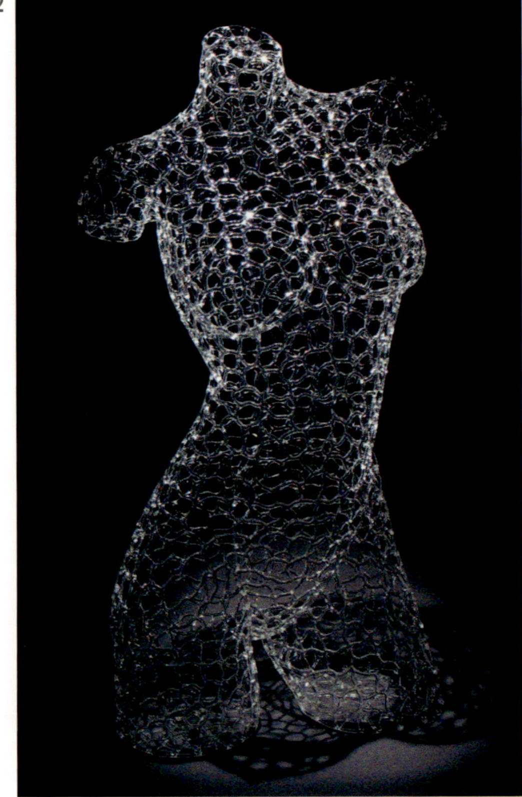

3

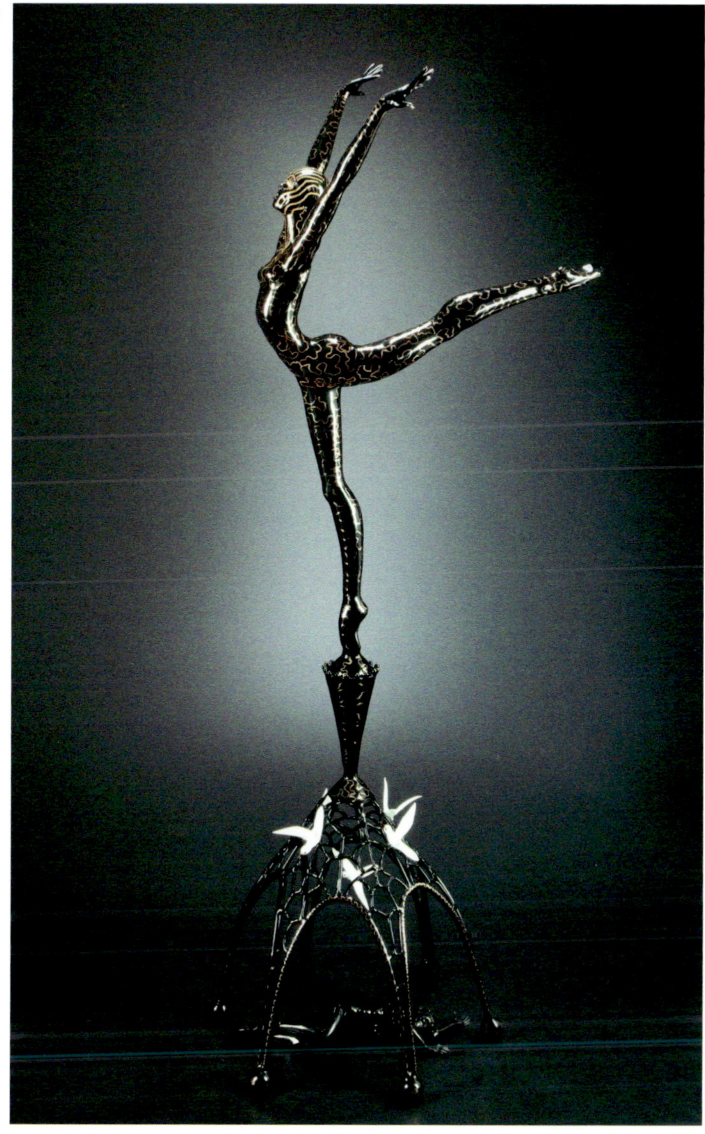

4

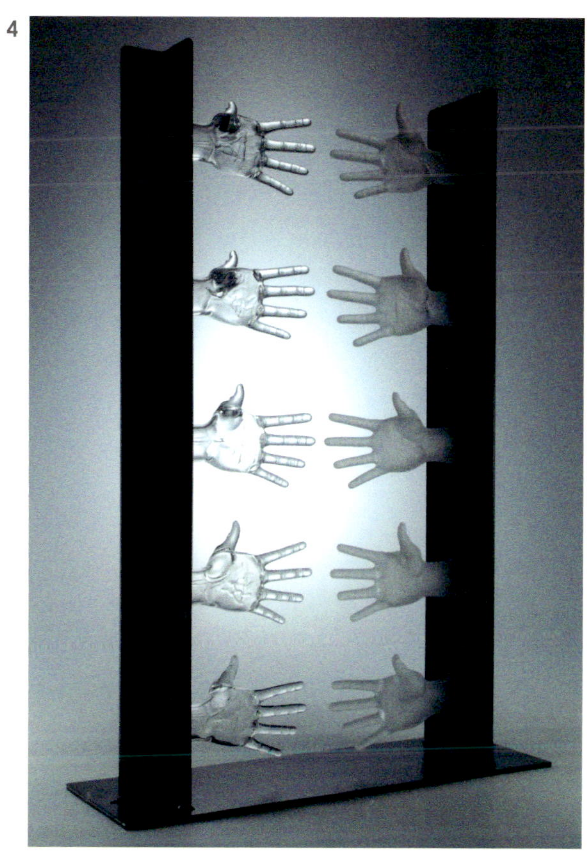

1 *Network Parasol*. Lampworked borosilicate glass. 33" × 34" × 34". 2009. Courtesy of Daniel Abbott.

2 *Network Venus*. Lampworked borosilicate glass. 29.5" × 9" × 15". 2009.

3 *Sueno Vuelo* (Dream Flight). Lampworked borosilicate glass, 24 carat gold. 35.5" × 12" × 15". 2012.

4 *Shake*. Lampworked borosilicate glass, steel. 34" × 8" × 24". 2008. Courtesy of Daniel Abbott.

5 *Swarm*. Lampworked borosilicate glass. 10" × 15" × 16". 2011.

5

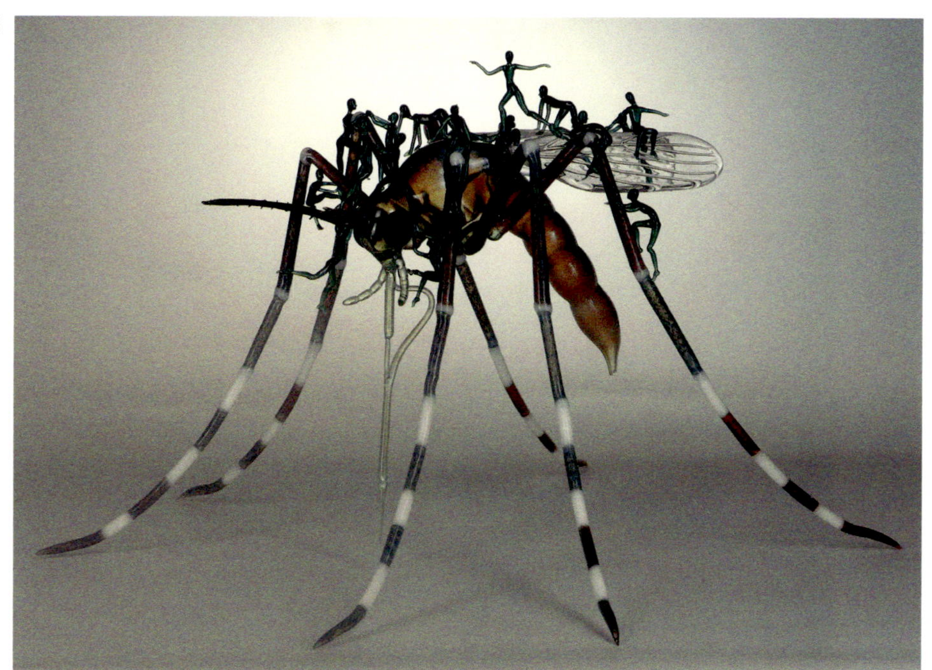

Michael Mikula

Cleveland, Ohio

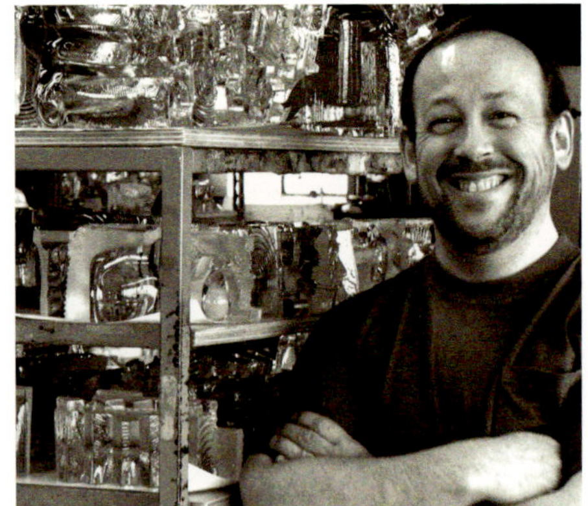

Courtesy of Uri Davillier.

I design and build multi-part graphite molds as a tool to shape the glass into positive/negative interplay. With a jazz-like sense of improvisation, I compose each mold from a large and ever-expanding library of interchangeable parts that I cut and carve by hand. As a result, no two compositions are ever alike. Once cooled, these dimensional blown forms are cut open and apart, polished, and recomposed in related sets within an integral metal armature of anodized aluminum and stainless steel. The genesis of the current glass and metal pieces was a series of related sculptural blown vessels and decorative objects.

Architectural details, the built environment, and the restless energy of cities and their cultural variations point the way for this body of work in blown glass. The unique decorative traditions of any culture tell us something about who they are or were, how they wish to be remembered, and what they valued or aspired to. These physical remnants connect us to the lives of those who created them.

As a designer-craftsman, I'm particularly drawn to the optimistic quality that these traditions reflect. Beyond my life-long obsession with anything architectural, the inherent qualities of glass fascinate me. Its transparent fluidity simultaneously captures light, rigid form, and sense of movement so beautifully. This and a well-developed vocabulary of material and form provide the framework in which I create.

1

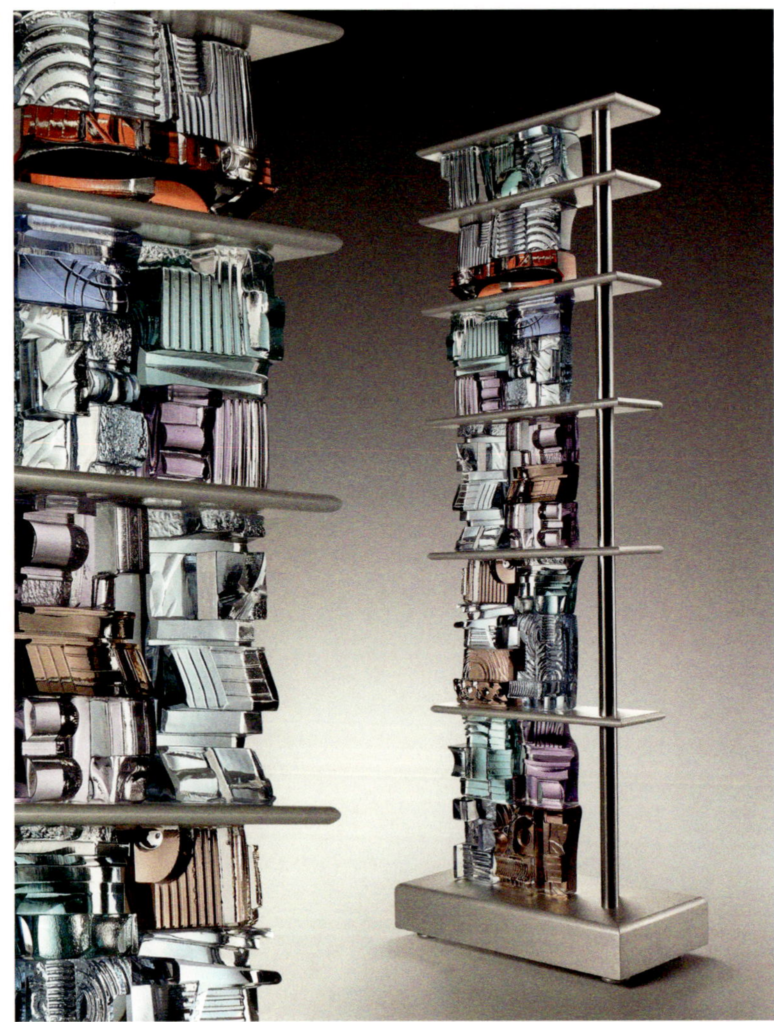

1 *Building Skyward.* Mold-formed, blown, cut, polished glass, anodized aluminum, and stainless steel. 34" × 3" × 13". 2013. Courtesy of Daniel Fox/Lumina Studio.

2 *Water Table.* Mold-formed, blown, cut, polished glass, anodized aluminum, and stainless steel. 16" × 5.5" × 32". 2014. Courtesy of Daniel Fox/Lumina Studio.

3 *Rio Rojo.* Mold-formed, blown, cut, polished glass, anodized aluminum, and stainless steel. 9" × 5" × 7". 2013. Courtesy of Daniel Fox/Lumina Studio.

4 *Cornerstone, Amethyst.* Mold-formed, blown, cut, polished glass, anodized aluminum, and stainless steel. 10" × 4" × 10". 2012. Courtesy of Daniel Fox/Lumina Studio.

5 *Finding True North.* Mold-formed, blown, cut, polished glass, anodized aluminum, and stainless steel. 40" × 6" × 9". 2014. Courtesy of Daniel Fox/Lumina Studio.

2

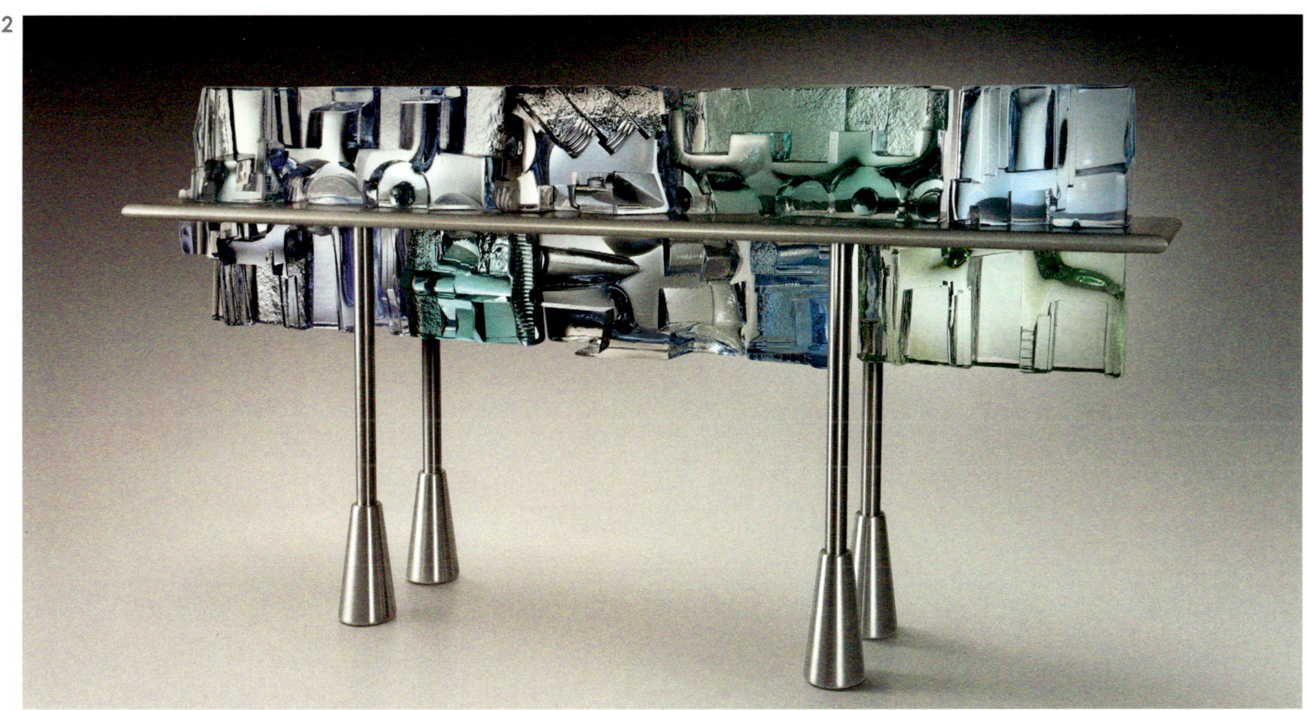

3

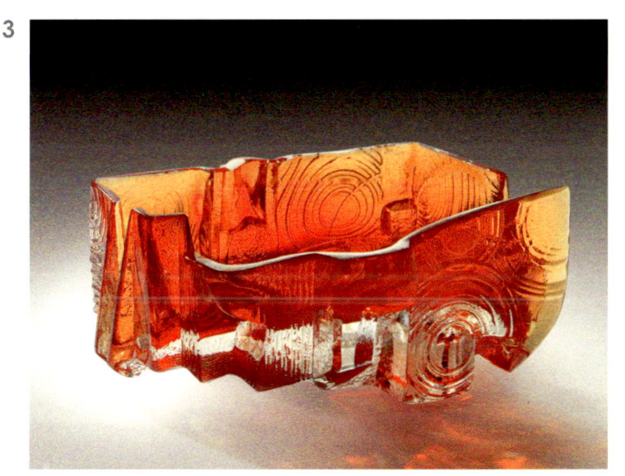

4

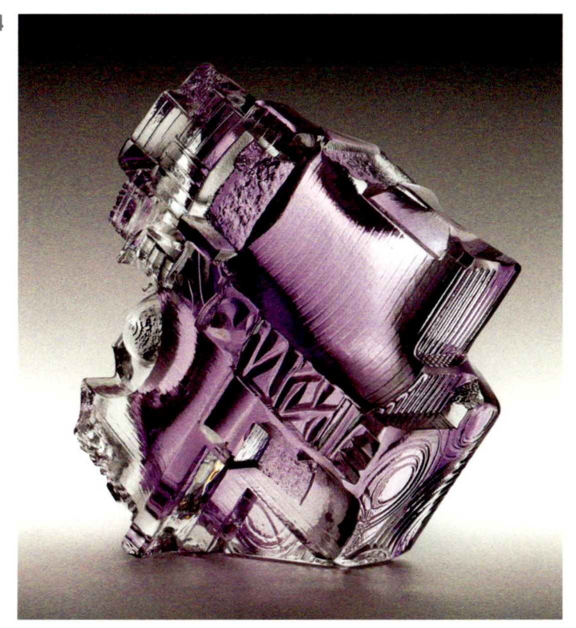

5

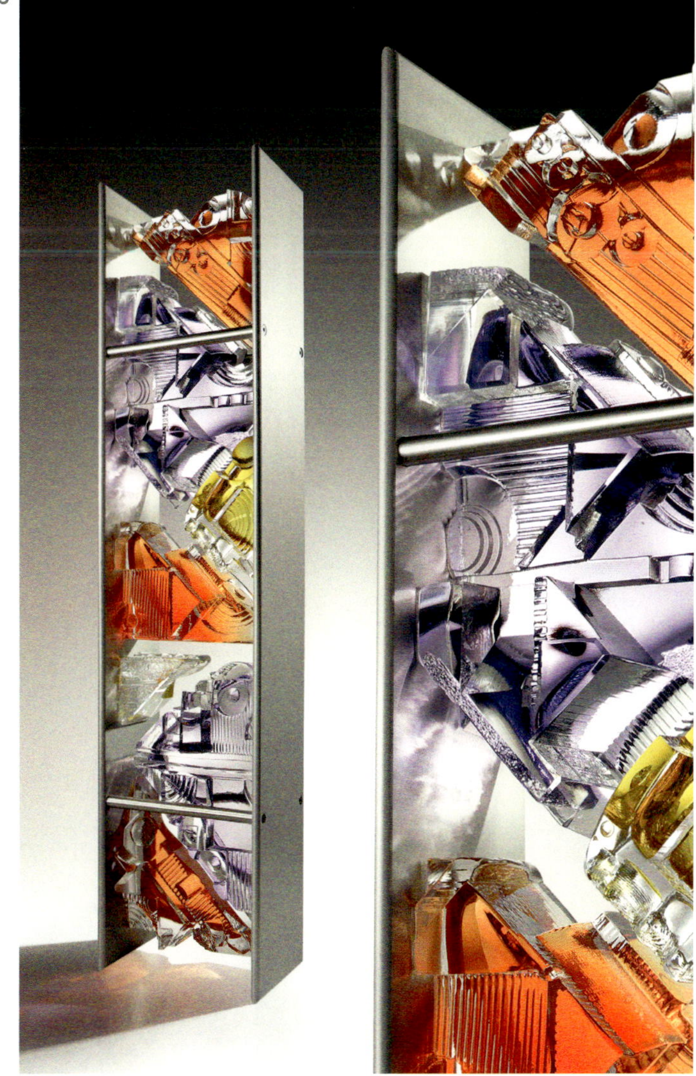

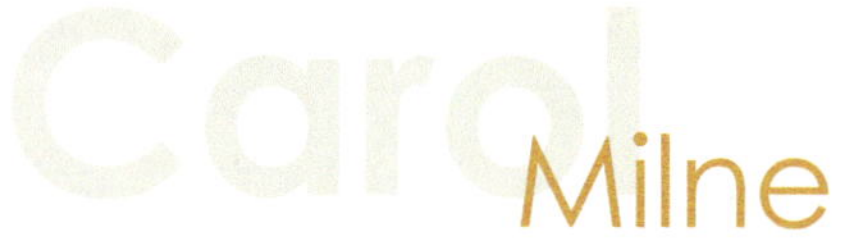

Seattle, Washington

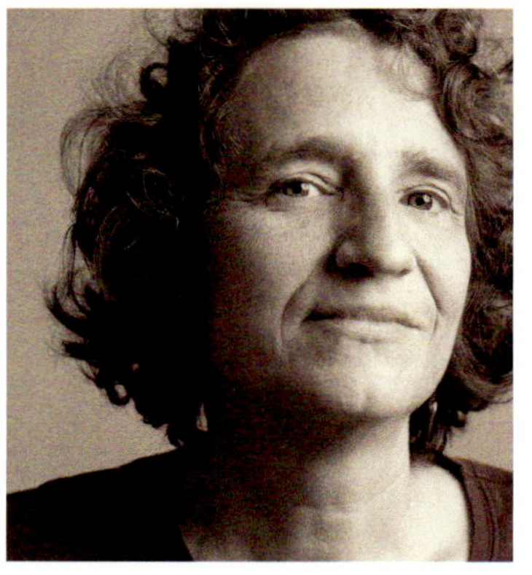

Courtesy of Andrew Imanaka.

I knit in glass. I see my knitted glasswork as a metaphor for social structure. Individual strands are weak and brittle on their own, but deceptively strong when bound together. You can crack or break single threads without the whole structure falling apart. And even when the structure is broken, pieces remain bound together. The connections are what bring strength and integrity to the whole and what keep it intact. The process of looping together and interlocking individual strands makes a solid object that is permeable, and yet it is constructed of many loops. It's like making connections in a fragmented world!

1

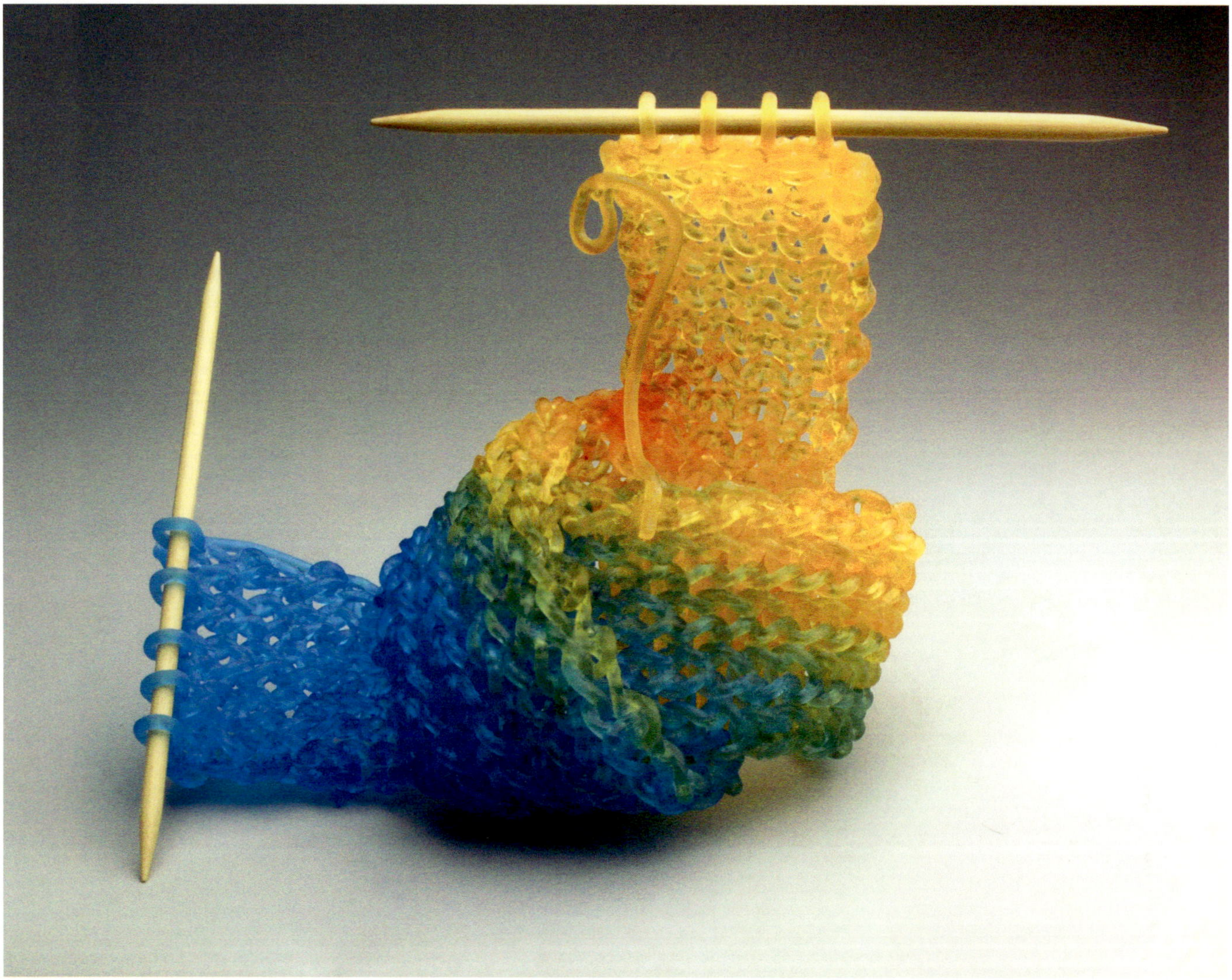

2

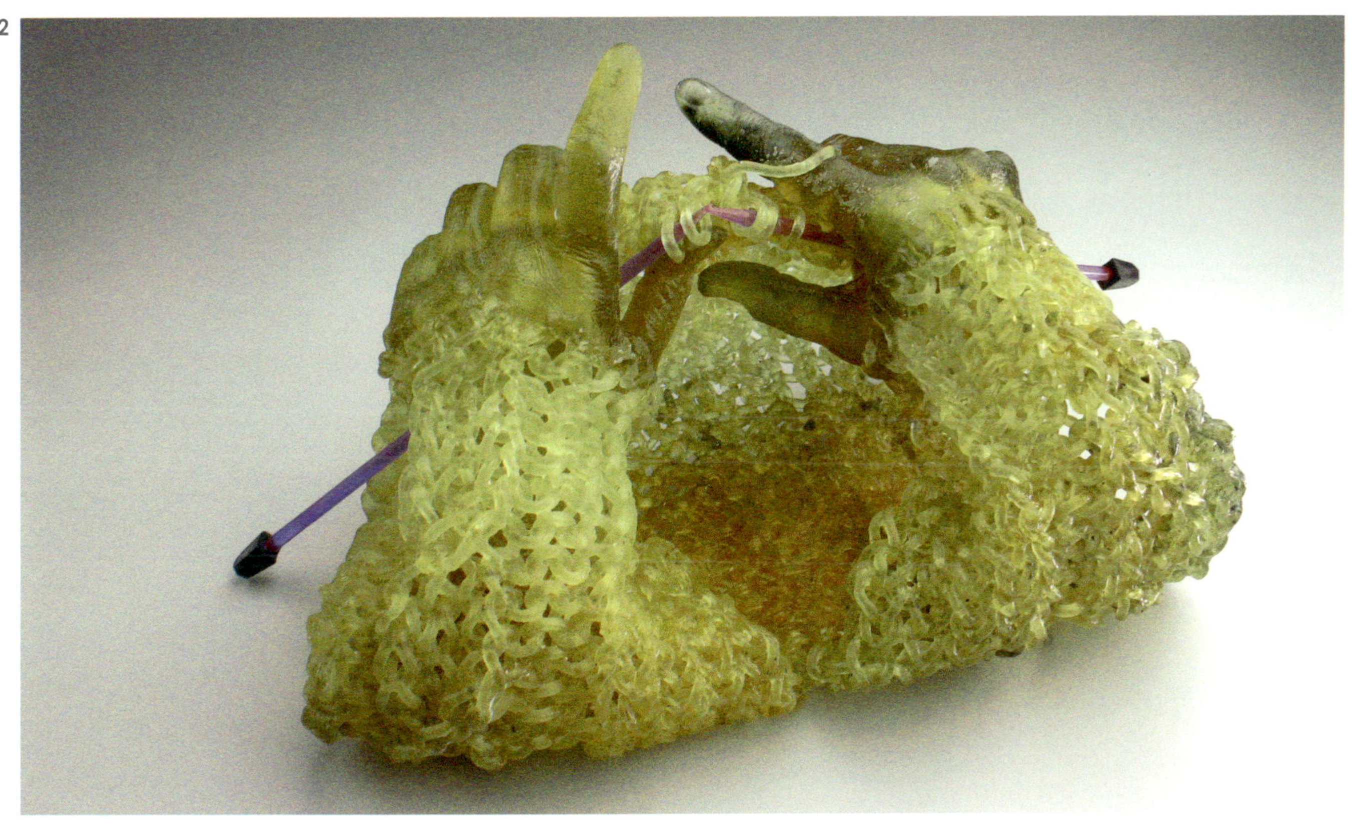

3

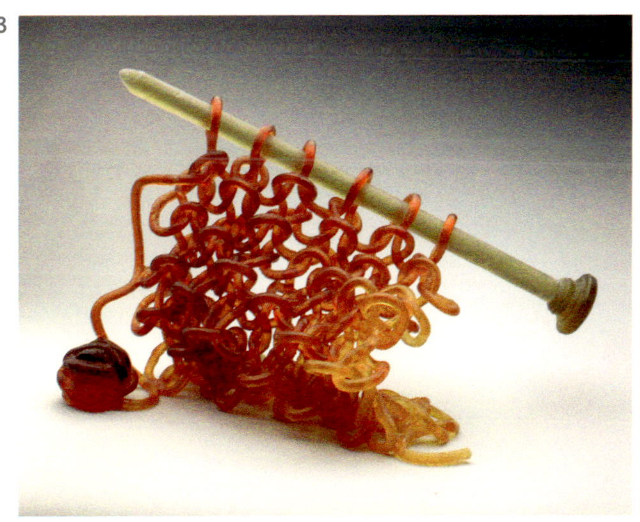

5

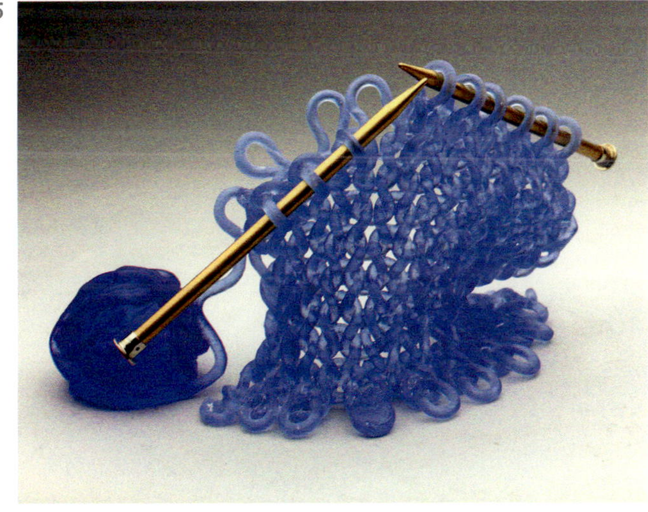

4

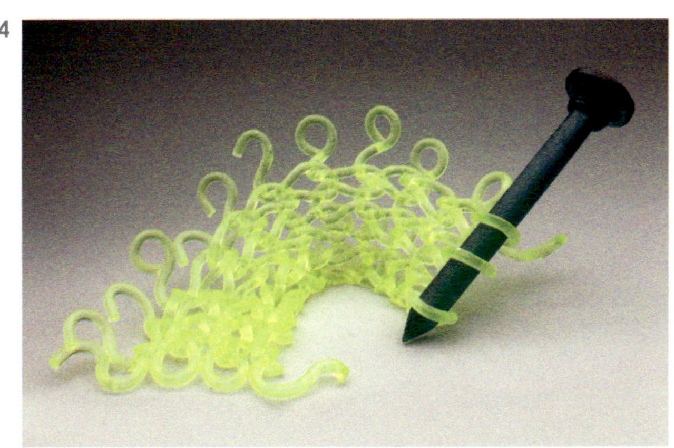

1 *Knit Knot*. Kiln cast lead crystal and knitting needles. 10"x 8" × 15". 2014.

2 *Handmade*. Kiln cast lead crystal and knitting needles. 9" × 9" × 16.5". 2013.

3 *Strike a Balance*. Kiln cast lead crystal. 13" × 9" × 21". 2013.

4 *Radiate*. Kiln cast lead crystal. 7" × 16" × 14". 2014.

5 *Blue*. Kiln cast lead crystal. 5" × 5" × 9". 2014.

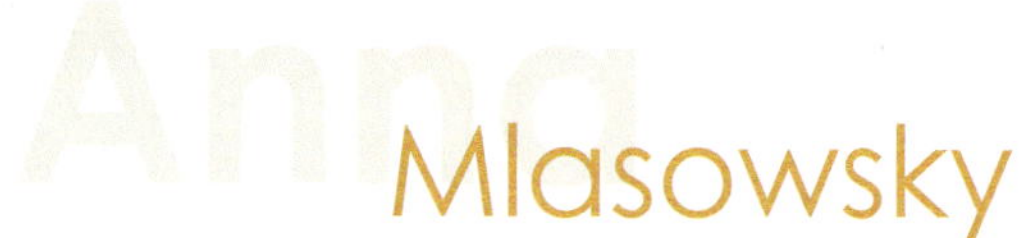

Anna Mlasowsky

Seattle, Washington

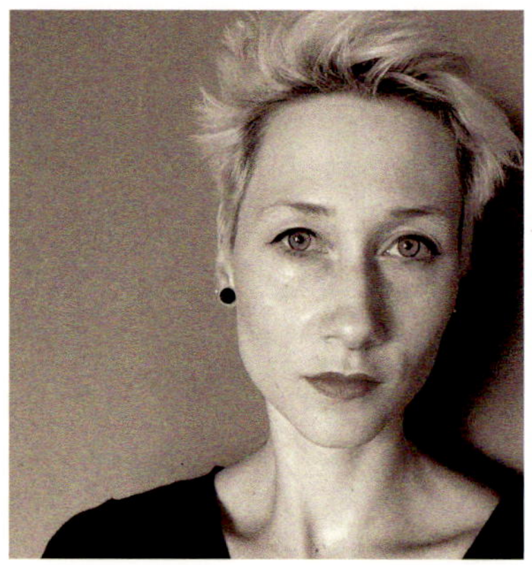

Describing reality is the hardest undertaking imaginable. In my work, I am interested in questioning common perceptions of reality and hope to critically observe the unconditional surrendering to facts approved by tradition and history. In glass, I have found a material deeply embedded in inherited ways of making and appreciating. This presents me with the challenge of pushing the boundaries of its perceived and physical reality. My work connects objects and techniques in new constellations to ask if things are what we think they are or if they might be more than we can perceive.

The results are experimental processes that approach the material in unconventional ways.

1

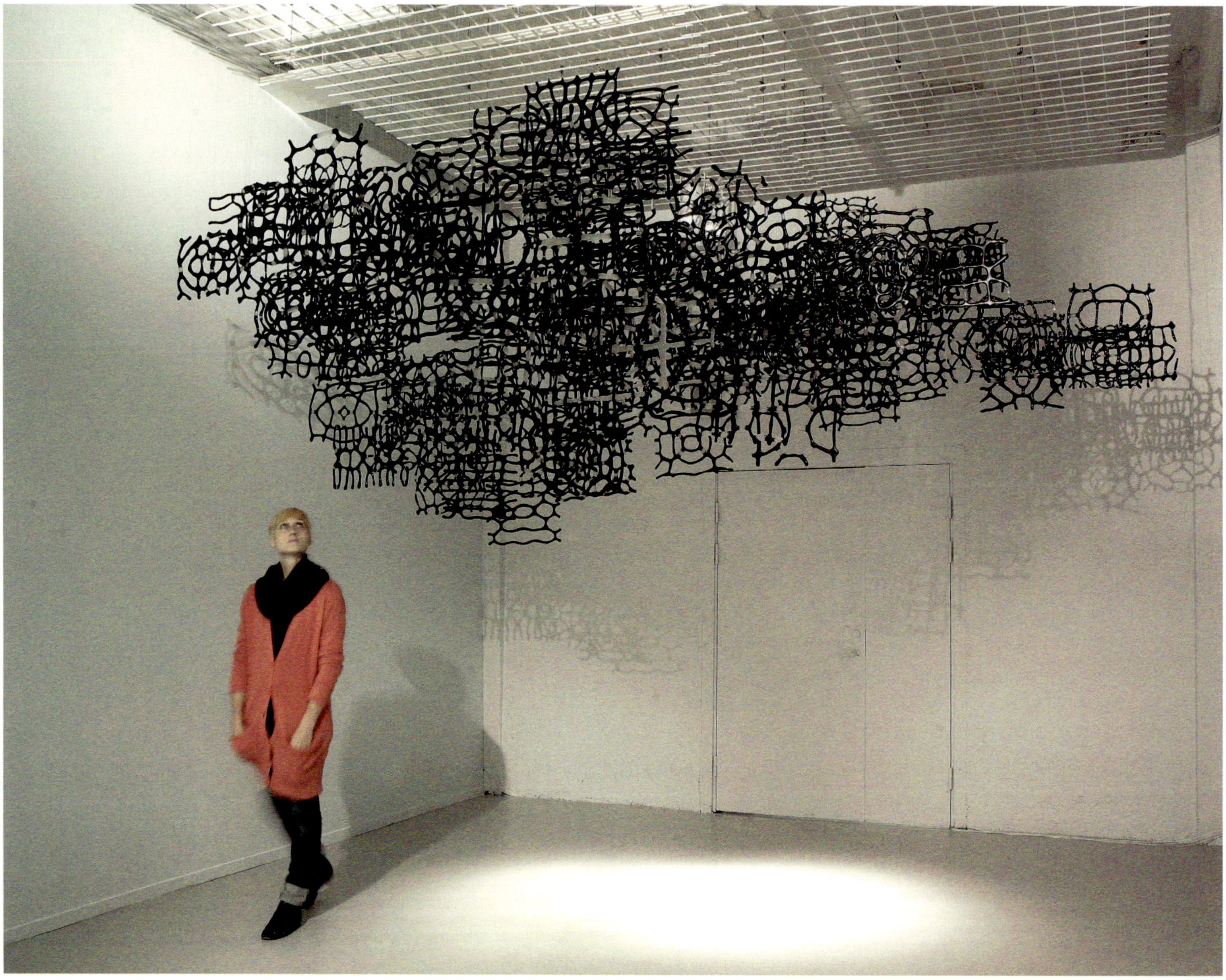

2

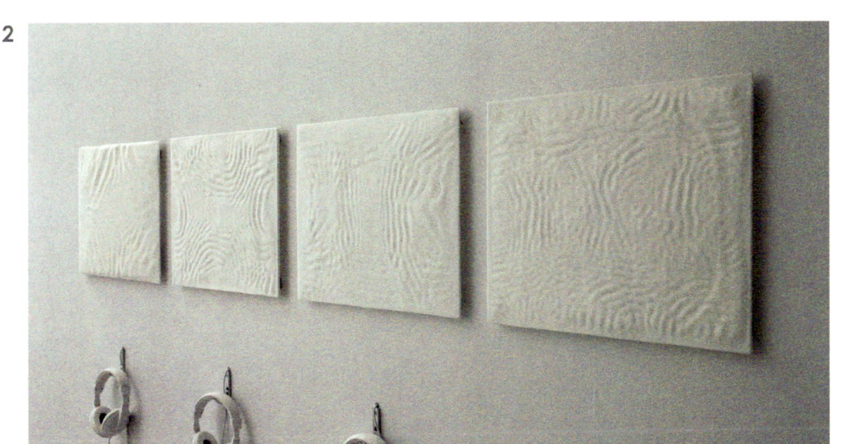

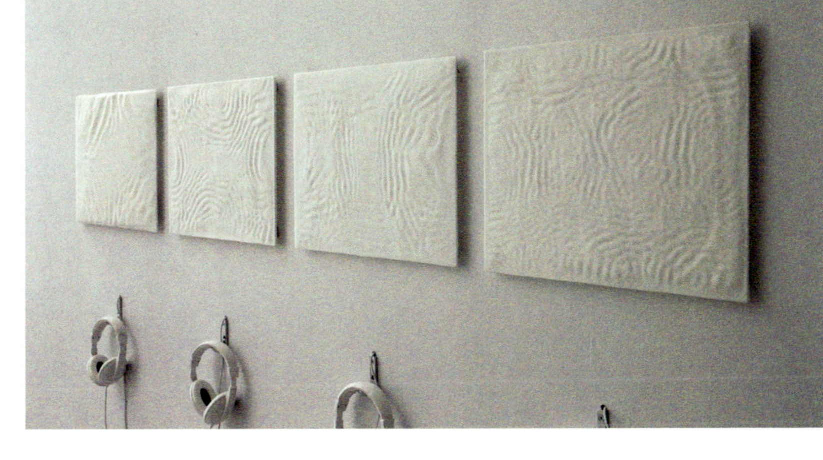

3

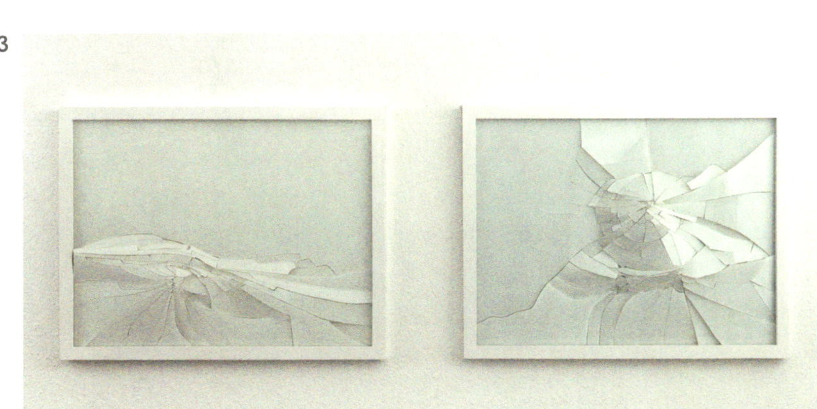

4

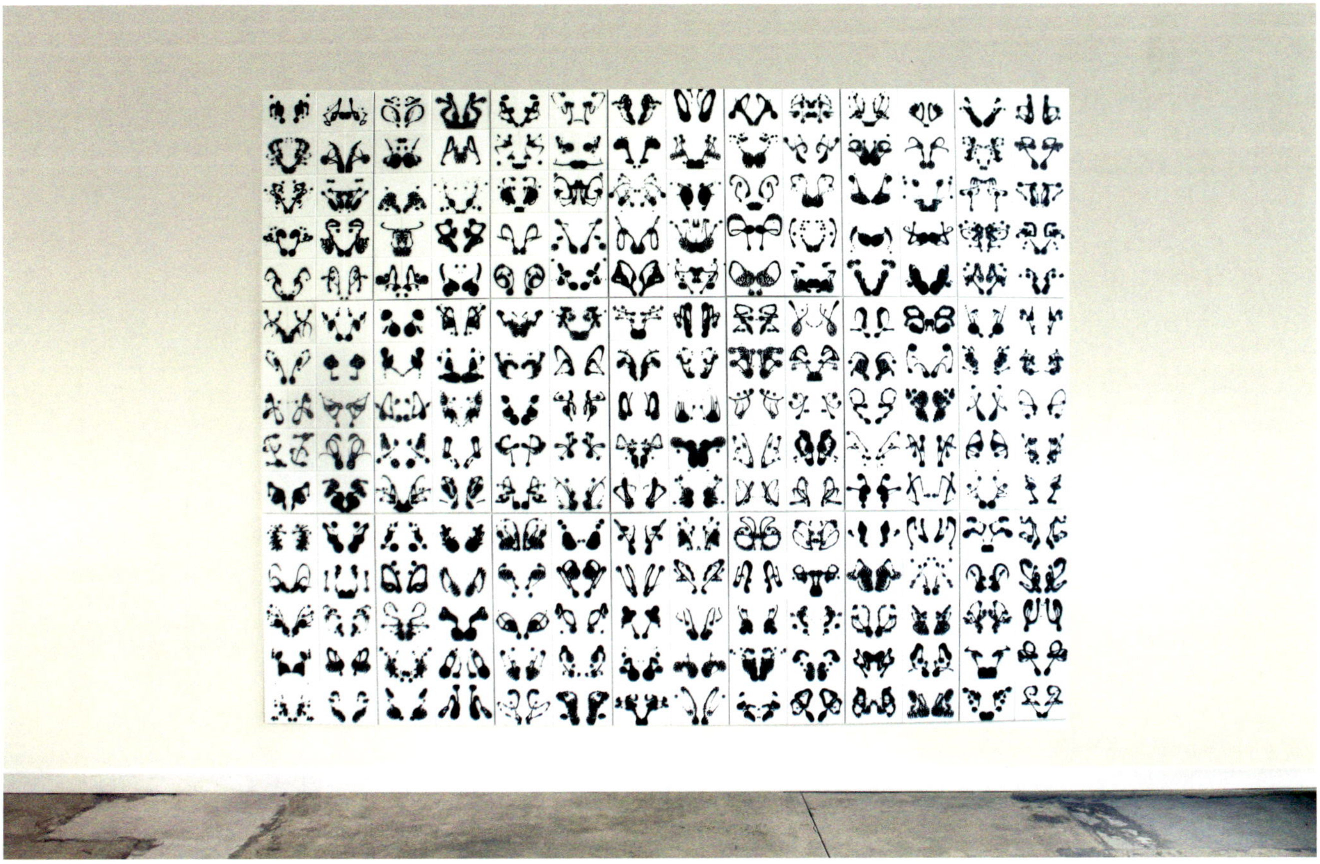

1 *Resonance*. Speaker, 11.8" × 15.7" aluminum plate, black glass powder, frequency generator, motion detector, video, and sound by Edmund Champion, The University of Berkeley, CA, Department of Music. 236.2" × 118.1" × 157". 2013.

2 *Sound-Visions*. Fused glass powder on sheet glass, AC sound recorder, and headphones. 15.75" × 0.79" × 19.7". 2013.

3 *Atlas No. 1 & 2*. Glass, lacquered wooden frames, resin, and fiberglass. 24" × 2.75" × 32". 2012. Fotografisch. de. Sven Claus.

4 *Rorschach*. Black enamel paint fused to 420 white sheets of glass, mounted in sets of 10 double images on plastic. 2014.

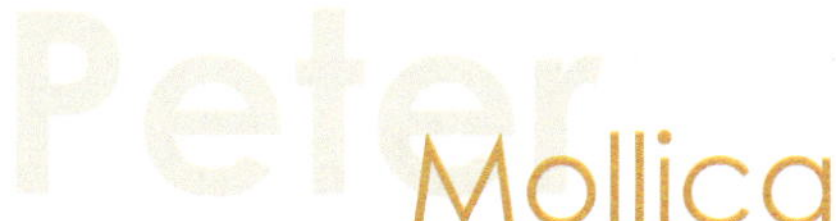

Peter Mollica

Walnut Creek, California

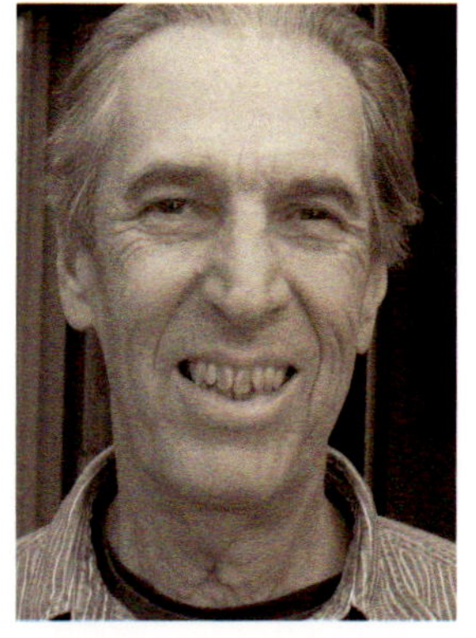

I was born in Newton, Massachusetts, in 1941. In 1964, I apprenticed to Chris Rufo in Somerville, Massachusetts, to learn all aspects of stained glass craft. We made windows mostly for churches in traditional Gothic style. We occasionally made "modern" windows, which meant in Mondrian style. In 1965, I found a book by Robert Sowers, which opened my eyes to windows made in Germany since the end of the war. I knew then that I had to learn to design. In 1968, I left Massachusetts and moved to Berkeley, where I opened a studio to make windows and free-hanging panels for homes and public buildings.

In 1979, I moved my studio to my garage in Oakland. In 1988, I was commissioned to fabricate two large clerestory windows, designed by Rowan LeCompte for the National Cathedral in Washington, DC. I needed a bigger studio so I moved to the studio I still have in Oakland, where I continue to make windows for libraries, churches, a synagogue, and homes, and free-hanging panels for a handful of faithful collectors and myself.

1 *Alia Red*. Leaded glass technique. 22" × 18". 2009.

2 *Jennie's Drip Window*. Leaded glass technique. 34" × 12". 1975.

3 *Rocks*. Leaded glass technique. 22" × 18". 2013. © Sam Halstead.

4 *Bieri Mtn*. Leaded glass technique. 24" × 18". 1991. © Sam Halstead.

5 *Catherine of Siena Chapel*. Leaded glass technique. 105" × 27". 2000.

1

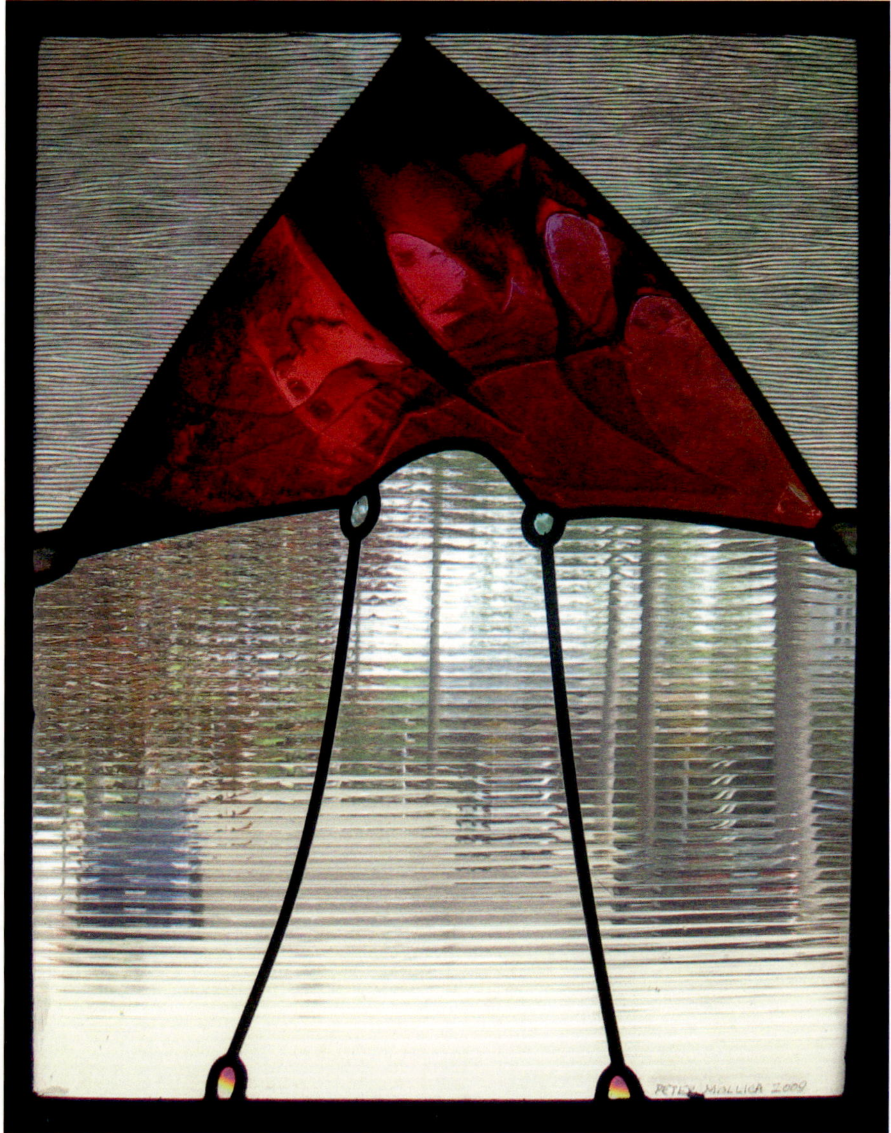

2

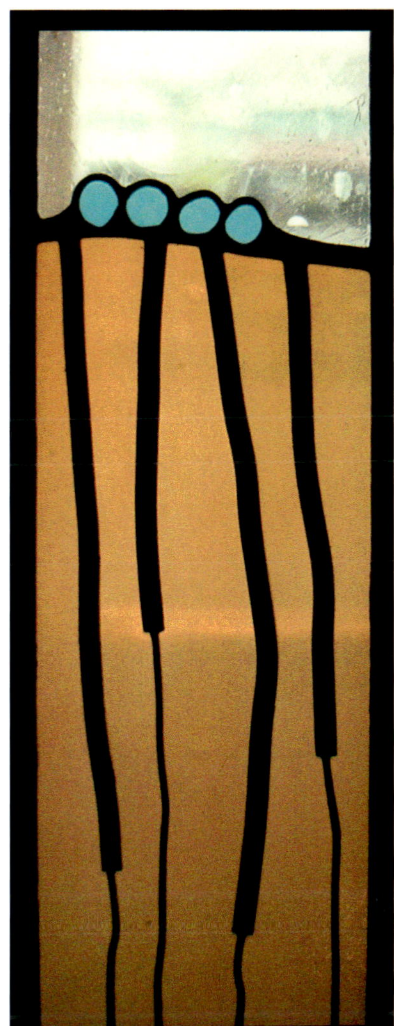

4

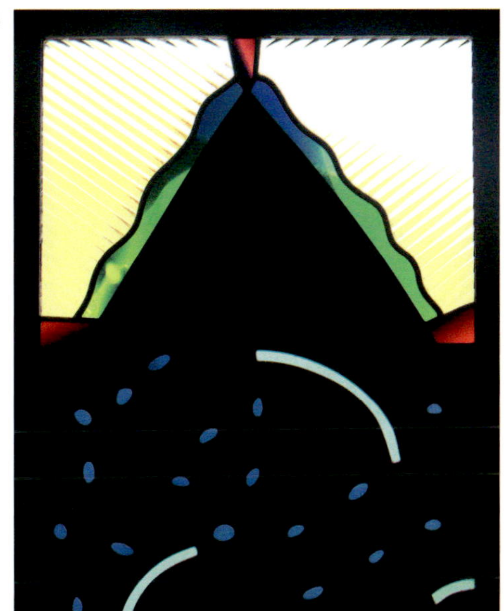

5

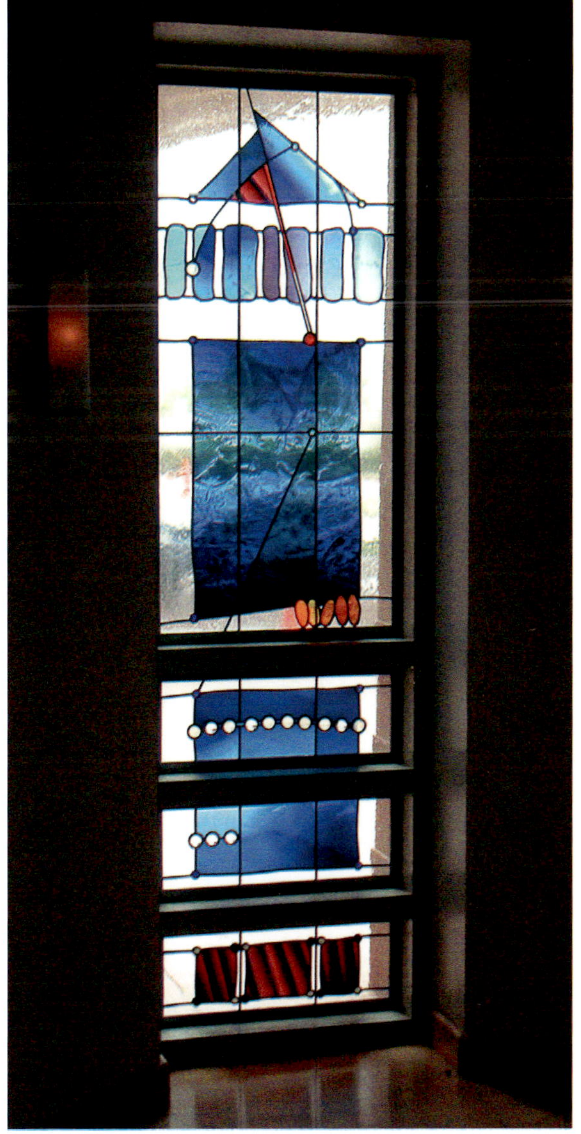

3

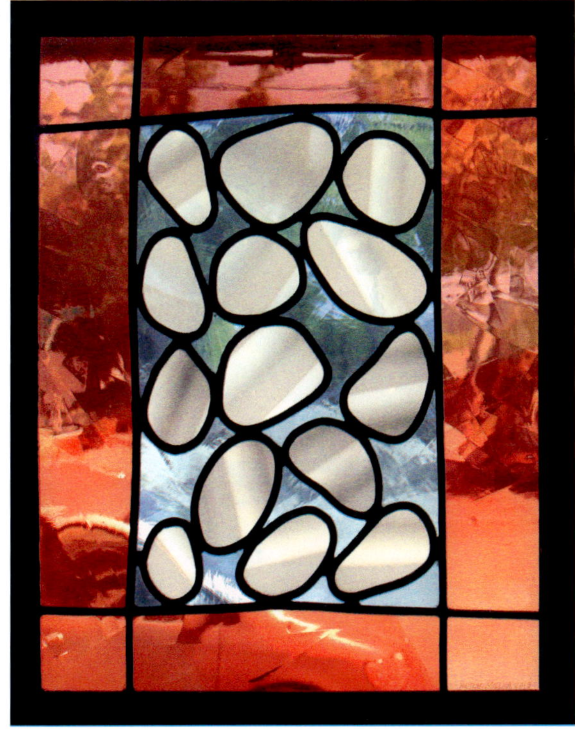

Benjamin Moore

Seattle, Washington

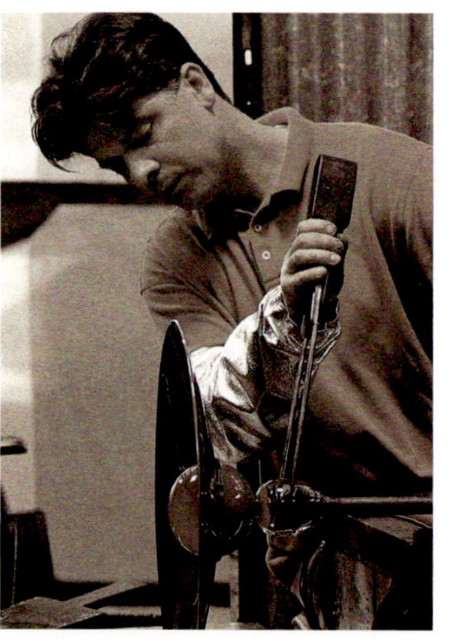
Courtesy of Russell Johnson.

The fundamental concern and focus of my work are to achieve simplicity, balance, and clarity of form. Simple geometric shapes, such as the sphere and the cylinder, are often referenced in the execution of my work. I use color generally to attract attention to contour, but utilize very little surface decoration that would take away from the purity of the object's form.

For me, the true challenge of creating an object is to give the piece a timeless presence or quality. To achieve this, I focus on the color, shapes, and proportions of the vessels by themselves and in groups and the way light interacts with the work. Opacity, translucency, and transparency are varied to create different impressions for each series of work.

1

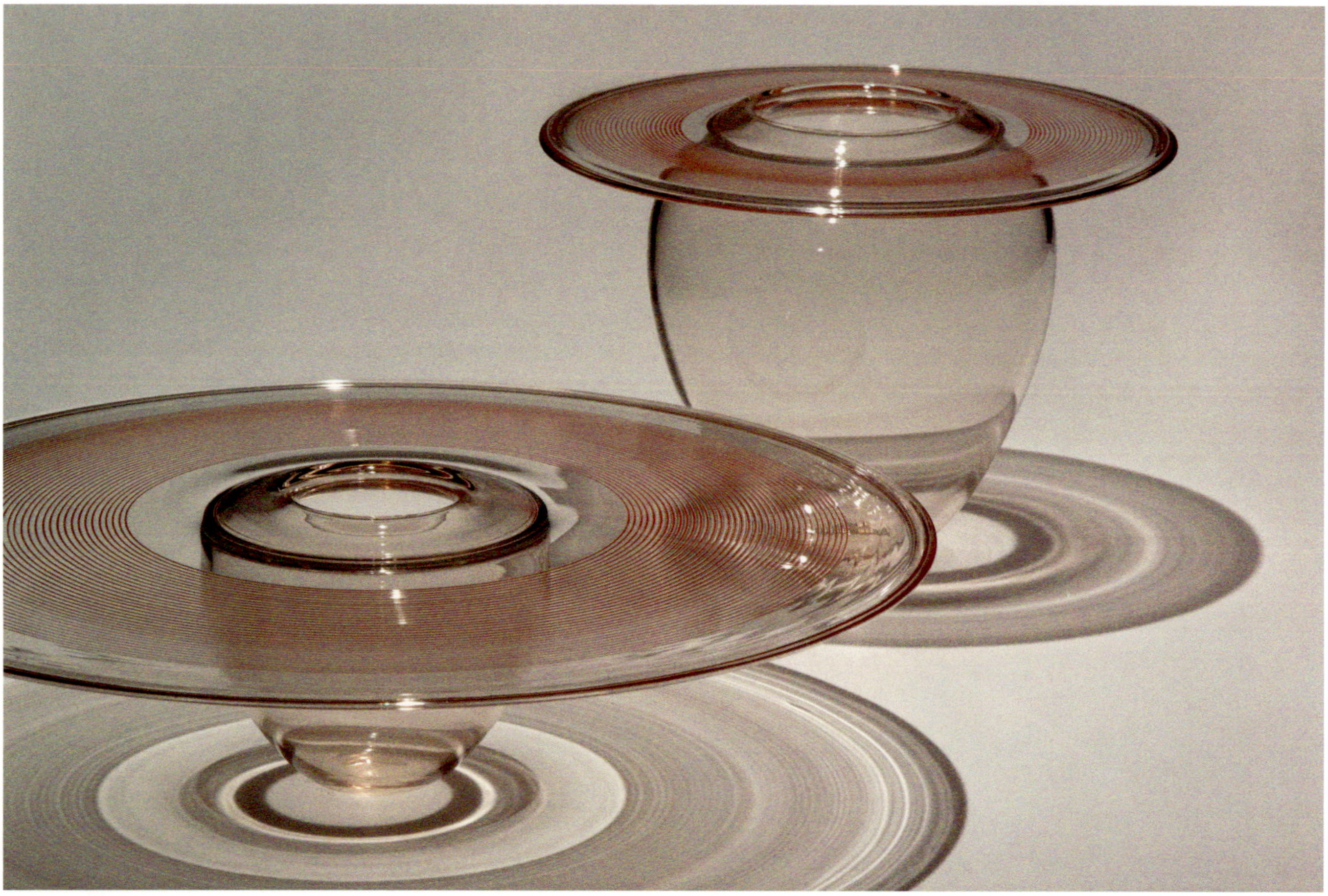

1 *Manganese Interior Fold Set*. Blown glass. Bowl: 4.5" × 19"; vase: 13" × 9.5". 1996. Courtesy of Russell Johnson.

2 *Lapis Palla Set*. Blown glass. Bowl: 4.5" × 16.25"; vase: 17.5" × 5". 2008. Courtesy of Russell Johnson.

3 *Amsterdam*. Blown glass and powder-coated bronze. 51" × 4" × 41.5". 2005. Courtesy of Russell Johnson.

4 *The Hungarian*. Blown glass and powder-coated bronze. 50" × 3" × 50". 2009. Courtesy of Russell Johnson.

2

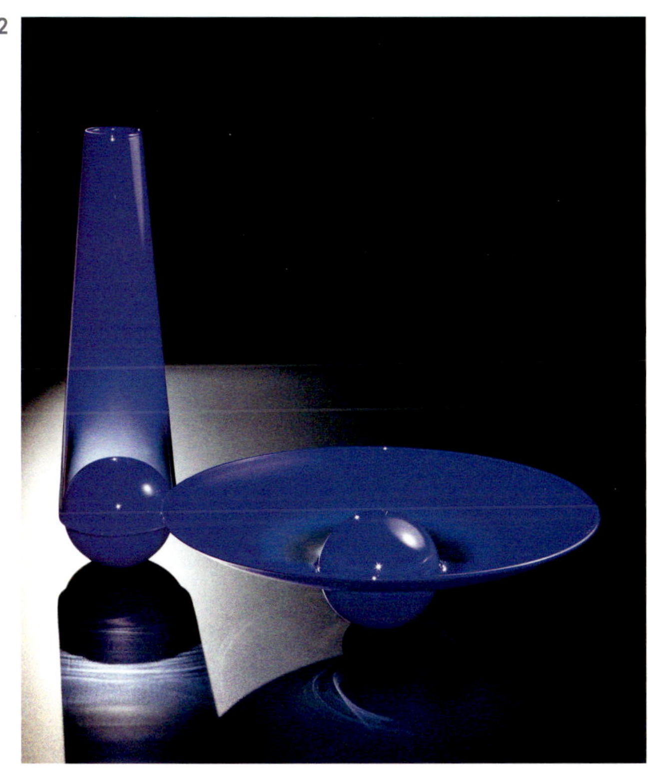

4

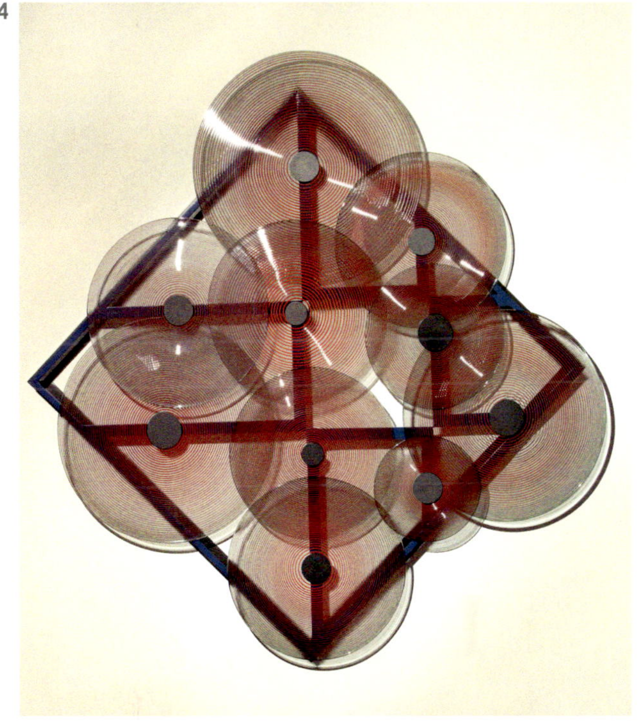

3

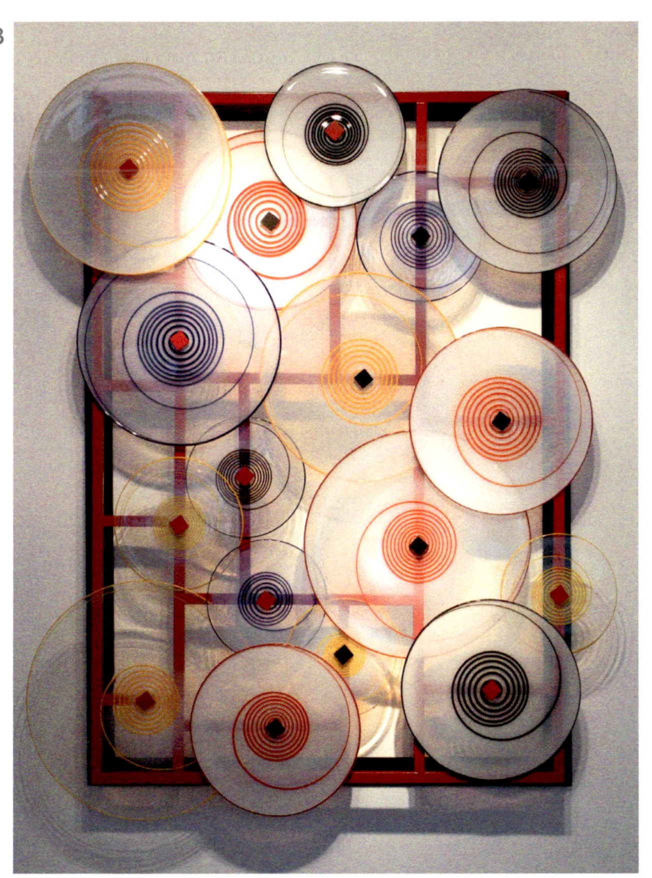

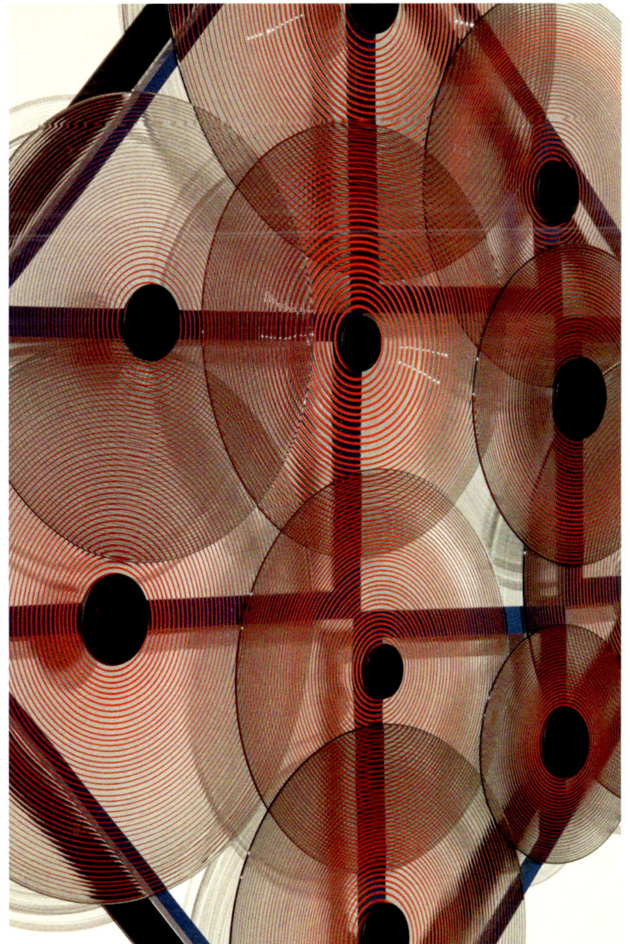

Kathleen Mulcahy

Pittsburgh, Pennsylvania

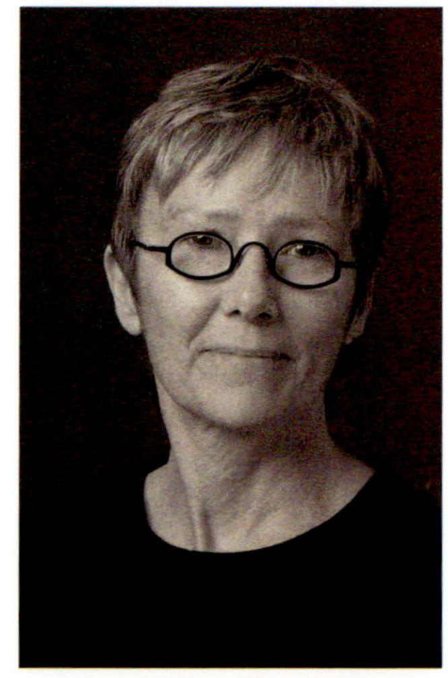

Courtesy of Mark Perrott.

I am floating along on the West Branch of the Susquehanna. It is a slow, wide river, and the riverbed is so close I can almost touch it from the edge of the canoe. My arm drops over the edge, and I let my fingers open to the cool sluice of water through my fingers. The colors are warm iron, orange, browns, sand, and dark shadows of the vessel quietly transporting us from campsite to campsite. I begin my work by recalling a body of water. It could be the deepest blue and high bright reflections of the open sea, the emerald green of an alpine lake, the horizon line at the Gulf, the shallow bed of a lazy river, or the tiny pond that we dug in our backyard.

Several things coalesce in my dreaming on water: the need to look deeply below the surface, below the skin, allowing the transparency and diffusion of the etching to obscure and reveal at the same time. This river or stretch of horizon that I am willing into being presents me with that perfect moment of a storm receding, the air clearing, and the feeling that everything has become new. Take a breath, it says, everything is listening.

1

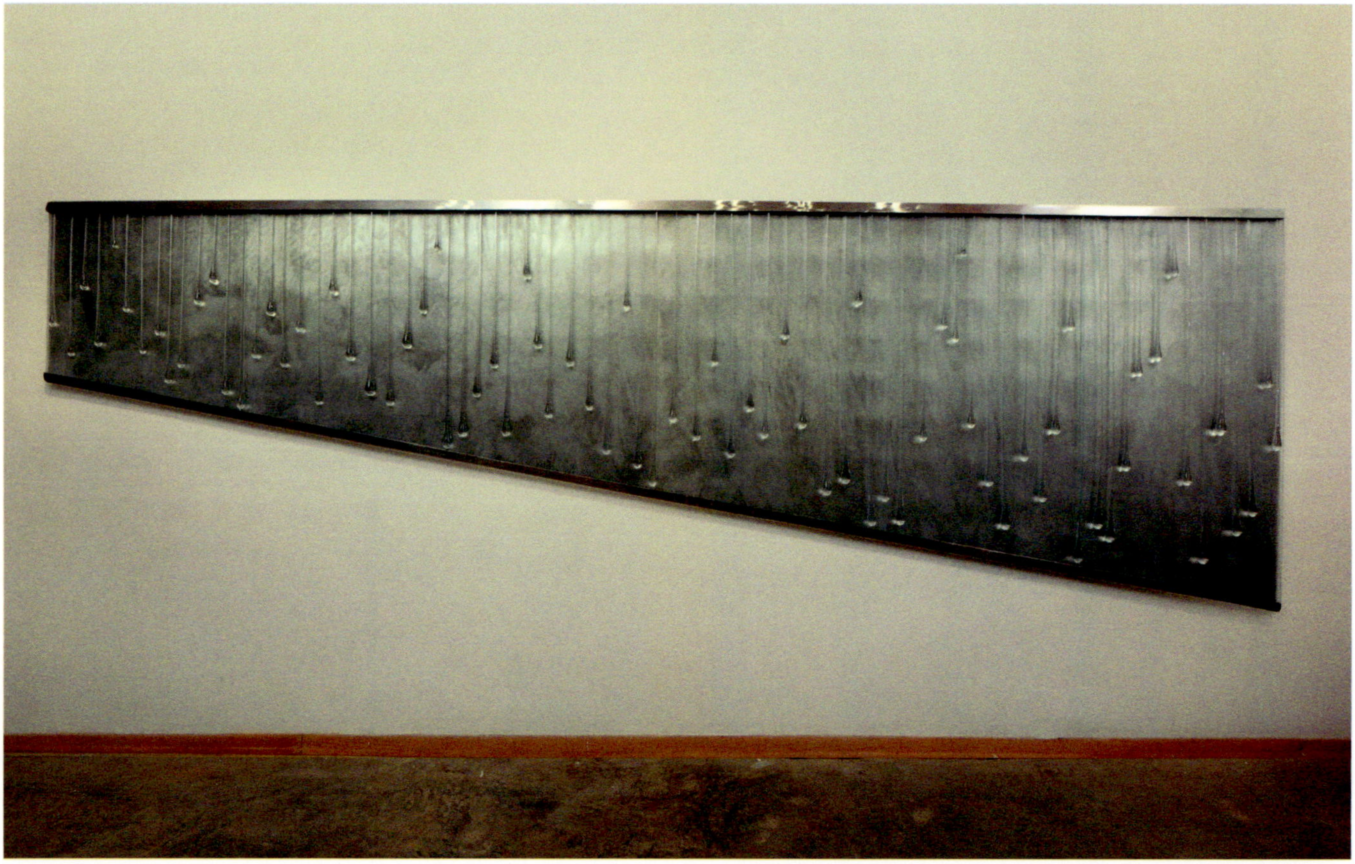

1 *Cascade*. Stainless steel with bent and etched glass and hotworked glass drops. 60" × 3" × 182" (wedge shape). 2013. Courtesy of Jim Judkis.

2

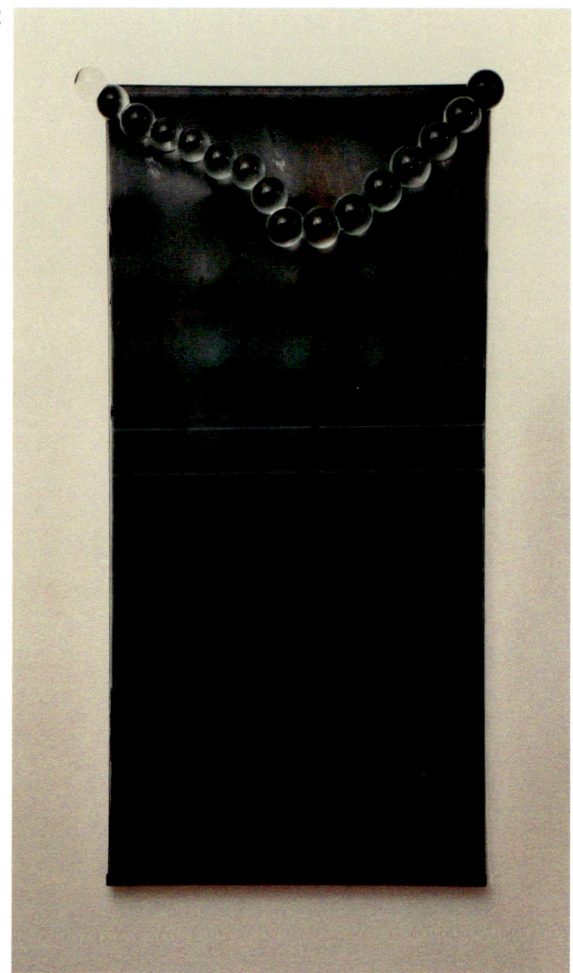

4

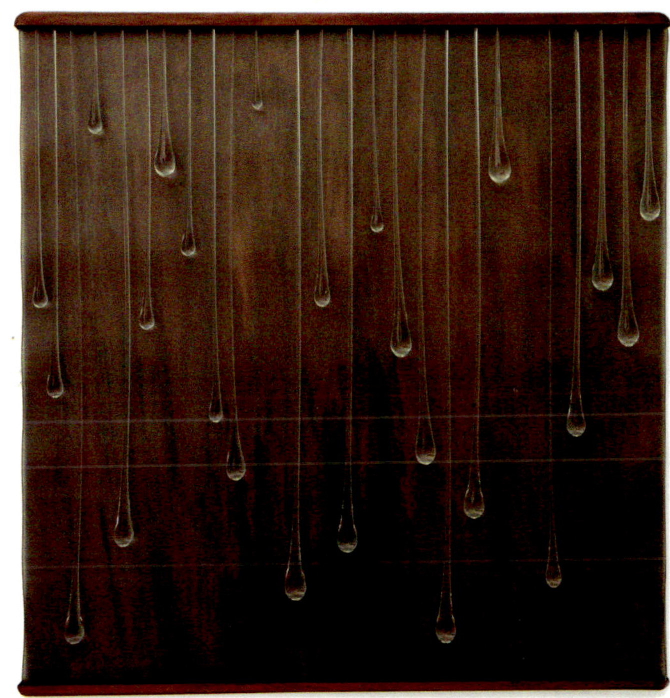

3

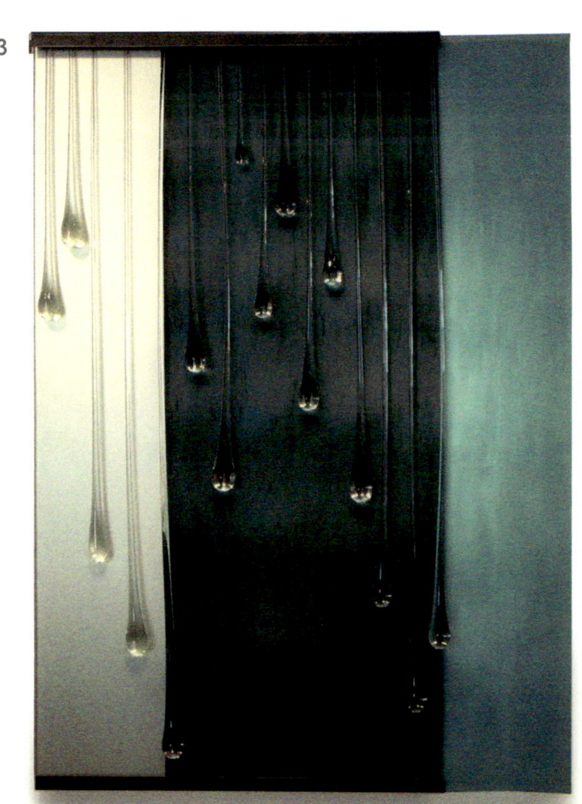

5

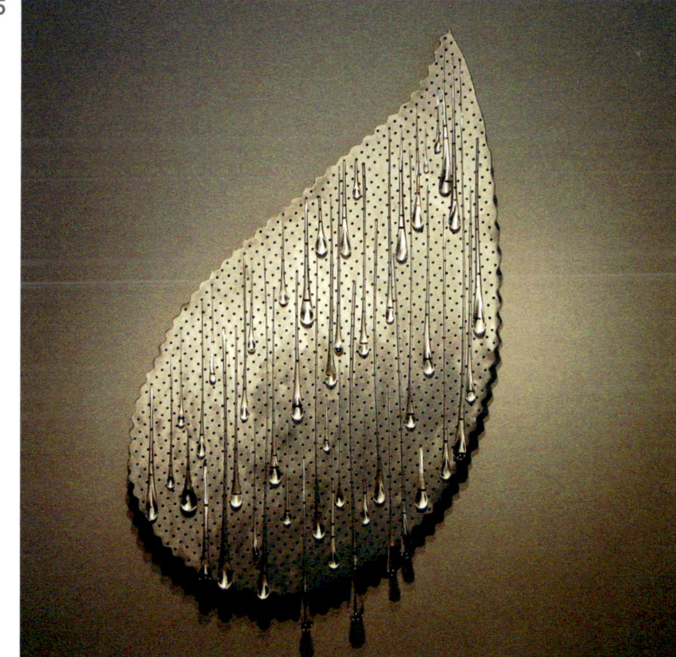

2 *Breakpoint.* Patinaed mild steel with bent and etched glass and fabricated solid glass spheres. 65" × 3" × 32". 2009.

3 *The Gulf at Noon.* Patinaed steel with etched mirror and bent blue glass and hot worked glass drops. 65" × 3" × 35". 2009.

4 *Susquehanna.* Patinaed mild steel with bent and etched glass and hotworked glass drops. 48" × 3" × 48". Courtesy of Jim Judkis.

5 *Tidal.* Fabricated aluminum with hot worked glass drops. 86" × 42". 2010.

Shelley Muzylowski Allen

Sedro-Woolley, Washington

By suspending figures in moments of tension, recalling myths and legends through animal forms, I hope to convey a place that different species have occupied over time. From the long and storied history of the horse, to medieval tapestries depicting the lure of the unicorn, to the mysterious disappearance of the Red Gazelle, animals have been associated with magic, legend, divinity, and mythology. They are symbols or icons of eras and cultures around the world, so it is important that I capture the inherent nature of these creatures in my work reflecting not just my own insights but inspiring an emotional experience and connection in the viewer.

To balance the dynamics of working in the glass hot shop, I spend time observing and drawing my natural surrounding. Trained as a painter, I use rich textures and understated colors to add depth to the sculpture being made and strive to bring the lushness of oil paint to this dynamic medium. Once it is cooled, I augment the glass with natural materials such as horsehair, leather, and stone. The hard unyielding surfaces of the hand-selected rocks contrast with the blown, sculpted glass and organic forms, enriching all of the materials' inherent beauty.

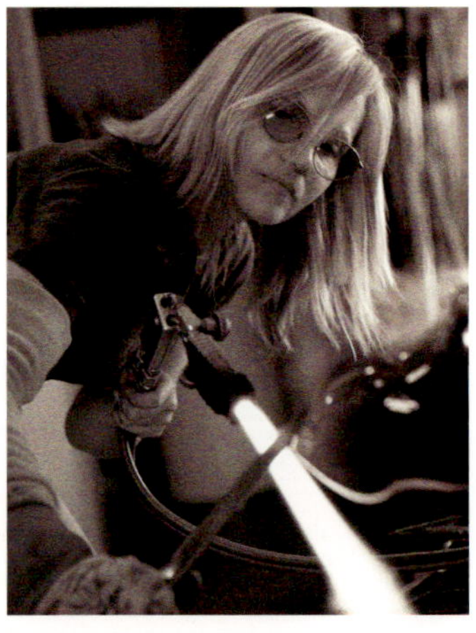

Courtesy of KP-Studios.com.

1

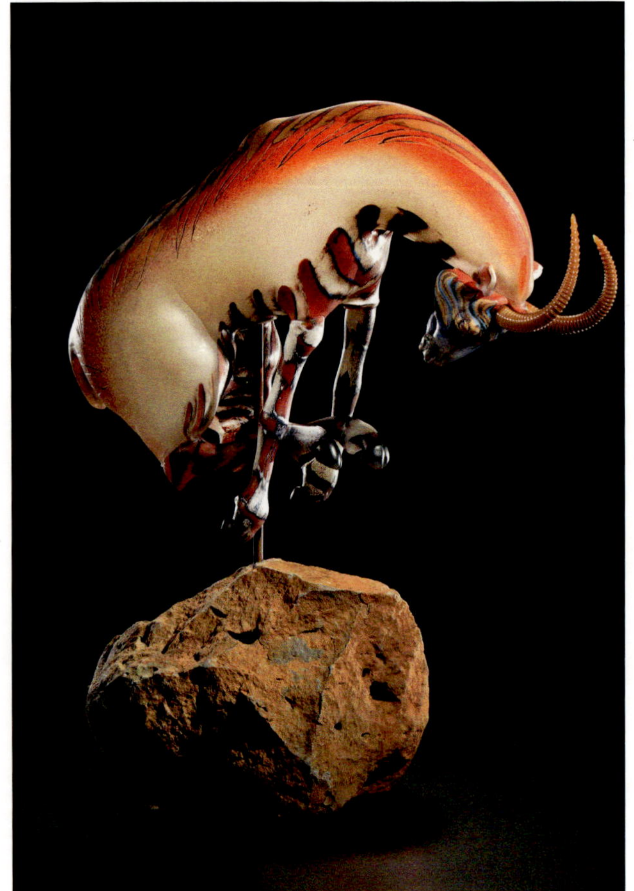

2

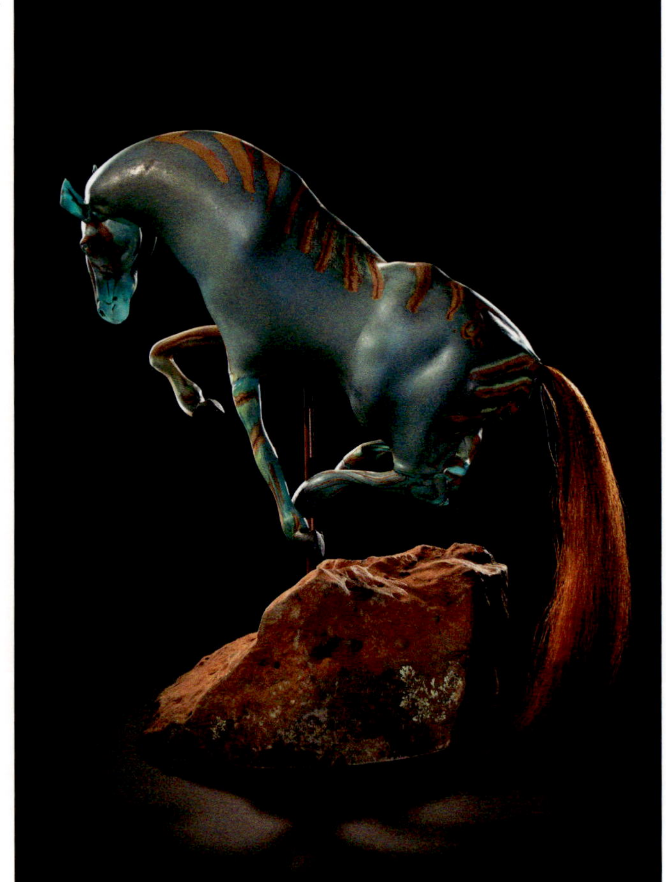

3

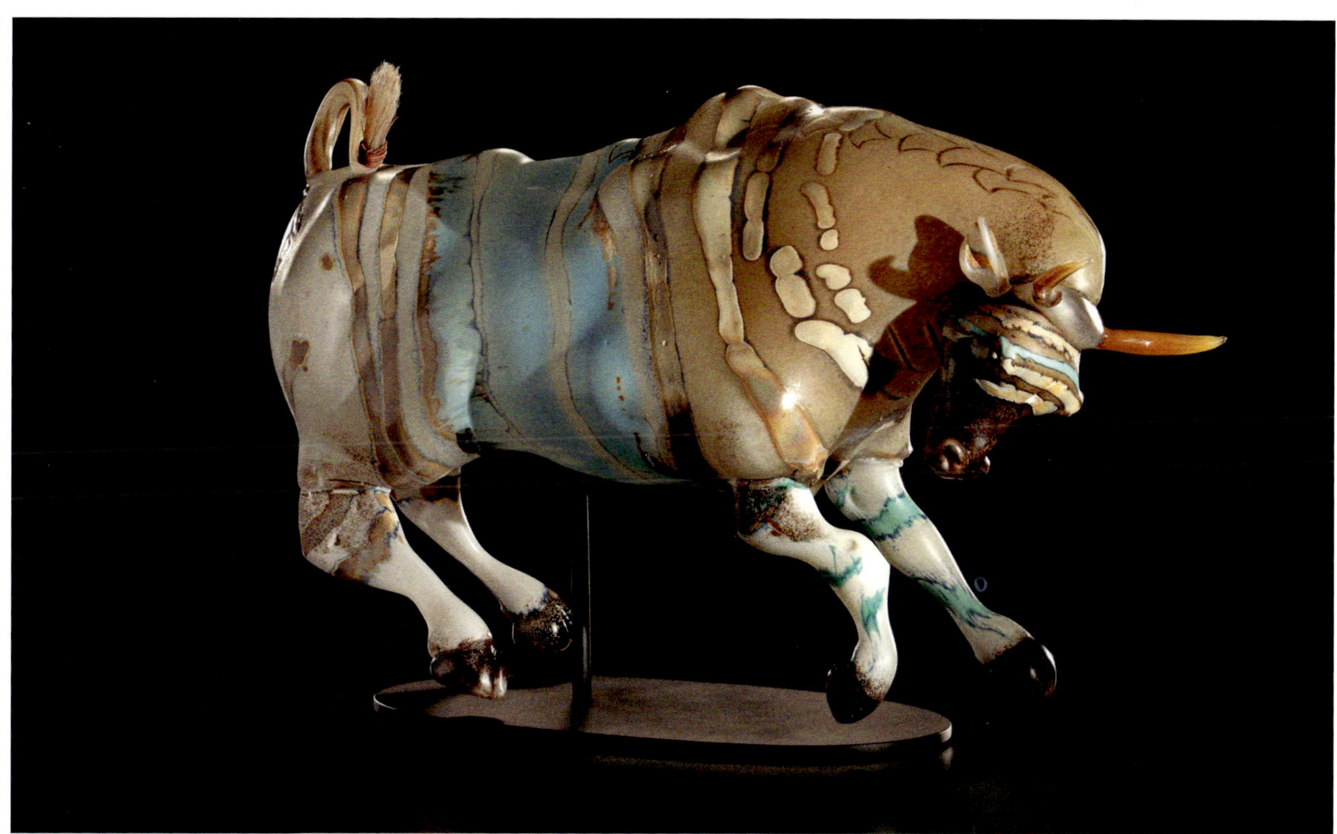

4

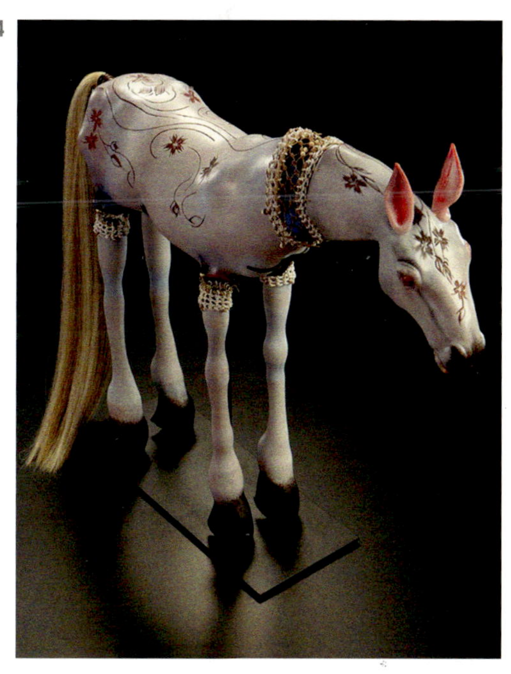

5

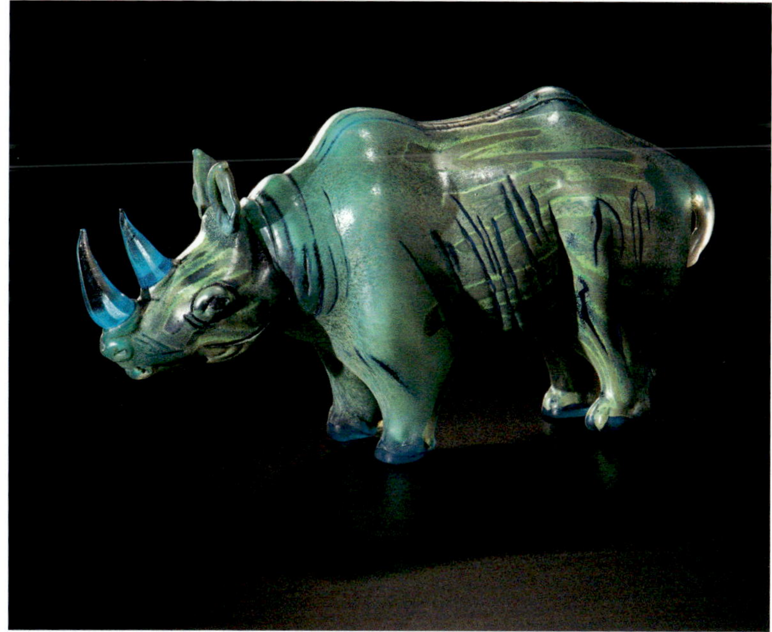

1 *Brio*. Blown, hand-sculpted and engraved glass, Arizona rock, and steel. 26" × 12" × 25". 2014. Courtesy of Russell Johnson.

2 *Under the Blue Blue Sky*. Blown, hand-sculpted glass, horsehair, Arizona rock, and steel. 26" × 18" × 26". 2014. Courtesy of Russell Johnson.

3 *Becoming the Bull*. Blown and hand-sculpted glass, human hair, mixed media, and steel. 13" × 8" × 20". 2011. Courtesy of Russell Johnson.

4 *Cherry*. Blown, hand-sculpted and engraved glass, horsehair, mixed media, and steel. 31" × 9" × 32". 2010. Courtesy of KP-Studios.com.

5 *Squire*. Blown, hand-sculpted and engraved glass. 7" × 5" × 12.5". 2014. Courtesy of Russell Johnson.

George O'Grady

Tesuque, New Mexico

I began working with hot glass in 1993. I am predominantly self-taught as a lampworker, with a great nod to my brother Kevin O'Grady and also to Lewis C. Wilson. In 1994, I first met Charles V. Miner, owner and founder of Tesuque Glassworks. This changed my world as I began exploring the wonders of off-hand glassblowing. While Charlie taught me most of what I know in this unique art form, I also gained a wealth of knowledge and experience from such fine artisans as Peet Robison and Marc Boute. This past year I have begun exploring, creating my own colors from scratch, in addition to buying my color from glass color manufacturers in Germany.

My creative art direction is strongly influenced by the art nouveau artist Louis Comfort Tiffany and the early twentieth-century art movement, which grew from impressionism, to cubism, and eventually into modern abstract. Those artists' use of color and shapes strongly inspires me as I work with hot glass. It is my fervent desire that those who purchase my work enjoy it as much I enjoyed creating it. "Hot glass is a gas!"

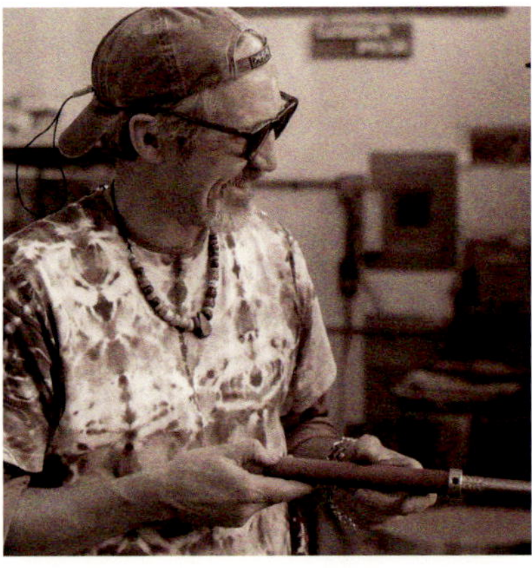

Courtesy of T. J. Nicholson.

1

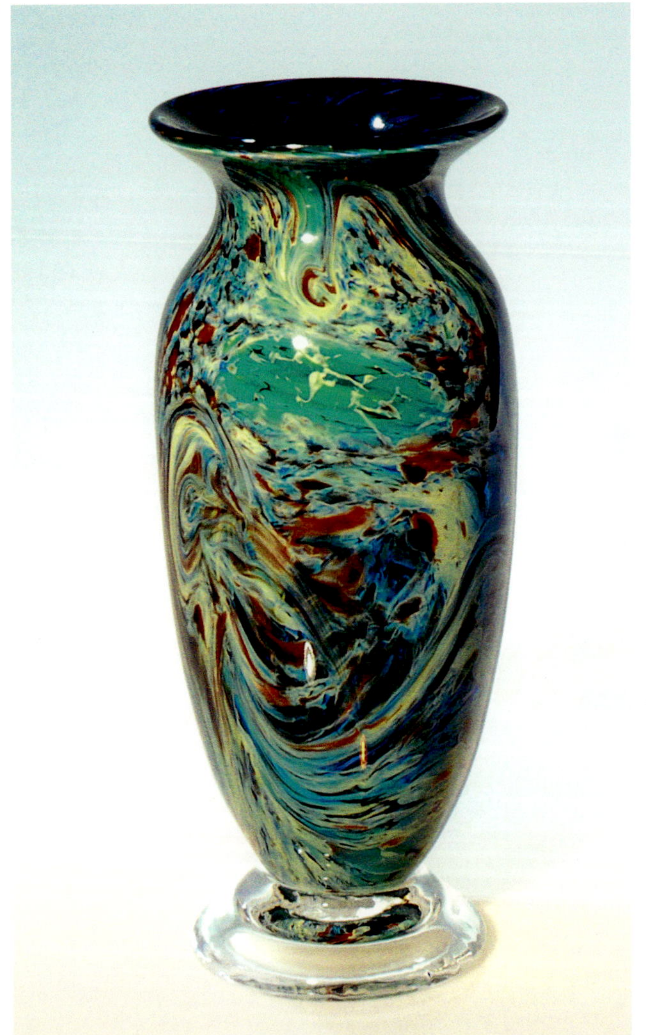

2

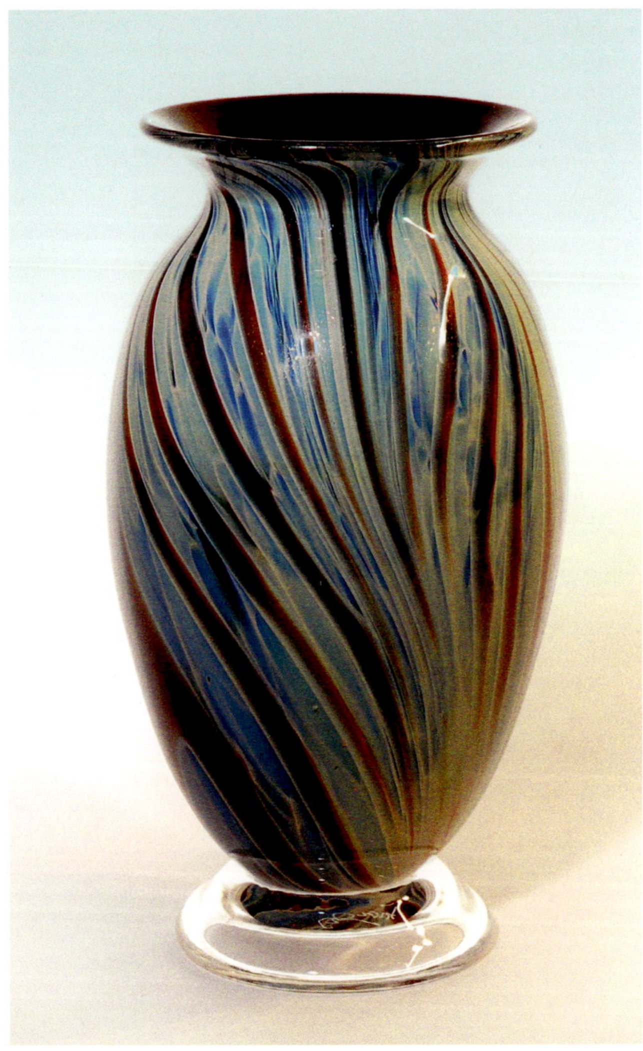

3

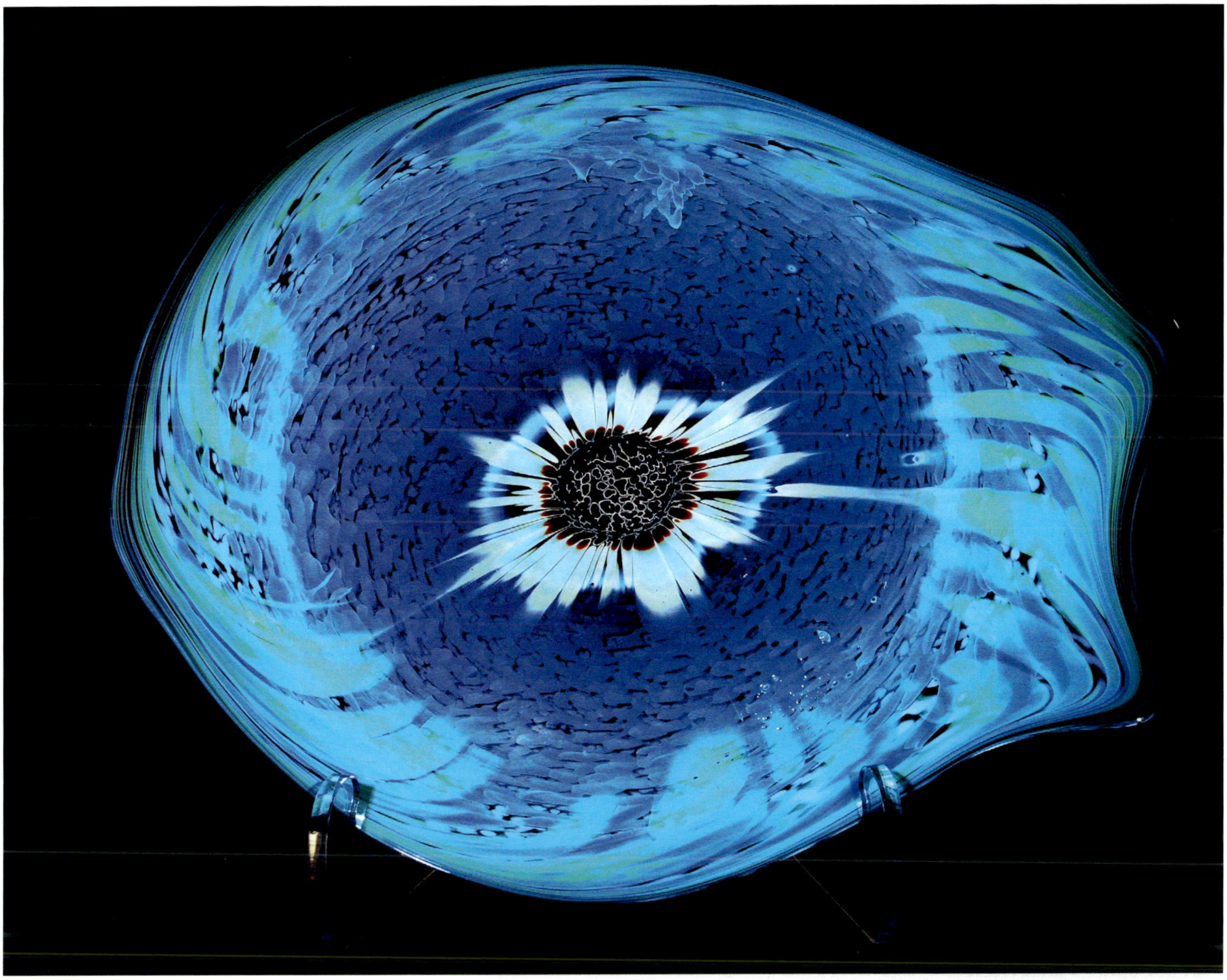

1 *Tie-dye Vase*. Green on deep cobalt. 10" × 4.5". 2014. Photo: Denny O'Connor.

2 *Garden vase*. Green-blue on black. Off-hand blown. 11" × 5.5". 2014. Photo: Denny O'Connor.

3 *Galaxy in Blue*. Off-hand blown. 5.5" × 23" × 26". 2014.Photo: Denny O'Connor.

4 *Beads and tops on the run*. Vase off-hand blown, beads and tops hand lampworked on torch. 2015. Photo: Denny O'Connor.

4

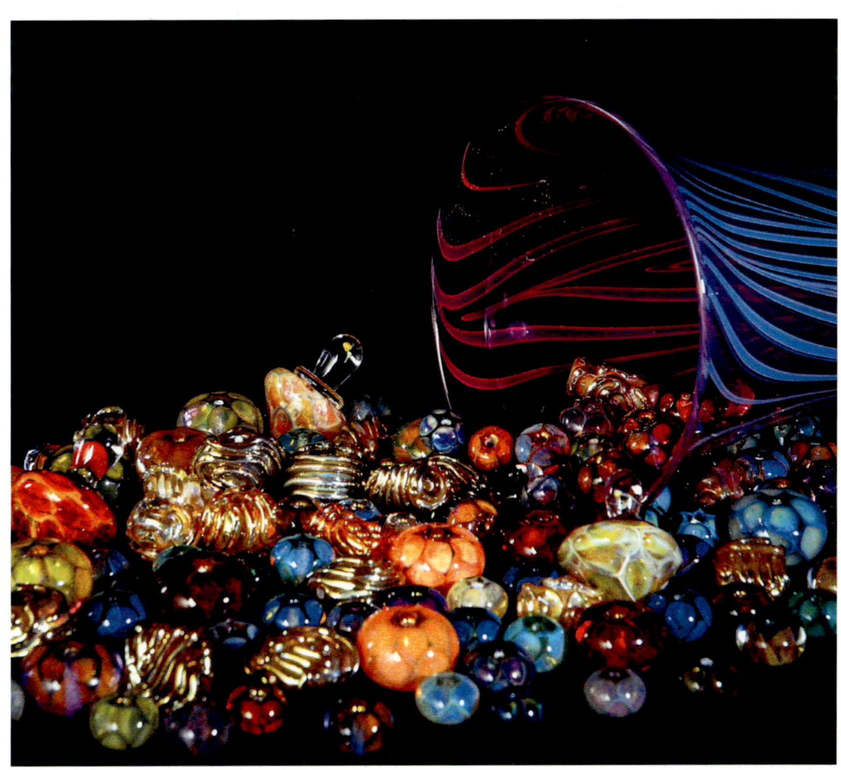

Joseph Pagano

West Nyack, New York

After spending many years in the urban environment of Brooklyn and New York City, I moved to New York's Hudson Highlands, which inspired me to get closer to the natural world. Nature's colors, shapes, and textures provide me with an infinite palette to create from. I will often clear my mind or work out ideas during a hike through the many trails and mountains that surround the area.

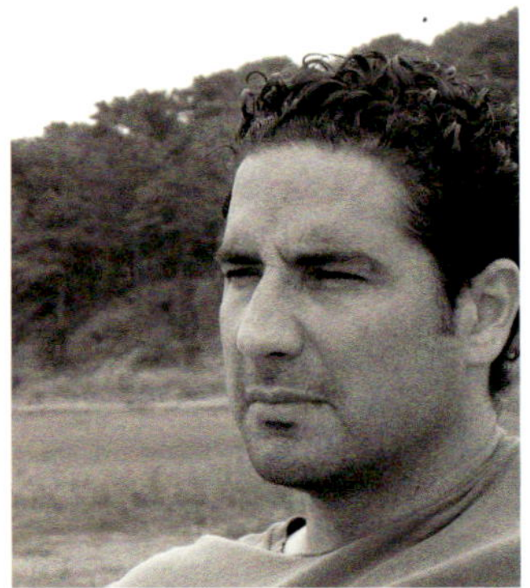

My vision is to combine old world craftsmanship with beautiful design. I have been classically trained in the various disciplines that encompass my work. Every piece I create is meticulously crafted and detailed. Joining elements like hand-blown and cast glass, distinctive woods, and metals, I produce works that can be custom tailored to meet the individual needs.

What is so fulfilling for me is working with so many diverse raw materials, merging the decorative arts with interior design, and in the process creating objects that excite and inspire me.

1 *Geometric Rosewood Desk Lamp.* Hand-blown glass, bronze, and wood. 2015. Courtesy of Kent Miller Studios.

2 *Umber Mantis Hanging Pendants.* Hand-blown glass, bronze fittings. 2015. Courtesy of Kent Miller Studios.

3 *Copperhead.* Hand-blown and carved glass. 24" × 5" × 16". 2013. Courtesy of Kent Miller Studios.

4 *Python.* Hand-blown and carved glass. 26" × 5" × 16". 2013. Courtesy of Kent Miller Studios.

1

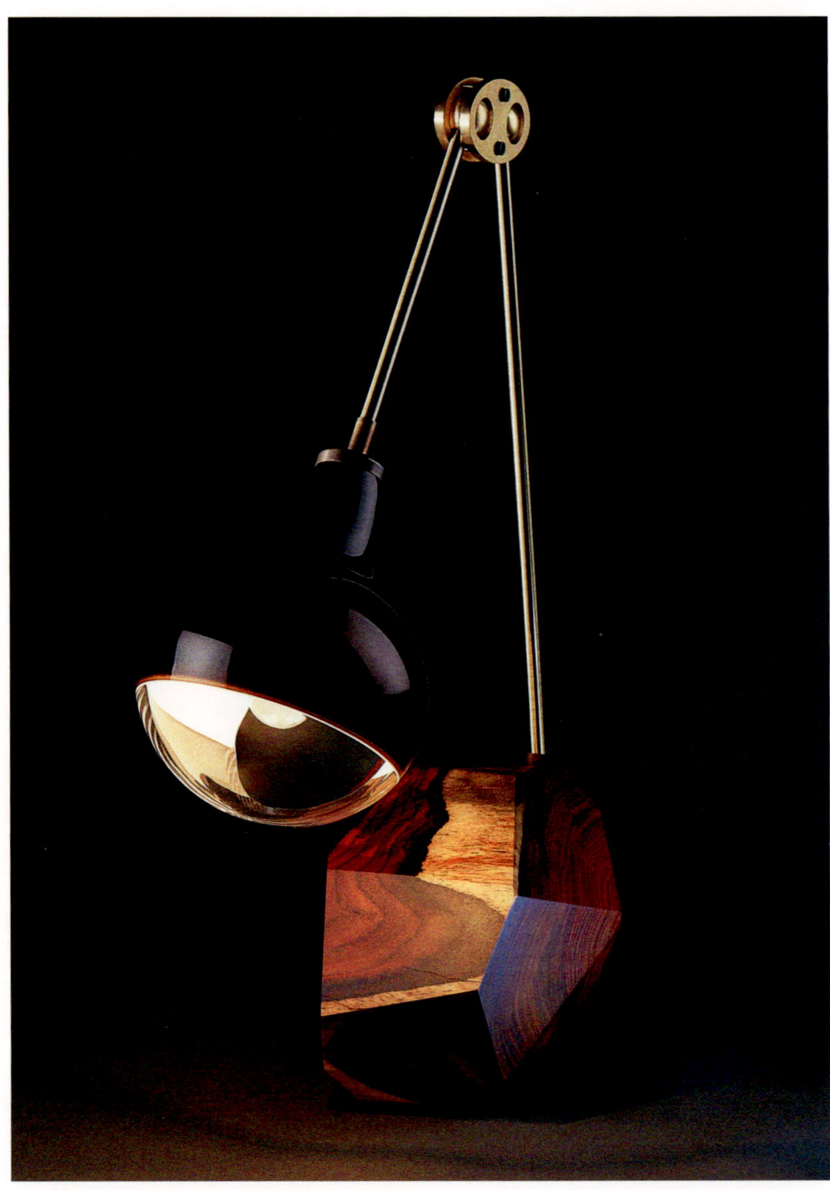

2

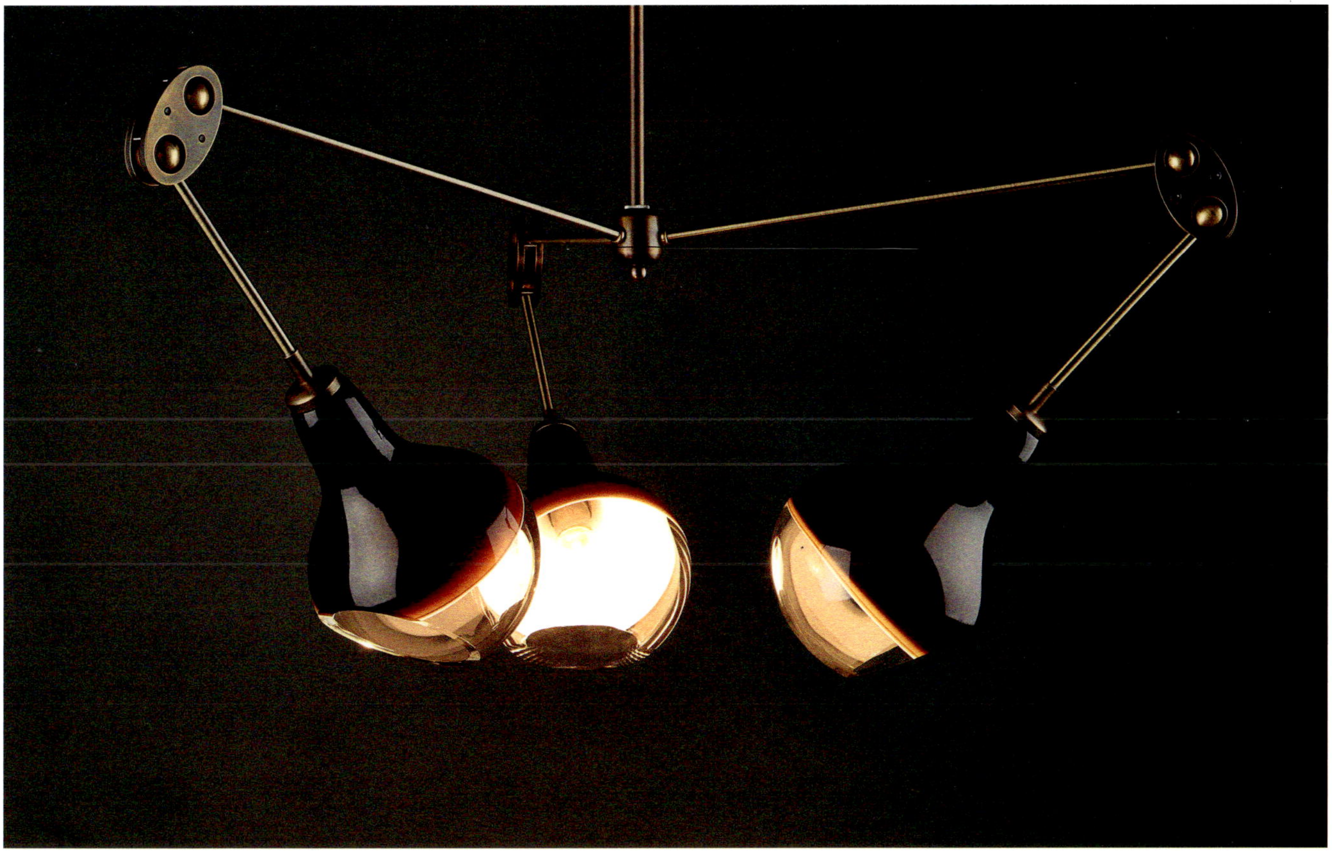

3

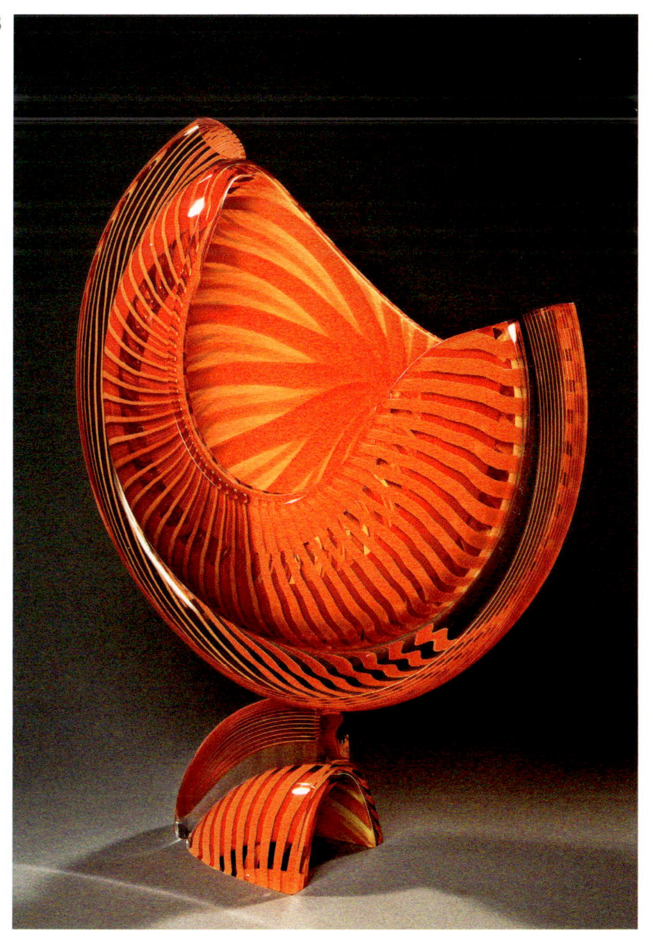

4

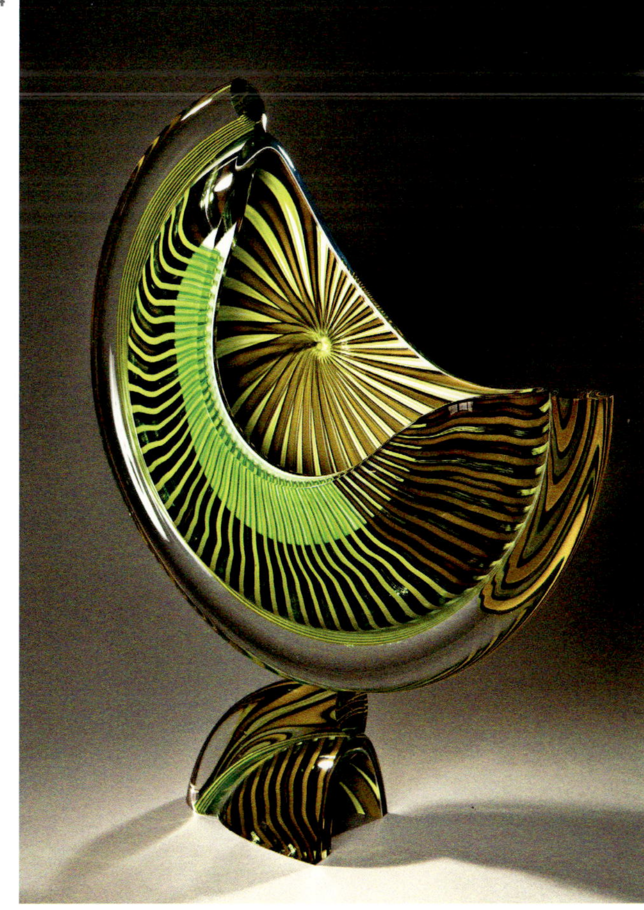

David Patchen

San Francisco, California

I find glass as seductive as it is challenging. A particularly unforgiving medium, it can provide an artist with endless creative opportunities to design; the only limitations are their imagination and skill in working with the material. I've always been captivated by how one can use this enigmatic material to achieve virtually any form, hold elements in suspension, and achieve great detail or soft abstraction. Its flexibility as a medium is matched by the difficulty it presents in using it to execute precise work.

Recently, I've been exploring a range of sculptural ideas that have evolved into a new body of work titled *Bloom.* Over the years, I have experimented with the concept of precious things hidden and revealed and only recently found an expression for these ideas. *Bloom* organic forms reveal something unexpected and precious that reward close inquiry. They are natural but non-representational and intentionally somewhat curious and hard to place. Since human brains are pattern-matching machines ("oh, that looks like x"), I wanted the work to feel vaguely familiar but lack a single point of reference, leaving it to the viewer to consider what it could be, how it evolved, what inspired it, what it communicates and what it could mean. *Bloom* one-of-a-kind works vary in color, texture, interior pattern, and overall form, but they are all of one "species."

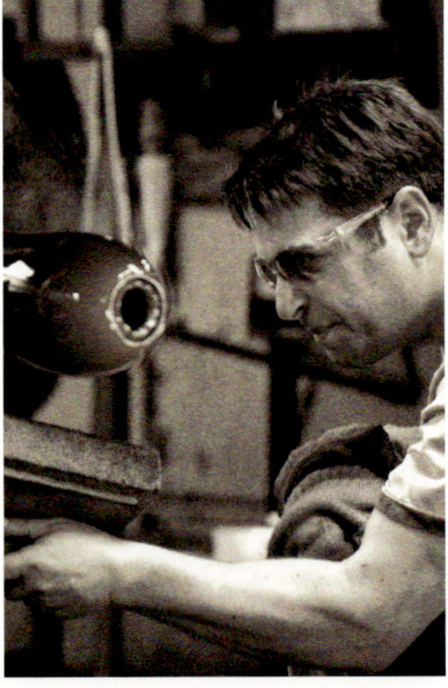

Courtesy of Erik Castro.

1

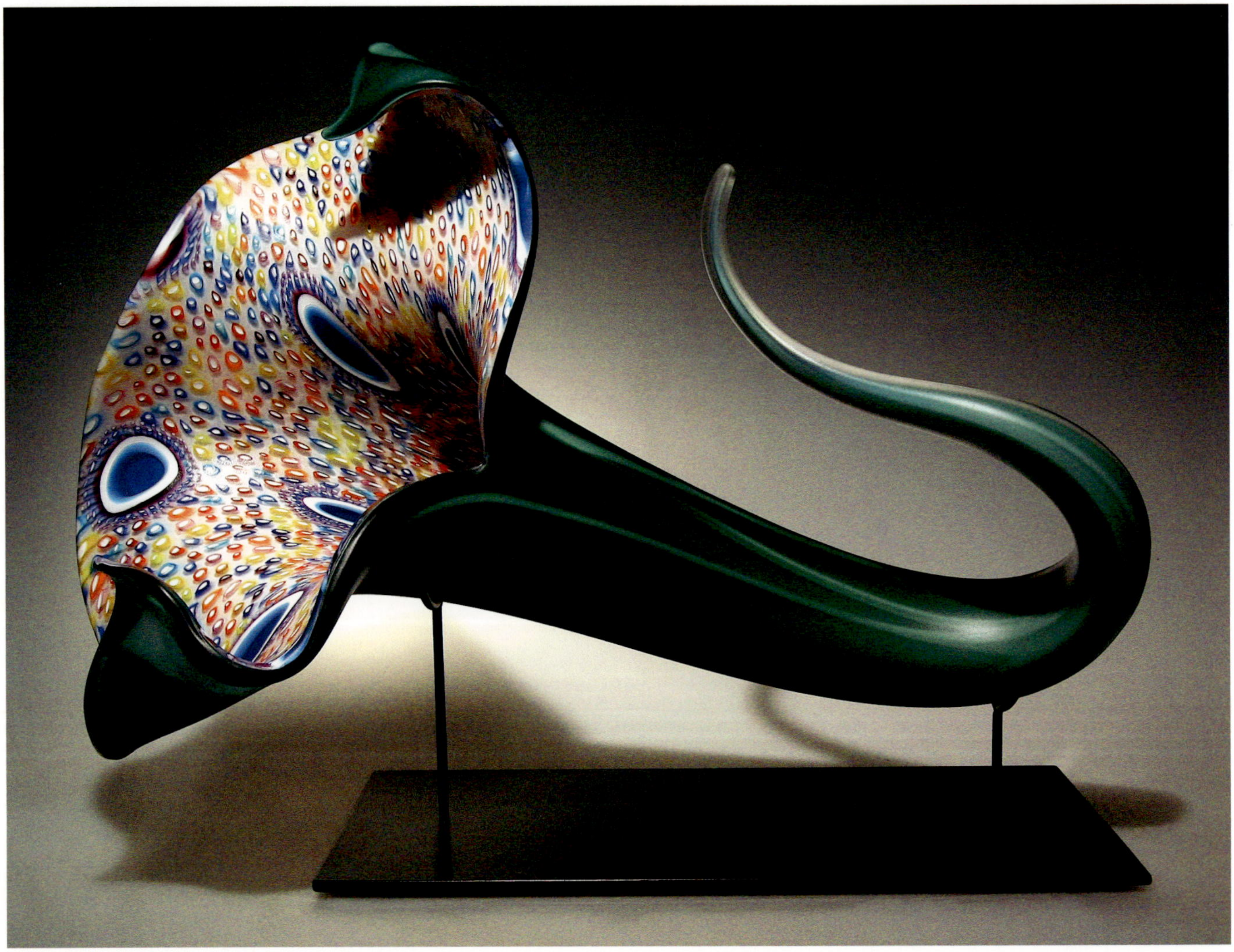

2

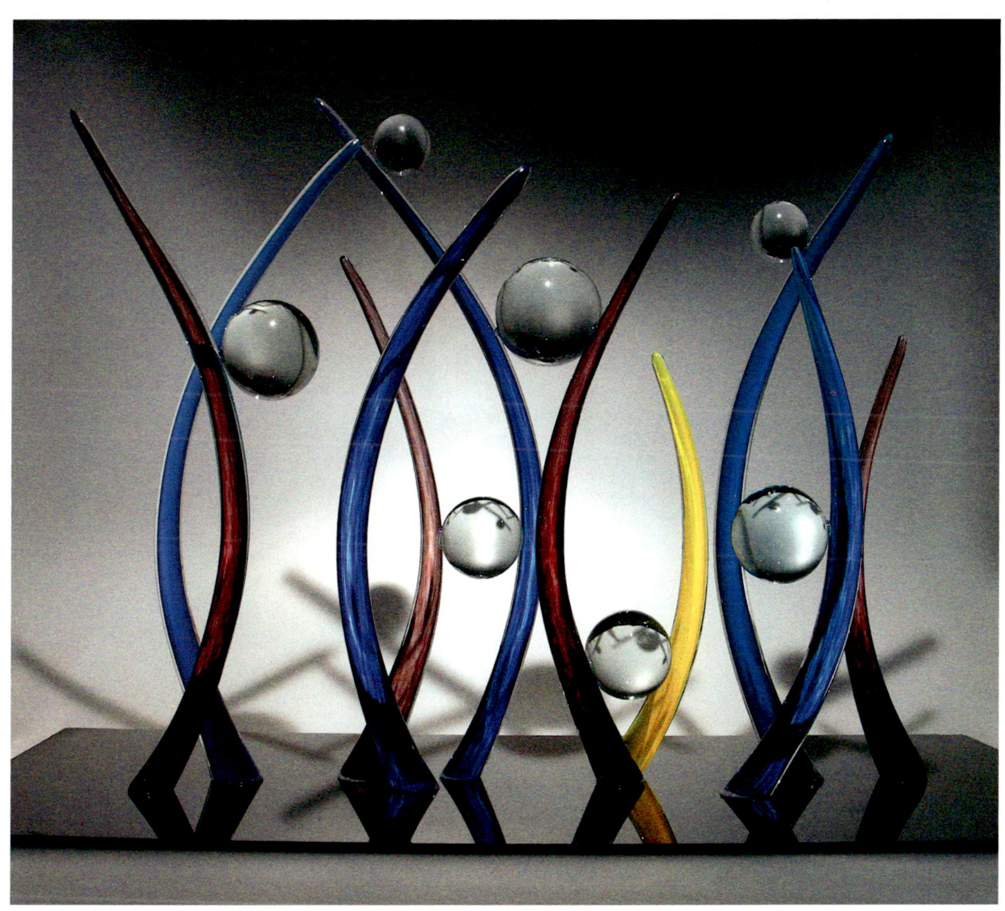

1 *Bloom*. Blown and hot-sculpted glass. 24" × 17" × 12". 2014.

2 *Dew*. Hot sculpted glass. 38" × 20" × 12". 2013.

3 *Sphere*. Blown glass, murrine. 13" × 13" × 14". 2014.

4 *Foglio*. Blown glass, murrine. 23" × 13" × 4". 2014.

3

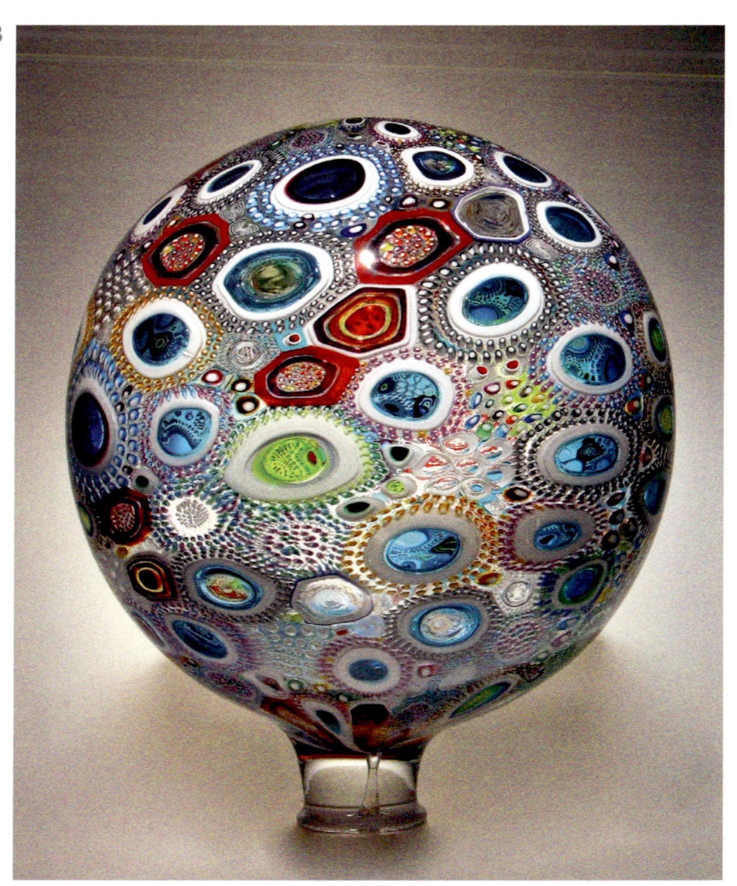

4

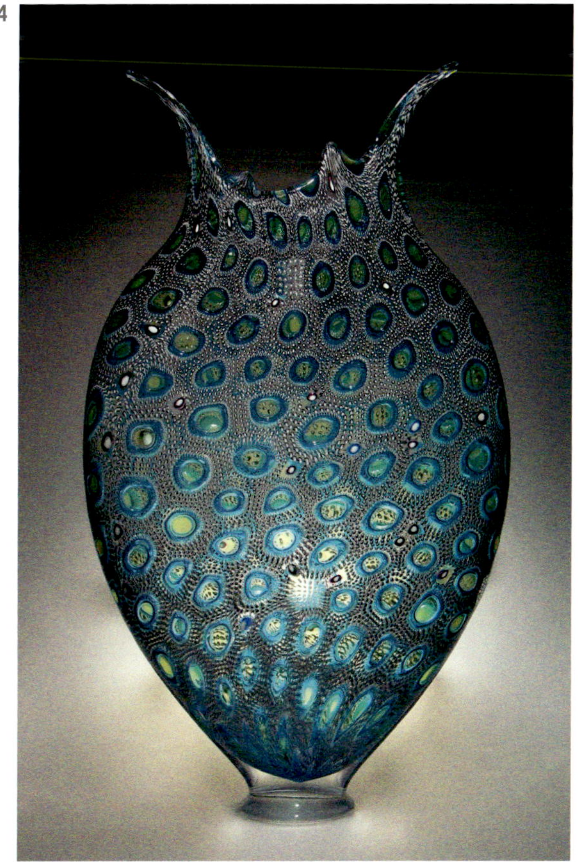

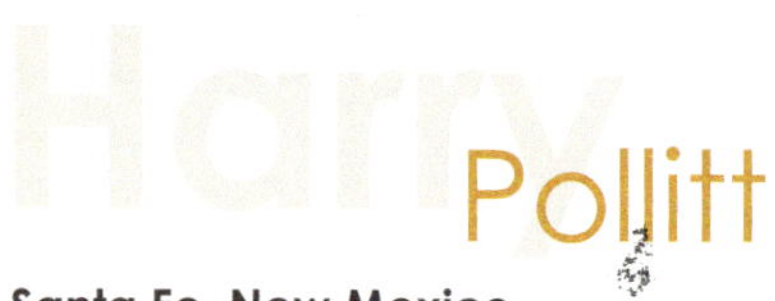

Harry Pollitt

Santa Fe, New Mexico

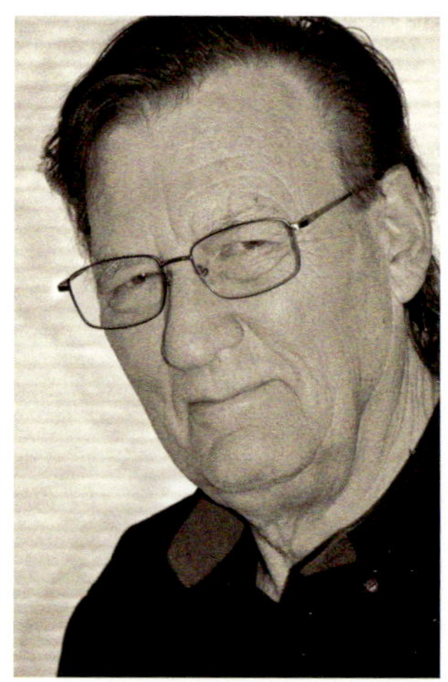

Courtesy of Gaye Gravely Pollitt.

People think that artists actively choose to become artists. It's not a matter of choice. We are compelled.

If there is such a thing as a gift, the gift is to participate in the universal force of creation. It's to muster enough courage to release oneself and slip the surly bonds of consciousness—to enter the realm of selflessness. It's leaving behind will and control and allowing the mind to drift into the ether of the eternal. And it's coming "back" after hours and wondering "where have I been?" There is, in that, a deep inexplicable mystery. The conscious self-observed hands moving and material being removed. But by what force did the form emerge?

Critics, curators, collectors, and galleries often want to see, read, and hear about the "intent" behind a work or body of work. But, in reality, intent, the activity of consciously setting out to do a thing, makes the thing "self-conscious." Makes it stilted. I can, and do, apply certain principles, logic, and engineering to a piece: line, form, balance, positive and negative space, rhythm, flow, etc. But the act of actual creation is still a mystery to me after forty-eight years as an artist. Something ethereal and inexplicable. To proclaim "I did that!" is arrogance. What I am is a participant.

1

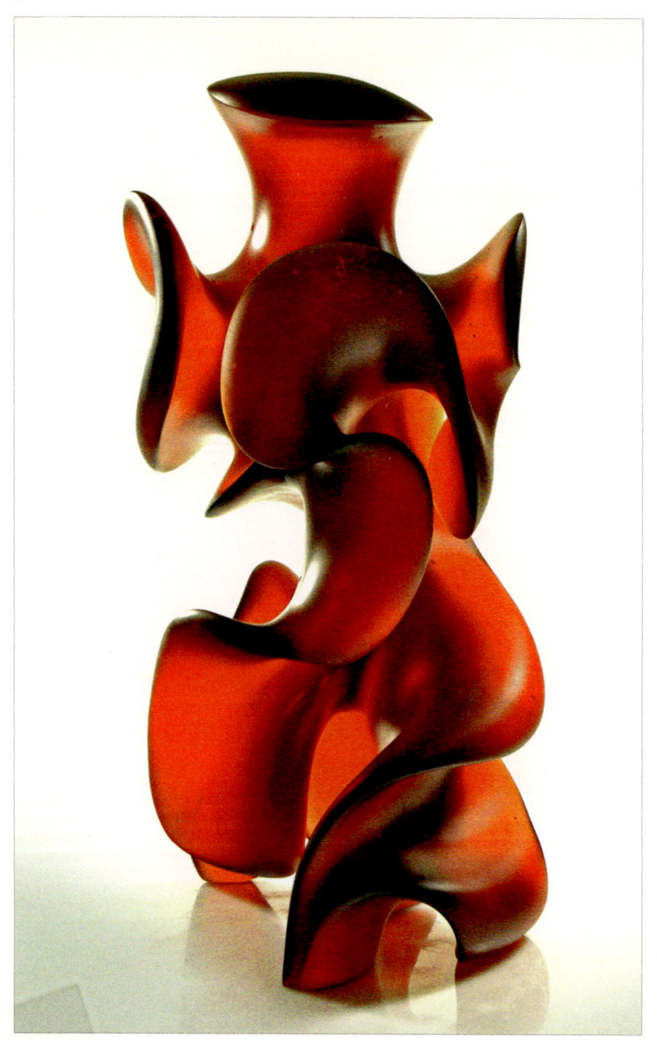

2

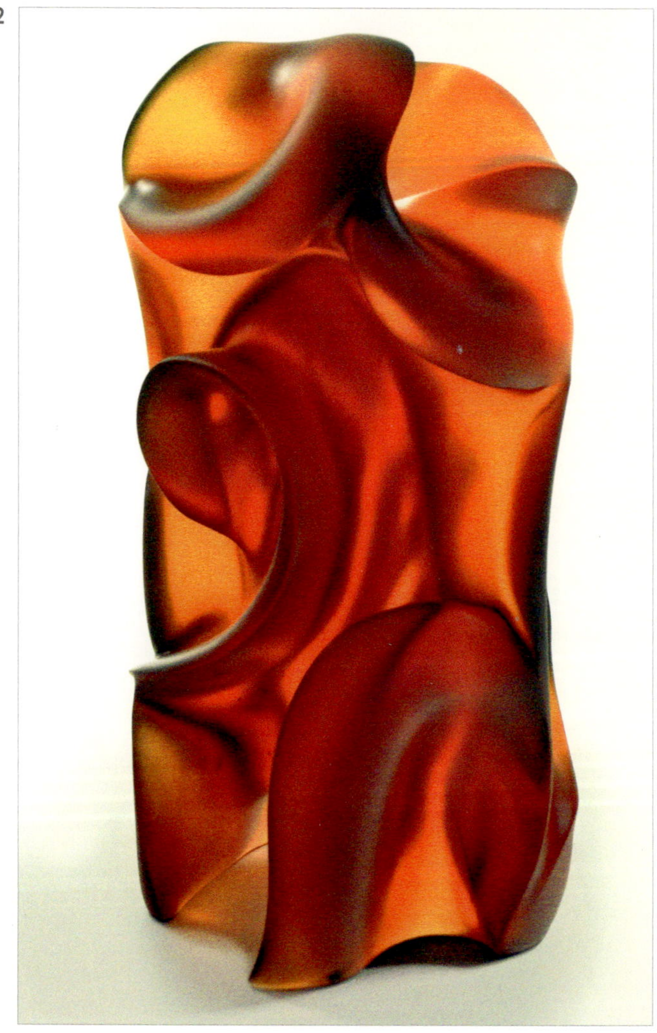

3

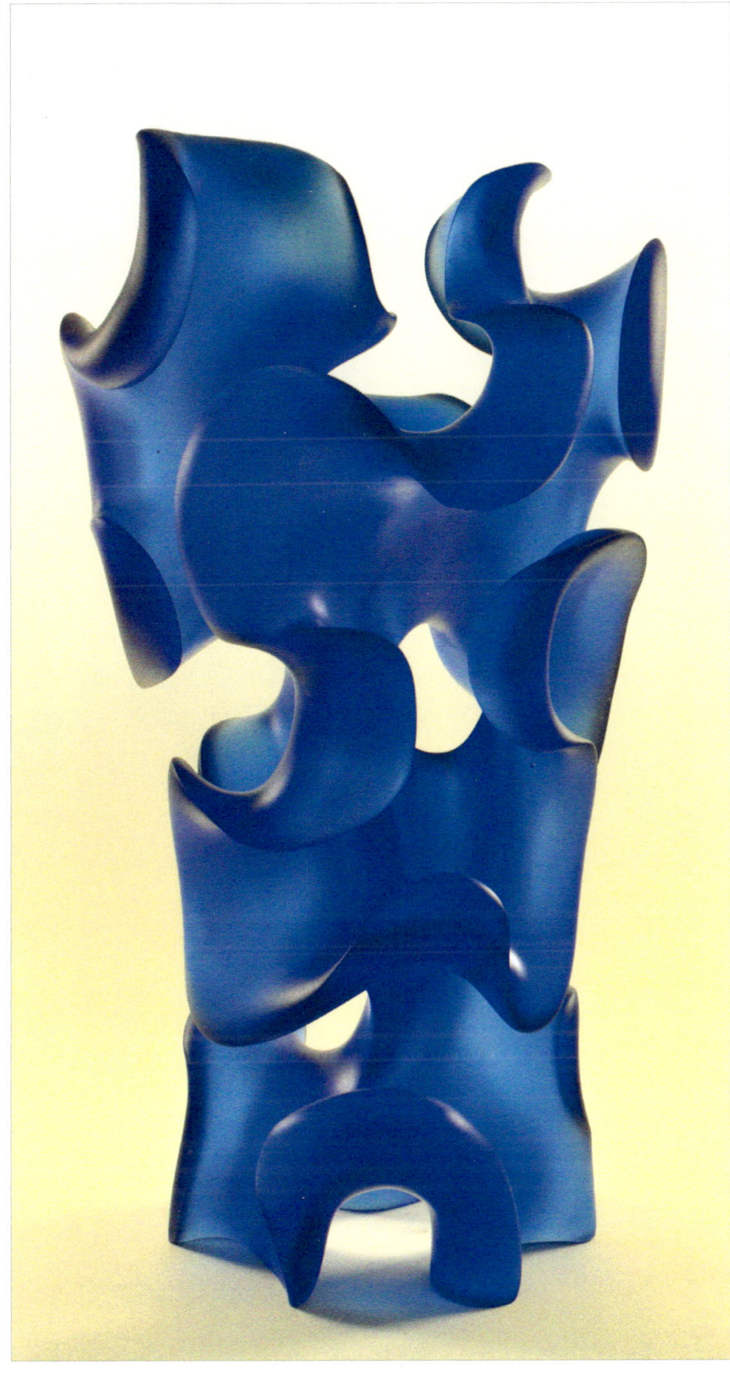

4

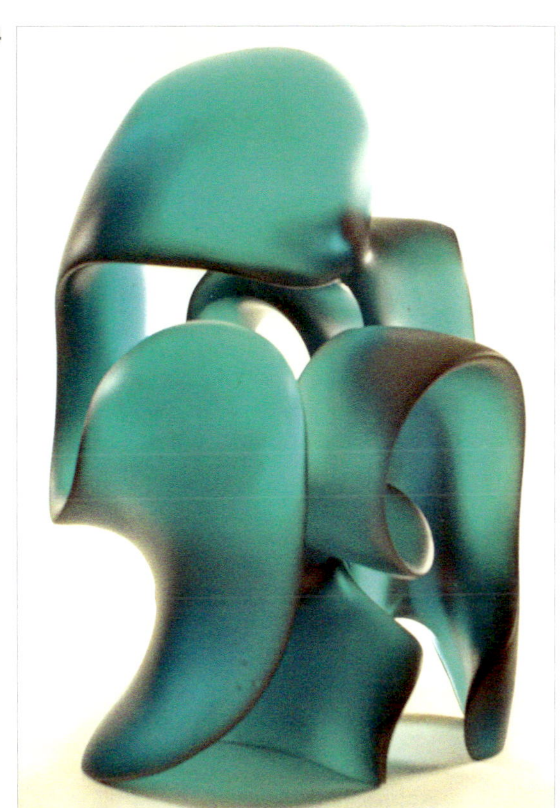

5

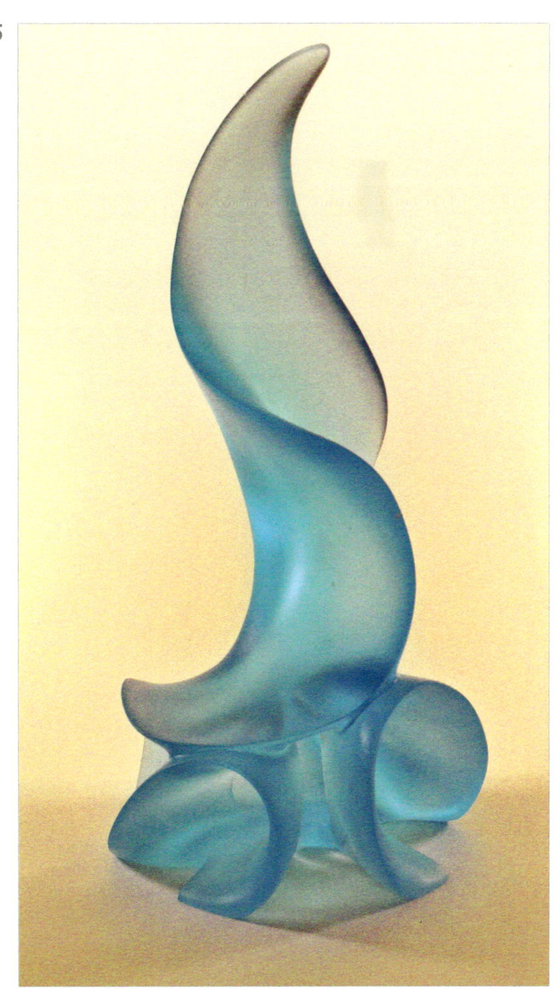

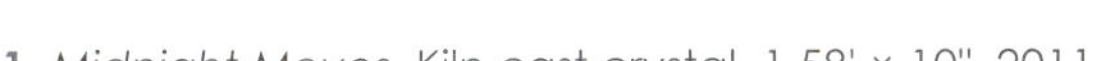

1 *Midnight Moves*. Kiln cast crystal. 1.58' × 10". 2011.

2 *Red Shift*. Kiln cast crystal. 1.25' × 8" 2012.

3 *Enigma*. Kiln cast crystal. 1.667' × 10" × 11". 2014.

4 *Splash*. Kiln cast crystal. 1.167' × 9" diameter. 2013.

5 *Escape Velocity*. Kiln cast crystal. 1.5' × 12". 2013.

Charlotte Potter

Norfolk, Virginia

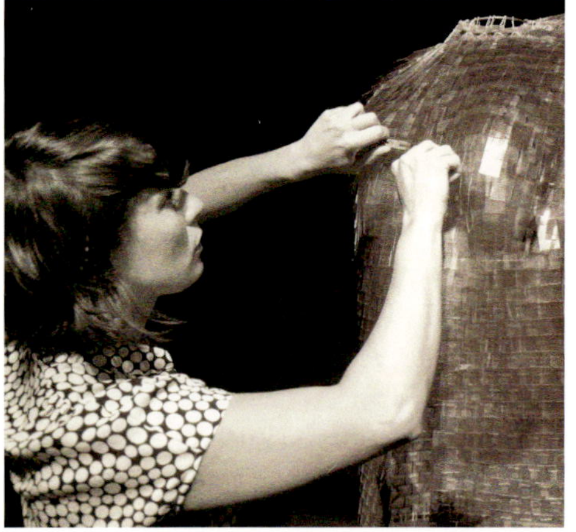

Courtesy of Echard Wheeler Photography.

Where is the break between my self and the rest of the world? My investigation begins with defining self through rigorous examination and comparison. My work discusses "the other" in terms of another person. However, my inquiry has also led me to consider the space between action, words, or meaning. I desire to articulate and name the liminal space between. It seems that there is an undiscovered intimate tie between us in this world that we share. In my works, I attempt to make these connections visible through apparatus, interventions, installations, and collaborations.

1

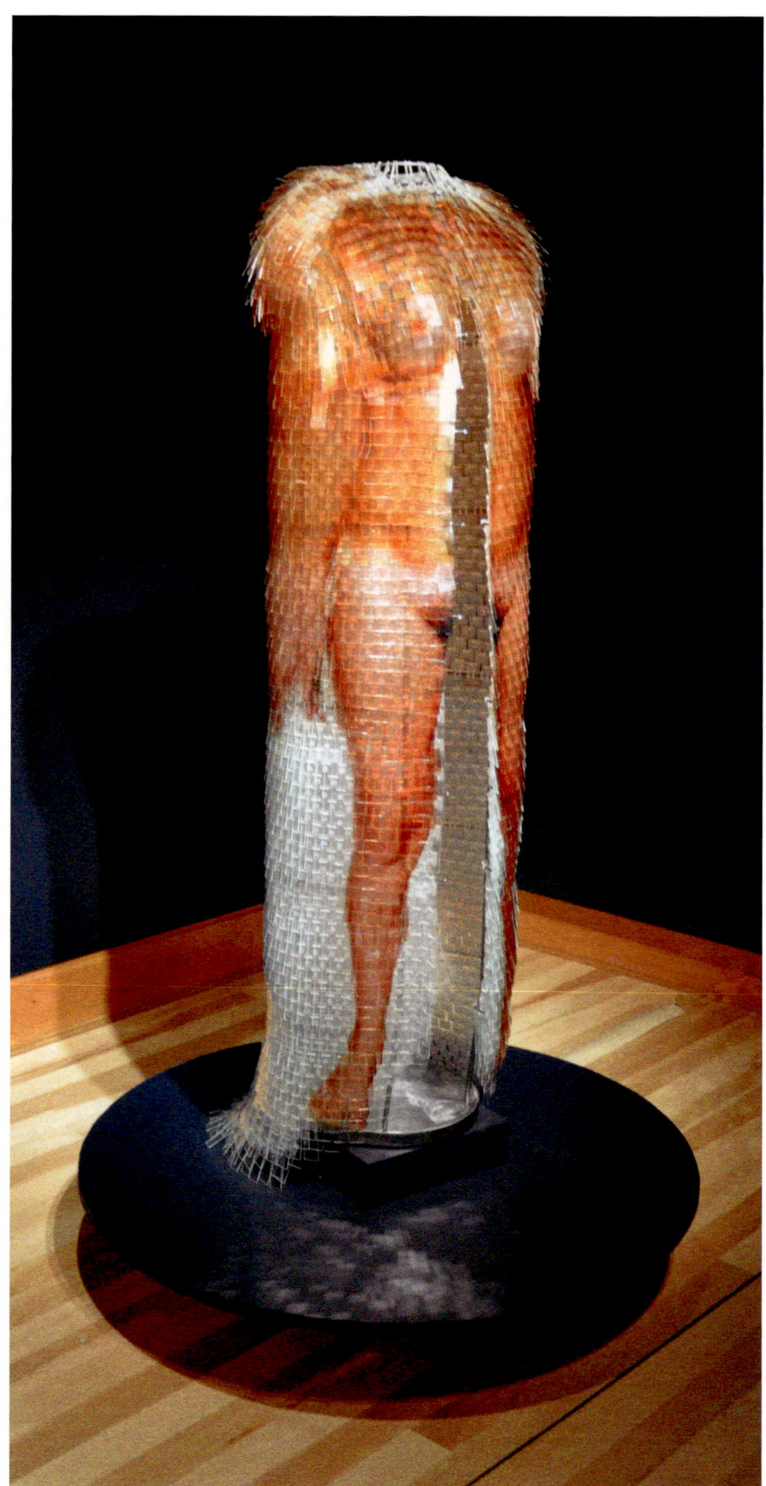

1 *Armor.* Microscope slides, photo decals of the artist's skin, urethane, and sterling silver. 60" × 14" × 48". 2014.

2 *Charlotte's Web.* Hand-engraved glass, images courtesy of Facebook, metal, and wax. 12' × 3" × 24". 2010–2012.

3 *Sideways Chandelier.* Glass, glue, mirror, metal, wax, and fire. 25" × 6" × 20". 2009–present.

2

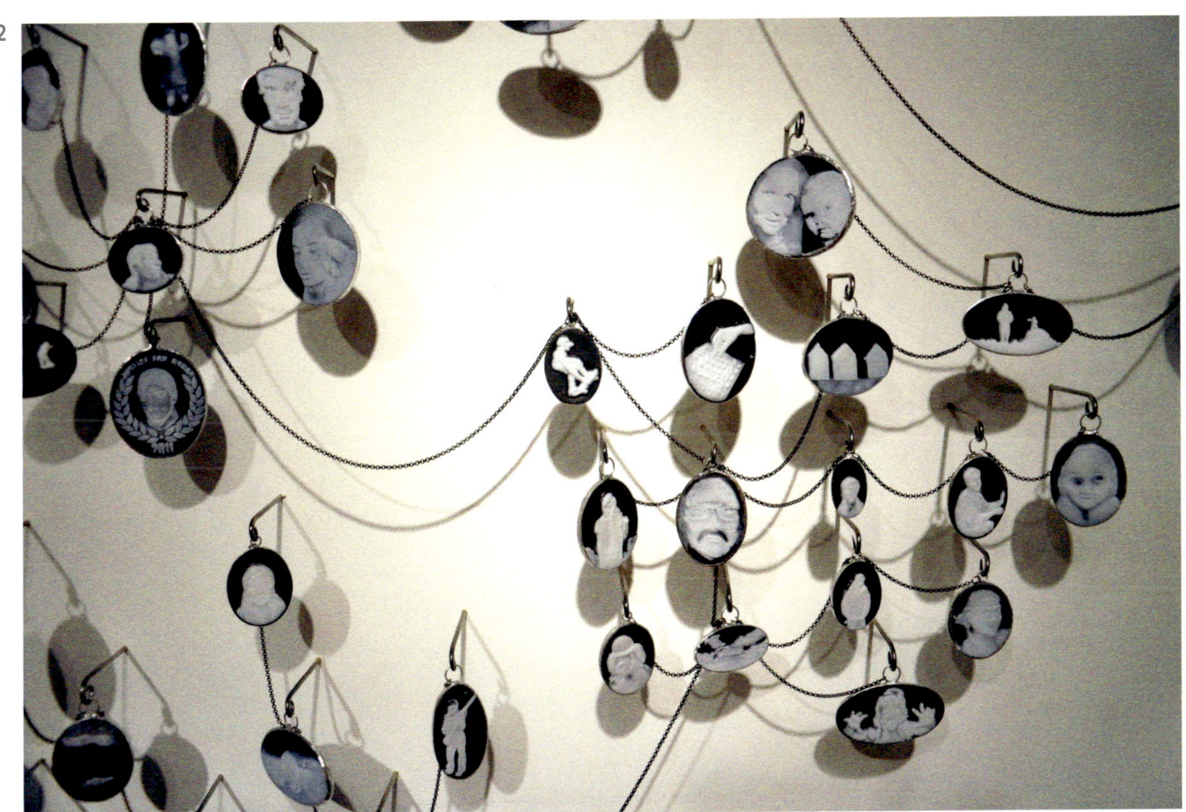

3

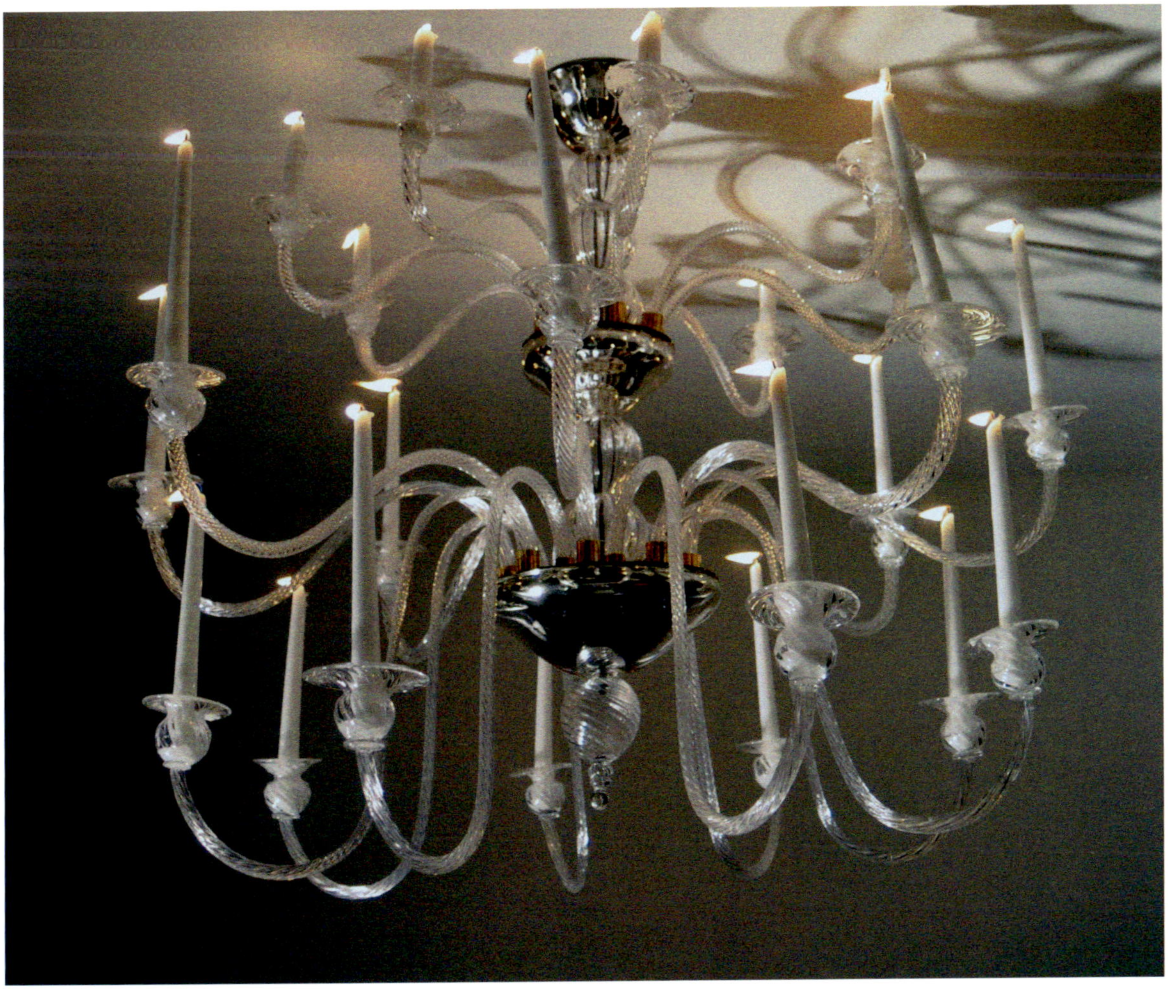

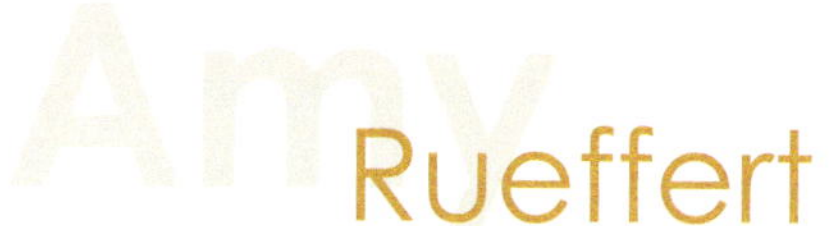

Amy Rueffert

Toyama City, Toyama, Japan

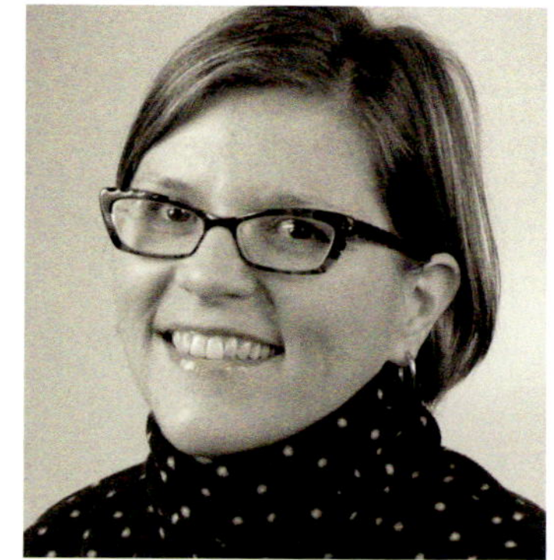

I started working with glass in 1994 at the Massachusetts College of Art in Boston. My roommate at the time was enrolled in a glassblowing class with Dan Dailey, a pioneer in the studio glass movement. She said to me, "Glassblowing is so hard, you won't like it." That was all the challenge I needed to sign up for a class. She was right, it was hard, and I didn't like it . . . I loved it, and almost twenty years later I'm still fascinated with the material.

For me, the medium of glass provides unique sculptural opportunities, especially optics that allow dynamic presentation of collaged imagery. These optics are also combined with traditional Italian glass patterning techniques such as *zanfirico* and *reticello*.

My work evokes aspects of the Victorian decorative arts period such as orderliness, ornamentation, and a mixture of Gothic, Tudor, and Elizabethan stylistic eras. The Victorian curio, an intriguing object presented for contemplation, provides an ideal context for the relationship between the viewer and my repurposed objects.

1 *Better Living Through Chemistry*. Found scientific glassware, decals, and flame worked borosilicate glass. 7" × 6" × 9.5". 2013. Courtesy of ChrisBrownphoto.com.

2 *Pear (Babies & Ingredients)*. Blown and fused glass, Vitrolite glass, found glass, and decals. 11.5" × 5" × 5". 2011. Courtesy of ChrisBrownphoto.com.

3 *Soft Fruit (Bears, Beans and Baby)*. Blown glass, zanfirico technique, doily, and decals. 6" × 6" × 6". 2008. Courtesy of ChrisBrownphoto.com.

4 *Bouquet*. Blown glass, decals, found glass, and ribbon. 10" × 4.75" × 4.75". 2013. Courtesy of ChrisBrownphoto.com.

5 *Little Patchwork Pill*. Blown and fused glass, found glass, decals, and Vitrolite. 9" × 4.5" × 8.5". 2011. Courtesy of ChrisBrownphoto.com.

1

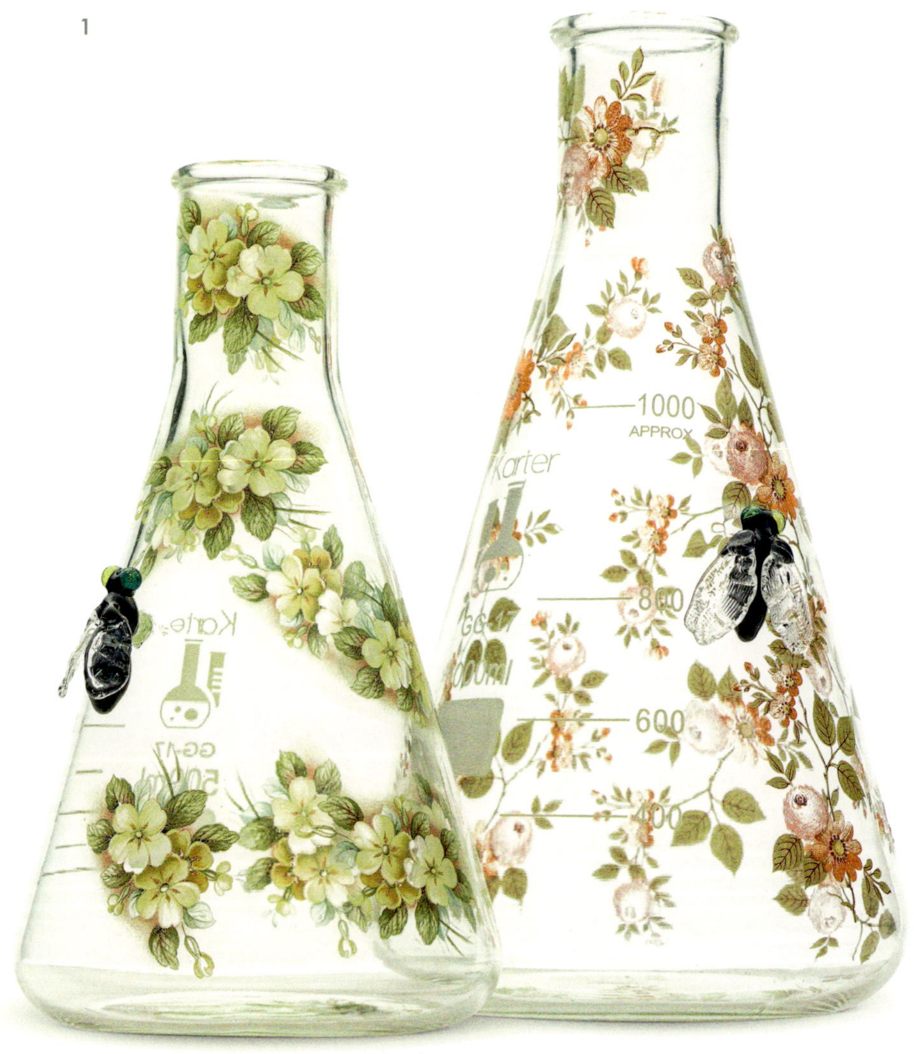

2

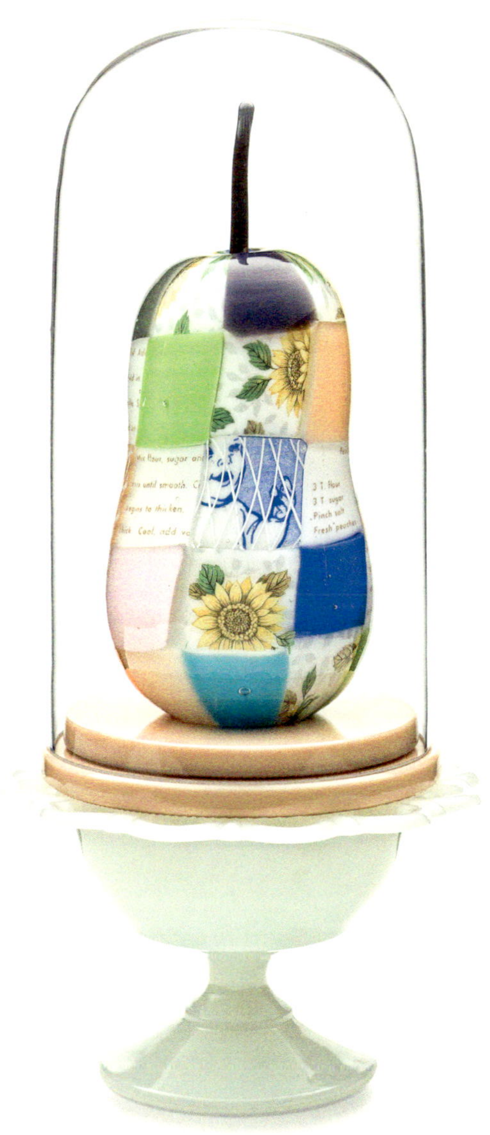

3

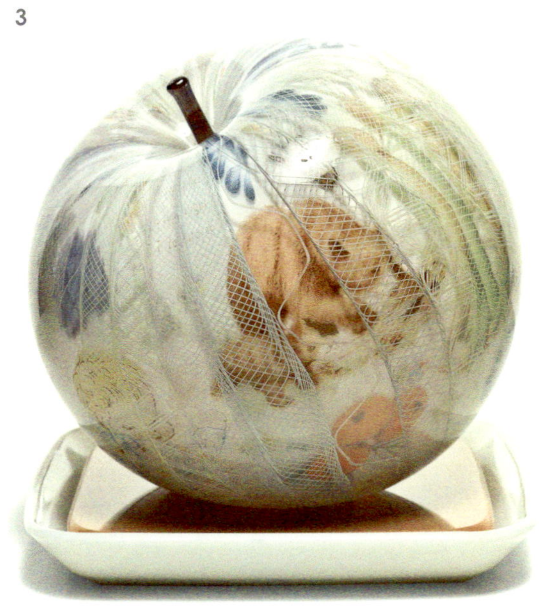

4

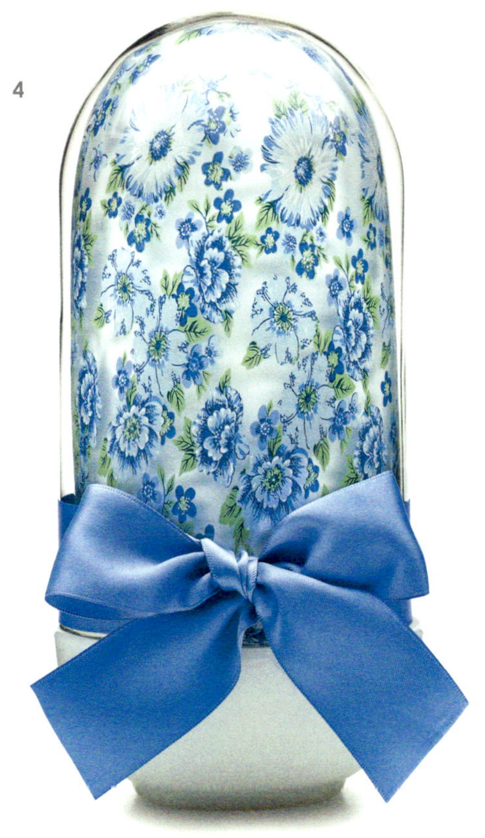

5

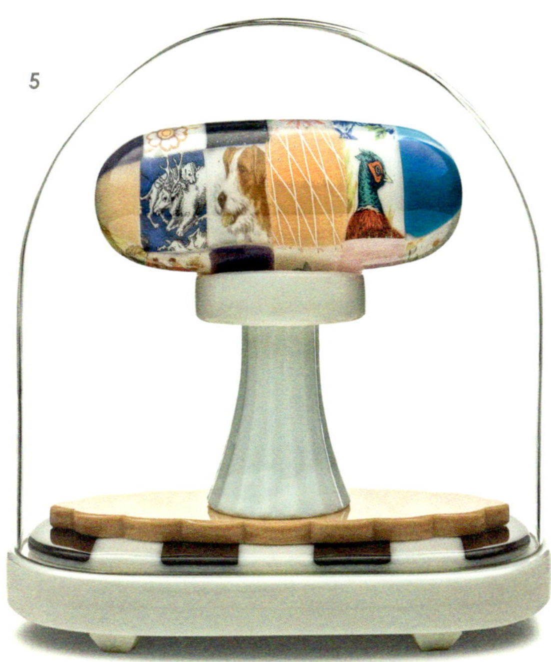

David Schnuckel

Rochester, New York

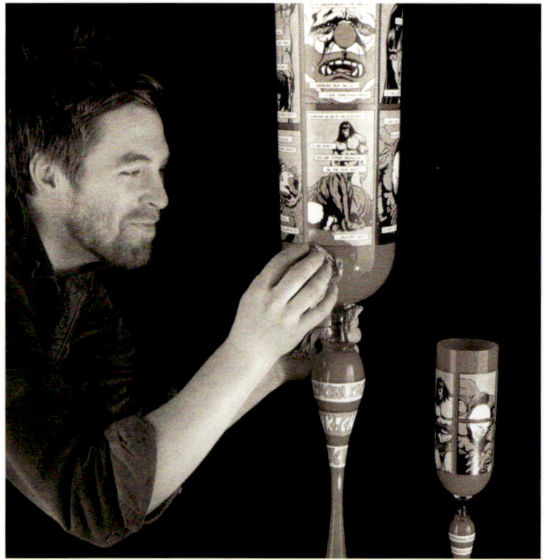

Courtesy of Elizabeth Lamark.

Life writes many stories upon us, stories that make us who we are. I was a shy, awkward boy who took interest and comfort in the fictional glories of favorite superheroes within comic books and animated television. At the time I believed my attraction was consciously toward an emphasis on color, simplistic shapes, and fantastical sequencing of both action and suspense. However, now in hindsight, I believe there was a subconscious response to the superhero as a model of the ideal . . . a being of thoroughly flawless characteristics physically, emotionally, intellectually, and morally. My boyish aspirations of developing into an equally perfect being dissolved gradually as maturity and experience revealed being human is actually quite the opposite of what I had once believed.

Today, I am drawn to issues regarding the human response to personal conflict. The content of my work reflects upon the presence of tragedy within the human experience in ambiguous narratives fictitiously rendered from personal experiences. In this way, I explore my attraction to the ironic beauty within struggle, humility, and failure . . . discomforting factors that allow us to continually redefine ourselves and, therefore, serve as highly transformative opportunities.

1

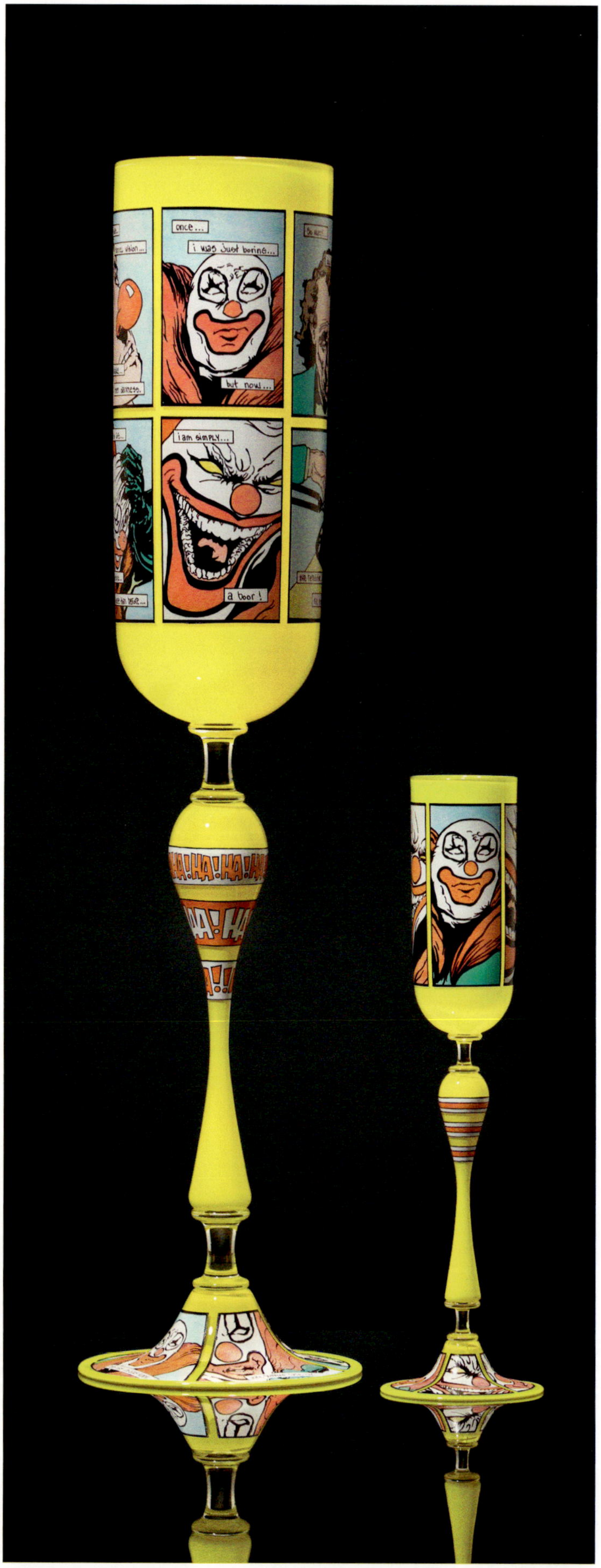

2

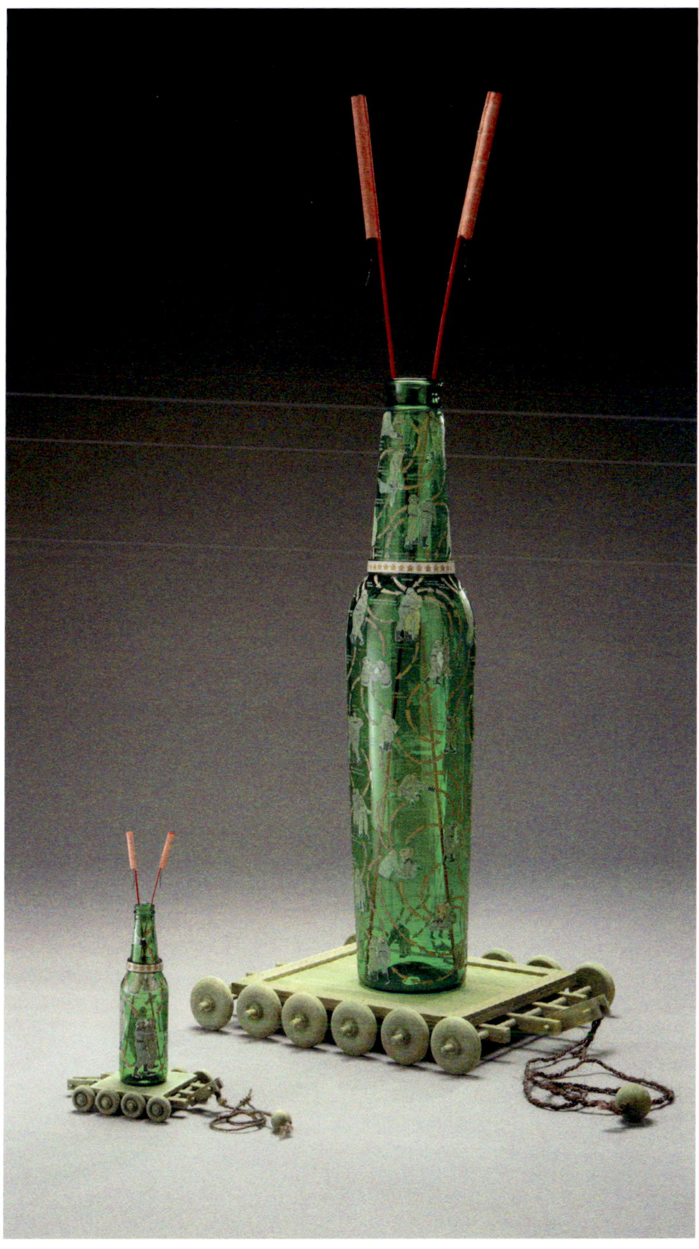

3

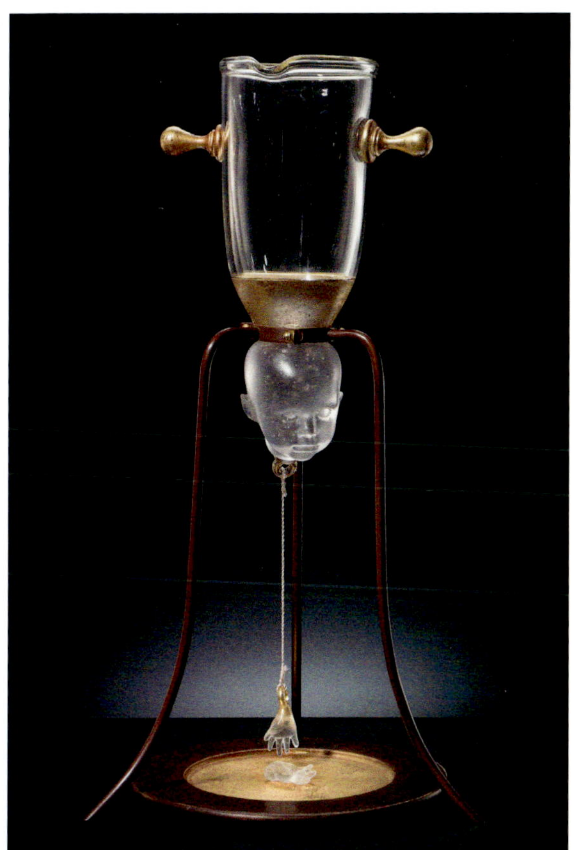

4

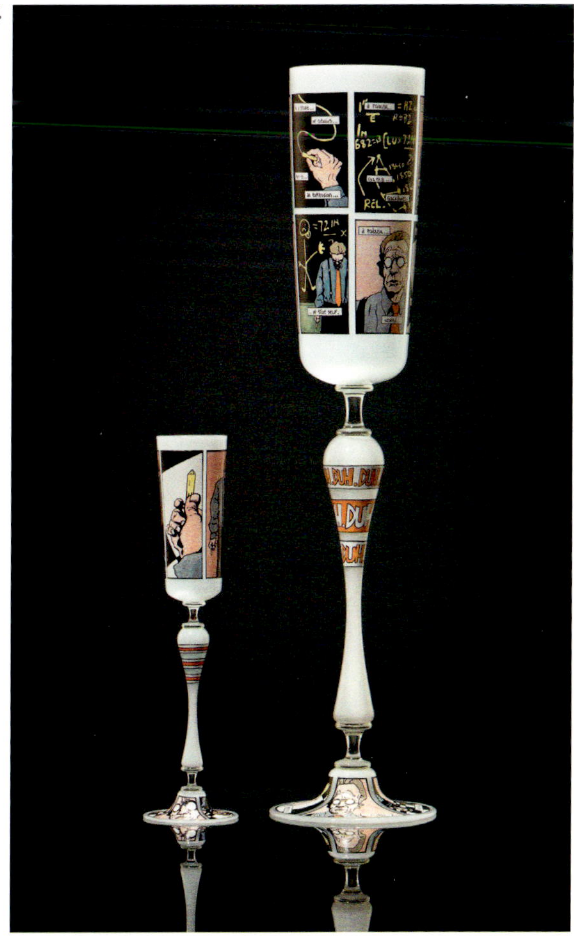

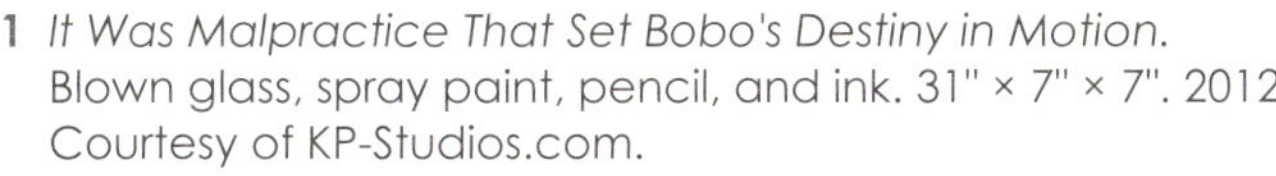

1 *It Was Malpractice That Set Bobo's Destiny in Motion.* Blown glass, spray paint, pencil, and ink. 31" × 7" × 7". 2012. Courtesy of KP-Studios.com.

2 *Tactical Discrepancy.* Blown and enameled glass, decal, and mixed media. 52" × 18" × 26". 2013. Courtesy of Elizabeth Lamark.

3 *hypothesis.* Blown and kiln cast glass, mixed media. 26" × 12" × 12". 2014. Collaborative work with Rebecca Arday (rebeccaarday.com). Courtesy of KP-Studios.com.

4 *The Inadequate Math Professor Put Two and Two Together.* Blown glass, spray paint, pencil, and ink. 29" × 6.5" × 6.5". 2012. Courtesy of KP-Studios.com.

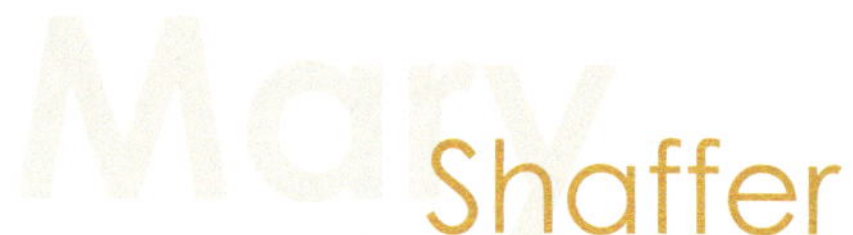

Mary Shaffer

Taos, New Mexico

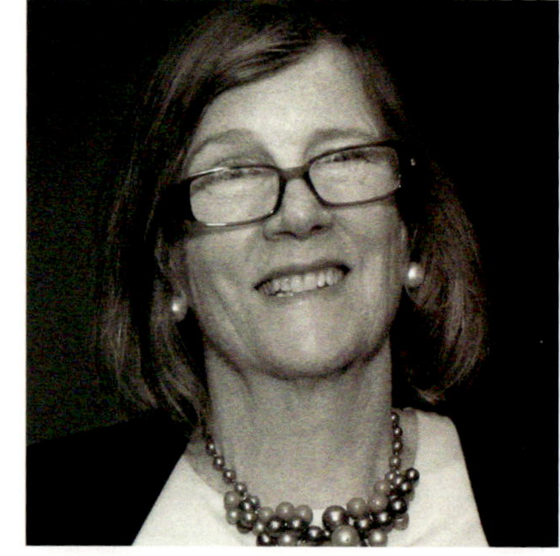

Glass with its responsiveness to light is inherently beautiful; I think any object professing to be art must have purpose or meaning—even when that meaning is a celebration of nature's perfection.

I am extremely lucky to have discovered a way of working in 1972 that no one had used before (at least to my knowledge and that of the glass artists in my circle), a way I called mid-air slumping. Also, I developed a technique I called dippy do and have made large-scale cast works. I especially like combining glass with other materials, pushing its limits in size or the extreme of its bend, to name a few approaches. Often I've been told by scientists and technicians that it couldn't be done, but it could! I'm even luckier to have made a living from doing what I love while raising two successful women.

1

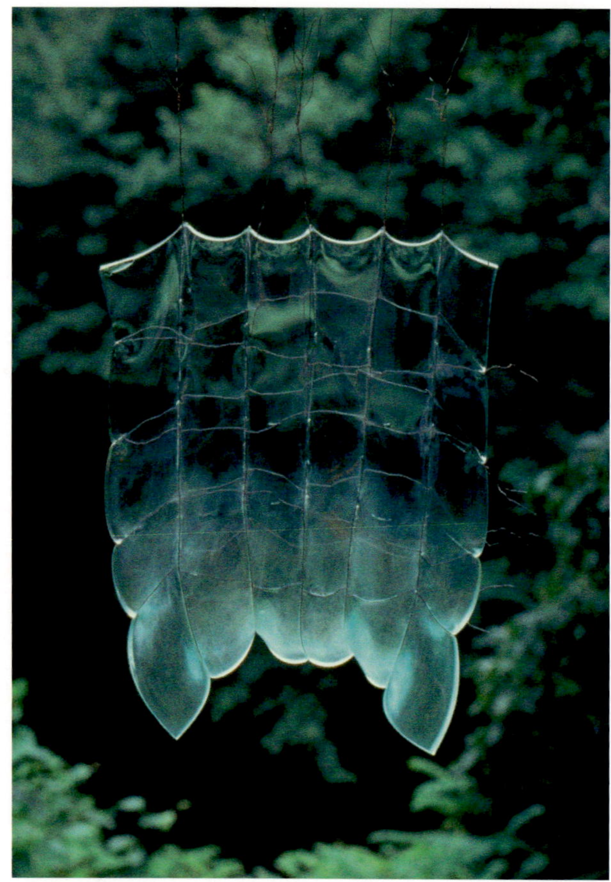

2

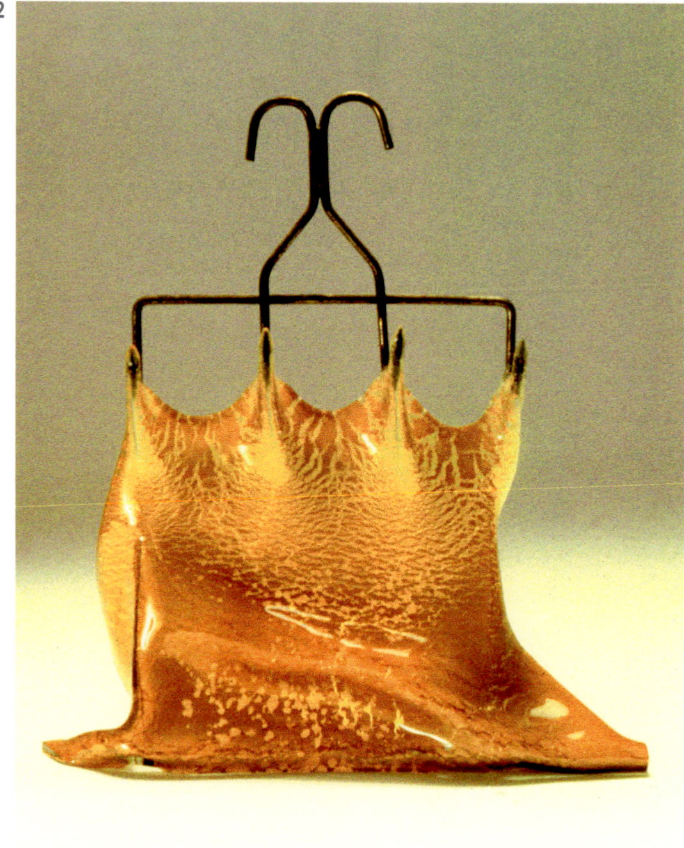

3

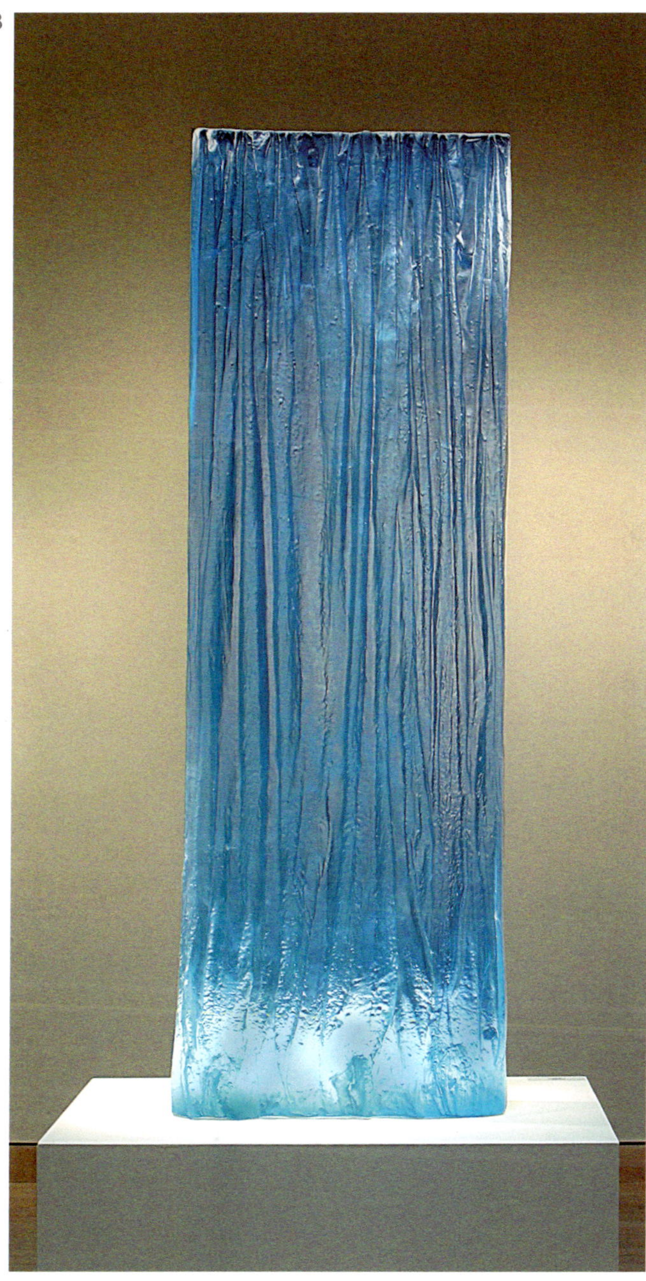

4

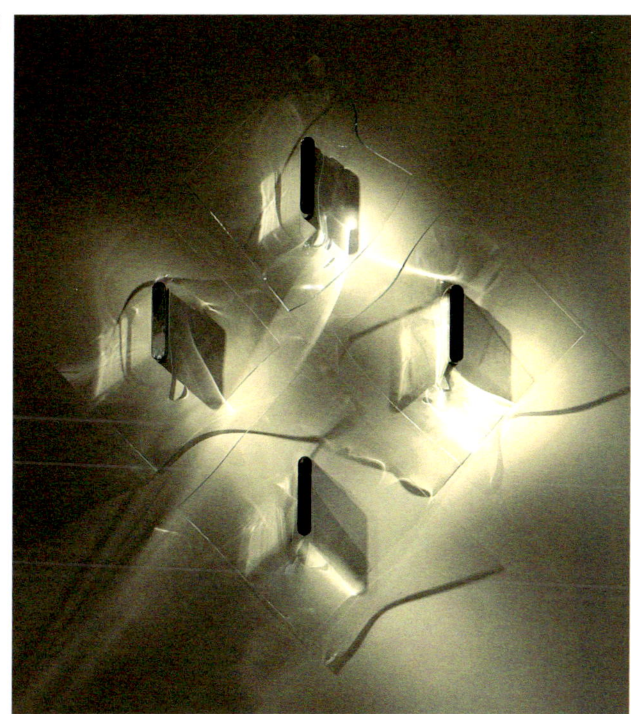

5

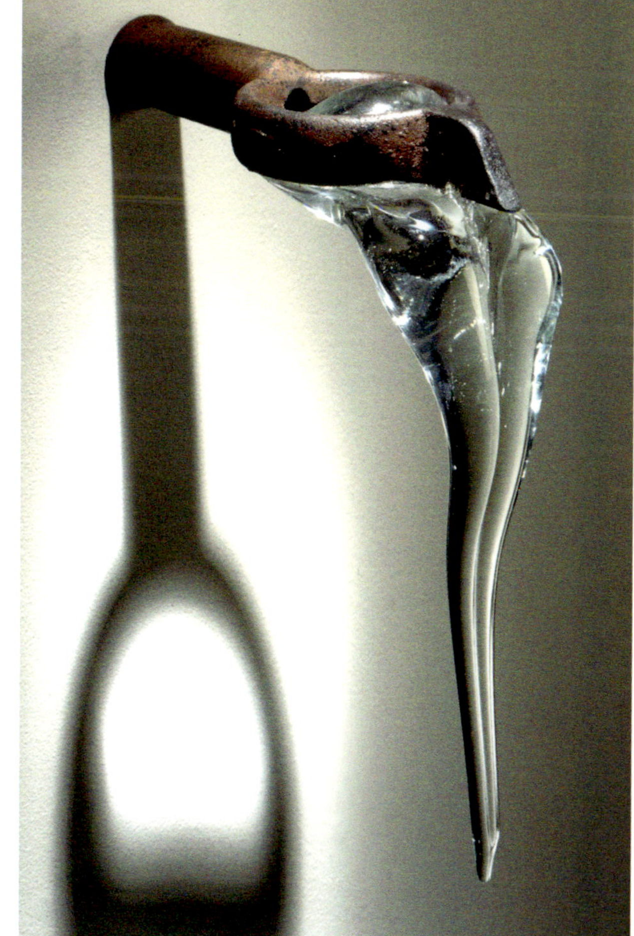

1 *Carrots*. Slumped glass and wire.
25" × 5" × 17". 1977. Courtesy of George Erml.

2 *Yellow Hook*. Slumped glass with found object.
11" × 3" × 9". 1972. Courtesy of Jay Langfitt Photography.

3 *Blue Rain Curtain*. Cast glass. 66" × 8" × 22". 2007.
Courtesy of Dan Morse.

4 *Reflected Diamond*. Slumped glass. 76" × 12" × 74".
2004. Courtesy of Dan Morse.

5 *Straight Out*. Dippy Do. 10" × 4" × 3". 1995.
Courtesy of George Erml.

Alison Sigethy

Alexandria, Virginia

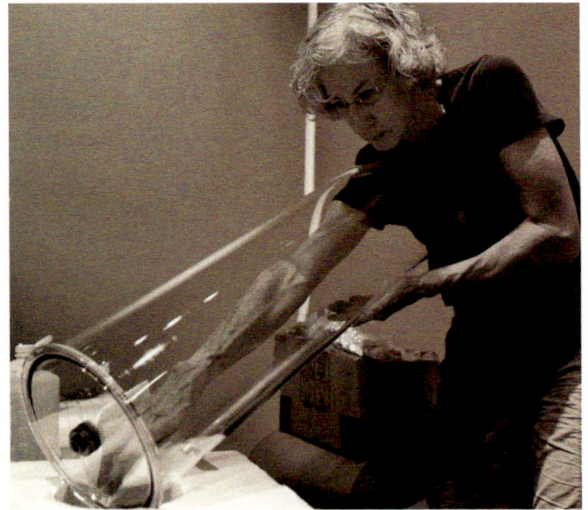

Courtesy of Cory Bush.

I think of my *Sea Core* kinetic glass sculptures as an oceanographic moment in time. Without attempting to be literal, I strive to capture the beauty and mystery of the sea, whose immense and ceaseless rhythms have captivated humanity for countless years. The constant motion of air and water through a *Sea Core* echoes this eternal ebb and flow, fascinating and mesmerizing the viewer. The *Sea Core* series also embodies the tranquility and the turbulence of the ocean, and reminds us of its fragile beauty. By using glass, a material that is permanent, yet delicate, I hope to inspire the viewer to look at our oceans with more caring eyes.

1 *Roe Sea Core*. Fused glass. 24" × 7.5" × 7.5". 2014. Courtesy of Pete Duvall / Anything Photographic.

2 *Baby Blue Sea Core* (detail). Fused glass. 19" × 6.5" × 6.5". 2014. Courtesy of Pete Duvall / Anything Photographic.

3 *Fossil Sea Core* (detail). Fused glass. 24" × 6.5" × 6.5". 2013. Courtesy of Pete Duvall / Anything Photographic.

4 *Exotic Sea Core* (detail). Fused glass. 30" × 9" × 9". 2013. Courtesy of Pete Duvall / Anything Photographic.

5 *Fossil Sea Core in Sushi Bar*. Fused glass. 24" × 6.5" × 6.5". 2013. Courtesy of John B. Spaulding.

1

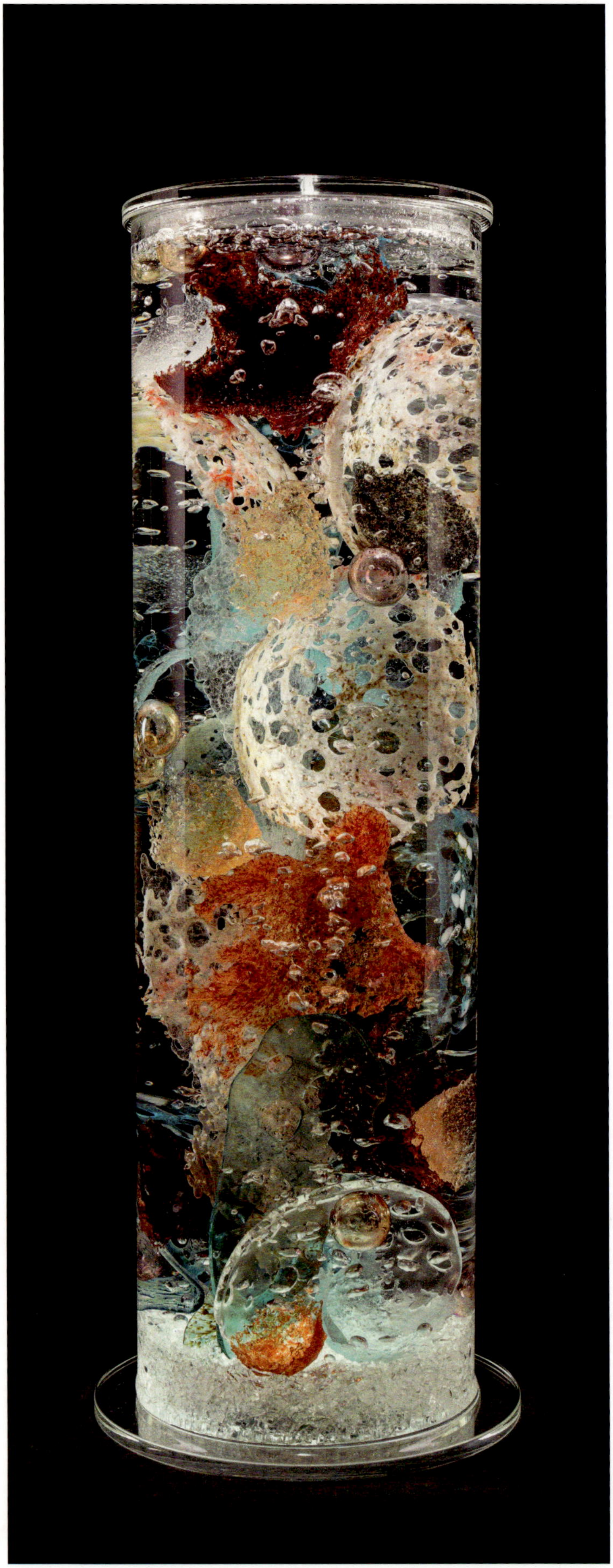

2

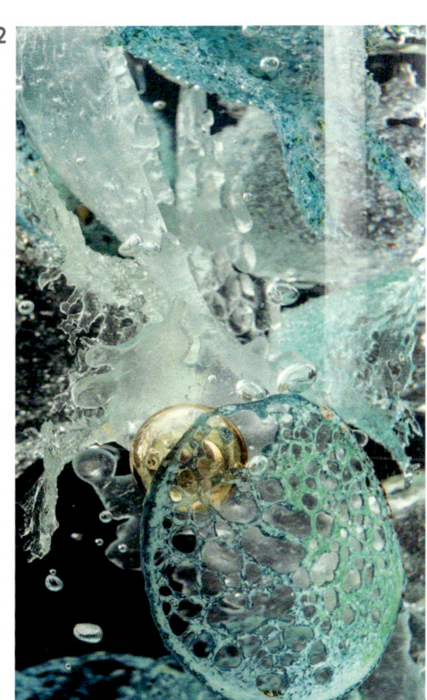

3

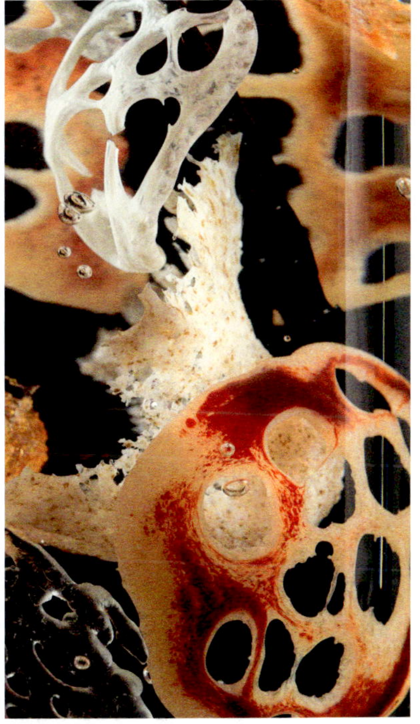

4

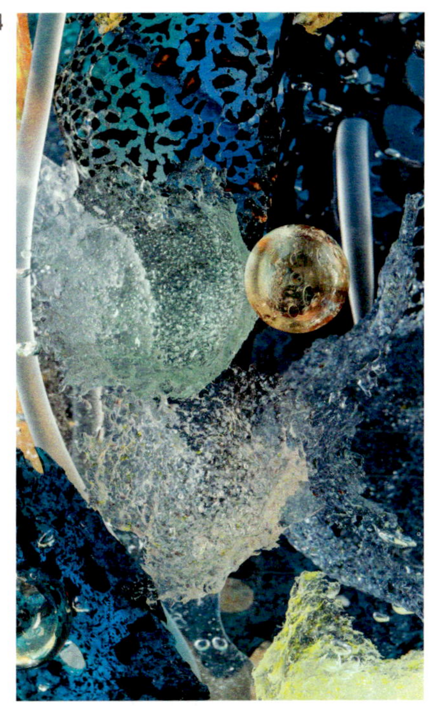

5

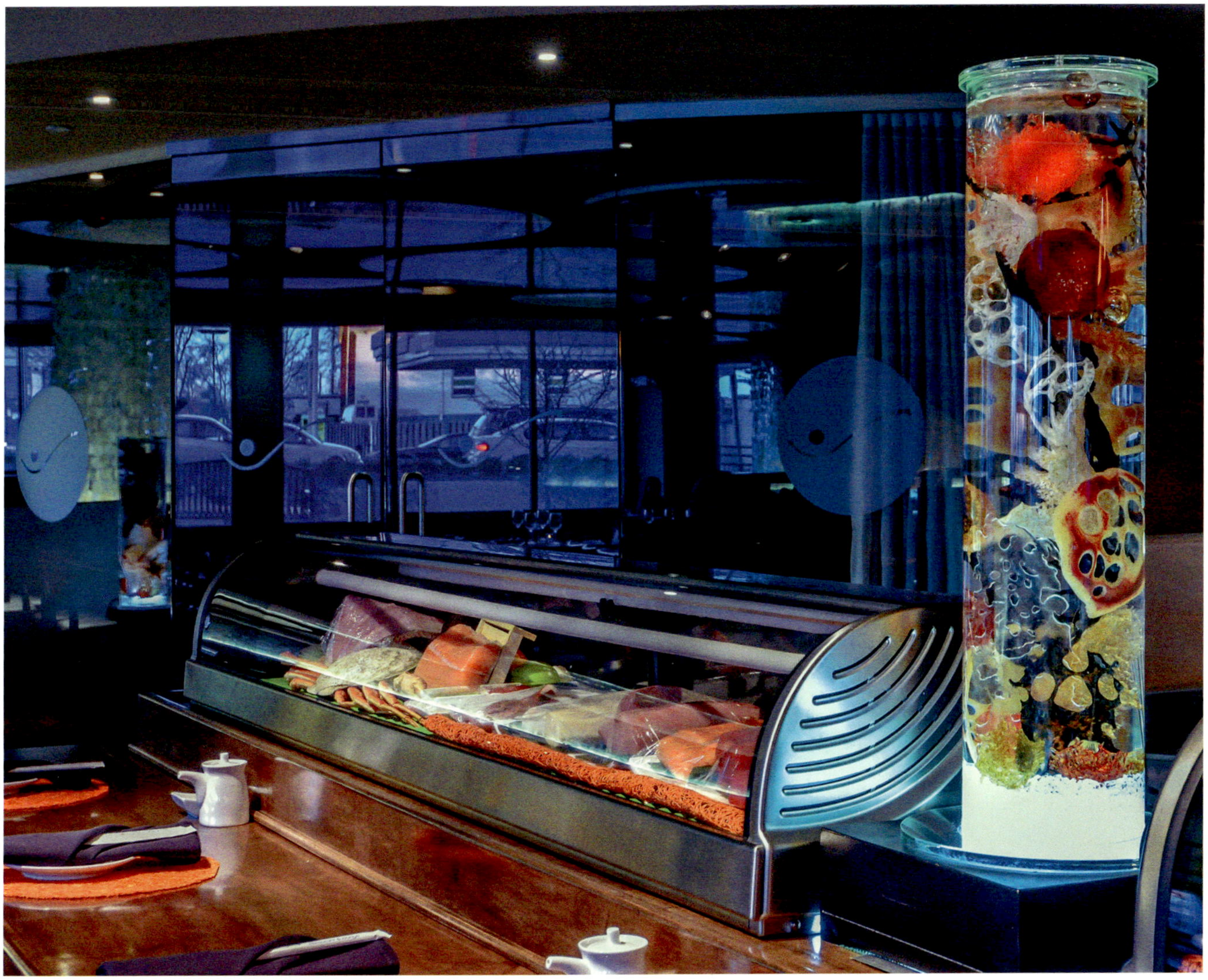

Raven Skyriver

Stanwood, Washington

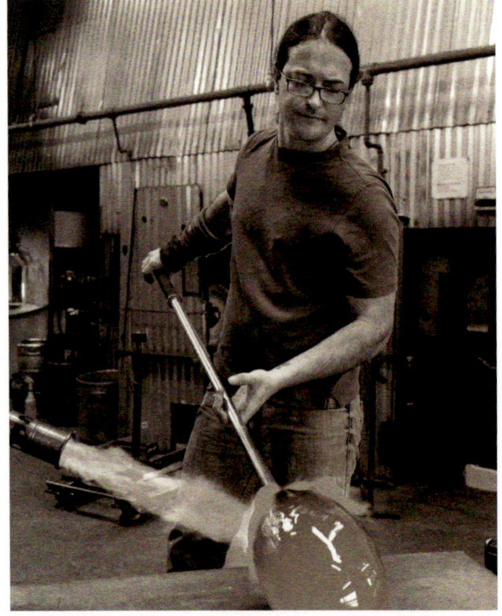

Courtesy of KP-Studios.com.

I started working in glass with my friend and mentor Lark Dalton during my junior year in high school. The process immediately enthralled me. In the beginning, I focused on Venetian cane work and functional forms, honing hand skills and ingraining the muscle memory that is required to be comfortable working with any medium.

After graduating, I was confident that I had found something that I was passionate about and resolved to continue working in glass. Between attending a workshop in Venice, assisting artists around the greater Seattle area, and setting up my own rudimentary glass shop, I was able to keep busy in my area of interest. In 2003 Karen Willenbrink-Johnsen asked me to work with her on the William Morris team. This was a dream come true, and a pivotal point in my life. Here, I met my wife Kelly O'Dell, with whom I share a child, and here I was introduced to the world of sculptural glass.

Working sculpturally has given me the ability to lend my own voice to the work, connecting my personal life experience and what I hold to be important to the pieces that I make.

1

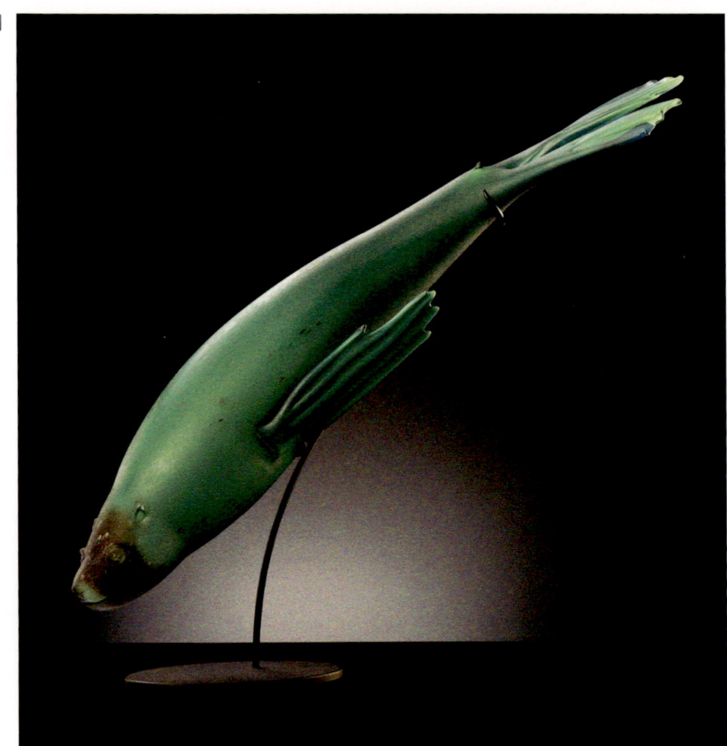

2

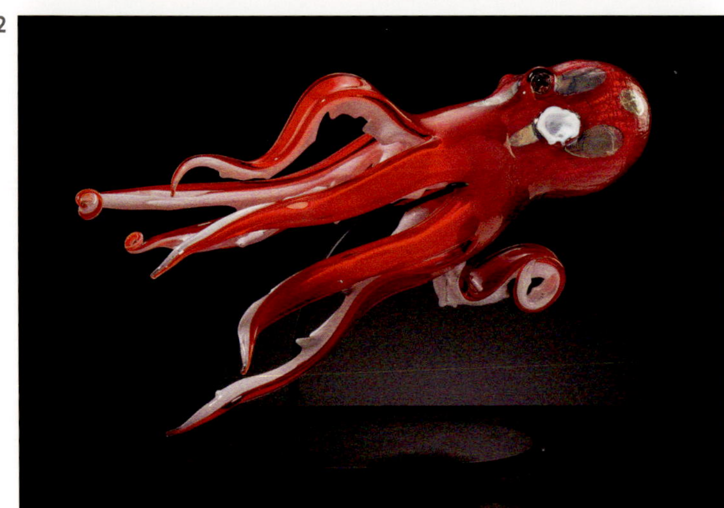

3

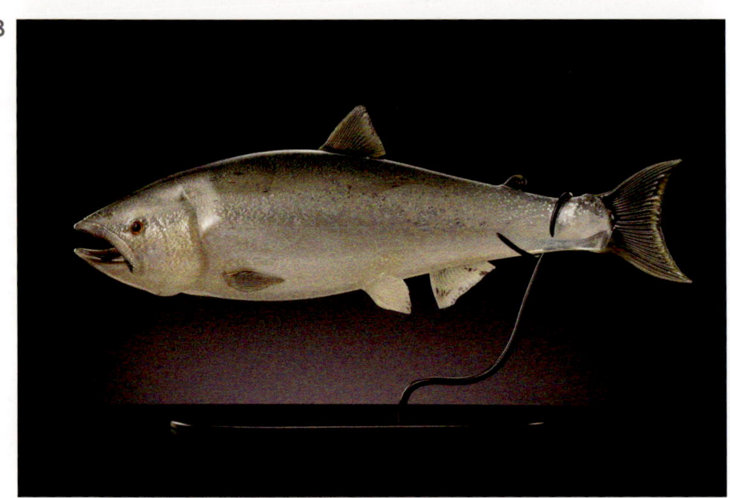

4

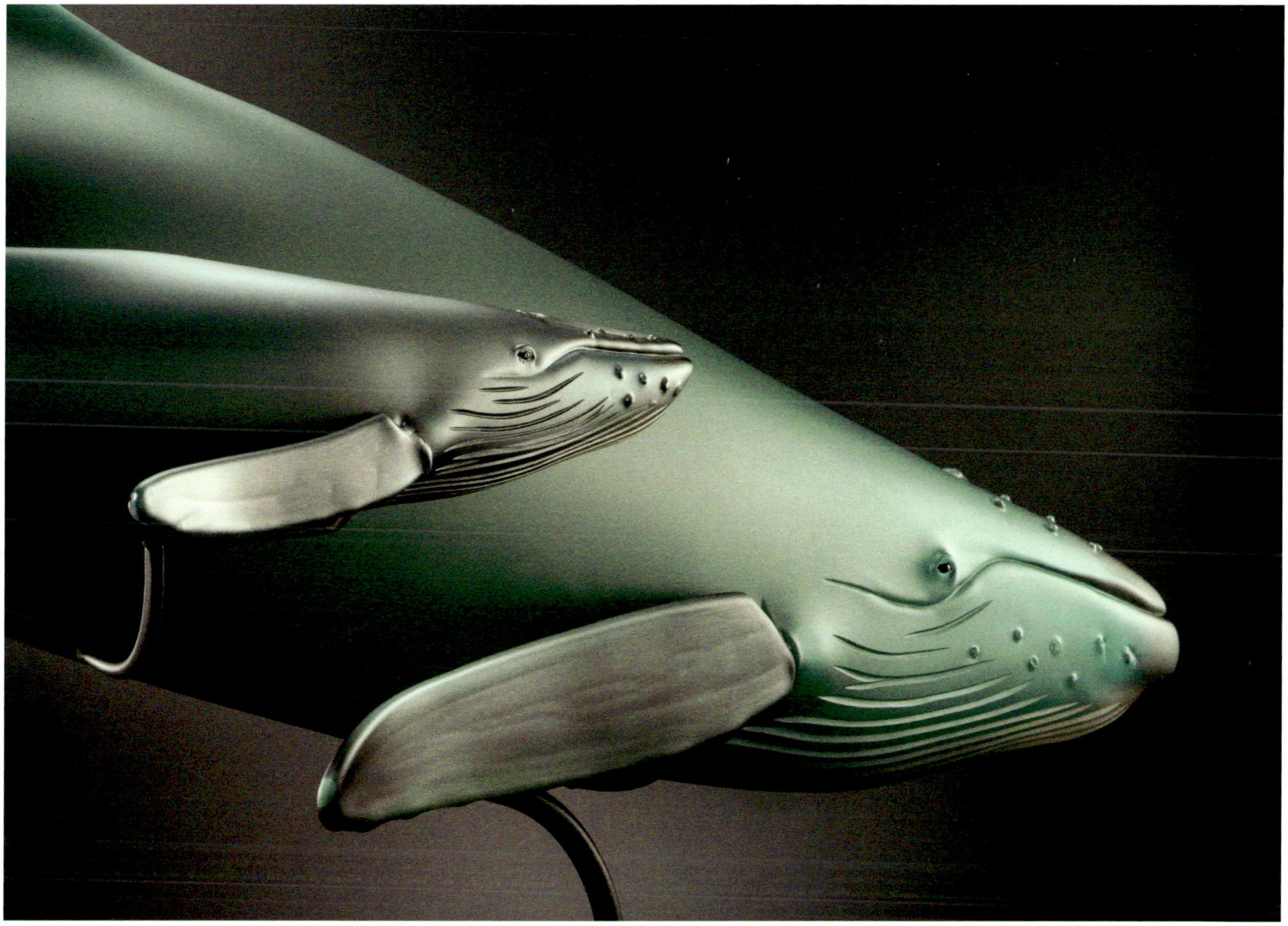

1 *Plunge*. Off-hand-sculpted. 30" × 12" × 34". 2012. Courtesy of KP-Studios.com.

2 *Intertidal*. Off-hand-sculpted glass. 16" × 14" × 24". 2014. Courtesy of KP-Studios.com.

3 *Tyee*. Off-hand-sculpted glass. 21" × 7" × 32". 2014. Courtesy of KP-Studios.com.

4 *Mother*. Off-hand-sculpted and carved glass. 27" × 46" × 14". 2014. Courtesy of KP-Studios.com.

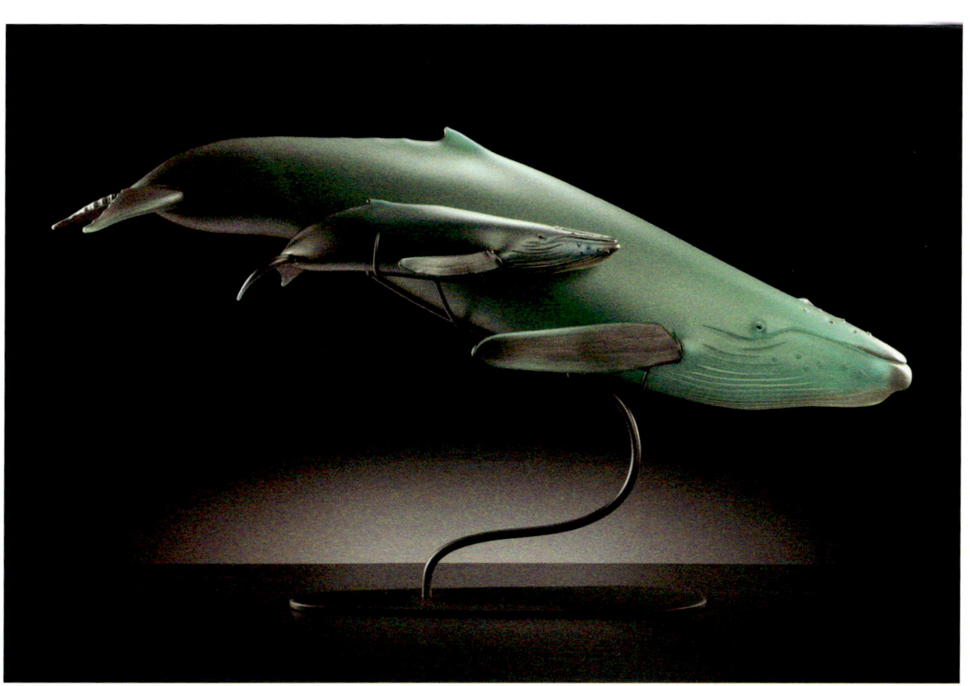

Aaron Slater

Lowell, Massachusetts

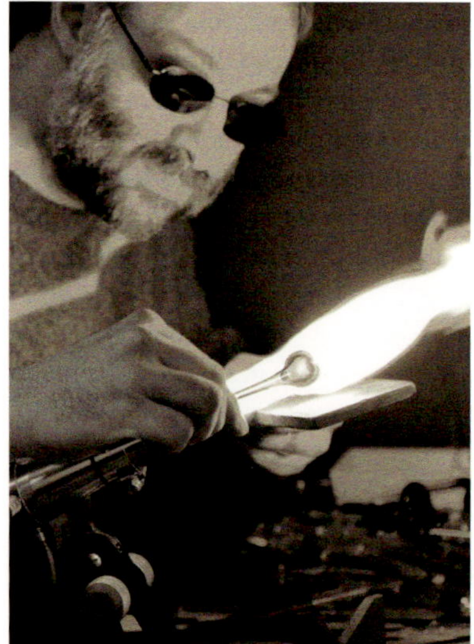

Courtesy of Celina M. Donis.

Inspired by the natural world and the natural properties of glass, I create glass art. As a flameworker, I use a torch to manipulate molten glass into detailed and dynamic forms. I let the physical limitations of the glass inspire my work. Glass has its natural flow and must be allowed to exert its will, or the work will look forced. I don't work glass; I work with it.

I am inspired by these technical limitations of the glass to push the limits of the medium and my ability. Physics and chemistry are my rhyme scheme, the wonders of nature my subject!

1 *Sea Nettle*. Flameworked glass. 1. 25". 2015. Courtesy of Celina M. Donis.

2 *Weblike Mollusk*. Flameworked glass. 3". 2014.

3 *Red Frosted Nudibranch*. Flameworked glass. 2". 2015. Courtesy of Celina M. Donis.

4 *White Lace Nudibranch*. Flameworked glass sphere. 1.5". 2015. Courtesy of Celina M. Donis.

1

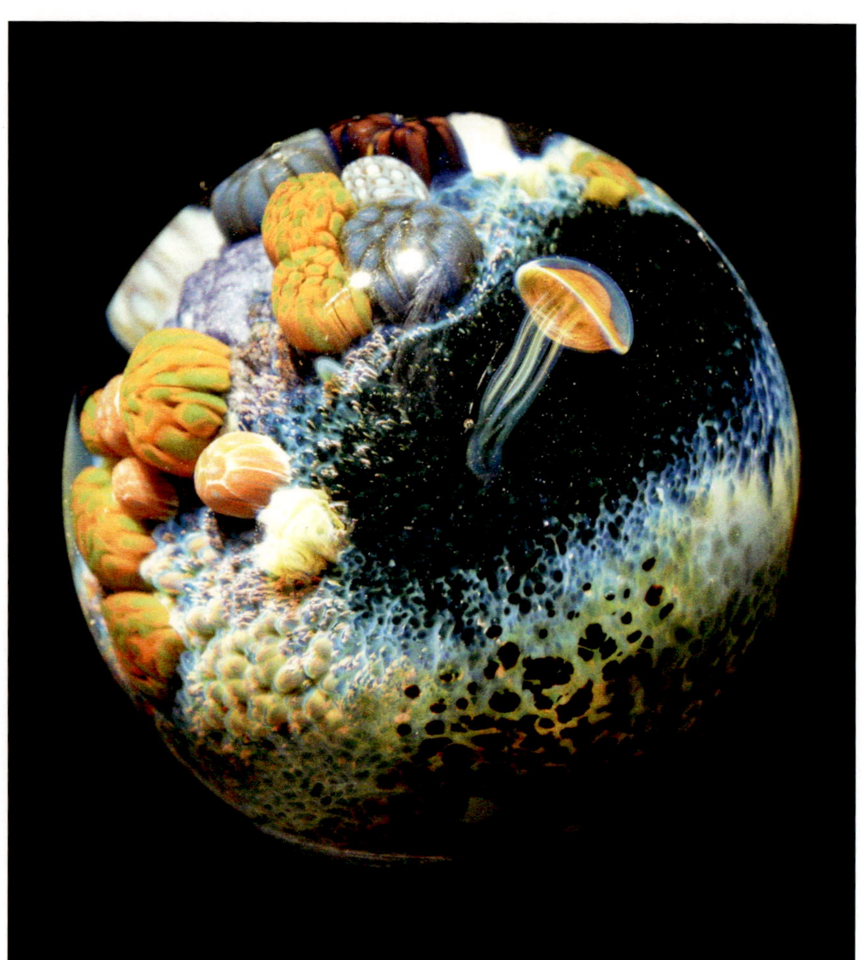

2

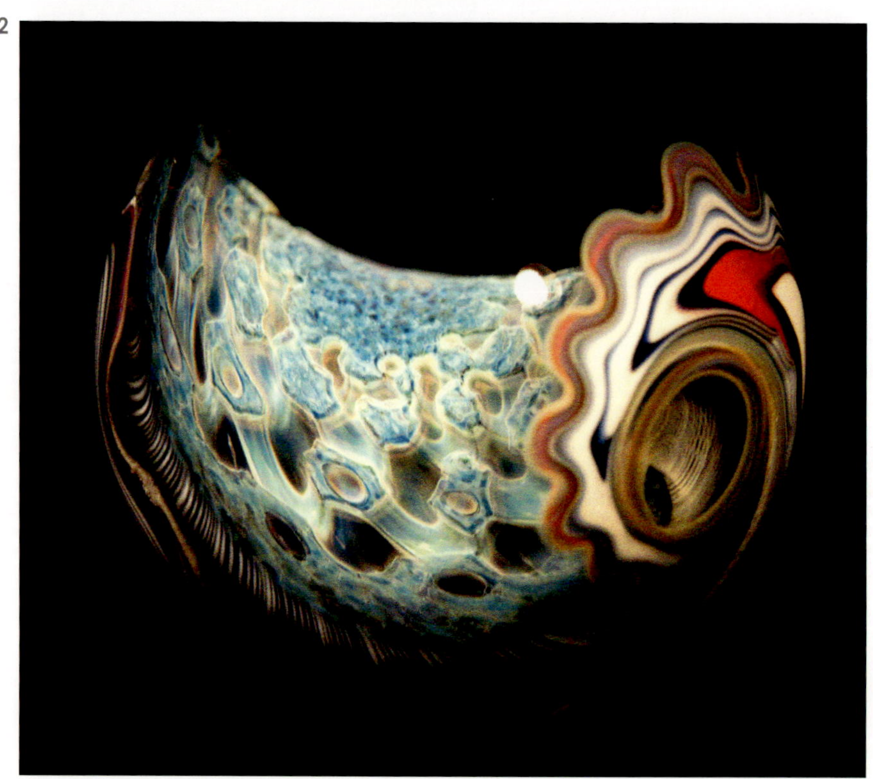

3

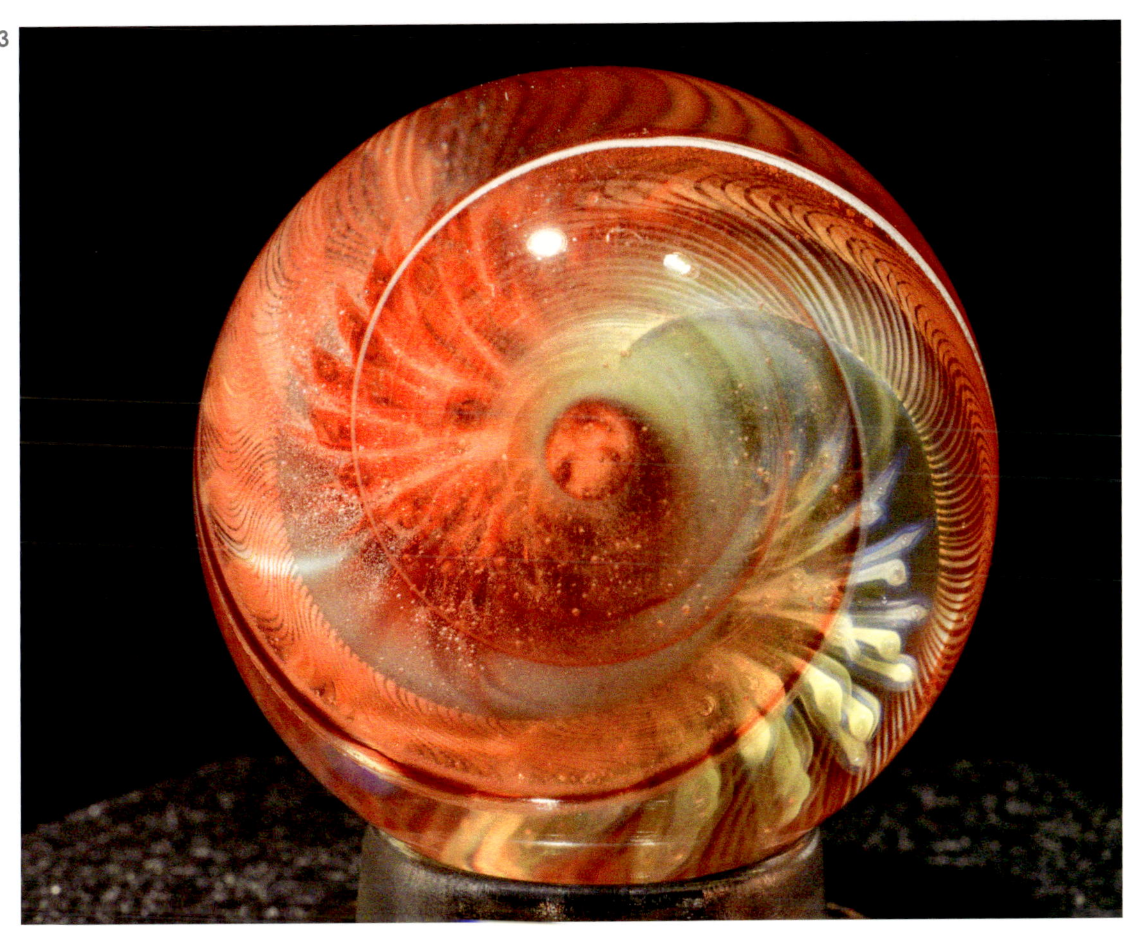

4

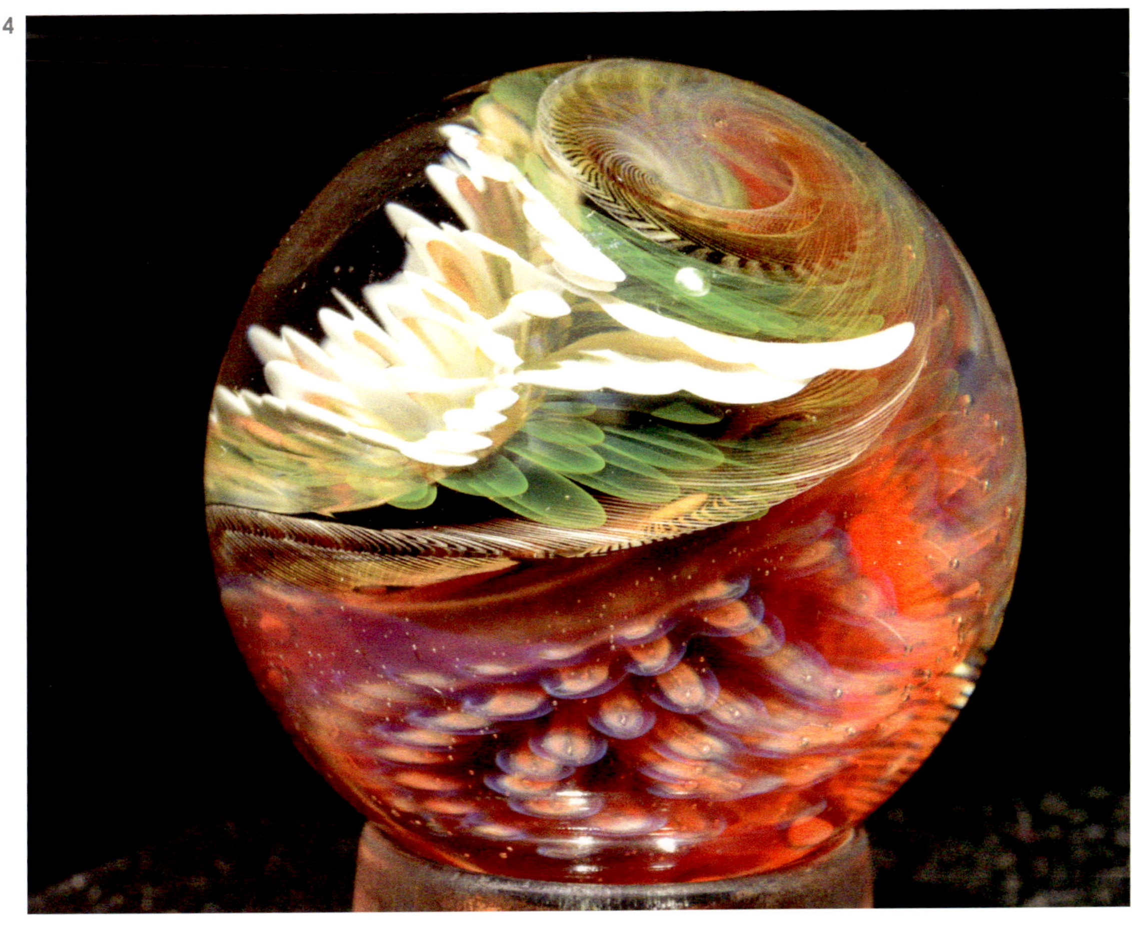

Lisabeth Sterling

Shoreline, Washington

I scribble on my glass with a marker while trying not to consciously impose an image upon the glass. It's much like looking up at clouds and describing what I see. Within my scribbles, I find people and objects. It often takes me a day or two to explore and refine the imagery before I start to engrave the glass.

Every detail in my compositions is symbolic because every person that I engrave on the glass means something to me. My goal is to find out who those people are, how they are interacting, and why the imagery is significant. I may work on a piece for weeks or even months before I realize how the imagery is relevant within my own life.

Throughout the engraving process, I keep a list of possible titles that I continue to add to as I gain additional insights into the story told by the piece. My understanding of the work changes over time. I frequently find the "true title" of the piece just as I finish engraving.

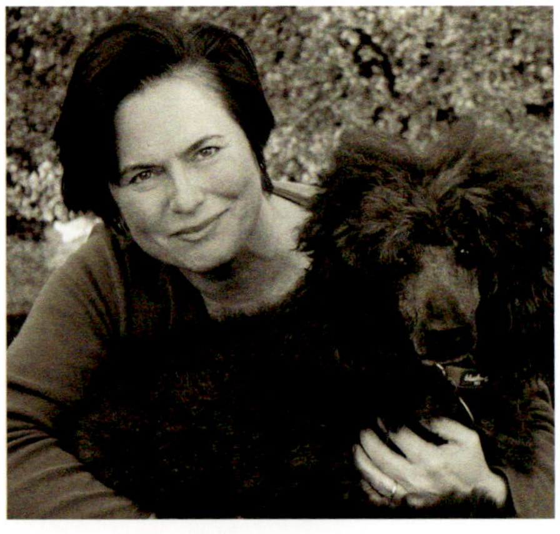

Courtesy of Tristan Levine.

1

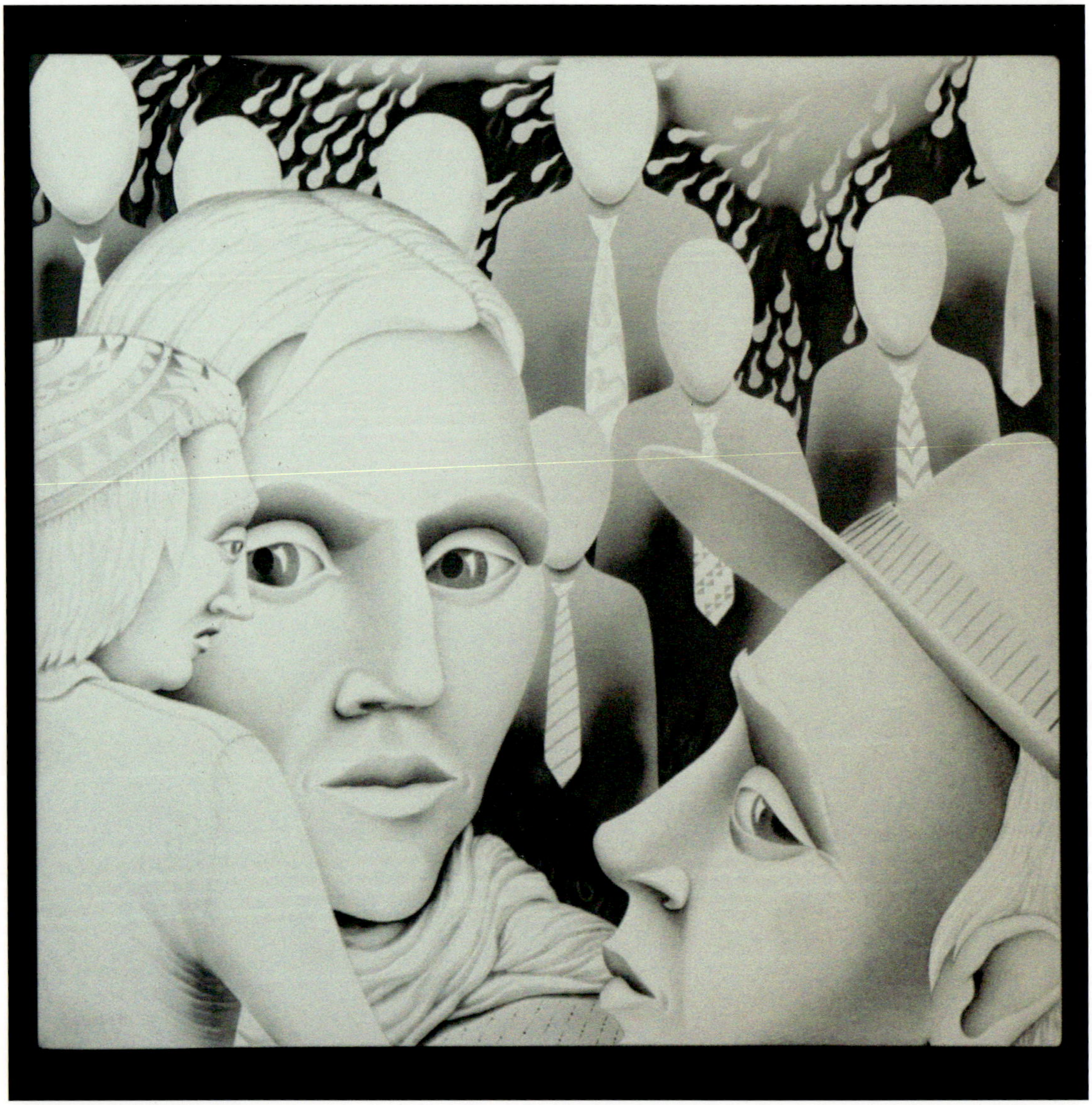

1 *Men With Ties*. White engraved cameo glass on steel. 20" × 20.5". 2011. Courtesy of Robin Sterling Brewer.

2 *Look and You Will See*. Yellow and green engraved cameo blown glass vessel. 16.5" × 5" × 11". 2014. Courtesy of Robin Sterling Brewer.

3 *Ascending Order*. Brown and yellow engraved cameo blown glass vessel. 8.75" × 5.5" × 5.5". 2014. Courtesy of Tristan Levine.

4 *Aroma Beyond Therapy*. Red and yellow engraved cameo blown glass vessel. 9" × 5.5" × 5.5". 2015. Courtesy of Tristan Levine.

3

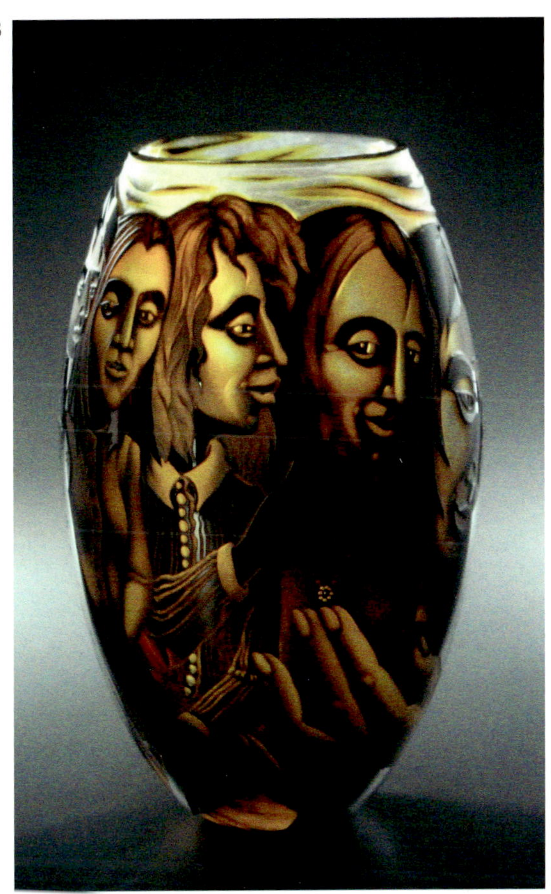

2

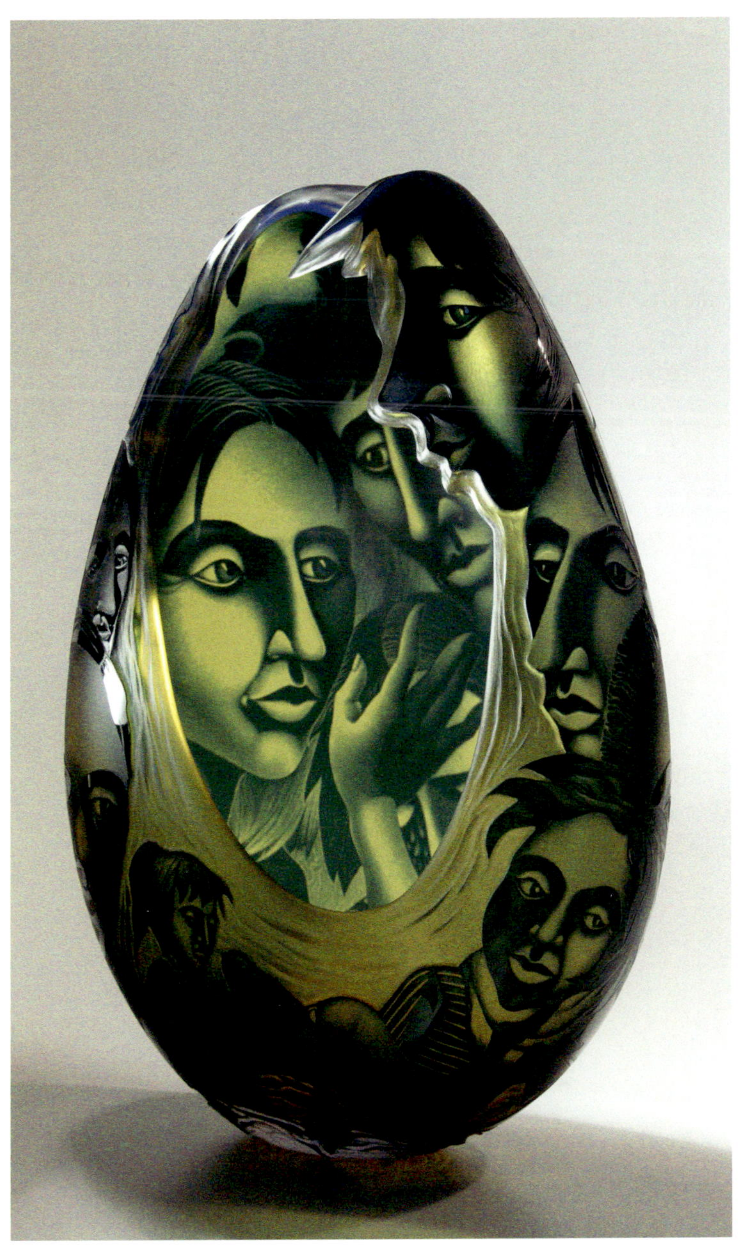

4

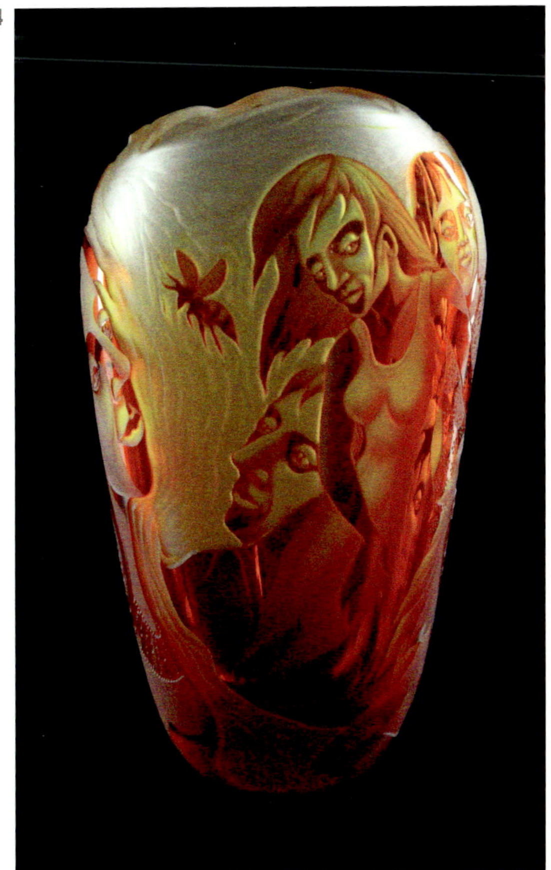

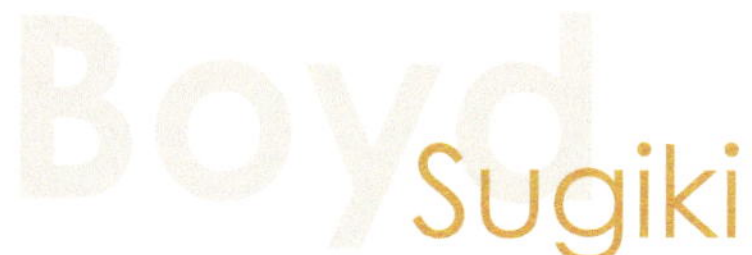

Boyd Sugiki

Seattle, Washington

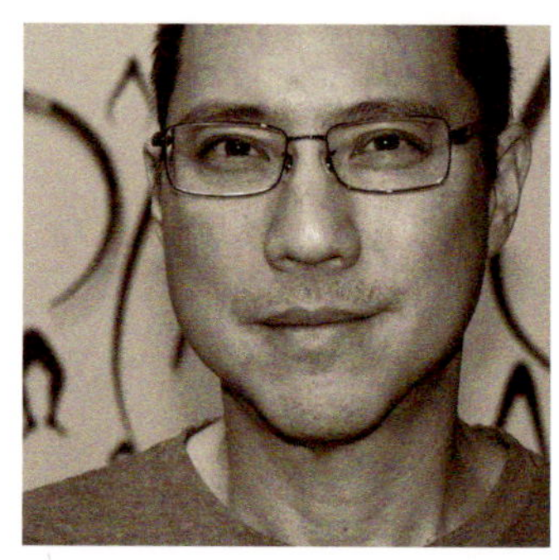

One of my primary objectives in glass is to create decorative objects that are both aesthetically pleasing and purposeful. The bowl is my favorite form to make because it requires the use of centrifugal force, gravity, and speed. They all come together, at the same time, to create volume and contour.

1

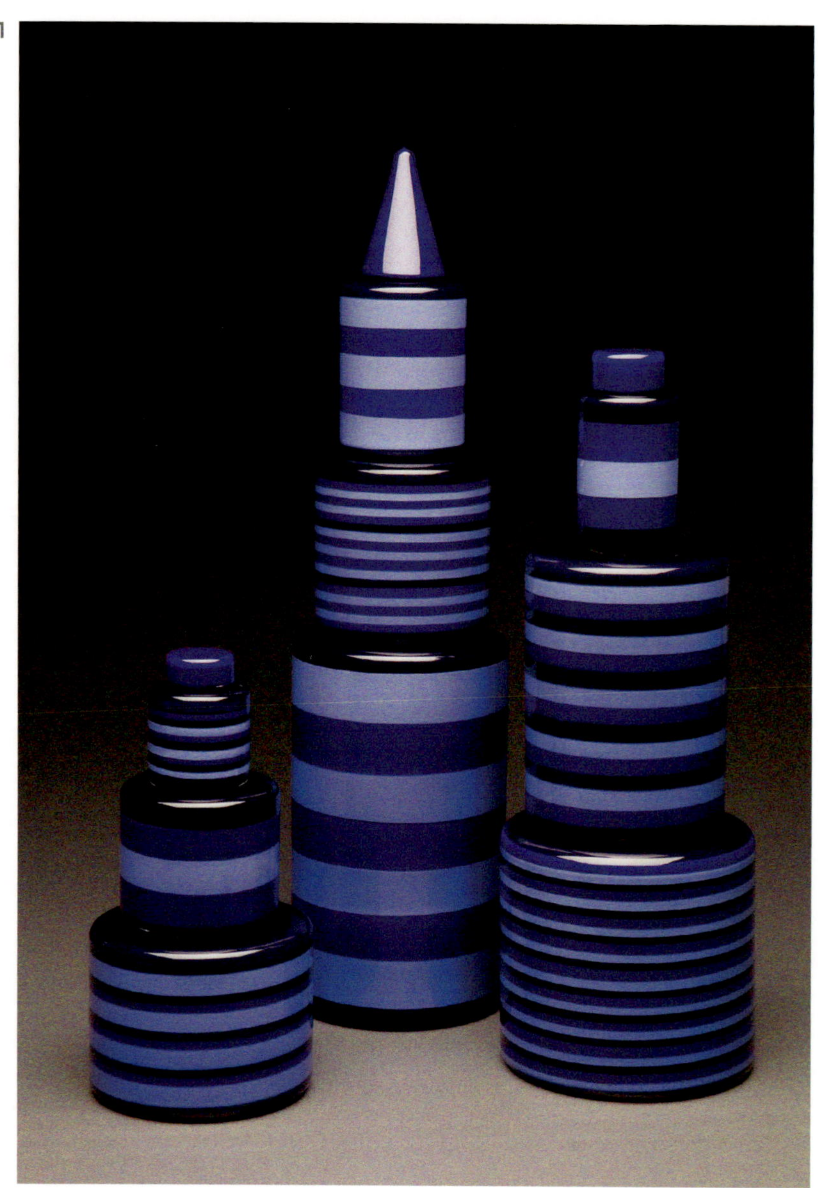

2

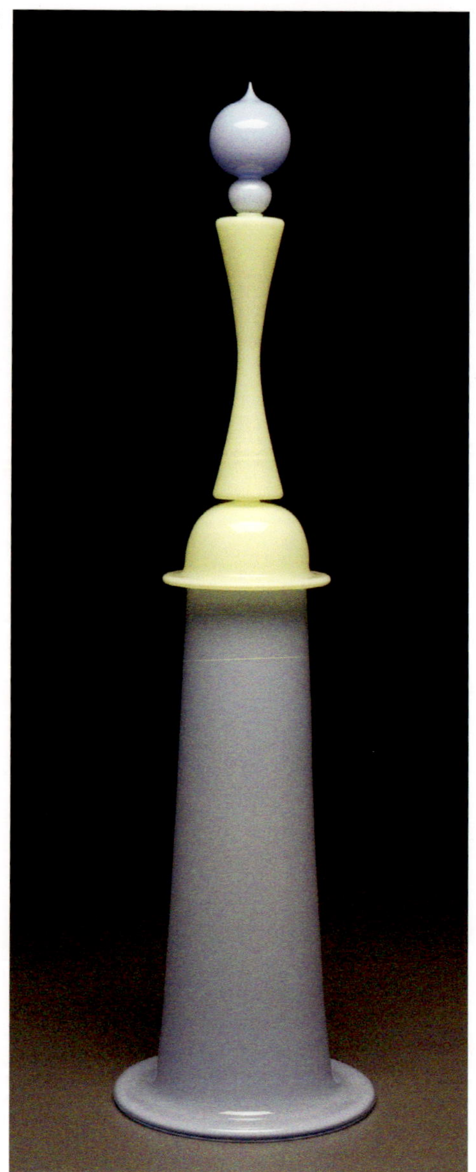

3

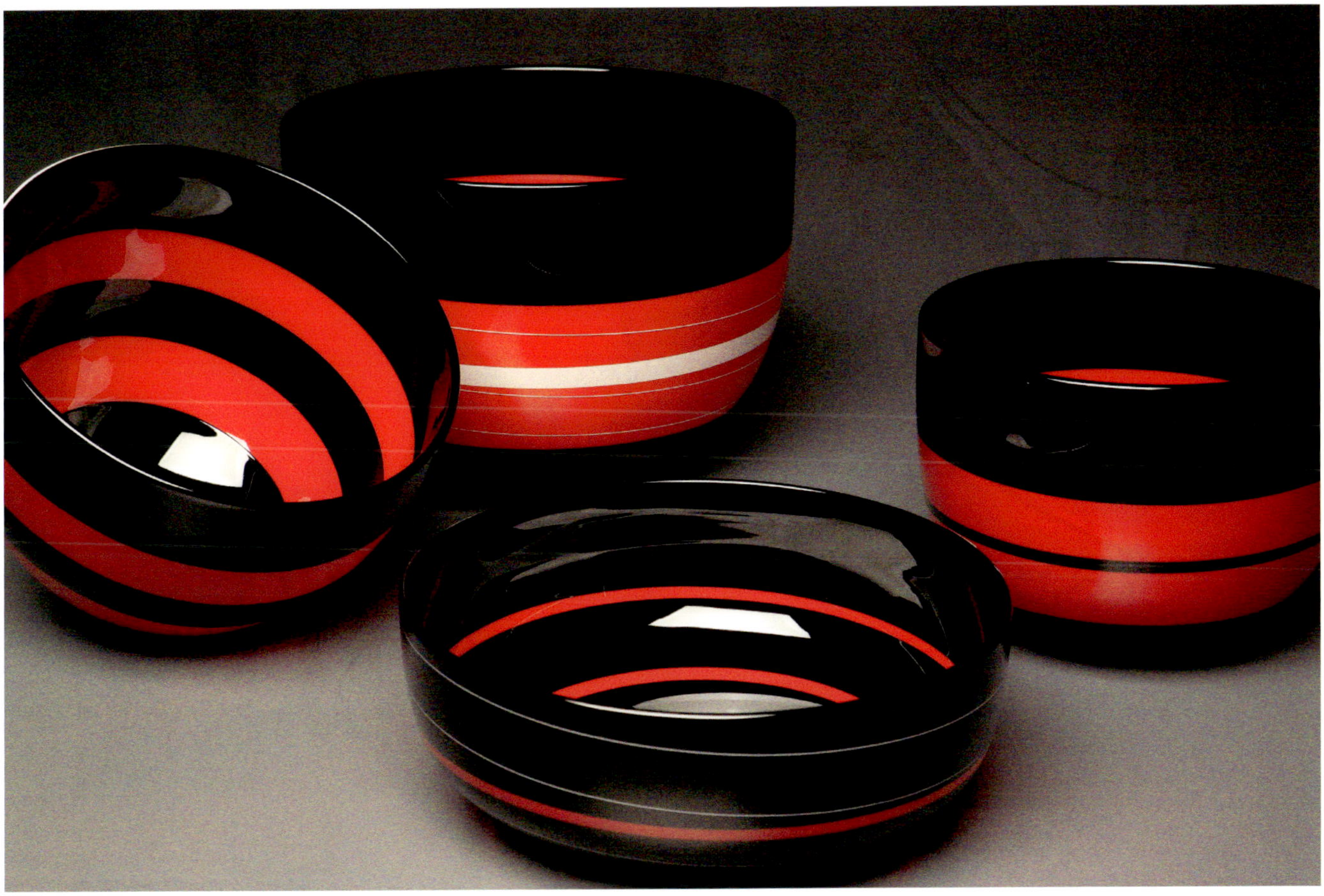

4

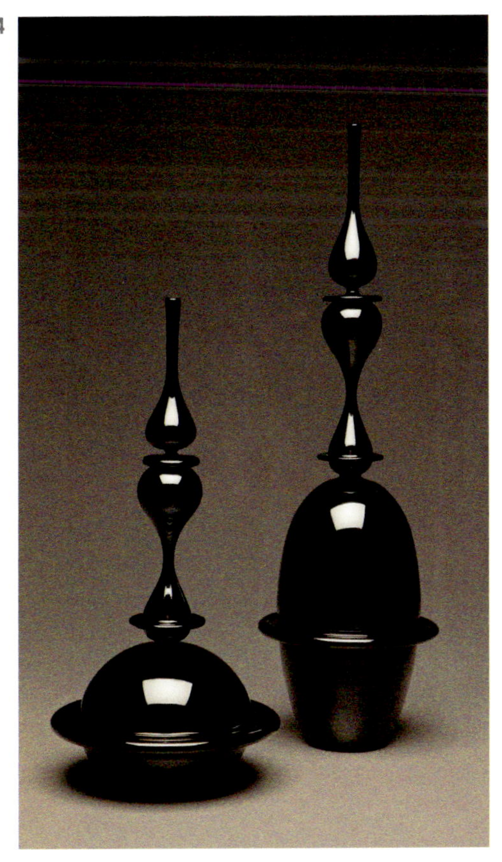

5

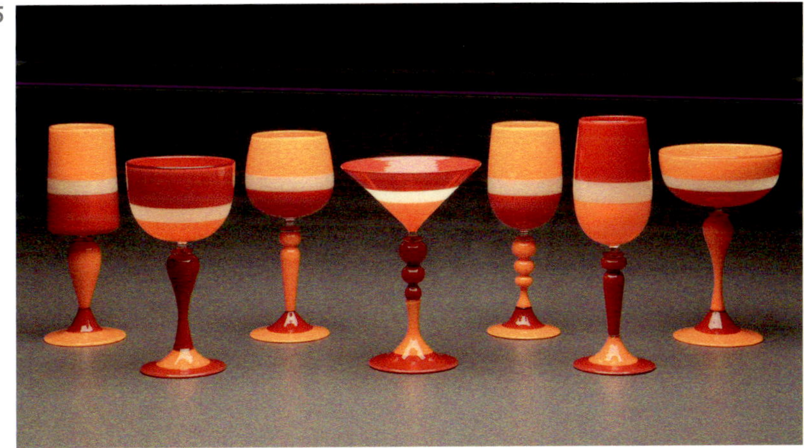

1 *Midnight*. Blown glass. 9" × 4.5" × 4.5"; 19" × 5" × 5"; 15" × 5.5" × 5.5". 2010. Courtesy of Mike Seidl.

2 *Balance*. Blown glass. 40.5" × 11" × 11". 2010. Courtesy of Mike Seidl.

3 *Striped Bowls*. Blown glass. 8.5" to 11" wide. 2010. Courtesy of Mike Seidl.

4 *Composition*. Blown glass. 17" × 8" × 8" and 23.5" × 7" × 7". 2009. Courtesy of Mike Seidl.

5 *Striped Goblets*. Blown glass. 7" to 9" tall. 2010. Courtesy of Mike Seidl.

Demetra Theofanous

San Francisco, California

In my work, I merge technique with narrative to express metaphorical bridges between nature and human beings. Inspired by the storytelling tradition of woven tapestry and basketry, I see myself as weaving with glass to connect the viewer with the story of the natural world. Through the delicate glass nests, flowers, branches, and leaves in each piece, I seek to depict the cycle of life: growth, discovery, change, and renewal. I utilize the fragility of glass as a material, to express the beauty, vulnerability, and challenges inherent in the human experience. My work also considers the tension between inner strength versus timing and circumstance and their impact on choice and personal growth. My eggs, buds, and flowers are key elements that evoke this notion of rebirth, becoming, and transformation of self.

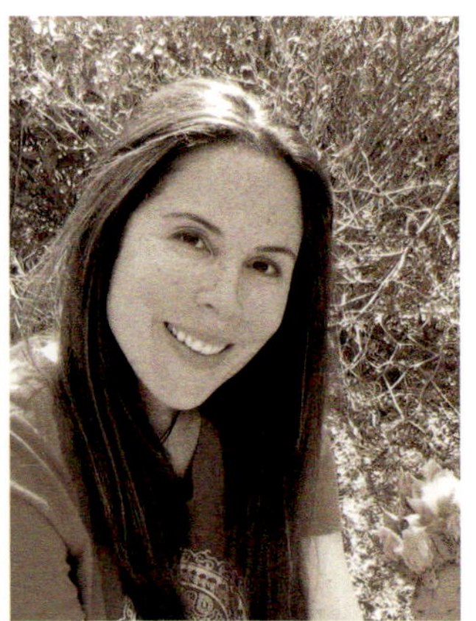
Courtesy of Keay Edwards.

My most recent work is an evolution from representational nests, or habitats, to vessels. The combination of nests and eggs, with vessel forms, builds upon the notion of transformation and the search for strength. I use container as a metaphor for the walls that contain us—whether true, or perceived—as we place the expectations of others above our own need to be authentic and true to self. *Liberate/Suppress* utilizes transparency to aid in this narrative, as the piece moves from opaque to a glistening clearness. Breaking free of containment and coming to life, the piece reflects this newfound vitality.

1

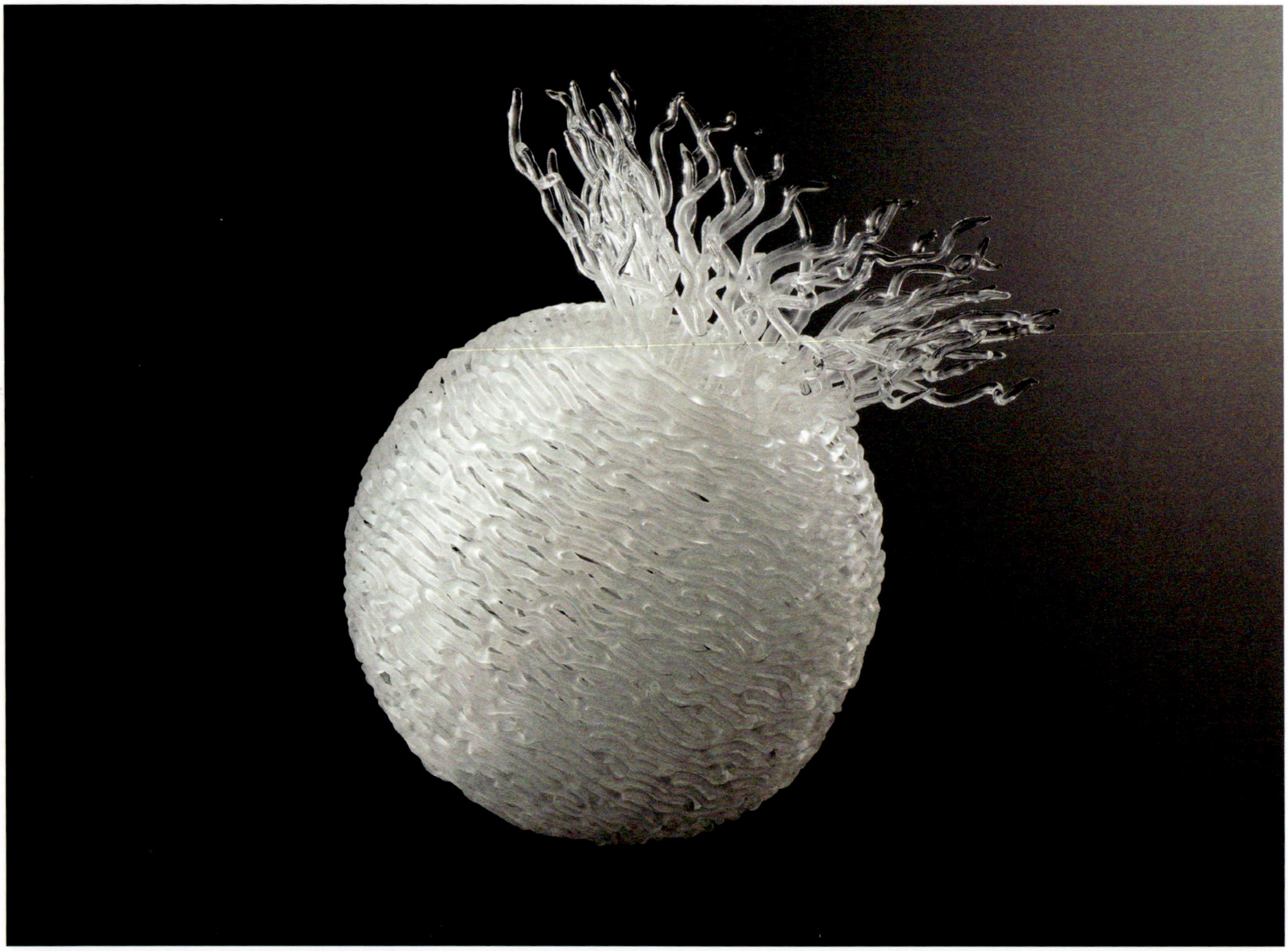

2

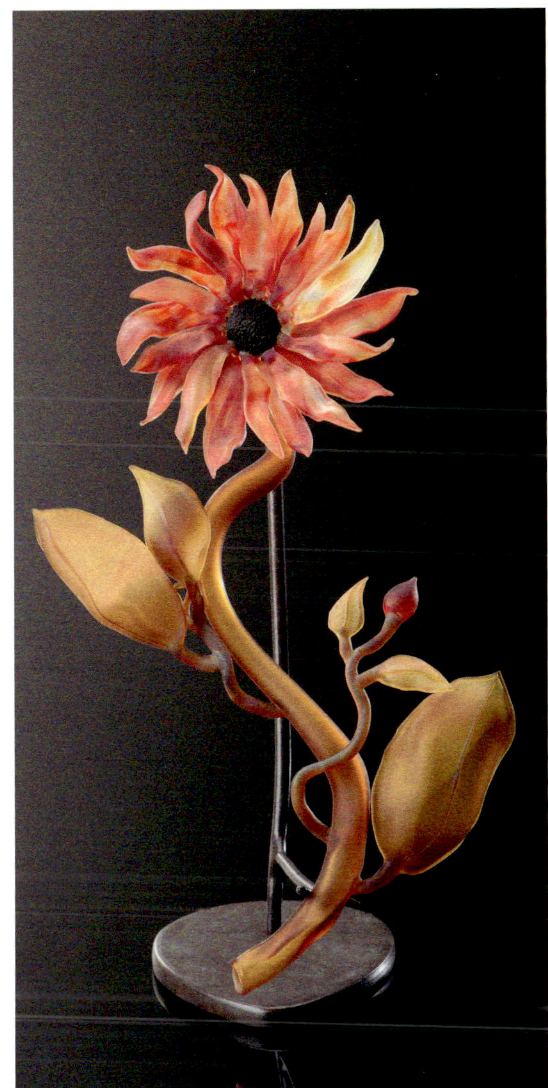

3

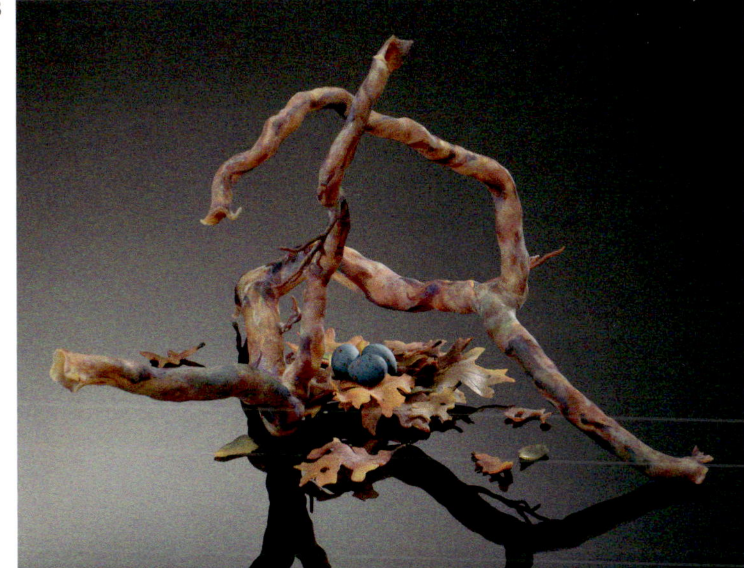

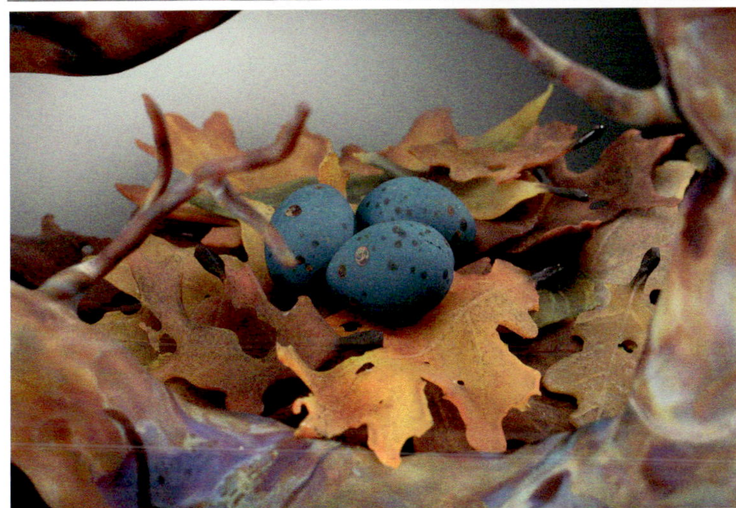

4

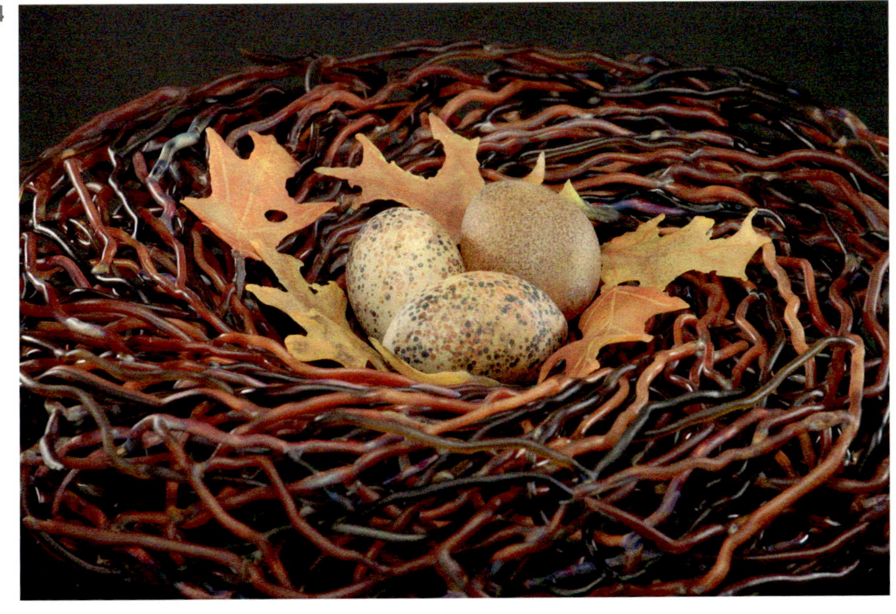

1 *Liberate/Suppress*. Flameworked glass, sandblasted. 8.5" × 7.5" × 8.25". 2014. Courtesy of Keay Edwards.

2 *Spirit*. Flameworked glass, sandblasted. 14.25" × 5.75" × 8.25". 2014. Courtesy of Keay Edwards.

3 *Repose*. Flameworked glass, pate de verre, and sandblasted. 14" × 18.5" × 20". 2014. Courtesy of Keay Edwards.

4 *Unfettered Spirit*. Flameworked glass, sandblasted, and pate de verre. 3.25" × 15.5". 2014. Courtesy of Keay Edwards.

Cappy Thompson

Seattle, Washington

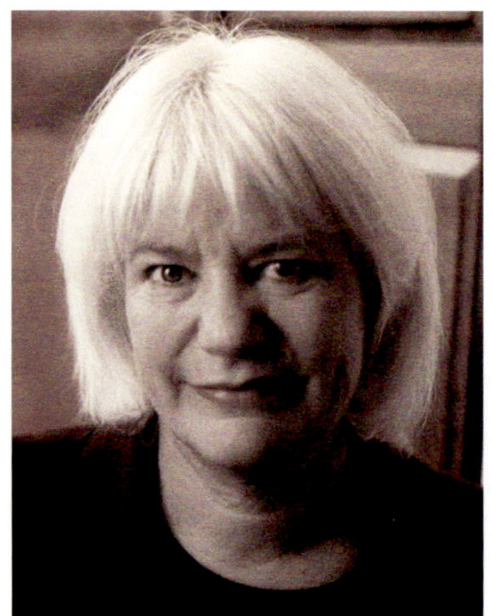

Courtesy of James Cheng.

I am a narrative painter, a storyteller. I have been painting on glass for almost four decades. Although the scale of my work changes, the themes of goodness, hope, and love remain constant. I work with a mytho-poetic process, drawing intuitively from the issues of my life, dreams, world myth, and spiritual traditions. Sometimes the drawings are simple with only a few elements, while others form a more complex narrative. I love the translucency of glass—it gives me the opportunity to bring an image to life with light.

1

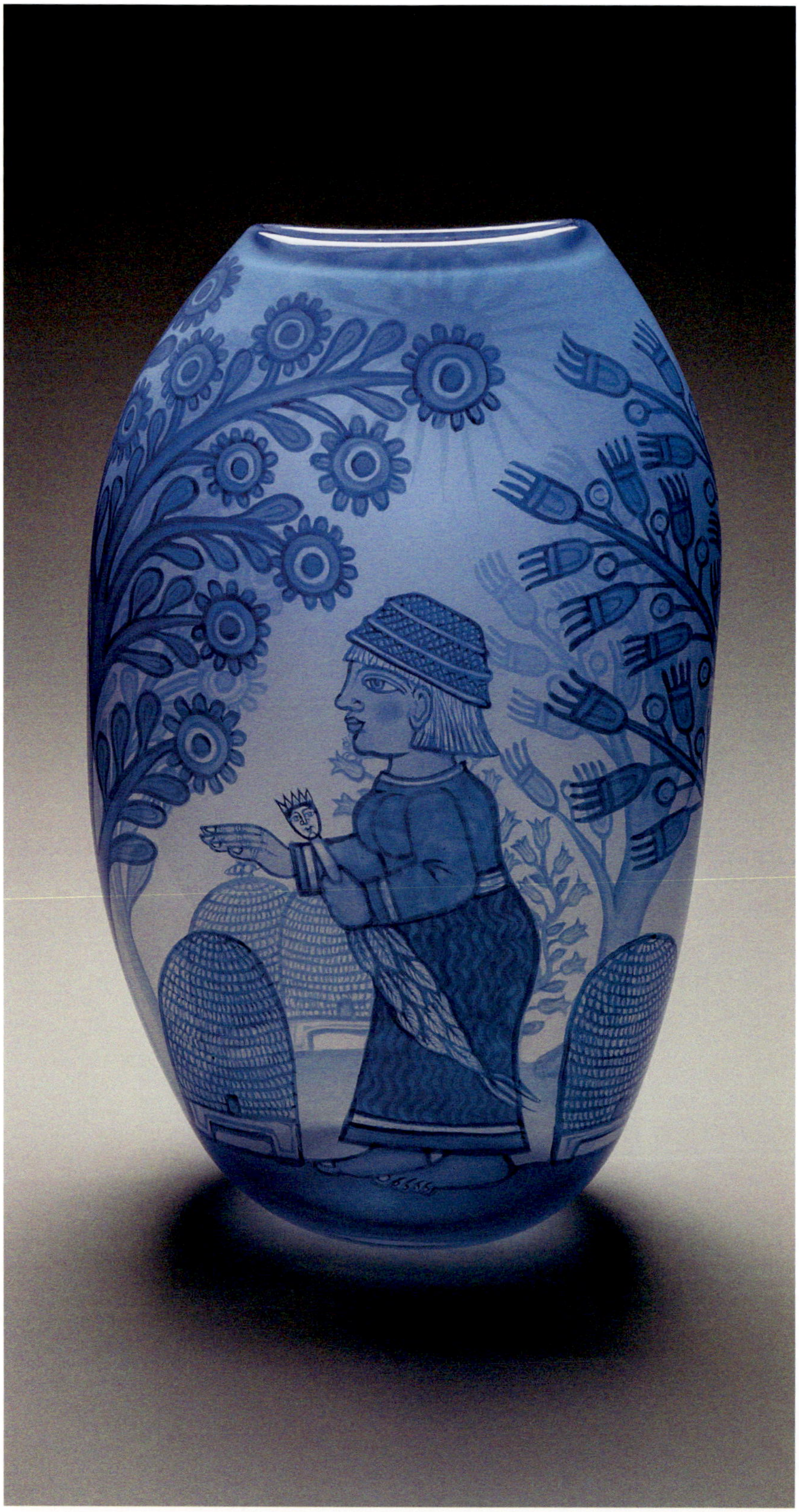

2

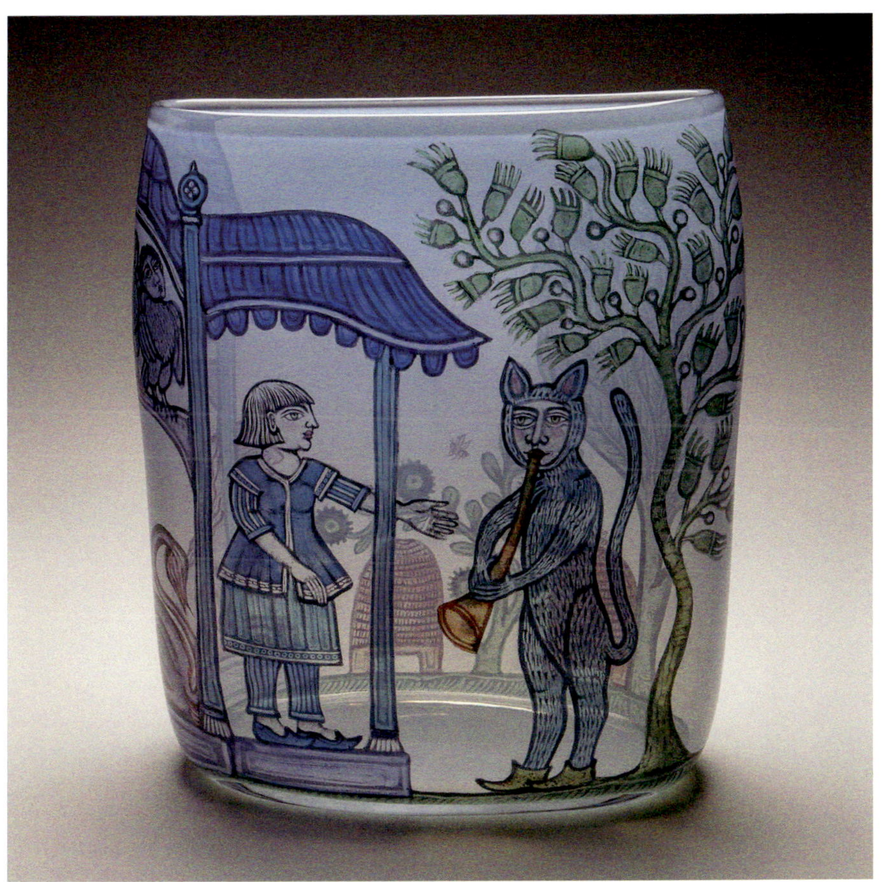

1 *Blue Sun.* Vitreous enamel reverse-painted on blown glass. 21" × 7" × 11". 2013. Photo: Lynn Thompson.

2 *Secret Garden: Welcoming My Animal Nature.* Vitreous enamel reverse-painted on blown glass. 15.5" × 5.5" × 13". 2013. Photo: Lynn Thompson.

3 *Tulip Mistress.* Vitreous enamel reverse-painted on blown glass. 19.5" × 7.5" × 13.75". 2013. Photo: Lynn Thompson.

4 *Tulip Master.* Vitreous enamel reverse-painted on blown glass. 19" × 8" × 16 ". 2013. Photo: Lynn Thompson.

3

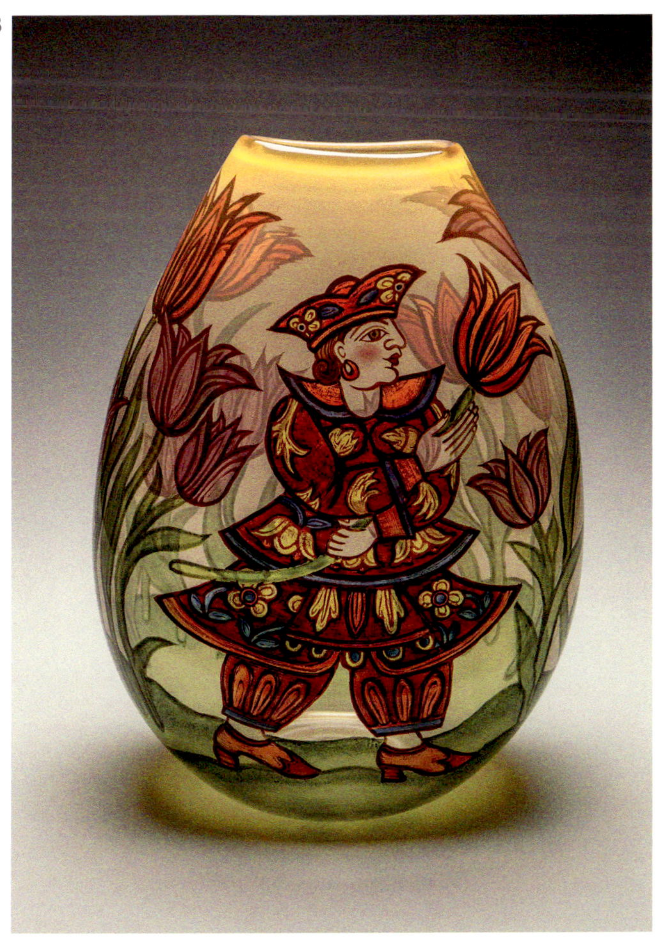

4

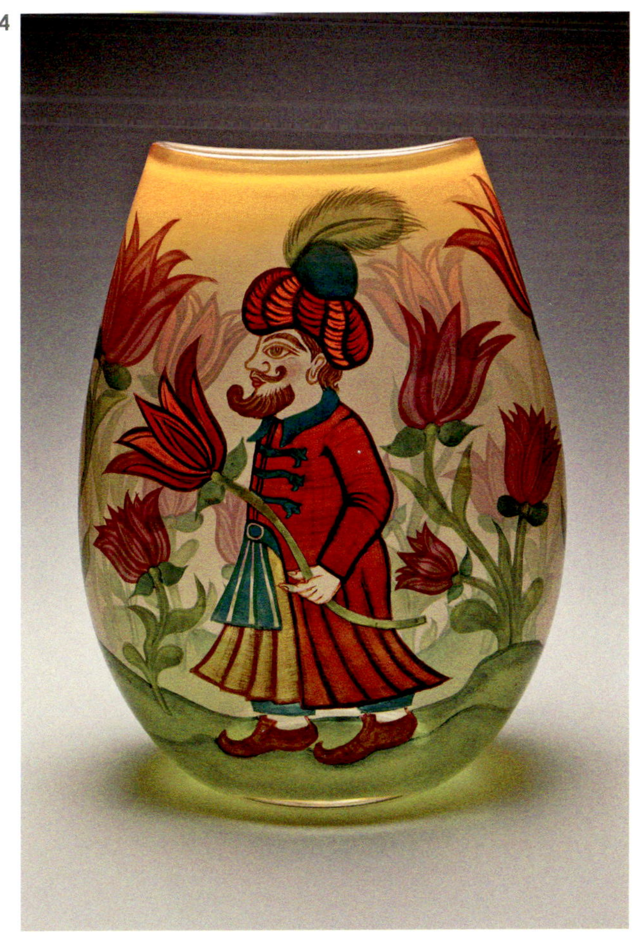

Cesare Toffolo

Murano, Venice, Italy

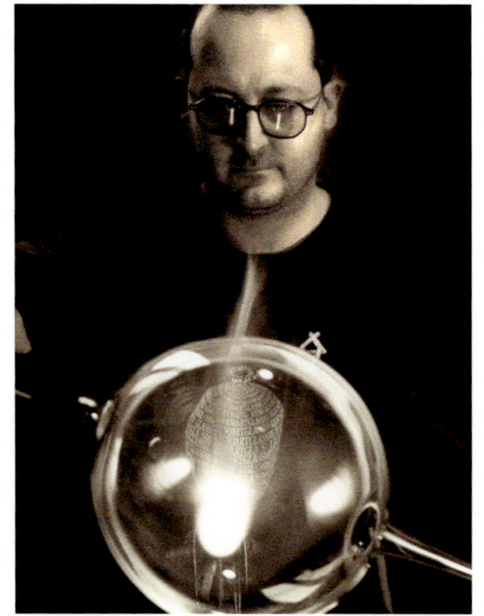

Courtesy of Studio Norbert Heyl.

Born in Venice in 1961, I come from a family of well-known Murano glass masters. At the age of fourteen, I started working in my father's studio, where I learned the fundamentals of lampworking. Today, I create avant-garde art glass pieces, many of which are internationally exhibited.

I don't create my works for others, but for myself. My works are the mirror of my soul, of how I am, of the environment in which I live, in which I breathe and have breathed in this life. They are my dreams and my nightmares. My works are instinctive expressions of thoughts, which crowd my mind; I don't seek out a subject or an idea to create; rather, they join me on their own. A work is a thought of the artist.

1

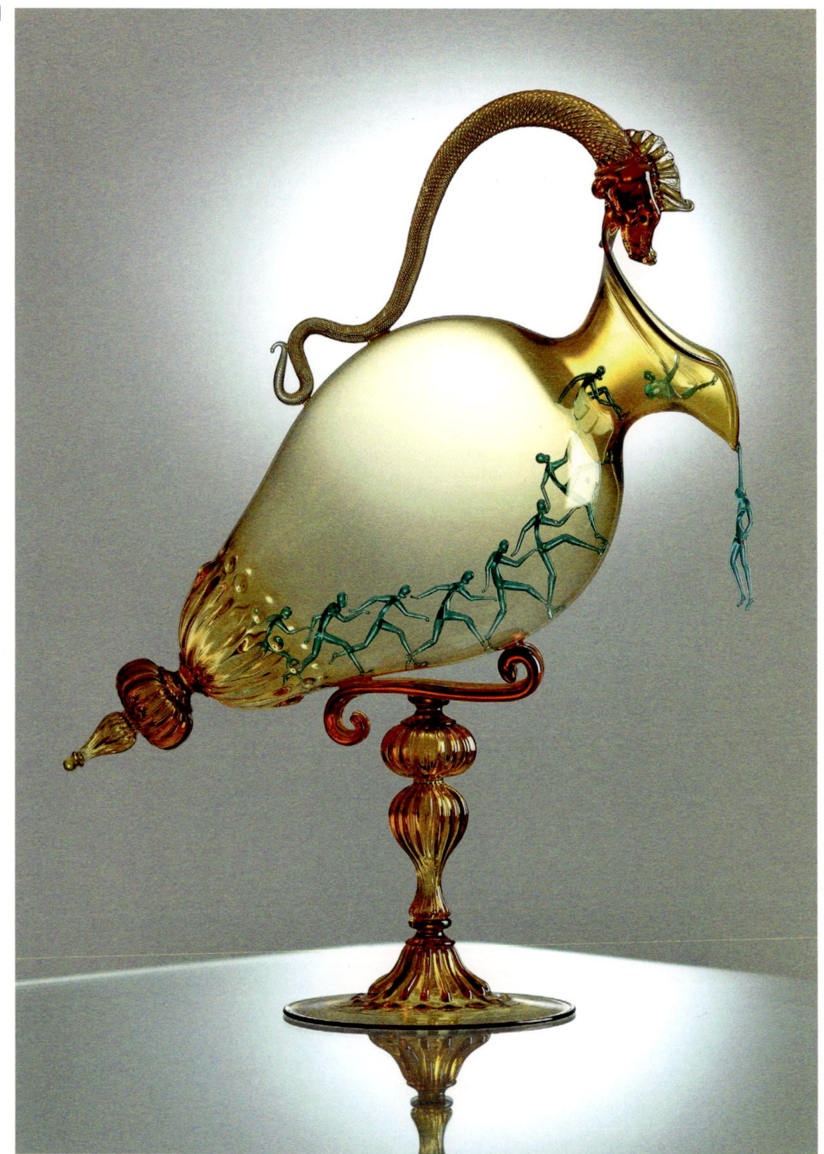

1 *Anfora amber*. Lampworked blown glass. 16" × 15". 2010.

2 *Piccoli Uomini black*. Lampworked blown glass, sandblasted. 10" to 14". 2009.

3 *Granelli Di Sabbia Gold*. Lampworked blown glass, gold leaf "graffito" technique. 17" × 12". 2009.

4 *Opera blue*. Lampworked blown glass, gold leaf "graffito" technique. 16". 2009.

5 *Natura Morta*. Lampworked blown glass, sandblasted, and gold painting. 20". 2000. Courtesy of Studio Norbert Heyl.

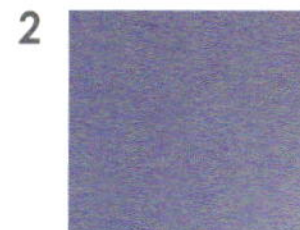

2

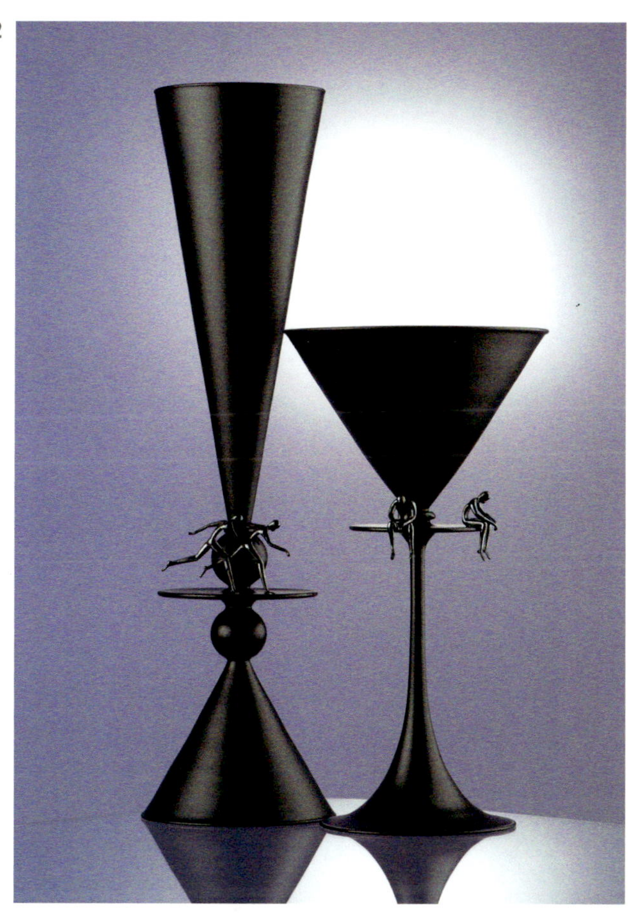

3

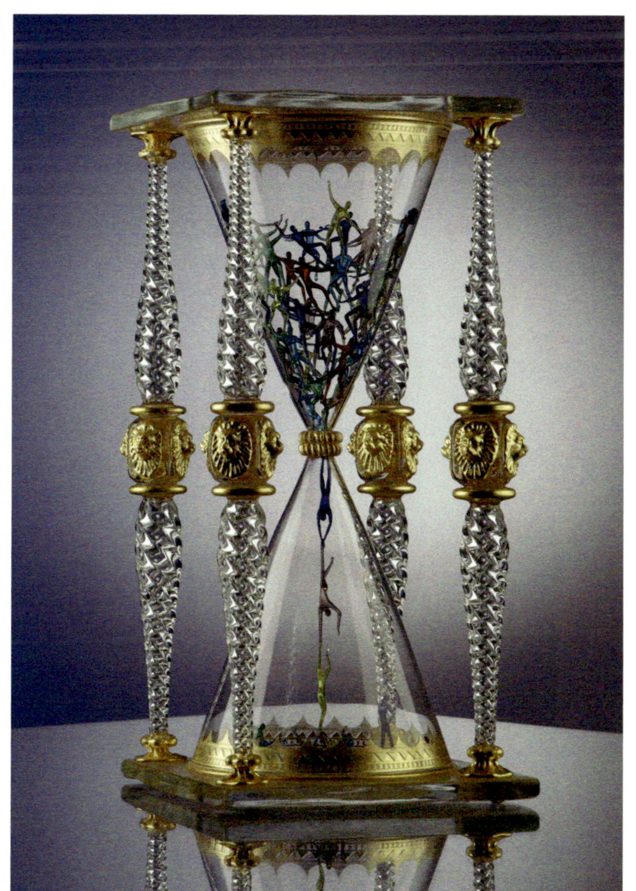

4

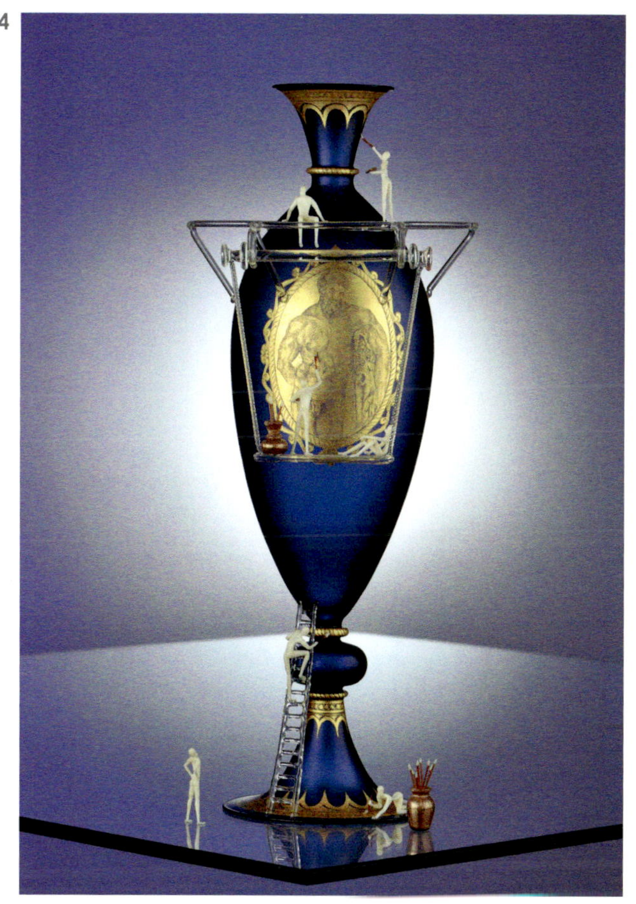

5

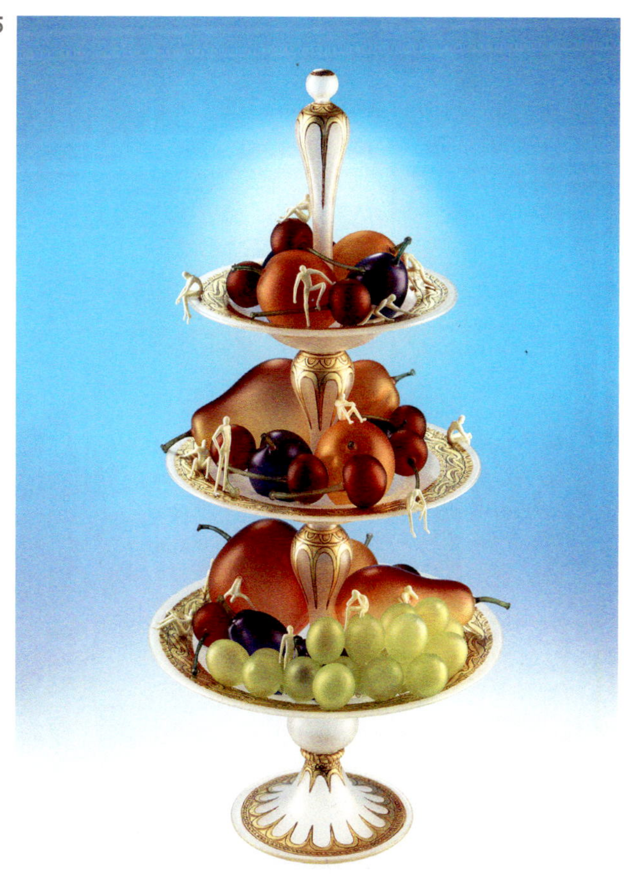

Emanuel Toffolo

Burano, Venice, Italy

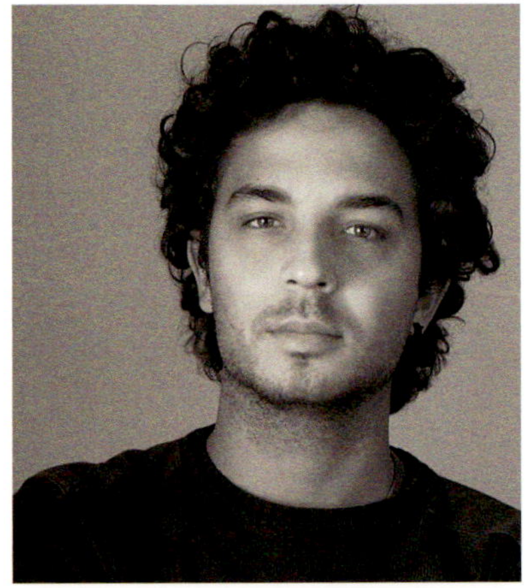

Born in Murano in 1982, I have followed in the footsteps of my father, Cesare, and a long lineage of celebrated glass artists. Upon graduating in 2001 from the High School of Art in Venice, I began flameworking glass. Thanks to my passion for natural subjects and particularly for the insect world, I focused on reproducing different kinds of insects in glass. What began as a pastime, without any special apprenticeship or training, quickly became my life passion—especially with the encouragement and suggestions of my father. Thus, inspired by the love and passion for this art, I continued, and it has become my career.

In 2014, I opened my own glass studio in Burano, Venice, where I continue to play with glass, exploring my life passion.

1

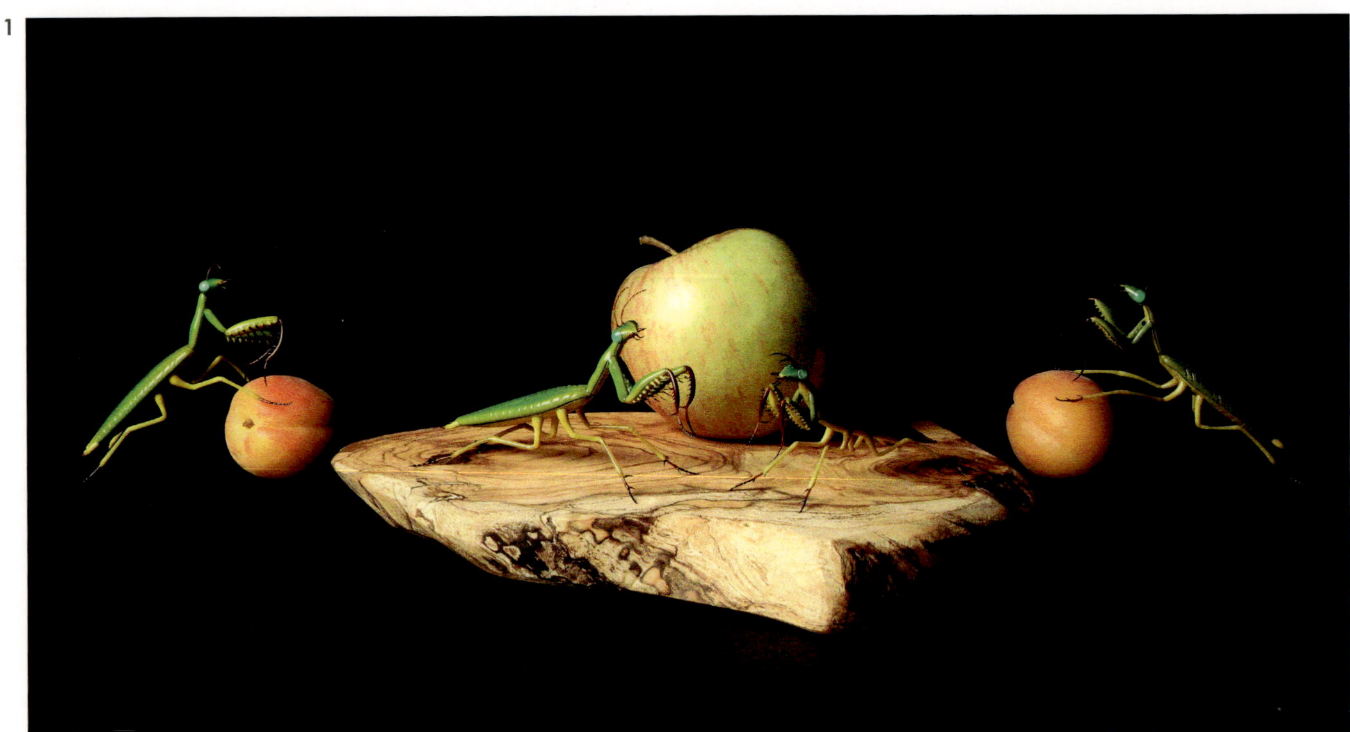

2

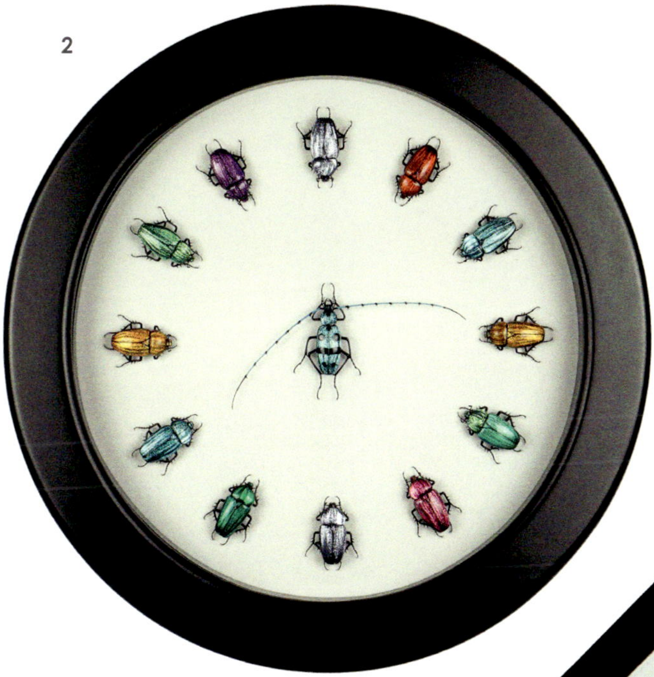

3

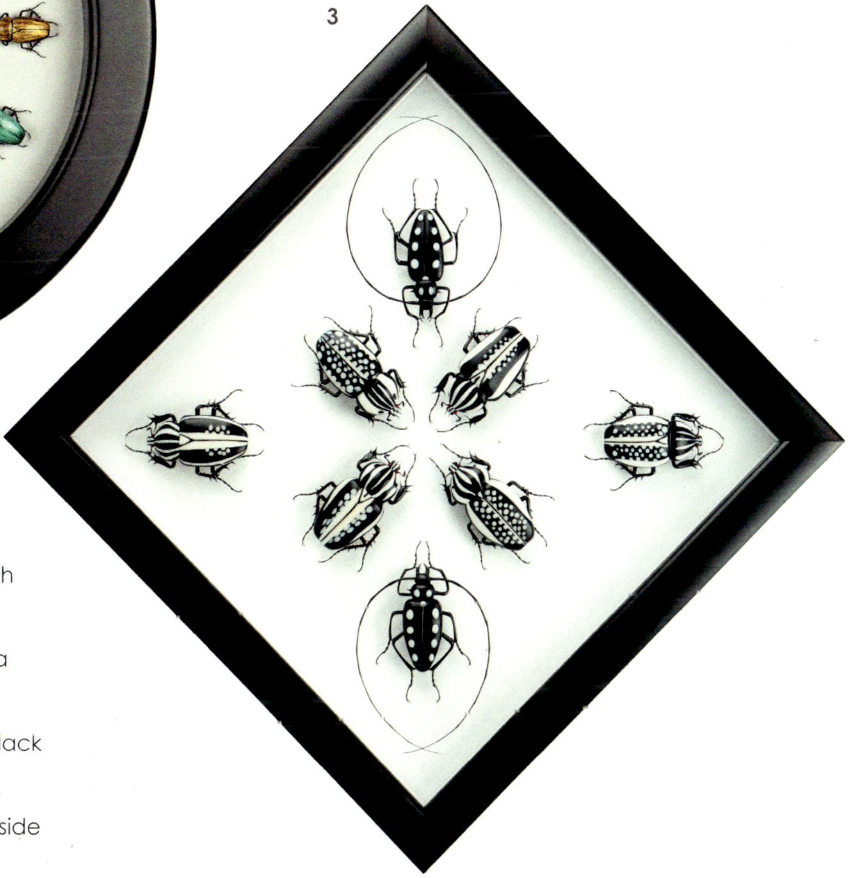

1 *Praying Mantis with Fruit*. Glass, wood, and fresh fruit. Each 2.5". 2013.

2 *Beetle Time*. Flameworked glass insects inside a black round wood frame. 19" across. 2014.

3 *Lozenge*. Flameworked glass insects inside a black wood frame. 12" across. 2014.

4 *Rainbow Scarab*. Flameworked glass insects inside a black wood frame. 5.5" × 15". 2013.

4

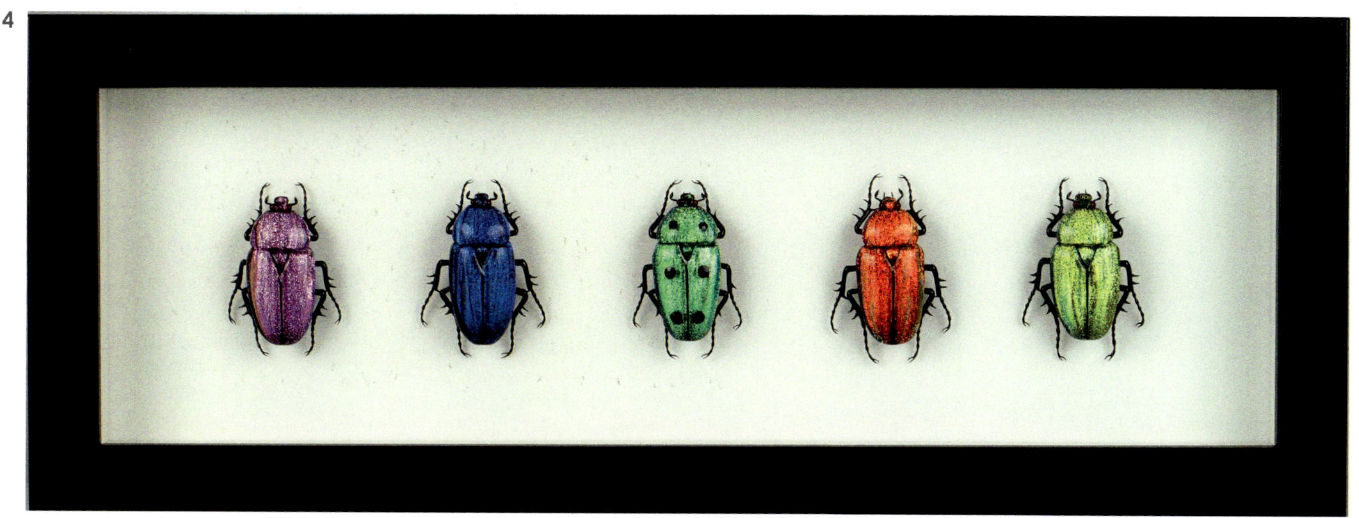

Mary Van Cline

Seattle, Washington

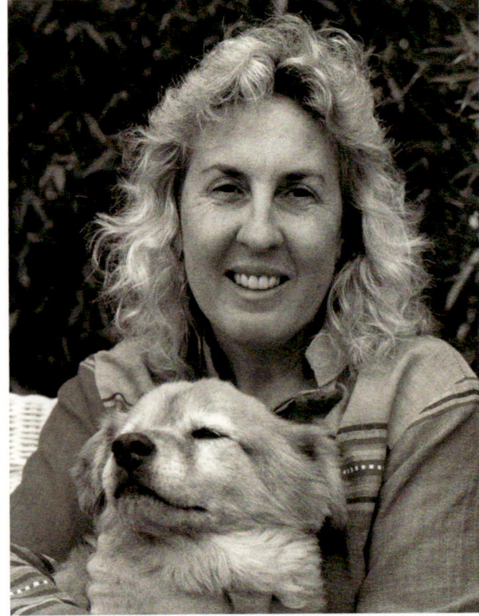

My process involves combining many contemporary hot and cold glass techniques. I worked with Kodak in the 1970s to develop a process of photosensitive glass, incorporating my own black and white photo images into my sculpture. I create life-size glass castings of the figures in my photography, using a sugar-like pate de verre glass-casting process.

My concept is that time is the riddle of human existence. It pushes one forward and leaves one behind. It exists beyond clocks, but humanity is constantly trying to measure it. Its boundaries can drive one to despair; its passage heals.

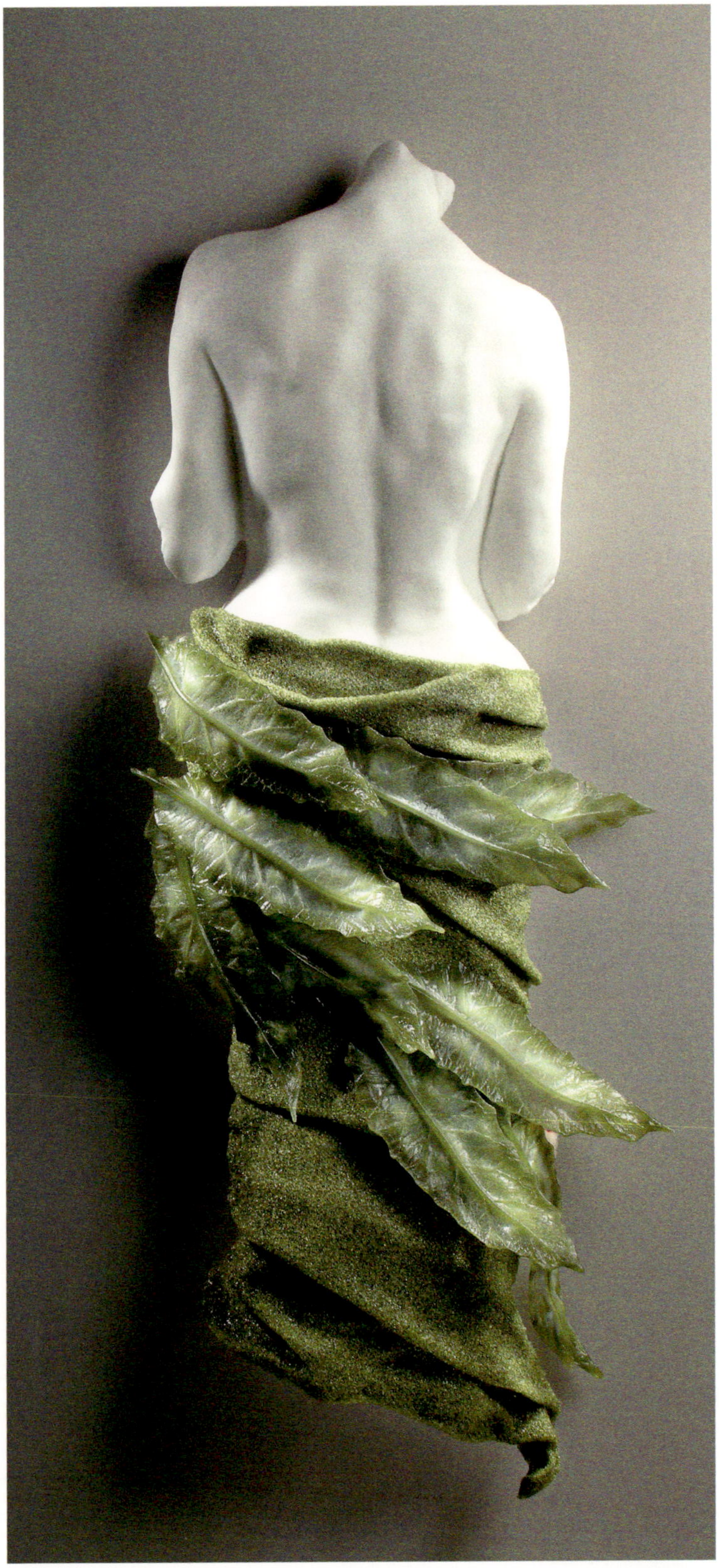

1 *Ivory Figure with Jade Leaves*. Ivory and jade pate de verre glass. 53" × 8" × 22". 2007. Courtesy of Douglas Schaible Photography.

2

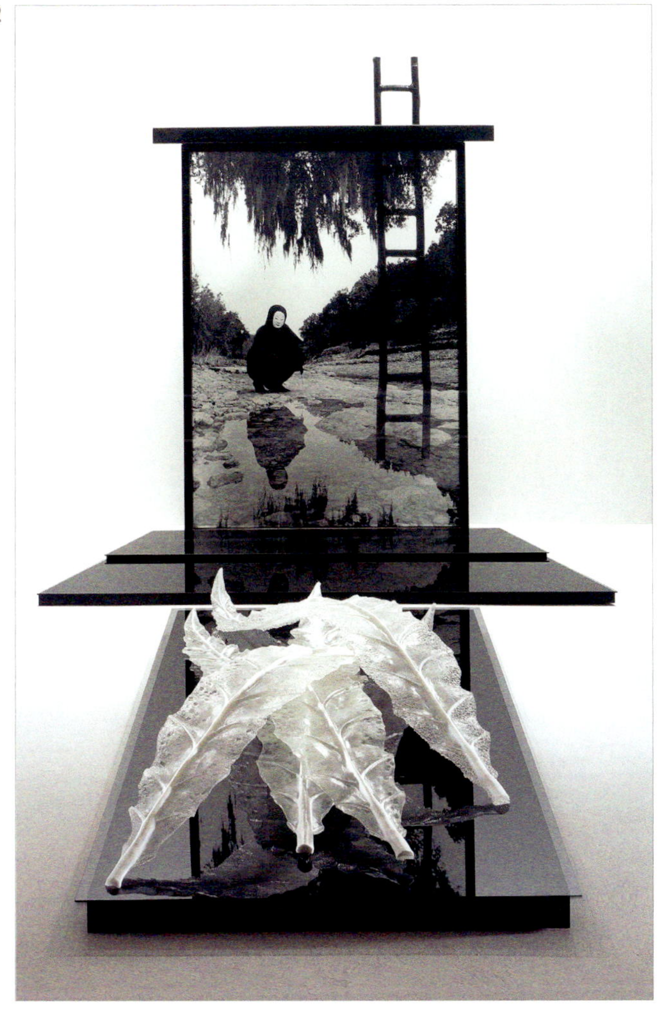

4

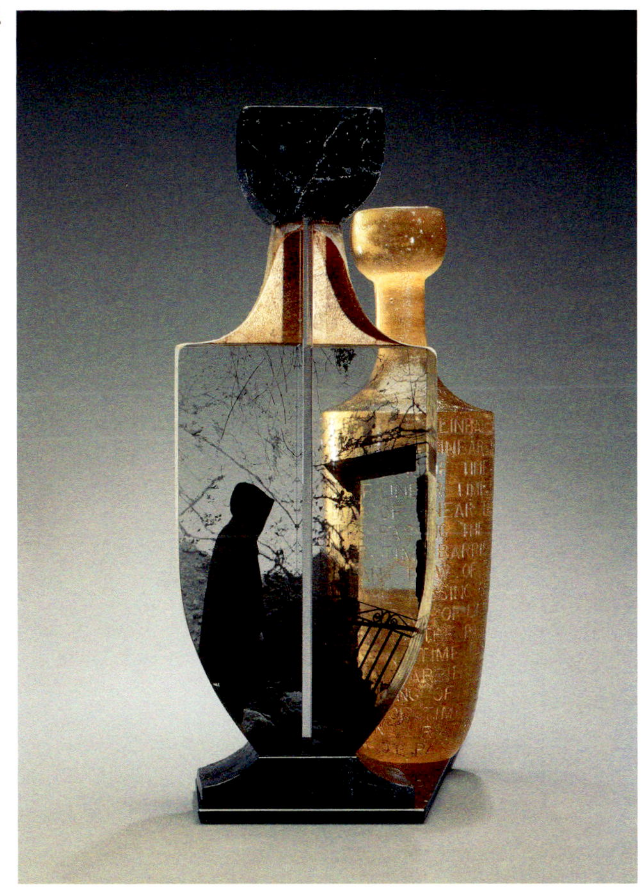

3

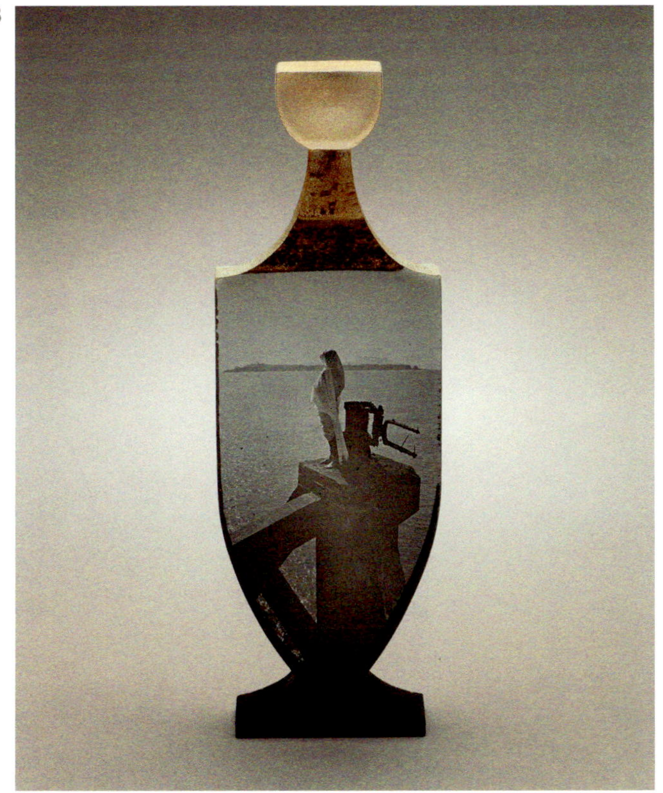

5

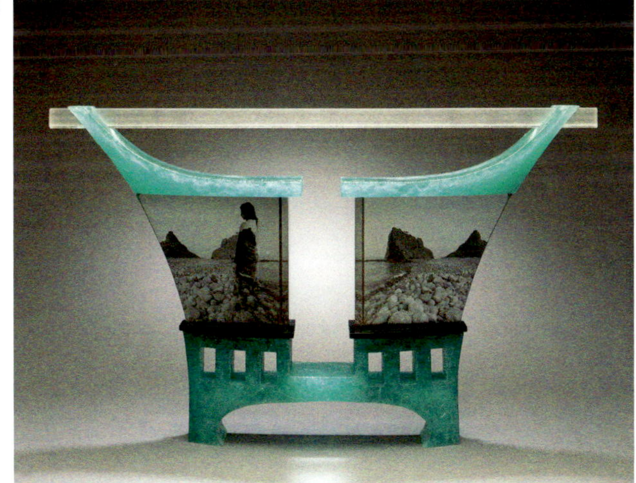

2 *Listening Point/Winter Ice Branches*. Photosensitive glass, ivory pate de verre glass. 6' × 18' × 8'. 1993-2008.

3 *Greek Vase Series*. Photosensitive glass, cast glass. 24" × 5" × 10". 1990 original series date.

4 *Linear Barriers Series*. Photosensitive glass, cast glass. 24" × 5" × 13". 1995 original series date.

5 *Ocean of Memory*. Photosensitive glass, jade pate de verre glass. 22" × 8" × 35". 2000 original series date.

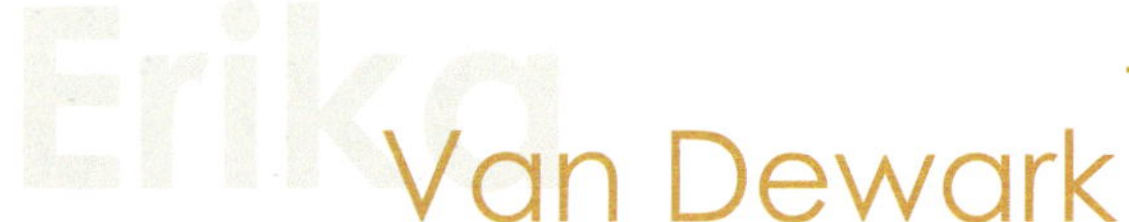

Erika Van Dewark

Vacaville, California

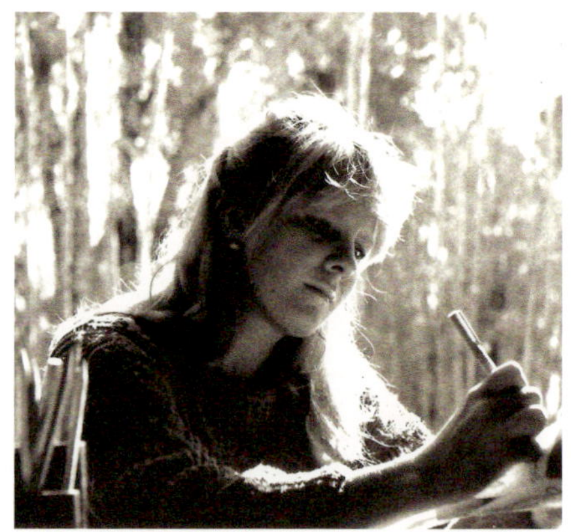

From a very early age, the beauty of the natural world inspired me to create. My childhood summers were spent in Ireland on my uncle's farm, where I began to develop a deep love for horses and other animals. They quickly became the subject matter of my sketches and paintings. As I got older, my passion for the outdoor world led me to a career with the US National Park Service as a wilderness ranger. Over the next ten years, I worked throughout the western United States. During this time, I was invited to partake in an apprenticeship at The Moving Glass Studio in Point Reyes Station. It was there that I learned the art of glass carving. Upon completing my apprenticeship, I returned to my work with The National Park Service.

Five years later, I combined my passion for glass carving with the years I had spent observing wildlife in North America, Europe, and Africa, and I opened my own studio. Ever since, my art has taken me many wonderful places and afforded me many exciting opportunities.

1

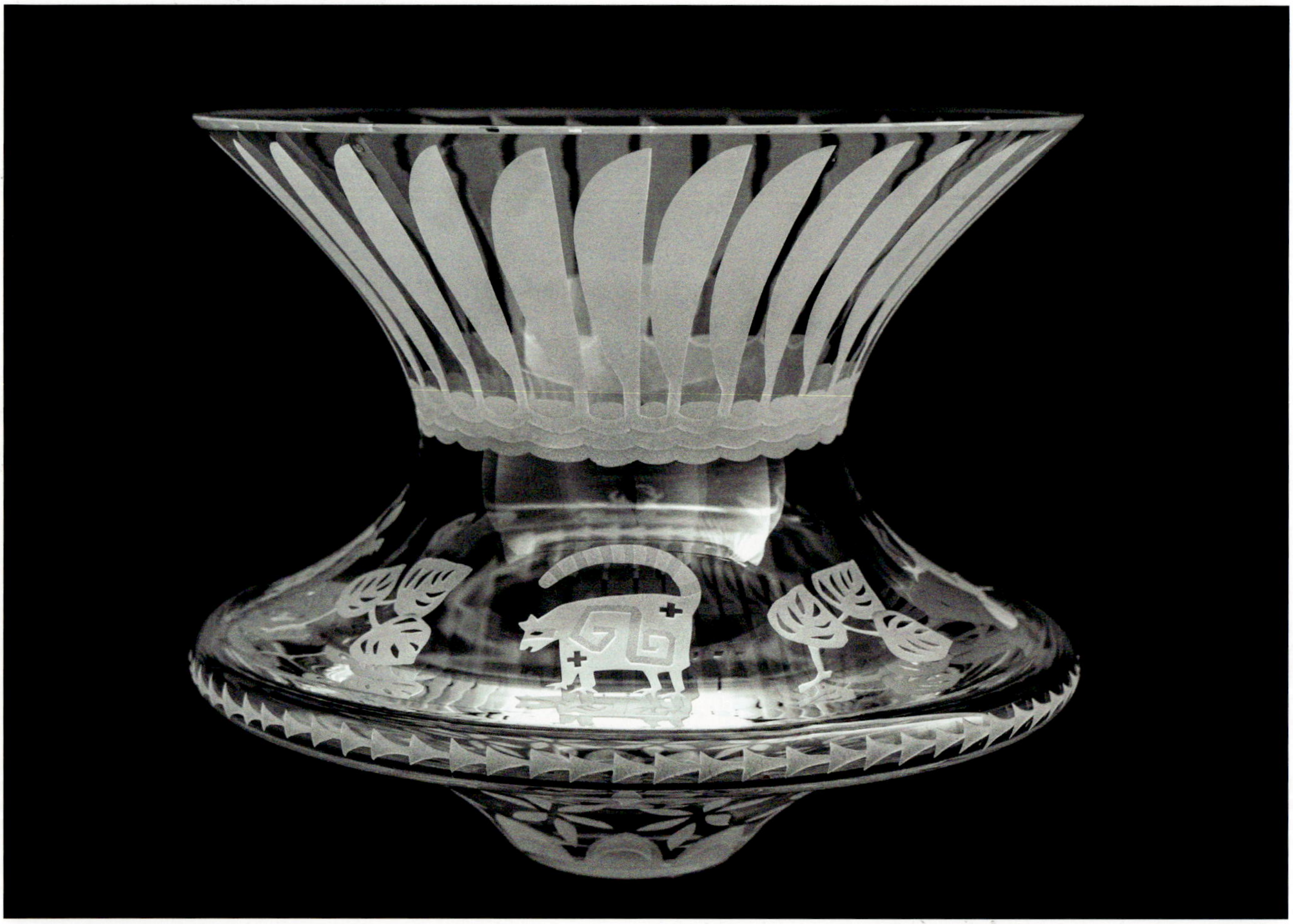

2

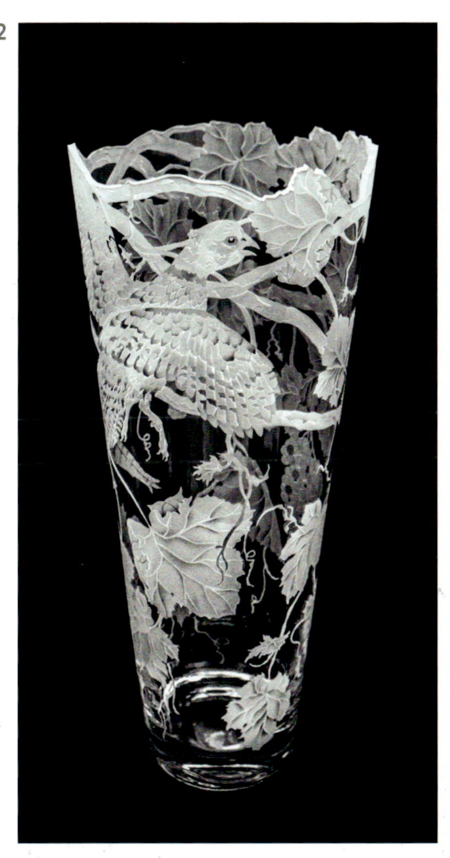

3

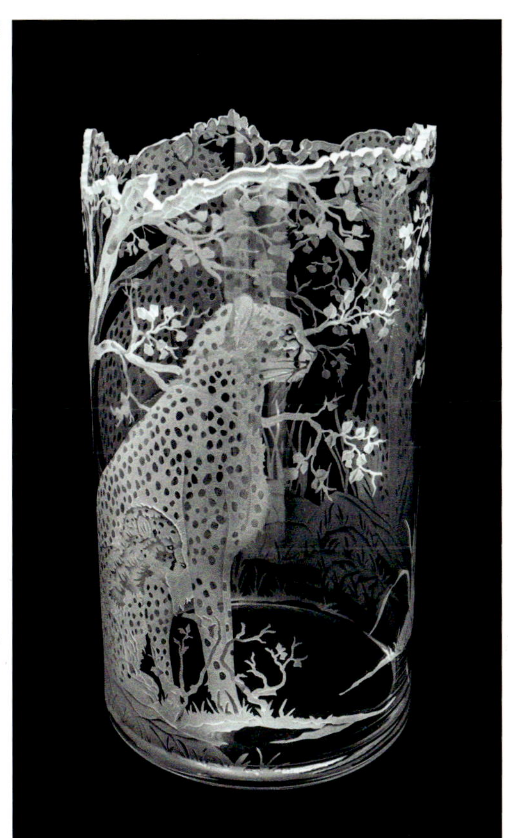

1 *Zia.* Carved. 14" × 14". 2014. Courtesy of Tracy Lukehart.

2 *Pheasant in the Vines.* Carved. 23" × 10". 2014. Courtesy of Tracy Lukehart.

3 *On Guard.* Carved. 15" × 9.5". 2012. Courtesy of Tracy Lukehart.

4 *Giraffe Screen.* Carved. Three panels. 0.50" StarPhire glass. 6.3' × 7'. 2010. Courtesy of Tracy Lukehart.

4

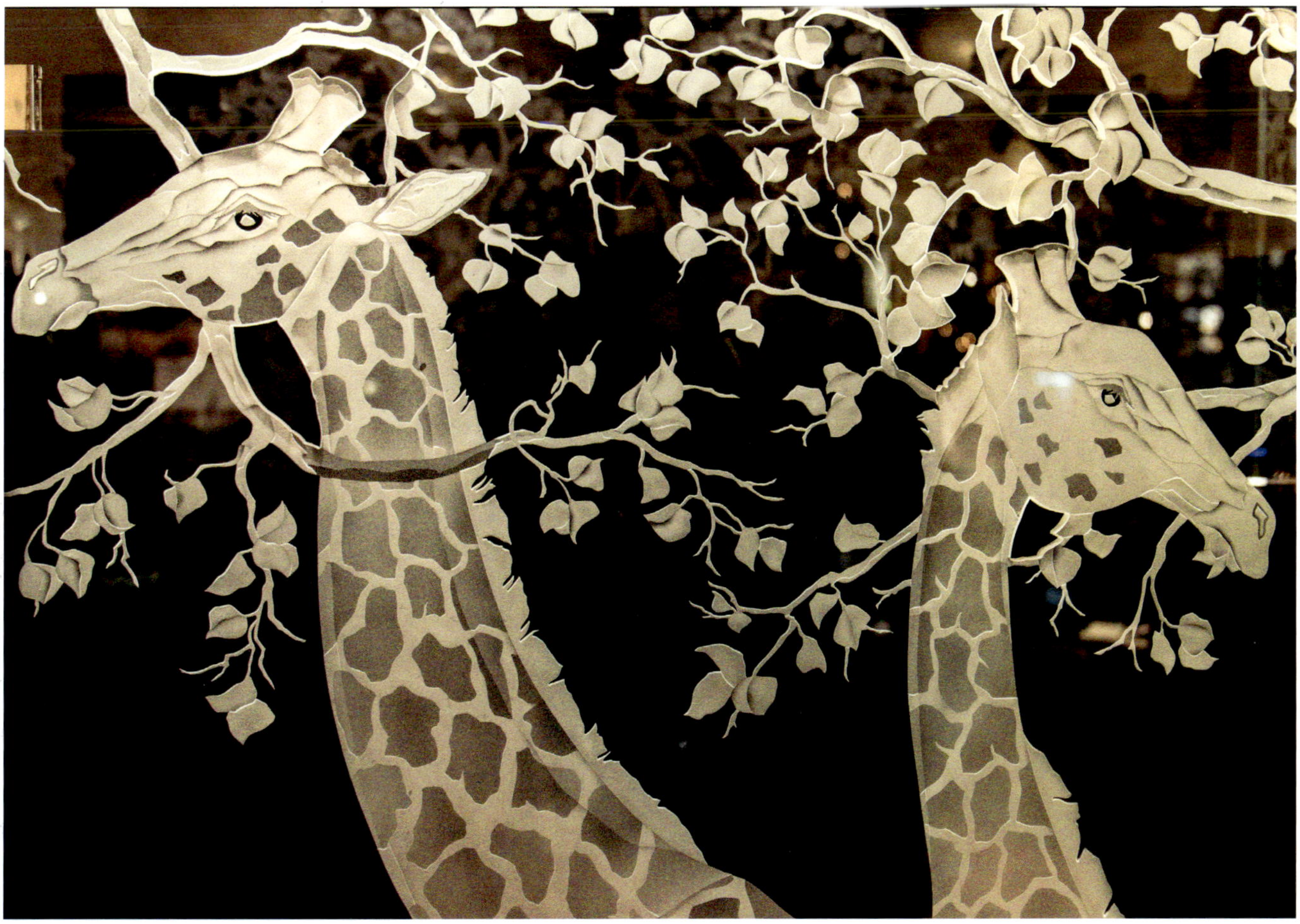

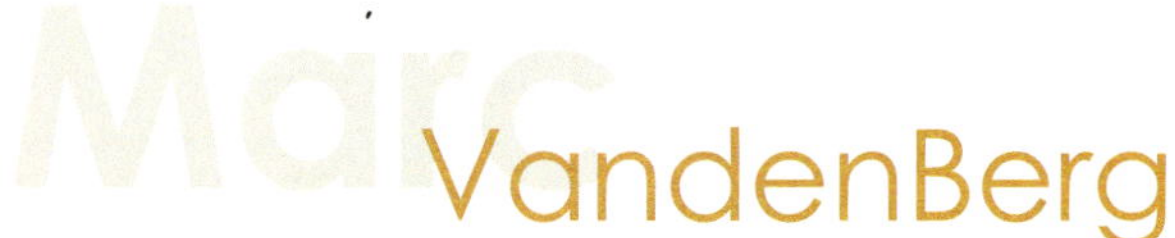

Marc VandenBerg

Dearborn, Michigan

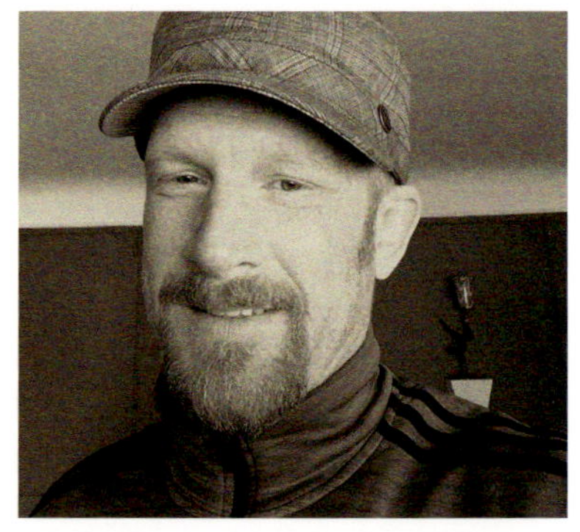

Working with glass has defined my life and purpose in the world. For me, glass means persistence, patience, perseverance, and introspection. The challenging material forces an understanding of failure as a pathway to success. Inspiration is everywhere; however, my difficult and painful life experiences have proven to be most powerful. I have found working with my hands therapeutic, allowing me to communicate thoughtfulness, self-reflection, honesty, and a pursuance of excellence.

1

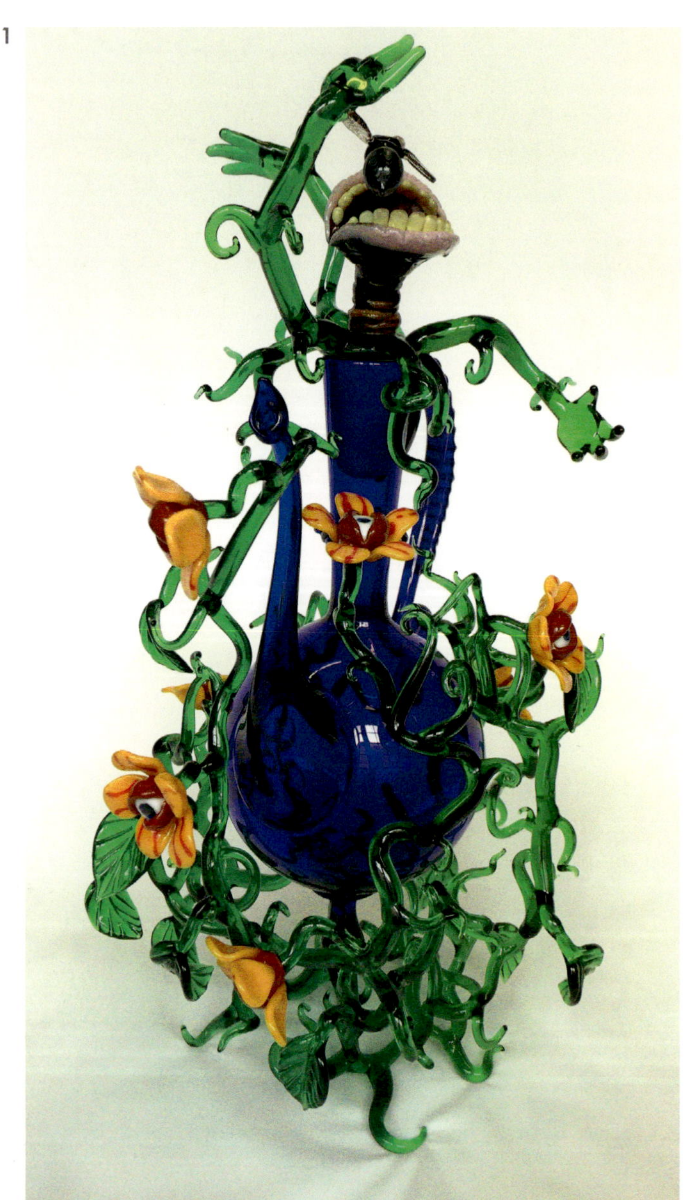

2

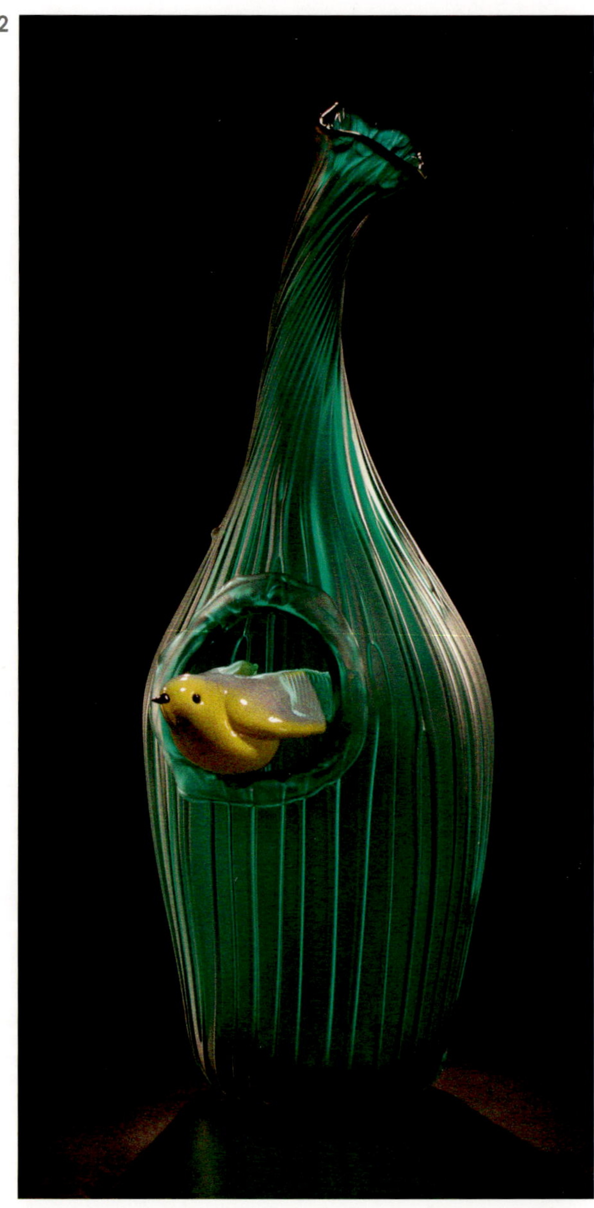

3

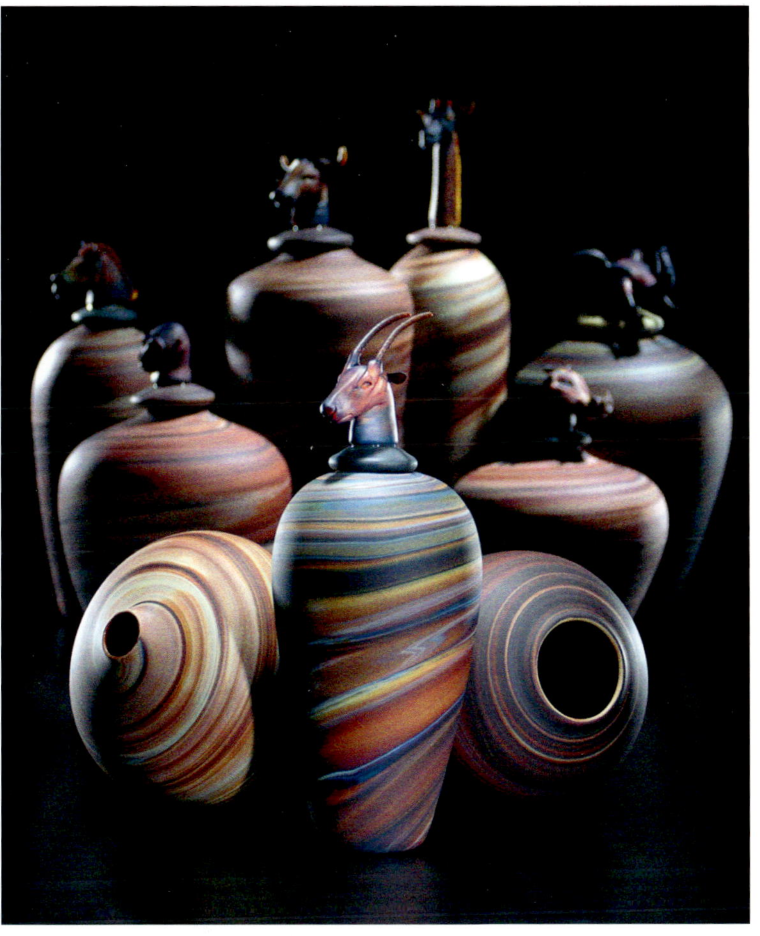

5

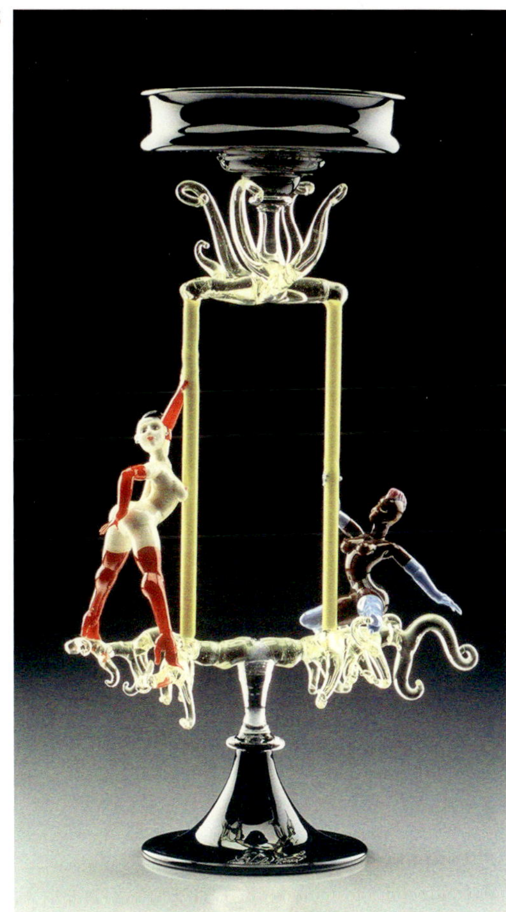

4

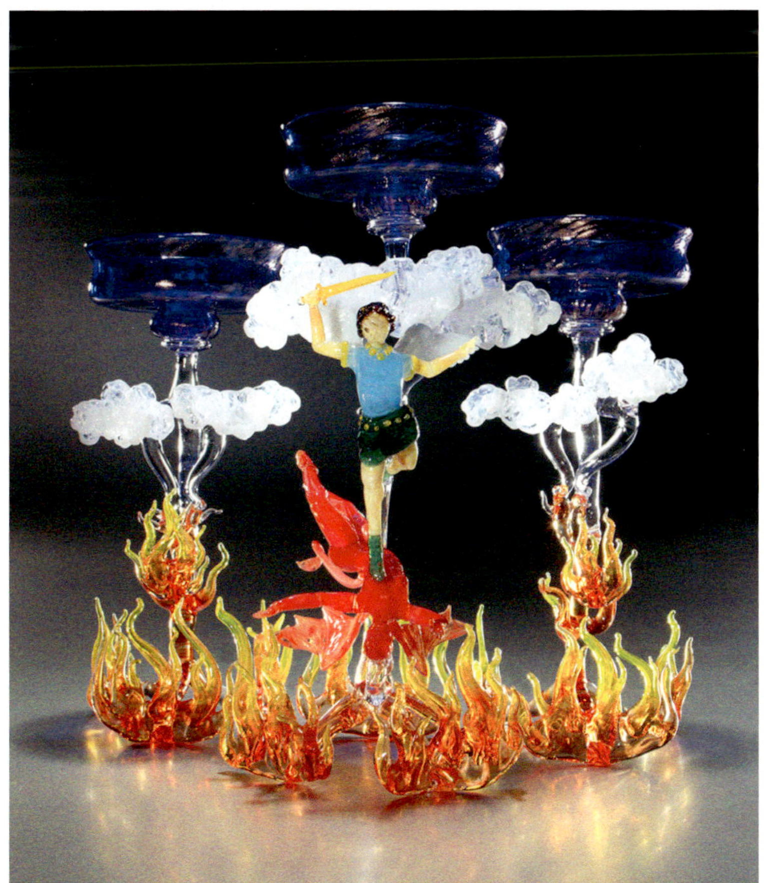

1 *Human Fly Trap*. Blown and flameworked glass. 15" × 7" × 7". 2013.

2 *Nesting Bird*. Blown and hot sculpted glass. 27" × 14" × 17". 2012. Courtesy of Leslie Patron Photo.

3 *Oryx Spirit Vessel*. Blown and flameworked glass. 15" × 6" × 6". 2012. Courtesy of Leslie Patron Photo.

4 *Fall of Lucifer* (Triptych). Blown and flameworked glass. 14" × 12" × 8". 2012. Courtesy of Leslie Patron Photo.

5 *Contemporary Fertility Goblet*. Blown and flameworked glass. 18" × 9" × 6". 2004. Courtesy of Leslie Patron Photo.

Teri Walker & Chad Ridgeway

New Orleans, Louisiana

Teri Walker graduated from the Ontario College of Art in Toronto, Canada, in 1994, in sculpture and glass. A year of painting in Florence, Italy, a summer at Toronto's Harbourfront glass studios, and a year at RISD in Rhode Island in the masters glass program reinforced her desire to pursue glassblowing full time. Chad's creative path began as a cook, first in Kansas City, then New Orleans, and culminating as a chef in Paris, France. While abroad, he trained in metalsmithing, sculpture, and foundry work.

We began combining our artistic talents in 2008. Together, we create beautiful, sometimes whimsical art that combines glass, metal, and mixed materials. We work out of our home in New Orleans. Inspired by birds, Mardi Gras Indians, costumes, skeletons, animals, and monsters, we have fused our love of New Orleans into all aspects of our lives.

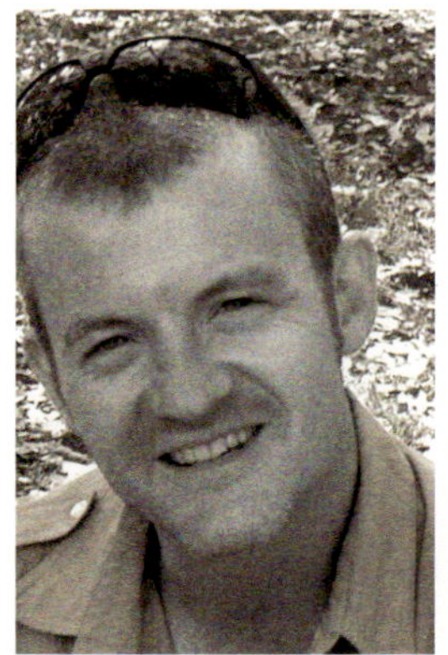

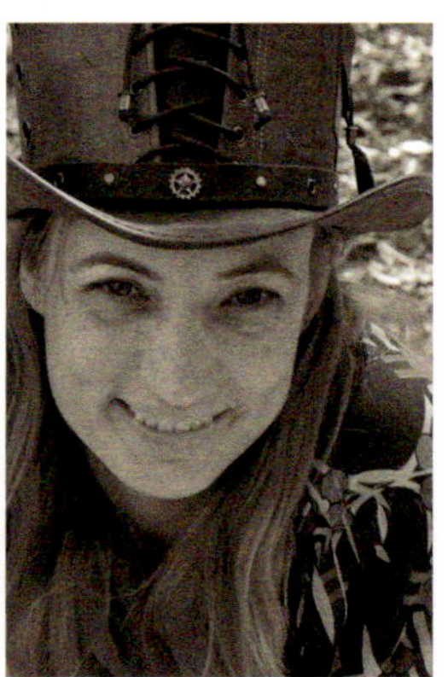

Courtesy of Rajo Photography.

1

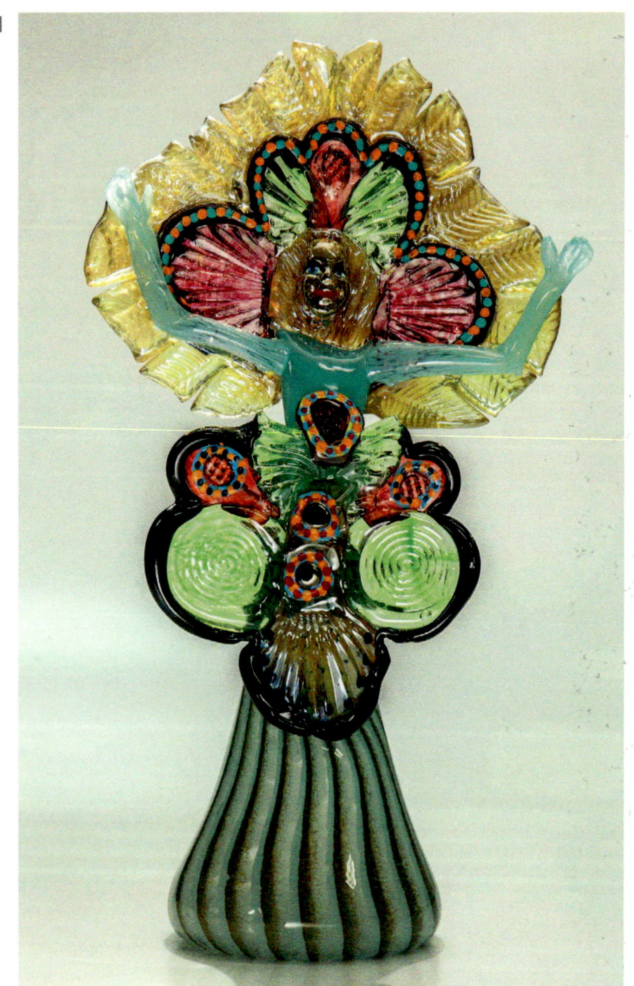

2

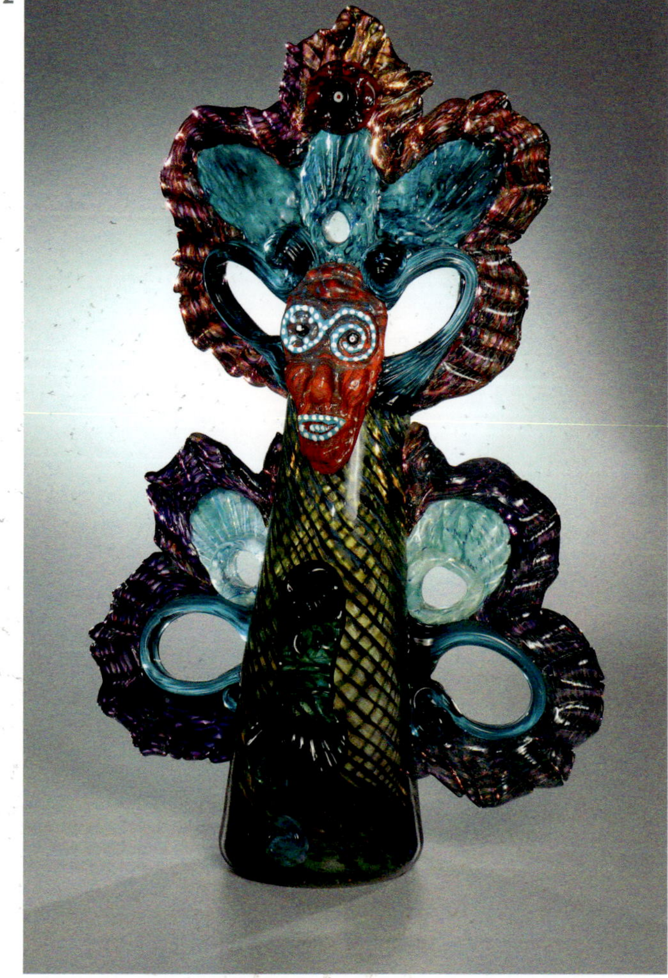

3

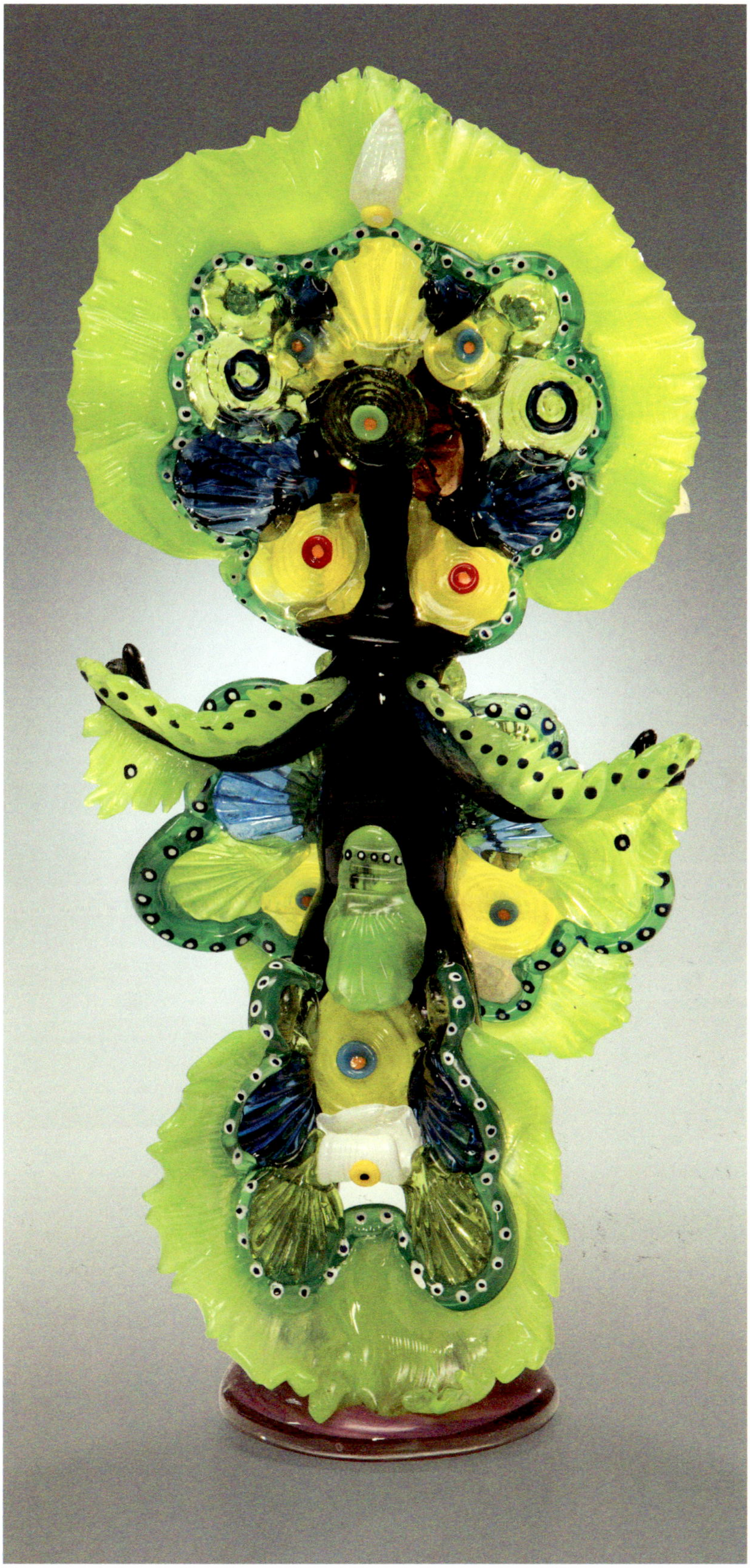

4

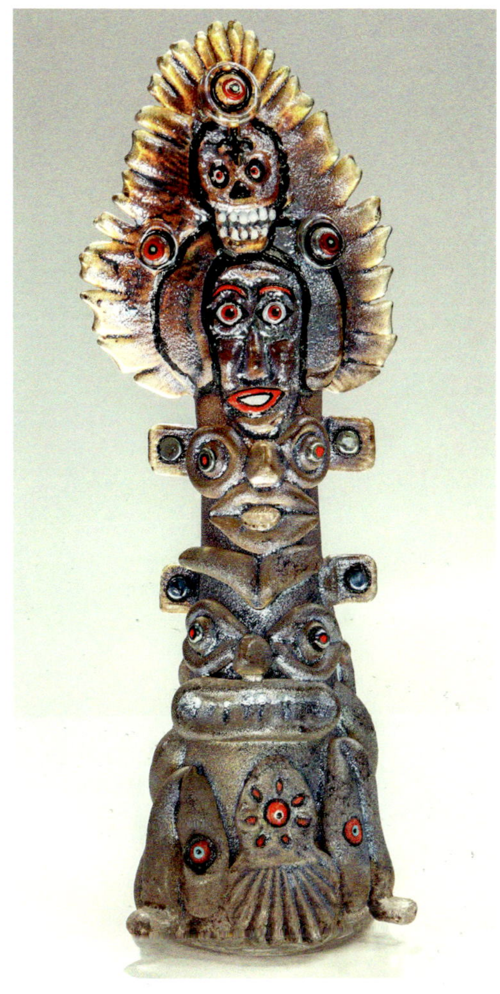

1 *New Orleans Spirit Lady*. Blown and sculpted glass. 14" × 9" × 5". 2014. Photo: Toby Armstrong.

2 *Mardi Gras Indian Vase*. Hot sculpted and blown glass. 14" × 12" × 6". 2013. Photo: Toby Armstrong.

3 *Green Glass Indian*. Hot sculpted glass. 23" × 12" × 6". 2013. Photo: Toby Armstrong.

4 *Totem Pole*. Blown and hot sculpted glass. 23" × 7" × 6". 2014. Photo: Toby Armstrong.

Maureen Williams

St. Kilda, Victoria, Australia

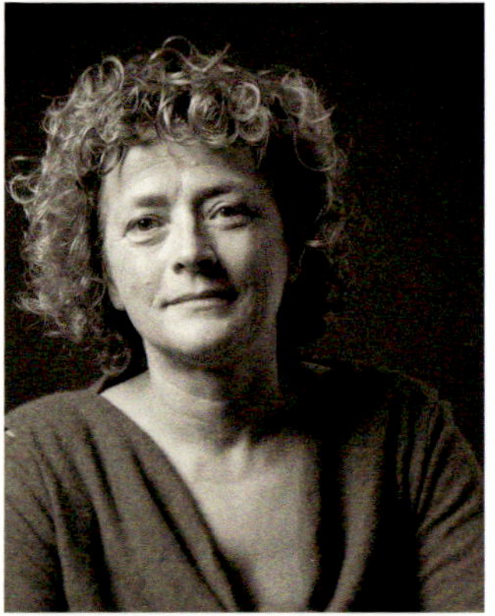

Courtesy of David McArthur Parallax Photography.

We weave endless journeys through our lives, and I weave my journeys, conscious and unconscious, in my art. I link them through the symbolic use of color and images, sometimes unbroken lines, like geographical contours, other times rocky outcrops. These are images of the imagination and cannot be read as literal representations of places. I use familiar objects and formats to allude to references from our relationships between the land and our selves.

After I was born, my family then moved around rural South Australia, which was very isolated. It is hardly surprising that journeys, actual and metaphorical, dominate my being.

1

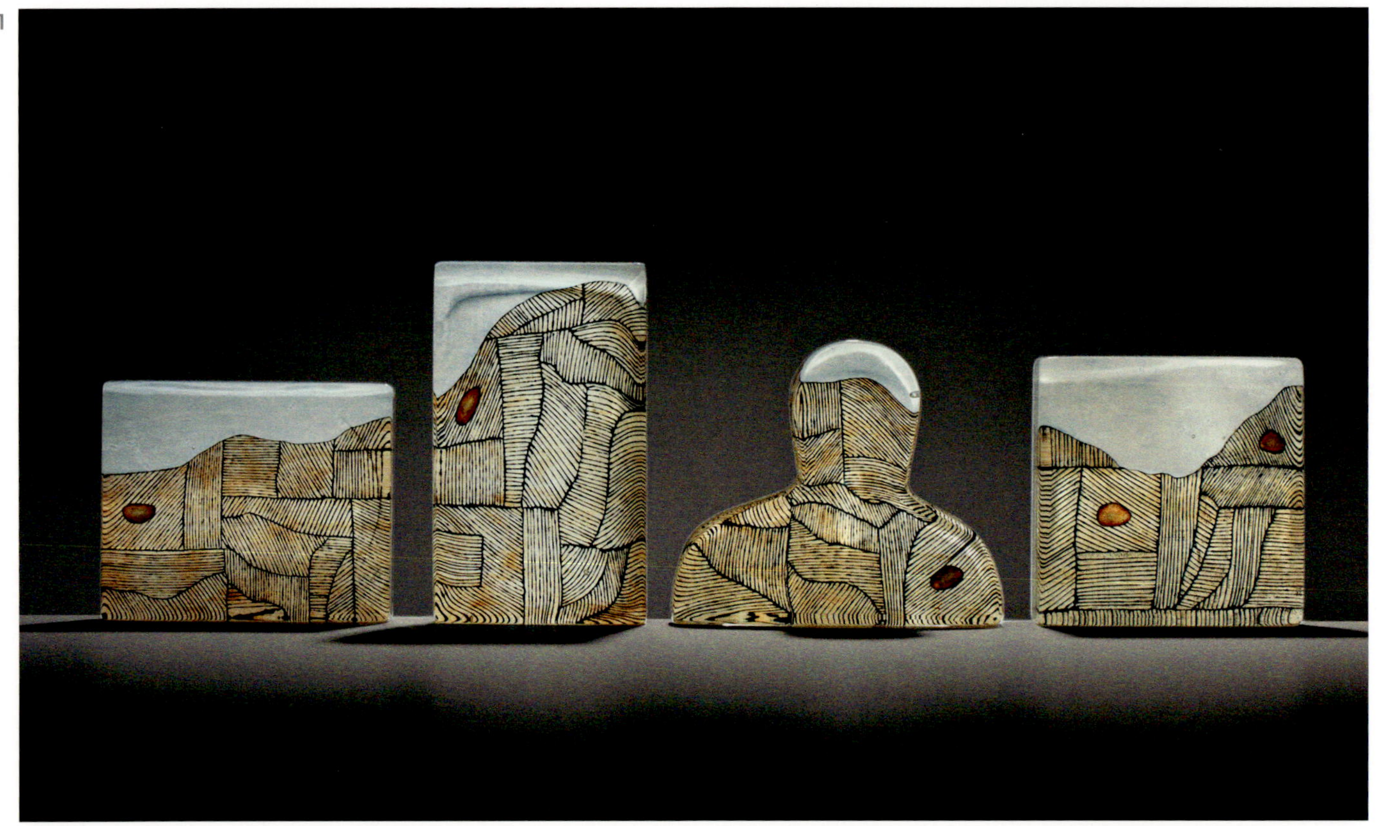

1 *Altered Landscape # 1*. Painted, cast glass. 5.91" × 1.18" × 18.90". 2011. Courtesy of David McArthur Parallax Photography.

2

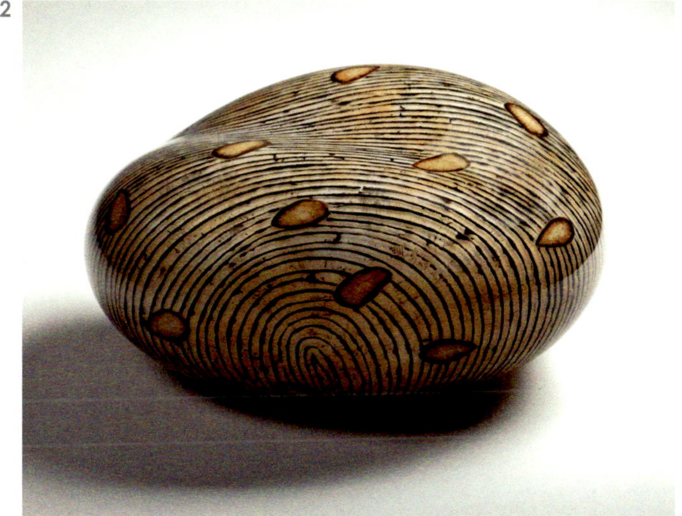

3

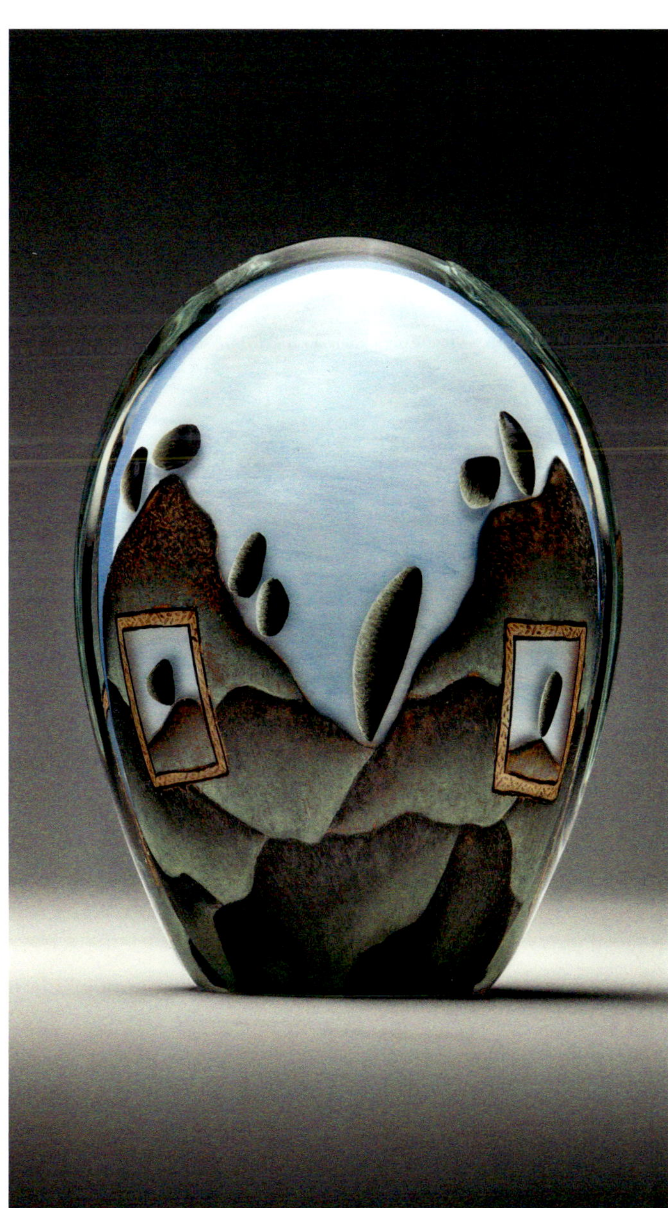

4

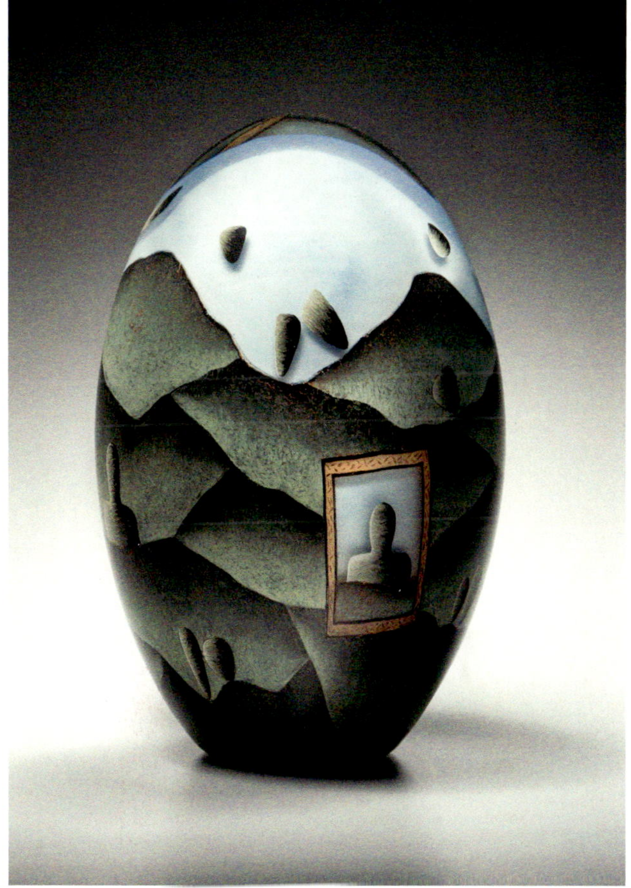

5

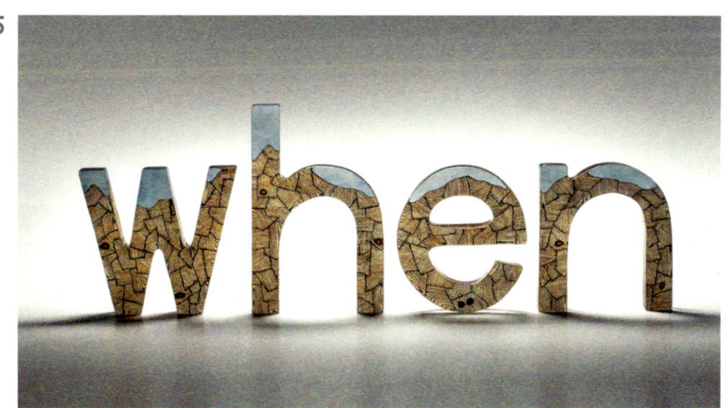

2 *Larapinta Series 29*. Painted, blown glass. 5.71" × 10.04" × 11.02". Courtesy of David McArthur Parallax Photography.

3 *Within & Without 31*. Painted, blown glass. 9.84" × 5.31" × 7.28". 2011. Courtesy of David McArthur Parallax Photography.

4 *Within & Without 21*. Painted, blown glass. 9.06" × 16.10". 2010. Courtesy of David McArthur Parallax Photography.

5 "*when*." Painted, cast glass. 10.63" × 1.38" × 32.68". 2014. Courtesy of David McArthur Parallax Photography.

John B Wood

Franklin, Michigan

My educational background is in engineering, and I think that training leads one naturally to an inherent appreciation of the Platonic solids, especially the cube. I am also a multi-decade collector of glass art and a practicing glass artist, so the Libensky *Cube in Cube* series is one well known to me and appreciated. Recently, I began to take another look at the cube in art, with the intention of putting my own stamp on that well-known form. My most recent work, the "Cut Cube" concept, was the result.

I am also a classical music listener and know and love Antonio Vivaldi's *Four Seasons* masterpiece. The idea of matching the organic flow of the four-part music and the solidity of the cubic geometric form in a single glass sculpture was irresistible. *Blue Cut Cube–Winter* is the first of four works in this series. The others (not shown) are in green/clear (*Spring*), yellow/clear (*Summer*), and red/clear (*Fall*). The other works shown here are from other recent series that have been important to me; all of them emphasize color, form, and narrative content as key compositional elements.

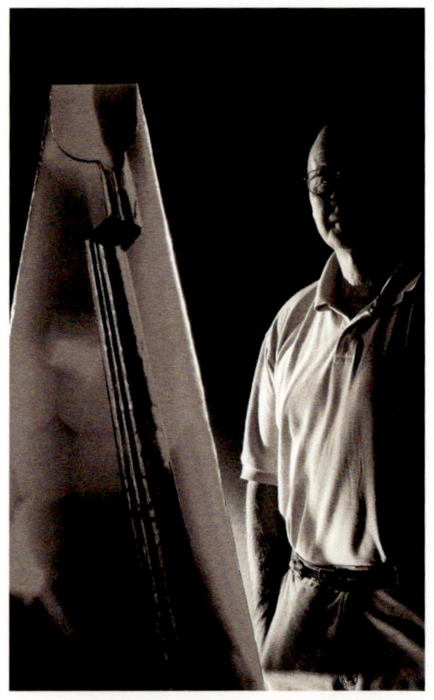

Courtesy of Douglas Schaible Photography.

1

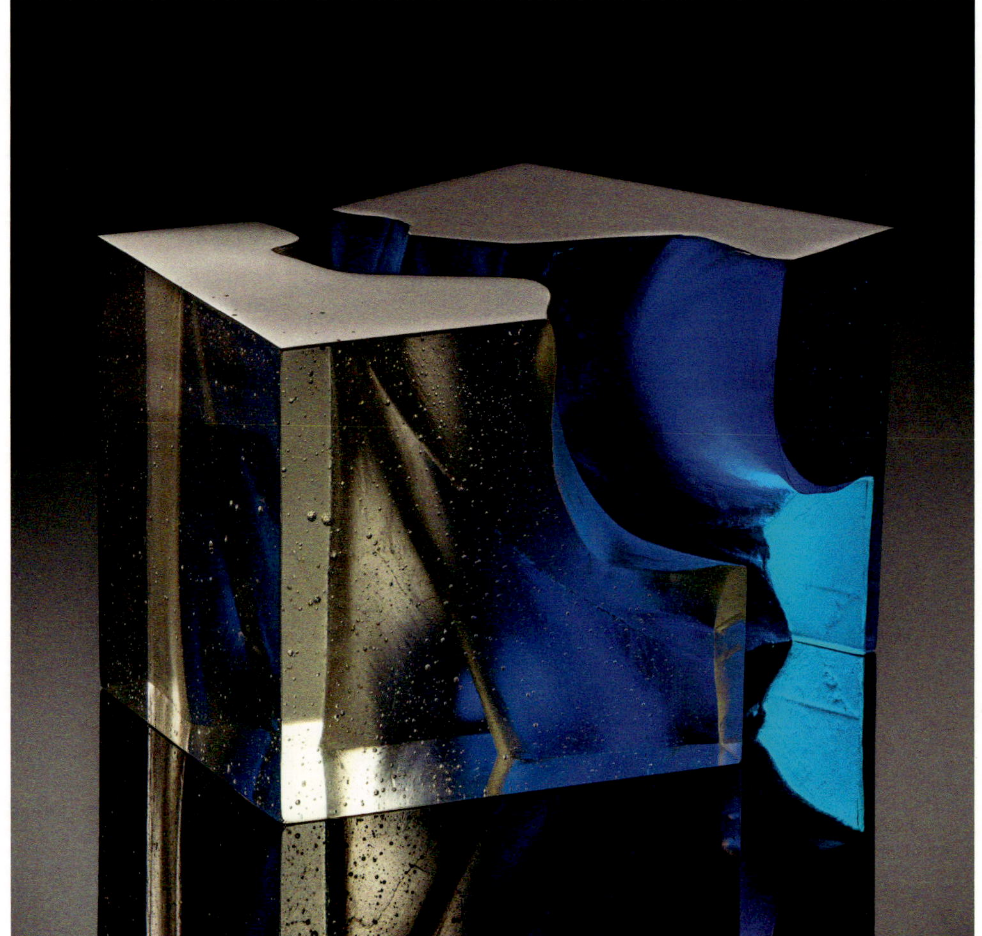

2

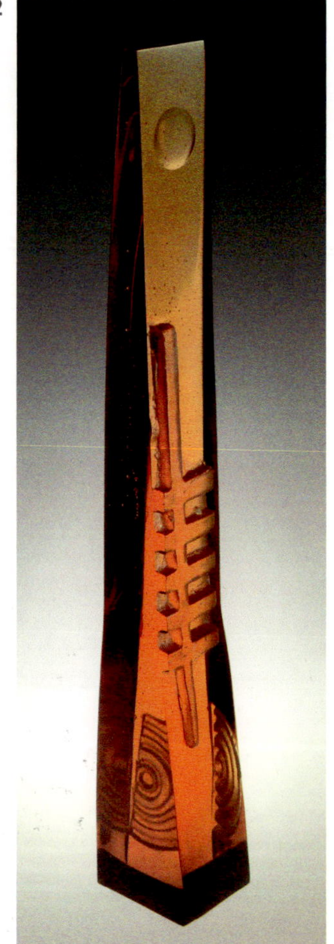

3

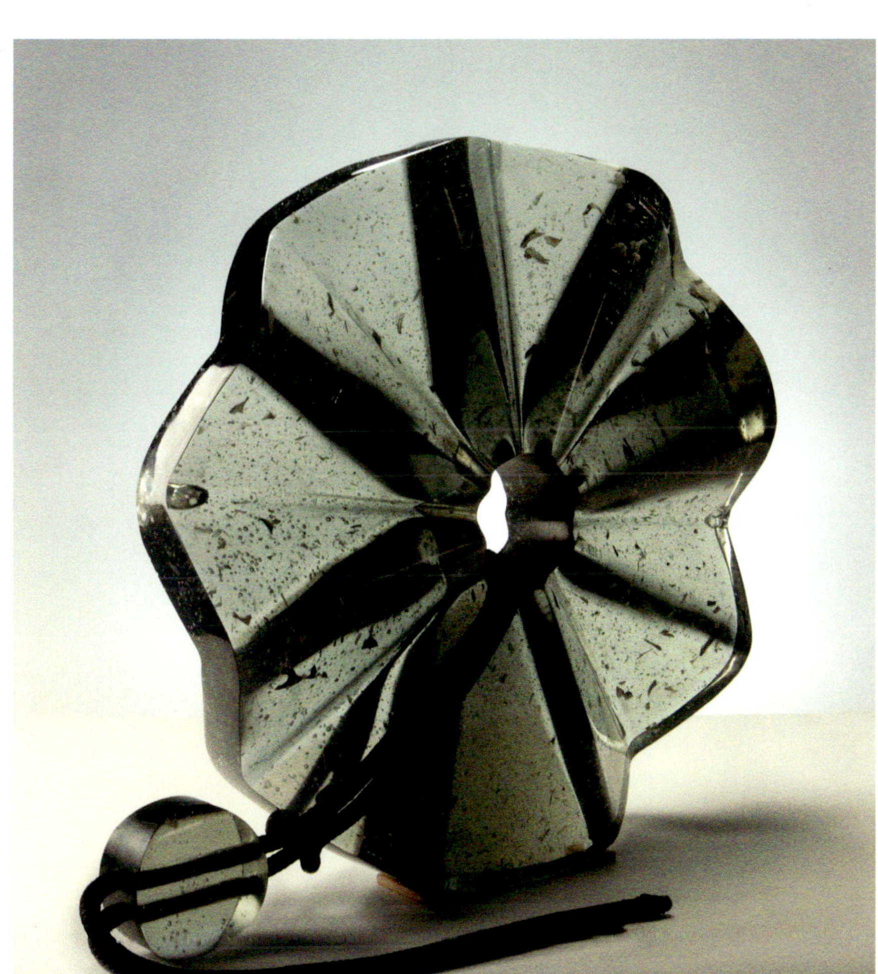

1 *Blue Cut Cube—Winter*. From the *Four Seasons* series. Cast soda glass. 10" × 10" × 10" (2 pieces). 2014. Courtesy of Douglas Schaible Photography.

2 *Nazca Spirits (Homage to Anonymous)*. From the *Earth Art* series. Cast lead crystal. 35" × 5" × 6". 2009. Courtesy of Ann Cady.

3 *Artifact No. 2; Dover, Flint and Chalk*. From the *Archeological* series. Cast soda glass. 23.125" × 4.5" × 23.125". 2012. Courtesy of Ann Cady.

4 *Crater (Homage to James Turrell)*. From the *Earth Art* series. Cast lead crystal. 24" × 5" × 38". 2009. Courtesy of Douglas Schaible Photography.

5 *Spiral Jetty (Homage to Robert Smithson)*. From the *Earth Art* series. Cast lead crystal. 28" × 3.5" × 14.5". 2009. Courtesy of Ann Cady.

4

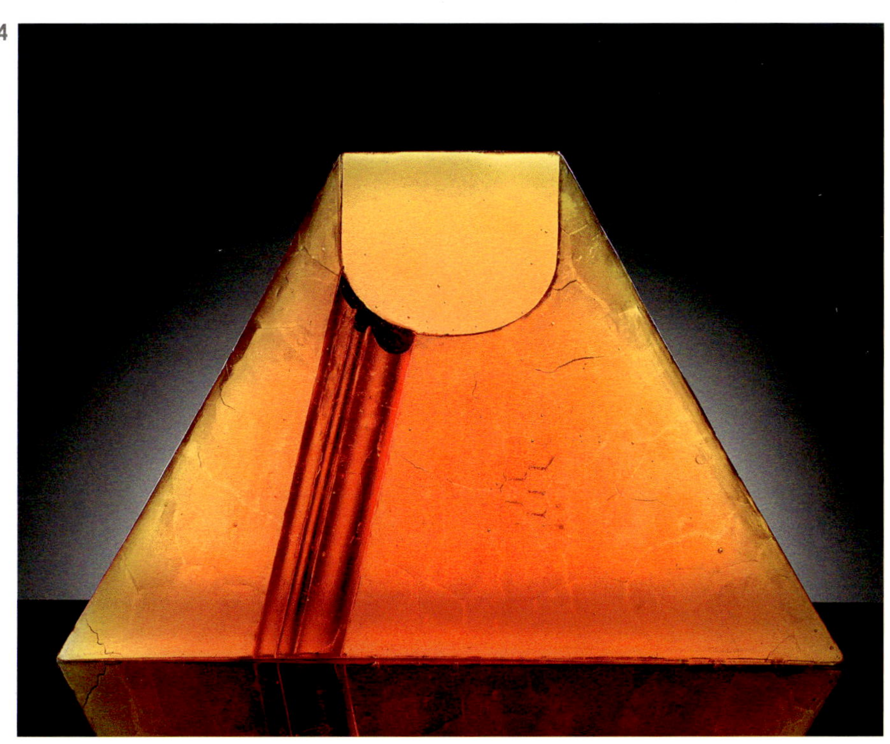

5

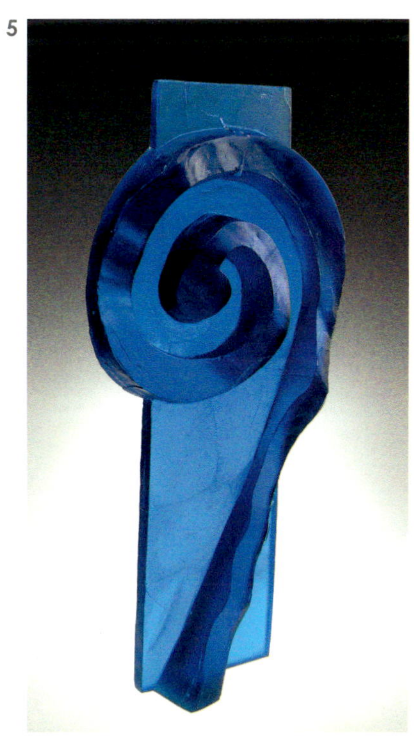

Wynia

Seattle, Washington

The mysterious qualities of glass have captivated me for decades. I began exploring glass in projects commissioned by architects, sandblasting geometric patterns and layering them for use as windows. Sun streaming through the layers projects one pattern onto the next; the patterns shift and change as one passes by. I have reached beyond my existing knowledge to manifest each client's vision, which has led me to innovate countless techniques that I now incorporate in my art.

I am seduced by beautiful surfaces—textures, patterns, colors—and have collected exquisite seedpods, beetles, and other gifts of nature over the years. They provide endless inspiration for my work. I explore ways to emulate these surfaces by sandblasting textures into the back of plate glass, then dyeing it with color, sometimes metal leafing it, sanding it off, working and reworking the surface until the alchemy is complete.

A recent commission for a multi-building development has reignited my passion for kinetic patterns on a large scale. My new work investigates working both sides of the glass to exploit its depth and transparency to its fullest effect. The arc of my creative work has curved from its geometric beginnings through organic forms and is now newly focused on integrated art in built environments.

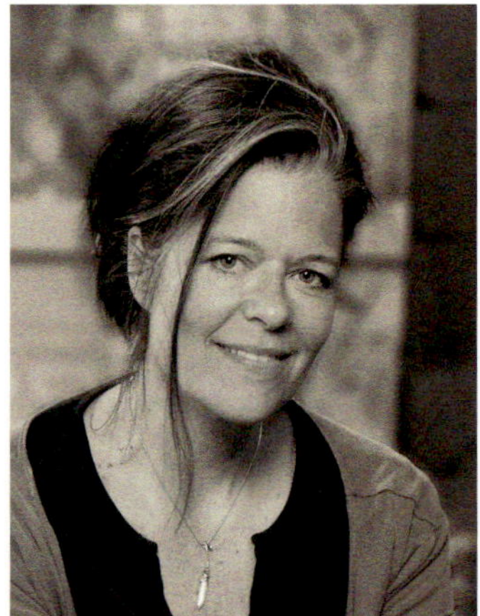

Courtesy of © Ric Peterson Photography.

1

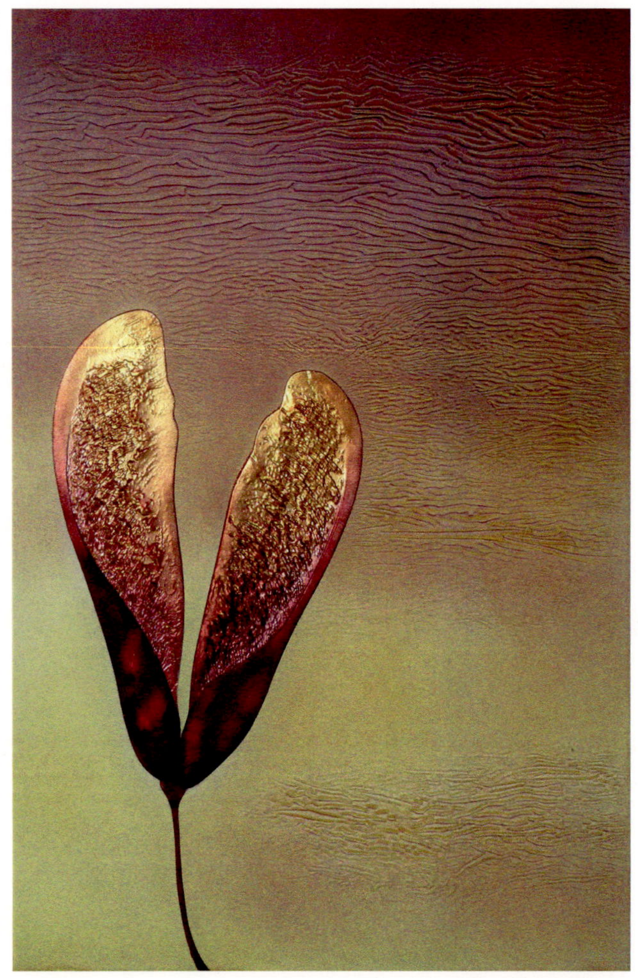

2

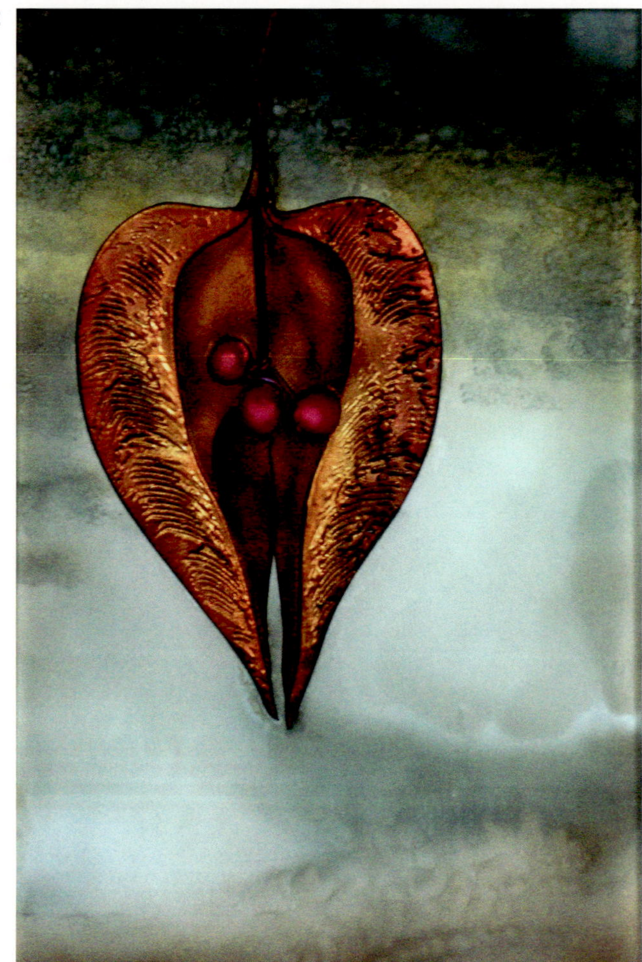

3

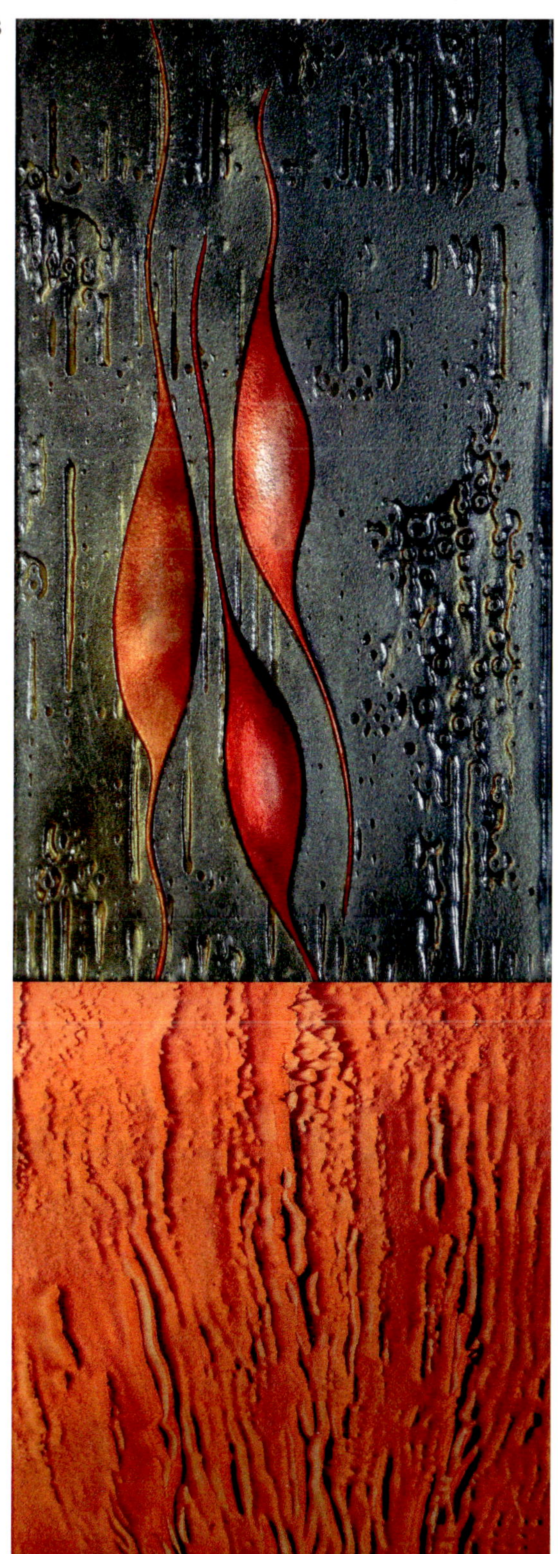

4

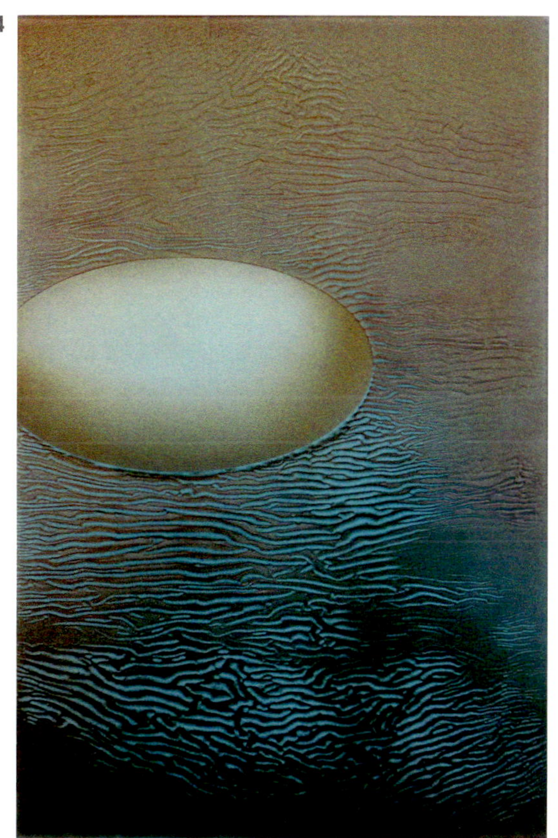

5

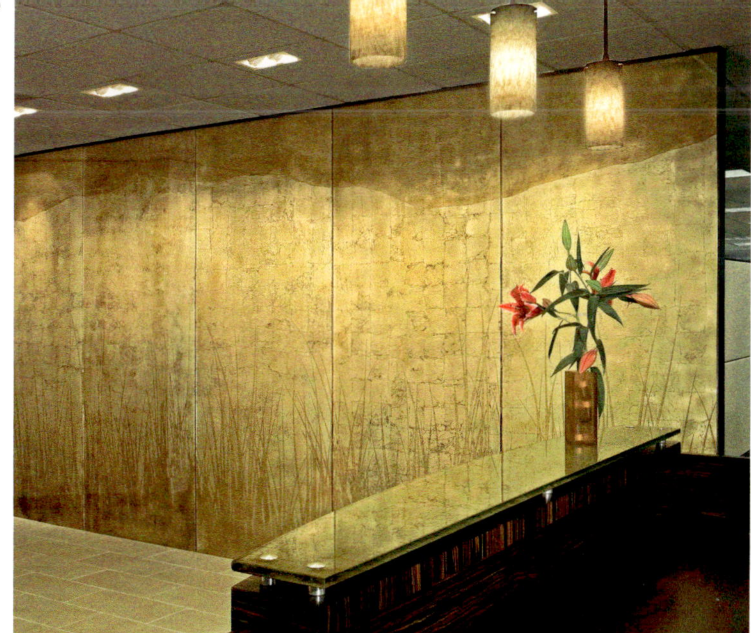

1 *Samara*. Sand carved glass, dyed, and metal leafed. 24" × 0.375" × 36". 2014.

2 *Lampa*. Sand carved glass, dyed, and metal leafed. 15" × 0.375" × 18". 2014.

3 *Depart*. Sand carved glass, dyed, and metal leafed. 9" × 0.375" × 24". 2014.

4 *Adrift*. Sand carved glass, dyed. 24" × 0.375" × 36". 2014.

5 *Serengeti*. Sand carved with Segredo treatment. 10 panels. 3.5' × 0.375" × 8.5'. Art glass permanent installation. 2010.

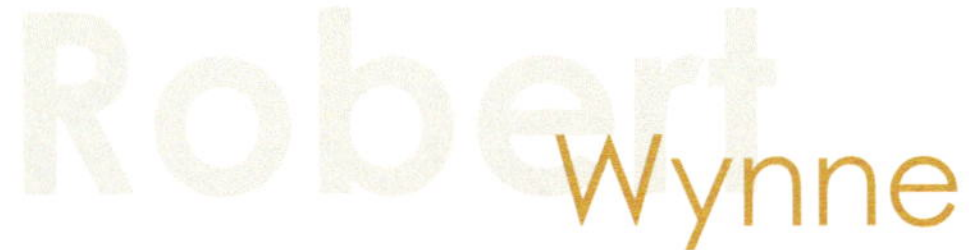

Robert Wynne

Manly, New South Wales, Australia

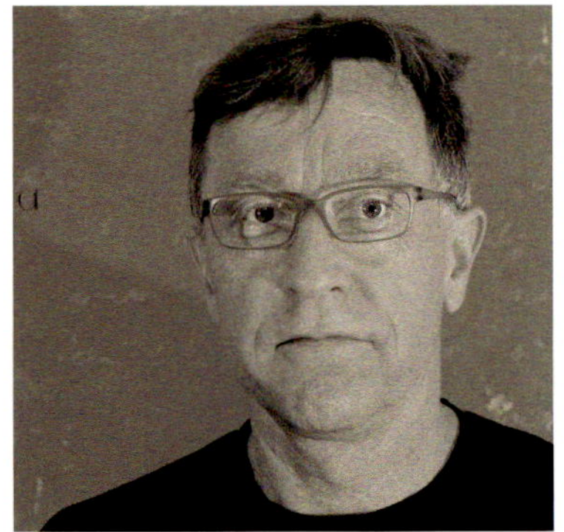

My work portrays contrasting impulses within. I love the challenge of technical precision, but I need to be able to play and explore. I enjoy making beautiful objects, but I am not afraid to create pieces that evoke emotions more complex than just aesthetic appreciation. In some ways, I'm an anarchist; I'm not happy when things are just comfortable. I am restless, always looking for an angle, and this is reflected in my diverse body of work.

On the other hand, common threads run through my work. I love the gorgeous glow of light through frosted glass and have a fascination with lustrous, iridescent finishes, particularly with the way that light is manipulated, reflected, and transmitted. I take inspiration from a broad range of influences including historical glassmaking practices and formal sculptural dialogue. My recent work featuring the Raven engages with themes of desire, the fragility of wealth, and the concept of security.

1

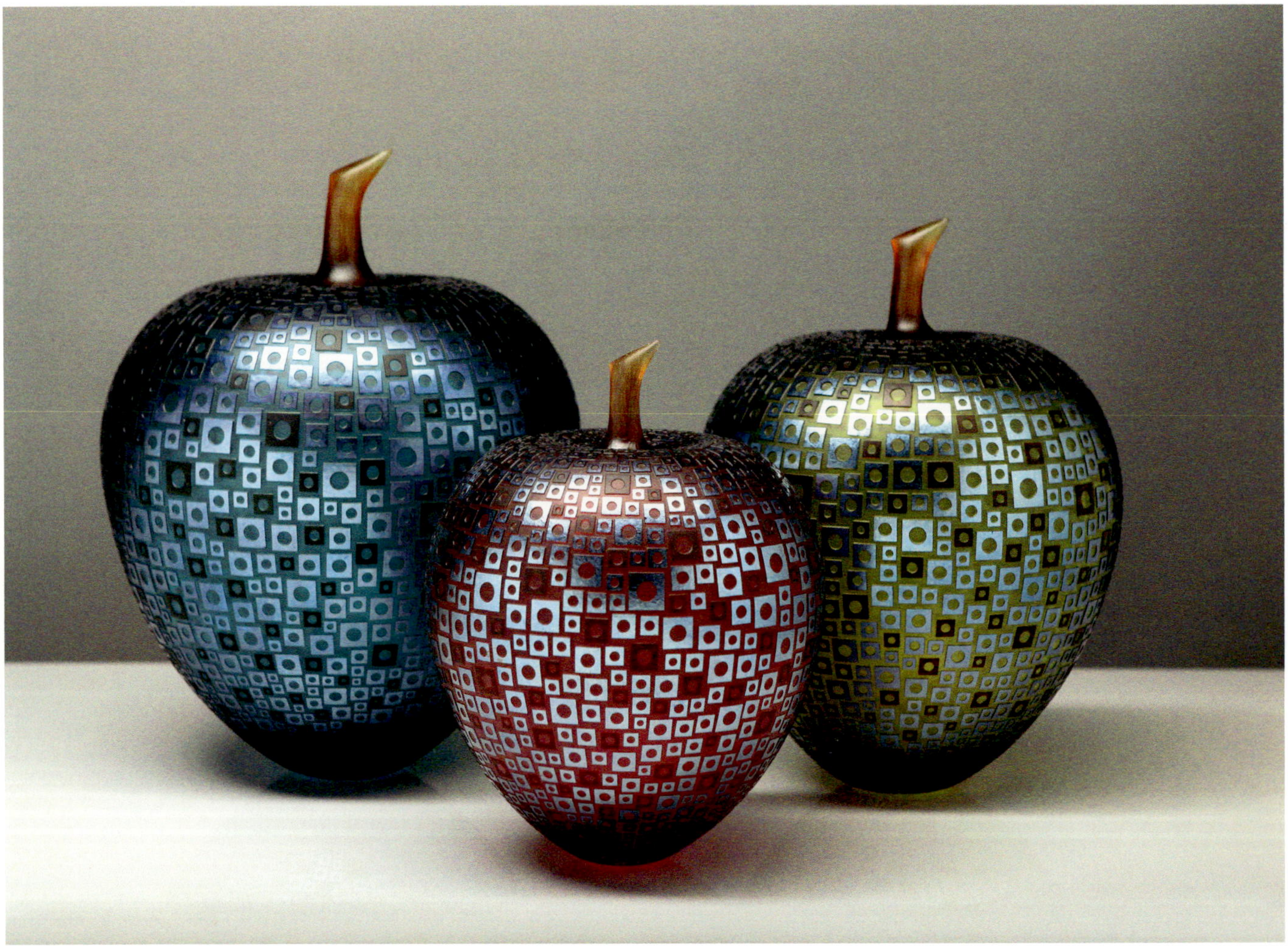

2

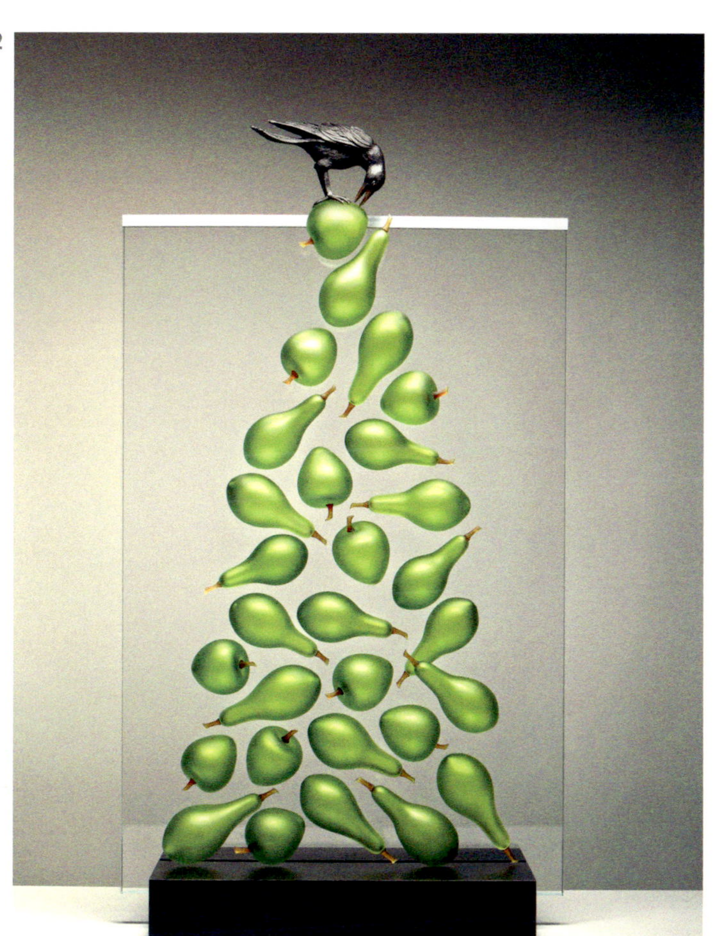

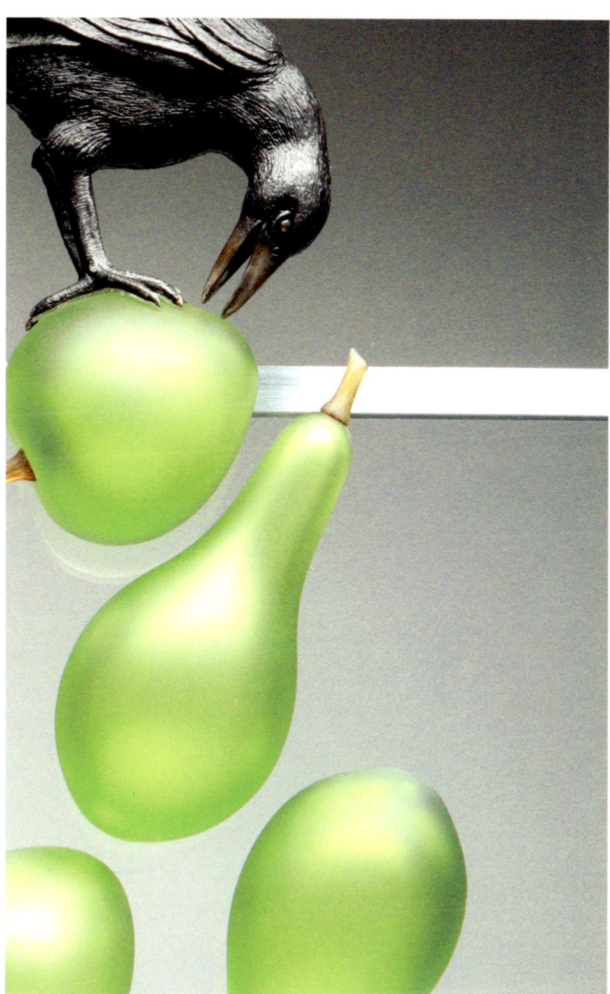

3

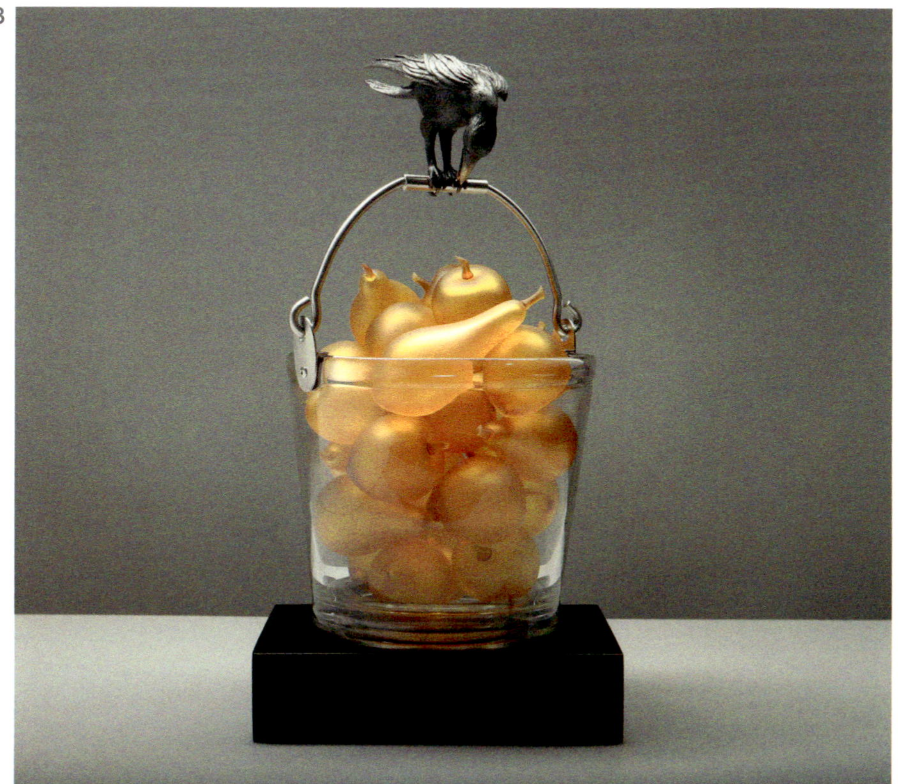

1 *Still Life*. 14" × 10", 12" × 9", 11" × 8". 2014.

2 *Raven's Clutch*. Blown and float glass, bronze and steel. LED light source. 44" × 9" × 25". 2014.

3 *Trove*. Blown glass, bronze, stainless and mild steel. LED light source. 19" × 9" × 11". 2014.

Nao Yamamoto

Seattle, Washington

The environment I grew up in allowed me to cultivate an appreciation for both contemporary art and traditional craft. Experiencing contemporary art based on a different society changed my perspective, and I felt like it took me beyond the narrow culture of Japan. Once I recognized my art as a way to represent myself, or even to have conversations with myself, I became devoted to a contemporary art practice.

The beauty of nature inspires me. When I am in nature, the simple, pure, clean force of life inspires me to just live, strongly but simply. I believe we have lost that notion in our complicated contemporary lives. What I am trying to do through my art is to reinterpret elements from nature to celebrate the power of life.

During the glassblowing process, I sometimes see the molten glass as a sentient creature that tries to challenge my skill or mastery. This idea helps me to create a different body of work that represents my experience or relationship with glass sculpture rather than the materiality of glass. Glass has become not only a material but also my fickle friend that reflects my inspiration and concentration.

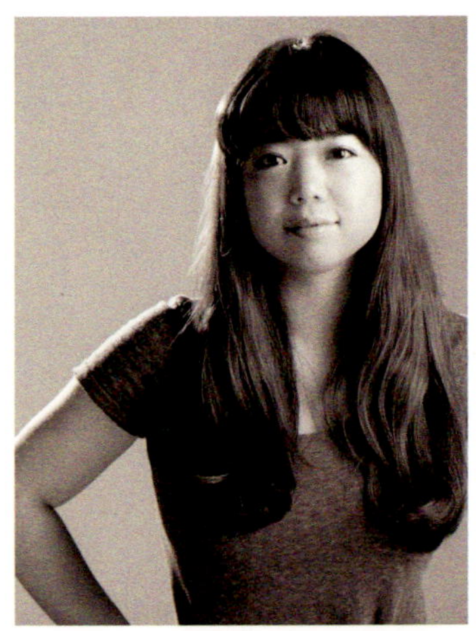

Courtesy of Alec Miller.

1

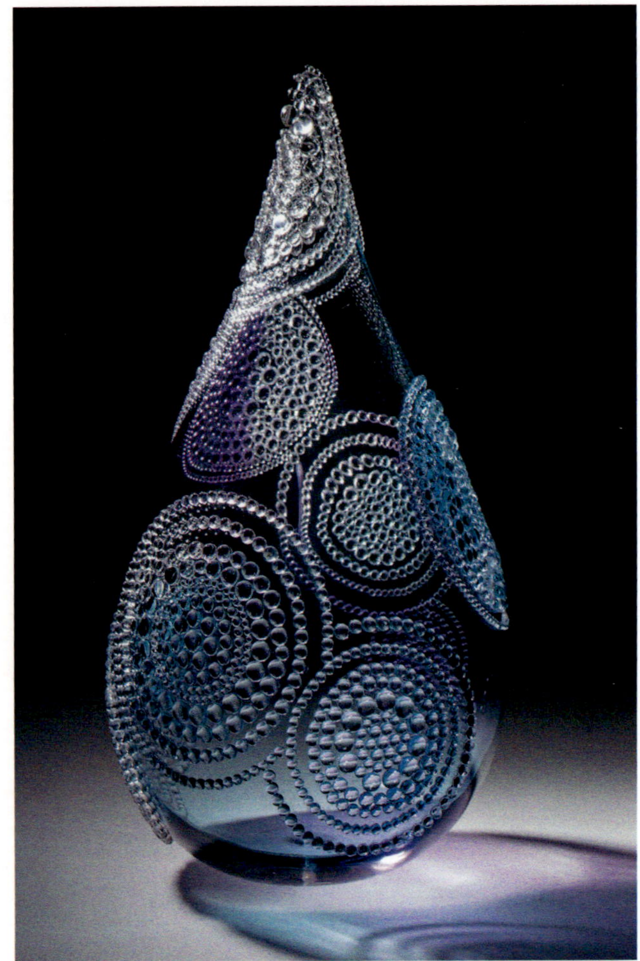

2

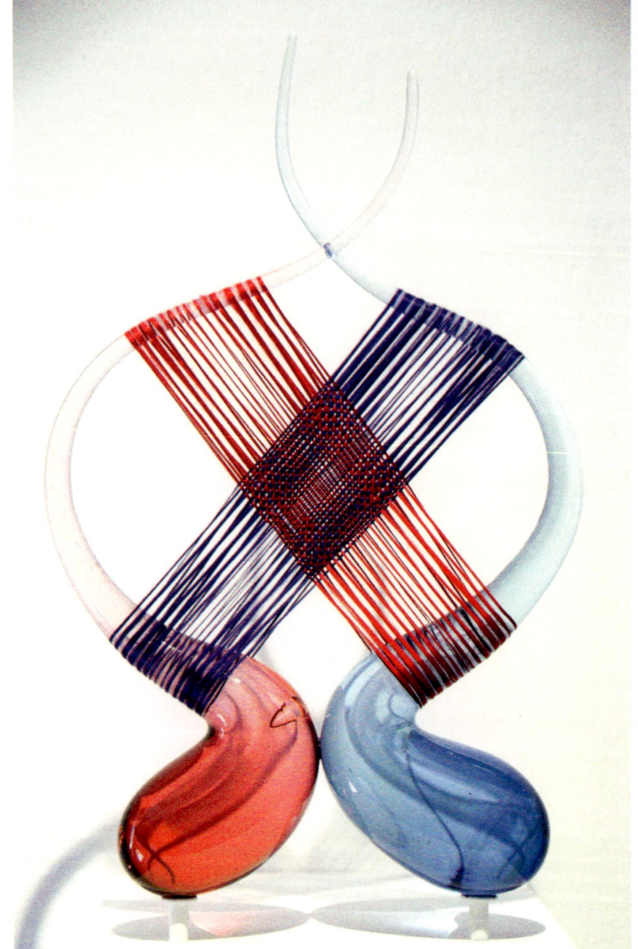

3

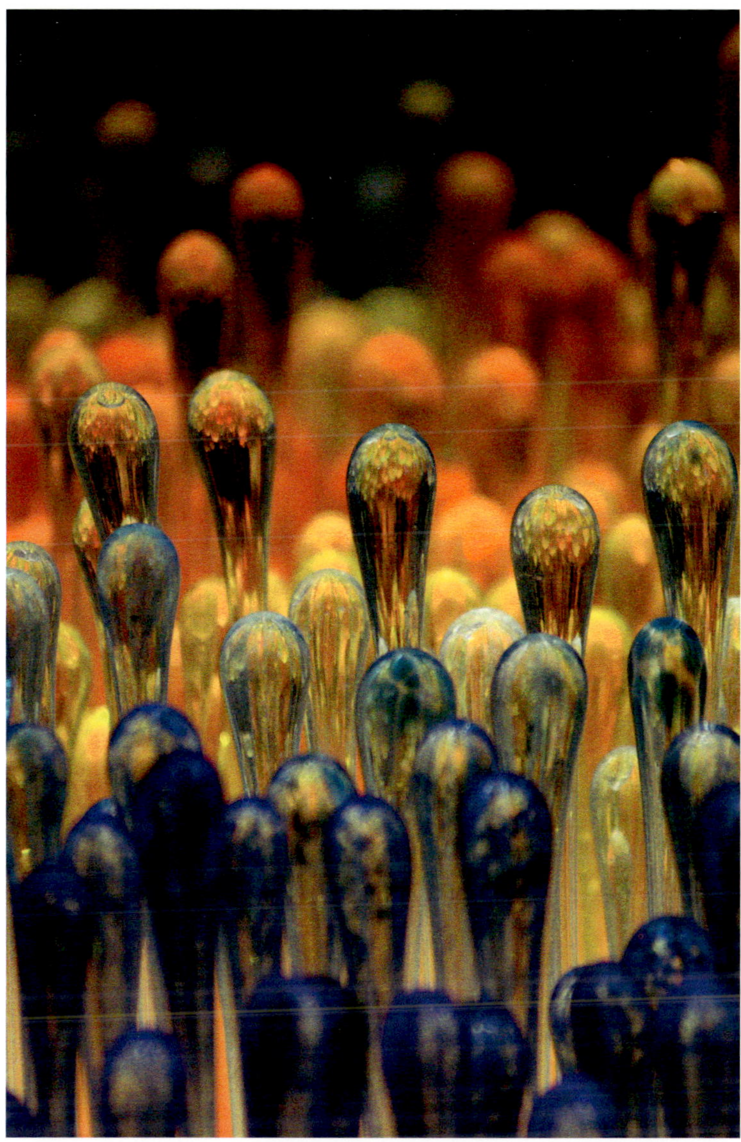

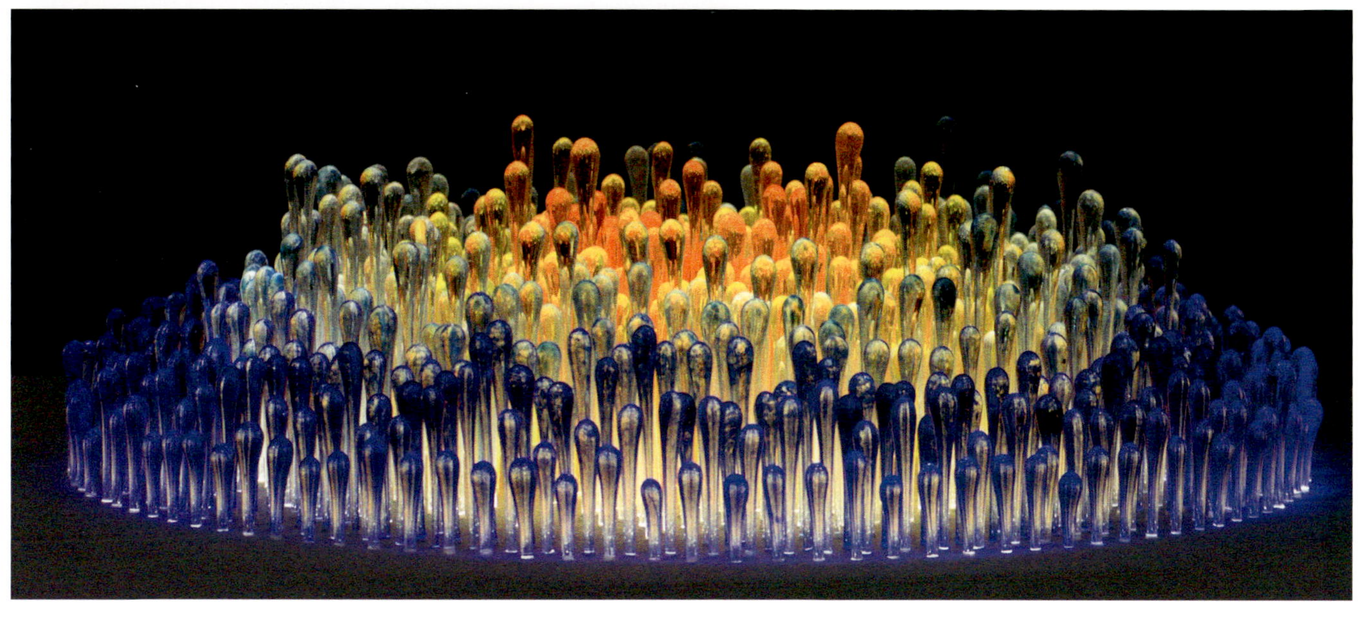

1 *Ripples.* Glassblowing, kiln glass. 17" × 8" × 8". 2014. Courtesy of Alec Miller.

2 *You & I, Lovers.* Glassblowing/mixed media, fiber. 15" × 2.5" × 10". 2014. Courtesy of Jason Charles Dawes.

3 *The Sun and Water.* Glass, fluorescent lights. 8" × 42" × 42". 2014. Courtesy of Steve Beswick.

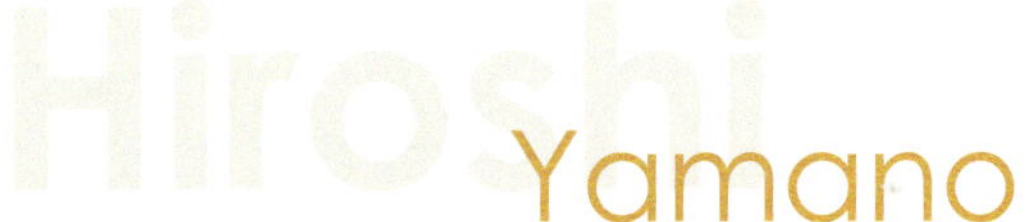

Hiroshi Yamano

Awara, Fukui, Japan

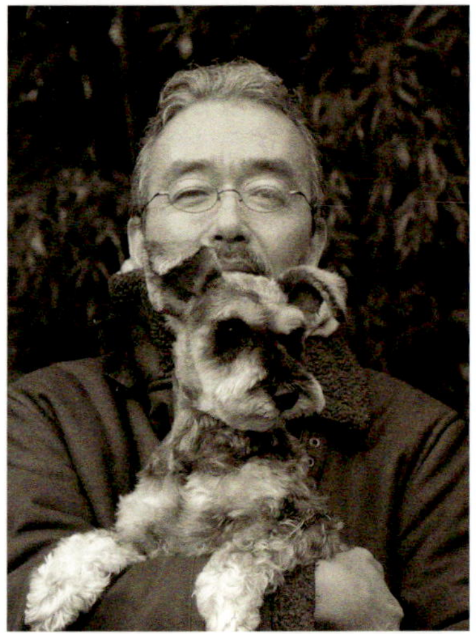

Born in Fukuoka, Japan, I spent six years in the United States, where I experienced new things and learned a lot about Western culture. I learned a lot about my culture too, and was able to compare both perspectives at a young age. In 1988, I started to make the series *From East to West*, reflecting the two cultures; I continued working on that series when I moved back to Japan in 1991. In 2010, I started the *Scene of Japan* series.

When I was over fifty and had spent many years in Japan, I felt my mind was changing. I was able to see the true beauty from the nature surrounding me. I have become more and more simple in my thinking. My mind is getting quieter and quieter, but still I am busy making art to live for. Through my works, I would like to share the quiet feeling I get from nature with my audience.

Last year, I started to draw my images onto glass panels. I used to paint when I was in high school. I hadn't had time to paint since then, but I'd always loved it. Now that I am almost fifty-nine years old, I would like to change myself again to become a "painter on glass."

1

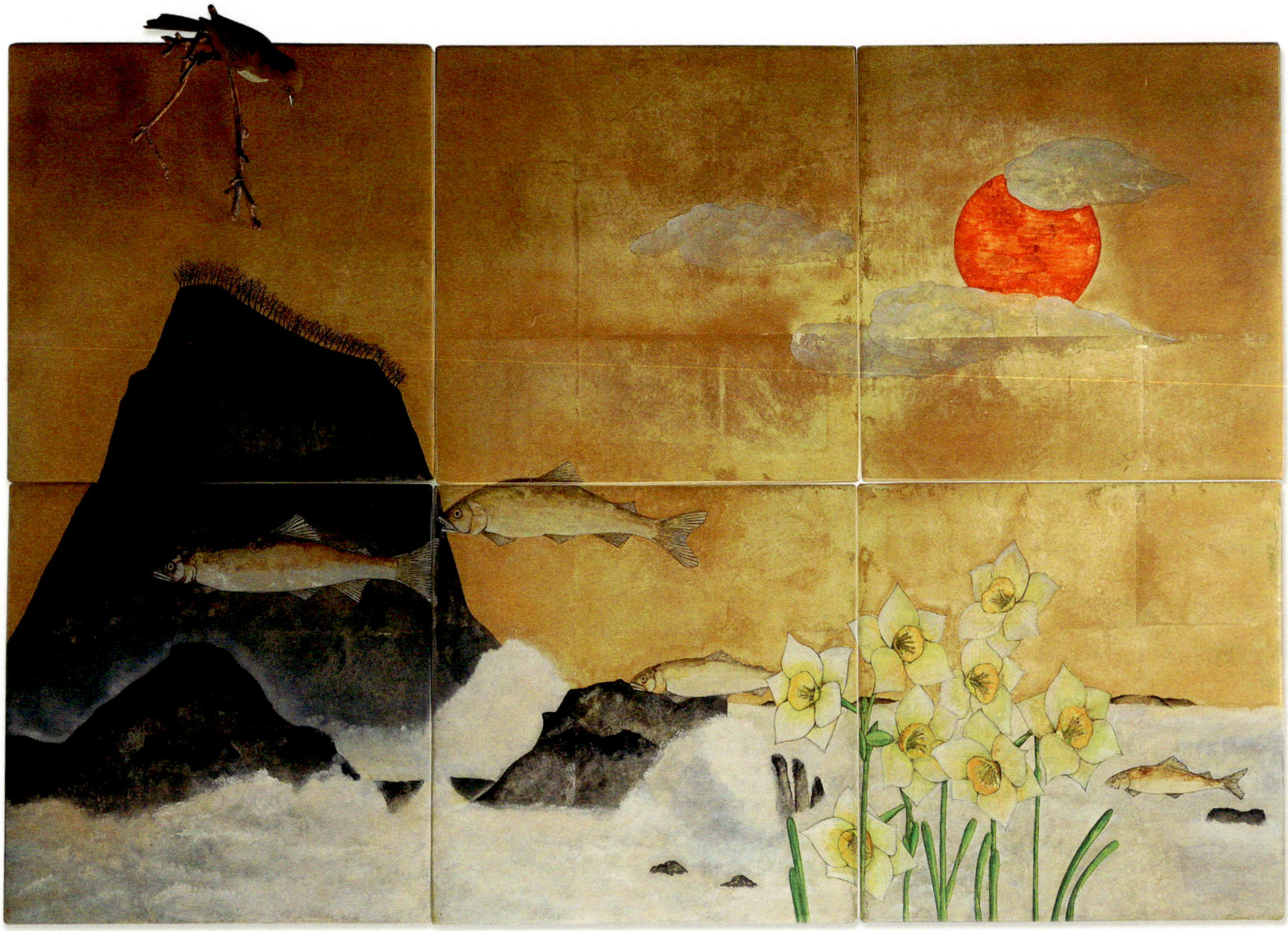

2

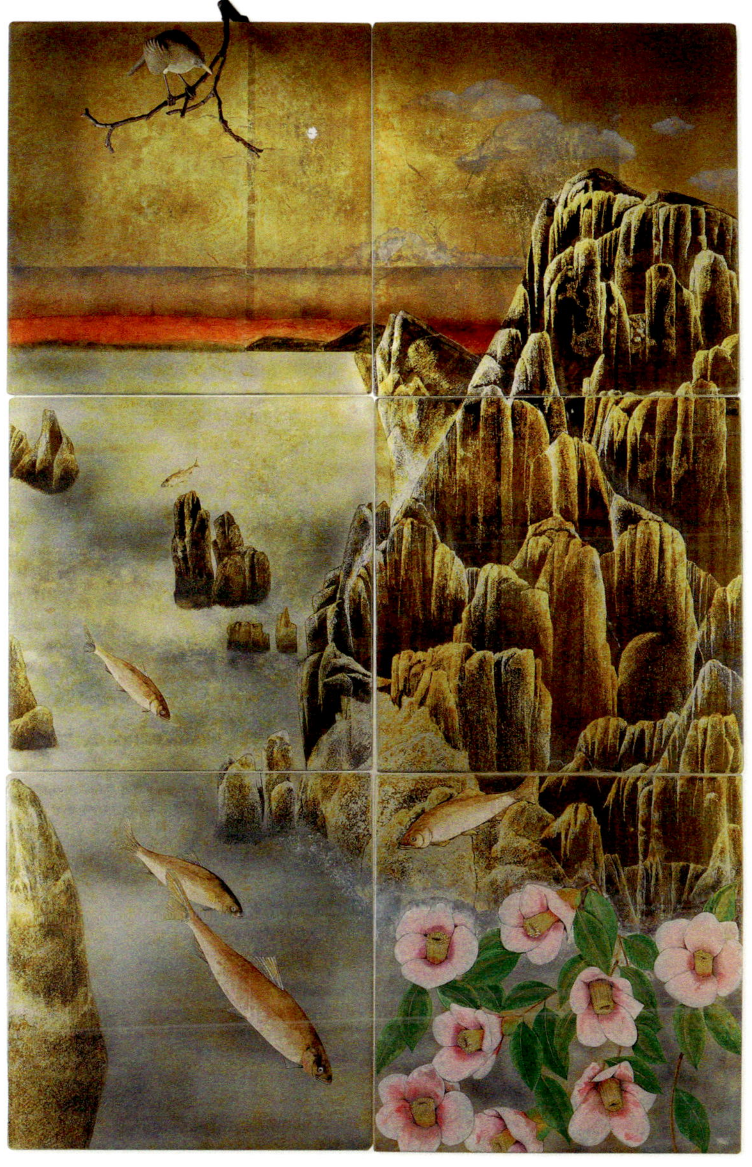

3

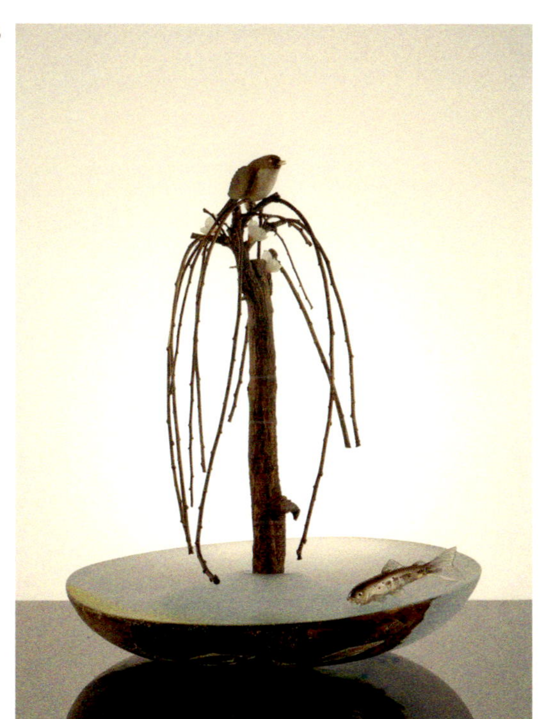

4

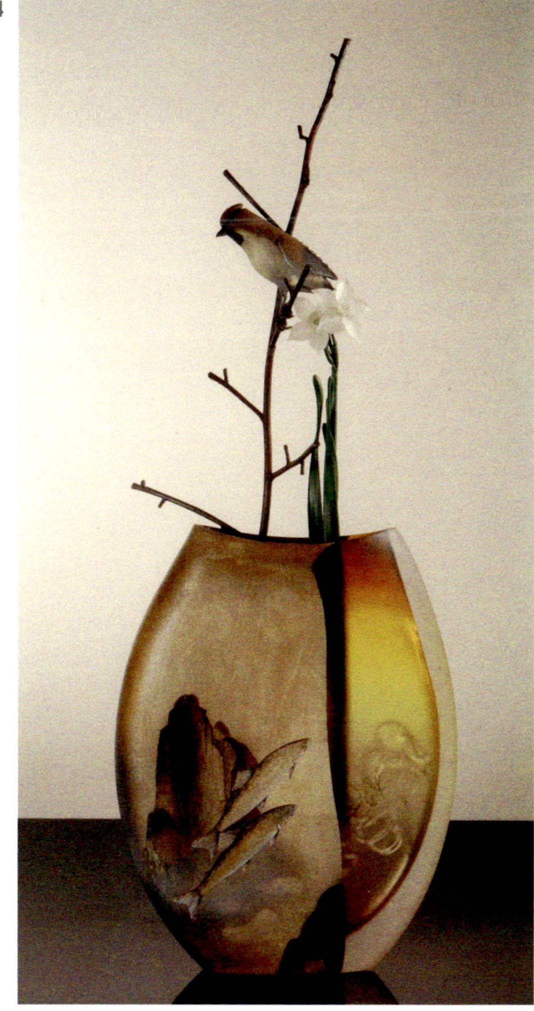

1 *The daffodils by the ocean in winter*. Kiln worked, blown, and painted. 26.97" × 6.3" × 40.55".

2 *The camellias by the mountain in winter*. Kiln worked, blown, and painted. 40.55" × 5.91" × 26.77". 2015.

3 *Scene of Japan*. Blown, cold worked, copper plated, and engraved. 19.69" × 16.14" × 16.93". 2014.

4 *Scene of Japan*. Blown, cold worked, copper plated, and engraved. 31.3" × 7.87" × 11.81". 2014.

Brent Kee Young

Cleveland Heights, Ohio

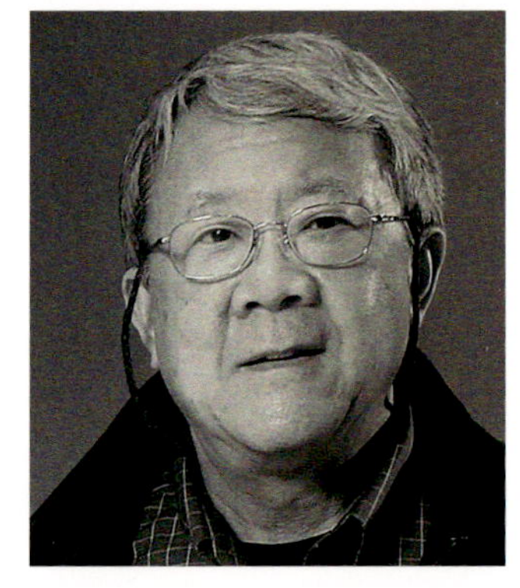

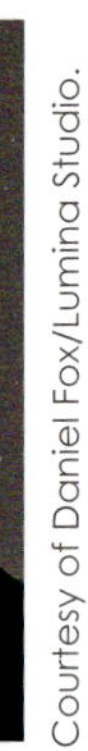
Courtesy of Daniel Fox/Lumina Studio.

As with other bodies of work with which I have been involved, my interests lie in the ambiguous nature of glass and the sense of space and volume one can create. Of course, the study of how light is controlled and affects form is an utmost curiosity. These new works in *The Matrix* series offer a fresh way of approaching inquiry into those mysteries as well as the objects that are represented.

All the sculptures are what I would consider in the realm of defining form with line and light. Glass does this so well. However simple or complex the structures, what is seen by the eye are a matrix of glints, short lines that are segments of light, which, when seen as a whole, define each form and speak to each idea.

1

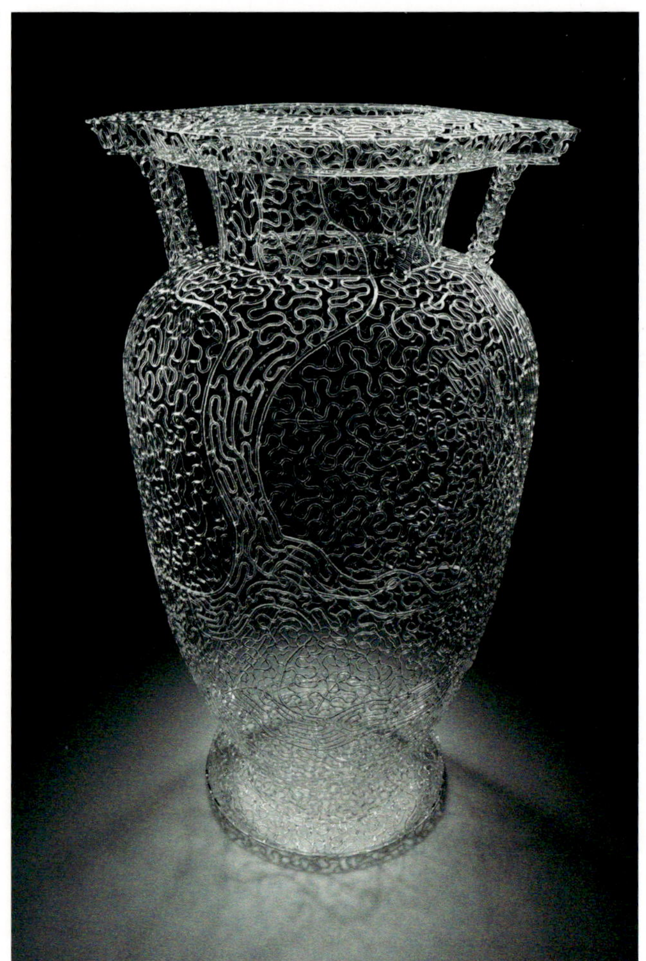

2

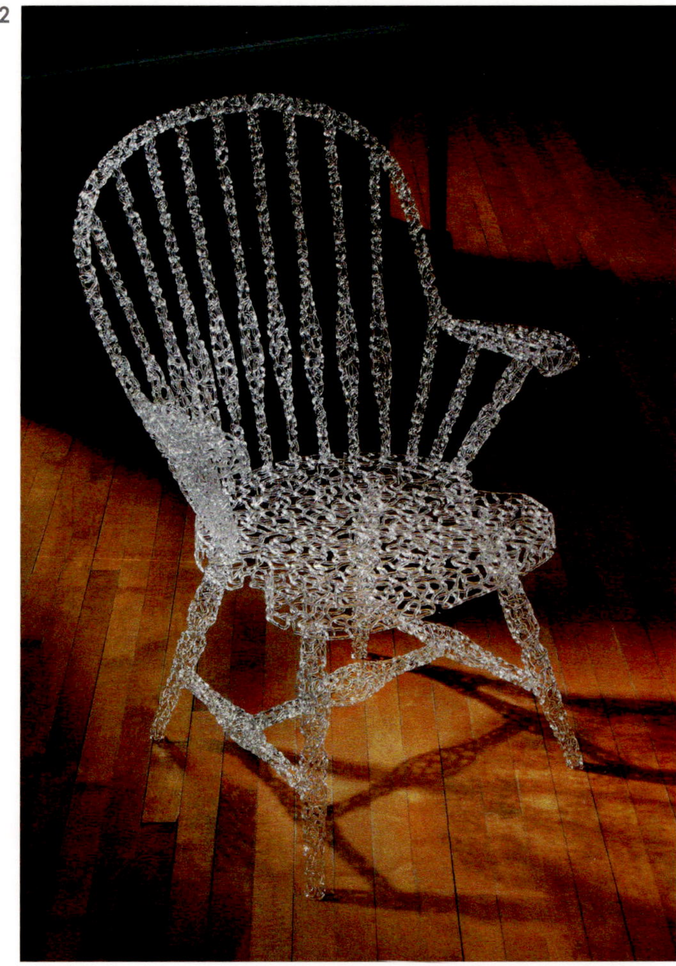

1 *Matrix* series: *It's Greek . . . To Me!* Flameworked borosilicate glass. 40" × 25". 2014. Courtesy of Daniel Fox/Lumina Studio.

2 *Matrix* series: *Across a Crowded Room . . . .* Flameworked borosilicate glass. 39" × 22" × 27". 2009. Courtesy of Daniel Fox/Lumina Studio.

3 *Matrix* series: *Quest* . . . . Flameworked borosilicate glass. 14" × 11" × 39". 2015. Courtesy of Daniel Fox/Lumina Studio.

4 *Matrix* series: *Learn One Thing Well* . . . . Flameworked borosilicate glass. 11" × 10" × 30". 2012. Courtesy of Daniel Fox/Lumina Studio.

5 *Matrix* series: *Catenary Ellipsoid* . . . . *Bi.* Flameworked borosilicate glass. Approx. 36" × 11" × 23". 2010. Collection of the Cleveland Museum of Art. Courtesy of Daniel Fox/Lumina Studio.

5

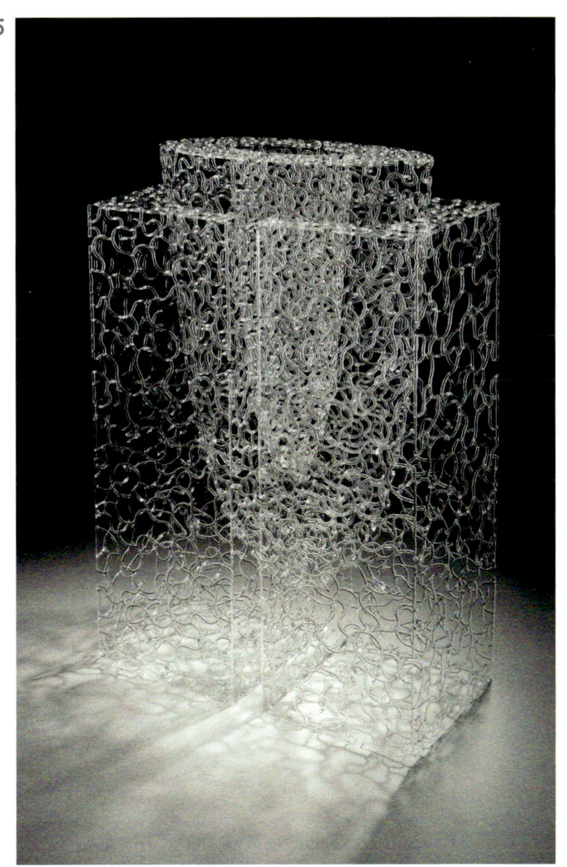

3

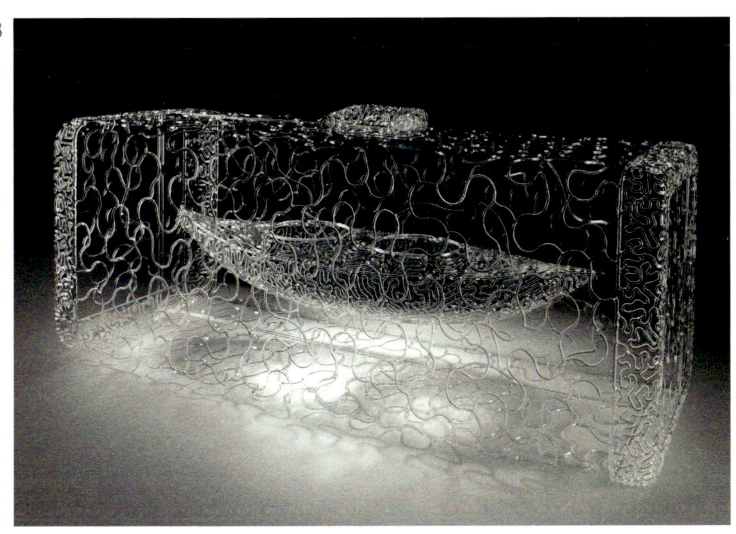

4

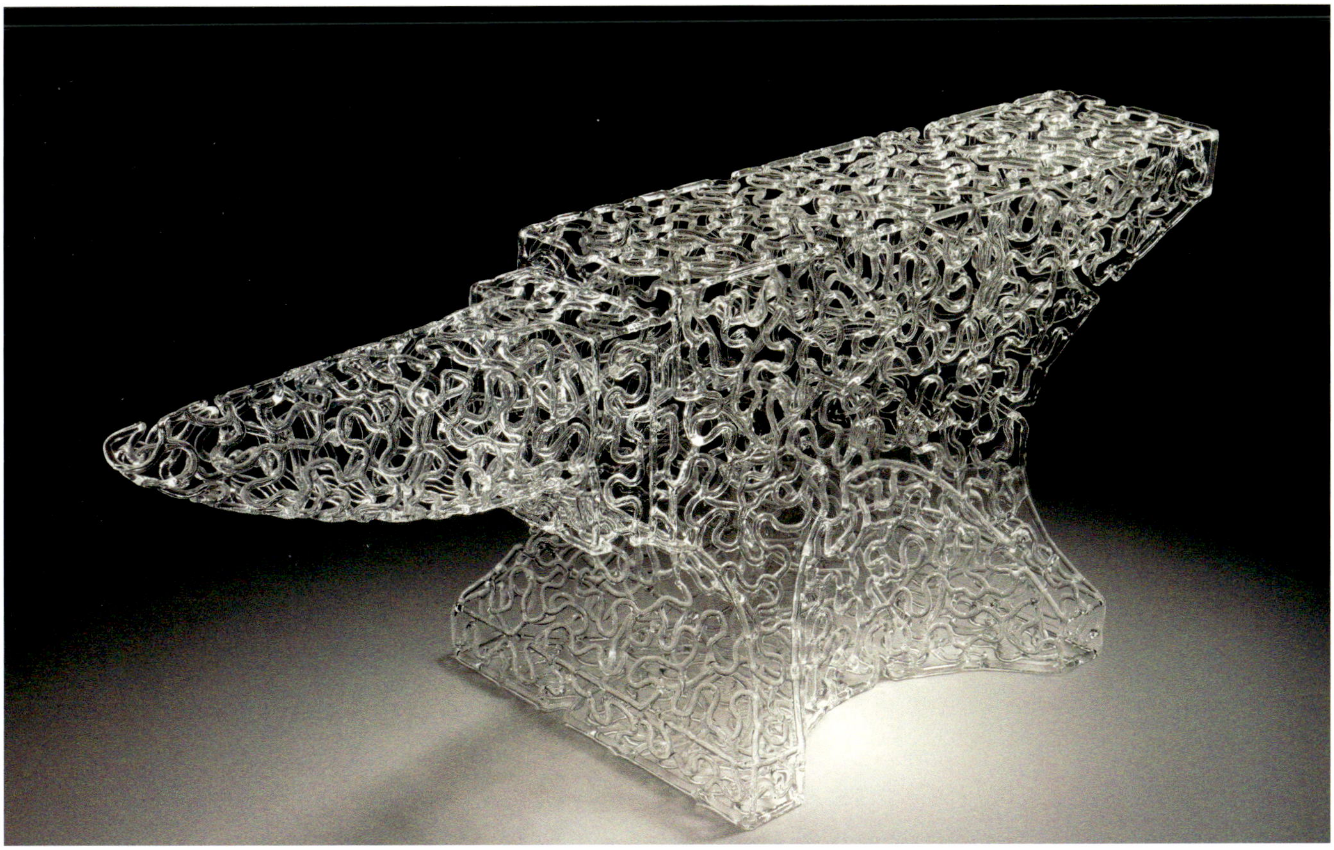

Teresa Young

Halifax, Nova Scotia, Canada

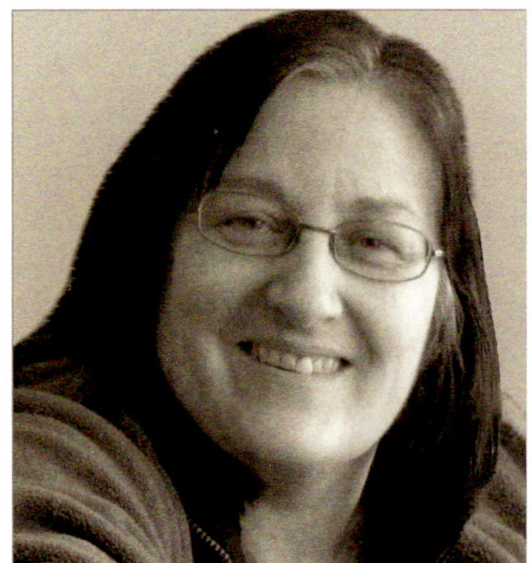

I started painting in traditional mediums and then found a new medium in glass art. I've been experimenting with creating artwork that differs from traditional stained glass. I feel that art should be dynamic and vibrant, a celebration of beauty and life that brings joy to the viewer.

1 *Fauvist Fantasy*. Painted glass. 11" × 13". 2010.

2 *Serenity*. Painted glass. 16" × 18". 2010.

3 *Siren Sighs*. Painted glass. 13" × 11". 2013.

4 *Frozen Frame*. Painted glass. 13" × 11". 2010.

5 *Something to Do With Creepy Staring Eyes*. Painted glass. 13" × 11". 2012.

1

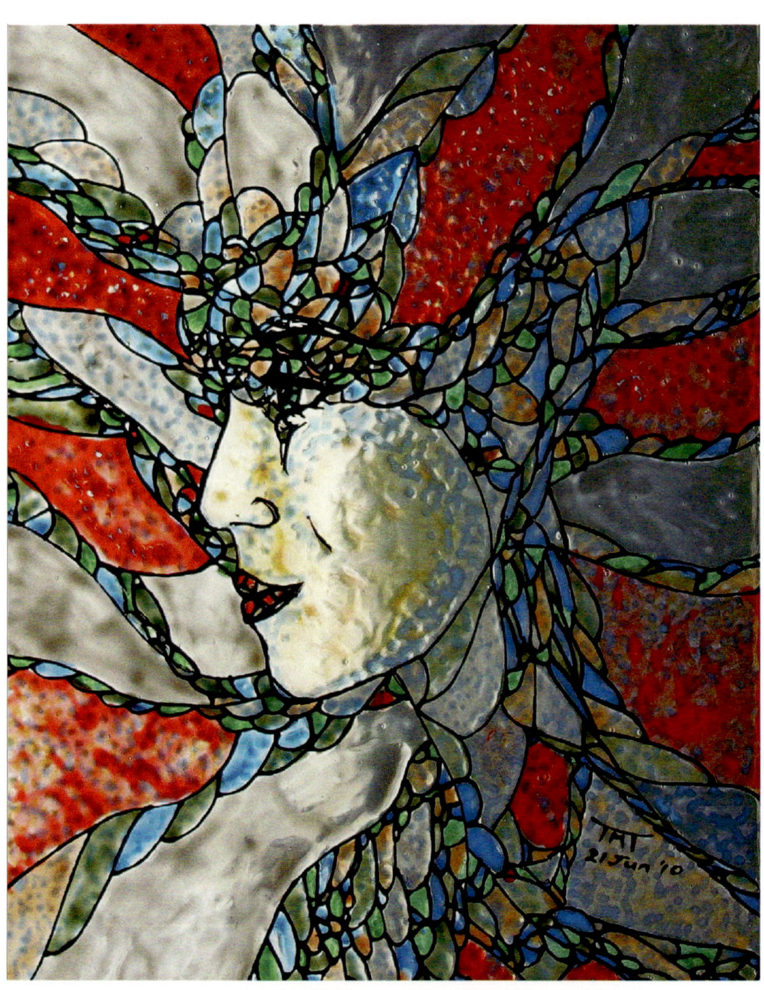

2

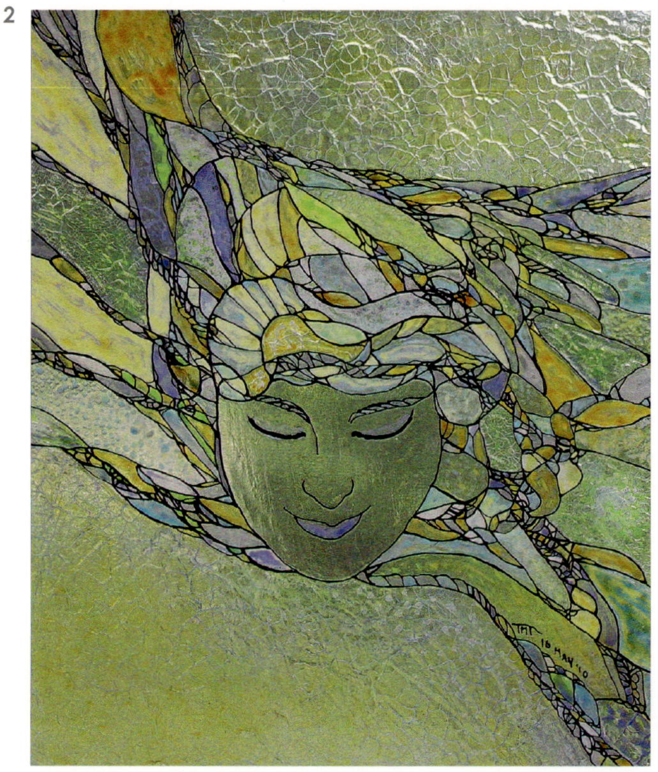

3

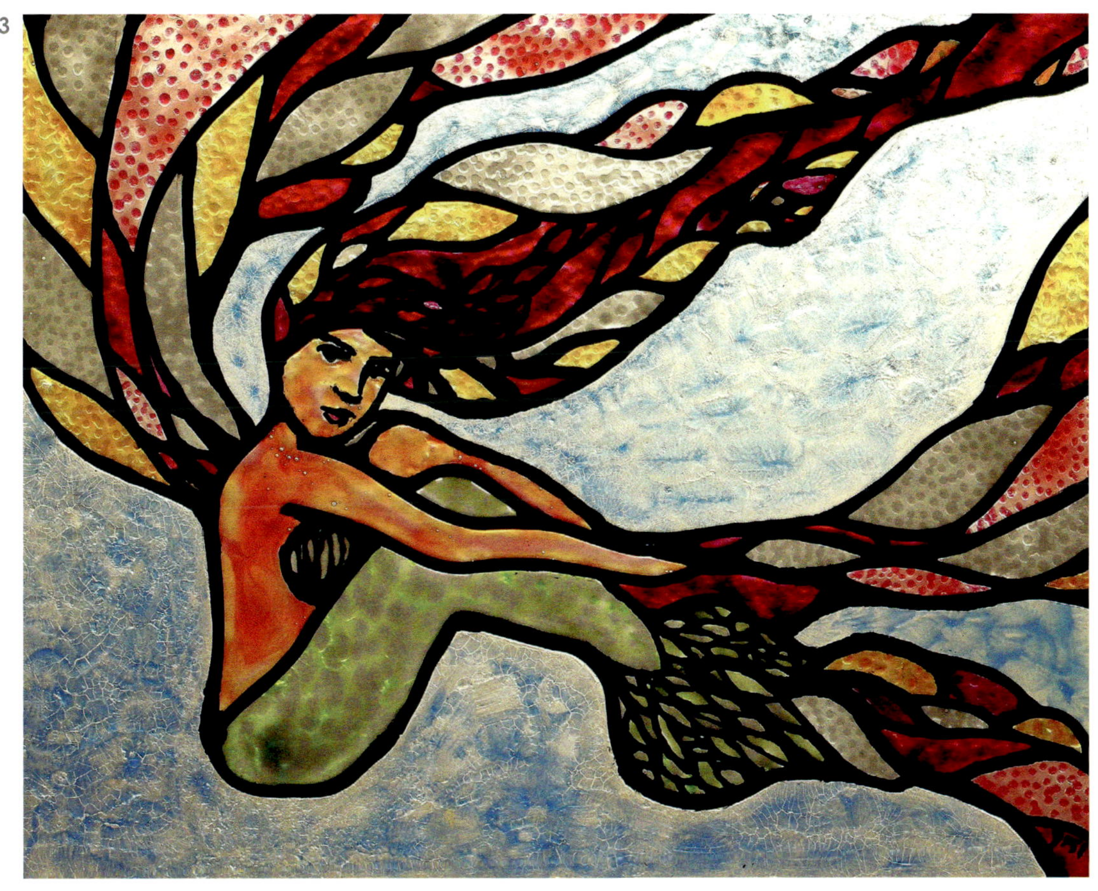

4

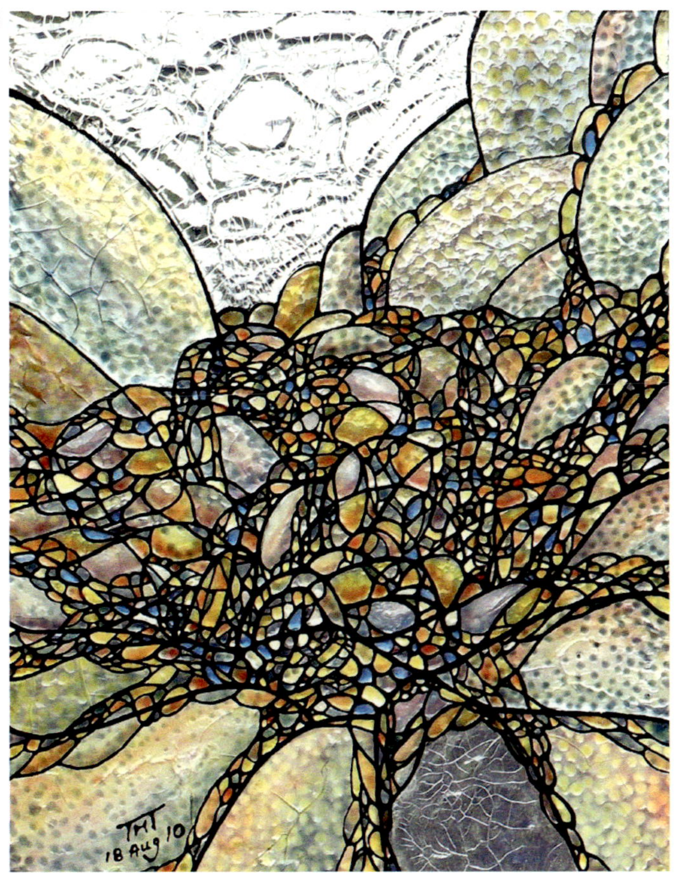

5

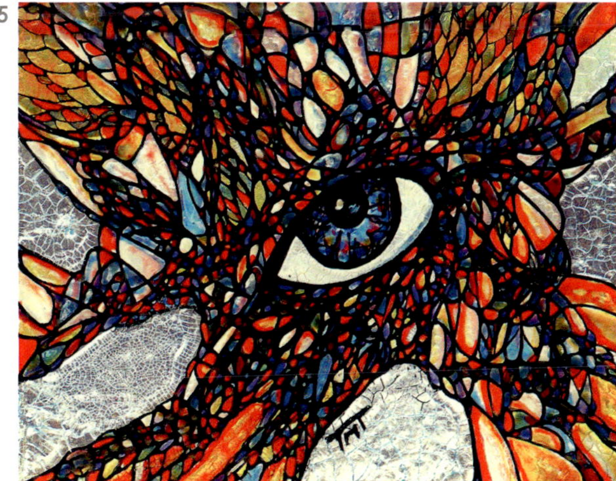

Betsy Youngquist

Rockford, Illinois

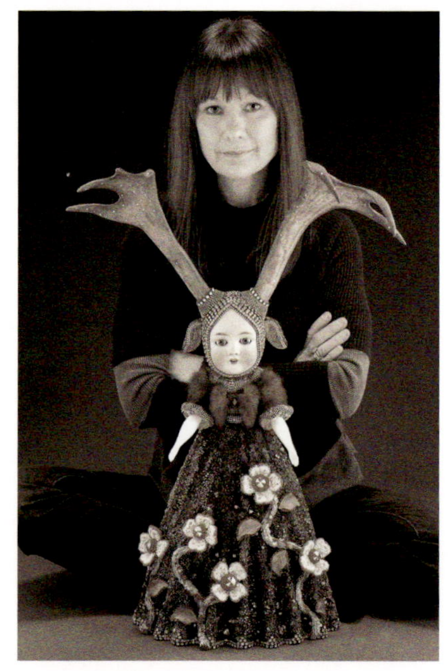

Photo: Larry Sanders.

I have always been fascinated with the intersection of humans, animals, and mythology. My creative pursuits are centered on exploring those connections.

Glass beads form the backbone of my materials. The colorful, textured, three-dimensional nature of beadwork allows me to immerse myself in surface detail. I am drawn to the quality of beads as a transcendent ceremonial material. There is an inherent magic with beadwork used in cultures where the mundane and the unseen merge. Eyes are my narrative center. When I begin a piece, I start with the eyes. In needing to meet a creature through the eyes, I begin to understand what each character wants to become.

The juxtaposition of beads with unorthodox materials led me into the world of mosaics. I am drawn to the visual effect of beads embedded in dirt. There is something mysterious and primal about a dirt-covered object. When creating these embellished objects, I collaborate with sculptor R. Scott Long in designing and constructing the forms. Each piece starts as a unique carving. The surfaces are encrusted with beads and found materials, often incorporating fragments of old porcelain dolls.

1

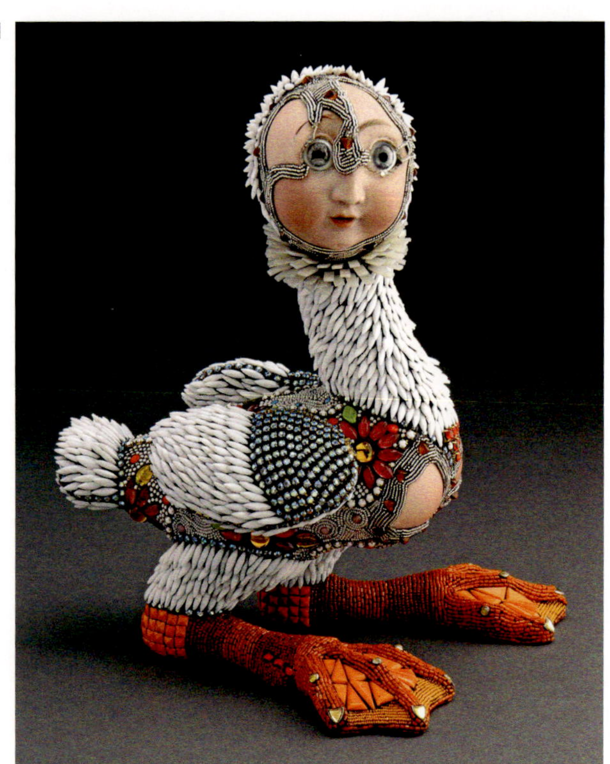

2

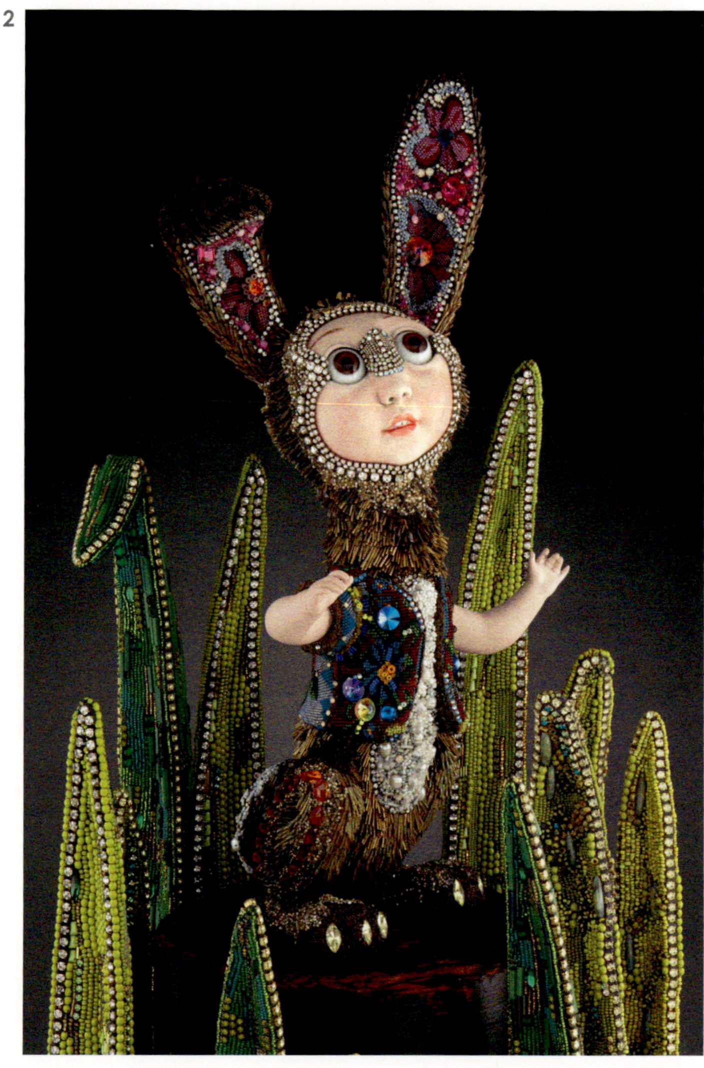

1 *Mr. Mothergoose*. Mosaic. 7" × 11" × 12". 2009. Photo: Larry Sanders.

2 *Peter in the Grass*. Mosaic. 15" × 15" × 28". 2015. Photo: Larry Sanders.

3

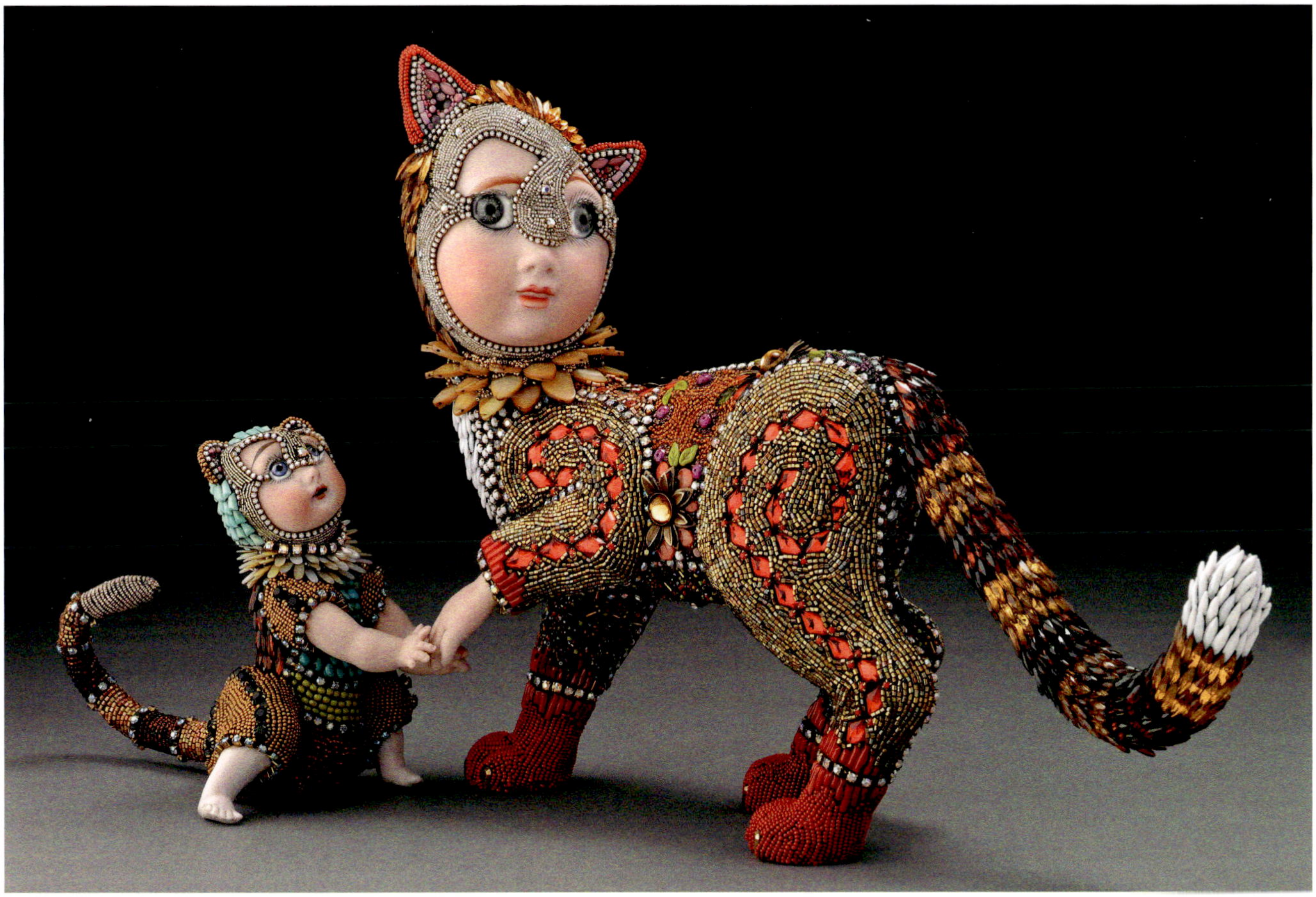

4

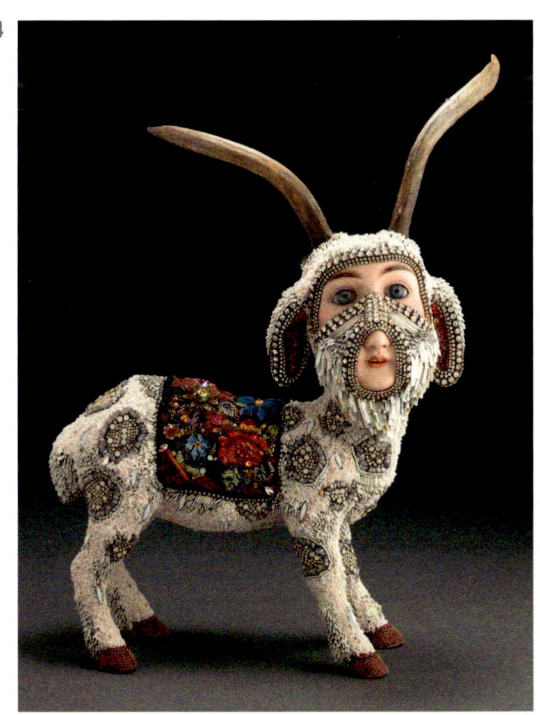

5

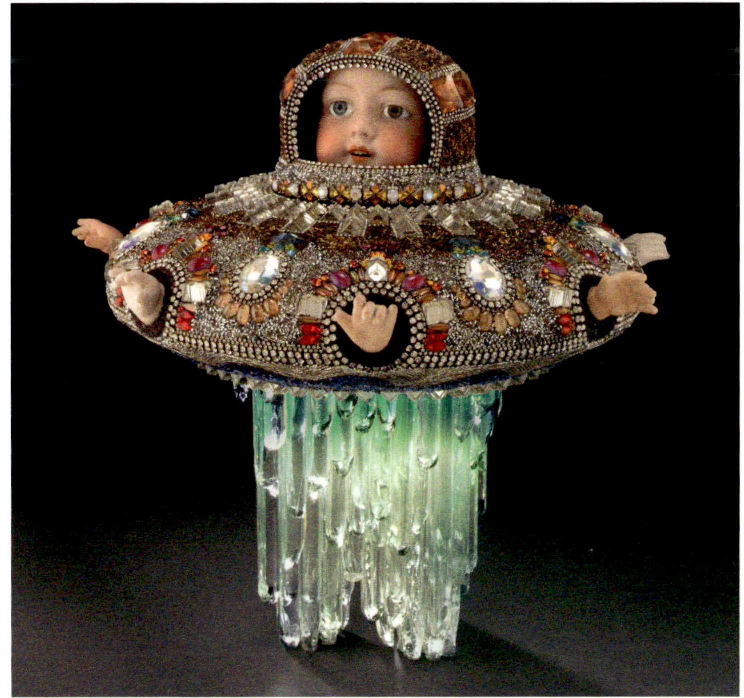

3 *Androcles and the Cat*. Mosaic. 8" × 22" × 12". 2009. Photo: Larry Sanders.

4 *Lost Rider*. Mosaic. 8" × 16" × 14". 2014. Photo: Larry Sanders.

5 *Hero*. Mosaic. 19" × 19" × 19". 2014. Photo: Larry Sanders.

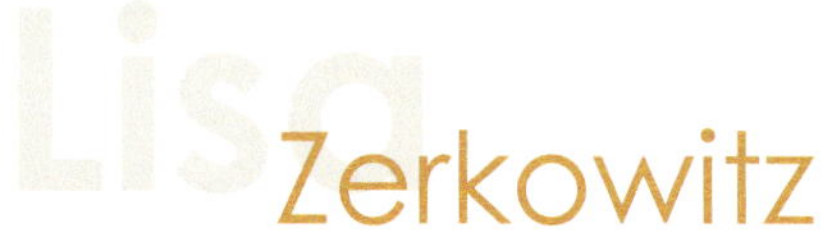

Seattle, Washington

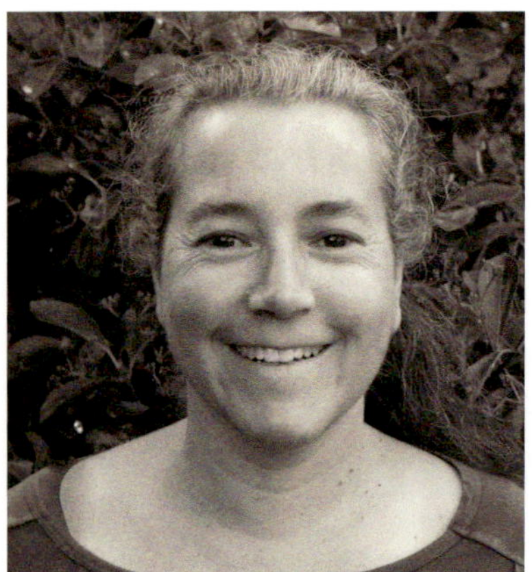

Courtesy of Boyd Sugiki.

My work is rooted in the exploration of the natural landscape. I celebrate nature by using it in my work as a means to express memorable moments in time that pass quickly and cannot be put into words. I seek to capture the light that transforms the forest at dusk or catch a snapshot of the shades of green that turn to gold and the quiet sounds of the forest. I am interested in transporting the viewer to a place they have forgotten or have never experienced—to a quiet moment that has no words, only feeling.

Living in Washington State has hugely influenced my work. I was and still am deeply affected by the lush foliage of the Pacific Northwest and its stark contrast from my native Los Angeles.

1

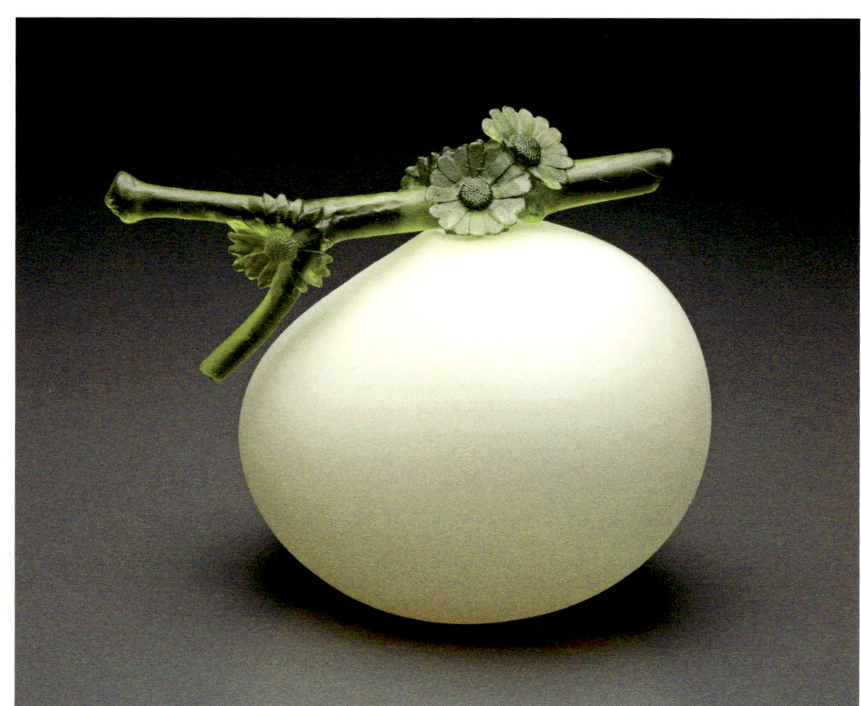

2

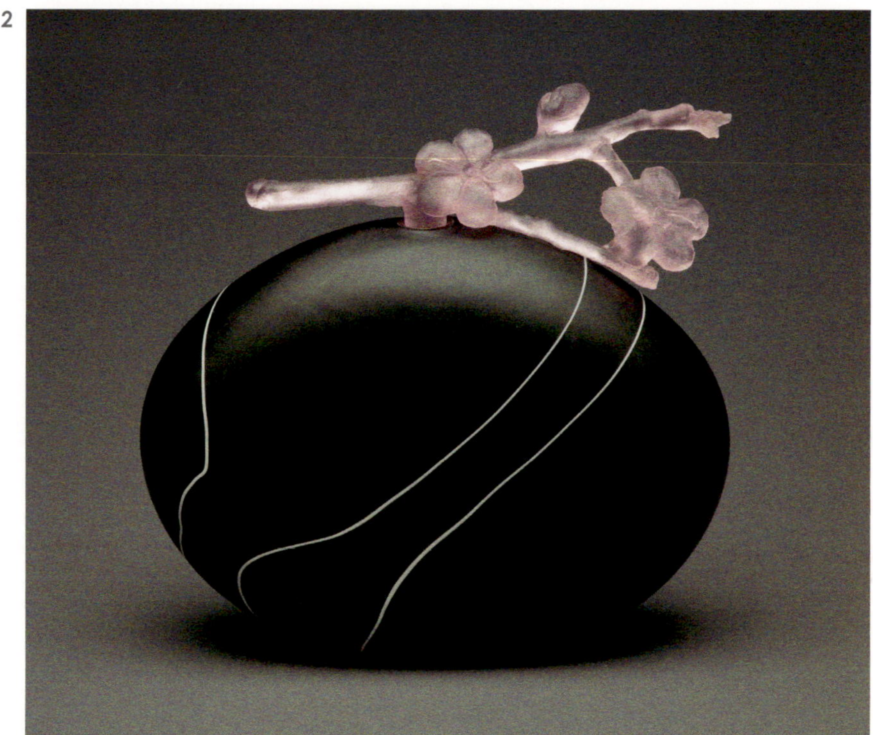

3

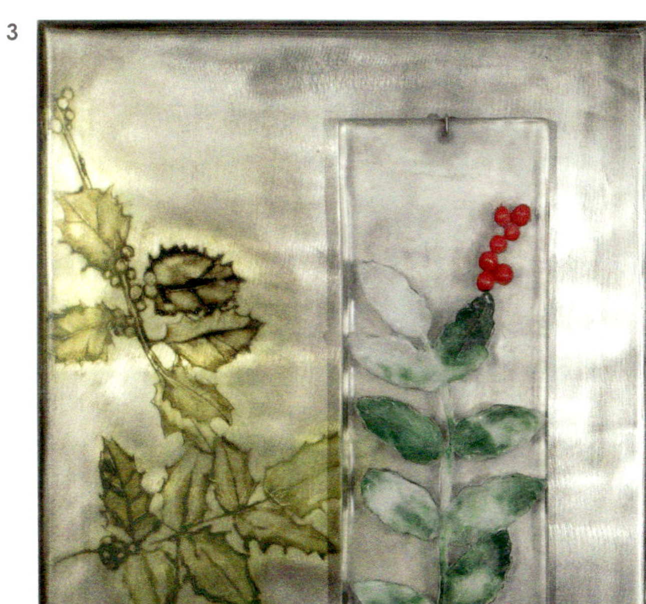

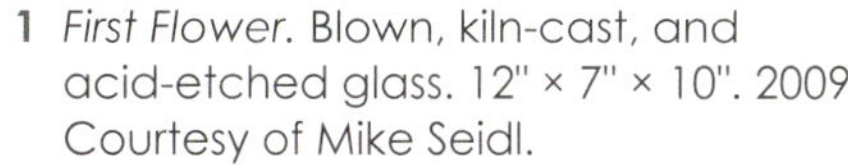

1 *First Flower*. Blown, kiln-cast, and acid-etched glass. 12" × 7" × 10". 2009. Courtesy of Mike Seidl.

2 *Haiku II*. Blown, kiln-cast, and acid-etched glass. 9.5" × 3.75" × 9". 2013. Courtesy of Mike Seidl.

3 *Winter*. Kiln-cast glass, pate de verre, steel, and ink. 15" × 2" × 12". 2013. Courtesy of Boyd Sugiki.

4 *Spring*. Kiln-cast glass, pate de verre, steel, and ink. 15" × 2" × 12". 2013. Courtesy of Boyd Sugiki.

5 *Harvest II*. Kiln-cast glass, steel, and ink. 15" × 3" × 12". 2008. Courtesy of Mike Seidl.

5

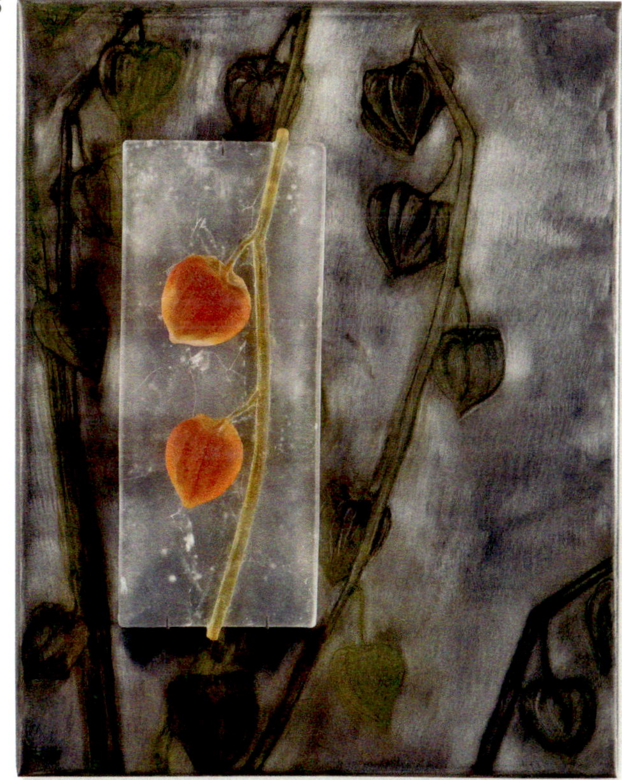

4

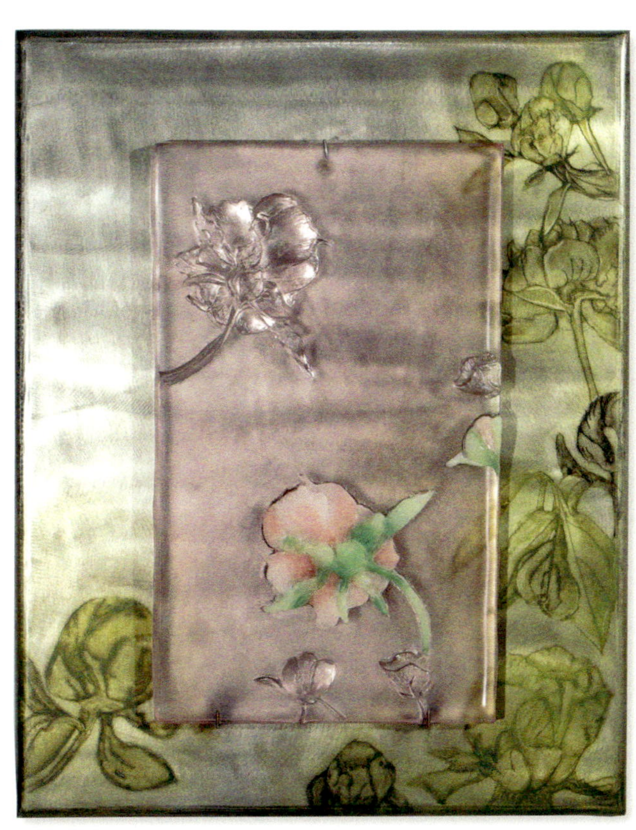

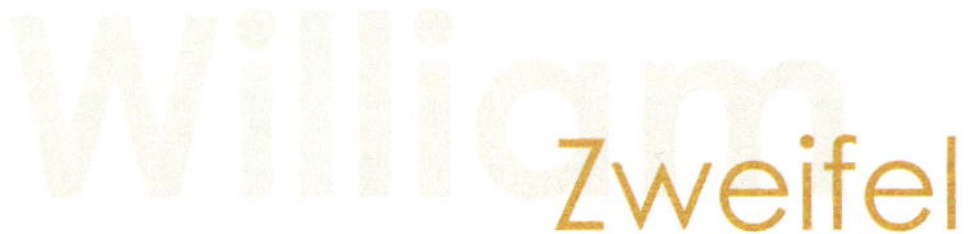

William Zweifel

Elkhorn, Wisconsin

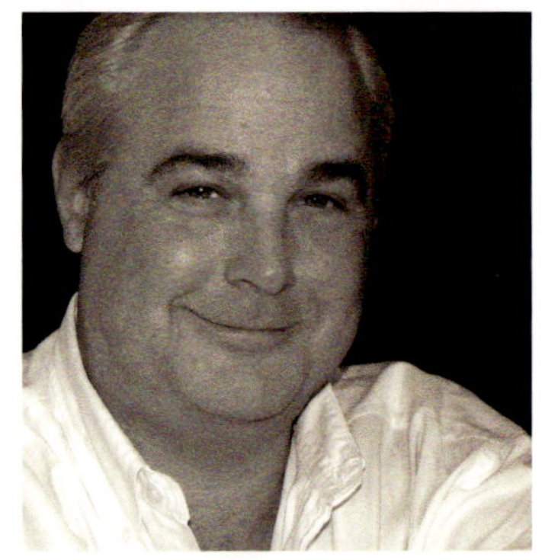

I seek to create in my work the feeling of calmness. Shape and structure are the tools used to evoke emotion. The shapes may appear simple and smooth, but they are composed of individual lines, working on different planes, and heading in different directions, yet interweaving in a way that they directly influence one another. Heat and gravity determine the final shaping. The strength with which they are applied determines whether the piece will be smooth and graceful or stark and angular.

I view life in much the same way. We are who we are as a result of the interweaving of many life experiences. The influences of outside pressures and our core beliefs determine our character. How much we allow these pressures to influence us will determine whether we will be in turmoil or at peace.

1

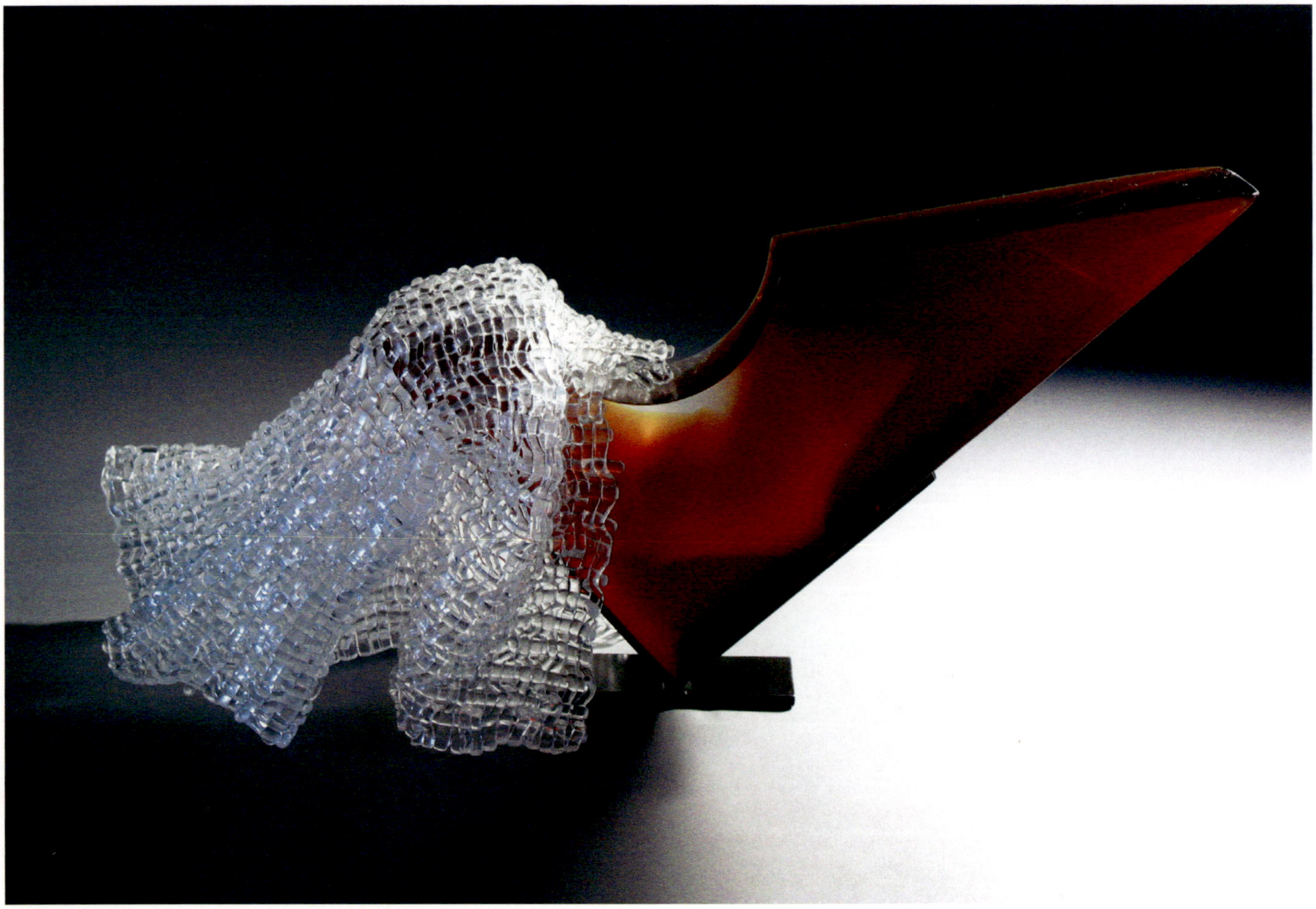

2

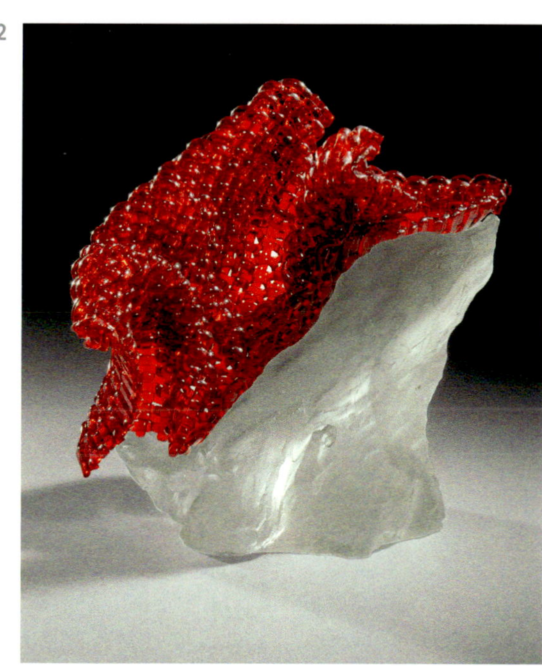

4

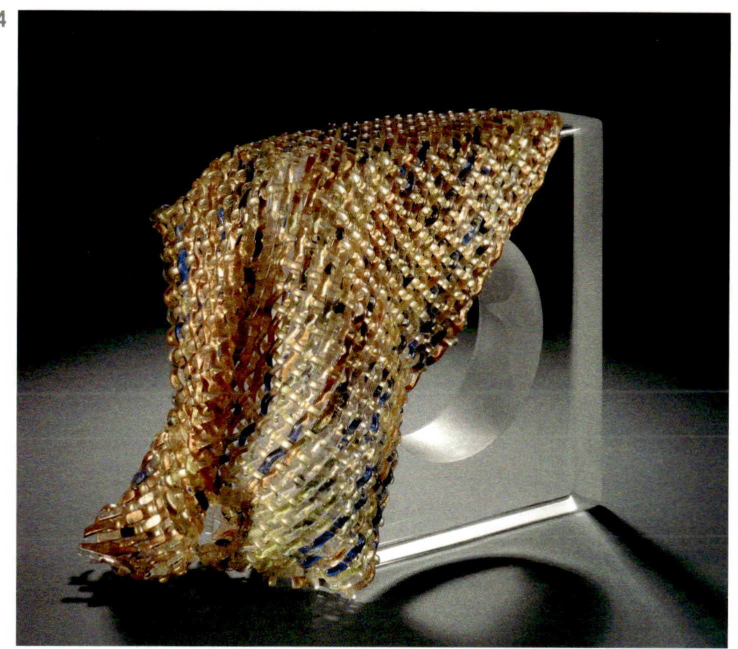

3

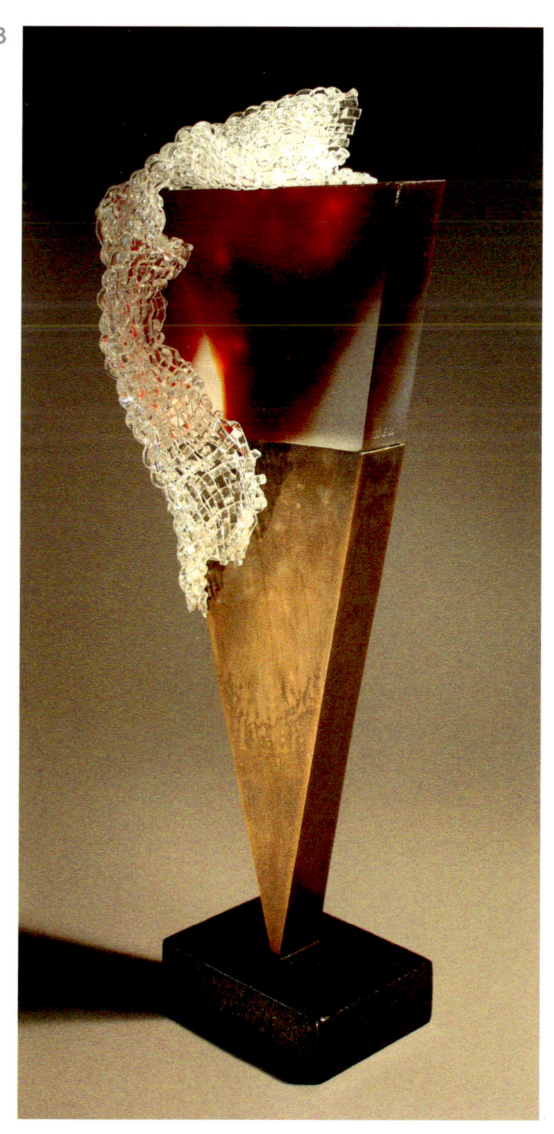

5

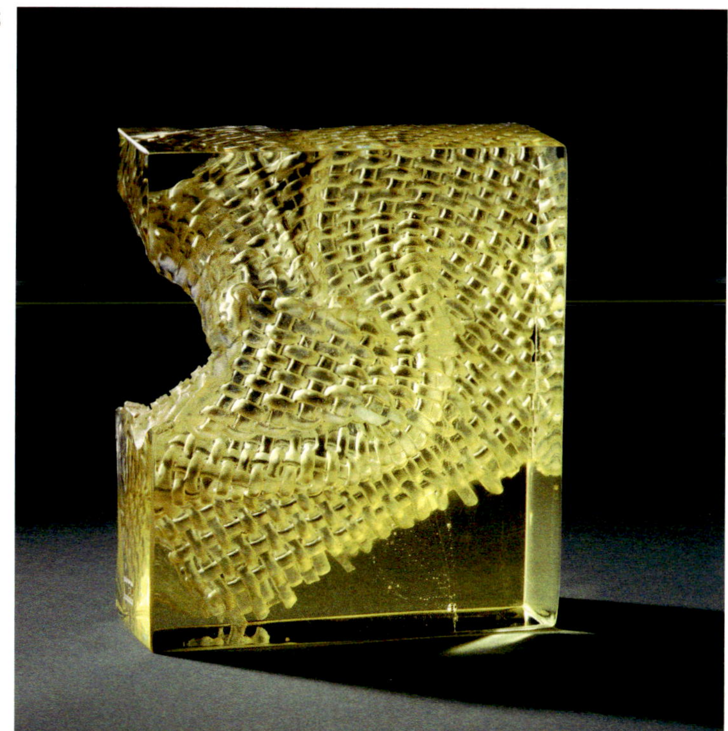

1 *Equanimity.* Cast and woven. 11" × 7" × 25". 2011.

2 *Betrayal.* Cast and woven. 10" × 6" × 12". 2013. Photo by Larry Sanders.

3 *Tangle.* Cast and woven. 22" × 8" × 12". 2012.

4 *Conceal.* Cast and woven. 13" × 5" × 15". 2009. Photo by Larry Sanders.

5 *Turmoil.* Kilncast. 9" × 3.5" × 8". 2008. Photo by Larry Sanders.

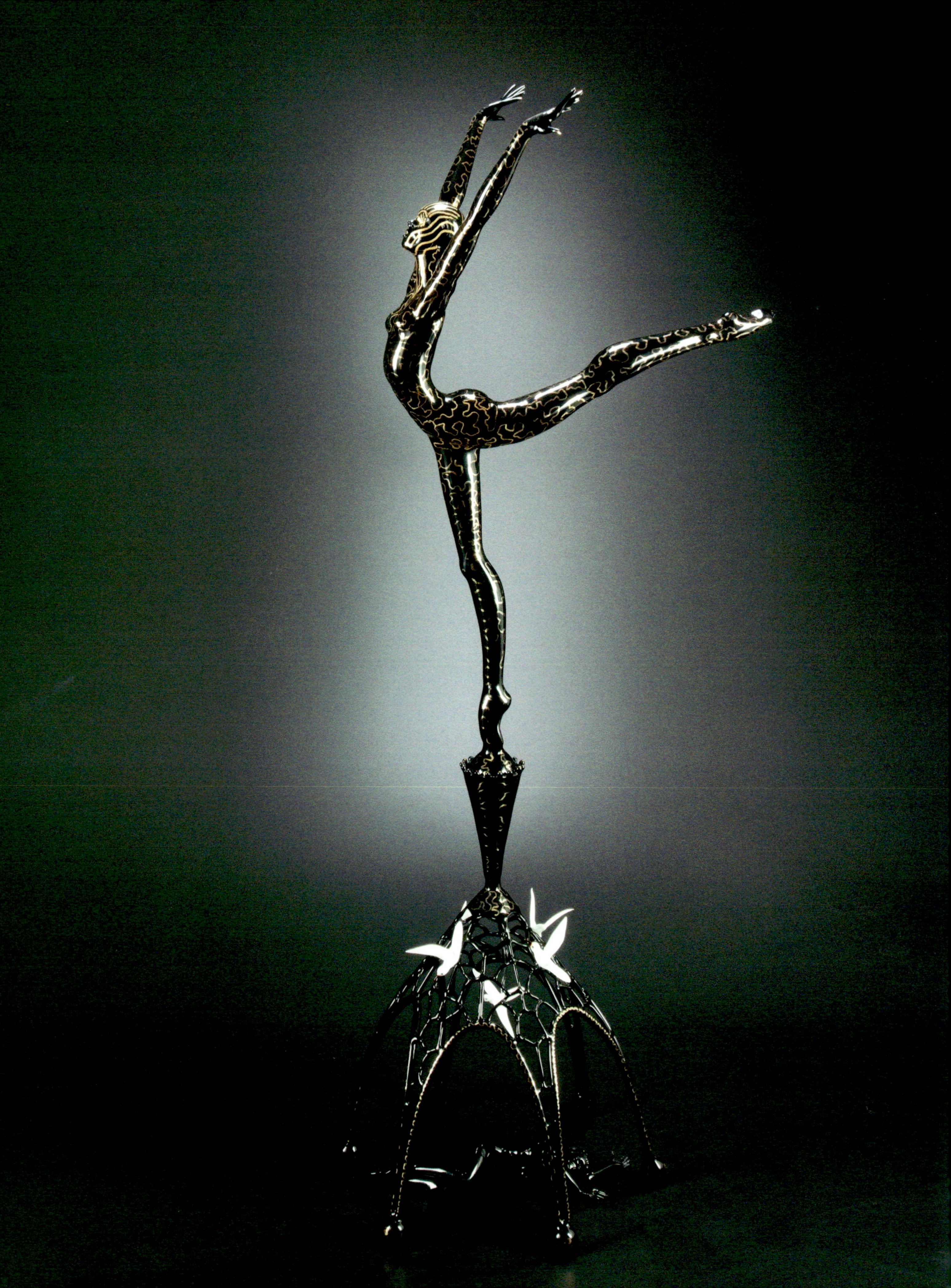

artists' websites

and Gallery Representation

Christian Arnold and Laurie Young
www.australianartglass.com
www.australianartglass.net

Shown at:
Kirra Galleries
Melbourne, VIC 3000, Australia

Herb Babcock
www.herbbabcock.com

Shown at:
Habatat Galleries
Royal Oak, MI 48073
and
West Palm Beach, FL 33401

Sandra Ainsley Gallery
Toronto, ON, Canada M4A 1B3

Rhoda Baer
www.rhodabaerglass.com

Shown at:
Gallery Sikabonyi
1010 Vienna, Austria

Morgan Contemporary Glass Gallery
Pittsburgh, PA 15232

Brian Berman
www.bermansculpture.com

Shown at:
A Gallery
Salt Lake City, UT 84108

Friesen Gallery Fine Art
Ketchum, ID 83340

Stewart Fine Art
Boca Raton, FL 33431

Third Dimension Gallery
Kamuela, HI 96743

Tina Betz
www.tinabetz.com

Shown at:
Gallery of Fine Craft, Wheaton Arts
Millville, NJ 08332

Morgan Contemporary Glass Gallery
Pittsburgh, PA 15232

Sandra Ainsley Gallery
Toronto, ON, Canada M4A 1B3

Philippa Beveridge
www.philippabeveridge.com

Shown at:
Contemporary Applied Arts
London SE1 0HX, UK

Jackie & Partners
Kobe, 658-0032, Japan

Lothar Böttcher
www.lotharbottcher.com
www.obsidianglass.co.za

Shown at:
Dimitrov Art Gallery
Dullstroom, Mpumalanga, South Africa

Ebony
Franschoek, 7690, South Africa

Edge Glass Gallery
Cape Town, South Africa

Latchezar Boyadjiev
www.latchezarboyadjiev.com

Shown at:
Habatat Galleries
Royal Oak, MI 48073
and
West Palm Beach, FL 33401

Sandra Ainsley Gallery
Toronto, ON, Canada M4A 1B3

Schantz Gallery
Stockbridge, MA 01262

Kathy Bradford
www.kathybradford.com

Rachel Bremner
www.rachelbremner.com

Charissa Brock
www.charissabock.com

Shown at:
Cavin-Morris Gallery
New York, NY 10001

Emily Brock
www.emilybrock.com

Shown at:
Habatat Galleries
Royal Oak, MI 48073
and
West Palm Beach, FL 33401

Hawk Galleries
Columbus, OH 43215

Susan Silver Brown
www.susansilverbrown.com

Roger Buddle
www.rogerbuddleglass.com.au

Shown at:
Kirra Galleries
Melbourne, VIC, 3000, Australia

Thor and Jennifer Bueno
www.buenoglass.com

Shown at:
Blue Spiral 1
Asheville, NC 28801

Consult Art
Atlanta, GA

Robert Carlson
www.robertcarlson.glass

Shown at:
Habatat Galleries
West Palm Beach, FL 33401
Traver Gallery
Seattle, WA 98101

Opposite: Robert Mickelsen.

Robin Cass
www.robincass.com

Maryse Chartrand
www.marysec.com

Shown at:
Art Works Gallery
Vancouver, BC, Canada V6B 4X7

Dimension Plus
Montréal, QC, Canada H4P 2S8

Espace VERRE
Montreal, QC, Canada H3K 2B3

Galerie Elena Lee
Montreal, QC, Canada H3G 1K4

Sandra Ainsley Gallery
Toronto, ON, Canada M4A 1B3

Lu Chi
www.luchiglass.com

Shown at:
Ai Bo Gallery
Rye, NY 10580

China Art Museum
Shanghai, China

Corning Museum of Glass
Corning, NY 14830

Habatat Galleries
Royal Oak, MI 48073

Maurine Littleton Gallery
Washington, DC 20007

Morgan Contemporary Glass Gallery
Pittsburgh, PA 15232

National Liberty Museum
Philadelphia, PA 19106

Victoria and Albert Museum
London SW7 2RL, UK

Deanna Clayton

Shown at:
Continuum Gallery
53639 Königswinter, Germany
Duncan McClellan Gallery
St. Petersburg, FL 33712
Habatat Galleries
Royal Oak, MI 48073
and
West Palm Beach, FL 33401

K. Allen Gallery
Sister Bay, WI 54234

PISMO Gallery at Aspen
Aspen, CO 81611

Sherrie Gallery
Columbus, OH 43215

Stephan Cox
www.stephancoxglass.com

Daniel Cutrone
www.danielcutrone.com

Shown at:
The Wexler Gallery
Philadelphia, PA 19106

Dan Dailey
www.dandailey.com

Robert Dane
www.robertdane.com

Shown at:
Dane Gallery
Nantucket, MA 02554

Gerald Davidson
www.geralddavidsonstudio.com

Ron Desmett
www.rondesmett.com

Shown at:
Kim Foster Gallery
New York City, NY 10011

Miriam Di Fiore
www.miriamdifiore.com

Shown at:
Habatat Galleries
Royal Oak, MI 48073

Laura Donefer
www.lauradonefer.com

Shown at:
Duane Reed Gallery
St. Louis, MO 63108

Habatat Galleries
Royal Oak, MI 48073

Sandra Ainsley Gallery
Toronto, ON, Canada M4A 1B3

Dina Priess dos Santos
www.dinapriessdossantos.com

Shown at:
First Glas Galerie
80798 Munich, Germany

Galerie am Museum
94258 Frauenau, Germany

John Drury
E-mail: simplefolktoo@hotmail.com

Eric Ehlenberger
www.ehlenberger.com

Shown at:
Venusian Gardens Art Gallery
New Orleans, LA 70117

Zenith Gallery
Washington, DC 20012

Shane Fero
www.shanefero.net

Wesley Fleming
www.wesleyfleming.com

Clouds Gallery
Woodstock, NY 12498

Kobe Lampwork Glass Museum
Kobe, Japan 650-0034

PISMO Fine Art Glass
Denver, CO 80206

Racine Art Museum Store
Racine, WI 53403

Tom Fuhrman
www.fuhrmanglass.com

Shown at:
Artlink
Ft. Wayne, IN 46802

Fuhrman Glass Studios Inc.
Oak Ridge, TN 37830

Locally Grown Gallery
Oak Ridge, TN 37830

McClung Museum
Knoxville, TN 37916

Serenity Glass
Clinton, TN 37716

York & Friends Fine Art
Nashville, TN 37205

Jason B. Gamrath
www.jasongamrathglass.com

Shown at:
Habatat Galleries
Royal Oak, MI 48073

Stephen Gartner and Danielle Blade
www.gartnerblade.com

Shown at:
See website for gallery representation.

Michael Glancy
www.michaelglancyglassworks.com

Shown at:
Barry Friedman, Ltd.
New York, NY 10001

Joe Grant
www.joegrantglass.com

Shown at:
Greenhill
Greensboro, NC 27401

STARworks Gallery
Star, NC 27356

Gabriel Greenlaw
www.gabrielgreenlaw.com

Shown at:
Centre St Arts Gallery
Bath, ME 04530

Gleason Fine Art
Boothbay Harbor, ME 04538

The Gallery at the Appalachian Center
for Craft
Smithville, TN 37166

Viles Arboretum
Augusta, ME 04330

York & Friends Fine Art
Nashville, TN 37205

Wilfried Grootens
www.wilfriedgrootens.de

Shown at:
Continuum Gallery
53639 Königswinter, Germany

Etienne Gallery
5061 HX Oisterwijk, Netherlands

Habatat Galleries
Royal Oak, MI 48073

Sandra Ainsley Gallery
Toronto, ON, Canada M4A 1B3

Jaime Guerrero
www.guerreroglass.com

Dorothy Hafner
www.dorothyhafner.com

Shown at:
Holsten Galleries
Santa Fe, NM 87501

Schantz Gallery
Stockbridge, MA 01262

Stewart Fine Art
Boca Raton, FL 33431

Marina Hanser
www.marinahanser.com

Karen Hibbs
www.hibbsartglass.com

Eric Hilton
www.hiltonglass.com

Shown at:
Habatat Galleries
Royal Oak, MI 48073

PISMO Fine Art Glass
Denver, CO, 80206

Schantz Gallery
Stockbridge, MA 01262

David Huchthausen
www.huchthausen.com

Shown at:
Habatat Galleries
Royal Oak, MI 48073

Schantz Gallery
Stockbridge, MA 01262

Scott Jacobson Gallery
New York, NY 10022

Sidney Hutter
www.sidneyhutter.com

Shown at:
Austin Art Projects
Palm Desert, CA 92260

Dane Gallery
Nantucket, MA 02554

Habatat Galleries
Boca Raton, FL 33431
and
Royal Oak, MI 48073

Hawk Galleries
Columbus, OH 43215

Hodgell Gallery
Sarasota, FL 34236

Holsten Galleries
Santa Fe, NM 87501

Ken Saunders Gallery
Chicago, IL 60654

Martha's Vineyard Glassworks
West Tisbury, MA 02575

Schantz Gallery
Stockbridge, MA 01262

Scott Jacobson Gallery
New York, NY 10022

Thomas R. Riley Galleries
Cleveland, OH 44122

Vlastislav Janáček
www.janacek-sklo.blog.cz

Shown at:
Mostly Glass Gallery
Englewood, NJ 07631

Elizabeth Johnson
www.elizabethjohnson.com

Shown at:
Copper Moon Gallery
Taos, NM 87571

Kittrell / Riffkind Art Glass
Dallas, TX 75254

Mark Payton Glass Center at Louisville Glassworks
Louisville, KY 40202

PISMO Fine Art Glass
Denver, CO 80206
and
Aspen, CO 81611
and
Vail, CO 81657

RAS Galleries
Napa, CA 94559

The Art Stop
Tacoma, WA 98402

Richard Jolley
www.richardjolley.com

Saman Kalantari
www.samankalantari.com

Sonia King
www.mosaicworks.com

Connie Kolman
www.kolmanartisanglass.com

Shown at:
Renjeau Galleries
Natick, MA 01760

The Drawing Room
Marion, MA 02738

Lynn Latimer
www.latimerglass.com

Shown at:
Artful Home
Madison, WI 53703

The Wit Gallery
Lenox, MA 01240

K. William LeQuier
www.kwilliamlequier.com

Shown at:
Habatat Galleries
Royal Oak, MI 48073
and
West Palm Beach, FL 33401

Schantz Gallery
Stockbridge, MA 01262

Robert Levin
www.robertlevin.com

Shown at:
Bill Hester Fine Art
Santa Fe, NM 87501

Blue Spiral 1
Asheville, NC 28801

Penland Gallery
Penland, NC 28765

Piedmont Craftsmen
Winston Salem, NC 27101

Shine on Brightly
Asheville, NC

Southern Highland Craft Guild
Folk Art Center
Asheville, NC 28815

Taupe Gallery
North Wilkesboro, NC 28659

The Design Gallery
Burnsville, NC 28714

Twisted Laurel Gallery
Spruce Pine, NC 28777

Village Smith Galleries
Winston-Salem, NC 27106

Steve Linn
www.stevelinnsculpture.com

Shown at:
Habatat Galleries
Royal Oak, MI 48073

Marvin B. Lipofsky
www.marvinlipofsky.com

Shown at:
Duane Reed Gallery
St. Louis, MO 63108

Habatat Galleries
Royal Oak, MI 48073

Marvin Lipofsky Studios
Berkeley, CA 94710

Micaëla Contemporary Projects
San Francisco Bay Area, CA

Schantz Gallery
Stockbridge, MA 01262

The Wexler Gallery
Philadelphia, PA 19106

John Littleton and Kate Vogel
www.littletonvogel.com

Shown at:
Blue Spiral 1
Asheville, NC 28801

Duane Reed Gallery
St. Louis, MO 63108

Edgewood Orchard Galleries
Fish Creek, WI 54212

Hodgell Gallery
Sarasota, FL 34236

Maurine Littleton Gallery
Washington, DC 20007

Melissa Morgan Fine Art
Palm Desert, CA 92260

Penland Gallery
Penland, NC 28765

Carmen Lozar
www.carmenlozar.com

Shown at:
Ken Saunders Gallery
Chicago, IL 60654

Tanya Lyons
www.tanyalyons.ca

Shown at:
A Gallery Fine Art
Palm Desert, CA 92260

Bender Gallery
Asheville, NC 28801

Kuivato Glass Gallery
Sedona, AZ 86339

L.A Pai
Ottawa, ON, Canada K1N 9M5

Morgan Contemporary Glass Gallery
Pittsburgh, PA 15232

Sandra Ainsley Gallery
Toronto, ON, Canada M4A 1B3

Stewart Fine Art
Boca Raton, FL 33431

West End Gallery
VIC, BC, Canada V8W 2A4

Linda MacNeil
www.lindamacneil.com

Caroline Madden
www.creativity.madden.com

Tom Marosz
www.tommarosz.com

Shown at:
Ai Bo Gallery
Greenwich, CT 06831

Chasen Galleries
Richmond, VA 93221

Contemporary Fine Arts Gallery
La Jolla, CA 92037

Freed Gallery
Lincoln City, OR 97367

Jim Miller Gallery
Carmel-by-the-Sea, CA 93921

NaPua Gallery
Kihei, HI 96753

The Third Dimension Gallery
Kamuela, HI 96743

Eileen Martin
www.martinglasscreations.com

Lin McJunkin
www.mcjunkinglass.com

Shown at:
Karla Matzke Fine Art Gallery and
Sculpture Park
Camano Island, WA 98282

Elizabeth Ryland Mears

Shown at:
Bender Gallery
Asheville, NC 2880

Stewart Fine Art
Boca Raton, FL 33431

Troika Gallery
Floyd, VA 24091

Zenith Gallery
Washington, DC 20012

Robert Mickelsen
www.robertmickelsen.com

Shown at:
Habatat Galleries
West Palm Beach, FL 33401

Hodgell Gallery
Sarasota, FL 34236

Morgan Contemporary Glass Gallery
Pittsburgh, PA 15232

Michael Mikula
www.mikulaglass.com

Shown at:
Collectors Corner Gallery
Toledo Museum Of Art
Toledo, OH 43697

Carol Milne
www.carolmilne.com

Shown at:
Karla Matzke Fine Art Gallery and
Sculpture Park
Camano Island, WA 98282

Anna Mlasowsky
www.annamlasowsky.com

Peter Mollica
www.petermollica.com

Shown at:
Stained Glass Garden
Berkeley, CA 94710

Benjamin Moore
www.benjaminmooreglass.com

Shown at:
Foster / White Gallery
Seattle, WA 98104

Holsten Galleries
Santa Fe, NM 87501

PISMO Fine Art Glass
Denver, CO 80206
and
Aspen, CO 81611
and
Vail, CO 81657

Schantz Gallery
Stockbridge, MA 01262

Kathleen Mulcahy
www.kathleenmulcahy.com

Shown at:
Borelli Edwards Gallery
Pittsburgh, PA 15201

Habatat Galleries
Royal Oak, MI 48073

Kim Foster Gallery
New York City, NY 10011

Shelley Muzylowski Allen
www.muzylowski.com

Shown at:
Blue Rain Gallery
Santa Fe, NM 87501

Habatat Galleries
Royal Oak, MI 48073

Schantz Gallery
Stockbridge, MA 01262

Traver Gallery
Seattle, WA 98101

George O'Grady

Shown at:
Tesuque Glassworks
Tesuque, NM 87574

Joseph Pagano
www.josephpagano.com

David Patchen
www.davidpatchen.com

Shown at:
See website for gallery representation.

Harry Pollitt
www.pollittstudio.com

Shown at:
Holsten Galleries
Santa Fe, NM 87501

Thomas R. Riley Galleries
Cleveland, OH 44122

Traver Gallery
Seattle, WA 98101

Winterowd Fine Art
Santa Fe, NM 87501

Charlotte Potter
www.charlottepotter.com

Shown at:
Heller Gallery
New York, NY 10001

The Wexler Gallery
Philadelphia, PA 19106

Amy Rueffert
www.amyrueffert.com

Shown at:
Traver Gallery
Seattle, WA 98101

David Schnuckel
www.davidschnuckel.com

Mary Shaffer
www.maryshaffer.com

Shown at:
Habatat Galleries
Royal Oak, MI 48073

Sculpturesite Gallery
Sonoma, CA 95476

Zane Bennett Contemporary Art
Santa Fe, NM 87501

Alison Sigethy
www.alisonsigethy.com

Shown at:
Zenith Gallery
Washington, DC 20012

Raven Skyriver
www.ravenskyriver.com

Shown at:
Dane Gallery
Nantucket, MA 02554

Duncan McClellan Gallery
St. Petersburg, FL 33712

Stonington Gallery
Seattle, WA 98104

Aaron Slater
www.aaronslaterglass.com

Shown at:
Cassidy Gallery
Jackson, NH 03846

Glass Orbits
www.pbase.com/bkbowden

L.H. Selman Ltd.
Chicago, IL 60605

Land of Marbles
www.landofmarbles.com

League of New Hampshire
Craftsmen Galleries
Statewide NH

Lisabeth Sterling
www.lisabethsterling.com

Shown at:
Duncan McClellan Gallery
St. Petersburg, Florida 33712

Hawk Galleries
Columbus, OH 43215

Ken Saunders Gallery
Chicago, IL 60654

Schantz Gallery
Stockbridge, MA 01262

Boyd Sugiki
www.boydsugiki.com

Shown at:
Traver Gallery
Seattle, WA 98101

Demetra Theofanous
www.sculpturebydemetra.com

Shown at:
Bender Gallery
Asheville, NC 28801

Morgan Contemporary Glass Gallery
Pittsburgh, PA 15232

PISMO Fine Art Glass
Denver, CO 80206
and
Vail, CO 81657

Vetri
Seattle, WA, 98101

Cappy Thompson
www.cappythompson.com

Shown at:
Traver Gallery
Seattle, WA 98101

Cesare Toffolo
www.toffolo.com

Shown at:
Cesare Toffolo Gallery
30141 Murano-Venezia VE, Italy

Emanuel Toffolo

Shown at:
Emanuel Toffolo Gallery
Burano VE, Italy

Cesare Toffolo Gallery
30141 Murano-Venezia VE, Italy

Mostly Glass Gallery
Englewood, NJ 07631

Mary Van Cline
www.maryvancline.com

Erika Van Dewark
www.vandewarkart.com

Shown at:
Safari Club International Annual Convention
Las Vegas, NV 89119

Van Dewark Fine Art Carvings LLC
Vacaville, CA 95688

Marc VandenBerg
www.marcvandenberg.com

Shown at:
Kittrell / Riffkind Art Glass
Dallas, TX 75254

Teri Walker and Chad Ridgeway
www.ridgewalkerglass.com

Maureen Williams

Shown at:
Beaver Galleries
Deakin ACT 2600
Australia

Kirra Galleries
Melbourne, VIC, 3000, Australia

Palette Contemporary Art & Craft
Albuquerque, NM 87109

Sabbia Gallery
Paddington NSW 2021
Australia

Thomas R. Riley Galleries
Cleveland, OH 44122

John B. Wood
www.jbwoodglass.com

Shown at:
Corning Museum of Glass
Corning, NY 14830

Habatat Galleries
Royal Oak, MI 48073
and
Habatat Galleries
West Palm Beach, FL 33401

Wynia
www.rhuby.com,
www.wyniafineart.com

Robert Wynne
www.robertwynne.com

Shown at:
Kirra Galleries
Melbourne, VIC, 3000, Australia

PISMO Fine Art Glass
Denver, CO 80206

Nao Yamamoto
www.naoyamamoto.info

Hiroshi Yamano

Shown at:
Duncan McClellan Gallery
St. Petersburg, FL 33712

Galleria Silecchia
Sarasota, FL 34236

Habatat Galleries
Royal Oak, MI 48073

Hooks-Epstein Gallery
Houston, TX 77098

Karla Matzke Fine Art Gallery and Sculpture Park
Camano Island, WA 98282

LewAllen Contemporary
Santa Fe, NM 87501

Lombard Contemporary Art
Orlando, FL 32836

Marta Hewett Gallery
Cincinnati, OH 45202

Maurine Littleton Gallery
Washington, DC 20007

Sandra Ainsley Gallery
Toronto, ON, Canada M4A 1B3

Schantz Gallery
Stockbridge, MA 01262

Stewart Fine Art
Boca Raton, FL 33431

Thomas R. Riley Galleries
Cleveland, OH 44122

Traver Gallery
Seattle, WA 98101

Brent Kee Young
www.brentkeeyoung.com

Shown at:
Habatat Galleries
Royal Oak, MI 48073

Melissa Morgan Fine Art
Palm Desert, CA 92260

RARE Gallery of Fine Art
Jackson, WY 83001

Thomas R. Riley Galleries
Cleveland, OH 44122

Teresa Young
www.teresayoung.artistwebsites.com,
www.surrealisticreflections.blogspot.ca

Shown at:
Art1274 Hollis
Halifax, NS, Canada B3J 1T6

Crouchers Pt. Gallery
Glen Haven, NS, Canada B3Z 2V6

Betsy Youngquist
www.byart.com

Shown at:
Tory Folliard Gallery
Milwaukee, WI 53202

Lisa Zerkowitz
www.lisazerkowitz.com

Shown at:
Bryan Ohno Gallery
Seattle, WA 98104

William Zweifel
www.midlandstudio.com

Shown at:
Stewart Fine Art
Boca Raton, FL 33431

The Bender Gallery
Asheville, NC 28801

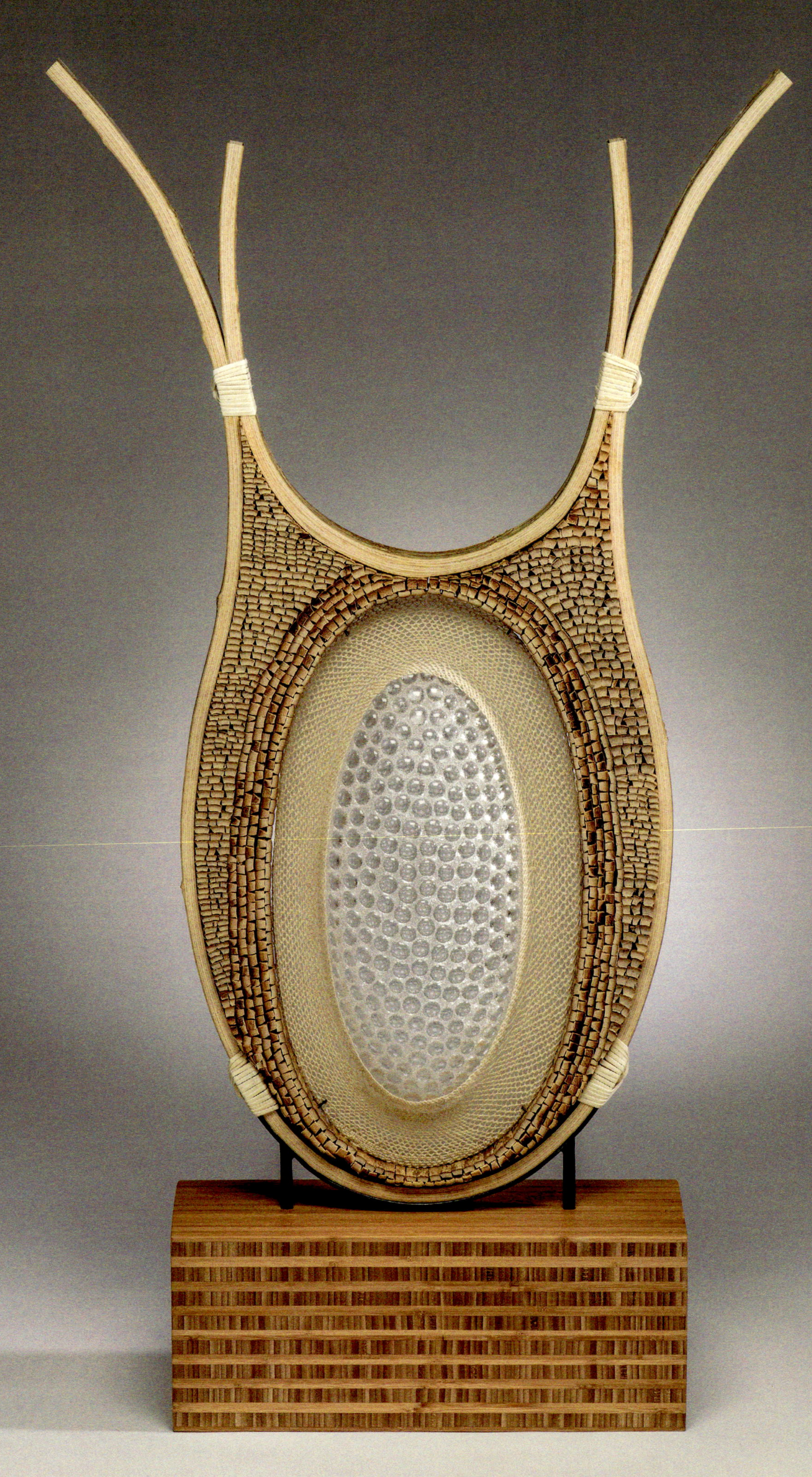

glass art galleries and museums

These galleries and museum collections represent the artists featured in this book.

Arizona

Kuivato Glass Gallery
336 Hwy 179, Tlaquepaque Suite B-125
Sedona, AZ 86339
kuivatoglassgallery.com

California

A Gallery Fine Art
73-956 El Paseo
Palm Desert, CA 92260
www.agalleryfineart.com

Austin Art Projects
44-651 Village Court, Suite 142
Palm Desert, CA 92260
www.austinartprojects.com

Contemporary Fine Arts Gallery
7946 Ivanhoe Ave
La Jolla, CA 92037
www.contemporaryfineartsgallery.com

Jim Miller Gallery
Ocean Ave
Carmel-by-the-Sea, CA, 93921
www.jimmillergallery.com

Marvin Lipofsky Studios
1012 Pardee St.
Berkeley, CA 94710
www.marvinlipofsky.com

Melissa Morgan Fine Art
73040 El Paseo
Palm Desert, CA 92260
melissamorganfineart.com

Micaëla Contemporary Projects
San Francisco Bay Area, CA
www.micaela.com

RAS Galleries
1109 Jefferson St.
Napa, CA 94559
www.rasgalleries.com

Sculpturesite Gallery
Cornerstone Sonoma
23588 Arnold Dr. (Hwy. 121)
Sonoma, CA 95476
www.sculpturesite.com

Stained Glass Garden
1800 Fourth St.
Berkeley, CA 94710
www.stainedglassgarden.com

Van Dewark Fine Art Carvings LLC
330 Merchant St.
Vacaville, CA 95688
www.vandewark.com

Colorado

PISMO Fine Art Glass
Cherry Creek North
2770 East Second Ave.
Denver, CO 80206
www.pismoglass.com

PISMO Gallery at Aspen
433 E. Cooper Ave.
Aspen, CO 81611
www.pismoglass.com

PISMO Gallery at Vail
122 E. Meadow Dr.
Vail, CO 81657
www.pismoglass.com

Connecticut

Ai Bo Gallery
27 Bowman Dr.
Greenwich, CT 06831
aibogallery.com

DC

Maurine Littleton Gallery
1667 Wisconsin Ave., NW
Washington, DC 20007
www.littletongallery.com

Zenith Gallery
1429 Iris St., NW
Washington, DC 20012
www.ZenithGallery.com

Florida

Duncan McClellan Gallery
550 24th St. South
St. Petersburg, FL 33712
www.dmglass.com

Galleria Silecchia
20 S. Palm Ave.
Sarasota, FL 34236
www.galleriasilecchia.com

Habatat Galleries
513 Clematis St.
West Palm Beach, FL 33401
and
608 Banyan Trail
Boca Raton, FL 33431
www.habatatgalleries.com

Hodgell Gallery
46 Palm Ave. South
Sarasota, FL 34236
www.hodgellgallery.com

Lombard Contemporary Art
1 Grand Cypress Blvd.
Orlando, FL 32836
www.lombardcontemporaryart.com

Stewart Fine Art
Gallery Center
608 Banyan Trail
Boca Raton, FL 33431
www.sfaglass.com

Georgia

Consult Art
Anne Lambert Tracht
Atlanta, GA
www.consultartinc.com

Hawaii

NaPua Gallery
3860 Wailea Dr. # 210
Kihei, HI 96753

Opposite: Charissa Brock (photo: Dan Kvitka).

Third Dimension Gallery
68-1330 Mauna Lani Dr.
Kamuela, HI 96743
www.thirddimensiongallery.com

Idaho

Friesen Gallery Fine Art
320 First Ave. North
Ketchum, ID 83340
www.friesengallery.com

Illinois

Ken Saunders Gallery
230 West Superior St.
Chicago, IL 60654
www.kensaundersgallery.com

L.H. Selman Ltd.
410 S. Michigan Ave., Suite #207
Chicago, IL 60605
www.theglassgallery.com

Indiana

Artlink
300 E. Main St.
Ft. Wayne, IN 46802
www.artlinkfw.com

Kentucky

Mark Payton Glass Center at Louisville Glassworks
815 West Market St.
Louisville, KY 40202
www.louisvilleglassworks.com

Louisiana

Venusian Gardens Art Gallery
2601 Chartres St.
New Orleans, LA 70117
www.VenusianGardens.com

Maine

Centre St Arts Gallery
11 Centre St.
Bath, ME 04530
www.centrestartsgallery.blogspot.com

Gleason Fine Art
31 Townsend Ave., PO Box 540
Boothbay Harbor, ME 04538
www.gleasonfineart.com

Viles Arboretum
153 Hospital St.
Augusta, ME 04330
www.vilesarboretum.org

Massachusetts

Dane Gallery
28 Centre St.
Nantucket, MA 02554
www.danegallery.com

Martha's Vineyard Glassworks
683 State Rd.
West Tisbury, MA 02575
www.mvglassworks.com

Renjeau Galleries
79 Worcester St.
Natick, MA 01760
www.renjeau.com

Schantz Gallery
3 Elm St.
Stockbridge, MA 01262
www.schantzgalleries.com

The Drawing Room
11 Spring St.
Marion, MA 02738
anthif.com

The Wit Gallery
27 Church St.
Lenox, MA 01240
www.thewitgallery.com

Michigan

Habatat Galleries
4400 Fernlee Ave
Royal Oak, MI 48073
www.habatat.com

Missouri

Duane Reed Gallery
4729 McPherson Ave.
St. Louis, MO 63108
www.duanereedgallery.com

Nevada

Safari Club International Annual Convention
Mandalay Bay Convention Center
3950 South Las Vegas Blvd.
Las Vegas, NV 89119
www.showsci.com

New Hampshire

Cassidy Gallery
95 Main St.
Jackson, NH 03846
www.cassidygallery.com

League of New Hampshire Craftsmen Galleries
Statewide NH
www.nhcrafts.org

New Jersey

Gallery of Fine Craft, WheatonArts
1501 Glasstown Rd.
Millville, NJ 08332
www.wheatonarts.org/museumstores/gallery

Mostly Glass Gallery
34 Hidden Ledge Rd.
Englewood, NJ 07631
www.mostlyglass.com

New Mexico

Bill Hester Fine Art
830 Canyon Rd.
Santa Fe, NM 87501
www.billhesterfineart.com

Blue Rain Gallery
130 Lincoln Ave., Suite C
Santa Fe, NM 87501
www.bluerain gallery.com

Copper Moon Gallery
105 Kit Carson Rd.
Taos, NM 87571
www.coppermoongallerytaos.com

Holsten Galleries
369 Montezuma Ave., #314
Santa Fe, NM 87501
www.holstengalleries.com

LewAllen Contemporary
1613 Paseo de Peralta
Santa Fe, NM 87501
www.lewallencontemporary.com

Palette Contemporary Art & Craft
7400 Montgomery Blvd. NE, Suite 22
Albuquerque, NM 87109
www.palettecontemporary.com

Tesuque Glassworks
1510 Bishop's Lodge Rd.
Tesuque, NM 87574
www.tesuqueglass.com

Winterowd Fine Art
701 Canyon Rd.
Santa Fe, NM 87501
www.fineartsantafe.com

Zane Bennett Contemporary Art
435 S. Guadalupe St.
Santa Fe, NM 87501
www.zanebennettgallery.com

New York

Ai Bo Gallery
10 Rockledge Rd.
Rye, NY 10580
www.aibogallery.com

Barry Friedman, Ltd.
110 West 30th St.
New York, NY 10001
www.barryfriedmanltd.com

Cavin-Morris Gallery
210 11th Ave. #201
New York, NY 10001
www.cavinmorris.com

Clouds Gallery
1 Mill Hill Rd.
Woodstock, NY 12498
www.cloudsofwoodstock.com

Corning Museum of Glass
1 Museum Way
Corning, NY 14830
www.cmog.org

Heller Gallery
303 10th Ave.
New York, NY 10001
www.hellergallery.com

Kim Foster Gallery
529 W. 20th St.
New York City, NY 10011
www.kimfostergallery.com

Scott Jacobson Gallery
114 East 57th St.
New York, NY 10022
www.scottjacobsongallery.com

North Carolina

Bender Gallery
12 South Lexington Ave.
Asheville, NC 28801
www.thebendergallery.com

Blue Spiral 1
38 Biltmore Ave.
Asheville, NC 28801
www.bluespiral1.com

The Design Gallery
7 S. Main St.
Burnsville, NC 28714
www.the-design-gallery.com

Greenhill
200 N. Davie St.
Greensboro, NC 27401
www.greenhillnc.org

Penland Gallery
PO Box 37
Penland, NC 28765
www.penland.org

Piedmont Craftsmen
601 N. Trade St.
Winston Salem, NC 27101
www.piedmontcraftsmen.org

Shine on Brightly
Asheville, NC
www.shineonbrightly.com

Southern Highland Craft Guild
Folk Art Center
PO Box 9545
Asheville, NC 28815
www.southernhighlandguild.org

STARworks Gallery
100 Russell Dr.
Star, NC 27356
www.starworksnc.org

Taupe Gallery
807A Main St.
North Wilkesboro, NC 28659
www.facebook.com/TaupeGallery

Twisted Laurel Gallery
333 Locust St.
Spruce Pine, NC 28777
www.insidenc.com/mountain/
twistedlaurel.htm

Village Smith Galleries
119 Reynolds Village #A
Winston-Salem, NC 27106
www.villagesmithgalleries.com

Ohio

Collectors Corner Gallery
Toledo Museum of Art
2445 Monroe St.
Toledo, OH 43697

Hawk Galleries
153 East Main St. #1
Columbus, OH 43215
www.hawkgalleries.com

Marta Hewett Gallery
1310 Pendleton St.
Cincinnati, OH 45202
www.martahewett.com

Sherrie Gallery
694 North High St.
Columbus, OH 43215
www.sherriegallery.com

Thomas R. Riley Galleries
28699 Chagrin Blvd.
Cleveland, OH 44122
www.rileygalleries.com

Oregon

Freed Gallery
6119 SUS 101
Lincoln City, OR 97367
www.freedgallery.com/oregon-coast/

Pennsylvania

Borelli Edwards Gallery
3583 Butler St.
Pittsburgh, PA 15201
begalleries@mac.com

Morgan Contemporary Glass Gallery
5833 Ellsworth Ave.
Pittsburgh, PA 15232
www.morganglassgallery.com

National Liberty Museum
321 Chestnut St.
Philadelphia, PA 19106
www.libertymuseum.org

The Wexler Gallery
201 North 3rd St.
Philadelphia, PA 19106
www.wexlergallery.com

Tennessee

Fuhrman Glass Studios Inc.
374 Warehouse Rd.
Oak Ridge, TN 37830
www.fuhrmanglass.com

Locally Grown Gallery
109 Towne Rd.
Oak Ridge, TN 37830
www.facebook.com/locallygrowngallery

McClung Museum
1327 Circle Park Dr.
Knoxville, TN 37916
mcclungmuseum.utk.edu

Serenity Glass
360 Market St.
Clinton, TN 37716
www.facebook.com/
SerenityStainedGlassStudio

The Gallery at the Appalachian Center for Craft
1560 Craft Center Dr.
Smithville, TN 37166
www.tntech.edu/craftcenter/gallery

York & Friends Fine Art
107 Harding Place
Nashville, TN 37205
www.yorkandfriends.com

Texas

Hooks-Epstein Gallery
2631 Colquitt
Houston, TX 77098
www.hooksepsteingalleries.com

Kittrell / Riffkind Art Glass
5100 Beltline Rd. #510
Dallas, TX 75254
www.kittrellriffkind.com

Utah

A Gallery
1321 S. 2100 E.
Salt Lake City, UT 84108
www.agalleryonline.com

Virginia
Chasen Galleries
3554 West Cary St.
Richmond, VA 93221
chasengalleries.com

Troika Gallery
203 South Locust St.
Floyd, VA 24091
www.troikacrafts.com

Washington

Bryan Ohno Gallery
521 South Main St.
Seattle, WA 98104
www.bryanohno.com

Foster / White Gallery
220 Third Ave. South
Seattle, WA 98104
www.fosterwhite.com

Karla Matzke Fine Art Gallery and Sculpture Park
2345 Blanche Way
Camano Island, WA 98282
www.matzkefineart.com

Stonington Gallery
125 South Jackson St.
Seattle, WA 98104
www.stoningtongallery.com

The Art Stop
940 Broadway
Tacoma, WA 98402
www.artstoptacoma.com

Traver Gallery
110 Union St., #200
Seattle, WA 98101
www.travergallery.com

Vetri
1404 1st Ave.
Seattle, WA 98101
www.vetriglass.com

Wisconsin

Artful Home
931 E. Main St.
Madison, WI 53703
www.artfulhome.com

Edgewood Orchard Galleries
4140 Peninsula Players Rd.
Fish Creek, WI 54212
www.edgewoodorchard.com

K. Allen Gallery
9991 State Highway 57
Sister Bay, WI 54234
www.k.allengallery.gallery

Racine Art Museum Store
441 Main St.
Racine, WI 53403
www.ramart.org

Tory Folliard Gallery
233 N. Milwaukee St.
Milwaukee, WI 53202
www.toryfolliard.com

Wyoming

RARE Gallery of Fine Art
60 East Broadway, 2nd Floor
Jackson, WY 83001
raregalleryjacksonhole.com

International

Australia

Beaver Galleries
81 Denison St.
Deakin, ACT 2600
Australia
www.beavergalleries.com.au

Kirra Galleries
Federation Square, Corner Swanston & Flinders Streets
Melbourne, VIC 3000, Australia
www.kirragalleries.com

Sabbia Gallery
120 Glenmore Rd.
Paddington, NSW 2021
Australia
www.sabbiagallery.com

Austria

Gallery Sikabonyi
Kohlmarkt 7
Wein, Austria
www.the-glassplace.com

Canada

art1274hollis
1274 Hollis St.
Halifax, NS, Canada B3J 1T6
www.art1274hollis.ca

Art Works Gallery
225 Smithe St.
Vancouver, BC, Canada V6B 4X7
www.artworksbc.com

Crouchers Pt. Gallery
5 Crouchers Point Rd.
Glen Haven, NS, Canada
www.crouchersptgallery.com

Dimension Plus
8110 Boulevard Décarie
Montréal, QC, Canada H4P 2S8
www.dimension-plus.ca

Espace VERRE
1200 Rue Mill
Montreal, QC, Canada H3K 2B3
www.espaceverre.qc.ca

Galerie Elena Lee
1460 Sherbrooke Ouest, Suite A
Montreal, QC, Canada H3G 1K4
www.galerieelenalee.com

L.A Pai
13 Murray St.
Ottawa, ON, Canada K1N 9M5
lapaigallery.com

Sandra Ainsley Gallery
The Warehouse, 100 Sunrise Ave,
Unit 150
Toronto, ON, Canada M4A 1B3
www.sandraainsleygallery.com

West End Gallery
1203 Broad St.
Victoria, BC, Canada V8W 2A4
www.westendgalleryltd.com

China

China Art Museum
No1 Xueye Rd
Shanghai, China
www.sh-artmuseum.org.cn

Germany

Continuum Gallery
Wintermühlenhof 11
53639 Königswinter, Germany
www.continuum-gallery.com

First Glas Galerie
Heßstrasse 58
80798 Munich, Germany
www.first-glas-galerie.de

Galerie am Museum
Grafenauer Strasse 8
94258 Frauenau, Germany
www.eisch-glas-galerie.de

Italy

Cesare Toffolo Gallery
F.TA Vetrai 37
30141 Murano-Venezia VE, Italy
www.toffolo.com

Emanuel Toffolo Gallery
S. Mauro 30141
Burano Ve Italy

Japan

Kobe Lampwork Glass Museum
79, Kyomachi, Chuo-ku
Kobe, Japan 650-0034
www.lampwork-museum.com

Jackie and Partners
Kobe Fashion Mart Office 7N-12
9-6, Koyocho-naka, Higashinada-ku
659-0032 Kobe, Japan
www.jackieandpartners.com

The Netherlands

Etienne Gallery
De Lind 38
5061 HX Oisterwijk, Netherlands
www.etiennegallery.nl

South Africa

Dimitrov Art Gallery
Dullstroom, South Africa
www.dimitrovartgallery.co.za

Ebony
Franschoek, South Africa
ebonydesign.co.za

Edge Glass Gallery
Cape Town, South Africa
www.capeglassstudio.com

United Kingdom

Contemporary Applied Arts
89 Southwark St.
London, SE1 0HX, United Kingdom
www.caa.org.uk

Victoria and Albert Museum
South Kensington
London SW7 2RL, United Kingdom
www.vam.ac.uk

Online Only

Glass Orbits
www.pbase.com/bkbowden

Land of Marbles
www.landofmarbles.com

Artist Index

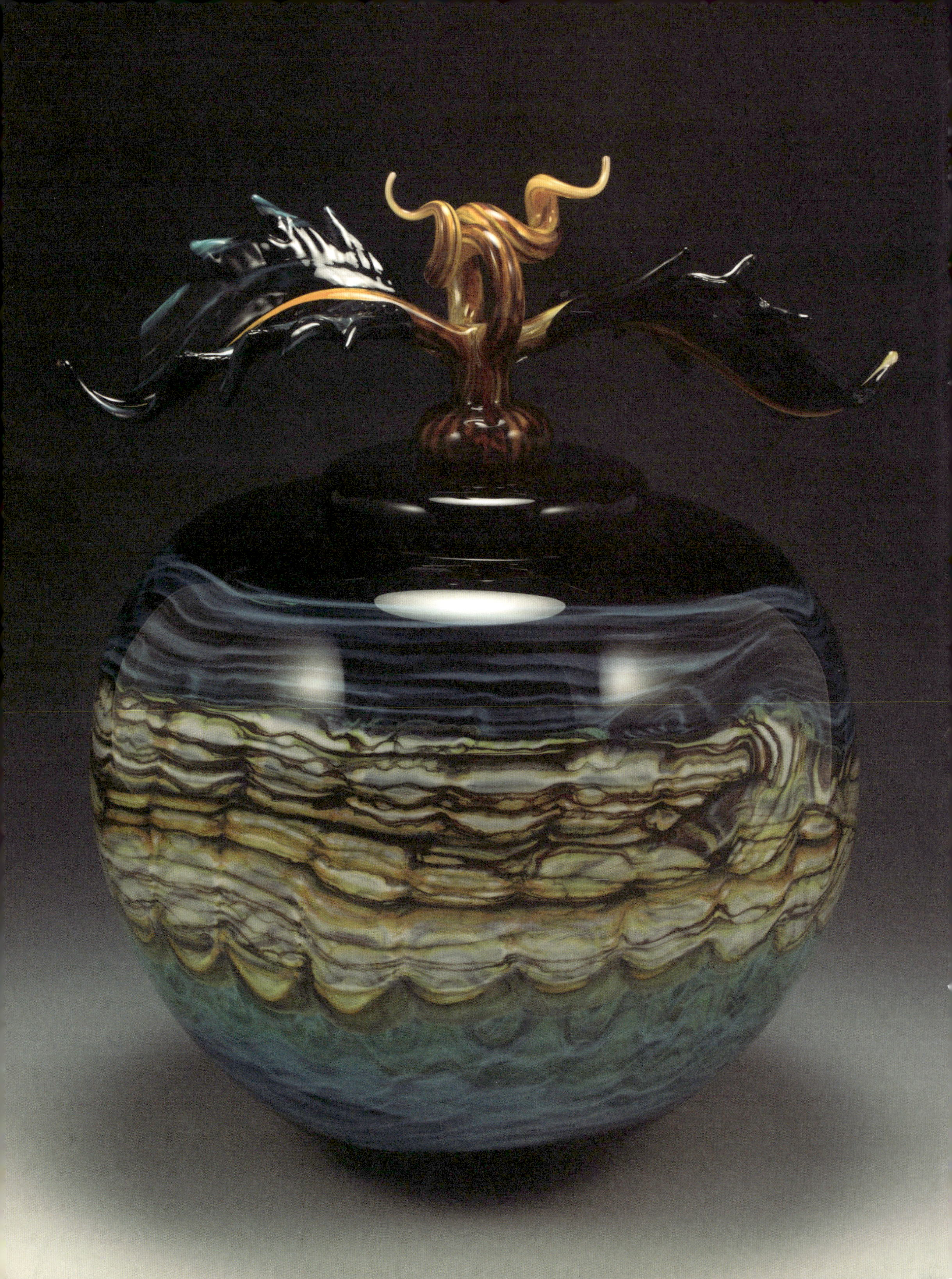